Seth Lerer is Avalon Foundation
in Humanities and professor of E
comparative literature at Stanfor

With essays from

Christopher Cannon, Cambridge University

Rita Copeland, University of Pennsylvania

Bruce Holsinger, University of Colorado

Ethan Knapp, Ohio State University

Seth Lerer, Stanford University

James Simpson, Harvard University

D. Vance Smith, Princeton University

Jennifer Summit, Stanford University

Stephanie Trigg, University of Melbourne

Deanne Williams, York University

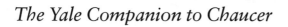

The Yale Companion to Chaucer

Edited by SETH LERER

The Yale Companion
to Chaucer

Yale University Press
New Haven
& London

Set in Sabon type by Keystone Typesetting, Inc.
Printed in the United States of America by Vail-Ballou Press, Binghamton, New
York.

Library of Congress Cataloging-in-Publication Data

The Yale companion to Chaucer / edited by Seth Lerer.
        p.   cm.
Includes bibliographical references and index.
ISBN-13: 978-0-300-10929-0 (alk. paper)
ISBN-10: 0-300-10929-6 (alk. paper)
1. Chaucer, Geoffrey, d. 1400 — Criticism and interpretation — Handbooks,
manuals, etc. I. Lerer, Seth, 1955–
PR1905.Y35 2006
821'.1 — dc22

                    2005025157

A catalogue record for this book is available from the British Library.

The paper in this book meets the guidelines for permanence and durability of the
Committee on Production Guidelines for Book Longevity of the Council on
Library Resources.

10 9 8 7 6 5 4 3 2 1

Contents

Acknowledgments

I am grateful to editors and staff at Yale University Press for their original invitation to prepare this volume and for their support throughout its preparation. In particular, I am grateful to Lauren Shapiro, who took over supervision of this project and has seen it through with grace and goodwill. I would also like to thank the referees for Yale University Press, who offered valuable comments on earlier versions of the volume, and David Bromwich of Yale University, without whose encouragement this book would not have been completed.

All of the contributors offered more than their chapters: they suggested areas of focus, offered advice on detail, and shared their comments on our work as it was being written. James Simpson, Jennifer Summit, and Deanne Williams were of special help in the planning stages of the volume and in the writing of my contributions.

Stanford University Library, the Huntington Library, and the Cambridge University Library were the places where I wrote my contributions and assembled this volume. The Stanford English Department supported this project in ways both tangible and intangible. My students of the past twenty-five years, both at Princeton University and at Stanford, have taught me a great deal about teaching literature and Chaucer in particular, and it has been with them in mind that I conceived this book. Among those students, I wish to single out

Mary F. Godfrey, Karen Gross, Amanda Walling, Deanne Williams, and Meg Worley for their insights. Lisa H. Cooper, a Mellon Postdoctoral Fellow at Stanford and now of the University of Wisconsin English Department, helped immeasurably with the final preparation of my contributions.

Last, I wish to acknowledge a long-standing intellectual debt to Joseph A. Dane, who knows more about the history of Chaucer editing and scholarship than anyone and who knows better than I what to do with that knowledge.

A Note on Editions and Abbreviations

Unless otherwise noted, all quotations and references to Chaucer's works are from Larry D. Benson, ed., *The Riverside Chaucer*, 3rd ed. (Boston: Houghton Mifflin, 1987). Quotations from the *Canterbury Tales* are cited by Fragment and line number.

Each chapter has a separate bibliography at the end of this volume. The following abbreviations are used in the notes and bibliographies:

CHMEL	*The Cambridge History of Medieval English Literature*, ed. David Wallace (Cambridge: Cambridge University Press, 1999)
EETS OS	*Early English Text Society, Original Series*
EETS NS	*Early English Text Society, Extra Series*
ELH	*ELH: A Journal of English Literary History*
JEGP	*Journal of English and Germanic Philology*
MED	*Middle English Dictionary*, ed. Hans Kurath et al. (Ann Arbor: University of Michigan, 1954–)
OED	*Oxford English Dictionary*, ed. James A. H. Murray et al. (Oxford: Oxford University Press, 1933; with Supplements)
PMLA	*Publications of the Modern Language Association of America*
SAC	*Studies in the Age of Chaucer*

Introduction

SETH LERER

The Claim for a New Companion

There is no dearth of companions to Chaucer. The past two decades have seen a spate of collaborative volumes, guides, and collections of essays (not to mention Internet sites) devoted to Chaucer study at the undergraduate and graduate levels. Much like any other major author, Geoffrey Chaucer has become something of an industry with his own scholarly society, his academic meetings, his journals and newsletters, and his encyclopedias and editions. For any student studying the poet for the first time, for any teacher looking to update a syllabus, or for any scholar seeking to enhance a footnote, resources abound.[1]

Why, then, produce another assembly of essays? In spite of the proliferation of materials and guides, no single-volume collection gives students up-to-date information on the history and textual contexts of Chaucer's work, on the ranges of current critical interpretation, and on the poet's place in English and European literary history in the large. The *Yale Companion* seeks to fulfill that need in three ways.

First, it presents the best in current scholarship and criticism by a generation of Chaucerians establishing themselves at the beginning of the twenty-first century. Most guides to Chaucer and companions to criticism draw on the familiar scholars of a quarter-century ago. Though updated with new contributions, the revised *Cambridge Companion to Chaucer* (2004) still has its anchor essays by contributors to the first edition of 1986.[2] Survey volumes by scholars who established themselves thirty or forty years ago are also still widely used.[3] By contrast, the *Yale Companion* assembles a group of younger contributors who will help chart the lines of future Chaucer studies: where its archival research, theoretical engagement, and critical idiom may be headed.

Second, although the *Yale Companion* brings together an international collection of contributors, it is designed primarily for an American audience. Most previous books of this type — the *Cambridge Companion,* the *Oxford Guides to Chaucer,* the *Oxford Companion,* the *Blackwell Companion* — reflect approaches developed in the British university system. The Oxford and Cambridge tradition of tutorials and final exams generates an approach to student criticism different from the American structure of seminar papers and class discussions. Certain theoretical lines remain firmly rooted in the British idiom: legacies, for example, of English practical criticism or of Marxist materialism or even of simple authorial celebration. American students tend to view these traditions differently from their British counterparts, and there remain certain theoretical and critical perspectives (for example, poststructuralism, psychoanalytic feminism, New Historicism) that have distinguished not just American literary criticism generally but American medieval literary studies in particular. Last, for American students who today receive little, if any, training in historical philology and Old English, who have little sense of regional dialect variation, and who have almost no awareness of the physical remains of medieval Britain — for these students, textbooks coming out of the United Kingdom may seem almost willfully out of step with both their classroom and their personal experience. The *Yale Companion* seeks to set a critical and pedagogical tone appropriate for students with an American background and, in the process, to provide those students with materials through which they can begin the study of philology, history, and textual criticism.

Third, therefore, the *Yale Companion* seeks to combine interpretation with information. Its mode is the long critical essay: an opportunity for authors to develop arguments at leisure, to present supporting evidence in detail, to linger, when necessary, over sources and analogues, historical contexts or philological details. Unlike the *Blackwell Companion*'s brief essays or the *Oxford Companion*'s encyclopedia-style entries, the *Yale Companion* illustrates to students how to pursue scholarship at length. More than just conveying facts or features of Chaucerian production, essays such as these reveal teachers and researchers at work. Readers will not find here bald surveys of plot or history. But we have not neglected information. These essays, together with this Introduction and the volume's bibliography, offer guides to scholarship and research. Maps and chronologies dovetail with details about language, manuscripts, and printed editions of Chaucer's writings to make textual and philological history accessible to students.

To fulfill these goals, the *Yale Companion* is organized in three major parts. Part I, "Contexts and Cultures," assays the historical, biographical, and socioliterary environments that shaped Chaucer's writing. Christopher Cannon's "The Lives of Geoffrey Chaucer" offers more, however, than a mere recitation of the facts of Chaucer's life or the details of his biography. It looks into the nature of the idea of the "life" itself: what that term meant in medieval literature and society; how Chaucer's many public roles feed into our impressions of his person; and how he explored the genre of the literary life throughout his fictions. The Chaucer that emerges from Cannon's account is a life lived in and through texts. As Cannon puts it, "There are not public and poetic lives to be contrasted, . . . but the progressive emergence of a new occupation in which one lived *by means* of texts (a job to which Chaucer, like us, would have given the name 'poet')." Chaucer's textual experiences shaped themselves against both European and English models, and the next two chapters reassess his work against those differing traditions. James Simpson's "Chaucer as a European Writer" stresses not simply the sources from the French or the Italian that he used but, also, the larger environment of medieval European letters that made Chaucer truly "European." In the process, Simpson reconsiders Chaucer's debts to Ovid — the preeminent classical *auctor* for European amorous and philosophical poetry and the one poet, as Simpson puts it, "via whose craft Chaucer can himself approach the classical and greater vernacular traditions." Translation, in all senses of the term, emerges at the fore of Simpson's account, whether it be the local issue of transforming French, Italian, and Latin narratives or the global matter of engaging with "republican letters as practiced in Italy" to introduce, in the *Canterbury Tales,* "an entirely new literary and cultural 'politics' into English writing." Chaucer, however, also appears as a thoroughly vernacular poetic craftsman in Simpson's account, and D. Vance Smith's "Chaucer as an English Writer" examines the nature of Chaucer's relationship to his English forebears and contemporaries. By examining the poet's debts to the romances, his relationship with John Gower, and his engagement with the lyric, Smith illustrates how "Chaucer uses English texts with the same kind of intelligent creativity with which he uses texts in other languages." Life and language come together in these essays, as they do especially in Rita Copeland's "Chaucer and Rhetoric." Her contribution, the first sustained assessment of Chaucer and the rhetorical traditions in over a quarter of a century, illustrates more than just Chaucer's debts to pedagogy or oration. It shows how certain fictive characters, the Wife of Bath in particular, can be "an embodiment of rhetoric" and how, in the invocation to Book 2 of *Troilus and Criseyde,* Chaucer demonstrates that "history *is* rhetoric."

Part II of this *Companion* turns to individual poems and forms in order to bring current critical interpretations to bear on the arc of Chaucer's literary career. Deanne Williams's "Chaucer's Dream Visions" shows how Chaucer used the form throughout his lifetime to "explore the idea of authorship itself." The dream poems, in her words, "illustrate the fundamental, yet fraught role of continental and classical sources in shaping Chaucer's work and his ideas about literary production." The *House of Fame*'s opening invocation, "God turne us every drem to goode," becomes, in the course of Williams's argument, a plea for literary making and interpretation. Such pleas chime throughout Chaucer's shorter poems: the many lyrics, ballads, complaints, and verse epistles that often reveal something of a personal and social poet, writing among friends or appealing to patrons. Bruce Holsinger's contribution on the shorter poems reveals the contours of a poet who had mastered all the forms of lyric utterance. But more than that, it shows how Chaucer, even in his longer works, was always conscious of the lyric moment — always ready to deploy those subjective outbursts or reflections that we find so palpably in, for example, the *Cantus Troili* of *Troilus and Criseyde,* or the laments of the *Book of the Duchess.* Holsinger's essay also raises methodological questions about the place of formal analysis in contemporary Chaucer criticism, and it provokes a new consideration of the place of form itself in Middle English literary history.

History and form, dreams and omens, lyric and narrative are all at work in Chaucer's longest and most complex single, complete poem, *Troilus and Criseyde.* Jennifer Summit argues that the claims for "literary ambition" in this poem dovetail with a heightened sensitivity to what she calls, following Jill Mann, "the woman question." *Troilus and Criseyde,* Summit shows, makes "questions of sexual ethics" into "problems of textual interpretation or storytelling, endowing acts of reading and writing with erotic or gendered significance." In her essay, Summit brings out Chaucer's Criseyde with a texture rarely found in either traditional, male-centered criticism or in recent feminist provocations. My contribution to Part II, on the *Canterbury Tales,* draws on the interests and the inspiration of my co-contributors to illustrate how Chaucer develops performing personae. His Tales bring together language, sex, and money to create performing selves, and my chapter's goal, as I put it, "is to explore how his narrators, characters, and dramatic interchanges question literary and social selves; how they interrogate language's ability to shape or describe the person and the world; and how they explore the *value* (in all senses of that word) of the imagination, both in public space and in private fantasy."

Chaucer's work had value for his later readers, scribes, publishers, teachers, and scholars, and Part III of the *Companion* illustrates the many paths along which his reception traveled. Stephanie Trigg's essay "Chaucer's Influence and Reception" argues that the poet's afterlife helped shape not only his personal reputation but a larger sense of English literary history. Genealogy, inheritance, achievement—such are the terms familiar to us from lifetimes of criticism; they are the terms set by the first writers and readers coping with Chaucer's example. By the late nineteenth century, those writers and readers began to be housed in college and university English departments, and the legacies of Chaucer criticism fall under the purview of Ethan Knapp's chapter. Knapp traces through the major lines of critical interpretation, but in the process he illustrates how Chaucer criticism, teaching, and scholarship reflect the larger arc of university literary study As he puts it: "In using Chaucer to substantiate literature as both an ethical pursuit and also a fit subject for scientific inquiry," nineteenth- and twentieth-century scholars "created a bifurcated and paradoxical Chaucer who still haunts the critics: on one hand, the distant object of philological and codicological detection and, on the other, the chummy poet who rides alongside, joking with us about a people and world that remains essentially recognizable."

That paradox remains with us, and if the purpose of this *Companion*'s essays is to chart future lines of inquiry into the poet—these days, far from simply chummy—those essays will remain as testimony to our present. Any volume such as this one is a product of its time. For many years, the study of Chaucer has moved away from critical appreciation, close verbal analysis, and source study (the defining modes of mid-twentieth-century academic teaching) to a more pointed, historical location in the politics, poetics, and personae of the late Middle Ages.[4] Chaucer's work has been assessed, of late, in the environment of religious dissent and ecclesiastical satire. Scholars such as Steven Justice, Andrew Watson, and Rita Copeland have illustrated how vernacular theology and politics shape Chaucer's literary idiom.[5] His contemporaries included the Lollard religious reformer and biblical translator John Wycliffe; the brilliant mystic Julian of Norwich; the leaders of the Rising of 1381; and the dynastically challenged King Richard II. Politics and religion are no longer seen as simply themes or backgrounds for Chaucer's writing. They are now understood to govern form and structure, drama and display. The Lollard movement, for example, may have textured the *Canterbury Tales,* where, in Nicholas Watson's words, "low- and highborn mix freely," and where dissent is never far from Harry Bailley's purview.[6] Some of the most familiar of Chaucer's poems, such as the *Miller's Tale* and the *Nun's Priest's Tale* (long taught as self-contained comic bravura performances) have been assessed anew as profound engagements with the Rising of 1381 and the insurgencies of vernacular politics.

Other critical changes have been similarly decisive. A mid-twentieth-century fascination with the French ambiance of Chaucer's poetry has given way to a preoccupation with its Italian contexts. David Wallace has done much, for example, to reveal Chaucer's debts to Giovanni Boccaccio, his responses to Petrarch and Dante, his knowledge of Florentine city-state despotism.[7] Texts and tales long relegated to the margins of study have become central to this newer contextualization: the *Monk's Tale* and the *Melibee,* for example, are now read as case studies in the Chaucerian response to Italian humanist identity. But works that have long been appreciated as the most "Italianate" of Chaucer's work — the *House of Fame,* for example, considered even by medieval readers as "Dante in English" — have been reassessed in different contexts. Frank Grady, for example, imagines this poem as a response to Chaucer's English contemporary, William Langland and his *Piers Plowman,* in its transformations of the dream motif and its meditations on vernacular authority.[8]

Throughout Chaucer criticism of the past thirty years, there has been a profound recognition that he was, and remains, a poet of gender and power. Although no one would imagine the Wife of Bath as a historical woman, critics have seen how Chaucer adapts the discourses of female writing to his fictional character. His presentations of women characters and narrators throughout his poetry have been reread within a larger historical context of medieval women's writing: from Julian of Norwich through Christine de Pizan to Margery Kempe. But these presentations have also sparked reflections drawn from feminist theory of our time. Critics such as Louise Fradenburg, Susan Crane, Carolyn Dinshaw, Elaine Tuttle Hansen, and many others have revealed the striking ways in which contemporary theory resonates with medieval gender history.[9] There is, in Dinshaw's now-famous formulation, a "sexual poetics" to Chaucer's work and a fascination, as Louise Fradenburg has more recently put it, that the defining rituals of medieval life (chivalry, courtliness, public mourning, dynastic display) are all, to some extent, fantasies that contribute to the symbolic economy of Chaucer's narratives.

All of the essays in the *Yale Companion* work through (if sometimes also against) these lines of criticism. Though this collection is no monolith of argument or ideology, it is a compilation by smart, professionally active scholars, critics, and teachers of medieval literature, all in their early or their mid-careers. Among their many interests — history and power, gender and society, England and Europe, script and performance — they share a concern with Chaucer's writing *as literature:* as an imaginative response to lived experience, as a set of written texts acutely conscious of the modes and methods of their making and reception. Among the many Chaucers that may emerge from this volume, one may stand out: a Chaucer of verbal nuance and linguistic innovation, a Chaucer in control from the level of the single line to entire genre.

The Linguistic Condition of Chaucer's Work

Well, maybe not every single line. If anything emerges from Chaucer's writing it is the unsureness of language itself: the inability to control what anyone will think of what you say; how regional dialect variation or historical linguistic change will make it hard to write for people far away or in the future; the ways in which words are only "cousins" to the deed. An understanding not just of the Middle English of Chaucer's day but also of Chaucer's attitudes toward language is essential to the study of his writing. But it is not just English that matters. Chaucer lived at a time and place in which English, French, and Latin were all languages in regular use. Not everyone, of course, was tri-, or even, bilingual, and each language, by the close of the fourteenth century, came to be deployed for distinctive purposes. But, taken as a whole, England in the late Middle Ages was a country of three languages, and Chaucer's poetry and prose reflects the registers and ranges in which they all operated.[10]

The English language of the later fourteenth century was no monolithic tongue. It grew historically out of the contact between the Germanic dialects of the Anglo-Saxons (what scholars since the nineteenth century have called Old English) and the Norman, and later Parisian, French of kings, nobles, clerics, scholars, merchants, and townsfolk. Nevertheless, what modern scholars call "Middle English" was a language, for all its dialectical variations, governed by a certain set of syntactic, grammatical, phonological, and lexical features. Old English was a highly inflected language. It used case systems to indicate grammatical relations among nouns in sentences. It grouped its nouns in sets of declensions and its verbs in sets of conjugations. Although word-order patterns were established in its prose (and to a lesser extent in its verse), Old English was a language in which meaning, at the sentence level, was conveyed through word endings rather than through the sequence of words in that sentence. This grammatical feature was already shifting by the Norman Conquest, and it is an oversimplification to say that the importation of French altered an Old English that had been stable and unchanging for centuries. But it is true that, from the twelfth through the fourteenth centuries, English became more and more a language governed by word-order patterns: a language from which case endings gradually disappeared and in which the morphology of nouns, verbs, adjectives, and adverbs simplified.

A good example of this set of changes, revealed early in the history of post-Conquest England, can be found in the *Peterborough Chronicle*.[11] This text, from the Abbey of Peterborough, illustrates how Anglo-Saxon traditions of historiography continued in the century after the Conquest. Each year-by-year entry in the *Chronicle* begins with a statement of what happened in that year. The entry for 1083, for example, uses the opening formula in precisely grammatical Old English: "On þissum geare" (in this year). The -um and -e endings signal the dative masculine singular forms of the adjective and noun, following the preposition. As the case endings began to lose their prominence in the spoken language, they became harder to reproduce in the written. The entry for 1117 opens, "On þison geare." Here, the adjectival ending has leveled to an indiscriminate back vowel plus an indiscriminate nasal. Perhaps this spelling represents a scribe's attempt to preserve what he thinks is a grammatical ending. The entry for 1135 opens, "On þis geare." Here, we have a total loss of the adjectival ending, together with what may be thought of as a fossilized dative final -e in the noun. Concord in grammatical gender has obviously gone by this time. The last entry for the *Peterborough Chronicle*, 1154, opens, "On þis gaer." Endings have completely dropped away, but the preposition "on" still has its Old English sense of "in" or "at this point," not the more modern sense (emerging in Middle English) of spatial location.

This is but a small example of how the English language was grammatically changing apart from any direct influence of French. True, in other parts of England, French grammar and syntax were beginning to have an effect, and by the early fourteenth century, English idioms (even if they were made up completely of Old English phrases) were shaping themselves to French order. An expression such as "to hold dear" is modeled directly on the French *tenir chier*; "to put to death" comes directly from the French *metre a mort*. Even though the words are English, the idioms are French. So, too, verbs such as "do," "give," "have," "make," and "take" came to be used in their French equivalent senses: thus emerge the English idioms "do battle," "give offence," "have mercy," "make peace," "take pains," and so on.[12]

Another important change lay in word stress. Old English, as in all Germanic languages, had fixed stress on the root syllable of a word: that is, regardless of what prefixes or suffixes, or what grammatical category of the word, the stress remained fixed on the root. The Romance languages had variable word stress. The stress could fall sometimes on the root syllable, at other times on a prefix or suffix. Sometimes the stress could change in the word itself. Such changes in stress helped create the possibility of multiple meanings in single words. Notice for example how the word "record" can have two grammatical forms: *récord* as a noun, and *recórd* as a verb. Changes in word and sentence stress also facilitated the English adoption of continental verse forms. From the Old English alliterative line (where the number of stressed syllables alone mattered), verse moved to a quantitative line (where the number of alternating stressed and unstressed syllables mattered), and rhyme became the organizing principle. Look at the opening lines of the poem known as *The Owl and the Nightingale,* probably composed in the late twelfth century and preserved in two manuscripts of the mid-thirteenth.

> Ich was in one sumere dale,
> In one suþe diȝele hale.[13]

The lines are in iambic tetrameter and they rhyme. But every word is Old English, and several preserve inflectional endings. The Romance features of Middle English were emerging, then, even when no loan words were being used.

The Middle English vocabulary differed markedly from that of Old English, not simply in its voracity for French and Latin terms but also in how it formed word compounds and established different registers for usage. Like its compeer Germanic languages, Old English tended to rely on compounds based on native words rather than borrowing terms from other languages. Noun-compounding, in particular, became one of the defining features of the Old English poetic lexicon. The highly metaphorical compounds were known as "kennings." Calling the sea the *swan-rad* (swan road) or the *hwæl-rad* (whale road) were evocative ways of making the commonplace memorable — and, because Old English verse relied on alliteration for its metrical organization, having a multiplicity of terms for the same thing increased the alliterative possibilities for the poetic line. Even some of our most seemingly ordinary Modern English words come, originally, from Old English and Old Germanic imaginative compounds. "Nostril," for example, comes from the Old English *naseþyrel,* a hole or puncture in the nose (the verb "thirlen" survives in Middle English to mean "pierced with a sharp object"). The Old English word for "window" was the similarly compounded *eagþyrel,* a hole or puncture for the eye. This word was eventually replaced by the term of Old Norse origin, *vindauga,* an eye for the wind. Such was the poetry of the prosaic.

The Romance languages did not form compounds in this way, and Middle English relied on appropriating loanwords from Latin and French to enhance its vocabulary. It is a commonplace of linguistic history to note that the Normans brought new words for learning, commerce, administration, the church, technology, cooking, and the like. For the student coming to medieval literature for the first time, such words are easily recognized. They are often polysyllabic; often words for the institutions of the Conquest (for example, church, law, and government); words for things imported with the Normans (such as castles, courts, and prisons); and words distinguished by certain sounds and spellings. Old English and new French words survived in common use, often distinguishing shades of meaning or connotation. Sir Walter Scott developed, in his novel *Ivanhoe,* one of the most famous (if overstated) distillations of this verbal doubling in his analysis of words for food. The Anglo-Saxon raised the food, whereas the Norman Frenchman ate it. Thus, our words for animals remain Old English: "sow," "cow," "calf," "lamb," "deer." Our words for meats are French: "pork," "beef," "veal," "mutton," "venison."

By Chaucer's time, the vocabulary options were complex, and he could draw on words of different origin, juxtaposing them for literary effect. Take, for example, the famous opening lines of the *Canterbury Tales,* where words of French and Latin origin stand side by side words from the Old English lexicon. The pilgrims on their way to Canterbury travel, we are told, "The hooly blissful martir for to seeke." All the words but one in this line are Old English: only *martir* comes from French, a word that signals not just a religious but a distinctive social category for Saint Thomas's condition. The little birds that "slepen all the night with open eye" in Old English have not "hearts" but "corages"—a French term that had, by Chaucer's time, begun to shift in sense from simply meaning the bodily organ (heart) to the moral quality of heartiness (our Modern English word, "courage"). Thus, twenty-odd lines later, when the poem's narrator notes how he set out on his pilgrimage, "with full devout corage," he links together religious conviction with the idioms of Francophone desire: devout courage, now not simply a good heart but something approaching moral virtue.

These are but brief examples of a movement in the social history of Middle English that distinguished French and earlier English words and that, in turn, had become conscious of the social and the moral registers of language variation. Medieval English literature is rife with such evidence, but some of the most dazzlingly witty examples come from medieval drama. The play known as *Mankind,* probably written in the mid-fifteenth century but certainly reflecting dramatic idioms of decades earlier, shows us the rowdy characters Newguise, Nowadays, and Nought taunting the effete Mercy (notice, again, the difference between the English names of the fools and the French name of the moral character).[14] Early in the play, Mercy announces:

> "Mercy" is my name by denominacion.
> I conseive ye have but a lityll favour in my communicacion.

Newguise responds, tauntingly:

> Ey, ey, yowr body is full of englisch Laten!
> I am aferde it will brest. (Bevington, lines 122–25)

Mercy's polysyllabic, Latinate vocabulary and his periphrastic syntax easily become the butt of popular humor. Nowadays takes it one step further in his scatological abuse. Turn this into Latin, he mocks:

> I have etun a disch-full of curdys,
> Ande I have schetun yowr mowth full of turdys.

And then he offers up a bit of "Latin" of his own: "Osculare fundamentum!" (kiss my ass).

Such moments from the medieval drama resonate with similarly abusive episodes in the *Canterbury Tales*. The anger of the Host, say, at the Pardoner's request for him to open up his purse and buy a pardon has all the vigorous obscenity of the scene from *Mankind*:

> Thou woldest make me kisse thyn olde breech,
> And swere it were a relyk of a seint,
> Though it were with thy fundement depeint!
>
> . . . .
>
> I wold I hadde thy coillons in myn hond
> In stide of relikes or of seintuarie.
> Lat kutte hem of, I wol thee helpe hem carie;
> They shul be shryned in an hogges toord!" (6.948–55)

Harry's blunt English, when seen against the backdrop of the language that survives in *Mankind,* also makes the non-English terms stand out with glistening clarity. Words such as "collions" or "seintuarie" chime with the Old French of the *Romance of the Rose* (whose discussion of proper language and obscenity has long been seen by modern critics as informing this scene in the *Pardoner's Tale*). But now, they stand out against the background of a hog's turd. It is as if we can watch not just the drama of the pilgrim's ire unfold here; we can also watch the drama of Chaucer's linguistic experience transpire, as words from French poetry jostle against the timber of colloquialism.

Take as another case the scene when Chaucer, babbling on in his intolerable *Tale of Sir Thopas,* provokes the Host's interruption. "Myne eres aken of thy drasty speche" (7.923), he says, and he concludes his judgment: "Thy drasty rymyng is nat worth a toord." This is a tale of literary criticism told as an offense to the ear. It is the sound of English that offends the Host, and he presents two options for Chaucer the pilgrim: either tell something in "geeste" (that is, tell a historical romance in alliterative verse) or tell something in "prose." Rhymed verse, alliterative poetry, or prose are not just the generic but the oral and aural options for the pilgrim. Harry presents a catalogue of what can happen in the vernacular, and there is more than merely dirty humor here. These scenes, in *Mankind* as well as in the *Canterbury Tales,* reveal an aggressive English vernacularity taking a stance in the face of literary pretense or social offense. English asserts itself through curses, oaths, and an assertion of the ass over the mouth.

If medieval English audiences were aware of differences in language, they were, too, acutely aware of differences in dialect. The Northernisms of the *Reeve's Tale* from the *Canterbury Tales* are but the most obvious example of Chaucer's transformation of regional linguistic variety into literary argument. Again, the medieval drama offers up a good analogy. In the well-known *Second Shepherd's Play* from the Wakefield Cycle, the sheep-stealing Mak shows up, affecting the linguistic airs of a messenger of the King. He speaks in Southern dialect (in contrast to the Northernisms of the play's other characters) and with words redolent of Gallicism.

> Fie on you! Goith hence
> Out of my presence!
> I must have reverence,
> Why, who be ich?

The shepherds of the play find this speech "quaint," and one jousts back:

> Now take outt that Sothren tothe,
> And sett in a torde! (Bevington, lines 204–16)

The dialect tables are turned here, as the Northerners make fun of the pretentiousness of the Londoners. As John of Trevisa put it in his translation of Ranulph Higden's *Polychronicon,* the language of the North seems "so sharp, slyttyng and frotyng, and unschape, þat we Southeron men may that langage unneþe understonde." If the Southern men can barely grasp the gratings of the North, the Northerners bristle at the mock mellifluousness of Mak's southern tooth.

Language and dialect are more than just the object of humor. One of the most remarkable moments in the history of language in the fourteenth century appears in 1362, when Parliament was opened by a speech in English. Now,

English probably had been used in Parliament before then, but this is the first time that the clerks of the *Rotuli Parliamentorum* specifically admit it: "Au quell jour, esteanz nostre Seigneur le Roi, Prelatz, Countes, Barons, & les Communes en la Chambre de Peinte . . . monstre en Englois par . . . de Grene, Chief Justice le Roi, les Causes des Somons du Parlement."[15] And yet, the language of record still remains French—even in the face of this very same Parliament's statute that all court proceedings be henceforth conducted in English (*pledez & monstrez en la lange Engleise*) because the litigants could no longer understand French (*la lange Franceois, q'est trop desconu en la dit Roialme*) (Fisher, 45, 161 n.34).

French was the language of the court and government well through Chaucer's lifetime. The first time English even appears in the parliamentary records is in the petition of the Mercers' Guild in 1388, and English entries are rare for the remainder of the century. The first English king (after the Anglo-Saxons) to have a will in English was Henry IV, who died in 1421. The first English guild to record its accounts in English was the Brewers' Guild, and that was not until 1422. Chaucer's contemporary John Gower could write long poems in both French and Latin (*Le Mirour de l'Omme,* and the *Vox Clamantis,* respectively), clearly expecting them to have as wide a readership as his poetry in English (the *Confessio Amantis*).

Modern scholars have made a great deal of England as a trilingual culture at the close of the fourteenth century. But they have also recognized that English was emerging, not so much as a "triumphant" tongue, but rather as a language central to imaginative (as well as political and commercial) discourse. Middle English was becoming the venue for reflection on the nature of poetic authorship, the ideas of reading, and the ways in which private spiritual experience could be publicly conveyed. A writer such as Julian of Norwich, whose *Revelation of Divine Love* was composed in the 1380s, could use the vernacular to brilliant ends. Julian transforms a Latinate religious idiom into English; indeed, "revelation" becomes, in her text, the English "schewynge." Look, for example, at this brief passage from the so-called Short Text of her work: "Botte God forbade that ye schulde saye or take it so that I am a techere, for I meene nought soo, no I mente nevere so. For I am a woman, leued, febille, and freylle. But I wate wele that this I saye. I hafe it of the schewynge of hym that es soverayne techare. Botte sothelye, charyte styrres me to tell yowe it, for I wolde god ware knawenn and my eveynn-Crystenne spede, as I wolde be myselfe, to the mare hatynge of synne and lovynge of God."[16] Such a passage reveals the fluency of English as a theological tongue in Chaucer's day. Its sentences are short, evocative of everyday speech. Its vocabulary is local, native, even—at times, perhaps, to modern readers—naive. This is, as the editors of the recent volume, *The Idea of the Vernacular,* put it, a "language of equality," a language that constructs an audience of all English Christians (Wogan-Browne et al., 83). In such a language, the very word for the community of Christians is an old-fashioned, Anglo-Saxon-sounding compound: *eveynn-Crystenne,* fellow Christians.[17] There are few words from French or Latin here. *Febille* and *freylle* come originally from the Latin by way of French, but their juxtaposition here, in what reads as an old-fashioned, English alliterative pairing, calls attention away from their etymological origins and toward their native sound. But in this passage, there are two words of distinctively non-English origin, used for powerful effect. God is the "soverayne techare," a teacher who is not only the chief instructor of the faith but the very sovereign of doctrine; and the love of this God is very pointedly "charyte," a word that goes back to the *caritas* of Saint Paul, Saint Augustine, and the whole tradition of patristic theology.

Julian of Norwich has only recently been read and taught as a woman writer of remarkable vernacular imagination.[18] Her word-choice and her rhythms are more supple and compelling than, frankly, anything that Chaucer wrote in prose, and she stands as a good foil for those who would continue to aver that Chaucer somehow "invented" English as a literary language. Yes, he did use words in new ways; he did develop a decasyllabic line that, for all of its irregularities in his and later Middle English hands, would become a metrical standard for English verse; and he did wrest a poetic form out of the mix of available dialects and idioms. But the elevation of these activities into original invention lay with Chaucer's fifteenth-century imitators. From the poetry of John Lydgate at the beginning of that century to the prologues and epilogues of William Caxton's printed editions at its close, and well into the Tudor period, Chaucer appeared as the first founder of the language: the well of English undefiled. Christopher Cannon has brilliantly shown, in his important study *The Making of Chaucer's English,* that the Chaucerian accomplishment is less a linguistic fact than a rhetorical pose.[19] Chaucer, that is to say, took up the pose of linguistic innovation by presenting a poetic persona preoccupied with new words and overall vernacular command. Cannon shows, through massive statistical analysis: "By presenting traditional forms as alternatives and grading them, Chaucer presents *his* English as the salvific form that can extract the good from the bad and become the best. It is his general method . . . to evoke one linguistic mode scornfully and to present it as a platform from which 'drasty' speech will be repaired by 'murye' virtues. In this way, Chaucer everywhere presented himself as the poet who could save English from itself" (137). Chaucer's English gathers what Cannon identifies as the "*quality* of novelty to itself" (134). It seems new, and certainly feels new to the modern student. But many of those new-seeming words were already part of the documented Middle English lexicon before Chaucer used them. Many of his words appear in the work of writers such as Robert Mannyng of Brunne or Robert of Gloucester (both writing in the early- to mid-fourteenth century) or in the romances and lyrics that predate Chaucer's time. Resources such as the on-line *Middle English Dictionary* and *The Idea of the Vernacular* will make this information available to students at all levels — not to diminish Chaucer's literary accomplishment but to frame it in a linguistic condition characterized by English, French, and Latin; by a vigorous fourteenth-century imaginative vernacular; and by a popular idiom that understood the meaning of an utterance to lie, at least in part, in its resonances with regional speech and personal idiolect. That linguistic condition now seems far more complicated than it did a generation ago. But if it does, it makes Chaucer's work more fascinating for its nuance, and it opens up directions for research unthought-of by the scholars and teachers of that time.

The Textual Condition of Chaucer's Work

If the linguistic condition now seems more complicated than it did a generation ago, nothing seems more complicated than the textual condition of Chaucer's work. There was a time when manuscripts and printed editions were taken as but the vehicles for literature: as if the literary work existed in some prior, ideal state, where manuscripts and printed books were but representations (at times corrupt) of that state. Three decades of textual scholarship have revealed the immense complexity of late medieval manuscript culture and of early print history. Editors and paleographers have shown in detail how the meaning of a literary work may lie, at least in part, in the physical appearance of the text and in the social and economic conditions that produced and disseminated it. Chaucer, like all medieval literature, comes to us in highly mediated forms, but even among his contemporaries he may be unique for a poet of his stature.

There is no manuscript in Chaucer's handwriting, and there are no copies of his poetry or prose datable from the fourteenth century. Unlike his contemporary John Gower, he did not, apparently, supervise the copying and disseminating of his poetry. Chaucer's work survives in manuscripts produced during the decades after his death in 1400. And, with the exception of the *Prologue* to the *Legend of Good Women,* there is no set of surviving Chaucerian texts that indicates authorial revision. Chaucer was clearly different from Gower, who carefully recalibrated the *Confessio Amantis* to the changing political scene at the end of the fourteenth century, and from William Langland, who seems to have spent his entire creative life rewriting his one poem, *Piers Plowman*. To understand the nature of Chaucer's work, it is necessary to know something about how manuscripts were made and read in the late fourteenth and fifteenth centuries and, in turn, how relationships among scribes and patrons, booksellers and buyers, influenced the selection and presentation of Middle English literature.[20]

Medieval books were made by scribes. Scriptoria could be monastic or commercial, keyed to the production of religious or secular texts, and under the aegis of institutions ranging from the church to the university. Scribes may have written from authorial dictation; they may have copied from an author's own exemplar; or they may have copied from other copies, thus contributing to something of a genealogy of textual production. Often, large books were produced in smaller units and then bound together. Such units, known as fascicles or booklets, may have been written out by different scribes at different times and places and then assembled by a controlling scribal or editorial hand.

Until the later fourteenth century, all books in England were written on parchment (sheepskin) or vellum (calfskin), carefully prepared by stretching, scraping, sizing, cutting, and folding (paper does not appear in any quantity until the fifteenth century). Scribes wrote with quill pens and ink made from oak gall or from minerals ground and mixed with water. The act of writing was an act of physical labor, and a major work—a commentary on the Bible, a treatise on canon law, a poetic text such as the *Cursor Mundi* or the *Romance of the Rose*—could tax the patience and the stamina of those who copied it. The great paleographer Malcolm Parkes records this colophon from a fourteenth-century copy of the work of Saint Thomas Aquinas as evidence for the "demands upon the time and energy of scribes":

> Explicit secunda pars summe fratris thome de aquino ordinis fratrum predicatorum, longissima, prolixissima, et tediosissima scribenti: Deo gratias, Deo gratias, et iterum Deo gratias.
>
> Here ends the second part of the *Summa* of brother Thomas Aquinas of the Order of Preaching Friars, the longest, wordiest, and most tedious thing written: thank God, thank God, and one more time, thank God.[21]

Faced with such a labor-intensive task, scribes developed (from about the middle of the twelfth to the middle of the fourteenth centuries) forms of handwriting that enabled speed and fluency of copying. Different scripts were used for different purposes: works in Latin, for example, would be written using letterforms different from works in the vernacular. By the end of the fourteenth century, a distinctive script had been developed for copying English literary texts, and set against this norm, the idiosyncrasies of individual scribes could stand out in a way that enables modern paleographers to identify the people who actually wrote the manuscripts we read.

Manuscripts were made for many purposes, and literary works in English had a range of patrons. Some were clearly written for monastic or fraternal communities. Others may have been commissioned by members of the aristocracy or gentry wishing a particular new text or a copy of an existing work. During the late fourteenth and fifteenth centuries, the possession of a major work by Chaucer, Gower, or Lydgate came to be associated with a certain social status. The lesser aristocracy might wish to imitate the nobility in commissioning lavishly illustrated works of scribal artistry. The gentry might wish to imitate the aristocracy in commissioning carefully copied manuscripts of elegance and utility. Commercial bookmaking was on the rise, especially in London, and manuscripts might be assembled "on spec" for potential buyers.

Few, if any, English literary texts, however, appeared on their own. Literary works would be incorporated into large collections, sometimes keyed to particular themes or occasions, sometimes keyed to authorial aegis. Our best-known Middle English lyrics, for example, survive in anthologies made throughout the thirteenth and the fourteenth centuries — assemblies of poetry and prose, English and French (and sometimes Latin, too), that constitute canons of literature for lay or religious communities. Ralph Hanna III has characterized this form of production in ways that help us see the radically different nature of the medieval book from the modern:

> Miscellaneity breeds individuality, the unique volume. While such volumes should induce us to abandon many specifically print-centered literary conceptions, they also underwrite other, narrower historical discoveries. However important it may be to define the conditions of medieval "literariness," one must also recognize that these conditions were not universally the same. Miscellaneous books testify to acts at least analogous to canon-formation as we understand it, but these are most normally private, individual canons. There was no general late-medieval vernacular literary public, only a range or spectrum of literary communities.[22]

The idea of the anthology controls much of the English medieval notion of the literary, as it did the notion of medieval European literature generally. But distinctive in the English manuscript and early print tradition are the ways in which collections were created. The compilations, for example, of the German *Minnesänger* or the Old French and Provençal troubadours keyed themselves to narrative or thematic coherence or, more pointedly, to individual authorial expression. Volumes gave voice to writers and performers, providing readers with the names of poets, scribes, or patrons.[23]

By contrast, anonymity seems to characterize the early medieval English compilation.[24] Manuscripts may have been assembled by monastic or commercial scribes or commissioned by patrons, booksellers, or individual readers, but it is a mark of virtuoso scholarship to be able to identify them. The great assemblies of Middle English poetry float in a kind of mid-world between localizable dialect and script and conjectured literary production.[25] It is no wonder that their poems became the object of New Critical attention in the middle of the twentieth century. Such texts remained, as one anthology dubbed them, "poems without names," documents not so much of authorial prowess or of cultural context as of autonomous aesthetic value.

Even for the fifteenth century, when manuscripts were built around the poetry of Chaucer, Lydgate, and their imitators, much remains that is ambiguous. Some poems appear without authorial attribution; others are appropriated into the sphere of Chaucer himself (what we now call the Chaucerian Apocrypha); and the origin and dissemination of many poems, along with many manuscript assemblies, remain subjects of conjecture. Even though a good deal of recent scholarship has sought to restore the historical conditions in which early English poetry was produced and read, we still have little information that compares to what we know of the named poet-compilers or compiler-scribes for the continental European Middle Ages.[26]

And yet, much like their continental counterparts, medieval English narrators will often dramatize their acts of reading as acts of perusing an anthology. The Chaucerian dreamer of the *Book of the Duchess,* for example, reads himself to sleep with a collection comprising romances, fables, and "thinges, / Of quenes lives, and of kinges, / And many other thinges smale" (lines 57–59) — an action modeled on the habits of his French sources, Jean Froissart and Guillaume de Machaut. Perhaps the most famous act of critical reading in medieval fiction is the Wife of Bath's encounter with her husband's "boke of wikked wives." "And alle thise were bounden in o volume" (line 681) is her description of this book, one that recalls in brilliantly parodic form Dante's earlier vision of the world as something of a bound anthology of love in *Paradiso* 33:

> Nel suo profundo vidi che s'interna
> legato con amore in un volume,
> cio che per l'universo si squaderna:

> In its depth I saw going inside, bound by love into a single volume, that which is scattered as pages throughout the universe:[27]

But if the world could be imagined as a compilation, then so, too, were many literary works themselves. Long poems that we consider single entities were often read as anthologies of a sort, capable of being broken up and rearranged for individual readers' expectations (certain of the *Canterbury Tales* were copied separately, and passages from Gower's *Confessio Amantis*, Lydgate's *Fall of Princes*, and even Chaucer's *Troilus and Criseyde* were copied out and rearranged as compilations of *sententiae* for moral or amorous instruction).[28] Well into the first decades of print, the anthological impulse controlled much of the dissemination, marketing, and critical reception of vernacular English writing. Even when individual copies of major, authored poems were produced, they could be bound together (by either contemporary or later readers) with other works, creating clusters of literary writing. This is a habit occluded by modern libraries, which have routinely separated books that had once been bound together in order to catalogue them separately (a legacy of early-nineteenth-century collectors concerned with the individual artifacts of English printers, if not of English authors).

Chaucer was acutely conscious of the textual condition of his writing. Not only does he dramatize the act of reading an anthology, as I have just noted, but he also expresses throughout his writings a concern with textual fidelity. He wants attentive scribes, but he realizes that linguistic change and regional dialect variation may introduce confusions among readers and copyists. At the close of *Troilus and Criseyde,* he gives voice to this anxiety.

> And for ther is so gret diversite
> In Englissh and in writyng of oure tonge,
> So prey I God that non myswrite the,
> Ne the mysmetre for defaute of tonge. (5.1793–96)

Such sentiments resonate with those of the little poem known as "Chaucer's Wordes unto Adam, His Owne Scriveyn," a stanza preserved only in one mid-fifteenth-century manuscript.

> Adam scriveyn, if ever it thee bifalle
> Boece or Troylus for to wryten newe,
> Under thy long lokkes thou most have the scale,
> But after my making thow wryte more trewe;
> So ofte adaye I mot thy werk renewe,
> It to correcte and eke to rubbe and scrape,
> And al is thorugh thy negligence and rape.

At moments such as these, Chaucer may well articulate a common medieval concern with the preservation of the author's text (Petrarch, for example, was also famous for his complaints about scribal inattention and the pirating of works in manuscript he had not formally released for distribution). But at such moments, Chaucer also takes textual production as a literary theme. It is not simply that the textual condition of his work gives us a context for exploring the dissemination of his writing. It is that this condition is itself a matter of Chaucerian drama: that Chaucer's poetry is, to some extent, about problems of correctness and error, about the problem of reader response and social dissemination, about the ways in which the written word may, or may not, represent the author's thought. In his various narrators' constant appeals for "correction" — by clerks, by readers, by named authorities — we may find a Chaucerian voice that knows (as he put it in the *General Prologue*) that words are only cousins to the deed, especially when those words are written down.

What, then, is the historical condition of Chaucer's texts? His major poetry survives in many copies from the fifteenth century. There are eighty-three manuscripts, complete or fragmentary, of the *Canterbury Tales;* sixteen manuscripts of *Troilus and Criseyde;* and dozens of copies of the shorter poems scattered throughout fifteenth-century anthologies (the most popular of these short poems, "Truth," survives in twenty-three copies, though only one has the final, fourth stanza addressed to Chaucer's friend Vache).[29] These manuscripts tell stories about readership and patronage, scribal making and literary criticism in late medieval England. Among the many manuscripts of the *Canterbury Tales,* for example, two stand out for their age, textual importance, and possible links to Chaucer's authorship or to the earliest circles of his readers.[30] The Ellesmere Manuscript (now at the Huntington Library) is a beautiful production: a large folio volume, carefully written, rich with Latin marginal annotations, and illustrated with portraits of each pilgrim on horseback. Even a cursory glimpse at its opening page reveals a guiding literary and aesthetic hand at work. The large, ornamented W of the poem's first word splays out into a floral border enclosing the column of verse. Each verse paragraph has a smaller, ornamented initial. When each pilgrim appears, the name is written in the margins, signaled by a large blue pilcrow (or paragraph marker). A. I. Doyle and Malcolm Parkes, in their definitive study of the early manuscripts of the *Canterbury Tales,* identify these features as the marks of *ordinatio:* the medieval system of organizing texts for visual access. "Layout and decoration" in the Ellesmere Manuscript, they write, "function like punctuation." They offer markers of meaning, and the pictures, apparatus, and marginalia in Ellesmere, they note, emphasize "the role of the Tales as repositories of *auctoritates.*" The *Canterbury Tales* appears here — visually and textually — as a *compilatio,* an assembly of authoritative sayings or moral exempla. The marginal annotations and textual apparatus of the Ellesmere Manuscript are designed to grant the reader easy access to those sayings and exempla: to create a literary text rich with doctrine. In Ellesmere, therefore, someone (continue Doyle and Parkes) "has emphasized his own interpretation" of Chaucer's poem. This manuscript may thus reflect not so much Chaucer's own, authorial intentions as it may embody a later editor's or patron's sense of how the poem should be understood and used.[31]

The Hengwrt Manuscript (in the National Library in Aberystwyth, Wales), by contrast, is at first glance an unattractive little thing. There are no illustrations, the *Tales* seem garbled in their order, things are missing (the *Canon's Yeoman's Tale* is absent, and the manuscript ends without the *Retraction*), and many of the lines of the poem seem, unlike those in Ellesmere, to scan coarsely. But Hengwrt is a fascinating document for many reasons. First, it has been shown (most recently by Ralph Hanna) that this is a manuscript made up of booklets. It comes down to us not, in Hanna's words, as "a continuous copy of the poem," as Ellesmere does, but as "five large chunks, bibliographically discrete in execution."[32] It is a kind of "partially planned codex," a miscellany put together as the scribe received portions of the text. "The physical form of Hengwrt," writes Hanna, "indicates that the director and scribe had no clear sense of the plan of the whole at the beginning of production."[33] This feature makes Hengwrt a radically different kind of textual entity from Ellesmere. It illustrates the ways in which a text could circulate in the early fifteenth century, and it illustrates the ways in which Chaucer's poem was a kind of unstable phenomenon in the decades after his death.

But what is equally fascinating is that both the Hengwrt and the Ellesmere Manuscripts were written by the same scribe (in the summer of 2004, Linne R. Mooney of the University of Maine claimed to discover that this scribe was a certain Adam Pinkhurst, perhaps the very Adam of Chaucer's little stanza to his scribe).[34] The ways he formed his letters are identical in both texts, and Doyle and Parkes describe his handwriting in such detail that even to an untrained eye his writing is unmistakable. That one scribe could produce such markedly different manuscripts of the *Canterbury Tales* reveals that there were multiple ways of dealing with Chaucer's poem after his death. In one manuscript, we see a bit-by-bit assembly of stories, a kind of loose anthology of Chaucerian fictions. In the other, we see a carefully prepared and guided book, planned and executed under a guiding critical and interpretive intelligence.

Nearly all modern editions of the *Tales* are based on Ellesmere, but some scholars have argued for Hengwrt as a more authentic text: less carefully constructed and, so, in a sense, less edited.[35] Are the elaborate forms of organization that make Ellesmere so attractive authorial in origin, or do they reflect the controlling patterns of a later editor or patron? Is Hengwrt really more Chaucerian because of its roughness, or is it simply less concerned with an overarching plan and purpose than the Ellesmere — is one, in other words, a complete work and the other but a loose collection of stories?

Scholars have argued over such points with exacting detail for the past three decades, and in Chaucer studies there has emerged a renewed awareness of the textual condition of his poetry: not just its various transmissions by scribes but the recognition that the meaning of a literary work lies as much in its physical and visual condition as in what we might think of as its content. The layout of a page, the organization of a volume, the very handwriting of a scribe, the use of illustration, of running heads, of titles, of marginalia — all contribute to a poem's meaning. Students may find rich arguments in scholarly debates about the primacy of certain Chaucer manuscripts. But at the least, they should recognize that such debates are more than mere turf wars of the editor or pedant. They strike at the heart of what medieval readers understood medieval literature to be: a made thing, a physical object, wrought by scribal hands on media laboriously shaped from plants and animals.

Among the laborers who made the manuscripts of Chaucer's works, a few fifteenth-century figures stand out. One is Thomas Hoccleve, a clerk of the Privy Seal and a self-described poetic disciple of his "maister Chaucer." In addition to writing poems in a Chaucerian vein (and, in his *Regiment of Princes,* presenting a limned Chaucer portrait and a verse encomium), he also wrote part of a copy of John Gower's *Confessio Amantis.* He was clearly part of an early-fifteenth-century circle of scribes, some of whom also produced manuscripts of Chaucer's poetry. There is some modern scholarly speculation that Hoccleve may, too, have had a role in the revival of Chaucer's reputation itself: that, in the early fifteenth century, he may have been part of a kind of Chaucer circle who assembled and disseminated Chaucer's poetry as part of a larger project of vernacular poetic politics — a way of offering a founding English poet for an English political world, under King Henry V, concerned with making the vernacular a "king's English" in a new and defining way.[36]

Another important figure in Chaucerian production was John Shirley, a scribe and book collector who claimed to have had direct acquaintance with the poet and who, late in life (he died in 1450, probably at the age of ninety) produced about half a dozen manuscripts containing Chaucer's poetry and prose (he wrote out, for example, the only manuscript that attributes the *Boece* by name to Chaucer). Shirley's texts are often oddly spelled. He may be writing from memory, which may explain the differences between his manuscripts and other surviving texts of certain poems. But Shirley's work is valued most of all because he attributes works to Chaucer. His long historical and biographical headnotes to the texts seek to locate their making in particular political or personal circumstances. For example, his copy of the lyric now known as "Lak of Stedfastness" appears in one of his manuscripts with the note that it was written in Chaucer's "laste yeeres." The poem known as "Truth" is titled "Balade that Chaucier made on his deeth bedde."[37] Is any of this information true? Scholars have long recognized that Shirley enhanced the veracity of his productions by locating himself in the Chaucer circle: that, in other words, he sought to place himself in a position of unique knowledge of the circumstances in which certain poems were composed. Perhaps he was in such a position, perhaps not. For anyone who studies Shirley's manuscripts, however, the conclusion reached by Julia Boffey and John J. Thompson is obvious: "Shirley produced a peculiarly random assortment of fragments which might have emerged in roughly associated fashion from the recesses of his memory."[38] To read Shirley's manuscripts, in other words, is to read Shirley. His headnotes to the poems are not designed to construct a canon of Chaucerian production or to locate their origin in object history. Instead, they compose a personal biography, a narrative of Shirley's bibliographic life and memories.

Though much may be unclear about Shirley's world, what is clear is that by his time, a group of texts had come to be associated with Chaucerian authority for little reason other than that there *was* a Chaucerian authority. By the end of the fifteenth century, a body of work we now call the Chaucerian Apocrypha emerged — partly on the belief that any good poem in Middle English must be by Chaucer, and partly on the belief that Chaucer's name would be enough to qualify any poem as good. Such poems as the *Assembly of Ladies, The Flower and the Leaf,* and a collection of proverbial sayings, lyrics, and allegories were included in the manuscripts. Some poems which we now know to be by Lydgate similarly passed under Chaucer's name. Chaucer had become, by the end of the fifteenth century, a writer of simply everything: no genre had escaped his pen, no subject his imagination.

This sense of Chaucer as *the* defining English writer was well established by the time William Caxton, England's first printer, began to publish his works in the late 1470s. An edition of the *Canterbury Tales,* of the *Boece,* of the *House of Fame,* of the *Parlement of Foules,* of *Troilus and Criseyde,* of assorted shorter poems, and then another edition of the *Canterbury Tales* had all issued from Caxton's press by the mid-1480s. Together with the poetry of Lydgate and Gower, Sir Thomas Malory's *Morte D'Arthure,* and other English writings, Caxton's Chaucer helps make up the canon of medieval English literature for early modern readers. Although modern editors have found his texts unreliable, and although he modernized, to some degree, the spelling and the idiom of Chaucer's Middle English, Caxton's publications reveal a new place for Chaucer in the emergent literary culture of early Tudor England. On one hand, they testify to the printer's sense of the market: a taste for English authors, for encyclopedic long works, for varieties of genres, and for blending virtue with delight. On the other hand, they reveal what Chaucer had become for early

English literary history: a founding "father" of poetic form and a linguistic innovator, purging the vernacular of its "rudeness" and "purifying" and "ornamenting" its language with new words from Latin and French.[39]

Caxton's successors — the printers Wynkyn de Worde and Richard Pynson — continued his program of vernacular publication, and they added new Chaucer editions for a buying public. They also came to print the spurious apocryphal texts circulating under Chaucer's name, so that by the time that William Thynne published his *Works of Chaucer* in 1532, it could be touted that this volume contained "dyuers workes whiche were neuer in print before." These early Chaucer editions make fascinating reading for the modern student (they are all available, by now, on Early English Books Online, and there is an excellent facsimile of Thynne's edition, together with materials from other sixteenth-century printings, put together by Derek Brewer). One sees, immediately, how the early English typefaces were modeled on the scribal hands of fifteenth-century manuscripts. The layout of the pages looks remarkably like that of manuscripts, though woodcuts replace hand-drawn illustrations. Thynne's volume is distinguished, in particular, for its important preface (written by the courtier Brian Tuke), dedicating the book to King Henry VIII and, in the process, associating English authorship and English rule. These were popular volumes in their own time. For example, in the 1530s, members of the Howard family copied stanzas out of Thynne's edition into a personal commonplace book (now known as the Devonshire Manuscript) to construct little assemblies of love verse out of Chaucer's lines.[40] There was clearly a market for Chaucer's works, and editions followed quickly in the sixteenth century. The antiquarian and historian John Stowe edited an important edition in 1561 (still with the familiar apocryphal texts, but now also containing some material seen in print for the first time, notably the stanza to "Adam Scriveyn"). Thomas Speght produced what may be the first "scholarly" edition of the poet's work in 1598 (reprinted in 1602 and then again in 1687). Speght offered "arguments" to each of the *Canterbury Tales:* brief summaries and critical assessments. He pared down the apocrypha to seek a volume of the authentically Chaucerian. And he gave readers a glossary and interpretive notes — windows to a literary vocabulary that, by Shakespeare's time, had become opaque to English men and women.

Significantly, all of these editions, right up to that of 1687, print Chaucer's verse in "black letter": the typeface modeled on the older medieval handwriting. Even when the notes and prefatory matter are in roman type (beginning with Speght), and even when roman and italic are used for Latin textual material and titles (as in Stowe), Chaucer's own words are in old type. Clearly, these volumes send a visual signal to their readerships. Chaucer is, quite simply, old. His language is no longer modern. But more than simply age, these typefaces evoke the feel of manuscripts: they visually represent a kind of literary making far from the ken of the late-sixteenth- or seventeenth-century reader. It is not Latin, it is not a modern European vernacular: it is Middle English, and on these printed pages one can see an idea of the "Middle Ages" taking shape for early modern England.

The eighteenth century saw many new editions, too — these now in roman typeface, with new annotations and scholarly materials. Chaucer, in these volumes, now appears on a par with the Greek and Latin classics. His poetry is explicated, his life is explained. He becomes one of the *auctores* of the classic past, an English Virgil or Homer (in fact, this classicizing of Chaucer had already begun in the seventeenth century, when such associations began to be made and attempts to make Chaucer into a classical *auctor* were being tried — perhaps the weirdest of which was Thomas Kynaston's Latin translation of *Troilus and Criseyde* of 1638). By the nineteenth century, the development of historical philology and stemmatic textual criticism had inflected the publishing of Chaucer, now making it an intensely scholarly rather than a purely popular project. Manuscripts came to be available to scholars, in part through the resources of the British Library and the Cambridge University Library, and in part, too, through auctions of the great old noble and aristocratic book collections throughout the late eighteenth and the nineteenth centuries. Late-nineteenth-century scholars such as Frederick Furnivall and Walter W. Skeat were able to produce editions grounded in manuscript research. In the United States, F. N. Robinson edited the *Riverside Chaucer* (first edition, 1933, second edition, 1957), a monument to classic editorial method and historical annotation.[41]

Chaucer's poetry and prose have appeared, then, in many forms. There is no unassailably pure or authoritative text. What we have, instead, is a history of copying and publication. Modern scholars have attempted to produce editions that may reflect a Chaucerian original. But behind all of their editions are aesthetic judgments and technical decisions. To understand Chaucer in history is to understand the history of his texts: their copying, reception, editing, and visual appearance. His is a literature of and in the textual condition: a literature aware of what it means to write and read, and of how the media of literary making may inflect the meaning of our texts and the responses of their audiences.

NOTES

1. Among the resources, the New Chaucer Society publishes *Studies in the Age of Chaucer* annually; each volume has a full bibliography of the previous year's work. Derek Pearsall inaugurated the Harvard Web site for Chaucer studies; there are good, if selec-

tive, bibliographies and summaries of major texts (http://www.courses.fas.harvard.edu/
~chaucer/). The University of Oklahoma Press has been publishing individual volumes
of the *Variorum Chaucer* since the late 1970s. Each volume is devoted to a single *Canterbury Tale,* or group of shorter poems (editions of other poetry have yet to appear), with
complete textual apparatus and reviews of criticism. Students may find bibliographical
and linguistic resources in most Chaucer editions. Further resources for studying Chaucer's language are listed in this introduction's bibliography. The *Chaucer Review* appears
quarterly and is sponsored by the Chaucer Division of the Modern Language Association
of America.

2. Boitani and Mann, eds., *Cambridge Companion to Chaucer,* 2nd ed.; the first edition was published in 1986.

3. Pearsall, *Life of Geoffrey Chaucer;* Brewer, *New Introduction to Chaucer,* 2nd ed.;
Mann, *Geoffrey Chaucer: Feminist Readings;* Wetherbee, *Canterbury Tales.* To this list
one should add the "Oxford Guides to Chaucer," volumes devoted to summaries of plot,
context, and criticism and keyed to the teaching habits and critical environments of late-
twentieth-century British universities: Cooper, *Canterbury Tales;* Windeatt, *Troilus and
Criseyde;* Minnis et al., *Shorter Poems.*

4. See Patterson, *Chaucer and the Subject of History* and *Negotiating the Past;* and
Strohm, *Hochon's Arrow* and *Social Chaucer.* For a review of these developments in the
history of Chaucer criticism and some broader contexts for the shifts in teaching and
writing about Chaucer in the twentieth century, see Ethan Knapp's chapter in this *Companion.*

5. Watson, "Politics of Middle English Writing"; Justice, *Writing and Rebellion;* Copeland, *Pedagogy, Intellectuals, and Dissent.*

6. Watson, "Politics of Middle English Writing," 342.

7. Wallace, *Chaucerian Polity.*

8. Grady, "Chaucer Reading Langland."

9. Fradenburg, *Sacrifice Your Love* and "Wife of Bath's Passing Fancy"; Dinshaw,
Chaucer's Sexual Poetics and *Getting Medieval;* Crane, *Gender and Romance in Chaucer's "Canterbury Tales";* Hansen, *Chaucer and the Fictions of Gender.*

10. There are many accounts of Chaucer's language and the state of English in the
fourteenth century. Standard histories of English include Baugh and Cable, *History of
English,* now in its fifth edition. The *Riverside Chaucer* has a good guide to the grammar,
vocabulary, and pronunciation of Chaucer's poetry, prepared by Norman Davis: "Language and Versification," xxix–xliv. For the history of England as a trilingual country in
the centuries before Chaucer, see Turville-Petre, *England the Nation.*

11. Clark, *Peterborough Chronicle.*

12. See Bennett and Smithers, eds., *Early Middle English Verse and Prose,* l–li.

13. Stanley, ed., *Owl and the Nightingale,* lines 1–2.

14. *Mankind* and *The Second Shepherd's Play,* in Bevington, ed., *Medieval Drama,*
cited by line number in my text.

15. *Rotuli Parliamentorum,* 1362, quoted in Fisher, *Emergence of Standard English,*
161 n.33.

16. I quote from the extract printed in Wogan-Browne et al., eds., *Idea of the Vernacular,* 81.

17. The *OED* calls attention to similar compounds in Old Frisian and Old High German and quotes examples in English from the mid-twelfth century (s.v. "even-Christian").

18. See the ongoing work of Watson, including "Composition of Julian of Norwich's *Revelation of Love*" and "Middle English Mystics."

19. Cannon, *Making of Chaucer's English.*

20. Among the many studies dealing with the history of the book, medieval scribal culture, and the place of English literature in its manuscript environments, the following are the best and most accessible: Griffiths and Pearsall, eds., *Book-Production and Publishing in Britain;* Hanna, *Pursuing History;* and Taylor, "Authors, Scribes, Patrons, and Books."

21. Parkes, *English Cursive Book Hands,* 9.

22. Hanna, "Introduction," in *Pursuing History,* 9.

23. See Huot, *From Song to Book.*

24. Material in this and the following two paragraphs is adapted from my "Medieval English Literature and the Idea of the Anthology."

25. See Pearsall, *Old and Middle English Poetry,* 119–49; Boffey and Thompson, "Anthologies and Miscellanies"; and Turville-Petre, *England the Nation,* 108–41, 181–221.

26. See Huot, *From Song to Book,* 211–41. On the identities of medieval French scribes and their impact on the dissemination of Old French poetry, see Huot, 34–55. For the ambiances of Middle English poetic assemblies, see the discussions in Pearsall, *Old and Middle English Poetry,* 119–49; Turville-Petre, *England the Nation;* and Boffey and Thompson, "Anthologies and Miscellanies."

27. *Paradiso* 33.85–87, quoted and translated in Ahern, "Binding the Book."

28. For chronicles of such transformations, see my *Chaucer and His Readers* and *Courtly Letters in the Age of Henry VIII.*

29. For a complete and detailed account of all the Chaucer manuscripts, see the Textual Notes to the individual poems in the *Riverside Chaucer.*

30. For a good guide to the scholarship on the Ellesmere–Hengwrt debates, see Hanna, "The Hengwrt Manuscript and the Canon of *The Canterbury Tales*," in *Pursuing History,* 140–57. The defining piece of scholarship on the manuscripts of the poem remains Doyle and Parkes, "Production of Copies."

31. Doyle and Parkes, "Production of Copies," 186–92.

32. Hanna, "Hengwrt Manuscript," 141.

33. Hanna, "Hengwrt Manuscript," 143.

34. Linne R. Mooney, "Chaucer's Scribe — On the Discovery of Adam Pinkhurst," paper delivered at the New Chaucer Society Conference, Glasgow, July 2004.

35. The most vociferous advocate for Hengwrt as the basis for a modern edition has been N. F. Blake. See especially his edition, *The Canterbury Tales Edited from the Hengwrt Manuscript.*

36. See Doyle and Parkes, "Production of Copies," and Fisher, "Language Policy for Lancastrian England."

37. For a full discussion of these and other manuscript details, and a larger argument (with bibliography) about Shirley's role in shaping the canon of Chaucer's poetry, see my *Chaucer and His Readers,* 116–46, esp. 128–29.

38. Boffey and Thompson, "Anthologies and Miscellanies," 306 n.43.

39. For more on Caxton, see my "William Caxton" and the important book by Kuskin, *Symbolic Caxton.*

40. For discussion, see my *Courtly Letters in the Age of Henry VIII,* 143–57.

41. For a survey of Chaucer editors and editions, see Ruggiers, ed., *Editing Chaucer.*

PART I

Contexts and Cultures

I

The Lives of Geoffrey Chaucer

CHRISTOPHER CANNON

In the fourteenth century the term "life" meant more or less what it means for us today, "animate existence" (what Chaucer called "an erthly livynge creature," *Legend of Good Women*, F.2118) or a "lifetime" (what Chaucer described as "our present worldes lyves space," *Parliament of Fowls*, line 53), but it also had a particular sense that we have lost. As the equivalent of Latin *vita*, Middle English "lyf" could also refer to the kind of text we now call "saint's life," those accounts of exemplary people whose devotion was particularly marked by sacrifice, miraculous occurrence, or both.[1] The connection was not strict, since other terms could describe such texts (Middle English "passioun" and "legend," for example), but it was also extremely well elaborated from the early part of the thirteenth century by the sheer number of such lives that were written (no other genre in English other than romance existed in such abundance by Chaucer's day).[2] The *Second Nun's Tale* is such a lyf and, before it was absorbed into the plan of the *Canterbury Tales*, Chaucer referred to this text as the "lyf . . . of Seynt Cecile" (*Legend of Good Women*, F.426). But the strength of the convention is best illustrated by those instances in the *Tales* in which the term is employed in order to invert expectations — as when the decidedly unsaintly wife in the *Shipman's Tale* says that, if she had time, she would "telle a legende of my lyf" (7.145) or when the Miller characterizes the bawdy story he is about to tell as "a lyf / Bothe of a carpenter and of his wyf" (1.3141–42). Inherent in even these more casual evocations is the proposition that a lyf is worth writing because the events it describes ought to remain in memory (that they are exemplary, if not in their piety, then in their wit). In this sense, these humorous uses of "lyf" also represent the emergent idea that *any* life could be worthy of textual commemoration.

Although they were not themselves described as "lives," the short biographies of unsuccessful men in Giovanni Boccaccio's *De Casibus Virorum Illustrium* (On the falls of great men, 1358) and the similar biographies of famous women in his *De Claris Mulieribus* (Concerning famous women, 1361) helped to generalize the possible exemplary subjects of Middle English lives.[3] Biographies of illustrious men and women had been a staple of chronicles for a long time, but, even though Boccaccio relied on the Bible for some of his material, the secular premise of the collections — the idea that an impious or merely famous lifetime might be worth knowing — was itself quite new. It is therefore as an aspect of the Monk's worldliness rather than his piety that Chaucer gives him a collection of *de casibus* stories to tell in the *Canterbury Tales* and also why, even as the Monk associates these stories with saints' lives, he is very clear that what recommends them is their unusual drama:

> I wol yow seyn the lyf of Seint Edward;
> Or ellis, first, tragedies wol I telle,
> Of whiche I have an hundred in my celle.
> Tragedie is to seyn a certeyn storie,
> As olde bookes maken us memorie,
> Of hym that stood in greet prosperitiee,
> And is yfallen out of heigh degree
> Into myserie, and endeth wrecchedly. (7.1970–77)

The Monk characterizes such drama as "tragedy," but what he actually offers is a particularly Boethian take on the tragic in which an arbitrary "Fortune" rather than any action of the fallen person causes each disaster, with the result that these lives recommend no set of actions or beliefs (only a stoicism of sufficient hardiness to cope with a cruel world). Chaucer's narratives of famous women are also associated with saints' lives (we now call them the *Legend of Good Women* because this is how the text refers to itself, for example, F.483–84, 549, 557, 579), but whereas this collection is interested in exemplary devotion (women "that weren trewe in lovynge al hire lyves," F.485) it more generally defines goodness as the quality possessed by women who are mistreated by "false men" ("that hem bytraien, / That al hir lyf ne don nat but assayen / How many women they may doon a shame," F.486–88). Such stories are therefore more lurid than moral in their import, and it is probably because they use the pose of exemplarity to teach so little that both the *Monk's Tale* and the *Legend of Good Women* are incomplete, the former as it is dramatically interrupted ("Hoo!," quod the Knyght, "good sire, namoore of this!" 7.2767), the latter because Chaucer seems to have abandoned it (at least nineteen stories are promised but only nine survive). And yet, such lives clearly fed and expanded a popular taste (in the generation after Chaucer, John Lydgate's *Fall of Princes* [1430] extended to 36,365 lines and survives, complete, in thirty-four manuscripts), and Chaucer certainly learned from such stories just how various were the lives a text might choose to remember.[4]

This broadening of the definition of the written "lyf" gave Chaucer the means to choose the kinds of life most immediately familiar to him for commemoration, and, in fact, the life that he chose most often was his own. The result is a set of poems that so frequently take on the attributes of a "life" in the Middle English sense of the word that the corpus of Chaucer's writing can be treated as something approximating a set of such *lives,* textual versions of lived experience that everywhere imply (and thus often exist by means of the illusion) that the experiences they record were actually lived. While Chaucer was still a young writer, other English poets began to experiment with similar modes of autobiography (although the allegories of John Gower [c. 1325–1408] and William Langland [c. 1330–1400] are both abstract and generalizing, they are presented as the personal experiences of particular men). If Chaucer was not the only English poet to be so bold, he was certainly the first and, in the end, the most committed to this literary form. Thus, even if it remains important to point out that every textual version of Chaucer's life is a false front, a "mask" or persona, which conceals as much as it shows (as it has long been common to emphasize in criticism), what we must also account for is the preternatural *strength* of this illusion—the general sense among readers and even the most cautious critics that Chaucer's writing creates a "man whom we feel that we know," a "real and living presence in his works."[5] In fact, from the moment of Chaucer's death (c. 1400) writers were trying to extend even further what Thomas Hoccleve called in his *Regement of Princes* (1412), the "lyflynesse . . . of his persone."[6] In recent centuries, Chaucer biography has become one of the most common modes of approving and valuing Chaucer as a writer.[7]

The various lives of Chaucer can be characterized by coordinating the forms of life Chaucer made in his poems with what can be reconstructed of his own life from the public record. This comparison makes clear that the richness of Chaucer's textual lives derives in large part from social circumstances that had made living unusually available to representation in texts: in Chaucer's period, in fact, texts were such an important instrument of social ambition that poetry was, in effect, no more than a particularly dramatic mode of social aspiration. But Chaucer's poetry was not only distinguished by the lives it traced on his behalf, for in near perfect reciprocity, these lives became a powerfully individualizing force in Chaucer's hands. In fact, these lives were not only what distinguished Chaucer from other people but, even as textual lives grew increasingly common in English poetry, they were what distinguished Chaucer's writing from the writing of others.

Court, Class, and the Speculative Life

Chaucer was born the son of a relatively prosperous merchant, John Chaucer, a London vintner, at a moment (c. 1340) when money was all a young man needed to be sponsored into the ranks of gentlemen.[8] In fact, we first meet Chaucer in the record as he crosses this crucial divide: in a fragment surviving from the household accounts of Elizabeth, Countess of Ulster, he is shown receiving funds in order to buy "livery" (*liberatus*) in the form of a "paltok" (or cloak), black and red hose, and a pair of shoes for Easter celebrations (*L-R*, 14). Although Chaucer's rank is unspecified in this entry or similar accounts, they suggest that he began his courtly service as a *pajettus* (page); by 1359 he is ransomed after capture in France for a sum that makes clear he has attained the rank of *valettus* (yeoman; *L-R*, 23–26); in 1366, his status is sufficient for him to marry Philippa, a lady of the queen's household and daughter of the knight Paon de Roet (*L-R*, 67–70); by 1367 he has been granted a life annuity of twenty marks and has himself moved into the court of Edward III (*L-R*, 123); in 1368 Chaucer is being paid in the royal court as an *esquier* (esquire), that is, at a rank just below that of a knight (*L-R*, 95). Such a rapid rise from relatively humble beginnings was by no means unusual, and yet even these outlines have what will become the characteristic shape of Chaucer's life in texts: although he is present for many momentous events, and although he is everywhere associated with the most powerful people, he is almost always an observer rather than a participant, very firmly at the margins rather than in the center.

Such marginality also characterizes the relationship between the various sorts of textual life Chaucer had in these early years for, although he must have written a great deal of poetry in his youth, no poem from before 1368 can be securely attached to his hand; by the same token, despite nearly five hundred surviving documents or entries referring to Chaucer in the public record, not a single one notes or acknowledges that he wrote poetry.[9] This disconnection is itself unremarkable in a culture in which the "amateur household poet" had only recently "usurped" the role of the "professional minstrel" and the ability to write and recite poetry had therefore become one of the necessary skills of every courtier, that which proved his place in the ranks of the "gentle."[10] In other words, even if Chaucer now has the distinction of being the "first English court poet," in his own time this would have seemed no distinction at all, since, in a courtier, the ability to write poetry was no more than "a useful social asset" unlikely to mark anyone out for "special treatment."[11] Since he had to perform so many other labors each day in his role as a courtier, it is also no surprise that Chaucer should have represented the making of poetry as difficult ("the lyf so short, the craft so long to lerne," *Parliament of Fowls*, line 1) or the product of fevered sleeplessness ("I may nat slepe, . . . I have so many an ydel thought / Purely for defaute of slep," *Book of the Duchess*, lines 3–5) compounded with fatigue:

> In stede of reste and newe thynges
> Thou goost hom to thy hous anoon,
> And, also domb as any stoon,
> Thou sittoot at another book
> Tyl fully daswed ys thy look;
> And lyvest thus as an heremyte,
> Although thyn abstinence ys lyte. (*House of Fame*, lines 654–60)

Such complaint makes clear that Chaucer's public and poetic life were also connected in these early days by the need to maintain social privilege through performance: as someone who could never lay firm claim to the social position he had attained (since, unlike many others in the court, he had not been born a gentleman), Chaucer's status depended on his ability to seem to *belong* to his rank. If the narrators of Chaucer's poems had lives that differed from the life led by the man who created them, in other words, Chaucer would have always had this feeling about his own life—and increasingly so, as his social rank progressively improved.

The proximity of the two kinds of performance also means that Chaucer's early long poems unfold as if they were no more than episodes in a courtier's life: all are narrated in the first person, describe a recent and spectacular dream, and address an audience of familiars (by implication courtiers of Chaucer's station or higher). This pose was conventional in poetry for the very reason that it was appropriate to Chaucer's situation (Chaucer would have learned it from the French *Roman de la Rose,* which he translated, at least in part, some time before 1368), but—Chaucer deployed this convention with characteristic ambition from the start. It is in this sense that the narrator of Chaucer's first original composition of any length, the *Book of the Duchess* (1368), presumes familiarity with John of Gaunt, Earl of Richmond and Duke of Lancaster, probably the most powerful man in England, and also takes up one of the more delicate of matters in Gaunt's life, the death of his young wife, Blanche, Duchess of Lancaster (on 12 September 1368):

> "Allas, sir, how? What may that be?"
> "She ys ded!" "Nay!" "Yis, be my trouthe!"
> "Is that youre los? Be God, hyt ys routhe!"
> (*Book of the Duchess*, lines 1308–10)

Of course it was in the nature of such courtly poetry to ensure that its author was "not directly committed to his work," and it is therefore crucial that it is *not* Chaucer (but a dreamer) who speaks here, that this narrator seems more stupid than brave, and that he speaks, not to someone called "Gaunt," but to a "man in blak" (line 445).[12] If such a structure blunts the force of any social striving, however, it is also typical of Chaucer that such circumspection should have yielded immediate, material results: in 1369 Chaucer turns up in the record as part of John of Gaunt's expeditionary forces in France (*L-R*, 31–32); in 1372 Philippa Chaucer is granted an annuity of ten pounds by Gaunt for services to Constance, Gaunt's second wife (*L-R*, 85–86); in 1374 Chaucer is himself granted a lifetime annuity of ten pounds by Gaunt for his "good service" (la bone et agreable service; *L-R*, 271). Precisely because the relationship between writing and courtly ambition had to look weak where it was most strong if it was to serve the writer's interests, biographers have not tended to believe that Chaucer's success in the court owed much to his capacities as a poet, and yet influence in the opposite direction is clear enough: Chaucer certainly exploited the opportunities courtly service and preferment gave him in order to obtain materials for his poetry. He learned of Dante's *Divine Comedy*, for example, when he was sent in the service of Richard II on a trading mission to Genoa in 1372 (*L-R*, 32–37) and he soon used it as a template for the *House of Fame* (c. 1378). Because his writing shows no awareness of Boccaccio's writings until he uses his *Teseida* (1339–41) as a source for *Palamoun and Arcite* (1380–81; later to become the *Knight's Tale*) and his *Filostrato* (1336–39) as a source for *Troilus and Criseyde* (1381–86), Chaucer must have obtained copies of these works when he was part of the diplomatic mission Richard II sent to Bernabò Visconti (lord of Milan) in 1378 (*L-R*, 54–60).

But Chaucer's poetry reflects his courtly life most strongly where it directly concerns itself with the possibility of — and the methods for — talking one's way up the social scale. In the *Parliament of Fowls* (c. 1380), for example, even though the relationships between different kinds of birds are said to be subject to the rigid dictates of the "noble goddesse Nature" (line 303), her "odre" (line

400) is shown to yield almost immediately to those birds capable of the most articulate self-advocacy:

> Another tersel egle spak anon,
> Of lower kynde, and seyde, "That shal nat be!
> I love hire bet than ye don, by Seint John,
> Or at the leste I love hire as wel as ye,
> And lenger have served hire in my degree;
> And if she shulde have loved for long lovynge,
> To me alone hadde be the guerdonynge." (lines 449–55)

The Eagle here employs the conventional language of courtly service, and the parliament of birds in which he speaks is certainly no vision of an open society. And yet, of the three common models for understanding social structure in Chaucer's day, it is telling that the *Parliament of Fowls* emphasizes neither the most permeable (the broad division of "gentle" and "churl" that Chaucer had traversed at seventeen), nor the most rigid (the theory of the three "estates" of knight, clergy, and plowman), but the most flexible, that infinitely divisible, endlessly partitionable scale of "degree," from the high to the low, which was "pragmatic" enough to recognize that rank based on distinctions of behavior could be earned (or lost) through effort.[13] By the time he wrote the *Parliament of Fowls* Chaucer had advanced himself beyond the more rigid ranks of the court into that more "civil" service where rank more or less *consists* of effort: he had been appointed controller of the wool custom in the port of London in 1374 (*L-R*, 149–50); in 1382 he added the control of the petty custom to this portfolio (*L-R*, 159); in 1386 he was returned as a member of the less avian Parliament in Westminster representing Kent (*L-R*, 364–69). Although it is now commonly believed that "class" is a "historical phenomenon," properly applied in Britain only to the relations that obtain between persons and "productive forces" in capitalism, Chaucer clearly lived at a moment (and in a segment of society) in which capitalism was emergent; it was therefore also possible for him to experience some of the revolutionary possibilities modern class structures provided when they emerged in a hierarchical society.[14] It is certainly as a reflection of such possibilities rather than, say, the Rising of 1381, that, in the *Parliament of Fowls,* Chaucer imagines a social ambition so great that it could amount to political insurgency ("For I wol of myn owene autorite / For commune spede, take on the charge now," lines 506–7). If, like Max Weber, we define class as a set of "life chances" ("possible, and frequent, bases for communal action"), then what Chaucer's steady promotion makes clear is that a courtier in his day could improve his chances through a life of hard work.[15]

It is *as* work, then, that Chaucer's public and poetic life tended to converge most fully, and indeed, the stipulation in Chaucer's appointment to the customs that he "write his records in his own hand" (rotulos suos . . . manu sua propria scribat; *L-R,* 148) means that he probably penned just as many lines as a civil servant as he did as a poet (as Derek Pearsall has remarked, Chaucer's daily work involved so *much* recording that it "might well have stopped a lesser man from writing poetry altogether").[16] Certainly Chaucer tended to represent the process of making poetry not only as difficult to find time for but arduous. This occurs, most famously, in that single exasperated stanza which calls down a "scalle" (rash) upon the head of the unfortunate "Adam Scriveyn," one of the scribes whose "negligence" in copying Chaucer's translation of Boethius's *Consolation of Philosophy* (1381–86) and *Troilus and Criseyde* put Chaucer to the "werk" of *re*-writing them ("so ofte adaye I mot thy werk renewe," line 5). In fact, the connection between literary aspiration and labor is strong enough in Chaucer's mind that he can even describe a text such as *Troilus and Criseyde*—which he is generally keen to place in the abstract realm of "poesye" (5.1790)—as a job of "werk":

> Wherefore I nyl have neither thank ne blame
> Of al this werk, but prey yow mekely,
> Disblameth me if any word be lame,
> For as myn auctour seyde, so sey I. (2.15–18)

Although this is a formulaic expression of modesty, it is weighed down by the size of what it apologizes for ("*al* this werk") and the concomitant sense of the smallness of its component parts (a great number of words). The connection is also made much more forcefully on the one occasion when Chaucer describes English society as a whole, for he chooses to do so in a poem that, as Jill Mann has shown, is fundamentally "about work."[17] Like the narrator of the *Parliament of Fowls,* the narrator of the *General Prologue* to the *Canterbury Tales* promises to set the Canterbury pilgrims in their "degree" (1.40), but he does so by means of an "enumeration of the daily duties of each occupation" unheard of in estates satire, and he also develops a moral vision of the whole of society in which "work as a social experience conditions personality."[18] The Franklin, for example, is a franklin only insofar as he does the kind of things that franklins do:

> At sessions ther was he lord and sire;
> Ful ofte tyme he was knyght of the shire.
> An anlaas and a gipser al of silk
> Heeng at his girdel, whit as morne milk.
> A shirreve hadde he been, and a contour.
> Was nowher swich a worthy vavasour. (1.355–60)

The *General Prologue* nowhere says that a person might alter his degree by changing the nature of his labor, but this possibility is inherent in a social vision that allows each person to be "worthy" of exactly the kind of work he or she performs. To emphasize the extent to which Chaucer's need to work actually distinguished him from those born to higher rank — to characterize him as "a bourgeois addressing his social betters" — is therefore to condescend to him anachronistically, and in fact, Chaucer would have experienced the work he did as a mode of social freedom.[19] When he reached the pinnacle of his career as clerk of the King's Works (*L-R*, 402), a post he held from 1389 to 1391, Chaucer had not only worked his way into the seat of government (in the Palace of Westminster) but, without any university training, secured his position in a "professional clerical bureaucracy."[20] The large favor he had earned placed him on the verge of the aristocracy, and his descendents made good on the opportunity by moving steadily upward: Chaucer's son, Thomas (b. 1367), was promoted by John of Gaunt into an even better marriage than his father, he was not only a member of Parliament but Speaker five times in the Commons, as well as a trusted diplomat of Henry V and, at one point, a member of the council of Henry VI; Chaucer's granddaughter, Alice (Thomas's only issue), married William de la Pole, Earl of Suffolk (later Duke of Suffolk); and Chaucer's great-grandson, John, was created Earl of Lincoln in 1467 and, for a short time, found himself heir presumptive to the throne.[21] These heirs achieved social advancement by the more traditional modes of blood and alliance, but they had access to such aristocratic privilege only because Chaucer had worked so hard. By the time he wrote the *General Prologue* it was what Chaucer had done *with* his life rather than where he had begun or who his father had known that made him as "worthy" as his own Franklin (who, like Chaucer, was also a "knight of the shire" and had served at judicial "sessions" [*L-R*, 375–83]) and, thus, just as free ("franklin" means "freeman").

If we are inclined to think of Chaucer as confined rather than freed by his class now, it is because class remains an important category in twenty-first-century Britain as a limit to, rather than chance for, bettering one's life. But it is also true that class set certain limits for Chaucer as well, and despite his success, he can also be seen to have been acutely conscious of a glass ceiling. This consciousness is best captured in the rhetorical parallel Chaucer creates for it in the *Miller's Tale* (1395–1400) where, after the lively and enthusiastic description of Alisoun's beauty and energy, a sudden scorn cruelly devalues her:

> She was a prymerole, a piggesnye,
> For any lord to leggen in his bedde,
> Or yet for any good yeman to wedde. (1.3268–70)

Although these lines have often been understood as a moment when Chaucer's snobbery got the better of his literary judgment (since the Miller, who is meant to be speaking here, could have no thought of this kind), as someone who himself never had rank above that of a "good yeoman," Chaucer would also have seen himself as the potential subject of such a remark. In fact, since social barriers consist of such sneering (by teaching their object her place, such scorn ensures that she will never even seek to advance her social position), this comment is designed to register the only social force that could restrain some-one with all Alisoun's capacity ("For she was wylde and yong," 1.3225) and optimism ("wynsynge she was, as is a joly colt," 1.3263). The bitterness inher-ent in the abrupt change of tone here cannot be directed at Alisoun, in other words, but at anyone who might make such an observation; its rhetorical violence provides a neat correlative for the real barriers of class that also governed Chaucer's social world.

In fact, in the decade before he wrote the *Miller's Tale,* not only had Chaucer watched many aspiring courtiers like himself put to death by the "Merciless Parliament" of 1388, but he had seen, among these, a writer, Thomas Usk, who had also secured the king's favor through hard work (he was a self-taught scrivener who became the king's sergeant-at-arms).[22] Although he took up literary writing only in his own defense, Usk claims in his *Testament of Love* (1385–86) that he had done nothing worse than tell the "sothe" (truth) of his "conscience" on his "kynges behalfe."[23] A more direct registration of the kind of social disaster Chaucer had every reason to fear is given in the *Manciple's Tale* (1396–1400), which also describes a faithful servant (in this case, a crow) who is put to death as a "traitour" (9.271) for no more than telling the truth to his lord (that Chaucer identified closely with the crow is obvious, for he, too, could "countrefete the speche of every man," 9.134). The public record never shows Chaucer in real danger of this kind, but at precisely the moment Usk blustered forward in his own defense, Chaucer had the wisdom to beat a hasty retreat. Just after things began to look grim for the king and his household in the Parliament of 1386, Chaucer relinquished the house in London he had lived in, by royal favor, since 1374 (*L-R,* 144–47); that December he retired from his positions as controller of the wool and petty customs (*L-R,* 268–69); and he seems to have removed himself at this point to Kent (*L-R,* 364–69). After the Merciless Parliament sat from February to June of 1388 Chaucer also resigned his royal annuities (*L-R,* 336–39). Chaucer did receive his most prestigious and prominent royal appointment in 1389, but this was only after Richard II had firmly regained the upper hand.

Although it is not usually understood in such terms, Chaucer can actually be seen to crash right into the glass ceiling himself in a deed of 1 May 1380 in which he is released from all culpability in the *raptus,* or rape, of Cecily Chaumpaigne (*L-R,* 341). As Derek Pearsall delicately puts the point, this document "has been something of a problem for Chaucer biographers" since it came to light in 1873, but in fact, few have extended themselves further than their own sexism in trying to explain it ("that [Chaucer] seduced Cecily we may well believe") even as the relentless attempt to mistranslate *raptus* as "abduction" has never managed to make its contents go away (this remains "the one biographical fact everyone remembers about Chaucer").[24] Many have wished to emphasize Chaucer's absolution from all culpability in the release, but the gravity of the matter is itself measured in the public record by the considerable sum (ten pounds) Chaucer paid Chaumpaigne in July 1380 (*L-R,* 344–45), as well as the trouble he clearly had coming up with a payment that was equivalent to the price of a house (*L-R,* 1–2, 49, 59–60, 77, 274, 319–20). Although it is also true that we will never know what event prompted the release, the resulting uncertainty cannot itself be evidence that this might not have been a case of rape (as it has also so often been argued), for uncertainty of this kind *defines* rape as a crime: both now and in the fourteenth century, what the law must discover to convict someone of rape is not that there was an act of sex (accuser and accused often agree that sex occurred) but that the accuser did not consent to this act at the time (what is at issue, in short, is a past — hence, vanished — state of *mind*). It may seem to be a different sort of trivialization to say that such a crime could ever be understood as a misappropriation of social degree (that rape could be punished as if it were a perpetrator's misplaced sense of entitlement), but feminism has taught us in recent decades that it is both legally and ethically helpful to victims to understand rape as an issue of social power rather than of sex; moreover, in Chaucer's day, where the law did not make prosecutions of rape at all easy, the only language available for describing power imbalances of this kind was the language of class.[25]

This is why Chaumpaigne made Chaucer *pay* for whatever he had the temerity to do to her (in this way striking at the foundations of his social degree), and this is also why Chaucer generally wrote about even good relationships between men and women as if they involved class distinctions (so even the egalitarian Arveragus in the *Franklin's Tale* is said to have "swich lordshipe as men han over hir wyves," 5.742). This is also why Chaucer provides the most precise textual version of what rape would have meant both to him (if he committed such a crime) and Chaumpaigne (if she was his victim) when he represents sexual violence as a manifestation of class insolence, what happens when a man feels so socially advantaged that, as in the first lines of the *Wife of Bath's Tale,* he can simply "take" a woman he fancies:

> And so bifel that this kyng Arthour
> Hadde in his hous a lusty bacheler,
> That on a day cam ridynge fro ryver,
> And happed that, allone as he was born,
> He saugh a mayde walkynge hym biforn,
> Of which mayde anon, maugree hir heed,
> By verray force, he rafte hire maydenhed. (3.882–88)

Cecily Chaumpaigne's degree was probably inferior to Chaucer's (she was the daughter of a London baker), but at issue is not their real social relationship but the one Chaucer erroneously construed for them by means of a particular action: that action finally warranted the name *raptus* because, to precisely the extent that what Chaucer did seemed right and proper to him, it was an unmitigated outrage to Chaumpaigne. It is in this sense that the Chaumpaigne release also punished Chaucer by insisting that he acknowledge his true status, forcing him to recruit men of much higher social rank in his defense (the document's witnesses include Sir John Philipot, collector of the wool customs when Chaucer was controller, Sir William de Neville and Sir John de Clanvowe, knights of the king's chamber, and Richard Morel, a member of the Grocer's Company; *L-R,* 343–47). It is also in this sense that Chaucer imagines justice being done in the *Wife of Bath's Tale* only when its overentitled "bacheler" agrees that he is socially inferior to his wife (by granting her "maistrie," 3.1236).

As the more sensational nature of this last set of observations will suggest to all readers, connections between lived and textual lives are always conjectural. Especially where the poetic record seems to bring lived experience into most vivid focus, our account is probably falling foul of what George Kane called the "autobiographical fallacy," the belief that the "speculative lives" of narrators and characters have some "historical necessity."[26] And yet, as Kane also made clear, it is particularly true of the kinds of life made by Chaucer and his most important Middle English contemporaries that they offer the strongest possible invitations to such error. Not only do Chaucer's narrators present dream visions as if they were a personal experience, but when they name themselves, these narrators turn out to be called "Geffrey" (*House of Fame,* line 729). Even though the narrator of John Gower's *Confessio Amantis* (1390–93) moves through an allegorical world inhabited by aspects of his own psyche ("Genius") as well as celestial gods (Venus), he is finally known by both of Gower's names:

> Whan I behield and sodeinly
> I sih wher Venus stod me by.

> So as I myhte, under a tre
> To grounde I fell upon mi kne,
> And preide hire forto do me grace:
> Sche caste hire chiere upon mi face,
> And as it were halvinge a game
> Sche axeth me what is mi name.
> "Ma dame," I seide, "John Gower." (*Confessio Amantis*, 8.2313–21)

The conflation of position was in fact so basic to literary making in this period
that a writer such as William Langland represented his efforts as a "never-
ending process" rather than a "finite production," not a book but the "labour"
that comprised the whole of a life:[27]

> When y ʒong was, many ʒer hennes,
> My fader and my frendes foende me to scole,
> Tyl y wyste witterly what holy writ menede
> And what is beste for the body, as the boek telleth,
> And sykerost for þe soule, by so y wol contenue.
> And foend y nere, in fayth, seth my frendes deyede,
> Lyf þat me lykede but In this longe clothes
> And yf y be labour sholde lyuen and lyflode deseruen,
> That laboure þat y lerned beste þerwith lyuen y sholde.[28]

Although the self-defense offered in these lines is immediately followed by
specifications suggesting that this narrator's real labor consists of saying prayers for people ("This y segge for here soules of suche as me helpeth"),[29] the
allegory in which such facts are provided necessarily conflates the whole of
Piers Plowman with spiritual work. Indeed, the conflation is so basic to this
poem that its narrator not only is named "Will" but describes his life in such a
way as to transform the manner of its living into an acrostic signature ("I have
lyved in londe," quod I, "my name is Longe Wille").[30]

Because they become so basic to the texts of which they are a part, it might
even be said that such lives gain a certain substance to the extent that they *are*
"speculative," that, insofar as they correspond to no lived experience these
lives *only* exist in texts. In Chaucer's case, then, it is not so much the richness of
the public record as its suggestiveness (in relation, say, to the *raptus* of Cecily
Chaumpaigne) or its more startling absences (failing ever to note, for example,
that Chaucer was a poet) that help most in the elaboration of the lives that
seem to fill his poems. Social degree in Chaucer's period helped to elaborate
such lives by providing a vocabulary of roles and positions that could be easily
recruited for such speculation. That is, in a period in which lived experience
unfolded itself by means of fixed positions (what Derek Brewer has character-

ized as "the rungs of a ladder") but where the quantity and extent of social climbing made it possible to move *between* those positions (thereby making those rungs both vivid and visible), it is possible to evoke or imagine a whole social world with reference to no more than a particular "degree" ("franklin," for example).[31] For Chaucer, then, it was not only the literary forms he took as his sources (in, say, Boccaccio) or may have seen in contemporary English writers (such as Gower and Langland) that helped him in the creation of textual lives but the very form of the society from which such lives were drawn. Chaucer lived at a moment, in other words, when speculative lives *had* historical necessity.

The Individual and the Public Poet

As I suggested at the beginning of this chapter, there is a second way to understand Chaucer's life and writing that does not negate the account I have so far given, but rather than emphasizing the conventional nature of Chaucer's textual lives, finds in them something both rare and new. This view also looks to Chaucer's court and class for the life chances they generally provided, and it understands the various lives Chaucer wrote to be a function of this grid, but it also emphasizes the unique shape that was traced by Chaucer's particular — and extraordinary — movements. Here, there is not merely movement along a social scale but a new social identity; there are not public and poetic lives to be contrasted (the one kind encouraging the speculation that produces the other) but a new occupation that merges the two (a job to which Chaucer, like us, would have given the name "poet").[32]

Crucial to the shaping of this new kind of life was a fourth view of medieval society that allowed for such innovation. This view was as common in Chaucer's day as the three theories of class so far mentioned — the distinction between "churl" and "gentleman," the theory of three estates, and the ladder of "degree" — but it left scope for individual action by understanding society as nonhierarchical, "composed of interdependent parts," "a site for the active reconciliation of diverse . . . interests."[33] Since it is "full of hierarchical systems, but . . . also full of contradictions which negate them," the *Parliament of Fowls* also neatly illustrates this theory.[34] Although the birds in this parliament are, as I have said, finally organized by a scheme "analogous to human classes," the poem's dreamer is first allowed to survey a natural environment organized "in terms of function," where difference actually produces a vision of perfect equality since each tree, for example, is like every other tree in having a particular use:[35]

The byldere ok, and ek the hardy asshe;
The piler elm, the cofre unto carayne;
The boxtre pipere, holm to whippes lashe;
The saylynge fyr; the cipresse, deth to playne;
The shetere ew; the asp for shaftes pleyne;
The olyve of pes, and eke the dronke vyne;
The victor palm, the laurer to devyne. (*Parliament of Fowls,* lines 176–82)

Detailed historical accounts of thirteenth- and fourteenth-century English society have also made clear that this was a real rather than a hopeful vision,
particularly for the "middle strata" where there were no "sharp edges of contrast" between social degrees.[36] In fact, the "merchant class" was itself distinctive in this period for having customs that actually "fostered ambition" and
the son of a merchant (such as Chaucer) was generally impelled "toward goals
that were not his father's."[37] Such circumstances led quite naturally to the view
that a person's rank in society owed nothing to his birth or achieved "degree"
and everything to the nature of his accomplishments, a view that Chaucer
devoted the whole of the poem *Gentilesse* to describing ("For unto vertu
longeth dignitee / And noght the revers," lines 4–5), and also set out in the
long speech given by the old woman to the knight in the *Wife of Bath's Tale:*

Looke who that is moost virtuous alway,
Pryvee and apert, and moost entendeth ay
To do the gentil dedes that he kan;
Taak hym for the grettest gentil man. (3.1113–16)

Because such valuations only applied to the society's middle, the glass ceiling I
have described must still be acknowledged in this view ("once he had entered
the lesser gentry a man's further efforts to rise encountered the full pressure of
conservative opinion"),[38] and yet it certainly helped Chaucer's sense of the
causal relation between "dedes" and social status that even kingship in this
period was subject to such evaluation: where even the king's performance
could be found wanting by powerful aristocrats (as it was from 1386 to 1389)
then every social position is vulnerable to individual action (as was proved
conclusively when Henry Bolingbrook deposed Richard II in 1399).

As the king's misfortunes also proved, Chaucer's position in the "turbulent
and ill-defined middle ranks of society" could be precarious, but that very vulnerability also made his position "more than ordinarily ambiguous," allowing
him to remain firmly on the ladder of degree, but mobile along quite a long area
of its length.[39] However much lower Chaucer's rank may have been than a
knight's, for example, he could still presume sufficient intimacy with Sir Philip

de la Vache to commiserate with him in his "wrecchednesse" (*Truth*, line 22) even as he warned him about the dangers of social climbing ("For hord hath hate, and climbing tickelnesse," line 3). He could also address a particularly rancid account of "the sorwe and wo that is in mariage" to Sir Peter Bukton (*Lenvoy de Chaucer a Bukton*, line 6) without fear of giving offense to Bukton or his potential spouse ("I wol nat seyn how that yt is the cheyne / Of Sathanas," lines 9–10). Chaucer's social position was finally supple enough for him for him to address a poem such as *Troilus and Criseyde* to peers such as John Gower and the Oxford logician Ralph Strode ("O moral Gower, this book I directe / To the and to the, philosophical Strode," 5.1856–57) as well Queen Anne herself ("Right as oure firste lettre is now an A," 1.171). Most important, however, this flexibility of position allowed Chaucer to shrug off even the most violent encounters with social limits by seeming to capitulate to his betters even as he forcefully exerted his own will. Such complexities can be particularly well observed in the *Legend of Good Women* (1386–87), Chaucer's last and most expansive dream vision, where the poem's narrator is accused of having committed a grave sin against courtliness by having "translated the Romaunce of the Rose" (F.329) and making "men to women lasse triste" by telling the story "of Criseyde" (F.332–33). Since the *Legend*'s charges are leveled by an autocratic "kyng" (F.431), and the poem presents itself as a royal commission (to be presented to "the queen . . . at Eltham or at Sheene," F.496–97), the scene suggests that Chaucer had incurred royal displeasure (as James Simpson has observed, the poem's *Prologue* describes the courtly author's nightmare, a "tyrannical and potentially violent environment" in which an "authorial will" is "suppressed" by an "imperious patron").[40] And yet, while the *Legend*'s narrator seems to be on the back foot even after Alceste has stepped in to defend him, the defense Chaucer writes for Alceste provides the occasion for a surprisingly assertive self-defense in the form of the first life of Geoffrey Chaucer ever written:

> He made the book that hight the Hous of Fame,
> And eke the Deeth of Blaunche the Duchesse,
> And the Parlement of Foules, as I gesse,
> And al the love of Palamon and Arcite
> Of Thebes, thogh the storye is knowen lyte;
> And many an ympne for your halydayes,
> That highten balades, roundels, virelayes;
> And for to speke of other holynesse,
> He hath in prose transated Boece,
> And maad the lyf also of Seynt Cecile.
> He made also, gon is a gret while,
> Origenes upon the Maudeleyne. (F.417–28)

Except for works that Alceste has already mentioned (the translation of the *Romance of the Rose,* the poem "of Creseyde"), this account is complete enough to include at least one work we now believe we have lost ("Orygenes upon the Maudeleyne"), and that comprehensiveness makes this an important biography of Chaucer in its own right. Although Chaucer represents his narrator (now fully conflated with himself) as in mortal danger from aristocratic displeasure (according to the *Prologue,* this narrator must now write a "legende" [F.549] of "goode wommen" [F.560] upon pain of his "lyf" [F.548]), Chaucer's very freedom is demonstrated in the way he parlays such vulnerability into an opportunity to insist on his paramount importance *as* a writer.

Since the stories that comprised the *Legend* were all chosen for their similar contours, they were themselves a surprisingly coarse instrument for commemorating lives (their very narrative homogeneity tended to render the extraordinary banal), and this inadequacy is almost certainly what caused Chaucer to abandon the project before it was complete. Chaucer had already begun to remove himself from public life when he began the *Legend* (by resigning his posts at customs in 1386), and the abandonment of the *Legend* coincides with an even more complete withdrawal (the resigning of his annuities in 1388). As I have suggested, political prudence would have formed the basis for these resignations, but there were other, more personal reasons for taking stock at this point in Chaucer's life (in particular, the death of his wife, Philippa, in 1387).[41] Even though Chaucer returned to a prominent position in the civil service from 1389 to 1391 (as clerk of the King's Works), the posture of the *Legend* and the circumstances of its writing also set the terms for most of Chaucer's remaining work-life: from 1391–1400, having firmly put aside all public labor, Chaucer lived his life *only* as a writer. Key to this change was the imagining of a social role in which this kind of activity was valuable; the view held by all of Chaucer's early narrators that writing was no more than a social accoutrement (a way of securing one's position as a courtier) had to be replaced by the view (first advanced in the *Prologue* of the *Legend*) that writing poetry was an end in itself. Rather than speak only of "the mode of living and personal values associated with the noble estate" ("Tho was I war of Plesaunce . . . And of Aray, and Lust, and Curteysie," *Parliament of Fowls,* lines 218–19) Chaucer's poetry now had to expand its subject to include the "entire community" ("To tell yow al the condicion / Of ech of hem . . . And whiche they weren, and of what degree," 1.38–40); rather than as a mode of entertainment defined by a particular "relation of speaker to audience" ("ye loveres . . . for me preieth . . . That I have myght to shewe . . . Swich peyne and wo as Loves folk endure," *Troilus and Criseyde,* 1.22–34), this poetry now had take this relation as its "subject" ("and after wol I telle of our viage / And all the remenaunt of oure pilgrimage," 1.723–24).[42] The text in which this new role was fully described as well as extensively pursued was the *Canterbury Tales*; and even though its scheme allowed Chaucer to incorporate earlier work into a larger frame (allowing *Palamon and Arcite* to become the *Knight's Tale* and the "lyf . . . of Seynt Cecile" to become the *Second Nun's Tale*), the composition of this collection seems to have been Chaucer's principal occupation throughout the 1390s. Other poets of the middle stratum such as John Gower and William Langland were also instrumental in elaborating this new occupation in their poetry, but the innovation is not only more marked in Chaucer's career (where there was also a rich body of more courtly poetry for the *Tales* to define themselves against) but more complete (since Chaucer had had such an extensive public life to abandon in favor of poetry as a different sort of public endeavor).

The narrator of the *Canterbury Tales* is not altogether different from the courtly narrator of the dream visions: even if he now inhabits real places (an inn in Southwark, the road between London and Canterbury) and has much more plausible social encounters (talking with fellow travelers on pilgrimage to the shrine of Thomas à Becket), he still has the courtier's ethical agility ("And I seyde his opinion was good," 1.183), and like any wise servant, he is always concerned to evade notice (as the Host observes, "Thou lookest as thou woldest fynde an hare, / For evere upon the ground I se thee stare," 7.696–97). But it is also true that the *Canterbury Tales* is a poem particularly rich in techniques for transforming the broad outlines of typical figures such as this into "an extraordinarily vivid *impression* of their existence as individuals."[43] These techniques are most fully on view in the portraits of the pilgrims in the *General Prologue,* but the same techniques are used to give the narrator an unusual vivacity throughout the frame narrative of the *Tales:* like each pilgrim, this narrator "calls forth contradictory responses" (as he is ridiculous in the *Tale of Sir Thopas* and sagacious in the *Tale of Melibee*), he leaves us "uncertain of the 'facts' that lie behind [his] social or professional façad[e]" ("he semeth elvyssh by his contenaunce," 7.703); he is not an abstraction "but affected by time" ("on a day, / In Southwerk at the Tabard as I lay / Redy to wenden on my pilgrymage," 1.19–21); and his responses outline a "point of view" of sufficient strength to give us a "sense of . . . independent life" ("the Millere is a cherl; ye know wel this," 1.3182).[44] The *Canterbury Tales* is about many things other than this narrator of course — it is in fact a poem so teeming with varieties of experience that it could hardly be equated with any individual life — and yet, in a gesture so beguiling that we want to miss it (and so subtle that most readers do), the narrator of the *Tales* retreats from view only in such a way as to make his textual life equivalent to every life he describes. He insists, in other words, that his character actually consists of "every word" of the Canterbury pilgrims *other* than himself:

> But first I pray yow, of youre curteisye,
> That ye n'arette it nat my vileynye,
> Thogh that I pleynly speke in this mateere,
> To telle yow hir wordes and hir cheere,
> Ne thogh I speke hir wordes proprely.
> For this ye knowen al so wel as I:
> Whoso shal telle a tale after a man,
> He moot reherce as ny as evere he kan
> Everich a word, if it be in his charge,
> Al speke he never so rudeliche and large,
> Or ellis he moote telle his tale untrewe,
> Or feyne thng, or fynde wordes newe. (1.725–36)

It is no accident that just before this promise to "speke" the "wordes properly" of every man this narrator has claimed to present the pilgrims according to their "estaat" (1.718) and that, just following these same words, he apologizes for *not* having "set folk in hir degree" (1.744), for this extraordinary figure is hard to see, not because he has fallen beneath our notice, but because he has become as large as the society he surveys. As Anne Middleton has put this point, it is not that this narrator is "chameleon-like," endorsing "whatever hobbyhorse his fellow travelers happen to be riding" (as he has so often been said to be) but that he "occupies the whole field of moral vision spanned by the several views of all the pilgrims"; he is, in this sense, "strech[ed] to the point of transparency."[45] Such a figure does not see social "degree" because he is constituted by the whole social world, and he is also in this sense differentiated — made unique — by his capacity for such expansiveness. He is a distinct individual, defined by the breadth of his social vision (the generosity of his attention to all of life's possible chances), *as* that vision has been contracted into the span of a single life.

Because of its particularity, this vision is not only Chaucer's narrator's, it is his own, and so the textual life in which it is lodged in the *Canterbury Tales* is as close an approximation to the life Chaucer lived outside of this poem as we probably could have. Obviously there were also many (and enormous) differences between the experiences Chaucer had and the experiences he was able to attribute to this narrator, and since Talbot Donaldson explained the importance of this distinction some decades ago, Chaucer criticism has been keen to insist on it.[46] But it is also a defining attribute of the kind of textual life Chaucer managed to invent for the *Tales'* narrator that insisting on this distinction also becomes a way of narrowing the gap even further. Thus, in the

Introduction to the Man of Law's Tale (a part of the *Tales* some have thought was Chaucer's first attempt at a prologue for the whole of the collection), the Man of Law provides a second biography of Chaucer, complaining that his tale-telling task has been made extremely difficult by Chaucer's prolific (if inept) productivity:

> I kan right now no thrifty tale seyn
> That Chaucer, thogh he kan but lewedly
> On metres and on rymyng craftily,
> Hath seyd hem in swich Englissh as he kan
> Of olde tyme, as knoweth many a man;
> And if he have noght seyd hem, leve brother,
> In o book, he hath seyd hem in another.
> For he hath toold of loveris up and doun
> Mo than Ovide made of mencioun
> In his Episteles, that been ful olde.
> What sholde I tellen hem, syn they been tolde?
>   In youthe he made of Ceys and Alcione,
> And sitthen hath he spoken of everichone,
> Thise noble wyves and thise loveris eke.
> Whoso that wole his large volume seke,
> Cleped the Seintes Legende of Cupide. (2.46–61)

The Man of Law goes on from here to describe many of the narratives that now comprise the *Legend of Good Women* along with other similar stories (perhaps lost items of the *Legend*), in this way simply filling in what had happened in Chaucer's career after the biography Alceste provided earlier. This life also bears traits of the old courtly modesty ("Chaucer . . . kan but lewedly"), although the defensive posture of the *Legend* is now gone and, in the more complex fiction of the *Tales,* self-assertion is now easily deflected into someone else's grudging praise ("if he have noght seyd hem, leve brother, / In o book, he hath seyd hem in another"); this new résumé also continues to insist that the work of writing is worth doing. But, as this biography equates Chaucer's life with such work — a progress from "youth," when he "made Ceys and Alcione" (what we now call the *Book of the Duchess*) to "sitthen," when he wrote the "Seintes Legende of Cupide" (or the *Legend of Good Women*) — it begins to understand poetry as an activity that can *make* a life unique, a "lyf" (in the strictest sense of that Middle English word) worthy of textual memory because it was itself lived in and by means of texts. Finally, in other words, even the life Chaucer led *outside* of his writing is individualized by that writing.

In his last years Chaucer certainly continued to write, but he also seems to have begun to think about the end of his life when he leased a tenement in the garden of the Lady Chapel of Westminster Abbey on 24 December 1399 (*L-R,* 535–40): among the privileges commonly granted to such tenants was burial in the abbey, and since the abbey had become the customary burial place of faithful royal officials, Chaucer was again securing his position by dint of shrewd effort.[47] It was at precisely this point, moreover, that Chaucer had to execute one of his more delicate social maneuvers in order to protect himself, since with the deposition of Richard II (in September 1399) he had not only lost his most powerful patron but was at least potentially aligned with the wrong side in a monumental power struggle. The short poem now called the *Complaint of Chaucer to His Purse* shows how Chaucer put everything right, for even as it begs Henry IV for the continuation of financial support, it insists that Henry has an absolute, and threefold, right to the English throne (that he is "verray kyng" as "conquerour of Brutes Albyon," "by lyne" and through "free eleccion," lines 22–24). Chaucer's annuity was duly received from the new king (*L-R,* 525–28), although he died quite soon afterward (Chaucer receives a payment on 5 June 1400, and then the public record goes silent; *L-R,* 54/), and yet this was still not the end. In 1556 Chaucer's remains were moved from under the pavement of the south transept of the abbey, where they were first buried, to a much more elaborate and prominent altar tomb, and the elaborately inscribed pieties on the new tomb show that this was done because Chaucer's textual life was ongoing:[48]

> Non tamen extincto corpore fama perit
> Viuet ineternum, viuent dum scripta poete.
>
> Yet even when the body is dead fame does not perish. It will live forever, as long as the poets' writings live.[49]

These words are part of a poem by Stephen Surigonus that claims to have been commissioned by William Caxton so that the "illustrious poet Chaucer . . . should live" (viuere . . . Chaucer clare poeta) not only in this "eulogy" (laudes) but in the "works" (opuscula) Caxton had so assiduously and successfully "printed" (compressit . . . formis).[50]

Caxton's attitude remains our own, since we continue to see Chaucer's writing as vivacious and measure Chaucer's achievement by commemorating the life we find in it, but it is therefore also crucial that we recognize such a conflation as Chaucer's idea in the first place. The *Retraction* is the key text here, for it seems to look back on the whole of Chaucer's life from the very boundary between life and death. It is always printed as Chaucer's last word in the *Canterbury Tales,* a coda to the *Parson's Tale* and a straightforward response to that text's lengthy insistence that eternal "lyf" may be purchased "by deeth and the mortificacion of synne" (10.1076–80). It is, in substance, a prayer to Christ for forgiveness, naming certain sins, with other good works entered in mitigation, yet it is also, in form, a list of texts, some of which are equated with good deeds, some with bad, but the sum of which transform the whole of Chaucer's lived experience into writing:

> Wherefore I biseke yow meekly, for the mercy of God, that ye preye for me that Crist have mercy on me and foryeve me my giltes; and namely of my translacions and enditynges of worldly vanitees, the whiche I revoke in my retracciouns: as is the book of Troilus; the book also of Fame; the book of the XXV Ladies; the book of the Duchesse; the book of Seint Valentynes day of the Parlement of Briddes; the tales of Caunterbury, thilke that sownen into synne; the book of the Leoun; and many another book if they were in my remembrance, and many a song and many a leccherous lay, that Crist for his grete mercy foryeve me the synne. But of the translacion of Boece de Consola-cione, and othere bookes of legendes of seintes, and omelies, and moralitee, and devocioun, that thanke I oure Lord Jhesu Crist and his blisful Mooder, and alle the seintes of hevene, bisekynge hem that they from hennes forth unto my lyves ende sende me grace to biwayle my giltes and to studie to the sal-vacioun of my soule. (10.1080–89)

This list of works is also full enough to tell us things we would not otherwise know about Chaucer's career (that he may have written twenty-five "leg-endes" in the *Legend of Good Women,* for example, or that he wrote a text called the *Book of the Lion,* now lost), but what it tells us most clearly is that Chaucer's final aspiration — in this case fully transcending any field we might call "social" — was to be, not just a poet, but poetry. The *Canterbury Tales* remains so variously incomplete that it is almost certain that Chaucer died with no opportunity to make an end to his literary affairs. And yet, in the *Retraction,* Chaucer had already fashioned the end of his life by writing the conclusion to his lyf, in this way, as in so many others, conflating lived and written experience so thoroughly that even now we have trouble telling the difference.

NOTES

1. On Middle English "lyf," see Strohm, "Middle English Narrative Genres," esp. 380, and Strohm, *"Passioun, Lyf, Miracle, Legende,"* esp. 155–58. See also *MED,* s.v. "lif" 5d.

2. An enormous collection of such lives, usually called the *South English Legendary,* was in existence from the beginning of the fourteenth century (it also survives in more than fifty manuscripts). See Boffey, "Middle English Lives," esp. 618–20.

3. See Boffey, "Middle English Lives," 617–19.

4. See Pearsall, *John Lydgate,* 250–51.

5. Howard, "Chaucer the Man," 337.

6. Hoccleve, *Regiment of Princes,* lines 4993–95.

7. The modern era of Chaucer biography was inaugurated in 1598 by Thomas Speght (see his "Chaucer's Life"). Other important biographies of Chaucer include Godwin, *Life of Geoffrey Chaucer* (1803); Lounsbury, *Studies in Chaucer* (1892); "Life of Chaucer" in *Complete Works,* ed. Skeat (1894); Hulbert, *Chaucer's Official Life* (1912); Chesterton, *Chaucer* (1932); Lowes, *Geoffrey Chaucer* (1934); Brewer, *Chaucer* (1953); Gardner, *Life and Times of Chaucer* (1977); Howard, *Chaucer* (1987); and Pearsall, *Life of Geoffrey Chaucer* (1992). The last of these is the most authoritative, and although I have cited it throughout this chapter wherever I have drawn directly on its observations, it has served as an invaluable general guide.

8. Crow and Olson, eds., *Chaucer Life-Records,* 1–2. Subsequent citations to this volume are by page number in my text and the abbreviation *L-R.*

9. Much of this early poetry must have been in French, and some texts that might be by Chaucer (they are attributed in their manuscript to "Ch.") survive. See Wimsatt, *Chaucer and the Poems of "Ch."*

10. Green, *Poets and Princepleasers,* 103.

11. Green, *Poets and Princepleasers,* 101 ("first") and 127 ("useful" and "special").

12. Burrow, *Ricardian Poetry,* 39.

13. Brewer, "Class Distinction in Chaucer," 197

14. Thompson, *Making of the English Working Class,* 9–10. For the strong argument that the concept of class must be linked directly to capitalism see Lukács, *History and Class Consciousness,* 55.

15. Weber, *From Max Weber,* 181.

16. Pearsall, *Life of Geoffrey Chaucer,* 180.

17. Mann, *Chaucer and Medieval Estates Satire,* 202.

18. Mann, *Chaucer and Medieval Estates Satire,* 15 ("enumeration") and 202 ("work").

19. Howard, "Chaucer the Man," 342.

20. Pearsall, *Life of Geoffrey Chaucer,* 210.

21. On Chaucer's descendents generally, see Pearsall, *Life of Geoffrey Chaucer,* 276–84.

22. On Usk at this moment (and in relation to Chaucer), see Strohm, "Politics and Poetics," 85–90 (on "Usk's career") and 97–106 (on Usk's advancement through writing).

23. Usk, *Testament of Love,* 1.6.627–28.

24. Pearsall, *Life of Geoffrey Chaucer,* 136; Plucknett, "Chaucer's Escapade," 35 ("seduced"); Dinshaw, *Chaucer's Sexual Poetics,* 10 ("one biographical fact").

25. On these issues generally, see Cannon, "Chaucer and Rape," 67–92.

26. Kane, *Autobiographical Fallacy,* 17.

27. Middleton, "Idea of Public Poetry," 103.

28. Langland, *Piers Plowman* (C-text), ed. Pearsall, 5.35–43. Subsequent quotations from the C-text are taken from this edition and cited by passus and line number in the text.

29. Langland, *Piers Plowman* (C-text), ed. Pearsall, 5.48.

30. Langland, *Piers Plowman* (B-text), ed. Schmidt, 15.152. See Middleton, "William Langland's 'Kynde Name,' " esp. 79–82 (for an appendix listing and analyzing Langland's many modes of signature). The identification may, of course, go the other way. and

"William Langland" may be the name adopted by a writer who was passionately interested in writing about the journeys of the human "will" (and its "long" life in the "land").

31. Brewer, "Class Distinction in Chaucer," 293.

32. See *MED,* s.v. "poete" n., and *Book of the Duchess,* line 54; *House of Fame,* lines 1483 and 1489; and *Canterbury Tales,* 3.1125, 4.31, 6.1732, and 7.1496 and 2460.

33. Strohm, *Social Chaucer,* 146–47.

34. Spearing, "'Al This Mene I Be Love,'" 175.

35. Spearing, "'Al This Mene I Be Love,'" 176.

36. Thrupp, *Merchant Class of Medieval London,* 314.

37. Thrupp, *Merchant Class of Medieval London,* 311.

38. Thrupp, *Merchant Class of Medieval London,* 309.

39. Strohm, *Social Chaucer,* 10–11.

40. Simpson, "Ethics and Interpretation," 83–84.

41. Pearsall, *Life of Geoffrey Chaucer,* 142–43.

42. Middleton, "Idea of Public Poetry," 98.

43. Mann, *Chaucer and Medieval Estates Satire,* 16. Emphasis Mann's.

44. Mann, *Chaucer and Medieval Estates Satire,* 189.

45. Middleton, "Public Poetry," 99.

46. See Donaldson, "Chaucer the Pilgrim."

47. Pearsall, "Chaucer's Tomb," esp. 52–53.

48. Pearsall, "Chaucer's Tomb," 54 and 59–60.

49. Text and translation taken from Brewer, ed., *Chaucer: The Critical Heritage,* 2:78–79.

50. Brewer, ed., *Chaucer: The Criticial Heritage,* 2:79.

Chaucer as a European Writer

JAMES SIMPSON

Chaucer became a European writer by, paradoxically, becoming an English writer. The sense of this paradox can be understood only by looking first to what might be called Chaucer's cultural and literary geography as he began his writing career. Chaucer's England and his English were "places" of lesser cultural significance and authority than their continental competitors. To enter the company of European poetic making, Chaucer's challenge was first to elevate English itself into a medium fit for making on a European scale. Even as he elevates the lesser category of English, however, Chaucer continues to give voice to the values of the "lesser" entity. He does so principally, though not exclusively, by drawing on the resources of Ovid, the great poet of the "lesser" and the belated. As Chaucer engages with French and especially Italian writing across his career, he maintains an Ovidian point of view. I begin by considering the challenges posed by Chaucer's place in space.

Chaucer's sensitivity to geographical relations is everywhere manifest in his poetry. The *place* of narrative has its own connotations that Chaucer is rarely slow to exploit. One suggestive feature of that sensitivity to place is a sharp awareness of the relations of small places to larger places, and (not necessarily the same phenomenon) of relatively insignificant places to places of powerful cultural resonance.

Many Chaucerian narratives occur, for example, in the suburbs of great or significant cities. Thus the *Second Nun's Tale* of Saint Cecilia begins in a noble household in central late-antique Rome; very soon, however, the action moves to a suburban site. Wishing that her husband convert to Christianity, Cecilia directs him to seek out Pope Urban, who hides away from the city center, among the sites not only of relative safety but also of more powerful spiritual energy, the tombs of saints. These are located outside Rome, in suburbs along the Appian Way, "That fro this toun ne stant but miles three."[1] The next tale, too, that of the Canon's Yeoman, gives voice to a figure who takes refuge in the obscurity of suburbia: asked where his master practices the suspect science of alchemy, the Yeoman replies thus:

> "In the suburbes of a toun," quod he,
> Lurkynge in hernes and in lanes blynde,
> Whereas thise robbours and thise theves by kynde
> Holden hir pryvee fereful residence,
> As they that dar nat shewen hir presence." (8.657–661)

The narratives of Miller, Reeve, and Shipman are all also set in towns (Osney, Trumpington, and Saint Denis) adjacent to much bigger and more significant centers (Oxford, Cambridge, and Paris, respectively).

When Chaucer's narratives represent a smaller place adjacent to a larger, or more significant, place, we might expect the values of the larger to predominate over those of the smaller. Such is not in fact the case. Occasionally, indeed, the values of the smaller entirely repudiate those of the larger: in the *Second Nun's Tale,* for example, the suburban and potentially revolutionary space of saintly tombs overpowers central, ancient Rome, populated as it is by idolatrously adored statues. For the most part, however, the smaller places in Chaucer's poetry do not overwhelm the larger; instead, they assert themselves as surprising, yet finally plausible competitors to the larger. We can see this in the very opening sequence of the *Canterbury Tales,* as the pilgrims set off from the Tabard in Southwark to the shrine of Thomas à Becket in Canterbury. Southwark is not a suburb of London but a separate urban entity just across the Thames River, south of London; it is nonetheless clearly a smaller, less culturally significant space than either the capital city just to its north or the religious center of Canterbury to the east. Its status is best expressed, perhaps, by the Tabard (the inn from which the pilgrims begin) — the space of chambers, stables, physical refreshment, and contingent conviviality. However much the existence of material need, and the values implied by contingent associations, might seem paltry beside the grand narrative of pilgrimage to Canterbury and "the righte wey of Jerusalem celestial" (10.80), those material values in fact continue powerfully to inform both the Canterbury pilgrimage and its narratives. Just as Geffrey in the *House of Fame* prefers the unpredictable, improvised, vernacular structure of the House of Rumor over the architecturally magnificent palace of Fame, so too in the *Canterbury Tales* does the improvised, street-level space of the Tabard exert its own irrepressible force across the entire pilgrimage.

For Chaucer, then, smaller places have the power to exert their own force field over larger competitors. This holds promise not only for smaller places within the narratives of Chaucer's poetry but also for England itself as a "small" geographical entity in relation to a larger, adjacent entity. For Chaucer, England was inevitably a smaller part of a larger continental cultural environment. Thus, at the beginning of the *Canterbury Tales,* he places Canterbury in relation to a much larger, continental movement of people in April pilgrimage. In spring, people throughout Christendom (and, no doubt, beyond) long to go on pilgrimage, "And palmeres for to seken straunge strondes, / To ferne halwes [shrines], kowthe [known] in sondry londes." Within, and wholly consonant, with that larger movement in Christendom is a more particular, English movement: "And specially from every shires ende / Of Engelond to Caunterbury they wende" (1.12–16).

It is true that England was engaged in military competition, with France, for more than a century (1337–1453) from just before Chaucer's birth. Only during and after the Reformation of the sixteenth century, however, did England begin sharply to define itself against what was now perceived as a *culturally* threatening European context. Only, moreover, with the rise and fall of the British Empire between the eighteenth and twentieth centuries could England build on the separations of the Reformation to develop a powerful narrative of its separate, national destiny. In some sense, indeed, it is only from the perspective of those post-Chaucerian centuries that the very subject of Chaucer as a European writer comes into focus as a subject at all: for Chaucer there was no question of being anything else. Thus already when Thomas Wyatt (1503–42) declares his satisfaction to be in "Kent and Christendom," his Kent is a very different place from the late-fourteenth-century Kent through which Chaucer's pilgrims travel to Canterbury.[2] Wyatt is writing after the Act of Supremacy (1534), by which England broke from the authority of Rome. He may locate himself in Christendom, but immediately before that self-placing, he repudiates all sense of cultural affiliation with the Continent. He is relieved *not* to be in France idly discussing fine wine or in Spain, where outer appearance is all, or in Flanders taking his "wit away / With beastliness they, beasts, do so esteem." Finally, and most significantly, he is relieved not to be "where Christ is given in prey / For money, poison, and treason at Rome — / A common practice used night and day."[3]

By contrast with Wyatt, Chaucer consistently sets England as a smaller place, but culturally very much part of the larger place of continental Europe. Perhaps the broadest placing of England is made in the *Man of Law's Tale*. Saints' lives are one genre where geographical consciousness is at its most acute, because the numinous power of the saint defines territorial jurisdictions of the Church. Accordingly, the saintly Constance, in this fictional version of English conversion to Roman Christianity, initiates the conversion of England. She traverses a geography that is at once realistically absurd and culturally coherent. Constance is the daughter of the Roman emperor (a Christian); she is first sent to "Surrye," where a failed marriage sees her pushed off to die in a boat on the open sea. The rudderless boat floats implausibly to Northumbria, where, after a further series of trials, Constance marries the local king and thereby converts him and many others to Christianity. From the perspective of realistic travel, the geography of the tale is little short of absurd. Implausibility aside, however, Constance's wanderings describe an entirely coherent cultural circuit. Christian Rome stands at the center of this wide sphere of influence; the narrative exposes those margins to the east that reject Roman influence, and those to the west of Rome that finally embrace it. As England is incorporated within the ambit of Roman influence, however, it does not escape its marginal status: after the death of her Northumbrian royal husband, Constance returns to her Roman father, begging him not to send her again "unto noon hethenesse" (2.1112).

The *Man of Law's Tale* imagines the moment, then, at which England moves from the outer edge of "hethenesse" into the realm, but still on the edge, of a larger Christendom. Some of the Canterbury pilgrims have themselves traversed the broader space, and occasionally the boundaries, of Christendom. War, commerce, and religion are clearly the primary motivations to travel to the Continent. Knight and Squire have fought abroad: the Squire in Flanders and northern France, while his father, the Knight, has campaigned around, and sometimes across, the very borders of Christendom, from Granada in Spain to (using modern country or area names) Morocco, Egypt, Turkey, Prussia, and Lithuania. The Merchant clearly trades with the Low Countries, the Shipman with western France and Spain. And while the Wife of Bath competes commercially with Flemish clothiers, she travels as a pilgrim thrice to Jerusalem, as well as visiting shrines in Rome, Boulogne in northern France, Santiago de Compostela in northwestern Spain, and Cologne in northwestern Germany. The Pardoner, too, is said to come "from Rome al hoot" (1.687). We know from surviving bureaucratic records that, among other voyages, Chaucer himself traveled to France (in 1360, when captured as part of a military campaign); to Spain (in 1366); to Italy in both 1372–73 and 1378, on diplomatic business; and (again almost certainly as a diplomat) to France and Flanders in early 1377.[4]

Chaucer's England, is, then, very much on the borders of the only large geographical unit to which it could have belonged. Certainly late medieval English travelers did travel extensively on the Continent, in large numbers, for military, religious, and commercial reasons. Before, however, the discovery of the New World in the late fifteenth century repositioned the westernmost countries of Europe in new sets of geographical relations, England remained very much on the geographical boundaries, a small if unified and relatively powerful unit adjacent to one large competitor (France) and a large landmass.

If that is true geographically, it is even more so culturally, especially in the realm of imaginative fiction. Writing in English had an especially low status in the cultural environment into which Chaucer was born. All European vernaculars had to contend with the immense cultural authority of Latin, the language of sacred texts and of learning more generally. In addition to that handicap, for historical reasons English had none of the status that French had enjoyed as a literary language since the middle of the twelfth century, and none of the status that dialects of Italian had gained as literary vernaculars from the middle of the thirteenth century. Chrétien de Troyes indeed, writing his romance *Cligès* in the 1170s, could already claim with astonishing confidence that chivalry and learning, having arisen in Greece, then moved to Rome, have now come to France, where he prays they may remain forever.[5]

To a poet aspiring to write in English in the 1360s, Chrétien's wish for French linguistic and literary predominance may have seemed a wish come all too true. Since the Norman Conquest of 1066 the language of polite society in England had been French, a situation that was only gradually changing in Chaucer's time. Not until 1362 was it permissible to plead law cases in English (legislation that appears to have had no practical effect for many centuries), and only in the same year did the clerks of Parliament admit that its proceedings were in English.[6] Even if English gained authority in certain discursive practices (Parliament, the law), French remained the language of preference for literary reading and, in some cases, writing, among royalty and the upper nobility of Chaucer's England. Even the French spoken in England would seem to have been regarded as inferior and less stylish than that of metropolitan France: thus Chaucer's Prioress is said to speak French according to the "scole of Stratford atte Bowe, / For Frenssh of Parys was to hire unknowe" (1.125–26). So the literary language of the English vernacular, in the middle of the fourteenth century, was itself a smaller "place" whose identity was overshadowed by larger competitors, a linguistic "suburb" beside the great linguistic "city" of French, and within reach of the newly developing literary metropolis of Italian.

In short, then, mid-fourteenth-century English literary culture was both marginal and belated: the great vernacular literatures had been created both elsewhere than and before any comparable literature in post-Conquest English. Chaucer's frequent deployment of the "modesty-topos" expresses as much his poetic discretion as the actual condition of English literary culture.[7] Lacking cultural credibility as they do, "suburban" figures must always struggle to find a voice. How did Chaucer confront this challenge? How did Chaucer become a European writer?

One solution would have been to write in French (or the dialect of French developed in England, Anglo-Norman). This dialect did have a long history of insular literary use and had flourished in the last half of the twelfth century particularly.[8] Chaucer's contemporary and friend John Gower made precisely this choice in his first large-scale poem, the *Mirour de l'Omme* (1376–78). Chaucer did not, apparently, make the same choice. He decided instead to deploy the lesser category of English by way of entering the field of European letters. He decided, that is, to become the "firste fyndere of our fair langage," as Chaucer's early-fifteenth-century admirer Thomas Hoccleve called him.[9] Hoccleve did not intend by this comment to make the absurd claim that Chaucer "invented" the English language. Much more accurately (setting aside the magnificent tradition of Old English poetry and some outstanding early Middle English texts about which Hoccleve was ignorant), he meant to say that Chaucer was the first literary "inventor" (a rhetorical term) in English. Chaucer decided to become a "finder," or *poeta,* by deploying his own language, using the lesser category to broach the larger.

The standard narrative of Chaucer's poetic engagement with European poetic making defines a French period as a kind of apprenticeship, followed by a profound engagement with Italian poetry. This narrative is indisputable, and in good part, I confirm it here. Chaucer's cultural interests may have been pan-European, but his literary affiliations were not: his geographical gaze is turned decisively south, to France and Italy especially. He does not mention Ireland or Scotland at all as separate entities, and Wales only once; his writing manifests no engagement with the literary traditions of those countries.[10] He had clearly traveled in Flanders, but the literary culture of the Burgundian court had no major impact in England until the reign of Edward IV (1461–70, 1471–83), and until the massive commercial translation project of William Caxton (d. 1492).[11] So, too, had Chaucer traveled in Spain in 1366, where the Black Prince (son of Edward III), and his brother John of Gaunt (Chaucer's first known patron), had powerful interests; Chaucer shows, however, no signs of Spanish influence. Neither does he show any sign of engagement with German literature: not until the biblical translation projects of the sixteenth century did German writing appear to have had any major influence in England.

If Chaucer shows few or no signs of engagement with Flemish, German, or

Spanish writing, his engagement with select examples of Latin, French, and Italian literature is, by contrast, profound. Faced with a literary vacuum of sorts in his own language, Chaucer turned to these continental literatures for the matter and models of his work. In every sense, Chaucer's entire oeuvre can be described as a project of translation (literally, a "carrying across"). Romantic and post-Romantic canons of literary value dismiss translation because, as is often said, the translator is by definition not the originary, creative, inspired source of meaning. Such canons of judgment also dismiss translation because, as is less often said, Romantic literary values are inextricably bound up with nationalist and often subliminally or explicitly racist projects. Within such a tradition, a national literature is thought to express the national character, and so critics repudiate or devalue works that derive from other national literatures.

However much nineteenth-century and earlier twentieth-century accounts of Chaucer did praise his poetry as the expression of an essential Englishness, the forces hostile to translation just defined did not exist in Chaucer's period.[12] Medieval literary theory for the most part steered clear of attributing originary creative genius to human authors, Just as medieval forms of nationalism in no way repudiated literary influences from other countries. English writers in particular were in no position to insist on exclusive commitment to a national tradition. Translation is the very lifeblood of Chaucerian writing no less than of late medieval English writing more generally, even for the "untranslatable" genres, such as lyric.

Chaucer, then, chose English and translation.[13] Most of the remainder of this chapter delineates the models and the materials of this wonderfully energetic, engaged career of translation from continental literatures. Before I turn to those various materials and competing models, it will repay us to define the guiding presence of Ovid across Chaucer's career. Too often Chaucer's "European" affiliations are taken to mean his affiliations with late medieval vernacular bodies of writing (that is, French and Italian). These engagements are treated separately from Chaucer's affiliations with classical writing. This account arbitrarily divides the community of dead (and some living) poets in whose company Chaucer moved. Certainly Chaucer is capable of making such a division himself. The writers named in Fame's palace in the *House of Fame* are, for example, primarily (though even there not exclusively) classical writers, and Chaucer's most explicit homage to a body of poets names only classical figures: "Virgile, Ovide, Omer, Lucan, and Stace" (*Troilus and Criseyde*, 5.1792). Even that profession of humility (and ambition) is made, however, in a text the bulk of whose narrative is derived from Chaucer's contemporary Giovanni Boccaccio (1313–75). Classical Latin and later medieval European vernacular and Latin texts are in constant dialogue in Chaucer's oeuvre. Thus the narrator of the *Parlement of Foules,* having read the narrative of Cicero's "Dream of Scipio," dreams that that text's own dream guide (Scipio Africanus) offers to repay Chaucer's narrator for having read the classical book so attentively.[14] This repayment issues in a new text, which is itself profoundly indebted to later medieval Latin and vernacular poets—Alan of Lille (d. 1203), Dante (1265–1321), and Boccaccio.[15] Chaucer's "continental" literary culture is as much classical and late classical as it is later medieval; it as much a Latin as it is a vernacular culture.

Ovid is the preeminent, approachable figure from the classical canon. Or, in other words, he is the poet via whose craft Chaucer can himself approach the classical and greater vernacular traditions. If, that is, Chaucer feels himself marginal in England, and belated as he uses English as a literary medium, he finds the perfect enabling poet in Ovid (43 B.C.–A.D.17/18). For, however much Ovid is himself one of the great classical poets, his own self-positioning in much of his oeuvre is also as a belated, marginal poet. He supplies Chaucer, that is, with a model of "subsidiary" writing *from within* the corpus of classical poetry. Ovid's amatory poetry presents itself as secondary to what he calls "tragic" verse (that is, classical epic). His amatory verse, what he calls Elegy (the writing of largely unfulfilled erotic love) is parasitic in fundamental ways, even borrowing yet deliberately deforming the verse form of "tragic" verse. The large, powerful "responsible" voice is, in Ovid's elegiac poetry, always (apparently) somewhere else. In *Ars Amatoria, Amores,* and *Heroides,* Ovid instead supplies the voice of experiential narrative, and often the female voice. This frequently female voice, often the victim and relic of empire, is invested, via small but immensely significant shiftings of perspective, with the power to unsettle and even undo the impersonal solidities of epic, and the assurance of accepted, masculine, imperial ideals. Ovid's poetic shapes a fundamentally skeptical viewpoint with regard to large-scale civic endeavor. There is always another perspective.

One compacted example of this Ovidian mode, generated from an Ovidian borrowing, will suffice to guide the following discussion. In Book 1 of *Troilus and Criseyde,* Pandarus attempts to persuade the suffering Troilus that, even if unsuccessful in love, Pandarus can still advise his suffering friend. A whetstone, he argues, is no instrument for cutting, but it sharpens tools; he caps this line of argumentation by referring (in a passage wholly original to Chaucer) to a letter, written by the Trojan shepherdess Oenone, to Paris:[16]

> I woot wel that it fareth thus be me
> As to thi brother, Paris, an herdesse
> Which that iclepid was Oënone
> Wrot in a compleynte of hir hevynesse. (1.652–55)

He asserts that Oenone argued in the letter that Apollo, even though he was the god of medicine, was incapable of curing himself when he fell in love.

Ostensibly the reference does no more than refer in passing to the letter as a kind of contemporary authority for an amatory maxim. Reflection on the reference reveals, however, very Ovidian (and Chaucerian) forms of both comedy and tragedy. Pandarus in fact refers here to Epistle 5 in Ovid's collection *Heroides* (*Heroines*), imagined as having been written by the shepherdess Oenone to Paris, after Paris has abandoned her for Helen. Chaucer cunningly works this citation from classical literature into the contemporary texture of his own fictional creation, and he has Pandarus insist on its contemporaneity: "Ye say [saw] the lettre that she wrot, I gesse?" (1.656). Within this very contemporary frame, certain kinds of comedy are possible: Pandarus can play up his comic inadequacy in love; Troilus can finally be persuaded to be less pathetically limp.

Chaucer is even, apparently, being playfully irresponsible with medieval traditions of understanding Ovid. A powerful medieval tradition of commentary on Ovid's *Heroides* has it that the text has a moral purpose. The *intentio* of this text, voiced as it is by abandoned women, is to praise or reprehend different kinds of love. Pandarus, by contrast, playing the role of the Ovidian amatory master ("*praeceptor amoris*"), himself disowns any moral interest in Troilus's case whatsoever: "For douteth nothyng, myn entencioun / Nis nat to yow of reprehencioun" (1.683–84).[17]

Once we stand back a little from the text, however, certain less comic resonances can be detected: this private and deeply painful letter to Paris is now, it would appear, public property among the aristocratic men of Troy, to be mined for handy amatory tips. Perhaps more disturbing, and certainly more dangerous, is the evidence of terribly foreshortened reading Pandarus displays: if he had read the entire (quite short) letter, he might have been struck not only by Oenone's pain but also by her report of Cassandra's prophecy concerning Troy's impending doom (*Heroides*, 5.113–20). Once Cassandra had seen Helen coming to Troy, she not only warned Oenone that she was wasting her time longing for Paris but prophesied Troy's doom: "What are you doing, Oenone? Why commit seeds to sand? You are plowing the shores with oxen that will accomplish nothing. A Greek heifer is on the way, to ruin you, your homeland and your home!"[18] So two men have been exceptionally poor readers here: Paris has ignored Oenone's letter, and Pandarus has ignored the prophecy of Cassandra embedded in that letter. His ignorance is even more shocking in the context of his offer, a few lines later, of working to help Troilus in love regardless of the woman involved. Even if it were Helen with whom Troilus had fallen in love, Pandarus would still help: " 'Be what she be, and love hire as the list [you desire]!" (1.679).

The pattern of allusion here is absolutely characteristic of Ovid's elegiac poetry: an allusion to myth is made in a way that both ignores, yet cannot help but expose, a dark and impending doom. A reference to the social comedy of a lover's malady ignores yet cannot help but expose the deep and potentially terrible connections between erotic passion and civic destruction. It is, as I say, entirely Ovidian, but here the shaping hand is entirely that of Chaucer himself. Chaucer has learned his craft from Ovid's allusive art, which positions itself in a secondary yet telling relation with the civic, "responsible" art of classical epic. Ovidian and Chaucerian art both hover between different perspectives, in this case the playful irresponsibility of Pandarus, the pain of the abandoned woman Oenone, and, in the distance, the destruction of the city. The world of both classical myth and epic are ultimately, for Chaucer, dark and destructive places. The shortened Ovidian perspective of Pandarus permits comedy provisionally to stay that violence; as we pause on the implications of that foreshortened comedy, however, we are ineluctably led to the longer perspectives of Oenone's suffering and Cassandra's prophecy of Trojan doom. This small, in-etched example might serve as a model for the whole of *Troilus and Criseyde* (c. 1381–86), as well as informing all Chaucer's poetry one way or another from his earliest dateable poem, the *Book of the Duchess* (c. 1368), to the *Legend of Good Women* (c. 1386–87). Even in the very different, predominantly "modern" world of the *Canterbury Tales,* the same Ovidian concerns with history and suppressed, usually female voices consistently resurface.

The Ovidian posture that Chaucer has absorbed, then, offers these possibilities: an understanding of the power and centrality of erotic desire; justification for dwelling on erotic narrative, even at the expense of the larger mythic and epic narratives; recognition of the pain of marginal, rejected, belated, experiential, and often feminine voices; and an understanding of the ways in which those experiential narratives can destabilize, through subtle changes of perspective, the apparent solidities of the masculine, imperialist, epic tradition. Chaucer exploits all these Ovidian possibilities, in different combinations, across his career, as he engages with the "moderns" of great French and Italian vernacular poetry closer to his time. To whatever great European writing Chaucer turns his penetrating gaze, he does so through a smaller, yet skeptical Ovidian lens.

Early Career

Ovid, then, is the underlying poetic presence across Chaucer's career; at one point, as we shall see, Chaucer even represents his own biographical situation on the template of Ovid's career as it was imagined in medieval commentaries. Within that larger frame, however, Chaucer makes many intense engagements with other, more modern continental texts, in Latin, French, and Italian. For the entirety of his visible career, these engagements were in English and did not for the most part consist of translations in the strict sense.

It *may* be that Chaucer composed in French in his earliest career. The "many a song and leccherous lay," to which Chaucer confesses in the Retractions to the *Canterbury Tales* (10.1087), might have been composed in French, as would have been consistent with literary practice in the environment of the court of Edward III.[19] And he *did* make some translations in the strict sense of that term. He certainly translated at least part of the great Ovidian thirteenth-century text, *Le Roman de la Rose* (written in two sections by two different authors, Guillaume de Lorris in c. 1230–35, and Jean de Meun in c. 1275).[20] Chaucer made this translation certainly before the mid–1380s; it is plausible to imagine him doing it early in his career, as a kind of apprentice work. Whenever he translated it, the *Romance of the Rose* (and especially Jean de Meun's trenchantly skeptical, subversive later section) provided Chaucer with a modern Ovidian text that, like Ovid's own works, taught Chaucer how to manipulate one voice within another, so as to destabilize received wisdom.[21] The Prologues to both the *Wife of Bath's Tale* and the *Pardoner's Tale* are in particular indebted to the unstable foundations of Jean's own text. Chaucer's liveliest, most verisimilar voices are in fact deeply indebted to this very lively but textual source.

In addition to that strict translation, Chaucer's other acts of more passive translation are generally philosophical or instructional prose works: the translation of Boethius's *Consolation of Philosophy* (written in Latin c. 530, translated by Chaucer, c. 1381–86, primarily from the French translation of Jean de Meun); the *Tale of Melibee*, translated (c. ?1390) from Albertanus of Brescia's *Liber Consolationis et Consilii* (1246), again via an intermediate French translation; and the *Parson's Tale,* translated at an uncertain date from two Latin penitential treatises from the first half of the thirteenth century, possibly although not certainly from French intermediaries. Chaucer made literary capital of sorts from all these translations: Boethius's work profoundly influenced *Troilus and Criseyde* especially, whereas the remaining two texts are worked, with slight or no creation of fictional voice, into the fabric of the *Canterbury Tales.*

At the beginning of his dateable career, however, Chaucer's work is not translation in the strict modern sense, however much he is indebted to, and engaging with, texts in French and Latin. The earliest known of Chaucer's literary engagements with continental making was with the courtly poetry composed in French by Guillaume de Machaut (1300–1377) and Jean Froissart (c. 1337–after 1404). In only the first of these poems, however (*Book of the Duchess,* c. 1368), does Chaucer remain within the coordinates of the preferred elegiac genre, the *dit,* of these poets. In this text Chaucer immerses himself in the dit and reworks it in his own language and his own courtly situation. Even as he reworks material from Machaut and Froissart into his own poetic narrative and structure, Chaucer nonetheless remains exceptionally deferential in this delicate, early work. He is deferential to the genre from which he borrows, to his patron, and to his readers.

As practiced by Machaut and Froissart, the dit is a courtly genre designed to ventilate, and tactfully to moderate, the dangerous melancholic excesses of aristocratic amatory pain. Poets overhear sensitive, languishing courtly patrons complain; through the resources of human art (not moralizing or Christian consolation) the poem produced offers therapy of sorts, principally by having allowed the subtle and sensitive patron to have done the painful and articulate talking. In Machaut's *Dit de la Fonteinne Amoureuse* (1360), for example, the poet overhears, and writes in its entirety, the complaint of a lord; later in the text, when the lord asks the poet for a complaint, Machaut produces the very text he had copied verbatim from the lord. This is a perfect strategy for poets writing for powerful patrons: the articulate patron is the sensitive one skilled in composition; the poet is a mere enabler. This delicate and inexplicit, not to say precious, relation between poet and patron is marked by allusive, coded references to the patron's actual name.[22]

Chaucer imitates all these subtle moves in the *Book of the Duchess:* once asleep, the apparently obtuse narrator, himself dazed into dull stupidity by long periods of sleepless love-longing, happens in a dream across the static, grieving aristocrat, dressed in black. Nothing, says the grieving lord, can help him, "Noght al the remedyes of Ovyde, / Ne Orpheus, god of melodye," nor any doctors (lines 567–72). Even less likely to offer serious therapy than Ovid and medical doctors is the zombie-like poet. His inaptitude is, indeed, underlined by the Ovidian story inset into the poem's larger narrative: by way of getting to sleep, the dreamer reads an abbreviated version of Ovid's story of Ceyx and Alcyone, from *Metamorphoses,* 11.410–748. In this narrative Morpheus, oafish god of sleep, is a psychological mirror image of the sleepless poet-dreamer, since Morpheus can hardly wake up. Once woken, he impersonates the dead Ceyx in a dream to the anxious Alcyone. His attempt at consolation results in the almost immediate death of Alcyone, from grief.

Whence therapy in such a situation? A psychologically static, black knight and an obtuse, melancholic poet-dreamer might seem like an unpromising base from which to generate psychological healing. The therapy is, nevertheless, enacted, principally by relying on the voice of the Black Knight himself to do the talking. He is painfully provoked to remember and reimagine his re-cently dead wife, and thereby homeopathically to begin his cure. The other great therapeutic resource here, however, is Ovid's text. That text gets the sleepless dreamer to sleep, and it provides a model of both aristocratic, femi-nine pain and consolation against which to measure, and through which to understand, the psychological pain of the present situation. Chaucer might borrow situations and whole blocks of lines from Machaut especially, but the poem's deepest debts are to the tradition of Ovidian remedy.

The *Book of the Duchess,* then, is a poem of subtle deference. Not only does it proceed with extreme deference to its powerful patron, John of Gaunt, who had recently lost his first wife, Blanche of Lancaster, to the plague of 1368. It also remains tactfully within the remit of the contemporary, courtly French form it adopts, including the use of its metrical form, the octosyllabic couplet, adapted to the four-stress couplet of English verse. Different kinds of transla-tional practice are on show, which Chaucer would have learned from school exercises. He paraphrases Ovid's narrative (which also appears, in different form, in *La Fonteinne Amoureuse*); he translates sequences more literally from French sources;[23] and he offers a comically bad gloss on the Ovidian narrative, when he responds by saying that he saw a tip in it about how to get to sleep, apparently having entirely missed the story's emotional force and sense (lines 231–69).

Such deference is unsurprising: Chaucer's position as young poet addressing England's greatest landowner would naturally incline him to a certain mod-esty; and as we have seen, Chaucer's cultural position, of writing sophisticated courtly verse in English, might also incline a socially cautious and adroit poet toward deference. What *is* very surprising is the engagement with European traditions we find in the next two poems, the dream poems the *House of Fame* and the *Parliament of Fowls.* These were both very probably written between Chaucer's first trip to Italy in 1372–73 and the period of large-scale poetic making in the mid-1380s. For even if deference of a kind survives in these poems, they remain works of extraordinary and prescient ambition. They stake out the poetic territories that Chaucer will inhabit for the rest of his career. And they use sources not as passive matter to be reworked into new poetic structures by a subtle poet, as had been the case in the *Book of the Duchess.* With these two poems, the narrowly "French" period of Chaucer's career was over before it had hardly begun, for here Chaucer moved out to survey the horizons of Italian and classical poetic making.

These texts initiate dialogues with their illustrious continental sources. They establish, indeed, a clear distinction to be made among Chaucer's "sources." On one hand, there are texts that Chaucer mines for material, without entering into dialogue with them (as had been the case with the use of the dits in the *Book of the Duchess* or as will be the case with Boccaccio's *Filostrato* and *Teseida* for *Troilus and Criseyde* and the *Knight's Tale,* respectively). On the other hand, there are writers and texts to conjure with, the invocation of whose names and titles establishes a standard to which vernacular making might aspire or from which it might distinguish itself. Virgil, Alan of Lille, and Dante are all, for example, figures of this last kind. Chaucer relies massively on the former kind of source for unacknowledged narrative material, while he cites sparingly from the latter kind, often from the beginnings or endings of texts, and often citing by name. Both the *House of Fame* and the *Parliament of Fowls* are manifesto poems, citing the authors against or by whom Chaucer defines his poetic enterprise.

These poems might, like the *Book of the Duchess,* appear deferential. In his *Art of Poetry,* Horace instructs the would-be poet to weigh his material on his shoulders, by way of knowing what those shoulders can bear.[24] The poets of Fame's palace do precisely this: they bear the weight of their respective matters, be it, for example, Troy, or Thebes, on their "shuldres hye" (line 1435). The *House of Fame* serves as an advertisement of sorts for the kind of matter of which Chaucer's own shoulders are capable of bearing. Deferentially, he declines the eagle's offer of going to the spheres: " 'No fors,' quod y, 'hyt is no nede. / I leve as wel, so God me spede, / Hem that write of this matere' " (lines 1011–13). Other writers — Martianus Capella, Alan of Lille, and more recently Dante — are capable of sustaining the brilliance of the planetary spheres, with all the poetic demands that such a journey entails.[25] If he cannot sustain the poetic challenge of an astral voyage, neither can he describe the underworld. In a matching disclaimer earlier in the poem, the poet-narrator Geffrey directs his reader to other poets for an account of "every turment eke in helle":

> Which whoso willeth for to knowe,
> He moste rede many a rowe
> On Virgile or on Claudian,
> Or Daunte, that hit telle kan. (lines 447–50)[26]

As Chaucer surveys the large places of European making in these texts, he stakes out his own claim to a poetic territory of "smaller" scale: he prefers the "vernacular," unstable, street-level space of the House of Rumor to the House of Fame, let alone to any trip to the celestial spheres. Rumor is the locus of "rounynges [whisperings] and of jangles" (line 1960), full of news, gossip, and background rumble. Or in the *Parliament of Fowls* he marks off the Garden of Nature by distinguishing it from the afterworld of Dante's great poem. Dante's Hell is marked by a gate whose forbidding inscription begins thus:

PER ME SI VA NELLA CITTÀ DOLENTE,
PER ME SI VA NELL'ETTERNO DOLORE,
PER ME SI VA TRA LA PERDUTA GENTE.
(*Inferno*, 3.1–3)[27]

[Through me one passes into the grieving city; through me one enters eternal suffering; through me one goes among the lost people].

Chaucer's Garden of Nature evidently recalls these terrible lines. Over the gate to Nature's park are written these lines: "Thorgh me men gon . . . Unto the mortal strokes of the spere / Of which Disdayn and Daunger is the gyde" (lines 134–5). This admonition is, however, only half the inscription. The other side of the *same* gate has the following encouragement written above it:

Throrgh me men gon into that blysful place
Of hertes hele and dedly woundes cure; [recovery]
Thorgh me men gon unto the welle of grace. (lines 127–29)

Clearly the space that Chaucer's narrator enters is *not* any afterworld, with its absolute, austere, eternal verities He enters instead the unstable, ambiguous poetic space of *this* world, which cannot provide any fixed and wholly reliable vantage point from which to survey and understand earthly existence. By this stage of his career Chaucer clearly knew from Dante's *Commedia* the heights to which vernacular poetry might aspire.[28] While expressing his intense admiration for that achievement, Chaucer chose a different path, remaining within the "selva oscura" (obscure forest) of this life.

Chaucer's decision not to assume the poetic burden of the afterlife may seem to be an act of wise discretion, the decision of a cautious poet who knows that he deals with "smaller" matters. This is partly true, I think. Much more interestingly, however, the decision to opt for the smaller poetic matter serves to critique the larger. A set of consistent oppositions runs throughout these two dream poems: on the one side stands (crudely stated) a masculine, politically directed project of fixing truth and repressing the claims of the body. The writers of this enterprise are, in Chaucer's field of vision, especially Cicero, Virgil, Alan of Lille, and Dante. On the other side stands a feminine posture whose politics are much more elastic, and which is skeptical of any claim to cognitive fixity; for this set of values, truth is always experiential and embodied. The pre-eminent poet of this posture in these poems is, for Chaucer, Ovid.

Chaucer aligns himself with Ovid's skeptical voice. This can be seen in many ways across both the *House of Fame* and the *Parliament of Fowls*. In the House of Fame the dreamer-poet begins reading Virgil's *Aeneid* inscribed on tables of brass but very quickly starts rewriting, and effectively critiquing,

Virgil's poem by adopting an Ovidian posture, sympathetic to the abandoned Dido. He rejects the locus of eternal poetic fame and opts instead for the porous bricolage of the House of Rumor, where "fals and soth" are inextricably "compouned" (line 2108). In the *Parliament of Fowls* he is left unmoved by Cicero's celebrated "Dream of Scipio," with its rejection of sensual pleasure and promotion of service to the commonwealth; instead he moves to the embodied politics of Nature's garden, in which erotic desire has a central place in any account of the "political." And in both poems Chaucer decisively rejects forms of absolute cognitive certainty. His dream guides may derive from authoritative sources (the Eagle in the House of Fame from Dante's *Purgatorio*, 9.19–33, and Scipio from Cicero's text), but they are either guides of uncertain status (the Eagle) or only take Chaucer so far but no further (Scipio). These poems may evoke models of unquestionable, divinely inspired dream knowledge; their own kind of knowledge is, by contrast, always grounded in earthly and bodily experience.

Chaucer stakes out, then, a "smaller," vernacular space in these poems, which nevertheless has the unexpected power to challenge its larger forebears. He also stakes out a rhetorical practice. Such explicit rhetorical theory as Chaucer had available to him had been developed in the cathedral schools of northern France in the last half of the twelfth century; it derived from fundamentally Neoplatonic sources. Chaucer certainly knew and used the *Poetria Nova* (c. 1200–1202) of Geoffrey of Vinsauf, for example.[29] The rhetorical practice promoted by this intelligent text is underwritten by Neoplatonic conceptions of creative conception and embellishment. Just as God makes the embellished world from an archetype in his mind, so too must the earthly poet begin with an archetype that contains the forms of *ornatus,* or embellishment, that such an archetype demands. The rhetorical microlevel of the resultant text will match its deepest creative sources. Throughout his career Chaucer's rhetorical practice with regard, for example, to abbreviation and expansion, or to his use of figures of thought, matches Geoffrey of Vinsauf's prescriptions closely. That said, Geoffrey's theory is based, as one would expect from a philosophical rhetoric, on a notion of "fittingness," *convenientia,* or decorum. Chaucer's philosophical predispositions led him inevitably away from any such strict practice of rhetorical decorum. Instead, his use of rhetorically mixed, adjacent styles better expresses his skeptical, multiperspectival understanding of earthly truth.[30]

Nowhere else is Chaucer's explicit engagement with a crowd of preexisting authors so busy as it is in these early poems, and especially in the *House of Fame*. These encounters are especially acute and vibrant as he finds his voice early in his career. This voice capitalizes on apparent weaknesses, as it finds a métier for an untried vernacular prizing the fluid and unstable over fixity and stability. The smaller space of the vernacular finds a way of addressing the larger place of continental poetic making, both classical and medieval, and it does so via the enabling example of Ovid especially.

Midcareer

Chaucer established the coordinates for the rest of his career with these early poems. In the next phase of that career, he addressed the great subjects of antiquity from these initial Ovidian, yet courtly perspectives. In the following, final phase, he largely abandoned courtly making about antiquity, in favor of a poetic modernity, as he headed for Canterbury on pilgrimage. In both these next phases, his inspiration remains that of continental, especially Italian poetry. As noted above, Chaucer certainly traveled to Italy in 1372–73 and again in 1378. He may also have been in Milan in 1368 for the wedding of his first master, Lionel, Duke of Clarence, to Violante, daughter of Galeazzo Visconti, lord of Pavia. As with many English travelers to this land, Italy had a profound influence on Chaucer.

Two aspects of the Italian scene in particular struck Chaucer. On one hand, he saw a set of polities at work in Italy entirely different from the political organization to which he was accustomed in England. Unlike the fairly unified and centralized kingdoms of France and England, "Italy" was, in the Middle Ages, a geographically and culturally disunified patchwork of states. Outside the Kingdom of Naples and the Papal States and in the south and center, respectively, many Italian states were republics and intensely democratic, from at least the early twelfth century. Thus Florence, Pisa, Lucca, Siena, Bologna, Genoa, Milan, and Venice were, for example, all city-states with republican, democratic government until they succumbed, at different times, to despotic rule by a single family, such as the Visconti in Milan (by the time of Chaucer's visit).

As long as they managed to preserve their republican status, these cities all had a vivid consciousness of and pride in their liberties, which we can see represented in the image of *Good Government* from Siena, painted by Ambrogio Lorenzetti. Here there is no single controlling principle, but many competing forces: the outer city walls are replicated by a complex pattern of defensive walls within the city. Cultural energy comes from below, from many different sites and jurisdictions. This diversity produced enormous energy, but it also produced very high levels of intra- and interurban violence. Those cities that succumbed to despotic rule, by contrast, produced a different and magnificent style of rule, in which power definitely emanated from above. Chaucer

witnessed both republican and despotic cities: he visited Florence in 1372–73
and Milan in 1378. Florence was at this period a republic, whereas Milan was
ruled despotically by the Visconti.

The other feature of the Italian scene that must have struck Chaucer with
lasting force was its new art and literature. One can only speculate that Chaucer was astonished by the vernacular art of Giotto (c. 1266–c. 1336) in Florence, an art whose combination of earthy, physical presence and great emotional intensity marked it off from the stylized, highly refined Byzantine style
of Giotto's master, Cimabue. What demonstrably did attract Chaucer with
compelling force was the new literature of both Florence and Milan, a literature that provided him both with models of vernacular poetic achievement
and with large bodies of narrative matter for translation and adaptation.[31]
Dante especially provided the model, while Boccaccio supplied the matter, in
massive quantity.[32] Both also supplied models of crucial metrical innovation
for the development of a more sonorous and flexible English line and stanza
form.[33] Petrarch (1304–74) was another Florentine, although employed by
the Visconti in Milan from 1353 and working largely under their patronage
until his death in 1374. Petrarch's vernacular influence is registered at one
remarkable moment in *Troilus and Criseyde* (1.400–420); his presence for
Chaucer is largely, however, a matter of Latin writing, with which Chaucer
engages later, in the *Clerk's Tale*.

In the middle period of Chaucer's career (1380–90), Boccaccio is the generous though unacknowledged source of Chaucer's narrative. Chaucer stepped
onto the European scene with real confidence and ambition by broaching the
two great city-state disaster narratives of classical civilization: those of Thebes
and Troy. He drew by far the greater part of his narrative material from two
works by Boccaccio, the *Filostrato* (1336–39) and *Teseida* (finished in Florence
in 1341), both written in Italian, and both begun while Boccaccio was resident
in Naples, then under the monarchical rule of the Angevins. If Dante was a
name to conjure with, Boccaccio seems at this stage to be an author to be
pillaged for narrative matter. This is precisely what Chaucer did, translating
and reworking the *Filostrato* and *Teseida* into *Troilus and Criseyde* and the
Knight's Tale, respectively, without naming Boccaccio as the source. He did so,
with extraordinary energy, as part of a single project, since material rejected
from the *Teseida* finds its way into *Troilus and Criseyde*.

Boccaccio, then, supplied Chaucer with the two foundational narratives of
classical and medieval literature: the stories of Thebes and Troy. In both cases,
though, Boccaccio supplies a narrative that sidesteps the destructive power of
these narratives: the dangerous forces of civic destruction are minimized in
favor of amorous narratives within the city walls. The subject of Chaucer's

treatment of Boccaccio is obviously a large one; I focus here on one aspect of the reception of Boccaccio. In both narratives, Chaucer alludes more insistently and powerfully to the dark undercurrents of these stories of civic destruction, and in particular to their consequences for women. In Chaucer's hands these great sources of narrative become microcosms of the larger destructive world that awaits, or has befallen, Troy and Thebes. Chaucer, writing after forty or more years of sporadic war with France, underlines both the forces of chivalric society that propel cities toward destruction and the sheer crushing emptiness behind chivalric splendor.

In 1932 C. S. Lewis published "What Chaucer Really Did to Boccaccio's *Filostrato*."[34] The argument of this celebrated essay is, in short, that Chaucer "medievalized" Boccaccio's text. Lewis means by this that Chaucer brought the narrative within what Lewis understood to be the ethos of "courtly love," an ethos in which the woman is idealized and adored by a subservient man. That understanding of courtly love was challenged in the twentieth century, but Lewis's position is still worth attending to. For what he means, more broadly, by "medievalizing" is that Chaucer roughened the smooth surface of *Filostrato*, both rhetorically and philosophically. Chaucer's *Troilus* presents a much less smooth and polished surface than Boccaccio's *Filostrato*, offering a much more varied range of philosophical and rhetorical positions. Chaucer practiced rhetorical expansion in his translation of the *Filostrato;* he inserted many passages of his own composition, and he inserted many passages from Boethius's philosophical work on destiny, free will, and suffering. The effect of these insertions and expansions is to break the smooth rhetorical surface of the smooth social environment depicted by Boccaccio. The effect is also to render the relation between Troilus's disaster and that awaiting Troy itself more pressing and serious. The catastrophic fate of Thebes awaits Troy; references to the great classical Theban narrative, Statius's *Thebaid,* become more insistent and irrepressible in Book 5 of *Troilus and Criseyde.*[35]

For the more broken rhetorical surface of Chaucer's fictional creation, consider these passages from both texts, the moment where the lovers finally enjoy the pleasures of the body. Boccaccio's passage describes a scene of frank eroticism, in which lovers, author, and readers are knowing players. Troiolo and Criseida enter the bedroom:

> It would be a long task to describe their happiness, and an impossible one to tell of the delight they shared when they were there. They undressed and entered the bed, where the woman, who still had one last garment on, asked him charmingly, "Shall I take off everything? Newly-wed brides are shy on the first night" . . . What a sweet and much-desired night it was for these two happy lovers! Even if I possessed all the skills that any poet ever had, I should

still be unable to describe it. Let those who have at any time advanced so far in Love's favor as these two had now think about it and they will have some notion of the lovers' joy.[36]

Compare that passage with some of the text Chaucer freshly composed to approach it, and his "translation," in *Troilus and Criseyde*. Troilus begins by praising the binding power of universal Love:

> "Benigne Love, thow holy bond of thynges,
> Whoso wol grace and list the nought honouren,
> Lo, his desir wol fle withouten wynges;
> For noldestow of bownte hem socouren
> That serven best and most alwey labouren,
> Yet were al lost, that dar I wel seyn, certes,
> But if thi grace grace passed our desertes" . . .
> [They kiss]

> "For certes, fresshe wommanliche wif,
> This dar I seye, that trouth and diligence,
> That shal ye fynden in me al my lif;
> N'y wol nat, certein, breken youre defence;
> And if I do, present or in absence,
> For love of God, lat sle me with the dede,
> If that it like unto youre wommanhede"

> "Ywys," quod she, "myn owen hertes list,
> My ground of ese, and al myn herte deere,
> Gramercy, for on that is al my trist!
> But lat us falle awey fro this matere,
> For it suffiseth, this that seyd is heere,
> And at o word, withouten repentaunce,
> Welcome, my knyght, my pees, my suffisaunce!"

> Of hire delit or joies oon the leeste
> Were impossible to my wit to seye;
> But juggeth ye that han ben at the feste
> Of swich gladnesse, if that hem liste pleye!
> I kan namore, but thus thise ilke tweye
> That nyght, bitwixen drede and sikernesse,
> Felten in love the grete worthynesse . . .

> But sooth is, though I kan nat tellen al,
> As kan myn auctour, of his excellence,
> Yet have I seyd, and God toforn, and shal
> In every thyng, al holly his sentence;
> And if that ich, at Love reverence,

Have any word in eched for the beste,
Doth therwythal right as youreselven leste. (3.1261–330)

Chaucer's text presents a set of much more clearly defined divisions, which are personal, literary, and discursive. The personal division between Troilus and Criseyde is much more pronounced; they do not inhabit an identical world; on the contrary, Lewis's point about the asymmetrical relations of "courtly love" is very apt. Or it is until Criseyde's confident and rhetorically abbreviated ("at o woord") response to Troilus's more rhetorically elaborate speech. Literary relations are divided, too. However much Chaucer clearly is *not* following the "sentence" of his author, Chaucer's fiction demands a strict division between an authorial and a narratorial voice. The narrator is a reader, not a direct witness, cut off as much from the fullness of the scene as he is from fully transmitting his author's text. So, too, is he not wholly at one with his audience: they are to judge the narrator's rhetorical success at this difficult narratorial challenge. Between characters, then, as much as among narrator, original author, and readers, Chaucer's passage represents and itself negotiates complex differences of status and knowledge, handling each area of difference with discretion and tact. Stylistically and discursively, too, the passage is much more variegated than Boccaccio's text at this point: the style of Troilus's speeches is much more elevated and syntactically complex than Criseyde's calm response. Troilus also appeals to different discursive realms: his speech about Love's grace surpassing the lover's desert is translated directly from the highest sphere of Dante's *Paradiso,* as Saint Bernard addresses the Virgin at the summit of heaven (33.13–18), and so evokes theological discourse. He also evokes a philosophical conception of Love as the binding force of the universe, drawn from Boethius (Book 2, metrum 8).

Chaucer's passage, then, deepens and divides his source in many ways. He not only "in-etches" new words, but whole realms of experience — emotional, philosophical, and theological — into the small space of this scene. So far from creating a knowing, easily confident scene as in Boccaccio, the divided perspectives of Chaucer's scene set the characters, the narrator and the reader "bitwixen drede and sikernesse," as they are all playing for much higher stakes.

This small example is characteristic of Chaucer's changes to the *Filostrato* more generally: Chaucer makes his text much more resonant by importing new and entirely different perspectives into Boccaccio's raw material. In particular, he introduces much philosophical material from Boethius, and he "in-etches" long passages about, or spoken by, Criseyde (see especially 2.610–931 and 3.806–40). These powerfully critique Boccaccio's framing of his story as a narrative designed to serve the interests of masculine suffering. Chaucer's text exposes the long perspective, a perspective in which Troy will be destroyed and in which philosophical reflection and persuasion might be all that can save us. And, in keeping with Chaucer's Ovidian commitments, *Troilus and Criseyde* creates a much more powerful account of female suffering and choice in difficult situations.

That microanalysis could be extended across the length of *Troilus and Criseyde*. Rather than pursue such an analysis now, let us look instead at how Chaucer received the *Teseida*. The *Knight's Tale* was written in the immensely fertile period before the *Canterbury Tales,* which is its final resting place (it is referred to by Alceste in the *Legend of Good Women* as "al the love of Palamon and Arcite / Of Thebes, thogh the storye ys knowen lyte" [F.420–21]). Whereas Chaucer practiced rhetorical and narrative expansion on the *Filostrato,* he abbreviated the *Teseida,* Boccaccio's long narrative of twelve books, to its essential narrative of the two lovers Palamon and Arcite.

Even as he abbreviated the narrative, however, he also reshaped and darkened it. The crucial addition he makes is to include, and grant a decisive role to, malign Saturn among the cast of gods. Chaucer constructs a narrative in which there is symmetry between humans and gods: the younger generation of Palamon, Arcite, and Emily are matched by the younger generation of gods (Venus, Mars, and Diana); the middle generation is represented by Theseus on earth and Jupiter in heaven; Saturn mirrors Theseus's father, Egeus, to make up the grandparental generation. Theseus and Jupiter are, ostensibly, the ruling figures here; governance on earth is, apparently, grounded on a cosmic scheme. The arena constructed by Theseus would make that claim, with its precise hierarchization of all spectators and its placing of temples to the younger, warring deities within its structure. Theseus presents himself, indeed, as a god to the spectators: "Duc Theseus was at a wyndow set, / Arrayed right as he were a god in trone" (lines 2528–29). At this point, however, Chaucer differs profoundly from Boccaccio, since he upsets the earthly-divine symmetry by giving Saturn the decisive influence. In Boccaccio's narrative, Mars and Venus sort the fight out themselves; in Chaucer, Saturn is the fixer; he is described, in a passage wholly original to Chaucer, as thoroughly malign and pitiless (lines 2453–69). Whereas Jupiter is unable to govern the strife between Venus and Mars (line 2442), only brutal and malign Saturn is capable of sorting it.

The upshot of this is that Chaucer's narrative is *much* darker than Boccaccio's. The world of antique (and, by implication, modern) chivalry as presented by the *Knight's Tale* is simultaneously magnificent and inescapably bleak. In the *Teseida,* the soul of Arcite flies up the eighth sphere, there complacently to behold human enterprise from a cool philosophical distance (Book 11, stanzas 1–3). Chaucer borrowed precisely this passage in his account of Troilus's ascent to the heavens (*Troilus and Criseyde,* 5.1807–27). In the *Knight's Tale,* by contrast, Arcite dies "Allone, withouten any compaignye" (line 2779), conscious of nothing so much as his solitude in the universe. The wholly Chaucerian account of his corrupting body is followed by this stubborn refusal to narrate his life beyond death:

> His spirit chaunged hous and wente ther,
> As I cam nevere, I kan nat tellen wher.
> Therefore I stynte; I nam no divinistre;
> Of soules fynde I nat in this registre. (lines 2809–12)

In sum, by stark contrast to Boccaccio's narrative, the *Knight's Tale* reveals that the claims of earthly power to ground itself in the pattern of the cosmos are no more than empty claims; they are grounded on nothing more, or less, than entirely human constructions. Once again the much more variegated rhetorical surface of this text reveals a world subject to darker, and more complex, forces than govern the world of Boccaccio's *romans antiques.*[37]

Chaucer's engagement with precisely or broadly Ovidian themes across the period of his career from the late 1360s to the late 1380s reaches a crisis with the *Legend of Good Women.* In the prologue to that work Chaucer represents himself as having been overtaken and cornered by that Ovidian inheritance. In a dream the God of Love arraigns Chaucer for having written *Troilus and Criseyde* and the *Roman de la Rose* translation. Both these works are, from the perspective of masculine desire personified by Cupid, "heresies" against his "law" (F.330). Medieval commentators on Ovid's works imagined that Augustus had banished Ovid because he was furious with the poet for having corrupted Roman matrons with his licentious poetry.[38] Chaucer develops this commentary tradition by figuring his own biography in Ovidian terms: he, too, is threatened with spectacular punishment by an outraged and imperial male reader. Chaucer's response is, as ever, to pretend compliance and deference, by writing stories of "good" women prepared to suffer patiently. In fact, however, the stories are inspired by, and evoke the Ovidian subtext of, the *Heroides;* despite the demanding patronal intention, Chaucer's obedient performance of literary penance cannot help but reveal both male oppression and female retaliatory violence.[39] Once again the "weaker" category responds in such a way as to critique the more ostensibly powerful. This claustrophobic text marks the dead end of Chaucer's "courtly" period, even if not of his commitment to Ovidian poetics, which Chaucer now relocates to a different social milieu.

Late Career

In the *Prologue* to the *Legend of Good Women,* Alceste restrains the violent impetuousness of her husband Cupid by recalling him to principles of monarchical justice; he should be a "ryghtwis lord,"

> And nat be lyk tirauntz of Lumbardye,
> That han no reward but at tyrannye.
> For he that kynge or lorde ys naturel,
> Hym oghte nat be tiraunt ne crewel. (F.374–77)

Whatever the actual conditions of Chaucer's patronage in the late 1380s, we know that court life in these years was, for those closely associated with Richard II (as Chaucer was, as a bureaucrat), dangerous. And even if Cupid in the *Legend* is restrained by Alceste, relations between patron and poet are at best narrowly defined and claustrophobic. Cupid may decide not to act like a despotic tyrant, but he could clearly have decided otherwise with impunity. Richard II was himself accused of acting precisely like a tyrant in the last decade of his reign. Chaucer avoided the especial dangers of too close an association with Richard II, possibly by making a strategic withdrawal from courtly household circles between 1386 and 1389, and retreating to alternative positions in Kent.[40]

At roughly the same time as the Canterbury pilgrims are imagined heading away from London, then, so too was Chaucer heading in the same direction. This geographical movement marks a decisive shift in the social milieu represented in Chaucer's poetry. True enough, the Knight's Tale is the first tale told on the way to Canterbury, but, as we have seen, that tale's account of chivalric life is by no means an optimistic one. And it is unexpectedly followed, out of the Host's socially ordered sequence, by the Miller's Tale, the first of many tales told by manorial, mercantile, commercial, or urban figures in the Tales, a range of figures with entirely different literary commitments and energies from those of the Knight.

Does this dramatic change of social environment for the audience and production of literature mark a change in Chaucer's affiliations with continental writing? In Fragment II of the *Canterbury Tales* Chaucer continues to mark himself out as a modern Ovid. The Man of Law, asked to tell a tale, modestly replies that Chaucer has already told all the tales: "For he hath toold of loveris up and dooun / Mo than Ovide made of mencioun / In his Episteles" (2.53–55). This is clearly a moment of stocktaking by a very confident Chaucer, who can now transfer the modesty topos onto the narrator, the Man of Law, attempting to imitate Chaucer's own achievement. This might suggest that Chaucer is prepared to claim the status of originary author now, the kind of poet whom others imitate. Such a view would be mistaken, as the Man of Law's closing reference to Ovid makes clear. He insists that he will not attempt imitation of Chaucer, for

> Me were loth be likned, doutelees,
> To Muses that men clepe Pierides —
> *Methamorphosios* woot what I mene.
> (2.91–93)

Through the Man of Law, Chaucer deliberately conflates two importantly distinct literary references here: the Muses are called the Pierides from their birthplace, Pieria. In an entirely distinct mythological narrative, the Pierides (daughters of King Pierus) challenged the Muses to a singing contest, of which the punishment for losing was transformation into magpies (*Metamorphoses,* 5.293–678). The point of the mistaken conflation is to dissolve Chaucer's claims to originary status as an author. At the very moment that such claims are made, they are reversed: the Muses become their exact opposite, mere chattering imitators, who unsystematically pick up scraps of discourse, birds known for "rauca garrulitas studiumque immane loquendi" (hoarse garrulity and the boundless passion for talk; *Metamorphoses,* 5.678).[41] The claim to originary purity of voice dissolves into its opposite at the moment of its utterance.

The model of Chaucer as literary magpie better describes his practice in the *Canterbury Tales* than the model of Chaucer as pure voice, fastidiously preserving its singular identity. But if the actual, detailed borrowings in the *Tales* are unsystematic and often drawn from many earlier texts, the whole is governed by a principle that Chaucer seems certainly to have drawn from the example of Italian vernacular writing. As we have seen, Chaucer visited Florence in 1372–73. Although his engagement with select works of Dante, Boccaccio, and Petrarch has never been in doubt, scholars have had difficulty in accepting that Chaucer borrowed from Boccaccio's *Decameron* for the conception of the *Canterbury Tales*. That situation is now rapidly changing, with many scholars now agreeing that the balance of probability is now very much in favor of Chaucer's having had serious contact with the *Decameron*, both for individual narratives and, more important, for the entire conception of the framed Canterbury sequence of narratives. Helen Cooper has articulated this case most forcefully and authoritatively.[42] She recognizes that no tale from the *Decameron* offers an indisputable source for any Canterbury tale but argues that the *Decameron* is "Chaucer's primary model for his collection of stories" under these heads: (1) Boccaccio's text is the only story-collection before the *Canterbury Tales* where narrators agree to tell the stories as a pastime and where these stories are the raison d'être of the work; (2) five Canterbury tales (those of Reeve, Clerk, Merchant, Franklin, and Shipman) have analogues in the *Decameron;* (3) in both works the "author remains as a first person presence alongside the storytellers"; (4) both collections offer a wider generic range of tales than "the typical single-genre medieval story-collection"; and (5) both authors create "connections of theme and motif between tales."

Boccaccio composed the *Decameron,* in prose, after his return to Florence in 1346 and after the plague had struck Florence so terribly in 1348. Although the young storytellers who people the frame of the work are exclusively well born (unlike the Canterbury pilgrims), the "politics" of the text are very much those of republican city life. Like Chaucer's pilgrims, who join the tale-telling competition "thurgh . . . free assent" (2.35), the members of Boccaccio's *brigata* become a corporate body through willing decision; they are citizens, not subjects.[43] The social standing of Boccaccio's characters is in any case equal, but that equality determines the structure of the entire period of narration. Just as the officeholders of republican Florence changed at short and frequent intervals to prohibit concentrations of power, so, too, does the power over Boccaccio's literary commonwealth change from day to day. Although Chaucer's pilgrims are definitely not social equals, they are equal in the eyes of the Host as literary judge and, often, in their own self-estimation: for the period of the pilgrimage, they are equal members of a new, associational society. And if a consciousness of moral equality of sorts pertains, in different ways, in both *Decameron* and the *Canterbury Tales,* so, too, does a strong sense of *literary* equality: one tale is potentially as good as another, whether it be a romance about the love of aristocrats or a fabliau about the wit of urban artisans and merchants (or their wives). This consciousness of literary competition is all the stronger in Chaucer's collection, where the generic range is much wider than is the case with Boccaccio's.

In short, Chaucer introduces an entirely new literary and cultural "politics" into English writing with the *Tales.* And he does so from his experience of republican letters as practiced in Italy. As with his contemporary Gower, Chaucer imports republican ideas and art into England and adapts them to monarchical conditions. In his *Confessio Amantis* (1390–93), Gower adapts republican political theory derived from Dante's teacher Brunetto Latini, and even goes so far as to relate the founding of the Roman Republic, in his narrative of Lucrece, which relates the expulsion of tyrannical and rapacious kings.[44] Chaucer's adaptation of Italian republican art is less explicitly political, but it remains the case that a powerful dialogue runs through the *Canterbury Tales,* with aristocratic, "top-down" models of political, social, and cultural authority pitched against bourgeois, "bottom-up" models. This competition is not exactly identical with a confrontation between two of Chaucer's principal

Italian sources in the *Tales,* Petrarch and Boccaccio, respectively. It does, none-theless, correspond in good part to Chaucer's reception of Petrarchan and Boccaccian sources. Crudely put, Chaucer champions nobility of soul above nobility of blood in the *Tales;* and even where the question of nobility is not at issue, he champions native wit against aristocratic models of success through the guiding hand of providence. For all his championing of these "bottom-up" models, Chaucer is, nonetheless, incapable of imagining the violence of re-publican politics.

Of course there are many non-Italian sources for separate Canterbury tales: Chaucer introduced, for example, the fabliau, in origin a French form, into English writing;[45] and he picks, magpie-like, from *Le Roman de la Rose* across the *Tales*.[46] And some of his Italian sources were not written by any of Boccac-cio, Petrarch, or Dante: the intermediate or ultimate sources of both the *Sec-ond Nun's Tale* and of *Melibee,* for example, are Italian, but written, in Latin prose, by Jacobus de Voragine and Albertanus of Brescia respectively. Texts derived from Dante, Petrarch and Boccaccio do nonetheless provide a very vibrant source of debate across the *Tales*. The following tales are in large part or in significant moments derived from, or closely analogous to, these writers: the *Knight's Tale* (Boccaccio's *Teseida*); *Wife of Bath's Tale,* lines 3.1109–64 (in good part from Dante, *Convivio*); *Clerk's Tale* (Petrarch, *Historia Grisel-dis*); *Franklin's Tale* (Boccaccio, *Filocolo*); *Shipman's Tale* (Boccaccio, *De-cameron*); and *Monk's Tale,* narratives of Zenobia (Boccaccio, *De Claris Mulieribus*) and Ugolino (Dante, *Inferno*).[47] Accordingly, I conclude this ac-count of Chaucer as a European writer with a brief description of the cultural "politics" of his reception of Dante, Petrarch, and Boccaccio from *Troilus and Criseyde* into the *Tales*.

In Book 1 of *Troilus and Criseyde* (1.400–420), Chaucer has Troilus utter what is in fact the first translation of a Petrarchan sonnet into English, even if Chaucer does not reproduce the sonnet form.[48] This close translation expresses a state of paralysis in which the voice is caught between opposed poles, the opposing pull of which is surprisingly desirable. Its rhetorical structure is built up of contraries ("good"/"woo"; "bona"/"effetto aspro mortale"; "wikke"/ "savory;" "ria"/"dolce"); finally though, however much the contraries provoke questions, this is a poem of *consento,* of accepting subjection to *tormento*. At its most tendentious, we might say that this is a poem of knowing consent to masochistic subjection, of delicious and excruciating subjection to a power that dominates and divides the self.

Petrarch's is, to be sure, a love poem, but love poems express power rela-tions in terms easily transferable to more explicitly domestic and political environments. The Chaucerian narrative in which the question of Petrarch's *dolce tormento* surfaces most powerfully is the *Clerk's Tale,* the story of patient Griselda, who apparently submits to her husband's sadism. Chaucer drew this narrative principally from Petrarch's Latin text (1373–74), itself translated from Boccaccio's Italian vernacular version in *Decameron* (10.10). Chaucer takes up the tale of Griselda, then, within a broad grid of oppositions: republicanism versus despotism, vernacular versus Latin.[49] How does he move within that grid?

Petrarch's way of reformulating yet preserving aristocratic authority and its demand for unswerving obedience is to allegorize the story, using the example of a woman only to deny that contemporary women could be capable of following her. He effectively makes God a despotic ruler, who tempts us not in order that he should know our souls, since he knows them already, but simply in order that we should know our own weakness. Chaucer retains this interpretative swerve away from the literal story: just as a woman was so patient "Unto a mortal man, wel moore us oughte / Receyven al in gree [good spirit] that God us sent" (4.1150–51). In the larger narration of the *Clerk's Tale,* however, this abstraction from the literal Griselda is unworkable. Chaucer consistently stresses Walter's pathological, tyrannical, and needless obsession with testing, no trace of which appears in Petrarch (for example, 4.456–62, 621–23, 696–700). If Walter is a God figure, then God is himself pathological, even more so since he already knows the result of his testing.

In exposing the implications of this theological allegorization, Chaucer may merely be bringing to light implications that are already embedded in Petrarch's version. The result of this new emphasis in Chaucer is, however, to incapacitate the allegorical reading and to return us to the literal level of the narrative. If we cannot avoid the literal level, then must we not also abandon any notion that this story can have a happy ending? Griselda's patience is to a despotic regime; the "happy" ending exemplifies nothing more, it could be argued, than the happiness of subjects who do submit themselves totally to the inscrutable desires of tyrants.

What distinguishes Griselda from everyone else in the tale is, however, her freely given commitment to stand by a given social order. By maintaining that commitment, it could be argued, Griselda not only preserves her dignity but also humanizes Walter. In this reading it is not Griselda who is helplessly obedient but Walter himself, who cannot help but submit to pathological and vicious desire; he is, by the Clerk's account, like those who "kan nat stynte of hir entencion, / But, right as they were bounden to that stake, / They wol nat of that firste purpos slake" (4.703–4). By this reading it is Griselda, not Walter, whose actions have divine resonances, but they do so most fully only as long as we read her actions literally. By this reading the tale is a radically Christian defense of passive resistance, whereby a fundamental faith in human goodness rides out and finally exhausts human pathologies.[50]

Such a reading of Griselda puts Chaucer firmly on the side of nobility of soul, the doctrine that defines nobility as a moral quality, and so opens the category to anyone, regardless of birth. In less extreme situations, Chaucer appeals to the same doctrine, and does so by reference to Italian authors. In the *Wife of Bath's Tale,* for example, the old woman cites Dante in her dismissal of the notion that "gentillesse" derives from "old richesse" (terms translated directly from Dante's *Convivio*): any such arrogant aristocratic claim "is nat worth an hen" (3.1109–12). Such a claim also underlies Chaucer's translation of Boccaccio's *Filocolo* in the *Franklin's Tale:* here, too, claims of nobility of birth are modified by equally persuasive claims to nobility made by the non-aristocratic figures.[51] The tale Chaucer himself tells (*Melibee*—also derived from an Italian source), although not explicitly concerned with issues of nobility of blood or soul, argues strenuously, through the mouth of a woman, for the mechanisms of civic reconciliation as opposed to avenging chivalric shame. And in all the fabliaux (the tales of Miller, Reeve, Merchant, and Shipman), the claims of the non nobly born are powerfully made. Even as May in the *Merchant's Tale* unpersuasively claims nobility of blood ("I am a gentil womman and no wenche," 4.2202), she underlines the superiority of her intelligence over her "noble" husband.

For all the broadness of Chaucer's welcome for implicitly republican poetics, however, we should also note his apparent incapacity to register the terrible violence of republican Italy. Among the tragedies of the *Monk's Tale*, the Monk relates the narrative of Hugelino, Count of Pisa (7.2407–62), material that Chaucer translated directly from Dante's *Inferno* (33.1–90). The Monk ends his narration by inviting his audience to read Dante, since in "nat o word wol he faille" (7.2462). When we take up that invitation, it is difficult to avoid the conclusion that Chaucer himself "failed" in his translation.

Chaucer focuses on the children, and on the pity their suffering provokes. His Hugolino is entirely innocent, a victim of a "fals suggestioun." The emotional energy of the passage derives from Hugolino's protective yet knowing adult consciousness, as he witnesses the entirely unmerited suffering of his children. Dante's Ugolino, by contrast, is set in a much darker environment, in the ninth circle of Hell, in which those who are treacherous toward their homeland are punished; it is covered in ice, and very near the "fondo a tutto l'universo" (the bottom of the entire universe. *Inferno,* 32.8). Dante first meets Ugolino at the end of *Inferno* 32, as Ugolino gnaws at the nape of a fellow Pisan's head. The scene is extraordinarily claustrophobic, but less so than the terrible story related by Ugolino, who tells of how he had been locked in a tower with his young sons, and without food, by the fellow citizen whose head he now gnaws. The story he tells of their death is deeply shocking: he had, apparently, cannibalized his sons. The account is pitched from a closed, agonized perspective (that of Ugolino), locked as he is in vicious hatred of his fellow citizen. The presence of cannibalism hovers over the whole scene, both literally and metaphorically as an image for civic strife, as one faction "eats" another.

The pathos of a father knowing what his children do not is at the margin of Dante's scene; in Chaucer's translation that pathos is central. As Dante approaches this circle he says that that it is not describable from a childlike perspective (not "da lingua che chiami mamma o babbo," a tongue that cries mummy or daddy, 32.9). This, however, is precisely what Chaucer does — his emphasis is almost entirely governed by pity for the children's hunger. This is powerful in itself, but it ignores the republican violence of Ugolino's story. Ugolino tells his story not primarily to provoke pity in his audience, but rather to inflict infamy on his enemy; once he is finished speaking, he turns back to his horrible meal, and the exiled Dante to a terrible execration of his fellow Italians, the Pisans. Italian republicanism may have been the source of the liberating, "bottom-up" models that Chaucer embraced so intelligently and energetically in his final decade. That republicanism was also, however, the source of a ferocious violence that Chaucer seems ill equipped to have comprehended.

In conclusion, then, Chaucer did have a French and an Italian "period." His powerful engagements with French and Italian texts cannot, however, be limited to the 1360s and 1370s, respectively. Throughout his career, he continued to draw on and engage with both French and Italian texts. But Chaucer's engagement with "continental" texts is not at all restricted to writers of the recent past. On the contrary, his textual world was overwhelmingly continental, and that world was peopled as much by recent as by classical and late classical writers. The presence who mediates all these engagements is that of Ovid. As belated Chaucer, writing from the margins, broached the great "places" of poetry (whether those were located in ancient Rome or in medieval France and Italy), Ovid allowed Chaucer to find his voice. With his sensitivity to what has been left behind, indeed, Ovid allowed Chaucer to rediscover the English vernacular as a medium for poetry of high ambition. Chaucer became a European writer by becoming an English writer, and it was Ovid who authorized the rediscovery of that vernacular voice.

NOTES

1. *Canterbury Tales,* 8.173.
2. Rebholz, ed., *Sir Thomas Wyatt,* Satire 1, no. 149.100.
3. Robholz, ed., *Sir Thomas Wyatt,* Satire 1, no. 149.89–99.

4. For Chaucer's travels, see Westrem, "Geography and Travel." For Chaucer's biography more generally, see Pearsall, *Life of Geoffrey Chaucer.*

5. *Cligès,* in Kibler, trans., *Chrétien de Troyes, Arthurian Romances,* lines 28–35.

6. See Fisher, "Language Policy for Lancastrian England."

7. For a brief history of the modesty-topos, see Curtius, *European Literature,* 82–85.

8. For the history of Anglo-Norman writing, see Crane, "Anglo-Norman Cultures."

9. Hoccleve, *Regiment of Princes,* line 4978.

10. For Wales, see *Canterbury Tales,* 2.544. Chaucer imagines a fictional influence from Celtic literature in the *Prologue* to the *Franklin's Tale,* 5.709–15.

11. This is not to say that Chaucer is not responsive to Flemish culture; see Wallace, "In Flaundres." He may have used a Flemish source for the Reeve's Tale; see Beidler, "*Reeve's Tale.*"

12. For which see Pearsall, "Chaucer and Englishness."

13. Elizabeth Salter makes a similar point about Chaucer becoming a European writer by choosing English; see "Chaucer and Internationalism."

14. Initially the closing portion of Cicero's *De Republica.*

15. The major source, once in the garden of Nature, is Alan of Lille, *De Planctu Naturae* (1160s).

16. For Chaucer's relation to Ovid more generally, see Fyler, *Chaucer and Ovid,* and Calabrese, *Chaucer's Ovidian Arts of Love.* Calbrese mentions Oenone's letter at 37. See also Dimmick, "Ovid in the Middle Ages."

17. For an example of this commentary tradition, see Minnis and Scott, eds., *Medieval Literary Theory,* 20–24.

18. The translation, slightly modernized, is taken from Showerman, trans., *Heroides and Amores,* rev. G. P. Goold, lines 114–118, p. 67.

19. See Wimsatt, *Chaucer and His French Contemporaries.*

20. For the details of Chaucer's likely authorship of a section of the surviving *Romance of the Rose* translation, see Benson, ed., the *Riverside Chaucer,* 1103–4.

21. For Jean de Meun as a modern Ovidian, see Minnis, "*Magister Amoris.*"

22. For a translation of *La Fonteinne Amoureuse,* see Windeatt, ed. and trans., *Chaucer's Dream Poetry,* 26–40.

23. For Chaucer's schooling, see Pearsall, *Life of Geoffrey Chaucer,* 29–34.

24. Horace, *De Arte Poetica,* 38–40; see Simpson, "Dante's 'Astripetam Aquilam.'"

25. The texts to which Chaucer refers are as follows: Martianus Capella, *Marriage of Philology and Mercury*; Alan of Lille, *Anticlaudianus*; and Dante, *La Divina Commedia.*

26. Claudian, author of *De Raptu Proserpinae.*

27. All references to Dante's *Divine Comedy* are to the edition of Sapegno; all further references are made in the body of the text.

28. For an overly skeptical survey of Chaucer's specific debts to Dante, see Schless, *Chaucer and Dante.* For a more literary critical treatment, see Taylor, *Chaucer Reads "The Divine Comedy."*

29. Chaucer cites the *Poetria Nova* in both *Troilus and Criseyde* (1.1065–71), and the *Nun's Priest's Tale* (7.3347–51).

30. The best account of Chaucer's style in relation to sources remains Muscatine, *Chaucer and the French Tradition.*

31. For the impact of Italian writing on Chaucer, see the essays in Boitani, ed., *Chaucer and the Italian Trecento.*

32. For Chaucer's indebtedness to Boccaccio's early works, see Wallace, *Chaucer and the Early Writings of Boccaccio.* For Boccaccio's decisive influence on Chaucer's conception of both antiquity and modernity, see Edwards, *Chaucer and Boccaccio.*

33. Chaucer's introduction of the five-stress line into English may be indebted to Dante's eleven-syllable line, used throughout the *Divine Comedy.* Chaucer also experimented with the terza rima he observed in Dante (see "Complaint to His Lady," lines 15–39). Boccaccio's ottava rima may also have influenced Chaucer's development of rhyme royal stanza for long narrative.

34. Lewis, "What Chaucer Really Did to *Il Filostrato.*"

35. For which see Patterson, *Chaucer and the Subject of History,* ch. 2.

36. The translation is drawn, slightly modified, from Havely, ed. and trans., *Chaucer's Boccaccio,* Book 3, stanzas 30–33, pp. 49–50. Close comparison of Boccaccio's Italian and Chaucer's English is made possible in the parallel text presentation in Windeatt, ed., *Geoffrey Chaucer: Troilus and Criseyde.*

37. For the genre of the *roman antique* and Chaucer's reception of it, see Nolan, *Chaucer and the Tradition of the Roman Antique.* For Chaucer's translation of the *Teseida,* see Anderson, *Before the "Knight's Tale,"* ch. 4.

38. For Ovid under attack from Augustus in medieval commentary traditions, see Copeland, *Rhetoric, Hermeneutics and Translation,* 188.

39. For which see Simpson, "Ethics and Interpretation."

40. For Chaucer's withdrawal, see Pearsall, *Life of Geoffrey Chaucer,* 205–209, and Strohm, *Social Chaucer,* 65.

41. References from the *Metamorphoses* are taken from the edition of Miller, rev. G. P. Goold.

42. Cooper, "Frame." See also the essays in Koff and Schildgen, eds., *The "Decameron" and the "Canterbury Tales."*

43. See Wallace, *Chaucerian Polity.*

44. For which see Simpson, *Sciences and the Self in Medieval Poetry,* ch. 7.

45. There is one earlier fabliau in English, *Dame Sirith;* see Hines, *Fabliau in English.*

46. For many examples, see Correale and Hamel, eds., *Sources and Analogues of the "Canterbury Tales."*

47. This list of sources omits analogues, a distinction that is not always easy to maintain.

48. See Cook, trans., *Petrarch's Songbook,* no. 132, p. 194.

49. See Wallace, " 'Whan she translated was.' "

50. See Mann, "Parents and Children in the *Canterbury Tales.*" My paragraphs on the *Clerk's Tale* are modified from Simpson, *Reform and Cultural Revolution,* 318–21.

51. For the Boccaccian source, see Edwards, "Franklin's Tale." See also Taylor, "Chaucer's Uncommon Voice."

3

Chaucer as an English Writer

D. VANCE SMITH

In his first truly invented scene (in the sense that it describes his *own* scene of invention rather than the treasury of European literature, as in the *Book of the Duchess*), Chaucer describes what can only be a peculiarly English vision of his poetic. It is, in fact, a scene of poetic invention in both senses, a place that Chaucer creates, apparently for the first time, and a scene that describes the act, the art, of poetic invention. This is the vast house made of twigs that the dreamer Chaucer goes to at the end of the *House of Fame,* where all the sounds of world arrive, crowding in together. From these reemerge the sounds that make up all human discourse, including, though Chaucer doesn't say it, the sounds of his poetry.[1]

Stumbling through the great and often ravaged scenes of the classical world on his way to the House of Tydynges, scenes where the traces of ancient authority are still sometimes evident and powerful, Chaucer here hints at one terminus of his writing, the hubbub of English noise, the noise that he will celebrate in the midst of a minisumma of rhetorical art in the *Nun's Priest Tale,* the "out" and "harrow" of the rural landscape and the sounds of angry rebels in 1381, crowding into the city where Chaucer lived, crowding in so closely and so indiscriminately that they seemed compounded of both truth and falsehood, human and animal.[2] That crowding of categories would become the mode of John Gower's poetic invention in his Latin account of the Rising of

1381, the *Vox Clamantis,* a taxonomy of the forms of animality and cacophony of which the unruly human is capable. The scene of English noise is always
there, and occasionally Chaucer stops briefly to listen to it, to show how its
noise is the all-too-often disparaged echo chamber of his poetic invention. In
the House of Tydynges, though, it seems to be the scene of invention itself that
stops him, a scene that so patently lacks an authoritative, authorizing, shape
that when one appears, the poem quite literally is terminated. All of the beings
in the House of Tydynges, the embodied sounds of utterances on earth, rush to
one corner of the house, frantically trying to glimpse a figure whom the narrator glimpses:

> And everich cried, 'What thing is that?'
> And somme sayde, 'I not never what,'
> And whan they were alle on an hepe,
> Tho behynde begunne up lepe,
> And clamben up on other faste,
> And up the nose and yën kaste,
> And troden fast on others heles,
> And stampen, as men doon aftir eles.
> Atte laste y saugh a man,
> Which that y nevene nat ne can;
> But he semed for to be
> A man of gret auctorite. (lines 2147–58)

It is difficult not to imagine this man of great authority as embodying anything other than the myriad forms of authority that silence, that terminate, the
cacophonous scene of domestic poetic production: the classical *auctoritates* to
whom Chaucer turns in the writing of other poems, and with which he will
embellish and support his later poetry, and the more modish trecento writers
whom Chaucer treats as modern auctoritates capable of reordering and re-
mapping their languages and countries, like Petrarch illuminating "al Ytaille"
(*Clerk's Tale,* 33).

But perhaps most important, this figure of great authority is the figure
silencing the echoes of this very scene, the suppression of what Chaucer quite
deliberately and unambiguously shows us is the messy and all-too-intimate,
even if rambling, house of his own language. This silent authority, perhaps the
most enigmatic figure in a body of poetry that has its share of enigmatic
figures, has continued to authorize how we read Chaucer, to see him as his
great French contemporary Eustache Deschamps did, a "grant translateur"
whose greatest work was to import a greater tradition, a greater diction, into
English than the one he found. The silent appearance of this figure of authority
at the end of Chaucer's most comprehensive and sustained attempt to imagine

an English scene of poetry marks, at least for the reception history of Chaucer's work, the disappearance of English authority, the termination of what might have been, because it was once, an English art of poetry.

To think about Chaucer as an English poet is, strange as it may seem, an unusual idea. As the preceding chapter by James Simpson in this volume demonstrates, Chaucer is deeply steeped in continental writing, and in terms of literary history Chaucerians have tended to think of him as a European writer who happens to write in English.[3] Even his Englishness is sometimes traced, paradoxical as it sounds, to the depth of his appreciation for European literature. As John Speirs put it in his book *Chaucer the Maker* (1951), "Chaucer, as the development of his poetry shows, became consciously an English poet — consciously a master of English — through his work of translating, paraphrasing and adapting from other European languages (French, Italian, and Latin) and thus assimilating essential European tradition."[4] To read Chaucer without having some idea of what these sources actually say is to miss a great deal of what happens in his work, in English as it might be. When Chaucer's characters refer to the sayings of "olde clerkes," as Palamon does in the *Knight's Tale*, it is almost universally a sign that comparative literature is afoot. Not to realize that the saying that Palamon quotes, "Who can give a lovere any lawe?" is what Boethius's Lady Philosophy says of Orpheus as he compulsively looks back at his beloved and into hell is to miss, well, almost all of the irony and moral horror of that line. And not to know that the Ovidian story of Ceyx and Alcyone that Chaucer reads to put himself to sleep at the beginning of the *Book of the Duchess,* and whose ending he tells us he can't be bothered to tell us, is to miss either a moving transformation or a movement toward transcendence in a poem that seems to deny the possibility of transformation or transcendence. More generally, we might not be able to reconstruct just what Chaucer expected his immediate readers, most of whom had not even heard of Dante, to make of the weird, wonderful pastiches of Dantean scenes and ideas in the *House of Fame;* but the delighted and ingenious references to Dante make it hard to read it as a Chaucerian poem rather than as a poem about the introduction of Dante into England. But where did Chaucer's subtle, sly, and witty citationality come from? Did he learn to use other texts in this way only from Latin, French, and Italian texts? My argument begins with the assumption that Chaucer uses English texts with the same kind of intelligent creativity with which he uses texts in other languages. For Chaucer does indeed draw from other English poetry, and our reading of Chaucer is enriched once we accord these texts, and Chaucer himself as an English writer, a respect and seriousness that they have often been denied.

There are three reasons for the powerful idea that Chaucer is a foreign writer who happened to write in English, that his greatest innovation was to use sophisticated courtly models in the local vernacular of England. The first is, simply, that Chaucer was, in fact, what his French contemporary Eustache Deschamps called him, a "grant translateur," whose knowledge of contemporary continental literature was, as far as we know, unparalleled in fourteenth-century England, a poet who admired and was raised in the tradition of the ballade, complaint, and elegant allegory. A second, related reason is that Chaucer's use of English consciously imitates an international trend, the emergence of a serious and literary mode for the vernacular in France and Italy, and that, as Elizabeth Salter put it, Chaucer's "use of English is the triumph of internationalism."[5] The third reason has more to do with the long afterlife of Chaucer's canon and the focusing of literary history increasingly on Chaucer while his contemporaries faded into the shadows.[6] This might seem to contradict my earlier assertion, that it's strange to think of Chaucer as an English poet. But he was, in fact, seen as such a powerful force of nature by his admirers that they found it hard to imagine the prehistory of English literature or to express their interest in a poetry before Chaucer. John Lydgate compares Chaucer to the sun at midday "in whose presence, no ster may a pere."[7] Chaucer, in other words, is imagined as an "English" poet because he is imagined by them to have invented the tradition himself, to have begun what others who came after him desperately imitated, or to have made other English poetry irrelevant.[8] It is not unusual for one of Chaucer's successors to interrupt a poem on a topic completely unrelated to anything Chaucer wrote about and to place it in terms of Chaucer's innovation, his particular kind of poetry, which seemed like the only kind to write. Thus Thomas Hoccleve's long poem the *Regement of Princes,* a so-called mirror for magistrates that he translates from Giles of Rome's *De Regimine Principum,* turns aside for a number of stanzas to lament Chaucer's death and the deprivation of the entire domain of English poetry:

> Allas! my worthi maister honorable,
> This landes verray tresor and richesse,
> Deth, by thi deth, hath harme irreparable
> Unto us doon; hir vengeable duresse
> Despoiled hath this land of the swetnesse
> Of rethorik; for un-to Tullius
> Was never man so lyk a-monges us. (lines 2080–86)

For Chaucer's successors, the death of this English Cicero also meant the end of the beginning of English poetry, the end of its invention. Chaucer's death was from that point on bound up inextricably with the foundation of English writing, and the relation between these two phenomena seemed more inevitable the more this idea was circulated.[9]

But is this account of Chaucer in relation to English writing before him true? Did Chaucer really not think about the brilliant poets working around him and the ones who came before him in the English Middle Ages? Like many histories, this one of Chaucer's legacy is motivated by a powerful myth, the myth that Chaucer was sui generis, that — even in an age when originality for its own sake was not especially valued — Chaucer had in fact done something original, unprecedented, and transformative to the language and literature of England. This myth seems to be borne out when one notices that Chaucer never cites as an *auctoritas* any English writer, no one born in England whom he cites as the source for any of his myriad retellings. But then Chaucer never mentions the name of the writer who was his most pervasive and immediate source for a great deal of his work: Boccaccio. Especially in the case of Chaucer, silence is eloquent.

"Winne Whoso May":
The Economy of Chaucer and Langland

Perhaps the most surprising silence in Chaucer's work after the absence of the name Boccaccio is the absence of any explicit reference to William Langland's *Piers Plowman*. Both are surprising because Boccaccio's *Decameron* and *Piers Plowman* are the most obvious, immediate, and compelling models for the narrative structures of the *Canterbury Tales*. The numerical similarity between the anthology structures of Boccaccio's and Chaucer's works — 100 stories for the *Decameron* and 120 stories projected in the *General Prologue* — is clear, and there is a vast literature on Chaucer's indebtedness to Boccaccio at more particular points.[10] Just as striking is the indebtedness of the *General Prologue* to the *Prologue* of *Piers Plowman*, a work that certainly circulated widely enough for Chaucer to have known it, although he never mentions it. Chaucer is clearly influenced in some, probably deep, way, by Langland, but readers of both poems have conventionally believed that it is hard to point to specific and local borrowings because, as Nevill Coghill put it, Chaucer's debt to Langland is "a debt of idea and not of phrase."[11] There is clearly a general relation, at least, between *Piers Plowman* and the *Canterbury Tales* at the level of both form and structure. Yet critics who have tried to express what this relation might be have tended to be concerned more with the questions of origin and indebtedness than with what it might mean for Chaucer to have thought about Langland's poem at all, what it might mean for us to read Chaucer's work as a response to Langland and not just as a redemption of it from English provincialism or alliterative insularity. From the perspective of Chaucer criticism, Langland has appeared important, not because his poem makes our understanding of Chaucer's work more complex or interesting, but because he is one of the sources of ideas that Chaucer makes more complex and interesting on his own. Perhaps the most extended appreciation of what Langland might have meant for Chaucer, J. A. W. Bennett's article of 1969, still finds Langland important because of *Chaucer's* accomplishment in seeing the "literary potentialities" of pilgrimage in *Piers Plowman*. It is true that it can be hard not to imagine Chaucer as the end of a progressivist history, as the culmination of a tradition of writing in which texts are lodged with tropes and ideas that wait for Chaucer to animate them fully. Even the most influential and important study of the *General Prologue,* Jill Mann's *Chaucer and Medieval Estates Satire,* tends to relegate *Piers Plowman* to the status of a more-or-less inert "source" for Chaucer's work, little more influential than other works in other languages.[12]

The form of the *General Prologue,* which Jill Mann first described as estates satire, certainly had antecedents, not least in John Gower's Latin *Vox Clamantis* and his French *Mirour de l'Omme.* But, as Helen Cooper says, the "work that has the strongest claim to being [Chaucer's] direct model is written in English: the early version, known as the A-text, of William Langland's *Vision of Piers the Plowman.*"[13] Not only is *Piers Plowman* the most extended estates satire in English before Chaucer's *General Prologue,* but it was the most famous. Indeed, it became one of the most infamous English works during the Rising of 1381, when the pseudonyms of some of the purported leaders of the uprising, and the language they used, were borrowed from the poem: "Peres Ploughman" himself, "Hobbe þe robbere" (from, Anne Hudson argues, "Robert þe robbour" in A.5.232),[14] an injunction to "do wel and better" (the central ethical worry of the second half of the poem), the opposition of "treuthe" and love to "falsnes" and "gyle," a précis of six of the seven deadly sins that mirrors the six listed in the first version of *Piers Plowman.*[15] The number of estates in each is close — twenty-seven in the A-text, thirty in *Canterbury Tales,* and in each the last described is the tavern keeper.[16]

Two additional evident influences are the plowman and the theme of pilgrimage. Readers of *Piers Plowman* and the *General Prologue* are struck by the saintliness of the plowmen, by their utter and complete irreproachability in works where no one (least of all the narrators) is left unindicted by their deep corruption and hypocrisy. But it's paradoxically their willingness to get their hands dirty, to be more (or less) than moral exemplars that distinguishes the absence of spiritual stain in these plowmen. As Elizabeth Kirk noticed, Langland carefully represents the plowman as the *bovarius* of medieval treatises on seneschaucy, the one laborer in the manorial economy "whose authority," as Kirk says, is derived "from the respect in which his knowledge and the quality of his work are held."[17] Yet the apotheosis of the plowman in *Piers Plowman,* as Kirk shows, is unprecedented in traditional representations of laborers, and it is so unusual, even shocking, that Chaucer's virtuous plowman must be directly indebted to Langland in its "point-by-point reversal of the almost universal contemporary criticism of laborers."[18] As Nevill Coghill first showed in 1935, perhaps the closest point-by-point correspondence between these two great fourteenth-century poems is in the representation of the plowman. His claim that every line of Chaucer's portrait of the Plowman has a parallel in *Piers Plowman* is excessive, but the point should not be, any more than it is with the portrait of, say, the Wife of Bath, that Chaucer's sources fully account for Chaucer's work, even at particular points. What is clear is that Chaucer drew a great deal from the representation of the plowman in Langland's poem and that Chaucer was a careful and synthetic reader of the poem.

Chaucer indisputably takes lines and phrases from *Piers Plowman.* Piers himself says, when the pilgrims on their way to find Truth ask what he does: "I dyke and I delue, I do that treuthe hoteth. / Some tyme I sowe and some tyme I thresche" (B.5.552). His labor comprehends the cycle of agricultural work, from start to finish, a cycle that Chaucer condenses to a single line: "He wolde thresshe, and therto dyke and delve" (line 536). And where Langland expects the reader to work out the temporal relations between the kinds of work that Piers lists and to deduce the centrality of the figure of Piers not only to the agrarian economy but to the economy of time itself, Chaucer, as we come to expect from his deployment of temporal adverbs in the *General Prologue* — the nested opening "whan" clauses followed by the "than" of human action, of pilgrimage — marks more strongly the intervention of the human in the work of time, with the single adverb "ther-to" linking planting and harvesting. The traces of the language of *Piers Plowman* itself, and not just its ideas, in Chaucer's portrait show us the rich economy of Chaucer's concision, his appropriation and distillation of an already powerful idea in the greatest English vernacular poem before his. Yet the second line of the Plowman's portrait shows us Chaucer reading *Piers Plowman* even more inventively, virtually in the technical, rhetorical sense of the word *inventio:* using the poem as a repository of ideas to be yoked together in new, yet recognizable utterances.

The Plowman's labor seems at first to be part of the *General Prologue*'s program of solidifying bodies and intensifying materialities. His work, in fact, is described in terms of the cartloads he's hauled of a substance that could hardly be more material: he has "ylad of dong ful many a fother" (line 530). But as the very nouns here suggest, the work of the Plowman is also indexed as

English work, not just the work of the bovarius or of Anglo-Norman manorial treatises, but also the work of *Piers Plowman*. Here I mean, not just the plowman in the poem, but the larger idea of labor that the poem thinks through in increasingly diverse ways. *Piers Plowman* ultimately embodies — one could say incarnates — the complex of ideas around work in the figure of Piers himself, and before his appearance in Passus V, labor is imagined in and through a number of allegorical guises. In the passus before Piers's first appearance, the figure of Reason counsels the King to avoid corruption (personified in the figure of "Mede") and to work for the "commune profit" rather than for the advancement of "Wrong." As that last piece of advice attests, Reason might be right, but not above stating the blindingly obvious. Yet the consequence of following a policy of reason would be recognizable, in a strange and unexpected way, to a reader of the *General Prologue:* "Lawe shal ben a laborer and lede afeld donge, / And Love shal lede thi lond" (B.4.147–48). What Chaucer seems to have done is to have taken this crucial, but still very abstract piece of regal counsel, whose effects would be to instantiate, at the level of a national labor policy, a love that would counteract the increasingly unruly labor market, and to have made it far more concrete.[19] He deflects, or even restricts, these lines to the singular Plowman, and the national allegorical love to the *amor Dei et proximi* of the New Testament (and, it should be said) also of the plowman in Passus V (lines 564–65): "God loved he beste with al his hole herte / At alle tymes, thogh him gamed or smerte, / And thane his neighebor right as hymselve" (lines 533–35). The portrait emphasizes the interiority of this nameless figure, focusing on the difficulties of the discipline of love in practice, and strips him of the larger allegorical and social registers that accompany, even determine, the plowman in Langland's poem. Yet Chaucer does more than merely convert Langland's plowman into a dutiful Robertsonian laborer, the exemplar of Christian *caritas*.[20]

Chaucer's embodiment of the work of Law in the figure of the Plowman anticipates what Langland does in the next passus, but in one sense, and perhaps an important one, *Piers Plowman* invites just the kind of identification that Chaucer makes. The passage from *Piers Plowman* that we are discussing follows a slightly cryptic passage in which Reason talks about the relation between economic rectitude and justice. Were I king, says Reason,

> Sholde nevere Wrong in this world that I wite myghte
> Ben unpuysshed in my power, for peril of my soule,
> Ne gete my grace thorugh giftes, so me God save!
> Ne for mede have mercy, but mekenesse it made;
> For "*Nullum malum* the man mette with *impunitum*
> And bad *Nullum bonum* be *irremuneratum.*"
> Late thi confessour, sire Kyng, construe this [on] Englissh. (B.5.139–45)

Readers of the poem will recognize that this problem is embodied in the figure of Mede, a figure that is never fully resolved. But, as with many of the poem's discussions of Mede, the problem is not helped with the incorporation of Latin phrases that can be read either as allegorical agents themselves or as the integuments of an underlying and more accessible meaning. That is why Reason says that this passage must be construed "on Englissh," a procedure the poem conspicuously avoids, at least at this point. But I'd like to suggest that what Chaucer does here is precisely to construe this passage in English. His Plowman is a specific and local instance of what Langland everywhere and massively associates with the very work of the poem itself, with the question of redemption and the possibility of representing in a written work an action that ranges from dutiful agrarian labor to the salvation of the soul, and a figure that ranges from the postplague unrooted laborer to Christ himself. What Chaucer gives us is a surprisingly economical construal of this figure in English, a material and strenuous *imitatio Christi* in thirteen lines.

It's possible, too, that the figure of the plowman in these two passages from *Piers Plowman* also works the other way, giving Chaucer the macrocosmic perspectives of the *Canterbury Tales* and not just a loose compendium of material for one portrait. Chaucer's Plowman not only threshes, dikes, and delves, but does it as an act of charity, when necessary, "for every povre wight / Withouten hyre, if it lay in his might" (line 538). And Langland's plowman, whose labor has also just been described in the passage we've examined, refuses payment ("huyre") not just from "every povre wight" but from pilgrims, specifically:

> "Ye, leve Piers," quod thise pilgrims, and profred him huyre.
> "Nay, by [the peril] of my soule!" quod Piers and gan to swere,
> "I nolde fange a ferthyng, for Seynt Thomas shrine!" (B.5.556–58)

The refusal of "huyre" here suggests that pilgrimage and payment are incompatible, that a "ferthyng" has nothing to do with "Seynt Thomas shrine." In the *Canterbury Tales,* which begins and ends on the way to visit the very shrine of Saint Thomas "the hooly blissful martyr," the charitable work of the Plowman must be suspended. But that is only incidental, if not irrelevant, to the deep and apparently inextricable involvement of economics in the Canterbury pilgrimage's way of telling things, where *afflatus* and farthing are convertible, where ultimately everything, in the admittedly diminished perspective of the Wife of Bath, "is for to selle."

While Langland's plowman might have suggested the way to Canterbury, his pilgrims, and Chaucer's, thread their way through a world that is not only involved in earthly commerce but is deeply constituted by it. The movement from the plowman to pilgrimage, in fact, might be more accurately described not as a movement from the microcosmic figure of the plowman to the macrocosm of the frame of the *Canterbury Tales* but as a movement from the charitable labor of the plowman to the world of the macroeconomic.

Where Chaucer's macroeconomics differs from Langland's is in the direction of this movement. In the *General Prologue* we find out that, despite the Merchant's apparent competence and prosperity, his true economic state is a putative secret: "Ther wiste no wight that he was in dette" (line 280), a fact that might well be kept from the other pilgrims but not now, at least, from us. In Langland's *Prologue,* however, social groups are sorted a priori by their economic activities and conditions, beginning, of course, with plowmen, who in "settynge and sowynge swonken ful harde, / And wonnen that thise wastours with glotonye destruyeth" (lines 21–22). Already we find the fundamental division of fourteenth-century vernacular economic thought, examined at length in the Edwardian poem *Winner and Waster.* That poem is incomplete, but it is still clear that, as late medieval encyclopedias sometimes did, winning and wasting could each be described in antithetical ways, *in bono* or *in malo.* Here at the beginning of *Piers Plowman* it seems to be a positive virtue, to oppose the ethics of the wastrel and the glutton. In the *General Prologue,* it has both a neutral and a negative connotation: the Merchant, we are told, speaks his "reasons . . . ful solempnely / Sownynge alwey th'encrees of his wynnyng," the profit by which merchants are motivated. But the Pardoner, by contrast, does his work solely to "wynne silver" (line 713). Perhaps the most famous example of the word is in one of the better-known lines from the *Wife of Bath's Prologue:* "Winne whoso may, for al is to selle." It describes what at this point of the *Prologue* is the Wife's thoroughly mercantile worldview, her reduction of all things to commodities.[21] We are not able fully here to examine the many ways in which the opposition of accumulation and expenditure extends throughout the *Canterbury Tales* and constitutes one of its important subjects. But we should notice that the entire narrative venture of the *Canterbury Tales* itself is framed as a contest in which there will be losers and one winner who will eat "at oure aller cost," and in which the aesthetic and moral judgment of the Host — such as it is — is guaranteed by the threat of having to "paye al that we spenden by the weye" (line 806). Where *Piers Plowman* begins by characterizing the social world by its economic practices, and indeed by suggesting that economic practices tie people together in profoundly indebted ways, the *Canterbury Tales* begins its own complex investigation of the world of secular economics by linking economics and narration, the reckoning of accounts and the telling of tales.

Indeed, the very linking of storytelling and pilgrimage appears near the beginning of *Piers Plowman,* in the poem's catalogue of human pursuits.

Pilgrymes and palmers plighten hem togidere
To seken Seint Jame and seintes in Rome;
Wenten forth in hire wey with many wise tales,
And hadden leve to lyen al hire lif after. (B.Pro.46–49)

Especially telling is Langland's evocation of pilgrims who gather at the beginning of their journeys and go forth telling "talis" or who "leiʒe" for the rest of their lives. The conjunction of penitential and narrative gathering virtually explains the shape, and provides the formal justification, of Chaucer's *General Prologue*. As readers of both works know all too well, the multifarious forms of pilgrimage and the elusiveness of the true way are deeply lodged ethical concerns in the larger bodies of both immense works. But where Langland's worry over the suitability of writing poetry in place of other activities — real, physical, honest, labor, or intense prayer — is refracted in the poem's many occasions of self-reflexive interrogation and doubt, Chaucer places himself at the level not of narration but at the level of all the various contingent and impeachable narrators (indeed, as we see in the prologues to *Sir Thopas* and the *Melibee*, he's the most impeachable of them).

This perplexity in the presence of his own works and the works of others, whether we are supposed to think of it as self-deprecatory or (less likely) as a serious statement of the relation between ethics and poetry, was something that seems to have halted the work of both Langland and Chaucer at more or less the same time, in the termination of the first of what was to be the three versions of *Piers Plowman* and in Chaucer's *House of Fame*, with the arrival of a "man of grete auctoritee" whose identity is never revealed and at the source of whose authority we can only guess. As Frank Grady has suggested in a provocative article, these two poems share such an intense concern with the status of narration and the ethics of poetry that it is hard to imagine that Chaucer had not read at least the earliest version of *Piers Plowman* by the time he wrote the *House of Fame*.[22] The appearance of several groups much like those in the *Prologue* of *Piers Plowman* suggests that there may be some connection between the man of authority and the authority of *Piers Plowman* — to be perfectly accurate, though, we should perhaps acknowledge that it's difficult to tell whether this authority is grammatically subjective or objective: the authority invested in the poem or the authority for which the poem searches. But in Chaucer's great vision of poetic origination in the *House of Fame* we see how the authority of *Piers Plowman* is both insistent and complicated. Langland's arrangement of human activities in social tropes certainly seems to have appealed to Chaucer, but this formal similarity can hardly be the whole story for the deeply intelligent and inventive reader we know Chaucer to be. The authority of Langland also lies in his compulsion to undermine the easy signs of authority in his own narrative. We have just discussed the connection that Langland draws between pilgrimage, narration, and lying and its appeal for Chaucer's comparably large project in the *Canterbury Tales.* But that passage also seems to be behind the smaller but scarcely less ambitious *House of Fame.* In the poem's last scene of poetic invention, the house of wicker in which all words end up, the narrator finds it

> . . . ful of shipmen and pilgrimes,
> With scrippes bret-ful of lesinges,
> Entremedled with tydynges,
> And eek allone be hemselve.
> O, many a thousand tymes twelve
> Saugh I eke of these pardoners,
> Currours, and eke messagers,
> With boystes crammed ful of lyes
> As ever vessel was with lyes. (lines 2122–30)

Here is the social plenty with which Chaucer would later begin the *Canterbury Tales,* the pilgrims bearing stories and lies, the shipman who would tell the tale first assigned to the Wife of Bath (the only serious "English" romance in the *Canterbury Tales*), the Pardoner with his "wallet . . . Bretful of pardoun" (*GP,* 689). Although Chaucer's tone here is scarcely that of the ironist in the *General Prologue,* it is a tone we recognize: that of Langland, in his *Prologue,* the tone of what Jill Mann identifies as "a greater concern to *evaluate* human activity than we find in Chaucer."[23] "Chaucer" here clearly refers to the Chaucer of the *Canterbury Tales,* not the Chaucer of the *House of Fame,* whose panoptical perspective he clearly shares with, or borrows from, Langland at this point in his career. With the authority of Langland behind us, we might identify it as a more "English" version of estates satire than the one Chaucer later writes. But the perspective of the ethnographic outsider that Chaucer adopts here does not mean that he stands outside and above his work any more than Langland does, unwilling to indict himself as a kind of messenger bringing before us "lesynges" and "tydynges."

Chaucer's Weak Englishness

Chaucer's "Englishness" until recently appeared to be the product of a bellelettristic, impressionistic assertion that he represented something irreducibly national or cultural, something like the genius of the place. This Englishness was the detritus or, more kindly, the remnant of the critical process of deducting the vast and undeniably powerful heritage of continental writing in Chaucer's literature. As recently as John Speirs's book *Chaucer the Maker,* whose title describes Chaucer with a term used generally for writers in the English vernacular, Chaucer's Englishness is the core that we glimpse after we strip away French and Italian writing, the exceptional and yet utterly characteristic nature of the writer, a genius in the archaic and Romantic senses of the word — both a local spirit and a sport of nature. The only book purportedly on the topic of Chaucer's Englishness, Ian Robinson's *Chaucer and the English Tradition* (1972), really concerns Chaucer more as a poet who invented a tradition out of disparate modes and haphazard occasions. So strong is the drive to see Chaucer as inventor that Robinson calls the period before Chaucer, by definition, "pre-literary."[24] Even as sensitive and erudite a reader as C. S. Lewis argues for the strongly originary force of Chaucer's poetry, even if on the strength of a single (though much-admired) line: "Often a single line such as 'Singest with vois memorial in the shade' seems to contain within itself the germ of the whole central tradition of high poetical language in England. It is not so much poetical as 'English poetry' itself — or what Englishmen most easily recognize as poetry."[25] The period in which Chaucer lived is sometimes represented in John Speirs's book as archaic in other ways, as a preindustrial utopia, where Chaucer's plenitude is really England's: "Chaucer's poetry . . . implies, perhaps the most nearly inclusive social order that has ever been implied in English and (despite the Peasants' Revolt), the most harmoniously integrated."[26]

We tend to be more suspicious of the purely mimetic claims of literature today and might even regard this attempt to assimilate the complex affirmations and subversions of Chaucer's writing to an uncritical and unproblematic political order as critical, if not political, bad faith. Yet we have to wonder how much of that bad faith lurks in many assessments of Chaucer's inevitable, unwitting Englishness. Charles Muscatine, who more than anyone is responsible for our notion of Chaucer as a poet dazzled by French models to the virtual exclusion of English ones, also seems to collapse class structure and literary style: "Some Continental critics have found Chaucer irreducibly 'middle class' on account of [his] language, but that is to be too pure as regards decorum. It is, rather, a great part of his delightful 'Englishness,' which must be acknowledged however much we may discover of his debt to the Continent in style, subject and genre. And it is even more than a source of easy geniality and of an appearance of artless spontaneity."[27] Derek Brewer, like many critics after the heyday of formalism, begins to acknowledge the importance of the writing that preceded Chaucer. But his metaphor for this relation, the "English taproot of Chaucer's poetry," "Chaucer grafts on to his basic English style, found in the romances, a new diction," suggests an unwitting vegetable love, the inarticulate drive that finds its expression in words it did not invent — that is, it finds its words as a symptom of what it cannot express.[28]

To be fair, however, as the generation following Chaucer began to make clear, Chaucer's legacy to English literature is far more important than are his influences. The stronger the claim that Chaucer invented something new, the harder it is to argue that Chaucer also began his career with a considerable body of English writing with its own tradition before him. As Ralph Hanna argues in *London Literature,* a writer could conceivably, already in the early years of the reign of Edward III, think his work important enough to worry about its legacy and to continue to shape it precisely because he realized that it would continue to be read and continue to influence other writing in English.[29]

As philosophers might say, we can make both a strong and a weak claim for Chaucer's Englishness. This distinction doesn't refer to the obviousness of the claim or even necessarily to its immediate validity. A strong claim may appear to be "weak" in conventional terms: it seems unlikely to be true, yet if evidence and logic demonstrate its truth, we would be forced to think differently about the thing it describes. But a claim that doesn't add much to what we already know or is obvious without the adducing of evidence is conventionally a weak one. I wish to suggest that, as the citations we have just been discussing attest, claims about Chaucer as an English writer have more often than not been weak ones.

Chaucer, obviously, is an English writer in the sense that he lived in England, spoke the language that would shortly after his lifetime be used in Parliament, and wrote in that language. To describe Chaucer's work as an English writer in terms of the "genius" or "spirit" of Englishness that he exhibited is simply to make this tautologous claim. But what is more interesting and revealing is the strong claim about Chaucer as an English writer. It's more interesting because Chaucer effaces much of the nexus of English vernacular literature in his writing; yet, and this is the most powerful paradox of Chaucer's English writing, this effacing of immediate traditions and sources is one of the peculiar properties of the tradition of romance in England.[30] Less obviously he's a writer steeped in a tradition that is, in every sense of the word, English — written in a vernacular that only then was beginning to be spoken in the court and involving a tradition that self-consciously asserts itself against, most immediately and obviously, the French tradition. The tradition of romance in England appears to be only slightly less tenuous than Chaucer's status as an English writer. It's a tradition that's often accused of debasing or wildly misunderstanding its more complex French sources, yet the turn away from the "romance" of the romance to other subjects — primarily economic and familial[31] — can be seen as an analogy to Chaucer's own reticence about English writing, a kind of national trope of modesty in which the vernacular is too insignificant even to be mentioned as a corpus. Where Chaucer does mention it, it's in the deprecating, disparaging references of *Sir Thopas*. Yet *Sir Thopas* begins with one of Chaucer's few undeniable and explicit references to contemporary English writing, a reference that touches on the deepest forms of poetic self-imagining.

Chaucer's Strong Englishness

Chaucer's *Tale of Sir Thopas* is usually regarded as the sole evidence that Chaucer had ever taken any interest in English romances, at least to the extent that he had even bothered to read them. In this short tale, which is one of the hilariously failed narratives of the *Canterbury Tales,* so awful and banal that it has a strongly somatic effect on its hearers — "Mine eres achen of thy drasty opeche," says the Host in interrupting the tale — Chaucer, or his inept alter-narrator, names at least five, and possibly six, surviving Middle English romances:

> Men speken of romances of prys,
> Of Horn child and of Ypotys,
> > Of Beves and sir Guy,
> Of sir Lybeux and Pleyndamour . . . (lines 897–900)

This is probably the only time Chaucer mentions English narratives, and certainly the only time he mentions them by name (or by those of their eponymous heroes). Of these romances, all but *Pleyndamour* can be easily identified, and they all contain or exploit the strange and uneasy rapprochement between vagueness and specificity that is such an important structural feature of *Sir Thopas.* "Horn child" is the subject of two romances, one of them perhaps the oldest surviving Middle English romance, *King Horn,* probably written toward the end of the thirteenth century in four-stress rhyming couplets, a form shared with a number of chronicles and pieces of didactic writing.[32] The other version, more likely to be the one referred to in *Sir Thopas,* is called "Horn Childe and Maiden Rimnild" where it appears in the Auchinleck Manuscript, the most important manuscript for purposes of understanding what Chaucer knew about Middle English romances. The Auchinleck version of "Horne Childe" is a tail-rhyme romance, the kind of loose, interlaced structure that Chaucer parodies in *Sir Thopas,* although it has the more common stanza of twelve lines, while Chaucer writes stanzas of between six and ten lines in *Sir Thopas.* The two *Horn*s are slightly different. In *King Horn,* Horn is exiled when his father is killed by Saracens, and he eventually marries the daughter of a neighboring king after having survived a treacherous companion, a campaign in Ireland, and another encounter with the Saracens in which he avenges his father's death. Apart from a few references to specific places, such as the Wirral near Liverpool, perhaps better known as the wilderness through which Sir Gawain wanders his way to Bertilak's castle, the geopolitics of this version are vague and sketchy. *Horn Childe,* however, like many of the texts in the Auchinleck Manuscript, carefully plots the journeys, expeditions, and battles against a fully conceptualized map of England, beginning not in the unnamed country of Horn's father but in Northumbria, where the invaders are not vaguely nefarious "Saracens" but, first, an army from Denmark, which is defeated, and then an Irish "host," which kills Horn's father. Yet there's something almost banal and trivializing about the names that appear: in a little under sixty lines, the Danes retreat to "Clifland bi Teseside" (line 54), and Horn's father goes first to Alerton More (line 65), then to Blakeowe More (line 110), then to Pikering for a feast (line 116). Nothing particularly happens at any of these places; indeed, the court moves on to York just two lines later. On one hand, this might give the romance the verisimilitude of a royal itinerary; on the other, their very inconsequence and particularity anticipates the kind of fussy, but ultimately pointless, precision with which Chaucer locates Sir Thopas "In Flaundres, al biyonde the see; / At Poperyng, in the place" (lines 719–20).

The second romance named here, "Ypotys," or *Ypotis,* is written, like the earliest version of *Horn,* in the four-beat couplets that were apparently the first verse-form Chaucer used in English. At first glance, it's a little difficult to see why this might be included in a list of "romaunces of prys," until one remembers that the romance was an extremely baggy concept in the fourteenth century.[33] Yet the list itself suggests that the narrative has something in common with the others. Most of the poem is a question-and-answer dialogue between Ypotis and Emperor Hadrian, who is interrogating him about Christianity yet who sometimes sounds more like a catechist than the catechumen. But that is certainly not the intent of the poem, because "Ypotis," a name reminiscent of Epictetus, is neither a Stoic philosopher nor a naive child—he turns out to be the child Christ. Indeed, the term "child" circulates in the poem with a frequency that comes close to matching that of *Sir Thopas*'s. "The emperour wyth wordes sterne / To þat chylde he sayde yerne: / 'Chylde, he sayde, I coniure þe'" (lines 587–89). It might be that it is not the *final* intent of the poem for us to think that the interlocutor is a mere child, but it is certainly a part of the poem's effect for us to be uncertain, as we read the poem, who the real figure of authority is. The disclosure that this "child" is actually a man, and the very man who is the subject of the poem's theological discourse, confounds the already strange nature of the *magister-discipulus* dialogue in the rest of the poem, reducing the adult, indeed the institutions of the Roman *imperium,* to the status of playthings, to the state of childhood. Where *Sir Thopas* differs is that it never really determines who the child is and leaves us with the strong, almost certain, impression that the word "child" in this poem is to be taken all too literally.

If nothing else, the inclusion of *Ypotis* in this list suggests that Chaucer intends for the English reader, the reader who knows many of these romances, to identify their central connecting feature: they all feature heroes who are children, even if they eventually, and in the cases of the very long romances Bevis of Hampton and Guy of Warwick, grow up.[34]

At the very least, these romances can tell us how we should understand words and terms that seem, in the context of Sir Thopas, deprecatory. One example is the description of these texts as "romaunces of prys," where it's all too easy to hear the antithetical sense of "prys" — precious. But Horn Child uses "priis" to refer exclusively to victory at arms, at tournaments, or in hunting, and so "romaunces of prys" is virtually a generic term, a description of a group of romances that concern the proving and establishment of the chivalric hero, who usually begins from nothing, as an abandoned or lost child.

As with many English romances, the list itself is more than an incidental feature. It is a microcosmic instance of the parataxis that makes up the mode of narration, the adjoining of one scene to the next, characterized, as Patricia Kean says, by "coordination rather than subordination."[35] More generally, the list reveals a governing principle in the absence of auctoritas, the evocation of a singular source behind the unfolding narrative, whether he is "Dant" or the fictional "Lollius," that would otherwise situate the poem generically and remind us that this poem, at least, has dimension, a contour, a goal.

Thus Chaucer frequently and playfully reminds us that he is following his "auctor" in narrating *Troilus and Criseyde* and in doing so often calling attention to the tension between his present work and the ideal, Platonic form of the work. In Book 2, for example, we witness a complex triangulation of knowledges and desires involving Criseyde, Chaucer, and Chaucer's "auctor": "what she thoughte somewhat shal I write, / As to myn auctor listeth for t'endite" (2.699–700). Although we are not entirely sure who is writing, and when they write it, we are sure, despite and because of this complexity, that this poem is unfolding according to a preordained design. But in the bulk of the English romance tradition, this form of classical, quasi-scholastic authority is simply not available, and the list does the same kind of work.[36] A list can be used to situate the poem generically, to enroll it in a series of which it will now form a part. One of the features of the Breton lay, as it exists in English, is precisely this opening list, so important, and so fundamental a part of the texts that we have, that it amounts to a trope of inception. The most famous example is from the beginning of both the *Lai le Freine,* a Middle English translation of Marie de France's lay, and *Sir Orfeo:*

> Sum bethe of wer and sum of wo,
> And sum of joie and mirthe also,
> And sum of trecherie and of gile,
> Of old aventours that fel while;
> And sum of bourdes and ribaudy,
> And mani ther beth of fairy.
> Of al thinges that men seth,
> Mest o love for sothe thai beth.
> In Breteyne bi hold time
> This layes were wrought, so seith this rime.
> When kinges might our yhere
> Of ani mervailes that ther were,
> Thai token an harp in gle and game,
> And maked a lay and gaf it name.
> Now of this aventours that weren yfalle,
> Y can tel sum ac nought alle. (*Lay le Freine,* 5–20)[37]

And the Franklin introduces his tale with a less compendious catalogue of topics that make up the Breton lay, a shorter list of generic signals, but a literary history that is recognizable from the openings of such Breton lays:

> Thise olde gentil Britouns in hir dayes
> Of diverse aventures maden layes,
> Rymeyed in hir firste Briton tonge,
> Whiche layes with hir instrumentz they songe
> Or elles redden hem for hir plesaunce. (lines 709–13)

As we might expect, Chaucer's version of a Breton lay prologue is far less paratactic, more complex syntactically than the example from the *Lai le Freine.* It's more than a simple list, partly because Chaucer tends not to use lists to situate his work in a generic or discursive setting. Most conspicuously, he does use lists to tell us that he doesn't, or won't, use them, deploying the device of *occupatio,* a formal rhetorical trope that designates something while claiming not to designate it. At the end of the *Knight's Tale,* for example, the Knight lists the kinds of destruction caused by the preparations for Arcite's funeral by listing what he says he won't talk about, a catalogue that takes up forty-five lines and that has a cumulative effect of inescapable horror rather than comedy, in which even "the goddess ronnen up and doun, / Disherited of hire habitacioun" (lines 2925–26). Such devices are a signal that Chaucer intends for this work to be taken seriously, to be read along with the comparable rhetorical effects of its source, Boccaccio's *Teseida*. But the degree to which Chaucer uses lists in the *Knight's Tale* to create the effect of unspeakable or otherworldly horror is remarkable and one of his conspicuous additions to the structure of the story. His list of the horrors to be seen in Mars's temple, for example, is more paratactic, closer to an unanalyzed list, than the descriptions in the *Teseida,* which are subordinated more fully to allegorical expressions of which each element is an example. This tendency is worked out most fully in the portrait of Saturn, which is Chaucer's addition to the *Knight's Tale*. The lines that Saturn speaks are some of the most chilling in Chaucer's work:

> "My cours, that hath so wyde for to turne,
> Hath moore power than woot any man,
> Myn is the drenchyng in the see so wan;
> Myn is the prison in the derke cote;
> Myn is the stranglyng and hangyng by the throte;
> The murmure and the cherles rebellyng." (lines 2454–59)

Here the list approaches the formal elegance of the figure in rhetoric known as anaphora, especially in the repeated "Myn," with its insistence on the utter power of Saturn. But this is not to say that we have to look beyond this passage, and the passage on Mars's temple, to classical rhetorical precepts to make sense of them. We find much the same kind of anaphora used to describe as powerfully morbid a scene in a romance we know that Chaucer read — *Sir Orfeo,* from the Auchinleck Manuscript, written in London in the first half of the fourteenth century.[38] In it, Orfeo finds a scene much like those we have seen when he makes his way to the kingdom of the otherworld, where he sees everyone who has been taken from the world, and who were

> þouȝt dede, and nare nouȝt.
> Sum stode wiþ-outen hade,
> & sum non armes hade,
> & sum þurth þe bodi hadde wounde,
> & sum lay wode, y-bounde,
> & sum armed on hors sete,
> & sum astrangled as þai ete. (lines 390–96)

The scene goes on for a few more lines, but this is enough to see how *Sir Orfeo* uses anaphora to describe the kingdom of the dead in just the way Chaucer was to use even more fully in the *Knight's Tale*. It's possible, too, that the vividness with which Chaucer describes the state of Palamon and Arcite when they are first found, "nat fully quyke, ne fully dede" (1015), derives from the liminality of the people in *Sir Orfeo,* who are "þouȝt dede, & nare nouȝt." More than this, perhaps, the introduction of Saturn in the *Knight's Tale* gives us a god of powerful destruction in England and in English, who is responsible for the most acutely English scenes of horror in recent memory, "the murmure and the cherles rebelling." This most powerful and most disregarded of all the gods is perhaps Chaucer's most malevolent vision of the insidious potential of English, an inescapable language that is coterminous both with the inarticulate "murmure" of the Rising of 1381 and with the very narrative that contains it.

Just where the foreignness of the tale, its exotic and classical paganism, with its troika of disputatious gods, seems irredeemably classical, Chaucer turns to this peculiarly English vision of the otherworld. More precisely, it's an otherworld that belongs to this world, a world of unalleviated suffering. The geography of *Sir Orfeo* is necessarily vague, but vague because the otherworld is a nightmarish vision of this world — no directions are necessary because we're already there. And rather than a Saturn who's ineffably remote, Chaucer gives us a Saturn insufferably close, who's responsible for what we all want to avoid, a Saturn who's present at the intimate moment of death. It's Saturn who is the least interventionist figure in the poem, but who's ultimately responsible for the poem's action, even if, actually, especially since, the Athenians and Thebans are finally unwitting of his presence. But this isn't the last time that Chaucer echoes *Sir Orfeo* in the *Canterbury Tales*.

Most famously, when the Host turns to Chaucer for his story he quotes exactly what the King of the Otherworld says to Orfeo: "What man artow?" (*Prologue, Sir Thopas,* 695). Riding along with his eyes downcast, staring like a hare, the figure most — actually, totally — responsible for the action of the *Tales* is among the least acute presences on the pilgrimage. Chaucer's appropriating the classical god makes him, in fact, less proper to Chaucer — the scene of the god is an English one, not a classical one, addressed to an English poem, an English otherworld that is already ambivalent, already purged of its property of the otherworldly. Where Chaucer knows perfectly well that the classical Orpheus goes to hell — as he says in his Boece, "He wente hym to the houses of helle" — in Orfeo the English Orpheus goes to a vaguely Celtic world that has little to do with the underworld and little to do with the afterlife. Chaucer is commenting on the afterlife of poetry, on the appropriations that take him further from the scene he intends to translate, commenting on an English poetic that turns the supernatural to the domestic, however unheimlich that domestic might be. Just where the figure of interminable authority might be lodged, the site of the god whose orbit and whose looking has the furthest to turn, we find the narrator whose eyes have the furthest to turn toward the community of English tellers with him.

Chaucer's "Ars-metrik"

Chaucer's representation of himself gazing at the ground, perhaps thinking of that other narrator who, like Amphiorax in Thebes, sinks through the ground to hell (*Troilus and Criseyde,* 2.104–5), suggests to us a great deal about the intensity and inwardness of Chaucer's historical gaze, his awareness of what lies under the ground beneath his feet. But it also shows how unaware, even willfully oblivious, of the living community of speakers around him he might be. That this downward gaze might be more than a reticent, modest withdrawal from the people around him is suggested by the pun that the Knight makes when Theseus orders the vast and glorious tournament lists to be built for the contest between Palamon and Arcite. He enlists the aid of the builders and architects who know the "ars-metrik" necessary to circumscribe the vast circle of ground he has his eye on for the tournament. But that metric art also describes the measuring eye of Theseus himself and, more precisely, the ambit of the poet Chaucer, who not long before had directed the construction of the famous tournament lists at Smithfield. And we won't have fully understood the intensity of Chaucer's downward gaze until we recognize that his body is included in that gaze, the body of poetry, that is, circumscribed by his metrical art. This stratified pun shows us, as do many passages in Chaucer, how complex Chaucer's representation of his own poetic could be. But it also shows how much it could neglect or willfully leave out. Indeed, it might be better here to talk about how much Chaucer disinherits, for that's precisely what the alter-poet Theseus does with his own native tradition. That tournament gives way to a space cleared for Arcite's funeral, a space that leaves the local gods running up and down, "disherited of her habitacioun." To say that Chaucer's elliptical description of his own English art of poetry effects a similar disinheritance because it depends on a Latin double meaning, and not an English one, might seem to be assigning a single phrase a greater degree of culpability than it can bear. But it's precisely the sly way in which Chaucer uses a single phrase to focus the intensity of our gaze, too, on the ground before him that leads us to forget how much is really around us and how much of a living English community really surrounds Chaucer.

Perhaps more than any single line in Chaucer's poetry, what the Parson says about alliterative verse has helped to shape what scholars have said about Chaucer's neglect of native English traditions. In his *Prologue,* the Parson says that it's because he's "a Southren man" that he cannot produce alliterative poetry, a style characterized by bombast and abecedarian formula, what he calls a "rum, ram, ruf by letre" (lines 42–43). Until recently, scholars accepted the Parson's version of literary history as accurate: as the note to the *Parson's Prologue* in the *Riverside Chaucer* glosses this very line, "Allusion is made here to the contemporary alliterative poetry mainly written in the north and west of England."[39] Yet as Ralph Hanna has demonstrated, much alliterative poetry may have been written not only in but about London and its environs — that is, the area in which a "Southren man" would have lived.[40] Even the Parson's putative snobbery could be read as a Saul Steinberg–like provincialism, with the Francophile ground of poetry looming so large that it makes the "provincial" terrain of alliterative poetry dwindle into insignificance. Yet this posture is one that the Parson shares with the narrators of some well-known alliterative poems: *Winner and Waster*'s narrator worries that all the young men are evacuating the western provinces by going south; Langland begins his poem by implying that the plains below the Malvern Hills are more or less the entire world. But in each case the poems eventually display a full and copious knowledge of London that belies their assertion of a provincial locale.[41]

What often is omitted in discussions of the Parson's — and by extension, Chaucer's — apparent dismissal of alliterative verse here is that the Parson goes on to say that he "holds of rhyme but litel better." It is important to remember that this passage is part of a larger disavowal — the Parson's of what Dante earlier in the century called the "beautiful lie," and the *Canterbury Tale*'s palinodic movement into prose and penitence at the end of the long day's journey. Rather than thinking of the Parson's comment as an expression of a Chaucerian disdain for a poetry putatively of the provinces, then, we should perhaps see the comment, on the level of literary history, as evidence of what Hanna calls "the developing Francophilia of the circumambient literary tradition," or as evidence of yet another Chaucerian narrator's turn away from those close to him.[42]

Even if the tradition of alliterative poetry may seem to have been disinherited in Chaucer's work, we can still see a good number of its vestiges running up and down in Chaucer's lines. It happens that alliterative poetry is particularly good at evoking the scenes of battle, with its onomatopoeic resources in which blow can be matched by counterblow, and alliterative poems such as the lengthy *Destruction of Troy* and the brilliant *Alliterative Morte Arthure* dilate such scenes at length, where they condense others. The necrophilic celebration of Hector's corpse in Guido delle Colonne's *Historia Destructionis Troiae,* for example, which goes on for three sentences, and which was so arresting that John Lydgate was to make a passage of more than a hundred lines out of it in his

Troy Book, is reduced to a single line, while the battle in which Hector is killed by Achilles is a little longer than in Guido's version. Even the *Alliterative Morte,* which is far more sophisticated lexically and semantically than the nearly contemporary version in the *Stanzaic Morte Arthure,* contains more, and much longer, battle scenes than the *Stanzaic Morte* does. It should not be surprising then, that when Chaucer *does* "geeste," briefly, in alliterating lines, he should do so in battle scenes. There are two of these, in the *Knight's Tale* and "The Legend of Cleopatra," in the *Legend of Good Women* (lines 637–49).[43]

I've used the term "alliterating lines" to describe what Chaucer writes in both of these passages, because technically he doesn't write passages of alliterative verse. Alliterative meter generally calls for the first three stresses in the four-stress line to alliterate, while the fourth stress usually doesn't alliterate. Only two of the lines from Chaucer's passages, however, "Ther shyveren shaftes upon sheeldes thikke" (line 2605), and "And he hym hurtleth with his hors adoun" (line 2616) exemplify these rules for a regular alliterative line. There are four other lines in these two passages (lines 2608, 641, 643, 644) that contain only two alliterating stresses, one in each half line (that is, one before and one after a metrical and grammatical "break" known as a caesura). All of the other lines would be considered unmetrical in alliterative poems. It's clear that Chaucer wasn't trying to write a technically unimpeachable parody, such as he writes in *Sir Thopas.* But it's not immediately clear what relation these passages do suggest between Chaucer and the repertoire of alliterative writing. Some scholars, indeed, have suggested that because so few of these lines conform to alliterative metrical patterns Chaucer might not have been familiar with alliterative romances at all.[44] Yet these lines, as most readers recognize, sound remarkably like passages from such romances, and the wide dissemination of other alliterative texts, notably *Piers Plowman,* which Chaucer probably had read, makes it unlikely that he would be completely innocent of the principles of alliterative meter. As Tauno Mustanoja said of the numerous incidental alliterating phrases in Chaucer's poetry, "One has reason to suspect that he took a keener interest in the native tradition than early Chaucerians were willing to admit."[45]

Some of Chaucer's alliterating lines might invite us to take a skeptical distance from such writing, especially when all of the stressed syllables alliterate: "He thurgh the thikkeste of the throng gan threste" (1. 2612). This comes close to the overstatement of parody, especially because the alliteration here joins an adverb, an adjective, a noun, and a verb — almost the whole gamut of grammatical functions, where conventional alliterative verse emphasizes nouns and verbs. But the other lines don't do the same thing, and they do have an undeniably visceral force — "And he hym hurtleth with his hors adoun" is compelling in a way that precludes parody. It may be impossible for us to sort out the complex relationships between Chaucer and alliterative writing from this distance, but this very mingling of several registers in such a short passage does suggest that Chaucer's relationship is, to say the least, complex and not altogether dismissive of the resources of alliterative writing. It's possible that Chaucer stumbled on the secret recipe that combines stress and onomatopoeia so effectively in alliterative poetry and which alliterative writers themselves propagated so well, but it hardly seems a closely guarded secret in the fourteenth century.

The Tydynges of English

Readers of the *House of Fame* will probably not have forgotten the "Three Stooges" comedy of "fals" and "soth" crowding through the same window together:

> And somtyme saugh I thoo at ones
> A lesyng and a sad soth sawe,
> That gonne of aventure drawe
> Out at a wyndowe for to pace;
> And, when they metten in that place,
> They were achekked bothe two,
> And neyther of hem moste out goo
> For other, so they gonne crowde,
> Til ech of hem gan crien lowde,
> "Lat me go first!" "Nay, but let me!
> And here I wol ensuren the,
> Wyth the nones that thou wolt do so,
> That I shal never fro the go,
> But be thyn owne sworen brother!
> We wil medle us ech with other,
> That no man, be they never so wrothe,
> Shal han on [of us] two, but bothe
> At ones, al besyde his leve,
> Come we a-morwe or on eve,
> Be we cried or stille yrouned."
> Thus saugh I fals and soth compouned
> Togeder fle for oo tydynge. (lines 2088–109)

Our discovery of the making of "tydynges" disturbs the very principles of the poem itself, which was undertaken precisely to supply Chaucer with more "tydynges" — of "Loves folk yf they be glad," of "fer contree: and of neighbours," in short, no less than everything "that God made" (lines 644–50). Not only the material but also the method of deriving it and, more important, of narrating it, are troubled by Jupiter's purported injunction (we know only that the Eagle claims that it has been sent from Jupiter) to Chaucer, an injunction that amounts to a discovery at the end of the poem of the mixed nature of all tidings. The verb that one of these figures uses to describe the mixing of truth and falsehood, "medle," indicates that what is at stake here is more than merely a description of the epistemological uncertainty of language. It's a word that describes, also, the mixing of "tydynges" and "lesynges" in the "intermedled" "scrippes" of the shipmen and pilgrims who return the inscribed forms of the compound to their origin in the wicker house. Only from this impossible perspective, from the perspective of Chaucer's vernacular house, can we see the indefatigable and self-sustaining economy of the narratives that go forth and return in the house of fame — that is to say, that go forth in the form of narratives of all kinds, only to return to the original question of which should come first in poetry, the lie or the truth, the diversion or the doctrine.

This might not be the most elegantly ironic description of the work of poetry in Chaucer's corpus, but it is an important one. It shows how Chaucer steps back from the most devastating kind of critique offered by the other most self-critiquing poet of the English fourteenth century, William Langland. If anything, Chaucer blames poetry more than himself for its lack of transcendence or meaningful termination. Langland, by contrast, implicates himself in the interminable and unfulfilled promise of poetry. For him, poetry is dangerous not because it is made of truth and falsehood "medled" together, but because *he* becomes a compound, that is to say confused, being by meddling *himself* and poetry. His interlocutor Imaginatyf tells him that he shouldn't be reading — or writing — poems (without stretching things very far, including poems such as this one): "thow medlest thee with makynges — and myghtest go seye thi Sauter" (B.12.16). This passage not only amounts to a critique of the vernacular work of poetry, of "makynges," but also of the poet, the "maker," for interrupting the kind of salutary, redemptive reading represented by the Psalter. The making of poetry, more generally, is defined here from the start as meddling, a criticism that is particularly trenchant in a poem characterized by fits and starts, by interruptions, and by the interference of its own characters, which often halt its development.[46] In other words, Langland's anxiety over the ethics of writing poems is, ironically, the subject of the poem he is writing or, more precisely, anxiety is the ethical mood of writing his poem. For Chaucer, however, meddling is simply what we begin with, a mixed relation between truth and falsehood that we encounter whether we turn to the primal scene of poetry, language, or fame or to the larger world. And Chaucer seems to be offering a way out of the Langlandian hall of mirrors in this passage, also. We have no choice but to turn to "tydynges" if we want to say anything at all. The utterance itself tells us that we humans are powerless to evaluate its truth claims, and moral indignation is quite literally beside the point:

> . . . no man, be they never so wrothe,
> Shal han on [of us] two, but bothe
> At ones, al besyde his leve. (lines 2103–5)

We might be justified in wondering which of the two "compounded" beings tells us this — "fals" or "soth" — and whether, as a consequence, what it says is, in fact, the truth. But the point is ultimately that we can't know, and that we have to proceed as if all "tydynges" contain the truth. Further, as the Man of Law tells us, with presumably unwitting irony, "tydynges" make up the wealth of narrative.

In the *Man of Law's Prologue and Tale* we see the confluence of the ideas we have been exploring in this section, the relation between the scene of commerce in England and the invention of narrative, the interrogation of poetic work in terms of the production of language at the local level. Indeed, the *Man of Law's Prologue* is an exemplification of the compounded narrative we've just been examining, quite literally a tiding made up of "fals" and "soth" together. It begins with what is largely a translation of Innocent III's famous encyclical *De Miseria Humane Conditionis,* also known as *De Contemptus Mundi* for its rigorous attack on the temptations of earthly wealth. But what the Man of Law does by sleight of rhetoric is to convert its ethic into its opposite, to champion the acquisitiveness of merchants — their "wynnynge" — precisely because it enables narratives:

> Ye seken lond and see for yowre wynnynges;
> As wise folk ye knowen al th'estaat
> Of regnes; ye been fadres of tidynges
> And tales . . .
> (lines 127–30)

And it turns out that the tale begins with a group of Syrian merchants who demonstrate just how this works, returning to their sultan to tell him "Tidynges of sundry regnes," which they have acquired along with their merchandise. Yet despite the wide cultural and geographical ambit suggested by the Syrian setting and the wanderings of the merchants, the tale's opening description of the activities of these foreign merchants is set clearly and insistently, not in the marketplace of international commerce and its lingua franca, which included its own body of law, the Lex Mercatoria, but in the marketplace of English vernacular.

> In Surrye whilom dwelte a compaignye
> Of chapmen riche, and therto sadde and trewe,
> That wyde-where senten hir spicerye,
> Clothes of gold, and satyns riche of hewe,
> Hir chaffare was so thrifty and so newe
> That every wight hath deyntee to chaffare
> With hem, and eek to sellen hem hire ware. (lines 134–40)

The naming of this group as "chapmen" obscures, if momentarily, their identi-fication with the "riche marchauntz" of the second-last stanza of the *Prologue*. The connection between these two groups of merchants is made blatant, any-way, two stanzas after this, where they are described, now, as "thise mer-chantz" (line 148). This insertion of a synonym where it does not seem neces-sary appears at first merely to be a case of what the great arbiter of style Henry Fowler called "elegant variation," a device used by writers who, he says, are "intent rather on expressing themselves prettily than on conveying their mean-ing clearly."[47] But if that is the case, then why does Chaucer repeat the word "chaffare," even if it is used in two different grammatical functions, twice in this single-sentence stanza? A partial answer is that both of these words are English, as opposed to French, terms of art in the domain of exchange. Indeed, both are from the same Old English etymon, "ceap," and have a specific and very detailed set of meanings in English commerce.[48] And as Chaucer's deft use of the word "chaffare" here shows, the language of English commerce was capable of carrying shades of meaning and of making distinctions that were, in every sense of the word, valuable. What Chaucer seems to be doing here, in other words, is not only to link "tydynges" and "tales," but to do so within the linguistic and cultural horizon of English, a horizon that doesn't seem to shift no matter from which part of the world we look out at it. The linguistic saturation of this stanza by English mercantile words suggests, too, the power of the vernacular not only to adapt to foreign substance but to translate it in recognizable terms. At this point of the tale, at least, Chaucer seems to be imagining a form of translation quite different from the formal and learned practice of *translatio,* the dominant mode of his own poetic art.

We are prepared for this strange elaboration of the power of English ver-nacular where we least expect it by the introduction to the *Man of Law's Prologue*. It contains one of Chaucer's best-known catalogues of his writing, listing the *Book of the Duchess* and virtually all of the stories in the *Legend of*

Good Women. It's a strangely deprecatory yet chauvinistic account of Chaucer as a vernacular hero. Although it's true that Chaucer, as the Man of Law claims, "kan but lewedly / On metres and on rymyng craftily," and that he can only muster "swich Englissh as he kan / Of olde tyme" (lines 47–50), yet he has still outdone Ovid. He has "toold of loveris up and doun / Mo than Ovide made of mencioun / In his Epistles, that been ful olde" (lines 53–55). At some point the two kinds of age here must be indistinguishable. The otiose forms of Chaucer's English that signal his obsolescence (an important concern in a tale where merchants depend on the newness of their wares for success) and the archaic stories of Ovid that constitute the longevity of his authority blend into one another. But we shouldn't let the antiquity of Ovid overwhelm the antiquated nature of Chaucer's writing, although the deprecatory evaluation of Chaucer's style and "lewedness" makes it happen almost imperceptibly. I would suggest that the very association of the antiquity of English with the antiquity of Ovid suggests a discursive possibility for the vernacular that has usually been overlooked in this passage. It's well known that the Man of Law goes on to mention two stories told by Gower (although he doesn't mention Gower's name) that both involve incest. It's possible, although probably not likely, that these references amount to a kind of literary dispute between Chaucer and Gower.[49] And given this passage's insistence on the belatedness of what Chaucer has narrated, it doesn't quite add up. We shouldn't forget that the story the Man of Law does go on to tell is conspicuously outdated. The story, recycled a number of times by the end of the fourteenth century, is one that the Man of Law is given by a merchant and is set, in the words of David Wallace, "in the sixth century: this predates 1066, the year that marks the maximum historical depth of the Man of Law's professional competence, by half a millennium."[50]

The "olde tyme" of Chaucerian English narrative, it turns out, will be, in the story the Man of Law unfolds, the period before the obliteration of Anglo-Saxon memory, or at least its overwriting by the Francophone Normans after the Conquest. It is, in other words, a period more authentically "English," if also pagan, than the Man of Law's present. This complex relation between an unknowable past and the many kinds of "diversitee" that the story narrates (of religion, language, desires) is also the relation between Chaucer and his English. The stories that the Man of Law says that Chaucer *doesn't* narrate — about Canacee and the daughter of Antiochus — show up in Gower's English *Confessio Amantis* and, under the name, at least, of Canacee, in the *Squire's Tale.* That the Man of Law should list stories that end up in important English versions indicates that this passage at least implicitly concerns the relation between the promulgation of stories in English and the theme of incest, which, as anthropologists argue, is simply not admitting a great enough degree of "diversitee" into sexual relations. Even if explicitly disavowed by the Man of Law at the tale's beginning (and Freudians know that disavowal is really a form of identification), the specter of incest haunts the tale in its endogamous appropriation of stories in terms of what is already deeply familiar — the logic and language of English mercantile exchange.[51]

The location of the story at a point of historical oblivion (at least from the point of view of the Man of Law's legal memory, a memory that takes its warrant from the historical extent of the English law of possession) indicts the tale with, at the least, a deep epistemological uncertainty. And from the *Prologue* proper, in which the Man of Law remembers most of Innocent III's *De Miseria* but seems to have forgotten its main point, to Canacee's claim that "she forgat hir mynde" when she washes up on shore, the tale seems to hold out the possibility that uncomfortable information might be suppressed, but that it never is consigned to real oblivion. It remains familiar, if not too familiar, just as the disavowal of incest at the beginning compels us to wonder what has been forgotten in this story.

It would be remarkable, for all of the moral fuss the Man of Law makes in his *Prologue,* if Chaucer had been completely unwitting of any of the numerous versions of the story that begin with a father wanting to marry his daughter. It's likely, as I'll suggest, that these narratives, and one in particular, are what the Man of Law refers to Chaucer writing about in "Englissh as he kan / Of olde tyme" (lines 49–50). What Chaucer and the Man of Law seem intent on forgetting as much as incest is the particular English familiarity of this story, a familiarity, as we've seen, that implicates Gower's work. But it also implicates Chaucer's. The second example of the kind of incestuous story Chaucer *doesn't* tell is that of Antiochus, who "Birafte his doghter of hir maydenhede" (line 83). It's somewhat surprising, then, that this phrase should appear in the fragment that usually follows this one, at the infamous beginning of the *Wife of Bath's Tale,* where a knight casually rapes a woman: "maugree hir heed, / By verray force, he rafte hire maydenhed" (lines 886–87). The virtual *rime riche* of this couplet suggests one of the tale's important themes: the thematic permutations of heads, from the seat of judgment to virginity to the life of the knight. And although one thing that the *Wife of Bath's Tale* doesn't include in its disturbing account of relations between sexes is incest, this very overdetermination, the "thrifty" properties, of the head derive from another Middle English text that does entertain the prospect of incestuous catastrophe. It is yet another of the romances in the Auchinleck Manuscript, *Sir Degare,* which recounts Degare's long search for, and near-marriage with, his mother and his hilariously oedipal encounter with his father. That story's fascination with heads of numerous kinds — spearheads, giant's heads, sleeping heads, the boars' heads that are the heraldic device of Degare's father — needs extensive analysis (of the psychoanalytic kind), but Chaucer clearly diverts the poem's overdetermined heads to his own thrifty and acerbic use. More significantly, the *Wife of Bath's Tale* repeats the beginning of *Degare* with a difference. Degare's mother, lost in the forest, is raped by a "fairi knyghte," who "anon gan hire at holde / And dide his wille, what he wolde. / He binam hire here maidenhood" (lines 111–13).[52] Where it isn't "fairi" that is particularly problematic, troublesome, or interesting in *Degare*, it's precisely "fayerye" that remains potent and enigmatic in the *Wife of Bath's Tale,* partly because it is so clearly associated with femininity (presided over as it is by the elf-queen), in a tale told by such a powerful avatar of femininity, and, partly with a rapacious sexuality that *Degare* represents in terms of the realm of "fairi."

The forgetting of incest in the *Man of Law's Tale* also implicates another romance, the only other Middle English version of this story, at least that survives, the late-fourteenth-century *Emaré*.[53] That romance begins with an emperor falling in love with his daughter, whom he then sends to sea in a boat when she refuses to marry him (despite a dispensation from the pope). In its own way, that story is as self-conscious as is the *Man of Law's Tale;* the central object is a robe that is, among other things, a figure for the text itself, a *textus* woven with stories of difficult and impossible loves. Where the robe becomes a figure for narrative and the sense of wonder that gives this poem its unexpectedly philosophical register (we are expected to notice the different form of illumination that the poem describes, for instance — the light of heaven and the mere confounding of the senses that the robe inflicts), the *Man of Law's Tale* strives deliberately and ostentatiously for the same effect:

> In sterres, many a winter therbirforn,
> Was written the deeth of Ector, Achilles,
> Of Pompei, Julius, er they were born;
> The strif of Thebes; and of Ercules,
> Of Sampson, Turnus, and of Socrates
> The deeth; but mennes wittes ben so dulle
> That no wight kan wel rede it atte fulle. (lines 197–203)

The gesture of showing us things that we *could* know about but won't, or can't, learn about from him is one we have seen before, in the Man of Law's disavowal of the Chaucerian topic of incest. It might also be seen as a cosmological version of the worry that Chaucer expresses about his book of English, *Troilus and Criseyde,* at the end of that poem.

And for ther is so gret diversite
In Englissh and in writing of oure tonge,
So prey I God that non myswrite the,
Ne the mysmetre for defaute of tonge;
And red wherso thow be, or elles songe,
That thow be understonde, God I biseche! (5.1793–98)

Here Chaucer's concern is that the vagaries of English in practice will obscure the intent of the poem, another way of claiming that "mennes wittes ben so dulle," except here a claim refracted through the lens of English contingency.

The *Man of Law's Tale* offers a way out of this impasse by placing the origin and intent of the story beyond the reach of human memory and putatively beyond the confines of mere English and Englishness. Yet it does this, as we have seen, by turning to the internationalism of the mercantile imaginary. For example, the tale replaces Emaré's subtle references to the circulation of the robe as "nurture," as the form of civilization itself, with, as we have seen, a much more pragmatic and commercial view of the way circulation really operates in the world. But the *Man of Law's Tale* may have taken its cue from the man who saves Emaré, a merchant who just happens to take a daily constitutional outside of Rome, where he sees Emaré wash up on shore. His occupation might be incidental, but the poem registers his reaction deep in the perceptual apparatus of the poem: he, too, is dazzled by the robe and

was aferde of that syght,
For glysteryng of that wede;
And yn hys herte he thowghth ryght
That she was non erthyly wyght. (lines 698–701)

He responds, that is, exactly as Emaré's father did, seeing her as "non erthyly wyght," and presumably, therefore, further away than the four degrees of consanguinity mandated by canon law. *Emaré*, in other words, equates the derangement of perception of an incestuous father with the derangement of a merchant who sees a fabulous commodity. Without having to look at what Karl Marx says about the allurements and phantasmatic quality of all commodities, we could say that what Chaucer does is to associate the allure of the commodity with both the Man of Law and the Chaucer of the opening of the tale, to associate it, in other words, with the derangement of narrative that simultaneously claims its place in a world of cosmopolitan, predictable, and valuable action, and denies its rootedness in a tradition that is unknowable because forgotten in a host of ways: through the precise and technical definition of the extent of legal memory, the denial of the prurient content of an inherited tradition, the disparagement of the resources of English:

I kan right now no thrifty tale seyn
That Chaucer, thogh he kan but lewedly
On metres and on rymyng craftily,
Hath seyd hem in swich Englissh as he kan
Of olde tyme, as knoweth many a man. (lines 46–50)

English, that is, threatens to become unknowable, not because of its transcendence, but because of its apparently unmotivated "diversitee," its ungovernability, even its antinomian tendencies. Despite the apparent inadequacy of English, or at least Chaucer's declared failure to use it well, Chaucer sometimes becomes an English writer precisely by denying that he is one.

NOTES

1. Although my argument does not depend on this point, I am assuming that the *House of Fame* is Chaucer's second major poem, written in 1379–80, an assumption that has been the consensus among Chaucerians. But several critics have suggested that the poem might have been written after the *Parliament of Fowls* (John Fisher) or even *Troilus and Criseyde* (Alastair Minnis). See Fisher, *Complete Poetry and Prose,* 564, and Minnis et al., *Shorter Poems,* 171. In a paper given at the Institute of English Studies (6 October 2004), Marion Turner argued that the poem should be seen in the context of the Mercers' Petition of 1388.

2. For the noise, and the bestial cry in particular, of the rising, see Gower, *Vox Clamantis,* and Knighton, *Chronicle,* 208–30.

3. Although this chapter will not consider the linguistic details of the language Chaucer uses, an excellent study of the nature of his English is in Cannon, *Making of Chaucer's English.*

4. Speirs, *Chaucer the Maker,* 29.

5. Salter, "Chaucer and Internationalism," 79. This passage is borrowed from Pearsall, "Chaucer and Englishness," 90.

6. A useful account of this history is Trigg, *Congenial Souls.*

7. *Life of Our Lady,* 3.1640.

8. On "father Chaucer," see Spearing, *Medieval to Renaissance,* and Lerer, *Chaucer and His Readers.*

9. For a study of the equivalence of Chaucer's death and his poetic legacy, see Prendergast, *Chaucer's Dead Body.*

10. See James Simpson's chapter in this volume. Chaucer's indebtedness to Boccaccio depends largely on works other than the *Decameron.* Two books by David Wallace are among the best examinations of this relation: *Chaucer and the Early Writings of Boccaccio* and *Chaucerian Polity.*

11. Coghill, "Two Notes on Piers Plowman," 90. A lively study of the ways in which the two poets interanimate each other, at least in our reading of them, is Bennett, "Chaucer's Contemporary." Another useful comparison is Kane, "Langland and Chaucer."

12. Although Mann's book ends with a five-page discussion of the parallels between Chaucer and Langland, and despite her attestation of the humane and capacious interests

of both writers and the broadly similar narrative interests of both, her account of Langland still necessarily gauges him against Chaucer. Langland is "capable," for instance, "of a non-moralising delight in human variety," capable, that is, of being like Chaucer, of being unlike the didactic moralists around them, capable of being unlike himself. Mann, *Chaucer and Medieval Estates Satire,* 209.

13. Cooper, *Canterbury Tales,* 30.

14. Hudson, "Piers Plowman and the Peasants' Revolt," 87.

15. These are listed, along with citations, in Cooper, "Langland's and Chaucer's Prologues," 73, n.4.

16. Cooper, "Langland's and Chaucer's Prologues," 74. References to a Miller and Reeve in Passus 2 of the A-text, Cooper points out, describe them, as Chaucer does, as dishonest, "and it is a curious coincidence of detail that both reeves should be given a name and a provenance, Randolf from Rutland [A.2.75], Oswald from Norfolk" (75).

17. Kirk, "Langland's Plowman," 4–5.

18. Kirk, "Langland's Plowman," 7. For more on plowing and the manorial economy, see Dyer, "Piers Plowman and Plowmen."

19. For a comprehensive discussion of the relation between *Piers Plowman* and labor legislation of the late fourteenth century, see Middleton, "Acts of Vagrancy."

20. For a brief discussion of how this operates, see Robertson, *Preface to Chaucer,* 365–90.

21. Patterson, "Chaucerian Commerce," examines the cash nexus of late-fourteenth-century England and economic tropes in the *Merchant's Tale* and the *Shipman's Tale* as irresistible examples. For further examples, and texts outside Chaucer, see Smith, *Arts of Possession.*

22. Frank Grady examines the ways in which Langland and Chaucer "both use the grammar of the dream vision in the same way." Grady, "Chaucer Reading Langland," 11. This exploration of the formal and structural similarities of the two poems is a playful but finally serious attempt to find more than a mere relation of synchronicity between the work of these two poets, a kind of appraisal that goes back to J. A. Burrow's important study *Ricardian Poetry,* esp. 35–41.

23. Mann, *Chaucer and Medieval Estates Satire,* 210.

24. Robinson, *Chaucer and the English Tradition.* Robinson's history is clearly evaluative, not diachronic. It's because Langland, for instance, represents a "development . . . comparable with Chaucer's" that there is, in Robinson's words, "some potential point in seeing Langland as contemporary with Chaucer" (218).

25. Lewis, *Allegory of Love,* 201.

26. Speirs, *Chaucer the Maker,* 20. In many ways, the cultural agenda of this book is similar to that of Ian Robinson's. As Christopher Cannon has pointed out, Speirs's has a clear and unabashedly Leavisite program, signaled by the use of D. H. Lawrence, particularly, as a standard against which to measure Chaucer. Cannon, *Making of Chaucer's English,* 53 and n. 30.

27. Muscatine, "Canterbury Tales," 98.

28. Brewer, "English and European Traditions," 15, 17.

29. For a fuller exploration of how the singularity of Chaucer and the weight of tradition have been treated, see Cannon, *Making of Chaucer's English,* 179–220.

30. For examples of this phenomenon, see Riddy, "Middle English Romance"; Hanna, *London Literature.*

31. For more on this, see Field, "Anglo-Norman Background"; Crane, *Insular Romance;* and Smith, *Arts of Possession.*

32. For a summary of evidence about the date of *King Horn,* see Allen, "Date and Provenance of King Horn."

33. See Strohm, "Origin and Meaning of Middle English *Romaunce,*" and "Storie, Spelle, Geste, Romaunce, Tragedie."

34. A deeply useful study of the function of *Sir Thopas* in relation to the rest of the *Tales* is Patterson, " 'What Man Artow?' " For further citations of Middle English romances in *Sir Thopas,* see Loomis, "Sir Thopas."

35. Kean, *Chaucer and the Making of English Poetry,* 62.

36. For the vernacular use of the scholarly exordium, see Minnis, *Medieval Theory of Authorship.*

37. In Laskaya and Salisbury, eds., *Middle English Breton Lays.*

38. For the history of the manuscript and its relation to Chaucer, see the important articles by Loomis, "Chaucer and the Breton Lays," and "Chaucer and the Auchinleck MS." More recent studies have qualified some of the claims that Loomis made: see Shonk, "Study of the Auchinleck Manuscript," and Hanna, "Reconsidering the Auchinleck Manuscript." See also Turville-Petre, "English in the Auchinleck Manuscript."

39. See Turville-Petre, *Alliterative Revival,* 29–36.

40. Hanna, "Alliterative Poetry."

41. For these examples, see Hanna, "Alliterative Poetry," esp. 498, 510–11.

42. Hanna, "Alliterative Poetry," 502.

43. A third, brief, passage is in *Troilus and Criseyde,* 4.39–42 (pointed out in Barney, "Langland's Mighty Line," 108 n.14).

44. See Blake, "Chaucer and the Alliterative Romances," 163–69, esp. 166, 168. Blake suggests that Chaucer may have in mind the kind of rhythmic prose represented in the fourteenth-century *A Talkyng of the Love of God* and the earlier *Þe Wohunge of ure Lauerd,* or the kind of prose treatise described in manuscripts as either a "carmen rythmicum" or a "carmen prosaicum," Richard Rolle's highly alliterative prose. See Turville-Petre, *Alliterative Revival,* 21–22; for more on what is sometimes called "cursus" or "cadence," see Morgan, "Treatise in Cadence," and Smedick, "Cursus in Middle English." For a good, brief discussion of Chaucer's metrical facility for metrical mimesis, see Everett, "Chaucer's 'Good Ear.' "

45. Mustanoja, "Chaucer's Prosody," 80–81.

46. For explorations of this idea, see Middleton, "Narration and the Invention of Experience," and Smith, *Book of the Incipit.*

47. Fowler, *Modern English Usage,* s.v. "elegant variation."

48. See Smith, *Arts of Possession,* 108–53.

49. For a summary of evidence for this, see the note to the Man of Law's Introduction in the *Riverside Chaucer* (854). On Chaucer's use of the Constance story in the *Confessio Amantis,* see Nicholson, "Man of Law's Tale."

50. Wallace, *Chaucerian Polity,* 205.

51. For a discussion of the relationship between marriage laws, exchange, exogamy, and "tidynges," see Dinshaw, *Chaucer's Sexual Poetics,* 88–112.

52. *Sir Degaré*, in Laskaya and Salisbury, eds., *Middle English Breton Lays*.

53. For a discussion of the many analogues of the story, see Schlauch, *Chaucer's Constance;* a comparison of the versions in Chaucer, Gower, and *Emaré* is in Isaacs, "Constance in Fourteenth-Century England." A few of the echoes of *Emaré* in Chaucer noted by Laskaya and Salisbury are: "He lette make a nobull boot, / And dede her theryn, God wote" (*Emaré*, 268–69), "in a ship al stereless, God wot" (*Man of Law's Tale*, 439); and "that wordy unthur wede" (*Emaré*, 250), "so worly under wede" (*Man of Law's Tale*. 917).

4

Chaucer and Rhetoric

RITA COPELAND

In the "General Bibliography" of the *Riverside Chaucer,* rhetoric is presented under the rubric "Style and Rhetoric." The entry is subdivided, the first twenty items relating to "style" alone and the remaining ten to rhetoric as a means of approach to literary style or poetics. Of this second group, only J. J. Murphy's *Rhetoric in the Middle Ages* (1974) and Robert O. Payne's *The Key of Remembrance: A Study of Chaucer's Poetics* (1963) are studies of rhetoric in a broadly comprehensive sense, and of these two exceptions, Murphy's book is the definitive study of medieval rhetoric from c. 400 to c. 1500 and is not specific to Chaucer studies. Five of the studies listed under "Style and Rhetoric" are of the mid–1980s; the rest range from the 1920s (J. W. Manly's *Chaucer and the Rhetoricians* [1926]) to the 1970s. The principle of selection in the subsection devoted to rhetoric seems to be that these studies (with the obvious exception of Murphy's history) defined "rhetoric" in tandem with "style" or "poetics." More generally, we can say that the "Style and Rhetoric" bibliography as a whole has carried forward a long critical tradition of narrowing the competence of rhetoric to style: in this scenario, "Rhetoric" is the subheading under the general heading "Style." Some historians of rhetoric (notably George Kennedy and Brian Vickers) would argue that this is a critical tradition that *began* in the Middle Ages, with the emergence of rhetorical manuals devoted to such specific topics as the "art of poetry."[1] Other historians, however, might argue that the restricting of rhetoric to verbal "color," decorative language, and various formal properties is more truly the product of the Renaissance, when the influential theorist Peter Ramus (1515–72) declared that rhetoric was nothing more than style and that all systems of argumentation and conceptual structure previously studied under rhetoric belonged properly to dialectic or logic. This narrow view of rhetoric as external or decorative form is the conception that was purveyed influentially by such Enlightenment philosophers as John Locke and Immanuel Kant, who reinscribed the Platonic binary between verbal style (rhetoric) and philosophical truth. Within the more limited terms of literary history, the editors of the *Riverside Chaucer* unknowingly also accept this binary by creating a bibliographical category, "Style and Rhetoric," in which stylistics is almost interchangeable with rhetoric or very nearly stands in for rhetoric, as genus to species.

Does this conflation accurately reflect how rhetoric was understood in the Middle Ages and how Chaucer would have understood it? More important, how does the history and theory of rhetoric exceed the scope of the *Riverside Chaucer*'s category, and how can we see the medieval expression of a broader conceptual picture in the work of Chaucer? The culture of medieval Christianity was profoundly informed by inherited and evolving systems of rhetorical thought. Rhetoric was not simply an "art" that was codified in the later Middle Ages and became important to literary authors: as a crucial legacy of classical culture, rhetoric was a fundamental way of thinking and constructing experience.[2] To begin to understand the outlook of medieval rhetoric, we need to grasp its history through the largest and most pervasive cultural themes that embodied rhetorical thought.[3] A more powerful and comprehensive understanding of rhetoric allows us to see that medieval poetry also articulated its rhetorical thought in synthetic and multifaceted ways.

How has rhetoric defined itself, as a competence, a field, a discipline? Rhetoric has always understood itself as a metalanguage, a language about how discourse functions under contingent situations, from the smallest units to the largest conceptual fields, from intention and the production of meaning to reception and understanding, from judgment to argument, from persuasion to action.[4] As one theorist has put it, "Rhetoric has to do either with the consequences of possessing the truth or with the difficulties that result from the impossibility of obtaining truth. . . . Lacking definitive evidence and being compelled to act are the prerequisites of the rhetorical situation."[5] The ancient definitions of rhetoric that we may still cite today as anchors in a vast theoretical history also resonated in the Middle Ages. Aristotle defines rhetoric as "an ability [or power — *dynamis*] in each case to see the available means of persuasion" (*Rhetoric*, 1. 2), a definition that was echoed by Cicero.[6] The *Rhetorica ad Herennium* (c. 90 B.C.) describes the task of the orator as being able to speak about the moral codes and laws that apply to civic matters.[7] Cicero's *De Inventione* (c. 86 B.C.), the ancient rhetorical text that was most widely known in the Middle Ages, insists on the mutuality of eloquence and wisdom (without its counterpart, the one is meaningless, the other ineffective); Cicero calls rhetoric "artificiosa eloquentia" and defines it as a "branch of civil science."[8] Quintilian's *Institutio Oratoria* (c. A.D. 95) defines rhetoric as "bene dicendi scientia" (the knowledge or art of speaking well), which must be paired with the moral training of the orator.[9]

The practical proficiencies of rhetoric would be described as the control and effective use of the system of composition and presentation, the canons of rhetoric: *inventio,* or invention, the conceptual spinal cord of rhetorical theory, which the *Ad Herennium* defines as "excogitatio rerum verarum aut veri similium, quae causam probabilem reddant" (the devising of matter, true or plausible, that would make the case convincing,1.3); *dispositio,* or arrangement, which is the structuring of the composition; *elocutio,* or style, which is the verbal expression, through appropriate language and figures of thought (*sententiae*) of the matters "invented"; *memoria,* or memory; and *pronunciatio,* or delivery. In antiquity, at least, technical proficiency would also involve mastery of the parts of an oration. Most ancient and medieval rhetorical treatises would present the mastery of these technical elements, including the topics (*topoi,* or commonplaces) of invention, the divisions of the speech or oration (*exordium, narratio, partitio, confirmatio, refutatio,* and *conclusio/ peroratio*), or the established lists of figures and tropes, as the core knowledge from which any rhetorical proficiency must proceed. But the fact that medieval rhetorical treatises rehearse much the same technical information across the centuries does not mean that the understanding of rhetoric was limited to narrow technical rules. We would not assume this about other fields of knowledge, such as theology or law, which were similarly characterized by the transmission of technical precepts. Such technical rules are the points of departure for what might be called "rhetorical competence," not the point of arrival. These theoretical prescriptions are the products of observation about how discourse acts in the face of contingency, and they have constituted the material form of the art or discipline of rhetoric.[10] But they are also the means — we might say the topoi, places, or fields of reference — for returning to observation about judgment and knowledge in uncertain ethical and political circumstances. These fields of observation constitute the largest dimensions of rhetoric, the cultural, hermeneutical, and textual problems shaped through the disciplinary concerns of rhetoric.

The question that accompanies rhetoric throughout its history, the story that is told of it and the story that it comes to tell of itself, is of its quarrel — perhaps even mortal enmity — with philosophy. Philosophy's suspicion of rhetoric originates with Plato's attack on the Sophists, whose teachings about the power of discourse to move and persuade an audience, and about timely judgment in the face of changing circumstances (*kairos*), Plato was to call for the first time *rhetorike,* thereby imputing to the Sophists the claim that they taught a coherent art.[11] It was the formal coherence as well as the philosophical integrity of this so-called art, or *techne,* that Plato would then refute, repeatedly and interminably, throughout his writings. This is the binary between truth value and representation, philosophy and rhetoric, that passes into the Christian Middle Ages and through there into the long history of Western thought about language. It is with this ancient problem that we can begin to address the dimensions of rhetoric in Chaucer's writing. Chaucer and other medieval poets did not simply accept the Platonic binary between truth value and representation, philosophy and rhetoric: rather, they worked with that binary, using rhetoric as the site from which they would negotiate the conflicting claims over the authority of knowledge and the power of representation.

Because rhetoric is a site for negotiating the largest categories of thought, representation, and social being, the very history of rhetoric's representation as a discipline is also a political and cultural script. Rhetoric thus speaks through the history of social identities such as sexuality and gender; or we can say that gender and sexuality are part of the political text of rhetoric's institutional history. There is no better textual site from which to begin looking at the history of rhetoric's representation as a discipline, its metadisciplinary dimensions, than Chaucer's Pardoner. The Pardoner offers a dramatic embodiment — in every sense of the term — of the ambivalence and contestation in the history of rhetoric's claims to be a body of knowledge, a discipline. We can say that Chaucer builds the Pardoner out of this tradition, which goes back to Plato's *Gorgias* and the critique that devolves from it that rhetoric appeals to mere appearances, contingencies, appetite, will, and belief over conviction. On the terms of this critique, which became implicit to all theoretical reflection on rhetoric, rhetoric is no science at all but just a knack — fragmentary, shifting, and unregulated. So, too, the Pardoner is recognized or, more accurately, recognizes himself, as a speaker whose efficacy depends, not on a moral condition grounded in a priori truths, but on an ability to manage discourse under changing circumstances and to project a persuasive *ethos,* or character, in his preaching performances: "For though myself be a ful vicious man, / A moral tale yet I yow telle kan" (6.459–60). The Pardoner's body, with its notorious sexual ambiguity or hypothesized lack (the narrator's comment "I trowe he were a geldyng or a mare," *GP*, 691), most clearly associates him with an ancient and medieval tradition representing rhetoric through images of bodily fragmentation, transgression of gender boundaries, and the threat of unregulated or diseased sexuality.[12] The history of rhetoric is inextricable from the representation of sexuality: these discourses give the theoretical problem of representation its very vocabulary in Western thought.

This is the connection that Chaucer brilliantly realizes in the figure of the Pardoner. The *Pardoner's Prologue* makes rhetoric speak the history of its own condemnation. The Pardoner gives us no less than a manifesto on ethos, the Aristotelian principle of a speaker's representation of his own character as one of the forms of proof or means of persuasion.[13] In so doing, the Pardoner also manifests the very constructedness of character, the fact that a speaker's efficacy need be tied to no moral foundations or truth value. Defenders of rhetoric had taken on this problem through a kind of denial, erecting an idealized "good rhetoric" that would triumph over the rhetoric that Plato had condemned. Thus Quintilian exhorts, "Let us banish from our hearts the delusion that eloquence, the fairest of all things, can be combined with vice. The power of speaking is even to be accounted an evil when it is found in evil men; for it makes its possessors yet worse than they were before" (*Institutio Oratoria*, 12.1.32).[14] The Pardoner expressly inverts this triumphant defense: "Thus spitte I out my venym under hewe / Of hoolynesse, to semen hooly and trewe" (6.422–23). The Pardoner speaks as Rhetoric, the doomed protagonist in a tragic history who is compelled to rehearse his crimes, condemned to produce the truth of his transgressions and to internalize the censure that writes his history from the outside. And indeed, the Pardoner's "truth" is also revealed in his body, which is a locus of knowing for others — the Narrator, the Host, the other pilgrims. His body, like his rhetoric, yields up the truth about itself. In the "history" of rhetoric that Chaucer writes through the figure of the Pardoner, rhetoric's claims to disciplinary self-sufficiency, to the coherence that attends on being a "body" of knowledge, are undercut by the incompleteness and fragmentation of the Pardoner's body.

Are we to assume that Chaucer is affirming this antagonistic view of rhetoric, that reproducing the adversarial representation of rhetoric amounts to an acceptance of its terms? I would suggest that this is not a condemnation of rhetoric but rather an exploration of what that condemnation means. Staging the condemnation affords an opportunity of examining the implications of rhetoric as if from the inside. For the Pardoner shows us that rhetoric is the master discourse of experience: of temporality, circumstantiality, shifting interests, and moral ambiguity. The contingent, as viewed in rhetorical terms, is a distinct kind of knowledge; viewed in philosophical terms, it is close to what

Aristotle would call "practical wisdom," *phronesis*.[15] For example, at various levels in his discourse, the Pardoner does what we would now call "constitutive rhetoric," that is, constituting or constructing the identity of the audience as a collective entity in order for some kind of persuasion to take place.[16] The Pardoner details how, in his usual preaching, he manipulates the moral self-perception of audiences; but his immediate audience, the pilgrims who are hearing his present performance, he constitutes as knowing participants in the secret of rhetoric or, as others might argue, as the recipients of his confession,[17] but in either case, as a group that possesses the same knowledge that he has about language. It could be objected that in the Pardoner's hands, such constitutive rhetoric produces disastrous results: having let the pilgrim audience in on his methods, he has also delivered to them the power to call his game, to expose the hollowness of his ritualistic call for them to buy his false relics and pardons, to visualize his emasculation, and to reduce him to stuttering silence (6.919–57). But this proves only that the Pardoner has not mastered the knowledge of contingency, and we in turn can see that. The knowledge that rhetoric gives us about shifting circumstances, choosing the appropriate moment (*kairos*), and knowing the souls and the psychology of one's audience allows us to take the lesson a step beyond the Pardoner's circumstantial limitations. His example of rhetorical inefficacy has empowered his audience, constituting it as a social body capable of judgment, clarifying by negative example the positive efficacy of rhetoric as a social discourse of contingent situations. The Pardoner fails to know his audience, but through the kind of teaching that rhetoric provides, his audience can know him and ultimately know itself. Thus we see that it is the Pardoner's performance that "cures" the Host's "cardynacle," or cardiac arrest, after the Physician's sickening tale of Virginia, restoring the company's interpretive and ethical powers after the deadening effect of an arbitrary patriarchal law in the *Physician's Tale*.

As a theoretical system, rhetoric is built on the analysis of circumstances: the systematic calibration of person, action, time, place, and cause that transforms a loose assembly of incidents and motives into narrative. The theory of the *circumstantiae*, the questions that need to be asked of any case to be argued, formed a key component of invention, the conceptual nerve center of rhetoric. Two texts of Latin antiquity provided the fundamentals of circumstantial theory that was incorporated into virtually all rhetorical teaching throughout the Middle Ages, Cicero's *De Inventione*, and Boethius's *De Topicis Differentiis* (early sixth century A.D.). Both texts address a point that was to remain crucial to understanding the domain of rhetoric: the kind of question that rhetoric asks is always limited by a multitude of circumstances, which Boethius lists as "who," "what," "where," "when," "why," "in what manner," and "by what means."[18] Rhetoric is focused, not on the general question or "thesis" ("Is it good for a man to marry?"), which is the province of dialectic, but on the particular question or "hypothesis" ("Should Cato marry?"). Boethius uses the scheme of the circumstances to represent the art of rhetorical invention as a whole and thereby also to define rhetorical method. The inventional scheme of the circumstantiae takes many forms in medieval theories of composition, argument, and even textual interpretation. It is found embedded in medieval arts of poetry, especially in teaching about how to produce a vivid description (*descriptio*) of a person based on the attributes of physical and moral character and of the person's actions;[19] it is found as a device for inventing one's argument in arts of preaching;[20] it even appears in confessional manuals, as a device for investigating the sinner and the sin (for example, "who, what, where, with whom, how often, why, in what way, when") and in penitential writings for lay people, such as the *Ancrene Riwle*.[21] Perhaps surprisingly, it is also found as a device of textual interpretation, as a basic structure for introducing and commenting on important literary and philosophical texts: the scheme of the circumstances allows the medieval commentator to introduce all the essential information about an author and text ("who wrote it," "what is the title of the work," "when did he write it," "why did he write it," and so on) and, more important, to produce new arguments about the text, especially about authorial intention and the work's intended meaning for its designated audience (answering the question "why?" or the topic "cause"). The absorption of this scheme into medieval literary exegesis dramatizes the performative, topical, and indeed inventional force of the interpretive act.[22]

The rhetorical doctrine of the circumstances enables the construction of narrative, and we see its clearest application in the realization of character, as in the pilgrim portraits in the *General Prologue* of the *Canterbury Tales,* with their vivid descriptions grounded in specific topical details of person, act, cause, manner, and so forth (such circumstantial topics are described in Cicero's *De Inventione* as the attributes of the person and the act).[23] But Chaucer also gives it a theoretical realization, that is, he theorizes the very principle of rhetorical circumstances, exploring another dimension of rhetoric as the discourse of contingency in the figure of the Wife of Bath. Like the Pardoner, the Wife is a figure who embodies rhetoric and its constitution through the languages of gender and sexuality: more than a product of rhetorical technique, the Wife figures forth rhetoric as the body, that is, as material, social, and historical entity governed by a "multitude of circumstances." The Wife's circumstances are well known to us: her life story is the matter of her own exposition, or *narratio,* an account of the multitude of circumstances attending her five marriages that offers up more topical detail than any of the other pilgrims' narratives. The Wife is also rhetoric realized through certain attributes of the feminine body, another convention of long lineage in the representation of rhetoric: dress that is ornate and luxurious, high color, garrulousness and digressiveness, willfulness and opportunism, and unrestrained sexual appetite.[24] Martianus Capella depicts Lady Rhetoric as a noisy, imposing, martial figure, pompous, public, and grandiloquent.[25] The Wife's speech is characterized as excess, as the Friar's joke at the end of her *Prologue,* "This is a long preamble of a tale" (3.831), suggests. These are the most visible attributes of rhetoric, or of rhetoric gone bad, defying regulation.

But it is easy enough to castigate rhetoric as woman, woman as rhetorical excess, and both rhetoric and woman as carnal, along the conventional lines of medieval clerical antifeminism and ingrained suspicion of rhetoric. The Wife of Bath's text demands more, because it takes these discourses beyond their conventional framework, and uses its realization of rhetoric to think about the interpretive conditions of "being in the world." If the Wife's *narratio* is a manifestation of the inventional system of the circumstances, her opening words, "Experience, though noon auctoritee / Were in this world, is right ynogh for me / To speke of wo that is in mariage" (3.1–3), announce the claims of rhetorical knowledge, the pragmatic conditions of experience.[26] On one hand, this can be read as a critique of rhetoric's particularity as against the universality of authority, a reduction of knowledge to mere experience.[27] But on the other hand, her *Prologue* converts the claims of experience into a program of textual interpretation that is largely consistent with medieval hermeneutical practices. The *Wife of Bath's Prologue* works along multiple and often contradictory lines. She uses standard interpretive programs, such as quotation, glossing, and compiling of authorities; but her arguments also nullify the force of these interpretive practices in favor of direct appeals to common opinion:

> Men may devyne and glosen, up and doun,
> But wel I woot, expres, withoute lye,
> God bad us for to wexe and multiplye;
> That gentil text kan I wel understonde. (3.26–29)

Her discourse is a tissue — indeed, a compilation — of the very clerical reasoning that would exclude her from the privileged sphere of clerical reasoning; she is at once a voicing and a refutation of the clerical posture that women and books don't mix.[28] Her interpretive moves, her appeals to the experience or common opinion of marriage over the "divining and glossing" of clerical authority, can be seen as opportunistic and willful, and thus as evidence of the insufficiency of feminine hermeneutics.[29] But they can also be read on the legitimate terms of a pragmatic tradition of interpretation that always had a rhetorical and circumstantial outlook.

If the Wife is an embodiment of rhetoric, she also embodies rhetorical competence: her interpretive practices share in this tradition. The Wife's discourse participates in the same interpretive program that allowed medieval exegetes to "discover" a text's meaning in the circumstances of its production, to consider the positioning of a text among a multitude of circumstances — "who," "what," "where," "when," "why," "in what manner," and "by what means." On this view, it is not so important to ask whether the Wife's reading of authorities on marriage is "right." For her discourse deploys the very strategies of the commentary tradition out of which she is formed, in which theoretical knowledge or abstract rules are accommodated to conditions of experience that are ambiguous. Her appeals to common opinion, as in the lines quoted above, are of course underwritten by the rhetorical tradition, in which general opinion — a topic or "commonplace" — is recognized as a valid source of argumentation.[30] Similarly, her invocations of our own judgment as an interpretive standard are underwritten by a traditional notion of rhetoric as a kind of practical wisdom:

> I woot as wel as ye, it is no drede,
> Th' apostel, whan he speketh of maydenhede,
> He seyde that precept therof hadde he noon.
> Men may conseille a womman to been oon,
> But conseillyng is no comandement.
> He putte it in our owene juggement;
> For hadde God comanded maydenhede,
> Thanne hadde he dampned weddyng with the dede. (3.63–70)

Here, the immediate references to 1 Corinthians 7:25–26 and to Jerome's treatment of the scriptural passage in his *Adversus Jovinianum* also need to be seen in the framework of the pragmatic, reader-centered hermeneutics that Augustine had set into motion when he assimilated rhetoric into his system of scriptural interpretation in his *De Doctrina Christiana*, giving readers the equipment, but also the ethical responsibility, for "discovering" the truths that are to be understood in scripture. Augustine asks us to adduce various circumstantial considerations when we are determining the meaning of a passage in Scripture — and asks us ultimately to rely on our own capacities of judgment which will be informed by divine laws of love: "Therefore in dealing with figurative expressions, this rule will be followed: the passage in question should be turned around in our minds with diligent attention until the interpretation is led to the law of love. But if this is already clear from the literal sense, the expression is not to be considered in any way figurative."[31] What the

Wife's discourse demonstrates here is nothing less than the prudential wisdom that Augustine asked of scriptural interpreters. The fact that such reasoning is here given voice through the character of a libidinous wife who adduces as many circumstances as possible in defense of serial marriage is simply another layer in Chaucer's mise en abyme. It can be seen within its ironized framework as "feminine rhetoric" or on the terms of the supposed dangers of an unregulated vernacular hermeneutics;[32] but it is also recognizable on its own terms as a statement of an ethical tradition of reading informed by the pragmatic knowledge of rhetoric.

Rhetoric carries with it the largest questions of cultural authority (that is, whose voice is authorized to speak through history) and cultural transmission. Rhetorical thought (which includes, but is not limited to, particular rhetorical precepts) provides a framework within which to explore the capacity of language to "manage" history, to bring it within our comprehension. Rhetoric lends its conceptual apparatus to the creation of narrative form, whether in the "truthful" genre of historiography or the fictive genres of romance and fable. And of course it is through narrative form that we apprehend history, with all of the conflict between truth value and representation that this may entail.[33] In antiquity, rhetorical teaching supplied a theory of narrative form or of language mastery that could be applied to the construction of historical as well as fictive narrative. In his *De Oratore,* Cicero poses the question: "What class of orator and how great a master of language is qualified . . . to write history?" and proceeds to consider the difference between the mere recording of fact and the elevation of chronological record into literary art form: "Do you not see how great a responsibility the orator has in historical writing? I rather think that for fluency and diversity of diction it comes first."[34] G. W. F. Hegel spoke of the "prose of history," approaching history as a formal concern: our "history" comes into being through the very form through which it is constituted.[35] Can history become a rational inquiry into human events without the literary or rhetorical structure of narration, that is, outside of the formal narrative arrangement of events that rhetorical theory treats under the heading of *dispositio*?[36] On the terms of medieval thought about this question, sacred history occurs outside narrative; or it sums up and transcends narrative time because it occurs outside human temporalities. But the scale of human events — empire, war, conquest, the birth and death of peoples and nations — is to be comprehended only through narrative. It is this comprehension, its limits and possibilities, that Chaucer explores throughout *Troilus and Criseyde,* as he moves the narrative in and out of epic-historical time, romance and lyric time, compressing and expanding narrative time, abbreviating and amplifying: "to encresse or maken dymynucioun" (3.1335).[37]

In *Troilus and Criseyde,* Chaucer famously draws our attention to the construction of narrative, to the artifice by which events are made to seem natural,
inevitable consequences of a structure of cause and effect. At the end of Book
1, Pandarus undertakes to bring about a liaison between Troilus and Criseyde
and formulates a plan to engage Criseyde's attention and interest. Pandarus is
engineering a plot, both a concatenation of events and the sequential structure
of those events that will lend itself to narration (whether prediction of what
will happen or recounting of what has happened). He leaves Troilus to medi-
tate on his plans:

> And went his wey, thenkyng on this matere,
> And how he best myghte hire biseche of grace,
> And fynde a tyme therto, and a place.
>
> For everi wight that hath an hous to founde
> Ne renneth naught the werk for to bygynne
> With rakel hond, but he wol bide a stounde,
> And sende his hertes line out fro withinne
> Aldirfirst his purpos for to wynne.
> Al this Pandare in his herte thoughte,
> And caste his werk ful wisely or he wroughte. (1.1062–71)

Pandarus plots the affair on the recognizable terms of narrative emplotting
borrowed from the opening of the *Poetria Nova* by Geoffrey of Vinsauf, the
most popular medieval rhetorical treatise:

> If a man has a house to build, his hand does not rush, hasty, into the very
> doing: the work is first measured out with his heart's inward plumb line, and
> the inner man marks out a series of steps beforehand, according to a definite
> plan; his heart's hand shapes the whole before his body's hand does so, and his
> building is a plan before it is an actuality. Poetry herself may see in this
> analogy what law must be given to poets: let not the hand be in a rush toward
> the pen, nor the tongue on fire to utter a word. . . . Let the mind's inner
> compass circumscribe the whole area of the subject matter in advance. Let a
> definite plan predetermine the area in which the pen will make its way or
> where it will fix its Gibraltar.[38]

Lines 1065–69 in Chaucer's text are directly taken from the opening lines of
the *Poetria Nova.* Pandarus's meditations on how to bring about a meeting
and ultimately a love affair are presented in conspicuously rhetorical terms:
Pandarus imagines his "matere" (*materia*) and establishes the references of
time and place; and he projects forward to imagine the linear and causal
structure of the narrative that he is about to produce. Pandarus's "narrative" is
the plot within a plot, for his very emplotting of the lovers' encounter will

form the core plot of Chaucer's "tragedye." This double plotting defines the space of two temporalities in the poem: narrative action as seen from within the small contingencies of human interactions on a local scale, and the containment of this narrative within a historical time seen from above and outside the local scale that broadens into the largest events of human history (war, conquest, empire) and ultimately a cosmic history presented in both philosophical (Neoplatonist) and theological terms (5.1807–69). At this moment, at the end of the poem, celestial time is foreshortened narrative time:

> And down from thennes faste he gan avyse
> This litel spot of erthe that with the se
> Embraced is, and fully gan despise
> This wrecched world . . .
>
> . . . .
>
> . . . and at the laste,
> Ther he was slayn his lokyng down he caste,
>
> And in hymself he lough right at the wo
> Of hem that wepten for his deth so faste (5.1814–22)

Celestial time is simultaneity, and we are asked to recognize how artificial has been the "real" narrative time of the poem, including the extraordinarily skillful descriptions of time that is lengthened by the tedium and suspense of futile expectation, human time slowed almost unbearably by desire, as Troilus and Pandarus await Criseyde's return (5.1100–309). Yet it is with the very artifice of human history, rhetoric's narrative domain, that the poem is most concerned. The secularity of rhetorical time reaches its limits against the broad expanse of cosmic-sacred time; yet we operate through the rhetoric of history, in all of its limitations of mutability and contingency, and in all of its technical effects of selection, arrangement, and ordering, retrospectively defining cause and effect.[39]

Troilus and Criseyde thematizes narrative time against the pressure of historical time by variously calling attention to historical change and to language itself as both the site of loss and the engine of recovery. At the opening of Book 2, launching into his (and Pandarus's) matter, the narrator invokes Clio, the muse of history (2.8), in imitation of Statius's *Thebaid* (1.41). It is worth noting that a gloss in one manuscript of the *Troilus,* MS B.L. Harley 2392, calls Clio "domina eloquentie" (lady of eloquence).[40] Perhaps the glossator recognizes that in addition to her identification with history, Clio also has an association with rhetoric, notably in Martianus Capella's *Marriage of Philology and Mercury,* where Clio is given a speech about the power of rhetoric to unlock and multiply linguistic meaning (2.122).[41] Thus in the figure of Clio, history is rhetoric, and the two are appropriately linked at this moment in the poem, when the narrator makes his most important pronouncement about the mutability of language throughout historical time:

> Forwhi to every lovere I me excuse,
> That of no sentement I this endite,
> But out of Latyn in my tonge it write.
>
> Wherfore I nyl have neither thank ne blame
> Of al this werk, but prey yow mekely,
> Disblameth me if any word be lame,
> For as myn auctour seyde, so sey I.
> Ek though I speeke of love unfelyngly,
> No wondre is, for it nothyng of newe is;
> A blynd man kan nat juggen wel in hewis.
>
> Ye knowe ek that in forme of speche is chaunge
> Withinne a thousand yeer, and wordes tho
> That hadden pris, now wonder nyce and straunge
> Us thinketh hem, and yet thei spake hem so,
> And spedde as wel in love as men now do;
> Ek for to wynnen love in sondry ages,
> In sondry londes, sondry ben usages. (2.12–28)

In these verses, a commonplace about the faithful translator's duty ("as myn auctour seyde, so sey I"), here predicated on the fictive claim that the *Troilus* is translated from a classical Latin source ("But out of Latyn in my tonge it write"), broadens into a statement about historical distance and historical inquiry. Language is here the sign of mutability through time that places the past outside the powers of accurate representation; or perhaps it is through language that we register historical loss. Language — the language of literary or persuasive narrative — is that "paynted proces" that Criseyde decries when Pandarus's beguiling and digressive tale of Troilus's heroism suddenly reveals its ulterior purpose, that she should accept Troilus's love (2.120–428, especially line 424). Yet it is also through the powers of eloquence that the poem stages one possibility for overcoming historical alienation, as it claims to perform the work of translation from ancient Latin to modern vernacular. This is the poem's central beguiling fiction, its own "paynted proces"; but it is also where the poem makes its most serious and sustained effort to come to terms with the gap between pagan antiquity and Christian modernity, and thus also with the two temporalities of secular and sacred history.

Rhetoric not only provides a structure for representing the historical past; it is also linked inextricably with the conduct of human affairs in the present, that is, with politics and with civil discourse. If rhetoric is an art of the contingent, it is truly the art of the politically contingent. The earliest systematic treatments of rhetoric (Aristotle, Cicero) treated it in relation to legal and political oratory, to forensic inquiry and political deliberation. Even though the political structures that gave rise to the golden ages of Athenian and, later on, Roman oratory had no direct equivalents in the Middle Ages, rhetoric remained firmly associated with the conduct of civil affairs and with persuasive discourse in matters of state. Medieval writers would have had ready access to the most important articulations of this in Cicero's *De Inventione.* Cicero's treatise opens with a famous myth of the origins of rhetoric. In the earliest times, he says, men wandered the fields like animals, unconstrained by religion, duty, or law. Then one man emerged who was able to convince the people to regulate themselves: "He introduced them to every useful and honourable occupation, though they cried out against it at first because of its novelty, and then when through reason and eloquence they had listened with greater attention, he transformed them from wild savages into a kind and gentle folk."[42] Rhetoric is the original civilizing force: eloquent reasoning imposes social order. Having placed rhetoric at the beginning of human history, Cicero then establishes the definition of rhetoric that was to remain uncontested for more than a millennium: rhetoric is a part of the science of politics: "hanc oratoriam facultatem . . . civilis scientiae partem esse dicamus" (1.5.6). This definition of rhetoric is found throughout medieval treatises on the liberal arts, whether or not the culture in which rhetoric was being studied provided the conditions for political oratory.[43]

Two brief examples of political speech in Chaucer's writings can suggest the range of contexts in which rhetoric is understood as a system of civic discourse. One that is perhaps less obvious is the rhetoric of debate and counsel in the *Parliament of Fowls,* in which the notion of a commons assembled to deliberate the "commune profit" is mapped onto the traditional courtly scenario of the *debat d'amours.* The scene depicted in the *Parliament of Fowls* is not political oratory in its classical sense: it does not present a sustained formal speech that persuades a popular assembly or a law court but rather represents the participation of heterogeneous voices (common, aristocratic) in a polity.[44] But the point of thinking about it in this context is that a classical theory of rhetoric as civic discourse persists into the Middle Ages where it can be assimilated to — and diffused among — political forms that are quite remote from the Greek and Roman political systems that originally defined civic rhetoric. Chaucer gives us a spectacle of counsel, consent, and finally judgment (Nature's) that takes place within the fantastic space of a Ciceronian vision of a political order subordinate to cosmic order (the *Somnium Scipionis* with which the poem opens).

But another example from Chaucer's writing can bring us closer to the theoretical core of rhetoric as politics. The *Tale of Melibee* presents the governance of the household on analogy with the governance of the state, an analogy derived ultimately from Aristotle's *Politics*. Based on a French adaptation of Albertanus of Brescia's *Liber Consolationis et Consilii*, it stages a dissuasion, as the wife, Prudence, deploys all of her argumentative skill to convince her husband, Melibee, not to take revenge on his enemies and so initiate a cycle of vendettas. As David Wallace points out, "The *Tale* will last just as long as (is synonymous with) the wife's rhetorical performance."[45] Melibee must turn from the bad advice of the friends, neighbors, and associates he has called in to advise him, most of whom counsel him to make war on his adversaries, to the salutary advice of Prudence, who urges self-restraint and reconciliation. Prudence's performance is a long one, because her arguments must cover every ethical-political category, from self-governance to household management to statecraft, but she knows her audience, and her dissuasion is successful:

> Whanne Melibee hadde herd the grete skiles and resouns of dame Prudence, and hire wise informaciouns and techynges, / his herte gan enclyne to the wil of his wif, considerynge hir trewe entente, / and conformed hym anon and assented fully to werken after hir conseil, / and thonked God, of whom procedeth al vertu and alle goodnesse, that hym sente a wyf of so greet discrecioun. (7.1870–73)

In what does Prudence's discretion lie? Her performance is not a formal speech before a public audience but is embedded in dialogue with her often intransigent husband, so that the genre of the *Melibee* is more obviously akin to advice literature (the mirror for princes tradition) than to oratory. But the strategy that governs her performance is deeply rooted in rhetorical thought: it is timeliness, the measuring of speech to the appropriate conditions of the moment.[46] This is the principle of kairos, adjusting speech — argument, diction, arrangement, voice, verbal ornament, level of style — to the immediate circumstances at hand, judging the emotional condition of the audience, as well as any other factors. The principle of kairos applies to the right or critical time, not to time in general. The Greek term *kairos* is nowhere defined conclusively, even according to ancient authorities,[47] but the concept is used in Greek and Roman rhetorical writings, and it is diffused throughout rhetorical thought.[48] The judge Albertanus of Brescia, author of the original version of the Melibee story, wrote an advice treatise, *Ars Loquendi et Tacendi* (The art of speaking and staying quiet), a practical guide to the appropriate rhetorical circumstances for speaking in public life, which is also suffused by the spirit of kairos. The narrative of Prudence's discourse also calls attention to her strategies of silence and speech. At critical moments in the narrative, the phrase "whan she saugh her tyme" appears to mark the discretion of her speech:

> For which resoun this noble wyf Prudence suffred hir housbonde for to wepe and crie as for a certein space, / and whan she saugh hir tyme, she seyde hym in this wise: "Allas, my lord," quod she, "why make ye youreself for to be lyk a fool? / For sothe it aperteneth nat to a wys man to maken swich a sorwe. (7.979–81)

Prudence's timeliness, her adjustment to circumstances, governs not just the way that she seizes the right opportunities for speaking but her choice of *sententia* at given points in her dialogue with Melibee, her appeals to different authorities.[49] Prudence inhabits circumstantiality in much the same way that the Wife of Bath does, and indeed "Prudence" as phronesis (Latin: *prudentia*) or practical wisdom is simply the positive valence of the same practical reasoning that the Wife of Bath embodies in such severely ironized ways.

I began by opposing a too conventional linkage between rhetoric and style. I will end by returning to that linkage, exploring it by casting it in a broader perspective: rhetoric and the teaching of literary form. The realm of rhetoric is not limited to style, as I have demonstrated; but rhetoric is the preeminent system for articulating a theory of form. That system was refined and replicated in classrooms across medieval Europe. The teaching of rhetoric was central to the elementary curriculum and, in some cases, in more advanced curricula. It was the system par excellence for the teaching of writing, that is, Latin composition, in the medieval classroom. Between the years 1175 and about 1230 there was a virtual explosion of rhetorical manuals, the *artes poetriae,* teaching verse and prose composition: from Matthew of Vendôme's *Ars Versificatoria* (c. 1175) to Geoffrey of Vinsauf's *Poetria Nova* (c. 1210), which was one of the most successful school texts in medieval Europe (more than two hundred manuscripts are extant), to Gervase of Melkley's *Ars Poetica* (c. 1215) and John of Garland's *Parisiana Poetria* (c. 1230). These texts are modeled on Ciceronian doctrine and clearly identify themselves with a rhetorical tradition.[50] The teaching of literary composition through rhetorical principles of invention, arrangement, and *elocutio,* or style, through imitation of literary models, and through the exercises of abbreviation and amplification, represented a higher stage in the acquisition of Latin literacy than the teaching of grammar.[51] There was considerable overlap between the grammatical teaching of reading and the rhetorical teaching of writing, and it is appropriate to think of the various artes poetriae as grammatical texts aimed at the production of new writing rather than at interpretation of texts (compare Murphy's term "preceptive grammars," indicating that the artes poetriae is aimed at the future text).

The artes poetriae constituted repositories of information, not just on how to write, but on the formal components of literary texts and the literary legacy of antiquity: the devices of eloquence, such as figures and tropes, diction, and levels of style; narrative order (natural and artificial) and narrative pace (contracted or amplified); the construction of character through vivid description, praise and blame, or attributes of the person and the act; the effects of meter, rhythm, and sound in verse, and of prose rhythms; and notions of genre and generic difference based on levels of style and social register. Taken together, the artes poetriae represented a complete education into form.

The *Nun's Priest's Tale* yields up the teachings of the artes poetriae in comically concentrated form. It is both product and illustration of the catalogues of precepts about form, a kind of distilled exercise in every formal possibility known to the literary curriculum.[52] It is an almost impossible experiment in amplification, a beast fable dressed up in virtually every literary and rhetorical genre: epic, romance, love lyric, *de casibus* narrative, epideictic, mythography, hagiography, satire, advice to princes, exemplum and proverb, history, contemporary chronicle, tragedy, prophetic dream, and philosophical discourse. Its breathless progress through rhetorical devices, trying on and discarding figures and tropes, narrative techniques (amplification, abbreviation, description), and forms of proof (citation of authorities, quoting proverbs, giving exempla), culminates in an arch illustration of the device of apostrophe, as the narrator addresses the poem's tutelary genius, Geoffrey of Vinsauf, the source of rhetorical precept:

> O Gaufred, deere maister soverayn,
> That whan thy worthy kyng Richard was slayn
> With shot, compleynedest his deeth so soore,
> Why ne hadde I now thy sentence and thy loore,
> The Friday for to chide, as diden ye?
> For on a Friday, soothly, slayn was he.
> Thanne wolde I shewe yow how that I koude pleyne
> For Chauntecleres drede and for his peyne. (7.3347–54)

The *Poetria Nova* contains a famous set piece illustrating the force of apostrophe, an address to England sorrowing for the death of Richard the Lion-Hearted. It is against the high standard of Geoffrey of Vinsauf's lament for Richard that the Chaucerian narrator measures his own rhetorical insufficiency for lamenting the abduction of Chauntecleer by the fox.

The *Nun's Priest's Tale* is an essay in the theory of form. It uses rhetoric to examine the question of literary form by assembling diverse rhetorical teachings and devices in a context that violates the very principles of decorum and self-consistency that rhetoric is supposed to teach. The comic effects of this heterogeneous collection of devices can really be appreciated only if we refer to what lies outside the poem, to the rhetorical and poetic manuals that the poem parodies with such skill. The poem is playing with the idea of decorum as organic form, because it violates decorum at every juncture while punctiliously observing the stylistic principles appropriate to each genre that it takes up. It violates representational propriety by making the lowly appear great and yet also calls attention to the way that rhetorical teaching enables one to inflate (and deflate) a subject. The result is artifact itself, exuberantly released from the pretense that literary texts imitate organic form.[53] Indeed, the *Nun's Priest's Tale* offers a perfect way to recapitulate the questions with which I began, the complex balancing of representation and truth value in rhetorical thought. The *Nun's Priest's Tale* takes the question of mimesis and truth to another level by suggesting that mimetic form may well be its own truth value: here the beast fable can be meaningful, not because it contains moral truths, but because even its meager structure can support a nearly infinite elaboration of formal possibilities. And the more that the formal choices are spun out, the greater the ambitions of the *Nun's Priest's Tale* to mean something greater than itself — to be a discourse about valor and kingship or about the truth of prophecies or about the purifying effects of courtly love or about predestination and free will. But do these flirtations with different genres really change the poem's meaning? The narrator's reminder: "My tale is of a cok, as ye may heere" (7.3252), punctures the multiple generic pretensions of the poem, returning us (if only provisionally) to the generic core, a beast fable.[54] But the tale derives its meaning not from its core but rather from its improbable formal aggrandizement, its preposterous violations of mimetic self-consistency. The *Nun's Priest's Tale* is a rhetoric laboratory. It sends us back to look again at the tight formal syntheses of *Troilus and Criseyde* or the *Knight's Tale,* which exclude extraneous elements and which subordinate part to whole and the whole to an intention manifest through formal contours.

For all of its comedy, the *Nun's Priest's Tale* is a distillation of Chaucerian and medieval thought about rhetoric. Rhetoric is not a secondary addition to a text: rather, it is through rhetoric that one thinks about language, truth, form, embodiment, time, history, intention, authority, the social construction of meaning, and the very human problem of being in the world. The *Nun's Priest's Tale* is a commentary of sorts on the very apparatus of thought that generated the Chaucerian corpus. To understand the pervasiveness of rhetoric as a cognitive structure in medieval culture is to understand how Chaucer conceptualized the power of language, the grounds of knowledge, and the possibilities of representation.

NOTES

1. Kennedy, *Classical Rhetoric;* Vickers, *In Defence of Rhetoric.* For a lucid account of twentieth-century scholarship on medieval rhetoric and an explanation of how the restrictive identification of medieval rhetoric with literary style came about, see Camargo, "Defining Medieval Rhetoric."

2. This is the key argument of McKeon's foundational essay, "Rhetoric in the Middle Ages," which traces the determining influence of rhetoric across the major intellectual traditions of the Middle Ages, including theology. On McKeon's contribution, see Camargo, "Defining Medieval Rhetoric." Carruthers makes some important corresponding arguments in two books, *The Book of Memory: A Study of Memory in Medieval Culture,* which explores the pervasiveness of rhetorical systems of memory, and *The Craft of Thought: Meditation, Rhetoric, and the Making of Images, 400–1200,* which considers how medieval conceptions of the very process of thinking were derived from rhetorical systems.

3. For comprehensive synoptic overviews of the various traditions of medieval rhetoric, the reader may consult the following texts: Murphy, *Rhetoric in the Middle Ages;* Camargo, "Rhetoric"; Copeland, "Medieval Rhetoric"; Ziolkowski, "Grammar"; and Copeland, "Trivium"; and the relevant chapters in Kennedy, *Classical Rhetoric.* References to more specialized comprehensive histories are found throughout the notes to this chapter.

4. See Struever, *Language of History,* 15.

5. Blumenberg, "Anthropological Approach."

6. The standard English translation of the *Rhetoric* is Kennedy, *Aristotle on Rhetoric: A Theory of Civic Discourse.*

7. [Pseudo-Cicero], *Rhetorica ad Herennium,* 1.2.

8. Cicero, *De Inventione,* 1.1, 1.6.

9. Quintilian, *Institutio Oratoria,* 2.15.33–38.

10. See Walter Jost and Michael J. Hyde, "Introduction: Rhetoric and Hermeneutics: Places along the Way," in Jost and Hyde, eds., *Rhetoric and Hermeneutics in Our Time,* 2–3.

11. See Schiappa, "Did Plato Coin Rhetorike?" and *Beginnings of Rhetorical Theory,* esp. 14–29.

12. For more details on the traditional imagery associated with rhetoric, see Copeland, "Pardoner's Body and the Disciplining of Rhetoric."

13. The theory of *ethos,* or character, of the speaker is outlined in Aristotle's *Rhetoric,* 1.2.1356a, 2.12–17.1388b–91b. On the theory of character articulated in the *Pardoner's Prologue,* see the unsurpassed article by Payne, "Chaucer's Realization of Himself as Rhetor." On the problem of ethos across the *Canterbury Tales,* see Camargo, "Rhetorical Ethos and the *Nun's Priest's Tale.*"

14. On the related rhetorical notion of appropriating the speech of others, or alienation from one's own speech, see Astell, "*Translatio* of Chaucer's Pardoner."

15. Farrell, "Knowledge, Consensus, and Rhetorical Theory"; Bitzer, "Rhetoric and Public Knowledge." On pragmatism or practical knowledge, see also Rorty, *Philosophy and the Mirror of Nature,* ch. 7, "From Epistemology to Hermeneutics." For Aristotle's notion of *phronesis,* see *Nicomachean Ethics,* 6.5; and for discussions of Aristotelian phronesis in connection with rhetoric, see Self, "Rhetoric and *Phronesis*"; Copeland, *Rhetoric, Hermeneutics, and Translation,* 14–21; and Kahn, *Rhetoric, Prudence, and Skepticism,* 30–36. But for a negative account of Aristotle's view of rhetoric and pragmatism, see Neel, "Degradation of Rhetoric."

16. Kenneth Burke considers this under the term "identification": see *Rhetoric of Motives,* 19–37, 43–46, 53–59. See the entry under "Constitutive Rhetoric" by Charland in Sloane, ed., *Encyclopedia of Rhetoric.*

17. Lee Patterson, "Chaucerian Confession: Penitential Literature and the Pardoner," in Patterson, *Chaucer and the Subject of History,* 367–421.

18. For Boethius's discussion of the circumstances, see Boethius, *De Topicis Differentiis,* trans. Stump, book 4, pp. 89–95; Latin text in *Patrologia Latina* 64, 1212B–16B. Cf. Cicero, *De Inventione,* 1.24.34–28.43. For a more detailed summary, see Copeland, *Rhetoric, Hermeneutics, and Translation,* 66–69.

19. See esp. Matthew of Vendôme, *Ars Versificatoria,* ed. Faral, *Les arts poétiques du XIIe et du XIIIe siècle,* 106–93, at 119 (no. 41); trans. Ernest Gallo, "Matthew of Vendôme: Introductory Treatise on the Art of Poetry," 51–92, at 66; and John of Garland, *Parisiana Poetria,* ed. and trans. Lawler, 1.84–380, 6.394–413. For one example of the system's presence in Chaucerian narrative, see Woods, "Chaucer the Rhetorician."

20. See, e.g., Thomas of Chobham, *Summa de Arte Praedicandi,* ed. Morenzoni, Pro. 164–201 (pp. 8–10). A translation of relevant parts of this treatise will be published in Copeland and Sluiter, eds. and trans., *Medieval Literary Theory.*

21. Robertson, "Note on the Classical Origin of 'Circumstances' in the Medieval Confessional"; see *Ancrene Riwle,* ed. Tolkien, 163.

22. For textual examples and discussion, see Copeland, *Rhetoric, Hermeneutics, and Translation,* 70–86. For another dimension of interpretive activity founded on inventional structures, see Carruthers, *Craft of Thought,* 7–115. For the role of this inventional system in Boethius's *Consolation of Philosophy* as it moves from forensic rhetoric to philosophical discourse, see Lerer, *Boethius and Dialogue,* esp. ch. 1.

23. See Olson, "Rhetorical Circumstances and the Canterbury Story Telling."

24. Alford, "Wife of Bath versus the Clerk of Oxford," gives substantial details of the literary tradition of rhetoric and feminine attributes; cf. discussions in Parker, *Literary Fat Ladies,* 8–35.

25. Martianus Capella, *De Nuptiis Philologiae et Mercurii,* ed. Dick, book 5 (paragraphs 426 and sq.); in *Martianus Capella and the Seven Liberal Arts,* trans. Stahl and Johnson.

26. Alford, "Wife of Bath versus the Clerk of Oxford," 123.

27. Compare Alford: the Wife "intends to reduce the question to the level of her own personal experience" ("Wife of Bath versus the Clerk of Oxford," 123).

28. See Hanna, "*Compilatio* and the Wife of Bath."

29. This problematic is explored in Patterson, "Feminine Rhetoric and the Politics of Subjectivity."

30. Aristotle, *Rhetoric,* 1.2.21 (1358a), 2.23 (1397a–1400b).

31. Augustine, *De Doctrina Christiana,* ed. W. M. Green, 3.15.23 (my translation); see also the edition and translation by R. P. H. Green, *De Doctrina Christiana* or R. P. H. Green's translation reissued in the Oxford World Classics series.

32. See Hanna, "*Compilatio* and the Wife of Bath"; cf. Copeland, "Why Women Can't Read."

33. On the long tradition of rhetoric and historiography, see the rich essay by Partner, "New Cornificius."

34. Cicero, *De Oratore,* 2.12.51, 2.15.62.

35. Hegel, *Philosophy of History,* 61.

36. See, e.g., *Rhetorica ad Herennium,* 3.9.16–10.18.

37. Chaucer's language here distinctly echoes the rhetorical terms *amplificatio* and *abbreviatio,* which could be virtually coextensive with the treatment of arrangement in late medieval compositional theory. See, notably, Geoffrey of Vinsauf's *Poetria Nova,* ed. Faral, *Les arts poétiques du XIIe et du XIIIe siècle,* at lines 219–736; translated by Kopp, *The New Poetics,* in Murphy, ed., *Three Medieval Rhetorical Texts,* at 41–60.

38. Translation by Kopp, in Murphy, ed., *Three Medieval Rhetorical Texts,* 34.

39. Valuable references here include: Auerbach, *Mimesis,* ch. 5, "Fortunata," which presents a reading of Tacitus's *Annals* against the Gospel narrative of Jesus' arrest and Peter's denial; Nichols, *Romanesque Signs,* ch. 1, "The Discourse of History"; Strohm, *Social Chaucer,* ch. 5, "Time and the Social Implications of Narrative Form"; and Patterson, *Negotiating the Past,* ch. 5, "Virgil and the Historical Consciousness of the Twelfth Century," on the nostalgia for a monumentalized past. See also Partner's essay, "New Cornificius"; and Ward, "Principles of Rhetorical."

40. See *Riverside Chaucer,* 1031 n. 8.

41. Translation in Stahl and Johnson, *Martianus Capella and the Seven Liberal Arts,* 42.

42. *De Inventione.* 1.2.2.

43. This is a commonplace in twelfth-century thought about rhetoric: see, for one prominent example, the commentary on Cicero's *De Inventione* by Thierry of Chartres, ed. Fredborg, *Latin Rhetorical Commentaries by Thierry of Chartres,* 50. It is also a commonplace in thirteenth-century thought: see, e.g., Kilwardby, *De Ortu Scientiarum,* ed. Judy, 162; and Vincent of Beauvais, *Speculum Historiale,* 1.55. On literary expressions of this notion of civil science, see Copeland, "Lydgate, Hawes, and the Science of Rhetoric," and Astell, *Chaucer and the Universe of Learning,* 71–83.

44. See Steiner, "Commonalty and Literary Form in the 1370's and 1380's"; Wallace, *Chaucerian Polity,* 66, 79, 235, 291; and Strohm, *Social Chaucer,* 125–30.

45. Wallace, *Chaucerian Polity,* 224.

46. See Wallace, *Chaucerian Polity,* 212–46, esp. 229–34.

47. Dionysius of Halicarnassus, *On Literary Composition,* in *Dionysius of Halicarnassus: The Critical Essays,* trans. Usher, 2:86–87.

48. For example, Aristotle, *Rhetoric,* 3.7.1408a–b; Quintilian, *Institutio Oratoria,* 3.6.26, 11.1.1; cf. Cicero, *De Oratore,* 2.85–120, and Augustine, *De Doctrina Christiana,* 4.19.38.

49. Wallace, *Chaucerian Polity,* 233.

50. The best short history and account of these texts is Kelly, *Arts of Poetry and Prose.*

51. On the medieval pedagogical contexts of these manuals for the teaching of poetic and prose composition, see Woods, "Teaching of Poetic," and the references there; and Camargo, "Towards a Comprehensive Art of Written Discourse," and "Where's the Brief."

52. In an important series of articles, Peter W. Travis has demonstrated the resonances of the *Nun's Priest's Tale* with another dimension of the curriculum, grammatical study, in its elementary forms (schoolboy exercises) and in its higher forms as academic theory about speech and signification; see especially "The *Nun's Priest's Tale* as Grammar-School Primer," and "Chaucer's Trivial Fox Chase and the Peasants' Revolt of 1381."

53. For a very different perspective on Chaucerian poetics of organic form, reading back through a Neoplatonist aesthetic of cosmic form, see Simpson, "*Ut pictura poesis.*"

54. On the exegetical ramifications of this implosive moment in the text, see Boitani, " 'My tale is of a cock.' "

PART **II**

Major Works, Major Issues

5

The Dream Visions

DEANNE WILLIAMS

God turne us every drem to goode! — The House of Fame

What does it mean to turn a dream to good? Dreams are subject to interpretation: they can be "turned" for the better or for the worse. As a literary genre, the dream vision requires the reader to work alongside the author to extract meaning from the dream: a process that can be done well, "to goode," or poorly. Chaucer's *House of Fame* opens with a prayer (perhaps closer to an oath) for a good — an accurate or benevolent — interpretation that acknowledges the difficulty of finding any stable meaning in a text. In other words: God help us. This noisy opening illustrates the dynamic relation between text and commentary, central to medieval literary theory, that motivates Chaucer's four dream visions: the *Book of the Duchess, House of Fame, Parliament of Fowls,* and *Legend of Good Women.*[1]

A dream vision is a poem that relates a curious dream as a pretext for an extended poetic and philosophical discussion of a more abstract subject: usually, but not always, the nature of love. One of the first medieval examples of the genre is the *Roman de la Rose,* an extremely influential Old French poem begun by Guillaume de Lorris circa 1237 and completed by Jean de Meun circa 1278.[2] An allegorical treatment of the art of seduction inspired by Ovid's *Remedia Amoris,* it concerns the efforts of Amant, the lover, to win the favor of his beloved lady, Rose, who is sequestered in a garden. The characters he encounters on the way have such names as Daunger (Resistance) and Bel-Accueil (Fair Welcome), representing different stages of courtship. Although the *Roman* reflects the love medieval poets had for classical literature, and especially for Ovid, its focus on love and courtship illustrates the growing demand by educated audiences at court for poems written in the vernacular that reflected themselves and their own concerns. The *Roman* was a major source and model for the fourteenth-century *dits amoreux* (love stories) by such French poets as Guillaume de Machaut and Jean Froissart, and it was extremely popular in England: Chaucer translated it into English as one of his first literary projects. Following the examples of Machaut and Froissart, Chaucer and his contemporaries such as John Gower and William Langland adapted the genre of the dream vision for their own poetic purposes.

Chaucer composed his dream visions at significant stages in his public as well as literary life. The *Book of the Duchess,* his first substantial poetic work, was written sometime between 1368 and 1372, when the twenty-something Chaucer was working as a member of the household of Edward III. The *House of Fame* and the *Parliament of Fowls* date from 1378–80, at the height of Chaucer's career as an international diplomat, during which time he made frequent trips to France and Italy on behalf of Richard II. The *Legend of Good Women,* written in 1386, represents a new phase: now living at some distance from the royal courts, serving as justice of the peace in rural Kent. Although each, in its own way, represents a milestone in Chaucer's successful career, a profound sense of self-consciousness, even diffidence, comes out in these poems. Chaucer is profoundly aware that he is using English to write poems that he associates with the French. Whereas such French dream visions as the *Roman de la Rose* adapt classical material to the needs of medieval readers, Chaucer's poems reveal the influence of both classical and French predecessors.[3]

The French origins of the dream vision genre were a constant reminder of the pervasive presence of French language and culture in England during the Middle Ages. After the Norman Conquest in 1066, the French language possessed high social, political, and literary status in England. For three hundred years, French was the language of England's royal and legal courts and the vernacular of choice in such institutions as the Church and the universities. Some of the most important literary works from this period were written in Anglo-Norman, the particular dialect of French spoken in medieval England. And many scholars believe that Chaucer's earliest poems were written in French.[4] In the *Book of the Duchess,* the Dreamer awakens in a chamber with walls painted with scenes from the *Roman de la Rose:* a powerful visual image of the feeling of being surrounded by French sources. The experience of immersion in French literature is dramatized by the bedtime reading that typically prompts Chaucer's dream visions: they call attention to Chaucer's initial experience as a reader and an observer of the genre of the dream vision, rather than a full participant. As a result, Chaucer's dreamers often seem insecure, painfully aware of their shortcomings, and passively willing to be led and guided by the authority of others.[5] They participate in the dream world, but they always remain a little detached from it.

An allegory of the processes of reading and writing, Chaucer's dream visions dramatize the experience of being a writer in late-fourteenth-century England. Raising questions concerning inspiration and transmission, as well as interpretation and authority, they destabilize tradition instead of reaffirming it. Highlighting the ongoing and productive tension between continental literary forms and the impulse to experiment with English poetry, and addressing the confusions as well as opportunities of cultural in-betweenness, Chaucer's dream visions explore the idea of English authorship. They move between imitation and innovation, carving out a space for Chaucer's unique contribution to the genre as an English author and, together, confronting the revolutionary idea of using the English language as a medium for courtly poetry

The Book of the Duchess: *Love and Death*

A dream vision, by definition, requires a dream. It comes as a bit of a surprise, then, that the *Book of the Duchess* opens with a discussion of insomnia, an affliction that is, in this case, tantamount to writer's block. Rather than marveling at the dream that he has just had (as he does at the beginning of the *House of Fame*), the Dreamer in the *Book of the Duchess* starts off by wondering why it is that he can't dream at all. The cause of his insomnia is an eight-year-long "sicknesse" (line 36) that only one "phisicien" (line 39) can cure: conventional metaphors for unrequited love or an unhappy love affair. These metaphors may have appeared tired or overused, even in Chaucer's day; nevertheless, Chaucer's account of his symptoms offers a strikingly up-to-date description of depression:

> . . . I take no kep
> Of nothing, how hyt cometh or gooth,
> Ne me nys nothyng leef nor looth.
> Al is ylyche good to me —
> Joye or sorowe, wherso hyt be —
> For I have felynge in nothyng. (lines 6–11)

With devastating simplicity, Chaucer's defines "melancholye," the medieval word for depression, as "felynge in nothing": an incapacity to be pleased, or roused, to any feeling at all. Chaucer's account of depression sets the stage for the poem's major theme: bereavement and the loss of love. It sets the Dreamer up for his encounter with the Man in Black, who shares his symptoms. The Dreamer's experience of insomnia, moreover, works as a metaphor for his relationship to the poetic process as a whole; it is an inauspicious beginning that expresses his sense of unsuitability to the genre of the dream vision and the feeling of being out of place in the literary tradition in which he seeks a place.

Such anxieties are understandable, considering that Chaucer is writing his first major work. The *Book of the Duchess* was written to commemorate Blanche, Duchess of Lancaster, who died of the plague in 1368.[6] Chaucer uses an anglicized version of her name, "White" (line 948), to identify her in the poem, and he encodes the name of her husband, John of Gaunt (who is known, throughout the poem, as the Man in Black) in the following riddling couplet: "A long castel with walles white, / Be Seynt Johan, on a ryche hill" (lines 1318–19).[7] Chaucer's lines refer to Gaunt's first name, John, and to his titles, Duke of Lancaster (the "long castel") and Earl of Richmond (the "ryche hill").[8] One of the seven sons of Edward III, John of Gaunt was one of the most important men in England during Chaucer's lifetime. Enriched by his marriage to Blanche, which also made him Duke of Lancaster, he was a gifted military strategist and, later, a trusted adviser to Richard II. Written early in Chaucer's career, at a time when he was working hard in the service of the king, the *Book of the Duchess* is likely a bid for attention or patronage from the court and aristocracy. Chaucer may have wished, at a purely personal level, to offer John of Gaunt consolation following his bereavement: he had served as part of John of Gaunt's army during the wars in France. However, he may also have written the poem from a distance, with the passing of the lovely Blanche providing the occasion for a more wide-ranging poetic meditation on love and death. Either way, Chaucer's efforts paid off: in 1374, John of Gaunt awarded him a life pension of ten pounds.

In the *Book of the Duchess*, Chaucer develops the narrative persona of the outsider, in but not of the world that surrounds him, naive and easy to underestimate. This persona dovetails with the poem's relation to its literary sources, as Chaucer consistently goes against the flow in his handling of the French dream vision. For example, to pass the hours before dawn, the Dreamer asks an anonymous "oon" (line 47)—a servant, perhaps—to bring him a book, "a romaunce" (line 48). The precise definition of the book is subject to scholarly debate. What Chaucer tells us is that it contains "fables / That clerkes had in olde tyme, / And other poetes, put in rime" (lines 52–54) and that these fables concern the lives of royalty: "Of queenes lives, and of kinges" (line 58). Based on this description, some scholars identify the book as Ovid's *Metamorphoses;* others propose that the book is actually the *Ovide Moralisé,* a medieval redaction of Ovid that combined the classical story with a moral, Christian interpretation.[9]

Regardless of whether he is reading Ovid or the moralized Ovid, Chaucer's account of his reading material contains changes, omissions, and apparent misunderstandings that work against the expectations of his readers. For example, Chaucer's account of the visit of Juno's messenger to the cave of Morpheus, the god of sleep, constitutes a rather inappropriate comic addition to the story of Alcione's dream, in which her husband makes an appearance in order to inform her that he has drowned at sea. Moreover, as Chaucer tells it, the story of Ceyx and Alcione has no obvious "moral." Where medieval authors typically included extended allegorical commentaries and descriptive set pieces, the Dreamer instead draws to an abrupt conclusion: "But what she seyde more in the swow, / I may not telle yow as now; / Hyt were to longe for to dwelle" (lines 215–17). Instead of presenting an interpretation of the story as an allegory of, for example, the soul's separation from Christ, the Dreamer reads it as a source of information concerning possible cures for insomnia:

> For I had never herd speke or tho
> Of noo goddes that koude make
> Men to slepe, ne for to wake,
> For I ne knew never god but oon. (lines 234–37)

It would appear, then, that Chaucer's Dreamer is simply not getting the point. He views a well-known tale of eternal love, in which faithful spouses are tragically separated by death, through the lens of his preoccupations. This prompts him to consider what kinds of offerings he might make to persuade Morpheus to bring him sleep: a feather bed, a pillow, a beautifully furnished bedchamber (lines 245–69)?

The Dreamer's omissions and misreadings do more than make him appear foolish: they call attention to the possibility of a variety of textual interpretations, and thus imply how an "English" reading of a certain text may differ from its "French" counterparts. The dream that follows dramatizes this experience of cultural alienation. The Dreamer encounters the Man in Black, whose mournful garb and demeanor make him utterly out of place in his sunny, lush surroundings. Their dialogue, moreover, proceeds from a misunderstanding: the Dreamer is unable to comprehend the Man in Black's poetic and allusive mode of speech. The Dreamer presents the events that unfold without couching them in any kind of allegorical interpretation.

Morpheus listens to his pleas, and the Dreamer finds himself lying in bed, naked, on a bright May morning (the typical time for dream visions). He stares at the painted ceiling, with sunlight streaming in through the windows, listening to the music that wafts in from outside. These pleasurable scenes and images signal the Dreamer's entry into the conventional world of the dream vision. The sound of a hunting horn prompts him to seize the horse that appears, out of nowhere, in his bedroom, and join in the chase, and a little dog leads him to a flower-strewn grove. These events have a symbolic meaning that is suited to the genre's thematics of love: hunting deer, with the Middle English pun on "hart" and "heart," was a popular medieval metaphor for courtship, and the dog was a popular image of constancy and, specifically, marital fidelity. These are dreamy symbols of the ideals of love and marriage addressed by the Ceyx and Alcione narrative; however, we cannot expect the Dreamer to make the connection: after all, for him, it was just a story about sleep aids. Chaucer here uses the cognitive gap between the Dreamer and his dream to play with the idea of a readership who can be expected to "get it" and a narrator who doesn't.

As Chaucer develops the notion of cultural alienation to address his relationship to his literary influences, he also applies it to the subject of death and bereavement. Although Ovid's story is about eternal love, it is also about the inevitability of pain and death, and Chaucer's opening account of separation from sleep, from love, and from the beloved prepares the reader for this major theme. The Dreamer finds himself in a grove from where the pains of winter appear to have been banished:

> Hyt had forgete the povertee
> That wynter, thorgh hys colde morwes,
> Had mad hyt suffre, and his sorwes;
> All was forgotten. (lines 410–13)

Among such images of growth and renewal lurks the Man in Black, his back to an oak tree (a symbol of long life and prosperity). When the Dreamer observes, "Hit was gret wonder that Nature / Myght suffre any creature / To have such sorwe and be not ded" (lines 467–70), he draws an intuitive connection between the experience of bereavement and death itself. Mourning his dead wife, the Man in Black appears, in terms that recall Chaucer's account of his own depression, close to death: "His hewe chaunge and wexe grene / And pale, for ther noo blood ys sene / In no maner lym of hys" (lines 497–99). Alienated from pleasure, and even from life as it swells around him, the Man in Black performs a series of poetic lamentations that for the most part directly translate the works of Machaut and Froissart.

It often comes as a surprise to readers of the *Book of the Duchess* that so much of it is a translation. It is a kind of poetic patchwork, with the *Roman de la Rose,* Froissart's *Paradys d'Amours,* and Machaut's *Jugement du Roy de*

Behaingne, Confort d'Ami, and *Dit de la Fonteinne Amoureuse* (among others) providing the main swatches.[10]

In the first long speech, the Man in Black's description of melancholy contains a catalogue of oppositions, such as "My song ys turned to pleynynge" (line 599), that the Italian poet, Francis Petrarch, developed to describe the experience of love-longing. He also uses the metaphor of having lost a game of chess with Fortune: a popular metaphor showcased in Machaut's *Jugement du Roy de Behaingne.* Chess jargon such as "draughtes" (aggressive moves, line 653), "fers" (queen, line 654), and "jeupardyes" (chess problems, the root of our modern "jeopardy," line 666), confirm the extent to which Chaucer is gesturing toward, and relying on, a set of borrowed lines and imported conventions to describe the Man in Black's experience.[11] Having reached a state of death-in-life, the Man in Black regards his world through the poetic vocabulary of past generations.

As the Man in Black's bereavement sets him apart from the wood, so his rarified language alienates him from the Dreamer. At first awestruck by the Man in Black's appearance and manner — "A wonder wel-farynge knyght, — / By the maner me thoughte so — " (lines 452–53) — the Dreamer's solicitous and deferential behavior toward a man who seems rather oblivious to him dramatizes their respective class identities. Mirroring, perhaps, Chaucer's behavior around John of Gaunt, the Dreamer is careful to mind, as it were, his p's and q's: "Y gret him as I best koude, / Debonayrly, and nothyng lowde" (lines 517–18). He immediately places himself at the Man in Black's service:

> ... yif that yee
> Wolde ought discure me youre woo,
> I wolde, as wys God helpe me soo,
> Amende hyt ... (lines 548–51)

However, his limitations are quite evident: although the Dreamer tries to show off his learning with a little collection of classical references to famous figures who have died for love — such as Dido, who killed herself for "fals" Aeneas, "which a fool she was!" (line 734) — he just can't figure out why the Man in Black is in such deep mourning for the loss of a chess piece. The Man in Black's recurring refrain, "Tho wost ful lytel what thou menest, / I have lost more than thou wenest" (lines 743–74, see also 1137–38 and 1305–6), protests that he is talking about more than the Dreamer could possibly know. At one level, this refrain refers to the Dreamer's literal-mindedness, which prevents him from understanding the story of Ceyx and Alcione metaphorically. On another, it calls attention to the larger lapses in understanding that take place when the Dreamer seeks to make sense of the Man in Black, who, apparently, can speak nothing but French poetry. The Dreamer cannot understand a literary and symbolic world that is far beyond his experience.

The Dreamer's inability to understand the Man in Black's chess metaphors forces the Man in Black to say more than he intended: had his interlocutor been less obtuse he could have left it at the chess pieces, with an unspoken understanding. However, the Dreamer forces the Man in Black to move out of the realm of literary allusion, and into vivid autobiographical detail. Thanks to the Dreamer's questions, we are treated to the details of her compelling eyes, swanlike neck, and perfect proportions, her intelligence, excellent manners, and, most important, of the sheer pleasure he derived from her presence:

> I sawgh hyr daunce so comlily,
> Carole and synge so swetely,
> Laughe and pleye so womanly,
> And loke so debonairly,
> So goodly speke and so frendly,
> That certes y trowe that evermor,
> Nas seyn so blysful a tresor. (lines 848–54)

She was the only one for him, she was his "soleyn fenix of Arabye" (line 982). But, because he was immature ("in my firste youthe," line 799), he could not speak his love, and worshipped her, for years, from afar. With details that bring this paragon to life, reflecting on her joie de vivre, "Therwith hir lyste so wel to lyve, / That dulnesse was of hir adrad" (lines 848–50), and recalling how she got more beautiful every day (line 906) the Man in Black explains how his beloved interfered with his will to death.

Many scholars discuss the extent to which the Dreamer is playing a role, and for whose benefit.[12] For some, the Dreamer is pretending to be a little daft in order to draw out the Man in Black; others believe it simply takes the Dreamer that long to understand what the Man in Black is saying. It seems that the Dreamer both knows and doesn't know: he understands about loneliness, but it is not quite the same as bereavement. He understands about not being able to have what you want (after all, he can't sleep) but he doesn't know what it is not to have whom you want, what it is to be separated from your lover forever. We can compare the Dreamer's situation to his bedtime reading: he may comprehend the words, but he doesn't necessarily get their meaning. However, the Man in Black also has something to learn from this encounter. The Dreamer's slow discovery that White is dead works in tandem with the Man in Black's psychological process of letting go. As he relives these joyous images of White, he is reconciled to the fact of her passing. When the Dreamer asks, "where is she now?" (line 1298), the Man in Black is forced to say, bluntly, "She ys deed!" (line 1309). The Dreamer has had to wring it out of him. But, finally, the Man in Black is speaking with an unadorned honesty that previously had eluded him.

A horn sounds, heralding the end of the "hert-hunting" (line 1313). This brings to a close the literal hunt that frames the poem, as well as the quest, on the part of the Dreamer and the Man in Black, for their heart's delight. As the Man in Black returns to his "long castel" on the "ryche hill," he responds to the harsh truth of love's impermanence by retreating behind the illusory permanence of lands and a title. As the Dreamer awakens with the book on his lap, he, too, returns to the life he momentarily left behind. But now he knows how to read the story of Ceyx and Alcione. He has learned that books are for more than curing insomnia: they teach us about life and death, love and loss, and about the connections between ecstasy and pain and between sorrow and sweetness. Most important, they show us the virtue of honesty.

The House of Fame: *Love and Lies*

The *House of Fame* and the *Parliament of Fowls* are generally believed to be the poetic products of a series of trips to Italy that Chaucer made in the 1370s.[13] Diplomatic affairs in Lombardy would have given him access to the great libraries of his hosts, the Visconti. In Florence on government business, Chaucer would have been exposed to the works of Petrarch (1304–74) and Giovanni Boccaccio (1313–75), as well as with those of the revered poet of the previous century, Dante Alighieri (1265–1321). It is tempting to imagine, however unlikely, that Chaucer actually met Petrarch and Boccaccio on his first trip to Italy, in 1373. They were alive and living in Florence at the time. At the very least, they all breathed the same air.

In the absence of more specific evidence, it is this tangible Italian influence that scholars use to date the *House of Fame* and the *Parliament of Fowls*. Details such as the "man of gret auctorite" (line 2158) who is supposed to deliver tidings of love at the end of the *House of Fame,* and the deferred marriage decision that concludes the *Parliament of Fowls,* have led scholars to suppose that the poems were written in response to the marriage negotiations of King Richard II to Anne of Bohemia in 1380, as well as, possibly, to discussions about the betrothal of John of Gaunt's daughter, Philippa, to King John I of Portugal.[14] This is a time in Chaucer's life when he was deeply invested in the events of court: his continental travels, to France as well as to Italy, and his involvement in high-level negotiations of everything from marriage to commerce produced poems that are worldly, sophisticated, and notoriously difficult to pin down.

A combination of Italian and French literary influences produce the mutually reinforcing preoccupations of love and empire that motivate the *House of Fame,* just as the international intrigue of an ambassadorial trip to Italy was complemented by the marriage issue at home in England.[15] The *House of Fame* is traditionally viewed as marking the end of Chaucer's "French" period, represented by the *Book of the Duchess,* and the beginning of his "Italian" period, which includes *Troilus and Criseyde.* Yet these poems reflect less a self-conscious movement away from the French and toward the Italian, than an accumulation of their influences. The *House of Fame* replaces the cozy bedroom and intimate forest bower of the *Book of the Duchess* with the landscape of the skies and desert. Although its interest in the allegorical depiction of emotional conditions retains the amatory preoccupations of the *Roman de la Rose,* its emphasis on external, epic action is more consistent with Chaucer's Italian sources. The poem's structure reflects the more expansive framework of Dante's *Commedia,* which narrates the poet's journey from a "selva oscura" (dark wood) to hell, through purgatory, and finally to paradise.[16] The strange tutelary relationship between Chaucer and the Eagle, who picks him up in his talons and carries him to the heavens, also comes from the *Commedia,* in which the poet Dante makes his journey in the company of his literary idol, Virgil, whose epic *Aeneid* charts the foundation of Rome. The Eagle, who symbolizes clarity of vision and power, reinforces the authority of the poem's classical roots.[17] Yet Chaucer is not content merely to emulate. The *House of Fame* transforms the formal, serious dialogues between Dante and Virgil in the *Commedia* into comic banter, as the Eagle complains about the weight of his charge and professes authority (albeit flimsy) on a variety of topics.

However, Chaucer uses the *House of Fame* not to switch allegiances from France to Italy but, instead, to make a declaration of literary independence. In the *Book of the Duchess,* Chaucer was content to translate and imitate literary sources; in the *House of Fame,* he calls these authorities into question. From the beginning, therefore, Chaucer distinguishes the *House of Fame* from the *Book of the Duchess.* Unlike his insomniac counterpart in the *Book of the Duchess,* the dreamer in the *House of Fame* accomplishes the task of getting to sleep in a mere couplet: "Whan hit was myght to slepe I lay / Ryght ther as I was wont to done" (lines 112–13). Whereas the Man in Black memorializes his dead wife with decorous metaphors in the *Book of the Duchess,* Chaucer describes the goddess Venus quite simply, even bluntly, as "naked fletynge in a see" (line 133) in the *House of Fame.* And while Chaucer expects the readers of the *Book of the Duchess* to recognize the Man in Black's allusions to the French dit amoreux, the *House of Fame* announces its intertextual relationship to Virgil's *Aeneid* explicitly. Chaucer's dreamer — whom scholars distinguish from Chaucer the author by referring to him as "Geffrey" — discovers the first lines of the *Aeneid* engraved on a brass tablet in the Temple of Venus: "I wol now synge, yif I kan, / The armes and also the man" (lines 143–44; in Latin, *Arma virumque cano*). With this engraving, Chaucer signals to his reader that the *Aeneid* will provide an important point of entry and interpretative framework for what follows. Whether you read "yif I can" as an expression of diffidence or of false modesty, the inscription signals to the reader that he is writing about the project of writing English poetry. Chaucer makes it clear that inscribed on the brass tablet is an English translation of the Latin original. But he is not translating the Latin to help his readers. Chaucer is very comfortable with sprinkling Latin phrases throughout his work, and in any case, these lines in Latin would have been familiar to anyone with a rudimentary education. Instead, he is calling attention to the fact that what follows offers an English perspective on Virgil, just as Dante composed an Italian one.

Chaucer proceeds to question the Virgilian source material that inspires the *House of Fame* While, like the *Aeneid*, the *House of Fame* addresses such grave and grand themes as war and the prehistory of the Roman Empire, what really interests Chaucer is the complexity of human relationships. He makes this clear by means of *ekphrasis:* an extended poetic description of paintings, or art.[18] The "curiouse portreytures" that adorn the walls of the Temple of Venus present a fairly straightforward account of the fall of Troy: an event that forced Aeneas, Virgil's hero, to flee and, eventually, to found a new Trojan colony in Rome. The walls depict the flight from Troy of Aeneas with his father, Anchises, and his son, Askanius, the storm they encounter at sea, and their arrival at Carthage (lines 140–238). However, this ekphrasis develops into a more extended commentary on the *Aeneid,* treating it as a love story rather than an imperial epic. Chaucer's focus on the amatory side of the story is anticipated by his encounter with Venus, whom he addresses as "my lady dere" (line 213) at the beginning of the *House of Fame*. The goddess Venus plays a major role in the *Aeneid,* as she is the mother of Aeneas, who directs him to the shores of Carthage, in North Africa. There he meets his lover, Dido, queen of Carthage. For Chaucer, Dido is the true hero of the *Aeneid,* and he proceeds from his dry account of the events of the Trojan War to a lengthy, sympathetic discussion of her plight: duped by Aeneas, who assured her that they would be married someday, she "let him doo / Al that weddynge longeth too" (lines 243–44). According to Chaucer, she acted like any woman in love. She trusted Aeneas, which gave him all the power: "Made of hym shortly at oo word / Hyr lyf, hir love, hir lust, hir lord" (lines 257–58). Yet Aeneas betrays her, leaving Carthage when duty calls, choosing his mandate to found Rome over his love interest.

Chaucer's lengthy digression on the subject of Dido, a character who appears in just one of the *Aeneid*'s twelve books, reflects the influence of the many translations of, and commentaries on, the *Aeneid* in the Middle Ages. Translations and adaptations of the *Aeneid* into vernacular languages assimilated the epic to the contemporary taste for literature about love. Scholarly commentary on the story of Dido and Aeneas prompted a centuries-long debate concerning the chastity of Dido and the virtue of Aeneas: Was Dido a loose woman? Was Aeneas a cad?[19] Orthodox Christian interpretations of the *Aeneid* viewed Aeneas's love affair with Dido as an allegory for the ensnarement of the human soul in sin: his abandonment of Dido represented the soul removing itself from sin to join the church, which, in the *Aeneid,* is symbolized by Aeneas's foundation of Rome.[20] Other commentators placed blame on Dido's morality: only a loose woman would allow Aeneas to anticipate the rights of marriage. However, many writers, notably Ovid, expressed deep sympathy for Dido. Ovid's treatment of Dido in his *Heroides* prompted many medieval authors to come down hard on Aeneas as an example of the worst kind of male cowardice. Influenced by the ideals of courtly love, they blamed him for what they considered to be his intensely unchivalrous treatment of his girlfriend/fiancée. This is the position Chaucer takes. As in the *Book of the Duchess,* his dreamer claims to know precious little of love:

> "What shulde I speke more queynte,
> Or peyne me my wordes peynte
> To speke of love? Hyt wol not be;
> I kan not of that faculte. (lines 245–48)

This gives him an edge as a (self-professedly) unbiased observer and a transparent, ingenuous writer. From this position, Chaucer makes his case for Dido. He sternly admonishes men who are only after sex, who will say anything to get it, and who flee silently — or make up some lame excuse when they find they are in too deep: "And swere how that she ys unkynde, / Or fals, or privy, or double was" (lines 284–85).

The story of Dido raises the issue of truth and lies. It is an opportunity for Chaucer to question the authorities who have written accounts of her. As Dido laments, "O have ye men such godlyhede / In speche, and never a del of trouthe?" (lines 330–31). Aeneas first lies to Dido, and then he lies about her mendacity in order to wriggle out of his responsibility to her. Dido, in contrast, insists that she has always been an open book to him: "We wrechched wymmen konne noon art" (line 335), and concedes that her one mistake was to put her trust in him before their relationship was formalized publicly. Moreover, she fears that their affair has ruined her reputation:

For thorgh yow is my name lorn,
And alle myn actes red and songe
Over al thys lond, on every tonge,
O wikke Fame! (lines 346–49)

The last thing she wants is to be known as Aeneas's ex-girlfriend. By raising the question of Dido's honesty, and Aeneas's lack thereof, Chaucer participates in a trend among medieval authors, and particularly vernacular ones, to defend Dido and seek to recuperate her reputation — a trend that responds to and reflects the growing audience of female readers and patrons.

Chaucer's defense of Dido is one of the reasons why Chaucer earned the reputation as "evere . . . wemenis friend" (ever friend to women): a phrase coined by the early-sixteenth-century Scottish poet Gavin Douglas.[21] Of course, it removes itself entirely from the narrative of war and empire-formation that Geffrey sees depicted on the walls of the Temple of Venus. While his ekphrasis may be intended as a corrective to the overtly masculinist focus of the paintings (and of the original narrative), Chaucer's alternative perspective on the events of the *Aeneid* develops the questions of interpretation, misunderstanding, and the potential for multiple interpretations that Chaucer raised in the *Book of the Duchess*. For the story of the *Aeneid* looks different, depending on one's perspective. Viewed through the lens of empire, whether earthly or spiritual, Aeneas is simply doing what was expected of him. Viewed through the lens of love, Aeneas is a faithless, heartless liar.

The idea that an event or text can have a variety of different, and competing, interpretations motivates Geffrey's subsequent adventures. In the poem's opening lines, the discussion of the diversity of dreams and their interpretations highlights the variety of words that can be used to describe the same phenomenon: "Why that is an avisioun / And why this a revelacioun, / Why this a drem, why that a sweven" (lines 7–9). Moreover, Chaucer's account of his dream offers a series of obscure details that fairly beg to be interpreted. For example, Chaucer ascribes to his dream the rather strange date of 10 December (line 111), a date opposite to the dream vision's typical May morning. According to the astrological calendar, 10 December falls in the middle of Sagittarius, a sign identified with the centaur, half-man, half-horse. This auspicious sign, associated with learning, friendship, and travel, is dominated by the benevolent planet of Jupiter. Jupiter's jovial aspect recalls Chaucer's opening prayer that every dream may be "turned to good," or given the best possible interpretation among the many that exist. Moreover, Sagittarius presides over the countries of Spain and Libya, which fits in with the desert surroundings in which Geffrey discovers himself after he leaves the Temple of Venus in Book 1:

> Then sawgh I but a large feld,
> As fer as that I myghte see,
>
> . . . .
>
> For all the feld nas but of sond,
> As smal as man may se yet lye,
> In the desert of Lybye; (lines 482–88)

Like 10 December, the desert is a contrarian move: it opposes the lush gardens that constitute the typical setting for a dream vision. However, Chaucer does not offer a specific explanation for his choice of 10 December, leaving it open to the interpretation of his readers or, perhaps, after the Sagittarian fashion, distancing himself from the conventions of the dream vision entirely and striking out on his own.

When Geffrey leaves the greenhouse-like Temple of Venus and finds himself in the desert, he makes a little prayer: "O Crist," thoughte I, "that art in blysse / Fro fantome and illusion / Me save" (lines 492–94). His prayer acknowledges the potential for the wrong interpretation of events to obfuscate the truth. He does not want to be like Dido, who believes in an impossibility. He just wants the truth. The Eagle appears as an answer to his prayers. When Geffrey describes the Eagle's appearance he insists that his account is "as sooth as deth" (line 502), and the Eagle appears to respond in kind, with an overwhelming list of facts. First, he lists the different kinds of information that they will encounter at the House of Fame: from lies to truth and from gossip to promises. He goes on to describe the house and its location (ideally situated between heaven and earth to catch all the information that flies up), concluding with a pseudo-scientific account of how speech, which is a kind of sound, travels up to the House of Fame, its rightful home, according to the laws of nature, or "kynde" (line 749). Yet the Eagle is not quite as knowledgeable as his impressive vocabulary and sheer loquacity would suggest. His frequent repetition of the words "kynde" covers up the fact that he has no real understanding of how, and why, sound moves up to the House of Fame. All he can do is assert that it just is that way, and insist that it is nature's way: "kyndeliche."

Ironically, the Eagle's rather nervous attempts to win his student's approval, and to get Chaucer to believe what he's saying, only confirm the capacity of language to deceive, and the limitations of the authoritative tradition that he represents. Just as Chaucer himself insists that he cannot celebrate love in flowery language (even as he pens a dream vision that accomplishes precisely that), so, too, does the Eagle, in long speeches rife with rhetoric, insist that he has sidestepped rhetorical flourishes to offer a simple proof. Geffrey is wise to agree with the Eagle: "Yis" (line 864). After all, he is flying through the air with only the Eagle's talons to hold him. Nevertheless, Geffrey's "yis" is no more honest than the Eagle's prolix speechifying. Its very simplicity, which recalls the Dreamer's "she ys ded" in the *Book of the Duchess,* calls attention to the absurdly comic lengths the Eagle has gone to make his point. It even inspires the Eagle to boast about his ability to adjust his speech to appeal to his listener, "I can / Lewedly to a lewed man / Speke" (lines 865–67), just like Shakespeare's Prince Hal can "drink with any tinker in his own language." When the Eagle crows, "Be Seynte Jame, / Now wil we speken al of game!" (lines 885–86) (as if what had preceded it were high seriousness), he barrels into a joking account of the Milky Way, comparing it to "Watlying Street" (line 939), the name of the ancient Roman road that goes through London. His references to the ill-fated flights of Phaethon, who crashes the sun chariot belonging to his father, Apollo, and of Icarus, who flew too close to the sun and fell into the sea, are explicitly designed to cast fear into the heart of his cargo, and are about as funny as an air traveler today making jokes about bombs. This is not the faithful Virgil on whose guidance Dante relied.

As the Eagle flits restlessly from one subject or opinion to another, refusing to alight on any perspective or position for very long, Geffrey's reaction ranges from the monosyllabic ("yis") to the concrete. His account of what can be seen as one flies through the air is highly plausible, if unsurprising: "Now ryveres, now citees, / Now tounes, and now grete trees" (lines 901–2). In the absence of a reliable guide or authority, Geffrey has only himself. His flight through the heavens makes him think, not of Dante, but of his own work. At this time, Chaucer's *Boece,* a translation of Boethius's *Consolatio Philosophiae,* might have been an incomplete project lying on his desk or, perhaps, was just occupying his mind:

> And thoo thoughte y upon Boece,
> That writ, 'A thought may flee so hye
> With fetheres of Philosophye,
> To passen everych element,
> And whan he hath so fer ywent,
> Than may be seen behynde his bak
> Cloude' — and al that y of spak. (lines 972–78)[22]

Chaucer recalls a passage in which Boethius describes how a thought can fly to the heavens in search of truth: it clothes itself in feathers and moves up, away from the earth, past the clouds, to behold the heavens. While these lines have been read as yet another indication of Chaucer's modesty about his own capacities, because he fails to mention how the thought can see God, we can also read Chaucer's omission as an indication of confidence in his own authority. "And al that y of spak" might even suggest that he expects the reader to know that he has translated the text, which would help scholars fix the chronology of Chaucer's work in the late 1370s and early 1380s. Note the slippage as the line begins with recalling what Boethius wrote and ends with referring to what Chaucer himself said. Ending with clouds at his back instead of with, as the passage reads in his translation, "the verray knowleche of God," Chaucer gestures toward the cloudiness of thinking that has characterized this section of the poem. Although the *House of Fame,* from its opening line to its classical roots, raises the expectation of firm, quantifiable facts and the solid truths that uphold historical tradition, the poem's first thousand-odd lines have succeeded in thwarting any kind of certainty or clarity. Moving from a position of indebtedness to French sources, Chaucer uses images such as being alone in a desert or flying chaotically through the air to express the terrifying, vertiginous feeling of being alone in the world.

Yet although we readers may accept, as authoritative, Geffrey's account of the Eagle's absence of authority, Chaucer refuses to allow us even this certainty. If we are questioning authority, we must also question him. Having established his legitimacy as author and as reporter, Chaucer makes the Eagle, finally, the sensible one. Ever the avid tour guide, the Eagle offers Geffrey the opportunity to see for himself the constellations of Arion and Castor and Pollux: constellations that he has read about in books: "How all these arn set in hevene; / For though thou have hem ofte on honde, / Ye nostow no wher that they stonde" (lines 1008–10). But Geffrey demurs: it would be too bright; it would ruin his eyesight. He is content with the knowledge he has received from his books and, if it weren't for the Eagle in this case, would have missed out on the experience. Chaucer thus refuses to allow his reader to feel comfortable anywhere or to fully trust anyone, even himself. Book 2 is the intellectual, or readerly, equivalent of having the ground removed from beneath your feet and finding yourself, suddenly, flying through the air.

The *House of Fame* has drawn attention to the different ways of processing a particular event, calling various forms of knowledge — literary, historical, experiential — into question. We have seen how events from the *Aeneid* are as pliable as play-dough, and how words themselves can be fashioned at will and mean the opposite of what they purport to say. Geffrey and the Eagle's interplay between plain words and prolix rhetoric illustrates the immensely unstable quality of speech itself. As they reach the House of Fame itself, words are reduced to mere sounds. The "tydynges, / Both of feir speche and chidynge, / And of fals and soth compouned" (lines 1027–29) that fly up to the house produce a kind of white noise that is compared to the "betynge of the see" (line 1034). With no apparatus to discern between true and false things, the information that is collected in the House of Fame resembles nothing so much as the Internet.[23] As the Eagle leaves Geffrey before the palace, he wishes him luck figuring the whole thing out: "And God of heven send the grace / Some good to lernen in this place" (lines 1087–88).

Fame's physical dimensions, however, are as fickle as her affections:

> Me thoughte that she was so lyte
> That the lengthe of a cubite
> Was lengere than she semed be.
> But thus sone in a whyle she
> Hir tho so wonderliche streighte
> That with hir fet she erthe reighte,
> And with hir hed she touched hevene. (lines 1369–75)

One moment shorter than a cubit (the length between the elbow and tip of the middle finger) and another long enough to touch heaven, Fame is difficult to visualize. Compounding the problem is the fantastic detail of her multiple ears and tongues: "fele upstonyng eres / And tonges, as on bestes heres" (lines 1389–90). With her countless tongues and unchartable size, Fame defeats Geffrey's capacity for description; a problem that plagues him throughout this final book.

Indeed, Geffrey appears to be defeated by language itself. In his account of Fame's palace, he spends more time explaining how he cannot reproduce its effect in language than on the details of its terrible beauty:

> . . . al the men that ben on lyve
> Ne han the kunnynge to descrive
> The beaute of that ylke place,
> Ne coude casten no compace
> Swich another for to make,
> That myght of beaute ben hys make,
> Ne so wonderlych ywrought;
> That hit astonyeth yit my thought,
> And maketh al my wit to swynke. (lines 1167–75)

And he goes on. The rhetorical term for this kind of passage is *occupatio*: the space intended for a description is filled — occupied — with complaints of unwillingness or inability to describe. It is one of Chaucer's favorite devices: we saw it in the *Book of the Duchess,* when Chaucer refused to elaborate on Alcione's reaction to her dream, or on the shipwreck that drowned Ceyx. It occurs with great frequency in this part of the *House of Fame.* The progressive erosion of certainty through the poem has infected Chaucer. This lack of confidence produces daunting, phantasmagorical images such as the twenty-foot-thick book that describes the embroidered coats of arms of the suppliants of the goddess Fame (line 1335) or the windmill under the walnut shell (lines 1281–82) — images that attest to his sense that language is unequal to the task of reproducing his experience. Reporting on the musical instruments played by the minstrels that surround the palace, Chaucer questions whether it is even worth his (and our) time:

> Of which I nyl as now not ryme,
> For ese of yow and los of tyme.
> For tyme ylost, this knowen ye,
> Be no way may recovered be. (lines 1255–58)

These impossible images, along with the rhetorical device of occupatio, subvert Chaucer's promise to describe his dream in language unclouded by fancy rhetoric or poetical turns of phrase:

> But for the rym ys lyght and lewed,
> Yit make hyt sumwhat agreable,
> Though som vers fayle in a sillable;
> And that I do no diligence
> To showe craft, but o sentence. (lines 1096–1100)

With phrases such as "yght and lewed" (easy and unsophisticated) and "o sentence" (just the meaning, just the facts), Chaucer is going to great lengths in this passage to distinguish his writing from the kind of allegorical, metaphorical language performed by the Man in Black in the *Book of the Duchess*. Yet Book Three not only lapses frequently into obscure metaphors, it operates in the realm of allegory by sheer generic affiliation. The dream vision derives its meaning, its "sentence," from symbolic language, a kind of poetic "craft." Chaucer's promise to pay homage to the laurel (line 1107) if he succeeds in communicating his dream relies on a well-known symbol for poetic achievement. Moreover, as Chaucer loads up on apparently extraneous details, he sets up the reader to look for meaning behind every little fact:

> And somme corouned were as kynges,
> With corounes wroght ful of losenges;
> And many ryban and many frenges
> Were on her clothes trewely. (lines 1316–19)

Even if it is not immediately clear what is intended by the lozenge-shaped crown, and the ribbon-bedecked outfit, the reader of the dream vision is expected to figure it out.

Chaucer cannot hold it all together. He starts off with a well-constructed and detailed account of the historians and poets who are the "pillars" of the House of Fame, but it just breaks down. The material that constructs the author's pillar is symbolically appropriate: for example, Ovid's pillar is copper, the metal of Venus; the metal of the Jewish historian Josephus is lead and iron, the former tied to a medieval association of the Jews with Saturn, whose metal is lead, and the latter to Mars, god of warfare. It begins with order and hierarchy: Josephus comes before Virgil on the basis of seniority; Virgil comes before Ovid because empire trumps love. Chaucer could go on like this forever. But the sheer volume of information he must convey and the poetic powers it requires defeat him:

> What shulde y more telle of this?
> That halle was al ful, ywys,
> Of hem that writen olde gestes,
> As ben on treës rokes nestes. (lines 1513–16)

Fame thus devolves into chaotic, ever-changing, multiplicity: pillars become trees, poets birds' nests.

This imagery of dissolution extends to the foundation of melting ice, which Chaucer observes is a "feble fundament" (line 1132) for such a structure. Famous people's names are engraved on the rock, but some have melted away, "so unfamous was woxe her fame" (line 1146), while others are "as fressh as men had writen hem here / The selve day ryght" (lines 1156–57). This image of the melting rock anticipates the arbitrariness of Fame, who decides randomly who will be spoken ill of and who will be remembered well or not at all. A group of idlers asks to be remembered as people who have accomplished a great deal (and as having been very attractive to women):

> Thogh we may not the body have
> Of wymmen, yet, so God yow save,
> Leet men gliwe on us the name —
> Sufficeth that we han the fame. (lines 1759–62)

Fame says, no problem. Yet when the next group asks for the same thing, she abuses them: "Ye masty swyn, ye ydel wrechches, / Ful of roten, slowe techches!" (lines 1776–77). She is completely aware that her choices lack coherence. When the next group of wicked traitors appears, asking for good fame, she responds: "Al be ther in me no justice, / Me lyste not to doo hyt now, / Ne this nyl I not graunte yow" (lines 1820–22). Fame is not a system where the just receive their due.

Chaucer's overarching concern with truth and lies hinges on the question of poetic reputation. His claim that authors are universally praised "folk of digne reverence" (line 1426) is undermined by a rumour about the reputation of Homer, a pillar of the House of Fame: "Oon seyde that Omer made lyes, /

Feynynge in hys poetries" (lines 4176–77). More importantly, the figure of Lollius (line 148) casts doubt on Chaucer's honesty. Even if Chaucer believed that Lollius was a genuine authority on the Trojan War (his name was actually derived from a misreading of some Latin verses in the *Epistles* of Horace), he knows perfectly well that he's never read a word of him.[24] The example of Lollius points out the extent to which all writing is suspect, given the universal temptation to invoke imperfectly known authorities in order to appear learned. What clinches it, at the end of the poem, is the swearing of a truth and a lie to eternal brotherhood. In the cramped House of Rumour, a veritable hothouse of speech, where everyone is whispering in everyone else's ears, a truth and a lie attempt to make a getaway. Stopped, as they would be if they were trying to escape an authoritarian regime, they are not allowed to leave: "Thus saugh I fals and soth compouned" (line 2108). Strange bedfellows, indeed.

Chaucer began his dream vision in search of good news. He opened his poem with the prayer "God turne us every drem to goode!" and at regular intervals throughout the poem, he has paused and repeated and clarified his intention. When asked what he is doing in the House of Fame, he states his benighted desire for glad tidings: "Somme newe tydynges for to lere, / Somme newe thinges, y not what, / Tydynges, other this or that, Of love or such thynges glade" (lines 1886–89). The idea of glad tidings (translated by some as good news) recalls the angel Gabriel's words to the Virgin: "I am Gabriel, that stand in the presence of God; and am sent to speak unto thee, and to shew thee these glad tidings" (Luke 1:119). But Chaucer doesn't get an angel; he only gets an eagle: longing for revelation, he remains stuck in the real world. When the Eagle reappears at the end of the poem, ready to take him home, Chaucer tries to buy himself more time: "For yit, paraunter, y may lere, / Som good theron, or sumwhat here / That leef me were, or that y wente" (lines 1997–99). But the good news never arrives. The poem's final line, which leads most readers to the conclusion that Chaucer left the poem unfinished, announces the appearance of "a man of gret auctorite" (line 2158). Even if the man of great authority did come up with a great annunciation of glad tidings, after Chaucer has called knowledge, language, and truth into question, who would believe him?

The Parliament of Fowls: *Love and Marriage*

The *House of Fame* opens with a positive, hopeful exhortation, and ends in cynicism and uncertainty. But the *Parliament of Fowls,* which exudes energy and good humour, starts off on a sour note: "The lyf so short, the craft so long to lerne, / Th'assay so hard, so sharp the conquerynge" (lines 1–2). Read as an account of the vocation of poetry, the speaker is marveling at how much work he has done, how much his accomplishments have fallen short, and how far his ambitions exceed his capacities. Yet this description of arduous labor and swiftly passing pleasures applies also to the difficulties of love, and these plaintive lines provide a somber point of entry for a poem that anticipates and celebrates the rites of marriage. Again Chaucer casts his speaker in the role of someone with more experience with books than with love: "I knowe nat Love in dede" (line 8). As the opening lines attest, however, this is a false opposition. Certainly Chaucer's sources would suggest that this is the case: the *Roman de la Rose* presents itself as a traveler's guide to seduction, and Dante's *Inferno* depicts the famous lovers Paolo and Francesca falling in love over shared reading. We read, in fact, to find out how to love. And when we love we compare our experience to what we have found in books. Yet love, like writing, disappoints as much as it rewards. Although a fantastic adventure promises to follow, Chaucer starts off the *Parliament of Fowls* with some sober home truths.

Amazing as it sounds, the *Parliament of Fowls* could be the first poetic treatment of Valentine's Day, a Hallmark-card holiday that to this day blends love with poetry. Yet a reader of the *Book of the Duchess* and the *House of Fame* will find much that is familiar. Like the *Book of the Duchess,* the poem begins with the dreamer reaching for a book in order to get to sleep. In this case, however, it is Cicero's *Somnium Scipionis*: a classical text known to medieval readers by the extensive commentary on it composed by the fifth-century grammarian Macrobius. Like the other dream visions, the *Parliament of Fowls* is the product of a mixture of influences. Dante's work informs the poem's very structure: Chaucer's movement from the dark Temple of Venus to the bright park where the birds have gathered for their parliament recalls Dante's pilgrimage from the terrifying circles of the *Inferno* to the revelatory *Paradiso*. This Dantean structure works alongside the French genre-within-a-genre of the bird debate, which inspired English poets since the twelfth-century poem *The Owl and the Nightingale*. And there are the unmistakable traces of the *Roman de la Rose*: the account of the Temple of Venus and its surroundings, with Cupid standing under a tree, his bow and arrow tossed aside in a classic emblem of submission to the exigencies of love and eros (lines 211–17), and allegorical figures such as Youth and Beauty adorn the idealized landscape (lines 225–31). For all its immersion in this continental heritage, however, the poem remains conscious of its Englishness. Praying for Venus's help transmitting the poem to verse, Chaucer requests: "As wisly as I sey the north-north west, / Whan I began my sweven for to write, / So yif me myght to ryme, and endyte!" (lines 117–19). While giving his French and Italian influences their due, Chaucer is placing his poetic production firmly in England, the "north-north west" of Europe. This view from the margins, from the north-north west, rather than from the center, reinforces Chaucer's status as an outsider: as a poet and as a lover.

The idea of a mixture — of literary influences as well as of emotions — motivates the poem. For just as love and authorship are mixed processes, so, too, is marriage: a mixture of blood, of families, of personalities and genders. Chaucer's use of rhyme royal, with its seven lines of iambic pentameter, in the *Parliament of Fowls* is an important example of this mixed style. Chaucer used rhyme royal for the first time in the *Parliament of Fowls.* Inspired by Boccaccio's ottava rima, the eight-line stanza of his *Teseida* and *Filostrato,* Chaucer went on to use it in *Troilus and Criseyde,* the *Prioress's Tale,* and the *Man of Law's Tale.* Whereas the octosyllabic rhyming couplets that Chaucer used for the *Book of the Duchess* and the *House of Fame* recall the French poetic tradition of the dits amoreux (and, hence, the tradition of love poetry), rhyme royal is associated with high seriousness. However, just as the *Book of the Duchess* and the *House of Fame* use the tail-rhyme to handle such serious topics as mourning, melancholia, and mendacity, the *Parliament of Fowls* brings the epic stanza down to the level of comedy. The elaborate, processional quality of the stanzas, mixed with the themes and conventions of love poetry, lends the poem an air of mockery, even parody. The sexual energy of the god Priapus and the goddess Venus, "naked from the breast unto the head" (line 269), along with the chattering birds, bring the aspirations of rhyme royal down a notch or two (although another way of looking at it is that rhyme royal dignifies the otherwise risible birds). And even if the classic comic conclusion of a marriage is deferred, as it is at the end of Shakespeare's *Love's Labour's Lost,* there is still the promise of a happy ending, which always feels a little cheeky.

For a poem that ends with courtship and talk of marriage in a sun-drenched field, the poem has a surprisingly bookish, even fusty opening. Chaucer may not know much about love, but he certainly knows his books: Cicero's *Somnium Scipionis,* written in 51 B.C., which Chaucer calls "Tullyus of the Drem of Scipion" (after Cicero's full name, Marcus Tullius Cicero) was one of the best-known classical texts in the Middle Ages. Whereas the rest of Cicero's *De Republica* (Concerning the Republic) was considered lost until the early nineteenth century, the *Somnium,* a portion of its sixth book, was preserved. The *Somnium* is a dialogue between the Roman consul Scipio Aemelianus and his grandfather Scipio Africanus the Elder, a hero of the Second Punic War between Rome and Carthage. It covers such matters as the structure of the cosmos, the harmony of the celestial spheres, the importance of patriotism and the virtuous life, and the immortality of the soul. Chaucer summarizes Scipio the Elder's feelings about the rewards for the just in the afterlife:

> . . . what man, lered other lewed,
> That lovede commune profyt, wel ithewed,
> He shulde into a blysful place wende
> There as joye is that last withouten ende. (lines 46–50)

Macrobius's much-studied commentary on the text pursues the discussion of the divinity of the soul with reference to contemporary Neoplatonist philosophy and astronomy. This is serious reading material for someone who has love on his mind: it would be more suited to the dreamer of the *House of Fame*.

Reflecting on the importance of his literary sources, "For out of olde feldes, as men seyth, / Cometh al this newe corn from yer to yer" (lines 22–23), Chaucer raises the key question of the *Parliament of Fowls*: What is the relationship between the grave preoccupations of Scipio and Chaucer's more light-hearted theme? Mentioned briefly as a dreamer in both the *House of Fame* and the *Book of the Duchess,* Scipio Africanus appears in the *Parliament of Fowls* as a guide, like the Eagle in the *House of Fame*. Like the Eagle, he regards his charge with a healthy measure of condescension. However, Scipio is a ghostly and taciturn presence, a far cry from the *House of Fame*'s caustic and irrepressible Eagle. He counsels the rejection of the pleasures that the world has to offer, a doctrine Chaucer takes the time to describe in detail: "syn erthe was so lyte, / And dissevable and ful of harde grace, / That he ne shulde hym in the world delyte" (lines 64–66). Yet the *Parliament of Fowls* offers a vivid account of a variety of pleasure zones, from the steamy Temple of Venus to the lush park, places "so attempre . . . / That never was grevaunce of hot ne cold / There wex ek every holsom spice and gras; / No man may there waxe sek ne cold" (lines 204–7). Many scholars have sought to reconcile this question by referring to the doctrine of "commune profit" (lines 47, 75, and elsewhere) that Chaucer ascribes to Scipio. The walls of the Temple of Venus are adorned with portraits of people who have wasted their time pursuing pointless relationships, such as Dido, whose lover couldn't commit, or Tristan and Isolde, the famous adulterers. Scipio's altruistic doctrine would harness the sexual instinct celebrated in the Temple of Venus to procreation, the creation of life, and hence, to Scipio's overall concern for cosmic harmony and the greater good. Yet we may also regard this tension as a productive contradiction, rather than as a potential synthesis. Chaucer's opening account of the pain of life and the eternity of the afterlife lends an important perspective on the festivities that follow. With commandments such as "Know thyself first immortal" (line 73) framing the "likerous folk" (line 79) as well as the cacophonous parliament, Chaucer offers a stern, serious corrective that makes the quest for everything from erotic pleasure to satisfying human relationships seem fleeting and fruitless.

This sense of a productive tension, with one side complementing and modifying the other, extends to the dream vision proper. Scipio leads Chaucer to "a park walled with grene stone" (line 122). In another example of the poem's indebtedness to Dante, Chaucer encounters two contradictory inscriptions over its gate. In terms that recall the *Roman de la Rose,* the first offers "the welle of grace" (line 129), complete with an eternally "grene and lusty May" (line 130) and promises of "good aventure" (line 131). The second leads to "Disdayn and Daunger" (line 136), a wasteland where "nevere tre shal fruyt ne leves bere" (line 137). Yet this does not place Chaucer "right as bitwixen adamauntes two" (line 148). For Scipio sees, as plain as the nose on his face, how an "errour" (line 156) in the past exempts Chaucer from either fate.[25] An outsider in the arts of love, Chaucer can observe but not fully participate in what he is about to see: "Yit that thow canst not do, yet mayst thow se. / For many a man that may nat stonde a pul / Yet liketh hym at wrastlyng for to be" (lines 162–65).

As Chaucer moves from the artificial atmosphere of the Temple of Venus, with its jasper pillars and painted murals, to the park where the goddess Nature presides, he is once again in but not of his surroundings. Of course, as Scipio points out, this is the best position for a writer: "And if thow haddest connyng for t'endyte, / I shal the shewe mater of to wryte" (lines 167–68). Yet Chaucer's account of his vision is very different from the impressionistic, almost offhand quality of the *House of Fame.* The high formality of rhyme royal contributes to Chaucer's detached, even analytical comments, such as his elegant account of Nature's flowery hill, which he implicitly contrasts with the "prive corner" of Venus: "Of braunches were here halles and here boures" (line 304). As a foil to the catalogue of ill-fated lovers, Chaucer presents a catalogue of birds choosing their partners on this lovely Valentine's Day. In this case, lovers are not longing for the forbidden or else simply unsuitable Other. Instead, like seeks like. The lengthy list of birds which proceeds in descending order from the "royal eagle" (line 330) to the "feldefare" (line 364), a kind of thrush, classifies the birds rather brutally as if according to social class: there is the "gentil falcon" (line 337), and the "cukkow ever unkynde" (line 358), a member of the lower orders. Chaucer draws on the time-honored attributes of folklore — "The stork, the wrekere of avouterye; / The hote cormeraunt of glotenye" (lines 361–62) — pairing his birds off, rigidly, according to their "kynde" (line 365).

The only bird with any choice in the matter is the formel (female) eagle, a perfect and beautiful specimen who must choose, with Nature's supervision, among three tercel (male) suitors. Many scholars identify the formel as Anne of Bohemia, the future wife of Richard II, who had two other suitors: Charles of France and Friedrich of Meissen.[26] The first tercel eagle, a worthy fellow, describes his feelings for the formel in the language of the Petrarchan lover: "For certes, longe may I nat lyve in paine" (line 424). A master of manners, this princeling performs the classic conventionry of courtship, for which the formel rewards him with another conventional response: a deep blush, "Right as the freshe, rede rose newe" (line 442). The royal eagle's courtly speech, however, opens up the issue of infidelity: if he ever proves untrue, he insists, let him be rent asunder: "That with these foules I be al torent" (432). The idea of being untrue to the formel returns us to the insecure shadow-world of the Temple of Venus and the *House of Fame*. And once raised, it requires the response of the next suitor. This tercel, of a lower order, cuts to the chase: "That shal nat be!" (line 450). His simple, monosyllabic speech protests: "At the lest I love hir as wel as ye" (line 452), and makes the age-old claim: I saw her first. Acknowledging, once again, the potential in marriage for lies and deception, the second tercel imagines, even promises, a violent end for himself if he should transgress (line 461).

Like Cordelia in Shakespeare's *King Lear*, the third bird says he can boast of "nothing" (line 470). He cannot compete in terms of the length of his devotion, but the depth of his feeling can compete with that of someone who has been lovelorn for twenty years. He can't compete in terms of service, either, but he promises there has been no truer love than his. Most important, he makes his marriage vow to her up front: "til that deth me sese, / I wol ben heres, whether I wake or wynke" (lines 481–82). As far as this eagle is concerned, he's already married. He made his commitment before the formel had even accepted him. Chaucer seems to approve of what he calls his "gentil ple" (line 485), which is disarmingly honest, and which, rather than projecting creative punishments for a potential infidelity, insists, simply, that he is "trewe" (line 483).

The debate that follows, however, undermines the validity of such speeches: some birds complain that they offer no concrete proof for their claims; others don't want to interfere in the decision at all. The waterfowls comment on the fickleness of men: "But she wol love hym, / Lat hym love another!" (line 566), while the turtledove is hopelessly idealistic: "Yet lat hym serve hir ever, til he be ded" (line 585). The falcon, chosen to sum up the position of the parliament, wants to abandon the contest: "I can not se that argumentes avayle: / Thanne semeth it there moste be batayle" (lines 538–39). As the responses to the eagles' speeches undermine the seriousness of the entire process, devolving into hilarious ad hominem invective, Nature intervenes. Words, once again, have accomplished little: "For I have herd al youre opynyoun, / And in effect yit be we nevere the neer" (lines 618–19). Although the choice rests (as it always did) with the formel eagle, Nature cannot resist making a plea in favor of the royal tercel: "As seyde the tercelet ful skylfully, / As for the gentilleste and most worthi" (lines 634–35). Her evaluation of the tercels places conventionality above passionate sincerity — an accurate reflection, perhaps, of the public, performative demands that such a high-level marriage makes on its participants. Or perhaps it is because, by being the most conventional, the tercel is also being the most honest.

While the *Parliament of Fowls* places the formal, ritualized rhythms of courtship and marriage at the forefront, its open-ended conclusion, in which the formel eagle remains "quyt" (line 663), or free, for another year, and in which Chaucer returns to his reading, resists the kind of closure that its structures lead us to expect. The self-destructive side of eros lurks in the background of the marriage negotiations, reminding us of the potent yet chaotic drives that marriage seeks to mitigate. The formel remains unfettered, and there is no telling what events might take place in the coming year that could, in a heartbeat, compromise her value in the marriage marketplace. As Chaucer gamely takes up his books, it is not clear that he has gained much from this dream vision, either. With the *Book of the Duchess,* the dreamer received an education in the arts of reading; with the *House of Fame,* he came to the startling but enabling discovery that nothing is reliable or certain apart from the self. With the *Parliament of Fowls,* the results are mixed, as the destiny of the formel remains open. Chaucer has cleared space for English poetry, yet he is still casting about, trying to figure out how to fill it. In the roundel, a short poem in which the first line recurs as a refrain in the middle and at the end, the summer overtakes the winter in the eternal cycle of the seasons: "Now welcome, somer, with thy sonne softe, / That hast thes wintres wedres overshake" (lines 695–96). Possibly based on the French lyric "qui bien aime a tard oublie" (those who love well are slow to forget), the roundel acknowledges the inexorable return of the winter with a glance back at insomnia: "longe nyghtes blacke" (line 692). Like the return of spring, the dream vision interrupts a long, black, sleepless night with sunshine and gardens. But this interruption is never permanent. And so, when Chaucer rises at dawn reaches for yet another volume, "I hope, ywis, to rede so som day / That I shal mete som thynge for to fare / The bet" (lines 697–99), he optimistically, yet hopelessly, continues his quest for eternal summer.[27]

The Legend of Good Women: *Love and Loss*

Think of the *Legend of Good Women* as a Janus face. The *Prologue* looks back at the three dream visions that precede it, and the nine stories of the "good women" that follow it anticipate the *Canterbury Tales,* a collection of stories that are distinct yet linked. The *Legend of Good Women* was composed in 1386, a number of years after the *Parliament of Fowls.*[28] Since the *Parliament of Fowls,* Chaucer had composed *Troilus and Criseyde* as well as a number of the poems that would become the *Canterbury Tales.* Perhaps it is this long lapse between dream visions that makes many readers find the *Legend of Good Women,* to put it bluntly, very dull.[29] A number of scholars explain its incomplete state by conjecturing that Chaucer himself got bored with the project and abandoned it. Its mixed critical reputation has meant that it remains the least well known and the least taught of Chaucer's dream visions. Indeed, sometimes a farewell or a finale can be a letdown. However, there are also many attempts to improve the poem's status, which argue that it cleverly bids farewell to the dream vision, and suggest that its attitude to the so-called good women offers a critical perspective on the traditional social structures and expectations for women, as the tales range from the earnest to the playful, the ironic to the satirical.[30]

Perhaps the germ of the idea for the *Legend of Good Women* came in the catalogue of unhappy lovers in the Temple of Venus in the *Parliament of Fowls.* Chaucer's lines, "and al here love, and in what plyt they dyde" (line 294), perfectly encapsulate what brings his good women together. For the *Legend of Good Women* attacks head-on an issue that is more occasional or tangential in his earlier dream visions: women who are unlucky in love. Dido, for example, appears in the *Parliament of Fowls* as one of the unhappy lovers painted on the walls of the Temple of Venus, and in the *Book of the Duchess* in the Dreamer's catalogue of women who have died for love. She provides an important example, in the *House of Fame,* of multiple, conflicting interpretations of the same event. Yet in the *Legend of Good Women,* her story gets the full treatment.[31] We have seen how interpretations of Dido's story shift according to the agenda of the author, and the *House of Fame* highlighted the fluidity of reputation and the contingency of historical narrative. Whereas Dido is a negative example in the *Parliament of Fowls* and the *Book of the Duchess,* in the *Legend of Good Women,* she is a paragon of loyalty and virtue.

The *Legend of Good Women* represents the culmination of Chaucer's dream visions. It contains all of the conventional structures of reading, dreaming, and supernatural encounters: the bookish narrator and his classical reading material; the royal dedicatee or pretext; the extensive continental influences (both French and Italian); and, most important, a self-consciousness about and affirmation of the potential of English. It is on this last issue that the *Legend of Good Women* has made the most progress. Rather than dwelling on marginality, as in the case of the *Parliament of Fowls,* or begging for inspiration, as in the *House of Fame,* Chaucer now thanks his lucky stars that he has English to use for his poetic purposes: "Allas, that I ne had Englyssh, ryme or prose, / Suffisant this flour to preyse aryght!" (lines 66–67). He seems to be saying, God only knows where I'd be without it.

The *Legend of Good Women* places particular emphasis on the priority of books: their status as source and inspiration, as the occasion for interpretation, and, now that Chaucer is more advanced in his literary career, as objects to be produced: "On bokes for to rede I me delyte, / And to hem yive I feyth and ful credence, / And in myn herte have hem in reverence" (lines 29–32). The poem addresses the importance of reading and the value of books: "Wel ought us thanne honouren and beleve / These bokes, there we han noon other preve" (lines 27–28). This opening note pays homage to Chaucer's literary sources, while also setting Chaucer himself up for his reception of his work by subsequent generations: we must take his word for it. The author of the *Legend of Good Women* is not the same man as the author of the *Book of the Duchess:* he is now someone with a reputation as a poet that he must promote as well as preserve.

The question of truth and falsehood, raised with such words as "credence," "beleve," and "preve," is, as we have seen, a longstanding Chaucerian preoccupation. Yet what is different in the *Legend of Good Women* is Chaucer's certainty about the value of books, and their potential for truth. The poem's opening lines, about "joy in hevene and peyne in hell" (line 2), concede that these are experiences that one only reads about in books. However, Chaucer goes on to point out that things are not untrue just because they haven't been witnessed: "thing is never the lasse sooth, / Though every wight ne may it nat ysee" (lines 14–15). Yet Chaucer tempers his case by stating that one should not consider books the only source of knowledge and, furthermore, that his esteem for books flies out the window in the month of May. It is at this time when he renounces the life of the mind and indulges in that of the body. Although Chaucer's opening validates books, which can transport him away from the quotidian world of sensory proof, it also offers a comment on the dream vision. Now professing not only the singularity of his vision but also, as it moves from the book to the body, the essential "truth" of its content, Chaucer claims for himself a kind of authority we have not seen in his earlier texts.

The *Legend of Good Women* proceeds out of Chaucer's existing reputation as an author. Writing books, however, doesn't exactly make him all-powerful. Chaucer is recognized by the god of Love, even though he is sitting unobtrusively, "as stille as any ston" (line 310). He is contemplatively sitting before Alceste, a representation of idealized, chaste femininity and, as a daisy, the central symbol of the marguerite poems, a subgenre of the French dits amoreux. We can imagine how this encounter could play out in the *Book of the Duchess,* with Chaucer meekly protesting his ignorance and incompetence before this daunting symbol of the French literary tradition. But here, Chaucer enters into active debate with the god of Love and Alceste, who each offer different interpretations of his texts. The god of Love is quite aggressive with Chaucer, addressing him as "my foo" (line 322) and accusing him of serious crimes against love:

> . . . of myn olde servauntes thow mysseyest,
> And hynderest hem with thy translacioun,
> And lettest folk from hire devocioun,
> To serve me, and holdest it folye
> To serve Love. (lines 323–27)

Why, he complains, couldn't he tell stories that emphasized women's goodness instead of their wickedness? Why not tell happy stories about love instead of sad ones? Chaucer's dream visions certainly fit the god of Love's description: in the *Book of the Duchess,* love ends in death; in the *Parliament of Fowls,* love is shown to go wrong, and even if it looks as though it might eventually go right, it offers no assurances. For the god of Love, however, the real culprits are Chaucer's translation of the *Roman de la Rose:* "an heresye," he insists, "ayeins my lawe" (line 330) and *Troilus and Criseyde,* "that maketh men to women lasse triste" (line 333).

The god of Love may have his problems with Chaucer, but it is Alceste, the queen, the daisy, who calls the shots. Widely considered to be a veiled and complimentary allusion to Queen Anne (the Anne of Bohemia represented by the formel eagle in the *Parliament of Fowls*), Alceste is not only a queen and a daisy but also a literary character: one to whom Chaucer has failed to do sufficient homage.[32] The god of Love reminds Chaucer that he has met Alceste once before, in a book: "Hastow nat in a book, lyth in thy cheste, / The grete goodnesse of the quene Alceste, / That turned was into a dayesye" (lines 510–12). Alceste is named for the wife of Admetus, whose love for her husband was so great that she chose to die in his place, in reward for which she was turned into a daisy. Alceste therefore symbolizes the completely selfless love that the *Legend of Good Women* is meant to celebrate. Of course, as a literary character, she, too, is subject to interpretation: Chaucer says of her, "I see wel she is good" (line 506), and the god of Love agrees, "That is a trewe tale, by myn hood!" (line 507). A faithful wife, a daisy, a literary character, a queen, and an object of desire (as Chaucer puts it, "myn owene hertes reste," line 519), Alceste's many hats gesture towards the multivalent acts of interpretation required of readers of the dream vision.

The discussion that proceeds shows how, in the same way that a text is defined by an interpretation of it, so, too, do people define themselves by their reading of a text. Just as, in the *Wife of Bath's Tale,* the knight learns that "maistrie" (3.1040) is what women want, so, in the *Legend of Good Women,* the god of Love gallantly turns over all authority to Alceste: "Al lyth in yow, doth with hym what yow leste" (G.339). However, even though she is in a "dream" scenario, with the author sitting right there in front of her, completely willing to tell her exactly what he meant by the book, Alceste closes discussion down.[33] Rather than consciously working against the interests of women and love, Alceste claims, Chaucer wrote: "Of innocence, and nyste what he seyde" (G.345). Although Chaucer stands his ground, ready to defend his work and his good intentions, his evidence, from the horse's mouth as it were, does nothing to sway their interpretation of his books. Alceste does not dispute the god of Love's reading of Chaucer's texts; she just takes exception to his violent response to them, which she finds tyrannical. Alceste also takes Chaucer's point, that his dream visions educate people in the glory of love, "He hath maked lewed folk to delyte, / To serven yow, in preysyge of youre name (G.403–4). Nevertheless, she does not shift her appraisal of the others. Anyway, as she pragmatically points out, Chaucer is someone who has written "many a lay and many a thing" (line 420). So it should be no problem for him just to sit down and write another book, this time "a glorious legende / Of goode wymmen, maydenes and wyves, / that were trewe in lovyng al hire lyves" (lines 483–85).

The *Prologue* of the *Legend of Good Women* exists in two versions: the F, named for the version in the Fairfax manuscript at the Bodleian Library in Oxford, and the G, named for the single manuscript of the revised version of the poem, Cambridge University Library MS Gg 4.27, completed about a decade after the poem's composition. Each version has its merits, and most editions of the poem present the *Prologue* as a parallel text. One of the key differences between the two versions, however, is in the final two lines. In the F version, Chaucer simply picks up his books and starts writing. He starts, at Alceste's request, with the story of Cleopatra, fitting what shall become a collection of tales into the genre of the dream vision. With the G version, however, Chaucer wakes up: "And with that word, of slep I gan awake / And ryght thus on my Legende gan I make" (G.544–45). Whether we read the tales that follow as part of the dream vision, or, following the revised version, as inspired by a dream vision (and composed in "waking life"), Chaucer's revision reflects the direction he had taken as a poet: the *Legend of Good Women* shows us how the dream visions gave birth to the *Canterbury Tales.*

NOTES

Author's note: I thank Christopher Cannon and Alfred Hiatt for their helpful comments and suggestions.

1. The classic study of Chaucer's dream visions is Spearing, *Medieval Dream Poetry*. See also St. John, *Chaucer's Dream Visions*, and Quinn, *Chaucer's Dream Visions and Shorter Poems*; Minnis, with Scattergood and Smith, *Shorter Poems*; Kruger, *Dreaming in the Middle Ages*; Edwards, *Dream of Chaucer*; Lynch, *High Medieval Dream*; Boitani, *English Medieval Narrative*; and Hieatt, *Realism of Dream Visions*. Also relevant are Windeatt, ed. and trans., *Chaucer's Dream Poetry*, and Ferster, *Chaucer on Interpretation*.

2. Guillaume de Lorris and Jean de Meun, *Romance of the Rose*, trans. Dahlberg.

3. On Chaucer and French literature, see Williams, *French Fetish from Chaucer to Shakespeare*; Calin, *French Tradition and the Literature of Medieval England*; and Wimsatt, *Chaucer and His French Contemporaries*.

4. On the French lyrics in University of Pennsylvania MS French 15, see Wimsatt, *Chaucer and the Poems of "CH."*

5. See, for discussion, Anderson, "Narrators in *The Book of the Duchess* and *The Parlement of Foules*."

6. On the historical circumstances surrounding the composition of the *Book of the Duchess* see Hardman, "*Book of the Duchess* as a Memorial Monument," and Palmer, "Historical Context of the *Book of the Duchess*." For a more wide-ranging discussion of Chaucer and mourning, see Fradenburg, " 'Voice Memorial.' "

7. On White's name, see Travis, "White."

8. For discussion, see Ellis, "Death of the *Book of the Duchess*."

9. On Chaucer's reading material, see Wimsatt, "Sources of Chaucer's Seys and Alcyone"; Minnis, "Chaucer and the *Ovide Moralisé*"; and Williams, *French Fetish from Chaucer to Shakespeare*, 23–24. On Chaucer and Ovid, see Fyler, *Chaucer and Ovid*.

10. The notes to the poem in *Riverside Chaucer* point out the passages that are direct translations; see, for discussion, Williams, *French Fetish from Chaucer to Shakespeare*; Calin, *French Tradition and the Literature of Medieval England*; and Wimsatt, *Chaucer and His French Contemporaries*.

11. See Connolly, "Chaucer and Chess."

12. See, e.g., Morse, "Understanding the Man in Black," and Cherniss, "Boethian Dialogue in Chaucer's *The Book of the Duchess*."

13. On Chaucer and Italy, see Wallace, *Chaucerian Polity*, and *Chaucer and the Early Writings of Boccaccio*; and Boitani, ed., *Chaucer and the Italian Trecento*.

14. See Benson, "Occasion of the *Parliament of Fowls*."

15. Bennett, *Chaucer's Book of Fame*; Delany, *Chaucer's "House of Fame"*; Boitani, *Chaucer and the Imaginary World of Fame*.

16. For a discussion of Chaucer's relationship to Dante, see Steinberg, "Chaucer in the Field of Cultural Production."

17. On the Eagle, see Leyerle, "Chaucer's Windy Eagle."

18. On Chaucerian ekphrasis, see John Watkins, " 'Neither of idle shewes, nor of false charmes aghast.' "

19. Important discussions of Dido include Ovid, *Heroides,* 7.7–14, and Augustine, *Confessions,* 1.13.

20. On literary appropriations of the *Aeneid* in the Middle Ages, see Desmond, *Reading Dido,* and Baswell, *Virgil in Medieval England.*

21. See Gavin, *Eneados,* 1.Pro.448.

22. This is the passage as it appears in Chaucer's *Boece:* "I have, forthi, swicfe fetheris that surmounten the heighte of the hevene. Whanne the swift thought hath clothid itself in tho fetheris, it despiseth the hateful erthes, and surmounteth the rowndenesse of the gret ayr; and it seth the clowdes byhynde his back" (4.Metrum 1).

23. See Evans, "Chaucer in Cyberspace."

24. See the classic essay on Lollius by Kittredge, "Chaucer's Lollius," and, for a more recent discussion, Millet, "Chaucer, Lollius, and the Medieval Theory of Authorship."

25. Scipio observes: "It stondeth writen in thy face, / Thyn errour, though thow telle it not to me" (lines 155–56). It is, however, possible that Chaucer's "errour" in this case is not ignorance but transgression. The Cecily Chaumpagne case was resolved in 1380 as well (likely the date of the *Parliament of Fowls*). See the discussion in Christopher Cannon's chapter, "The Lives of Geoffrey Chaucer," in this *Companion.*

26. See Benson, "Occasion of the *Parliament of Fowls.*"

27. On the poem's indeterminacy, see Leicester, "Harmony of Chaucer's *Parlement*"; Aers, "*Parliament of Fowls*"; and Sklute, "Inconclusive Form of the *Parliament of Fowls.*"

28. On the historical circumstances surrounding the composition of the *Prologue,* see Kellie Robertson, "Laboring in the God of Love's Garden."

29. See Muscatine, *Poetry and Crisis in the Age of Chaucer,* and the editorial comments by Skeat, *Legend of Good Women by Geoffrey Chaucer.*

30. See Robert W. Frank, Jr., *Chaucer and "The Legend of Good Women"*; Kiser, *Telling Classical Tales;* Dinshaw, *Chaucer's Sexual Poetics;* and Delany, *Naked Text.*

31. On Dido in the *Legend of Good Women,* see Gaylord, "Dido at Hunt, Chaucer at Work."

32. The F version makes it mores specific that Alceste is the queen with reference to royal residences: "And whan this book ys maad, yive it the quene, / On my byhalf, at Eltham or at Sheene" (lines 496–97).

33. On authorial intention in the *Legend of Good Women,* see Simpson, "Ethics and Interpretation."

6

Lyrics and Short Poems

BRUCE HOLSINGER

Thou pinchest at my mutabilitee. — *"Fortune"*

Throughout his career as a writer of long poems, from early works such as the *Book of the Duchess* to the great *Troilus and Criseyde* to the *Canterbury Tales,* Chaucer also composed, translated, revised, and adapted plenty of short ones. Although this chapter is devoted mainly to those Chaucerian works officially anthologized under the rubric of "short poems" (thus leaving aside some quite short nonlyric poems, such as the *Second Nun's Tale* and the *Tale of Sir Thopas*), the writing of lyric — that is, to adapt a conventional definition, the formal isolation of subjective feeling and emotional state into a single, unified expression in verse — was a central and enduring part of Chaucer's identity and profession as an English poet, and those who study this strange corner of his oeuvre have recognized that the lyric mode suffuses his writing in practically all genres he engaged (or, as one critic has put it more strongly, "literature began with lyric, and so did Chaucer").[1] Among other examples treated below, the so-called *Canticus Troili,* the poem that the lovesick Troilus recites in Book 1 of *Troilus and Criseyde* (and that Chaucer translated from a sonnet of Petrarch), is in fact a lyric insertion into a larger poetic framework, as is the roundel from the *Parliament of Fowls.* The first stanza of the *Prioress's Prologue* paraphrases the first two verses of Psalm 8, a biblical lyric that was an important part of the Church's liturgical ceremony in the late four-teenth century. Stanzaic narrative poetry is itself a kind of serial lyricism, demanding that the poet craft a long sequence of discrete poetic units in a prescribed number of lines, each one of which will ideally possess its own formal, thematic, or narrative integrity in relation to those that surround it. Chaucer's short poems proper, though numbering fewer than twenty, reveal a unique lyric imagination embodied in the specific genres and forms in which they are written as well as the personal, political, and social situations for which they were composed.

Despite his considerable abilities as a lyric poet, however, we understand Chaucer today primarily as a master of narrative and characterization, not as a poet of love in the tradition of the earlier troubadours or of his continental counterparts such as Petrarch, Guillaume de Machaut, and Eustache Des-champs, who, alongside their own considerable contributions to various nar-rative genres, left behind voluminous amounts of lyric poetry.[2] The inherent interest of Chaucer's lyric corpus notwithstanding, what is most surprising about his short poems is the remarkable narrowing of the formal, generic, and institutional spectrum of medieval lyric possibility they collectively represent. In this respect, the short poems stand in stark contrast to the breadth of literary imagination informing the *Canterbury Tales,* a work that translates and adapts from a stunning variety of forms and genres current in Chaucer's literary milieu. Estates satire, romance, fabliau, Breton lay, epic, saint's life, alliterative romance, political treatise, sermon, rhetorical handbook, homily, moralizing exemplum, preacher's manual: this is just a partial list of the writ-ten genres Chaucer appropriated in his writing of the narratives that make up his most famous work.

When he chooses to write lyric poetry, by contrast, whether apostrophe, ode, elegy, or complaint, Chaucer's relation to medieval written tradition be-comes constrained, even impoverished. In generic terms, these poems rely nearly exclusively (though, as we shall see, with a few important exceptions) on the tradition of courtly verse exemplified by the works of Machaut, a French poet of the fourteenth century whose career defined the emergence and consolidation of the *formes-fixes chansons,* the "fixed-form songs" that would become the bread and butter of French and English secular lyric for the next century (and inspire the putative attribution of many "balades, roundels, vir-elayes" to Chaucer himself in the *Prologue* to the *Legend of Good Women* [F.423]). Axiomatic in what follows will be the always creative tension in Chaucer's lyric poetry between a dogged reliance on French forms and a will to make English a language fully capable of the lyric innovations that French, Italian, and even Latin literatures had contributed to the European literary tradition writ large.

It will be worth beginning, then, by considering Chaucer's practice as a lyric poet within and against just a few of the medieval poetic traditions that obtained in his day. For only by understanding the kinds of lyric poetries that Geoffrey Chaucer chose *not* to produce — whether through adaptation, translation, or original composition — can we begin to comprehend the full significance of those poems that he did write within the larger framework of his oeuvre. Indeed, to write about Chaucer as a lyric poet is also to write about the status and fate of lyric within his longer works, which often avoid complex engagement with the various lyric modes available in his sources and the literary traditions from which they emerged. Most of the scholarship produced on Chaucer's short poems in this age of historicism has been topical, concerned with uncovering the social, political, and ideological resonances of specific lyrics within Chaucer's Ricardian milieu. Although I point readers (mostly in the notes) to suggested historical occasions for some of these poems as well as the scholarship that has most influentially articulated their historicity, my concern here is primarily with form — in other words, with the particular rhetorical, syntactical, metrical, stanzaic, and grammatical mechanisms that allow these writings to work and to be read precisely *as poems.*

As a result, there is a fair degree of technicality here that readers are asked to absorb as they follow the specific readings; an introductory guide to poetic analysis (John Hollander's *Rhyme's Reason* or Stephen Adams's *Poetic Designs* are among the best) and a good dictionary are recommended for those who might not be on solid ground with rhetorical and poetic terminology (words like "chiasmus" and "tercet"), the implications of syllable count and scansion, the idiosyncrasies of rhyme schemes (and the consequences of their abandonment), or, say, the distinctiveness of quantitative verse within the medieval history of English prosody.[3] This chapter aims not only to provide a synthetic overview of Chaucer's short poems, in other words, but also to *teach* its readers how to unpack a Chaucerian lyric poem and work in some detail through the formal intricacies that establish any and every poem as a unique historical artifact. The general avoidance of historicist engagement here, then, is not to be taken as part of an anti- or ahistorical argument. To the contrary: As a number of proponents of the so-called new formalism have been arguing in recent years, the false opposition between historicist and formalist analysis resulting from the "theory wars" of the 1970s and 1980s have left two generations of literary critics unequipped with the basic skills and vocabularies necessary to engage literary production at the level of the foot, the line, and the stanza — formal aspects of poetic language that are themselves profoundly and unavoidably historical, however much this remains unrecognized within the wider field of literary study. Though such a project is beyond the scope of this chapter, a close attention to poetic form may allow the specific metrical, prosodic, rhythmic, and rhetorical dimensions of Chaucer's lyricism to come alive in a way that will complicate yet also enrich the historical character of his poetic practice as we understand it in years to come.

Let us first consider the basic contours of Chaucer's relation to several European lyric traditions, both insular and continental. This relation entailed a series of formal and generic choices the consequences of which become most visible, paradoxically enough, in Chaucer's nonlyric writings. Accordingly, I turn here to what is surely Chaucer's least lyrical work: the *Boece,* his translation of Boethius's *Consolation of Philosophy,* a late Roman dream vision written by a high-level aristocrat, translator, and philosopher inhabiting the inner circle around the Gothic king Theodoric.[4] The *Consolation* belongs to a hybrid genre of late-classical and medieval writings known as the *prosimetrum,* which, as its name suggests, combines prose and poetry, usually in strict alternation from section to section. Other prominent examples of the genre (some of them certainly known to Chaucer) are Martianus Capella's *Marriage of Philology and Mercury,* Alan of Lille's *Complaint of Nature,* and Dante's *Vita Nuova.* As critics have long noted, Chaucer's most remarkable choice in translating the *Consolation of Philosophy* was to jettison entirely this prosimetrical affiliation, a choice signaled in his rendering of every last one of Boethius's lyric poems into prose.[5]

On one level, Chaucer's "prosing" of the *Consolation of Philosophy* seems relatively straightforward in both precedent and motivation. Jean de Meun, the French poet who cowrote the *Romance of the Rose,* had chosen not to render Boethius's poems into verse when he translated the *Consolation* in the previous century; since we know that Chaucer was consulting Jean's French version as well as the Latin original while working on his own translation, his subsequent choice not to retain Boethius's poetic apparatus may be a signal of respect for the work of a continental poet whose oeuvre he had engaged at length throughout his career. Dr. Johnson's assessment that Chaucer in the *Boece* "attempted nothing higher than a version strictly literal, and has degraded the poetical parts to prose, that the constraint of versification might not obstruct his zeal for fidelity" now seems unduly harsh; as the editors of the standard edition of the text put it, if the *Boece* is indeed "a version strictly literal," it is "ambitiously so," aiming to render the poem fully intelligible for an emerging English readership.[6]

Yet such impressionistic assessments fail to explain what Chaucer actually did to the Boethian short poems he had in front of him. Consider, for example, the fate of Boethius's Meter 2 from the second book, a twenty-line poem in which Lady Philosophy, speaking in the voice of Fortune, scolds the human race for its insatiable greed:

si quantas rapidis flatibus incites
pontus uersat harenas
aut quot stelliferis edita noctibus
caelo sidera fulgent
tantas fundat opes nec retrahat manum
pleno Copia cornu,
humanum miseras haud ideo genus
cesset flere querelas.
quamuis uota libens excipiat dues
multi prodigus auri
et claris auidos ornet honoribus,
nil iam parta uidentur,
sed quaesita uorans saeua rapacitas
alios pandit hiatus.
uae iam praecipitem frena cupidinem
certo fine retentent,
largis cum potius muneribus fluens
sitis ardescit habendi?
numquam diues agit qui trepidus gemens
sese credit egentem.

If Plenty with o'erflowing horn scatter her wealth abroad, abundantly, as in the storm-tossed sea the sand is cast around, or so beyond all measure as the stars shine forth upon the studded sky in cloudless nights; though she never stay her hand, yet will the race of men still weep and wail.
Though God accept their prayers freely and give gold with ungrudging hand, and deck with honours those who deserve them, yet when they are gotten, these gifts seem naught: wild greed swallows what it has sought, and still gapes wide for more.
What bit or bridle will hold within its course this headlong lust, when, whetted by abundance of rich gifts, the thirst for possession burns?
Never call we that man rich who is ever trembling in haste and groaning for that he thinks he lacks.[7]

The diminishing lengths of the four discrete sentences making up this twenty-line poem — eight lines, six lines, four lines, two lines — follow the verbal migration from two conditionals in the subjunctive through the interrogative to the moralizing proverb that concludes the lyric. The syntactical contrast between the acting agents of the first two sentences — the main subject *Copia,* "Plenty," is deferred until the sixth line of an eight-line sentence, while *deus,* or God, appears in the first line of the next — serves the poem's larger argument concerning humanity's insatiable greed, which turns from one source to another in an endless cycle of insatiability. The complex meter of this particular poem ("glyconic internally compounded with a choriamb . . . alternating with pherecratic," as a recent commentator on the text enthusiastically describes it) is but one of dozens of metrical arrangements chosen for the lyrics making up the poetry of the *Consolation,* an exercise in prosodic variety unparalleled in subsequent Latin writings.[8]

How might an English poet, writing near the end of the fourteenth century for a courtly audience, deal with the verbal economy, grammatical sophistication, and poetic intricacy of such a lyric work? Here is how Chaucer (closely following Jean de Meun) treated the remarkable lines above in his own rendition in the *Boece:*

> Though Plente that is goddesse of rychesses hielde adoun with ful horn, and withdraweth nat hir hand, as many richesses as the see torneth upward sandes what it is moeved with ravysshynge blastes, or elles as manye rychesses as ther schynen bryghte sterres in hevene on the sterry nyghtes; yit, for al that, man-kende nolde nat cese to wepe wrecchide pleyntes. And al be it so that God resceyveth gladly hir preiers, and yyveth hem, as fool-large, moche gold, and apparayleth coveytous folk with noble or cleer honours; yit semeth hem haven igeten nothyng, but alwey hir cruel ravyne, devourynge al that they han geten, scheweth othere gapynges (that is to seyn, gapyn and desiren yit after moe rychesses). What brydles myghte withholden to any certeyn ende the disorden covetise of men, whan evere the rather that it fletith in large yiftes, the more ay brenneth in hem the thurst of havynge? Certes he that qwakynge and dredful weneth hymselven nedy, he ne lyveth nevermo ryche. (*Boece,* 2m2)

Even allowing for prosaic license, Chaucer's English version suffers greatly by comparison to its Latin model. Boethius's punchy aphorism — "sed quaesita uorans saeua rapacitas / alios pandit hiatus" (wild greed swallows what it has sought, and still gapes wide for more) — becomes in Chaucer an exercise in superfluous verbiage that more than triples the length of Boethius's eight-word couplet: "but alwey hir cruel ravyne, devourynge al that they han geten, sche-weth othere gapynges (that is to seyn, gapyn and desiren yit after moe rych-esses)." Throughout the work, prose becomes indistinguishable from poetry, the purposeful oscillation of the *Consolation* between the two modes entirely abandoned; in the manuscripts of the *Boece,* rubricated headers like "Metrum 2" are thus rendered anachronistic indexes of the Latin poetic original even while they remind the reader of what has been lost in translation. Although it may be true that Chaucer's literalism is "ambitious," then, it can be argued that it is so only in strictly quantitative terms.

If the Latin prosimetrum modeled a particularly explicit presentation of lyric poetry as part of a broader literary enterprise, the medieval liturgy repre-sented a body of poetry always ripe for literary adaptation and appropriation, consisting in no small part of psalms, hymns, sequences, and numerous other verse genres to which Chaucer would have been exposed since childhood. Despite the liturgy's status as a constant (if most often implicit) source of allusion and cultural reference for medieval poets, the *Canterbury Tales* by and large denigrates the liturgical culture of medieval England through satire, parody, and an often condescending aloofness.[9] The *Prioress's Prologue and Tale* together provide one of the most striking instances of this abnegation of liturgical poetics. The first stanza of the Prologue is a paraphrased translation of the first two lines of Psalm 8, a biblical passage that served as both the opening of Matins in the Little Office of the Virgin and the introit to the Mass of the Holy Innocents. By invoking this fragment of devotional verse, Chaucer clearly means the Prioress to signal her piety through the medium of liturgical poetry, and we would expect the subsequent tale to maintain this sensibility — and indeed, the *Prioress's Tale* does focus on the performance of a Latin liturgical antiphon, the *Alma Redemptoris Mater,* which was used in praise of the Virgin Mary during a most significant part of the liturgical year. Yet in the tale itself, not only is the "litel clergeon" who performs the *Alma Redemptoris* unable to comprehend the meaning of the text he sings (he is unlettered in Latin, and an older student must assure him that the song is made "in reverence of our blissful mother dere"), but Chaucer provides his English readers with no translation of the very lyric poem that provokes all of the narrative's considerable violence.

The *Prioress's Tale* was written during Chaucer's so-called Italian period, a span of years in the 1370s during which he traveled twice to Italy and became acquainted, presumably for the first time, with the works and reputations of Petrarch and Boccaccio, both of whom were resident in Italy during Chaucer's visits (though there is no record that he actually met either poet). Chaucer's narrative debts to both poets were considerable — he adapted Boccaccio's *Teseida* into the *Knight's Tale* and the *Filostrato* into *Troilus and Criseyde,* while the *Clerk's Tale* is a stanzaic translation from Petrarch's *Seniles* (itself a Latin translation of the Italian prose version of the same tale from Boccaccio's *Decameron*) — and, in the case of Petrarch, self-conscious: a famous passage from the *Man of Law's Prologue* hails "Fraunceys Petrak, the lauriat poete" for his "rethorike sweete" while anxiously reassuring readers that the great poet is now "deed and nayled in his cheste" (4.31–32, 29).[10] Despite Chaucer's extensive engagement with Petrarch's Latin prose for the nearly twelve-hundred-line *Clerk's Tale*, however, Petrarch's Italian lyric — the works that would consolidate an entire European tradition of love poetry and become an enduring source of lyric invention across the continent for the next two centuries — inspires but a single effort from Chaucer. This is the *Canticus Troili,* the sung complaint performed by a lovesick Troilus in the first book of *Troilus and Criseyde.*[11] Writhing on his bed and making "a mirour of his mynde" in which to view the object of his desire, Troilus sings Petrarch's Sonnet no. 132 from the *Canzoniere*, "S' amor non è":

If no love is, O God, what fele I so?	S' amor non è, che dunque è quel ch' io sento?
And if love is, what thing and which is he?	ma s' egli è amor, per Dio, che cosa et quale?
If love be good, from whennes cometh my woo?	se bona, ond' è l'effetto aspro mortale?
If it be wikke, a wonder thynketh me,	se ria, ond' è sì dolce ogni tormento?
When every torment and adversite	
That cometh of hym may to me savory thinke,	S' a mia voglia ardo, ond' è 'l pianto e lamento?
For ay thurst I, the more that ich it drinke.	s' a mal mio grado, il lamentar che vale?
	O viva morte, o dilettoso male,
	come puoi tanto in me s' io nol consento?
And if that at myn owen lust I brenne,	
From whennes cometh my waillynge and my pleynte?	Et s' io 'l consento, a gran torto mi doglio.
If harm agree me, wherto pleyne I thenne?	Fra sì contrari venti in frale barca mi trovo in alto mar senza governo,
I noot, ne whi unwery that I feynte.	sì lieve di saver, d'error sì carca
O quike deth, O swete harm so queynte,	ch' I' medesmo non so quel ch' io mi voglio,
How may of the in me swich quantite,	e tremo a mezza state, ardendo il verno.
But if that I consent that it be?	
And if that I consente, I wrongfully	
Compleyne, iwis. Thus possed to and fro,	
Al sterelees withinne a boot am I	
Amydde the see, bitwixen wyndes two,	
That in contrarie stonden evere mo.	
Allas, what is this wondre maladie?	
For hote of cold, for cold of hote, I dye. (*Troilus*, 1.400–420)	

[If it is not love, what then is it that I feel? But if it is love, before God, what kind of thing is it? If it is good, whence comes this bitter mortal effect? If it is evil, why is each torment so sweet? / If by my own will I burn, whence comes the weeping and lament? If against my will, what does lamenting avail? O living death, O delightful harm, how can you have such power over me if I do not consent to it? / And if I do consent to it, it is wrong of me to complain. Amid such contrary winds I find myself at sea in a frail bark, without a tiller, / so light of wisdom, so laden with error, that I myself do not know what I want; and I shiver in midsummer, burn in winter.][12]

Although critics have generally contended that the *Canticus Troili* is a "fairly close rendering" of Petrarch's sonnet (notwithstanding a few minor errors in comprehension of the Italian), Chaucer chooses an often stretchy literalism over a graceful adherence to form, though here he may have felt cornered into this choice by the stanzaic structure of the *Troilus* itself.[13] Petrarch's fourteen-line "S' amor non è" follows the strict form of the bulk of his sonnets: two *abba* stanzas, the octet, are followed by the sestet, consisting of two tercets (often in tension with each other) rhyming *cde cde*.

But surely this presents a real puzzle. A Petrarchan sonnet, Chaucer knew firsthand, contains fourteen lines; rhyme royal stanzas, he experienced over years of crafting them, contain seven. Why, then, would Chaucer have chosen to expend *three full stanzas* on the *Canticus Troili* — twenty-one lines, a third again the number as in the Italian original — when two stanzas could have allowed him to match his model line for line? While Petrarch's metrically longer lines might have challenged Chaucer to squeeze more words into fourteen decasyllabic lines, this choice would at least have allowed him to avoid the extremely awkward arrangement of his three stanzas so as to correspond to the two quatrains of the octet and then the sestet.

As it stands, though, the English version twice dilates four lines of Petrarch into seven lines of Chaucer in order to render the octet. While the sestet more comfortably expands six lines into seven, the effect of the turn is greatly diminished, for Chaucer has abandoned the strictly interrogative voice of the octet in favor of the long embellished declarative in lines 4–7 (which displaces Petrarch's one-line plaintive question, "If [love] is evil, why is each torment so sweet?") and the confused improvisation in the middle line of the second stanza, "I noot, ne whi unwery that I feynte": a sentiment that perfectly encapsulates Chaucer's apparent queasiness in the face of the work of a superior lyricist. Nowhere are Chaucer's limitations more apparent than in his management of Petrarch's final line, "e tremo a mezza state, ardendo il verno" (and I shiver in midsummer, burn in winter). Chaucer's rendering — "For hote of cold, for cold of hote, I dye" — reduces Petrarch's physiological quandary to a nearly nonsensical chiasmus that leads to the speaker's metaphorical death: a too-easy solution to the Italian poem's agonized quest after the paradoxical nature of love and a drastic simplification of the "quike deth" (Petrarch's *viva morte*) apostrophized in line 411.[14]

To call attention in this way to the formal discrepancies between lyric source and poetic adaptation is not to deny the considerable beauty of Troilus's song as an English lyric poem in its own right. It is, however, to follow Chaucer's own rhetorical lead. In introducing the *Canticus Troili,* the narrator of the *Troilus* seems strangely worried that readers will doubt his skill as a translator of lyric poetry from another language:

> And of his song naught only the sentence,
> As writ myn auctour called Lollius,
> But pleinly, save oure tonges difference,
> I dar wel seyn, in al, that Troilus
> Seyde in his song, loo, every word right thus
> As I shal seyn; and whoso list it here,
> Loo, next this vers he may it fynden here. (1.393–99)

The second line of this stanza contains Chaucer's first mention in the poem of his alleged source for the *Troilus,* the Latin author "Lollius." What is so striking about this identification is its appearance just before the *Canticus Troili:* a lyric insertion that Chaucer precisely could *not* have taken from his actual source for the *Troilus* in Boccaccio. The narrator-poet seems particularly anxious that his audience believe, not simply that he has accurately translated every word from his source, but that he has crafted a lyric poem (a "song") worthy of its original. This strangely anxious and somewhat incompetent translation of "S' amor non è" thus casts in miniature the relation between Chaucer's short poems and the lyric production of Petrarch. Petrarch's *Rime Sparse,* the authorially sanctioned edition in which this sonnet appears, contains a variety of poetic forms and genres, including the sonnet, madrigal, canzone, sestina, and ballata, each of which, in Petrarch's hands, allowed for numerous variations within the constraints of its (often loosely) prescribed form. The result is a mixed collection that, in terms of its sheer formal range, more closely anticipates the *Canterbury Tales* than the corpus of Chaucer's short poems.

Despite its limitations, this Petrarchan sonnet as Chaucer translated it had a rich afterlife. The first stanza alone was copied out several times and apparently regarded as a discrete lyric poem — most fascinatingly in a fifteenth-century treatise for women religious called *Disce Mori,* which combines its catechetical, homiletic, and moral teachings with a fair measure of anxiety regarding the situation of its women readers in a religious community that also included men. As Lee Patterson argues, the writer's treatment of the *Canticus Troili* suggests that he regarded *Troilus and Criseyde* itself—quite surprisingly, given the moralizing and allegorical habits of interpretation that suffuse medieval religious writing in this period—"as a text to be read literally, i.e., as an exemplary instance . . . Troilus' Petrarchan song is read not as signifying a blasphemous homage to Cupid but as describing a psychological reality, the conflict and bewilderment brought on by love."[15] The short poem thus becomes a synecdoche for the entire romance, its lovesick bewilderment an image of what the *Disce Mori* writer condemns as the "furst token of carnal love," the desire of lovers to communicate their passion: "how she loveth hym, and he hir, and what he wol doo and suffre for hir and she for hym"—in other words, the precise discursive domain of lyric poetry.[16]

Although Chaucer's negotiation with Petrarch signals a constrained relationship to non-French continental lyric, perhaps the most profound of his lyric abnegations was his wholesale rejection of the indigenous vernacular lyric tradition of medieval England. From the thirteenth century onward, Middle English had developed a rich current of lyric invention, both sacred and secular, produced within a variety of institutions and surviving in a spectrum of manuscript sources. Those who come to Chaucer's short poems possessing any familiarity with this vernacular tradition will find his lyric corpus greatly limited in form, structure, metrics, mode, and theme by comparison to the hundreds of Middle English lyrics that survive from the thirteenth and fourteenth centuries.[17]

Two examples from this great lyric archive must have sufficed here. One of the most famous pre-Chaucerian Middle English lyrics (which is set to music in the unique source that transmits it) celebrates the dawn of summer and the transformations in the natural world that herald its arrival (much like the opening lines of the *Canterbury Tales*):

> Svmer is icumen in,
> Lhude sing cuccu!
> Groweþ sed and bloweþ med
> and springþ þe wde nu.
> Sing cuccu![18]

Immediately notable here in metrical terms are the trochaic thumps that begin the poem, a rhythmic feature that tends to distract from the intricate juxtaposition of vowel lengths on u- and i-syllables in the first stanza. I have placed these vowels in bold and italics, respectively, to highlight the density of both within the first two lines: "**Su**mer *i*s *i*c**u**men *i*n, / Lhude s*i*ng c**u**cc**u**!" With four distinctive i-sounds and five discrete u-sounds within just twelve syllables of verse, these opening lines purposefully foreground the variety of ways these two vowels can function, despite their varying lengths and pronunciations, as diverse yet unifying prosodic elements. What the poet is attempting here, I would suggest, is neither alliteration nor assonance but rather an experiment in quantitative verse. This basic convention of Latin prosody, exceedingly rare in English versification of any period, structures the poetic line, not in the syllabic, accentual, or accentual-syllabic terms familiar to students of English prosody, but rather by means of the differing vowel lengths structuring every word of the language. Despite his obvious facility with Latin, Chaucer never approached such prosodic ingenuity, settling instead, perhaps, for the contemporary French development of "natural music" as the metrical fabric of lyric poetry.[19]

Chaucer's relationship to his more immediate lyric environment was also less daring and innovative than it is often described. It has been accepted almost as gospel, for example, that Chaucer introduced the rhymed decasyllabic couplet into English poetry (a metrical form that would evolve into the heroic couplet in iambic pentameter); as the *Riverside Chaucer* insists, Chaucer's "greatest contribution to the technique of English verse was the arrangement of [the] five-stress line in rhyming couplets, which he adopted in the *Legend of Good Women* and most of the *Canterbury Tales*. No earlier model for this has been found."[20] Yet even this canard cannot stand up to a wider scrutiny of Chaucer's poetic milieu, as these six opening lines from a Marian lyric dating from around 1370 clearly demonstrate:

> A Sone! tak hede to me whas sone þou was,
> and set me with þe opon þi crosse.
> Me, here to leue, & þe, hennys þus go,
> Hit is to me gret care & endeles wo.
> Stynt now, sone, to be harde to þi moder,
> Þu þat were euer godliche to al oþir.[21]

Positively "Chaucerian" in their metrical sensibility, these lines oscillate between the iambic regularity of the first couplet and the emphatic spondee ("Me, here . . .") that begins the second, finding a great deal of prosodic flexibility within a five-stress devotional poetic that could easily find a place in the prologue to one of Chaucer's religious tales. These are just a few examples of a long native tradition of lyric making in England that Chaucer, for whatever reason, remained unwilling to engage throughout his career. This is not to say that Chaucer did not conceive of himself as an "English poet"; as many scholars have shown, he continually sought to locate his work within a wider domain of Englishness that determined much of the thematic and narrative material he treated. For Chaucer, however, to be an English *lyric* poet within his milieu was precisely to reject the actual tradition of English lyric and the boundless poetic variety it had embraced for centuries.

The existing corpus of Chaucer's short poems, then, represents a profound narrowing of formally diverse lyric traditions extending from the late Roman metrical experiments of Boethius through a panoply of lyric ingenuity in Chaucer's language and linguistic heritage. If Chaucer knew these traditions intimately and deeply, he nevertheless resisted their aesthetic complexities in favor of a lyric production that remained safely within the institutional and stylistic expectations of his immediate social arena. In stressing the lyric choices that Chaucer did not make, however, I do not intend to denigrate his extant lyric oeuvre: indeed, Chaucer's eschewal of much of the kind of short poetry he *could* have produced renders all the more remarkable the complexity of the lyrics he *did* write, almost of all of which draw on formes-fixes French poetry in the so-called Machaut tradition.[22] Unlike its English language counterpart, French courtly lyric of the fourteenth and early fifteenth centuries survives in massive quantities and is attributable to numerous identifiable poets living in both France and England. Chaucer almost certainly composed poetry in French early in his career (his contemporary John Gower wrote an entire long poem in Anglo-Norman), though none of these lyrics are known to survive.[23] As an anglophone poet he found varied and ingenious ways of disrupting the formal conventions he had inherited. Caught between the stiffening constraints of courtly convention and the poet's agonistic will to innovation, Chaucer struggled against lyric regularization even as he perpetuated it, producing a number of truly hybrid poems even while writing some of the most conventional lyrics imaginable.

We might consider in this regard Chaucer's roundel from the *Parliament of Fowls,* a lyric insertion into a larger stanzaic dream vision that likely represents the first literary celebration of Valentine's Day. Chaucer interpolates this lyric (a roundel is a poem of varying length in which the opening line or lines repeat as a refrain) just before the *Parliament*'s final stanza, in which the dreamer awakens and returns, seemingly unsatisfied, to the eternal "labour" of reading that had led to his dream.[24] Performed by a group of birds "at here departynge," this gorgeous example of a fixed-form courtly lyric articulates a broad metapoetic statement beneath a mask of birdsong and love:

> Now welcome, somer, with thy sonne softe,
> That hast thes wintres wedres overshake,
> And driven away the longe nyghtes blake!

> Saynt Valentyn, that are ful hy on-lofte,
> Thus syngen smale foules for thy sake:
> Now welcome, somer, with thy sonne softe,
> That hast thes wintres wedres overshake.
>
> Wel han they cause for to gladen ofte,
> Sith ech of hem recovered hath hys make,
> Ful blissful mowe they synge when they wake:
> Now welcome, somer, with thy sonne softe,
> That hast thes wintres wedres overshake,
> And driven away the longe nyghtes blake! (lines 680–92)

Although this self-contained lyric poem stands well enough on its own, the framing of the roundel within the *Parliament* is crucial to its wider relation to Chaucer's oeuvre. Just before the lyric begins, the narrator comments on its musical and linguistic affiliations: "The note, I trowe, imaked was in Fraunce, / The wordes were swich as ye may heer fynde" (lines 678–79). These lines are in effect a pronouncement of English poetic indigeneity, a rare paean to an English vernacular lyricism that, as we have seen, Chaucer elsewhere eschews.

It is peculiarly fitting, then, that the roundel would evoke the opening passages of the two most influential *non*-lyric English poems of the late fourteenth century, each of which would define a distinctive verse idiom for the respective social milieu in which it circulated. The first and most obvious of these is Chaucer's own *General Prologue* to the *Canterbury Tales,* which was probably composed within the same few years as the *Parliament of Fowls* (and in fact there is no good reason to date the *Parliament* before Chaucer's initial dabblings in the *Tales*). The roundel's middle stanza, with its depiction of an ad hoc Saint Valentine's liturgy sung by the formel eagles — "Thus syngen smale foules for thy sake" — brings to mind the middle couplet of the *General Prologue*'s celebrated first sentence: "And smal foweles maken melodye, / That slepen al the nyght with open ye" (1.9–10). These two choirs of "smale foules," one of them singing paeans to Saint Valentine, the other pricked by Dame Nature to sleep with eyelids propped open, make up a thoroughly conventional courtly tableau, though the language in which Chaucer describes these songs is politically self-aware to a surprising degree. As Seth Lerer argues in Chapter 8 in this *Companion,* the opening sentence of the *General Prologue* purposefully juxtaposes words derived from Anglo-Norman French with those originating in the language of pre-Conquest England, a feature that seems intended to highlight the status of the *Canterbury Tales* as an avowedly English poem.

Missing from the *Canterbury Tales* couplet, though, is the alliterative density that characterizes so much of the *Parliament*'s most interesting poetic matter, from its first line — "The lyf so short, the craft so long to lerne" — to the line above from the roundel to a panoply of hammeringly accentual lines and half-lines ("Berafte me my bok for lak of lyght," line 87) throughout the poem that often work against the five-stress syllabic rhyme royal that Chaucer supposedly first perfected in the *Parliament*. In fact, the more intriguing possible allusion here is to William Langland's great allegorical dream vision, *Piers Plowman,* which opens with an alliterative line that Chaucer may well have had in mind when composing the roundel as a musical conclusion to his own dream vision: "In a somer seson, whan softe was the sonne" (*Prologue,* 1). The density of alliteration in this short roundel (in addition to the first line, repeated as part of the refrain, we have the phrases "wintres wedres" and "syngen smale foules for thy sake") represents a poetic mode from which at least one of Chaucer's characters distances himself purposefully ("I kan nat geeste 'rum, ram, ruf,' by lettre," avows the Parson in his *Prologue* [10.43]). Here, however, a fully accentual alliteration is embraced as an integral part of a Chaucerian lyric poem.

Given his general avoidance of native rhythmic, prosodic, and stanzaic structures in favor of French poetic forms, Chaucer's few forays outside French lyric convention are perhaps worth more consideration than they have received. As we have seen, Chaucer drew on a sonnet of his contemporary Petrarch for the *Canticus Troili,* though it was an Italian poet of the earlier part of the fourteenth century who provided him with the formal matter for one of his least read poems, "A Complaint to His Lady." This 127–line work of uncertain date might be read as the formal counterpart to Chaucer's extended thematic use of Dante's *Divine Comedy* in the *House of Fame*.[25] Critics have generally contended that "A Complaint to His Lady" as we now have it remains unfinished, though this cannot explain the remarkable disjunction between its thoroughly conventional treatment of lovesickness and its radically hybrid form. The poem opens with two stanzas in rhyme royal in which a sleepless narrator complains about the "longe nightes" and the endless days in which the "sore spark of peyne" afflicts him. Nothing new here. The single stanza of Part 2, however, moves haltingly into an initially perplexing formal scheme: rhyming *abacacdc* (a nonce stanza in Chaucer's oeuvre) and extending the length of the preceding two stanzas by one line, Part 2 complains of Love's cruelty in setting the narrator in "such a place / That [his] desir" will never be fulfilled. In formal terms, however, the succeeding part of the poem does provide a kind of fulfillment, clarifying the principle that Part 2 had attempted to initiate as none other than the terza rima structuring the *Divine Comedy* — a rhyme scheme of which the following lines represent the first incarnations in the English language:

> Hir name is Bountee set in womanhede,
> Sadnesse in youthe and Beautee prydeles
> And Plesaunce under governaunce and drede;
> Hir surname is eek Faire Rewthelees
>   The Wyse, yknit unto Good Aventure,
>   That, for I love hir, she sleeth me gilteless.
>
> Hir love I best, and shal, whyl I may dure,
>   Bet than myself an hundred thousand deel,
>   Than al this worldes richesse or creature.
> Now hath not Love me bestowed weel
>   To love there I never shal have part?
>   Allas, right thus is turn me the wheel,
> Thus am I slayn with Loves fyry dart! (lines 24–36)

Terza rima has often been compared to the helical structure of the DNA molecule for its integration of inflexible constraint and endless transformation: no matter how distant from the first, all subsequent tercets will bear the trace of the opening tercet that initiates the entire sequence and ultimately determines the shape of all those to follow in a potentially infinite chain of rhyme (*aba bcb cdc ded* . . .). This experiment in terza rima represents one of the few moments in his lyric poetry at which Chaucer appropriates a radically foreign rhyme scheme, and although it may be accurate to see "A Complaint to His Lady" as "a series of metrical experiments," this characterization overlooks the potential interplay between the poem's unique formal provocation and the thematic treatment of its subject (and the fact that the "Complaint" was clearly regarded as a finished product by fifteenth-century audiences). Chaucer's introduction of terza rima here may have been as much an emotional experiment as a metrical one, an attempt to reveal in poetry the effects of lovesickness on human sensation and response: in the face of an unobtainable love, the lover will be eternally transformed while always rooted to the original constraint in which his desire has ensnared him. This paradoxical sense of the evolving stasis of love must be abandoned quickly, however, the shocking poetic innovation of Part 3 yielding to the tedious ten-line stanzas making up Part 4. Here allegory and personification are abandoned in favor of a self-pitying lament that takes up the bulk of the poem while contributing none of its formal or thematic originality:

> For I am not so hardy ne so wood,
> For to desire that ye shulde love me,
> For wel I wot — allas — that wil nat be;
> I am so litel worthy and ye so good. (lines 84–87)

The cagey manipulation of form characterizes as well two corresponding complaints of pagan divines that together articulate something of the complexity of the poeticization of love in Chaucer's lyric environment. "The Complaint of Mars" is in many ways Chaucer's most accomplished lyric poem, if indeed it deserves the designation at all (which should probably be reserved for the actual lyric complaint comprising its final section).[26] The poem consists of three parts: a proem of four rhyme royal stanzas in which the speaker, "in . . . briddes wyse," promises to provide the "sentence" of Mars's complaint on his "departyng / Fro fresshe Venus in a morwenynge" (lines 25–26); the narrative, which tracks the vagaries of the relationship between Venus and Mars through the conceit of astronomy and the celestial migration of planets and constellations; and the complaint itself, a tightly woven articulation of the narrator's situation in five ballade-like sets of three stanzas each, though without the through-rhymes characterizing the stricter Chaucerian examples of the genre. Here, Mars avows his "trewe servise" to Venus while acknowledging the perilousness of love and asking why God inflicts us with this necessary emotional evil: a madness hard to elude and nearly impossible to conquer.

Despite its conventional theme, in this poem Chaucer seems to be working deliberately against formal convention, particularly on the level of the stanza.[27] At the opening of the complaint itself, the raison d'être of the larger work, the poetic unit abruptly shifts to a nine-line stanza. Muddying the waters further, Chaucer inserts an introductory stanza to the complaint that can provide only the most awkward lead-in to a new rhyme scheme:

> The ordre of compleynt requireth skylfully
> That yf a wight shal pleyne pitously,
> Ther mot be cause wherfore that men pleyne;
> Or men may deme he pleyneth folily
> And causeles; alas, that am not I.
> Wherfore the ground and cause of al my peyne,
> So as my troubled wit may hit atteyne,
> I wol reherse; not for to have redresse,
> But to declare my ground of hevynesse. (lines 155–63)

Notable here are the extremely dubious rhymes on the *a*-lines: skyl*fully* / pit*ously* / fol*ily* / *I*. These hardly qualify for status even as slant rhymes, let alone pairings worthy of a Machautian ballade, and yet they serve as the foundation for all that follows. This is a peculiar way to launch a stanzaic form that Chaucer had never tried before and never would again; the contrast seems deliberate with the stanza that immediately follows and begins the first "tern" (or group of three stanzas) making up Mars's complaint proper. Here the *a*-rhymes on *wroght, broght, thoght,* and *boght* (lines 164–68) are conventionally secure, almost as if to emphasize the looseness of the preceding stanza: indeed, it is practically impossible even to diagram the rhyme scheme of the nine-line unit that makes up this section unless one proceeds to its second stanza. Genre, too, seems vulnerable in this poem. The proem to "The Complaint of Mars" sets the reader up to expect an *aube* or aubade, traditionally a courtly lament that expresses anger at the dawn for sundering a pair of lovers after a night of passion.[28] And we get nothing of militarism until the very last tern and only in a single stanza, addressed to "hardy knyghtes of renoun" ("I am your patroun," Mars announces, rather unconvincingly).

If "The Complaint of Mars" foils generic and formal expectations, "The Complaint of Venus" adheres strictly to convention. A triple ballade with through-rhymed sections (that is, in which the three stanzas of each tern share the same rhymes, for example *-aunce, -esse, -ure* in the first), the poem is written in eight-line stanzas that together provide a creatively free translation of several discrete ballades by the French poet Oton de Grandson, a retainer of the English aristocracy and royalty who is named in the poem's *Envoi* and whom Chaucer surely knew in person. Chaucer seems to have selected these ballades as a kind of study in contrasts, though it has been pointed out more than once that a coherent narrative binds the separate poems.[29] The first three stanzas (that is, the first ballade) voice the light banality of a lover admiring the loved one: "him whos I am al, while that I may dure," the speaker describes him. Full of virtues "more then any mannes wit can gesse" and formed "so wel" by Nature, his very presence provokes a prayer of thanksgiving ("I blesse wel myn aventure") for the simple pleasure of serving him. The second ballade darkens things a bit, as Jelousy rears her ugly head ("Jelosie be hanged by a cable!" the narrator avows). The gift of Love is "agreable" for a "lytel tyme," "But ful encomberous is the usying," and its ultimate effect is summed up in the refrain: "Al the revers of any glad felyng" (line 48). Nevertheless, as the third and final ballade makes clear, the narrator has no desire "t'escape out of youre [that is, Love's] las," for despite its ill effects, the "fraunchise" or nobility of love itself does enough good to make its pursuit worthwhile; as the final refrain emphatically avows, "To love him best ne shal I never repente" (line 72).

Commentators on this poem have long admired its adherence to the fixed form of the French ballade, but the more notable aspect of Chaucer's translation was his curious switching of the gender of the narrator's lover, who is clearly female in Grandson's original yet unambiguously male in Chaucer's translation.[30] This does not necessarily imply, though, that Chaucer's speaker is female — as indeed the entirety of the poem's critical tradition has insisted. The title identifying the speaker as Venus is a modern editorial convenience, not Chaucer's own, and two manuscripts of the poem dub it "a balade made by that worthy Knight of Savoye in frenshe calde sir Otes Graunson. translated by Chauciers," suggesting a more direct translation than Chaucer in fact produced.[31] This deliberate ambiguation of the speaker's sexual identity places "The Complaint of Venus" in a long line of medieval poems of *fin'amor* that explore the possibilities of gender inversion within the courtly relationship, possibilities heightened in this case by the realization that the "Complaint" represents Chaucer's only appropriation of an ostensibly "female" voice in all of his lyric poetry. Although this voice does not come close to questioning contemporary sexual politics in the way that the Wife of Bath does, the hyperbolic veneration of the male love object here does suggest a homoerotic connotation to the speaker's "pleasaunce" from the poem's first line. Accordingly, perhaps, the penultimate line of the third ballade — "Thus wol I ende this compleynt or this lay" (line 71) — suggests that the poem as a whole might be read generically as a "lay," a short narrative romance in the English tradition of the Breton lay of the twelfth-century Anglo-Norman poet Marie de France. With its structuring subtext of male homosociality that often erupts into overt accusations of homoerotic love, the lay seems perfectly suited to the speaker's refusal to divulge his or her gender to the reader through any identifying signs other than desire itself.

The poem's envoy only reinforces this aspect of the complaint's erotic ambivalence. Here, Chaucer's self-consciousness as an English poet becomes inseparable from his veneration for his francophone agon, Oton de Grandson. Addressed (like the ballade "Fortune") to an unidentified group of "Princes," the envoy asks them to receive the product of the poet's "endyting" while clearly raising the possibility that the "Complaint" has been dedicated all along to Chaucer's French poetic rival:

> For elde, that in my spirit dulleth me,
> Hath of endyting al the subtilte
> Wel nygh bereft out of my remembraunce,
> And eke to me it ys a gret penaunce,
> Syth rym in Englissh hath such skarsete,
> To folowe word by word the curiosite
> Of Graunson, flour of hem that make in Fraunce. (lines 73–82)

That the possessor of all the "manhod and the worthynesse" celebrated in the poem may be readable as Grandson himself seems all the more likely when we consider the narrative progression of the "Complaint" as a whole: the first stanza gives thanks for the comfort, pleasure, and humility inspired by a lover who is in turn bountiful, wise, knightly, and "gentil" "in word, in werk" (in, perhaps, the writing of poetry); the second laments the effects of jealousy, including the tendency of those suffering from it to "singe in compleynyng" (an apt description of a poetic complaint); and the third reconciles the speaker to the "servise" of love, a poet's pursuit, while also making clear that the narrator of these fused ballades has chosen "the worthiest in alle wise / And most agreable unto myn entente" as the poem's subject — *entente* representing one of Chaucer's favorite words for denoting the very purpose of writing poetry.

For a late-fourteenth-century English poet trying to model and surpass his continental contemporaries, the ultimate backhanded tribute to "Graunson, flour of hem that make in Fraunce" might be just such a poetic artifact: a sequence of translated French ballades fitted together precisely in order to advertise the ingenuity of English poetics as a medium capable of challenging the primacy of francophone love poetry in the European tradition.[32]

This self-conscious relation between poetic form and thematic purpose recurs throughout Chaucer's lyric oeuvre and may be seen as one of its unifying elements. It is especially evident in a set of four through-rhymed ballades (all but one with a closing envoy) that modern editors have titled "Fortune," "Truth," "Gentilesse," and "Lak of Stedfastnesse." These four works (along with "The Former Age," also considered in this section) have long been grouped together by modern scholars as Chaucer's "Boethian poems," a designation that reflects their philosophical debt to the *Consolation of Philosophy* and their close engagement with the themes of loss, the vagaries of fortune, and the cyclical character of life that Boethius explored in such great depth. But these poems can also be understood as proposing a kind of metapoetic axiom that emerges from their collective Boethian idiom: that the formal register of poetic language provides a unique means of engaging with human institutions and scrutinizing their simultaneous indispensability and fallibility as engines of identity, community, and change.[33]

The ballade "Truth," which survives in more fifteenth-century copies than any other Chaucerian lyric, has the distinction of being Chaucer's only poem written entirely in the imperative mood (and, if the ascriptions in several manuscripts are to be believed, a ballade that Chaucer "made on his death bedde").[34] "Flee fro the prees and dwelle with sothfastnesse," commands the first line: "Suffyce unto thy thing, though it be smal, / For hord hath hate, and climbing tikelnesse" (lines 1–2). If the reader will simply follow such sobering imperatives, though, the refrain promises salvation: "And trouthe thee shal delivere, it is no drede" (line 21). The poem employs a muscular prosody at a number of points to reinforce its injunctions, recognizing that a command is more effective when barked trochaically than suggested iambically. This is true above all of line 18, a highly unusual Chaucerian example of *geminatio,* the repetition of particular words in a single line of poetry: "Forth, pilgrim, forth! Forth, beste, out of thy stal!" The combination of these monosyllabic imperatives and the animalized addressee anticipates the envoy's direct address to a certain "Vache": perhaps Sir Philip de la Vache, who served in a number of royal households before and after the turn of the century.[35] Given the enormous disparity between the total number of surviving manuscript copies (twenty-two) and the number of these that contain the envoy (one), however, the envoy itself may be, not Chaucer's, but rather a clever scribal interpolation that puns on the "beste" in line 18 to confect a generic French addressee (*vache* is French for "cow").

"Truth" was itself a loaded word for Chaucer—"a keyword in Ricardian England" more generally, in Richard Firth Green's assessment.[36] Equally in flux was the definition of *gentilesse,* or nobility, an attribute that could be inherited by the lucky coincidence of aristocratic birth or—in the view of Chaucer's Boethian ballade "Gentilesse"—acquired and practiced as part of a moral character regardless of the circumstances of familial inheritance.[37] The poem's structure constantly puts these two forms of gentilesse in ironic tension from the opening lines:

> The firste stok, fader of gentilesse —
> What man that desireth gentil for to be
> Must folowe his trace, and all his wittes dresse
> Vertu to love and vyces for to flee. (lines 1–4)

The first line creates a tension between "natural" lineage and cultural construct in the apposition of "stok" and "gentilesse," a tension carried over into the third line's invocation of the "trace" (a term from the lexicon of hunting that can mean both animal tracks and spoor) that must be followed for "man" to assume gentility. Similarly, the intangible signs of moral living—shown by an individual full of "rightwisenesse, / Trewe of his word, sobre, pitous, and free, / Clene of his gost" (lines 8–10)—supersede the concrete, material symbols of worldly gentility mentioned in the refrain: a man lacking nobility of character is not gentil in any way, "al were he mytre, croune, or diademe" (line 7). And those full of vice may well inherit their family's wealth, the third stanza argues, "But ther may no man, as men may wel see, / Bequethe his heir his vertuous noblesse" (lines 16–17). "Gentilesse" thus articulates in a more complex way the sentiments behind a widely cited egalitarian proverb from this period—"Whanne Adam dalfe and Eve span, / Who was þanne a gentil man?" —that was featured in the Blackheath sermon of John Ball, one of the leaders of the Rising of 1381.[38] The coupleting conventions of rhyme royal serve here to oppose "gentilesse" to "dresse," "rightwisnesse" to "besinesse," and, most interestingly in the refrain, "deme" and "seme" on one hand to "diademe" on the other — as if to suggest that the outward accouterments of a blood-based nobility will always remain vulnerable to relativism and doubt. They are merely, the poem suggests, tokens of an outward nobility that may or may not (in Chaucer's day, we would suspect, mostly not) correlate to an inner gentilesse.

"Truth" is succeeded in three manuscripts by the similarly themed ballade "Lak of Stedfastnesse," which exploits the world-turned-upside-down motif adumbrated in the *Consolation:* "turned up-so-doun / Is al this world for mede and wilfulnesse, / That al is lost for lak of stedfastnesse" (lines 5–7). Inspiring this conceit is Fortune's wheel, the Boethian device determining the rise and fall of individual fortune with a paradoxical combination of inevitability and unpredictability whose interrelationship can be known only to God. Chaucer registers this lack of earthly stability in three lines that subject personified abstractions to the material results of ideological usurpation: "Trouthe is put doun, resoun is holden fable, / Vertu hath now no dominacioun; / Pitee exyled, no man is merciable" (lines 15–17). Unlike the Vache envoy in "Truth," though, this poem's envoy is integrally related both poetically and thematically to the ballade proper, which seems to have been written with its designated royal addressee, Richard II, explicitly in mind:

> *Lenvoy to King Richard*
> O prince, desyre to be honourable,
> Cherish thy folk and hate extorcioun.
> Suffre nothing that may be reprevable
> To thyn estat don in thy regioun.
> Shew forth thy swerd of castigacioun,
> Dred God, do law, love trouthe and worthinesse,
> And wed thy folk agein to stedfastnesse. (lines 22–28)

Far from a simple plea for those in power to value truthfulness, as Paul Strohm has argued, the poem bears an extremely complex relation to the ideological machinations that defined the closing years of Richard's reign.[39] A significant part of this relation, though, must lie in the particular poetic genre Chaucer's advice to the king assumes: in such fickle times, a fixed-form ballade with an immutable refrain can constitute a unique form of "stedfastnesse" in the face of social change and potential usurpation.

This combination of institutional inconstancy and formal stability comes to a head in "The Former Age," which has been described as "the bleakest poem

[Chaucer] ever wrote" due to its resigned comparison of an Edenic "former age" to "oure dayes," summed up in the parade of moral squalor making up the concluding lines: "covetyse, / Doublenesse, and tresoun, and envye, / Poyson, manslawhtre, and mordre in sondry wyse" (lines 61–63).[40] While some critics have read the poem as a scathingly pessimistic commentary on Ricardian England and the various social and religious forms of corruption it embraced, others have contended that its Boethian themes are rendered too generally to allow such a conveniently topical reading.[41] What nearly all critics have agreed on, though, is the rhetorical adeptness of the poem in defining its subject almost exclusively by negation. Far from telling the reader what the prelapsarian "blysful lyf" actually consisted of in the "former age," Chaucer instead constructs a catalogue of modern destructiveness that he then employs to set off the ancient, unsullied world his poem invents:

> Yit nas the ground nat wounded with the plough,
> But corn up-sprong, unsowe of mannes hond,
> The which they gnodded and eete nat half ynough . . .
>
> . . . .
> No coyn new knew man which was fals or trewe,
> No ship yit karf the wawes grene and blew,
> No marchaunt yit ne fette outlandish ware.
> No trempes for the werres folk ne knewe,
> Ne toures heye and walles rounde or square. (lines 9–11, 20–24)

Humanity's ravages of the natural world determine the poem's diction in the provocative subject and verb choices Chaucer makes here: the plough "wounds" the ground as it works, while ships "karf" the multihued waves they traverse.

In strictly formal terms, "The Former Age" appears highly idiosyncratic. The eight-line *ababbcbc* rhyme scheme of the individual stanzas clearly affiliates it with the French ballade, though the poem is the only one of the five Boethian lyrics that is not explicitly labeled as such in the manuscripts. The four other poems follow a generally strict pattern, with end-rhymes held over to succeeding stanzas (for example in "Truth," which repeats *a*, *b*, and *c* end-rhymes over its three central stanzas as well as the envoy). "The Former Age" is the only one of these poems that is not through-rhymed (in other words, in which end-rhymes do not repeat from stanza to stanza within a single ballade). Chaucer's two other non-through-rhymed ballades are the envoys to Scogan and Bukton (treated below), but in these two poems the ballade form is maintained: "Scogan" is a free double ballade (two sets of three thematically grouped stanzas plus an envoy), while "Bukton" is a simple ballade plus envoy. "The Former Age" is thus Chaucer's only lyric written in something approximating ballade form that is *neither* through-rhymed *nor* stanzaically conforming. Adding an extra stanza rather than the existing eight could have rendered the poem a free triple ballade, or we could simply choose to call it a complaint (though this might appealingly explain the puzzling structure, thematically and rhetorically this generic designation does not fit).

On one level, this failure to conform to ballade conventions may be explained by the ostensibly unfinished status of the penultimate stanza. "A line is obviously missing," the explanatory note to line 55 in the *Riverside* asserts; the textual note to line 54 agrees: "After this line, the syntax and rhyme scheme imply a missing line." The poem's critical tradition has long regarded "The Former Age" as incomplete: phrases such as "an incomplete rough draft," "clearly a fragment," and so on abound in the scholarship. The existing rhyme scheme in the seventh stanza — *ababbcb* — could be taken as an uncompleted eight-liner, though if the final *b*-rhyme were a *c*, the stanza would become a syntactically hybrid seven-line rhyme royal: a radical violation of form, obviously, yet one that would allow the poem to be read, not as an incomplete draft missing a line, but rather as a deliberate swipe at the rigid constraints of the formes-fixes chanson — at this point only a generation old — within which Chaucer was forced to work. The stanza itself begins by thematizing the lack of creativity of various sorts in the former age: forging, "fantasye," "debat," the artisanal equivalents of the three deadly sins listed in line 53. In an age before craftsmanship — an age before poetry — formal convention had yet to assume its tyranny over the sphere of human language; the final stanza's Jupiter and Nimrod, the pagan and biblical fathers of desire and greed — in other words, of poetry — have yet to come into existence. Perhaps this quasi-rhyme royal stanza right at the end of a quasi-ballade is a nose-thumbing gesture at Chaucer's French contemporaries and the oppressive formal convention they represent; Guillaume de Machaut, it goes without saying, does not pace on the same Chaucerian steps as "Virgile, Ovide, Omer, Lucan, and Stace," the quintet of classical poets hailed at the conclusion of *Troilus and Criseyde* as Chaucer's worthiest poetic forebears (5.1792).

What was it about the Boethian *aetas prima* theme, then, that provoked Chaucer to violate ballade conventions in the writing of "The Former Age"? Are we meant to take the poem as an "imperfect" ballade, a formal betrayal that symptomatizes the social conditions — "doublenesse, and tresoun, and envye" — endemic to "oure dayes"? With its eight stanzas rather than nine and its lack of through-rhyming, the poem is virtually begging to be read in terms of its formal violations — violations that embrace as well its peculiar textual history. In one of the two surviving exemplars, the poem is inserted immediately following the fifth meter of the second book of Chaucer's *Boece* and is there given the title "Chaucer upon the fyfte metur of the second book." Though much of the poem's language and imagery clearly derive from *Boece* 2.5 (which begins, "Blisful was the first age of men. They heelden hem apayed with the metes that the trewe feeldes broughten forth"), in at least one case "The Former Age" was thus read and understood specifically as a *gloss* on a portion of Chaucer's own translation. One of the three most reliable witnesses to Chaucer's *Boece,* Cambridge University Library MS Ii.3.21, is also one of only two witnesses to "The Former Age" (and, we might add, one of the most highly regarded texts of "Truth"); "The Former Age" survives here as a poetic gloss on a Boethian meter (*Consolation,* 2m5) that Chaucer translated in the *Boece* as prose. Particularly intriguing has been the suggestion in the textual criticism (never really pursued) that the scribe may have been following Chaucer's autograph in MS Ii: in other words, that Chaucer himself may have been responsible for the peculiar interpolation of "The Former Age" and "Truth" into the text of his Boethius translation. It seems at least possible, then, that the Boethian poems may be Chaucer's attempt to restore lyric integrity to one of the great vernacularizing enterprises of his career.

The longest of Chaucer's Boethian lyrics is "Fortune," which is given the strange and much-discussed subtitle "Balades de Visage sanz Peinture" (Ballades on a face without painting) in several sources.[42] Presented in the form of a legal complaint by the narrator, the "Pleintif," against the defendant, Fortune, the poem is a triple ballade in eight-line stanzas plus an envoy in rhyme royal. What makes this poem unique in relation to Chaucer's other similarly themed lyrics is the overwhelming prominence it grants to the voice of Fortune, the allegorical figure from the *Consolation of Philosophy* who is often cursed by Chaucer's narrators for her seemingly whimsical play with the lives of the individual beings whose fate she controls. "Fortune" does begin with the narrator's complaint, which laments this "wrecched worldes transmutacioun," governed by "Fortunes errour" and subject to the machinations of this "fals dissimulour" (line 23). The third stanza turns for momentary consolation to Socrates, the "stidfast champioun," who was never tormented by Fortune but instead was attuned to "the deceit of hir colour" (her rhetorical fakery, perhaps) and knew that "hir most worshipe is to lye" (lines 21–22). The initial complaint takes up the entirety of the first ballade, and the second follows suit with "La respounse de Fortune au Pleintif," as the sources dub it. Here Fortune replies to the narrator's complaint with a dismissive urbanity: it is she who has taught him the difference between true and false friends, and the narrator should be aware that his fortunes could well change for the better at any moment ("What wostow yit how I thee wol avaunce?" line 31). The second ballade concludes with fatalistic advice to the plaintiff to accept his lot as a cog in her wheel: "Thou born art in my regne of variaunce, / About the wheel with other most thou dryve" (lines 45–46).

The poem provides no resolution to the lawsuit it imagines, and in fact the strange imbalance of the remainder of "Fortune" suggests that Chaucer strongly favored the allegorical defendant over the human plaintiff. The third ballade grants a single stanza to the narrator, a mere eight lines of spitting anger ("Thy lore I dampne," the plaintiff begins) that hardly deserve the subtitle "La respounse du Pleintif countre Fortune" given to the stanza in the sources. The legal exchange is at its most gripping in this third ballade, however, as the plaintiff and Fortune both enlist the refrain that unifies the three stanzas — "In general, this reule may nat fayle" — even as the ballade is divided unequally between the two parties. Fortune finishes off with two stanzas that constitute her final response, which are a devastating exposure of the narrator's hypocrisy: "Thou pinchest at my mutabilitee / For I thee lente a drope of my richesse, / And now me lyketh to withdrawe me" (lines 57–59). The vagaries of Fortune are as inevitable as the tide, which "may ebbe and flowen more or lesse" (line 61); for what humans, "blinde bestes ful of lewednesse," curse as Fortune's mutability is but the will of God, "th'execucion of the majestee / That al purveyeth of his rightwysnesse" (lines 65–66). Adding insult to injury, Fortune gets the envoy, too, which enjoins an unidentified group of "Princes" (perhaps the three Lancastrian dukes) to "Lat nat this man on me thus crye and pleyne" (lined 74). On the whole, this triple ballade provides a fitting if rather dark rejoinder to the other Boethian poems, recapitulating their understandable human concerns while advocating earthly resignation in the face of cosmic inevitability: "The hevene hath propretee of sikernesse, / This world hath ever resteles travayle" (lines 69–70).

If Chaucer drew on a variety of literary traditions and genres in several languages for poetic inspiration, he also exploited many nonliterary materials in crafting his lyric style. As we have already seen in the case of "Fortune," one of the most creative aspects of his extraliterary purview was the law, which for Chaucer represented a constant source of written inspiration throughout his career. "An ABC," Chaucer's adept translation of an abecedarean or alphabetically acrostic prayer to the Virgin Mary from Guillaume de Deguileville's *Pèlerinage de la Vie Humaine,* follows its French model in drawing extensively on legal language for much of its narrative tension (as, for example, in its plea for intervention at the Last Judgment: "But merci, ladi, at the grete assyse / What we shule come bifore the hye justyse," [lines 36–37]).[43] In the eighth stanza, however, Chaucer departs from his source in Deguileville by imagining a very different kind of writing that will guarantee salvation for the penitent:

> He vouched sauf, tel him, as was his wille,
> Bicome a man, to have oure alliaunce,
> And with his precious blood he wrot the bille
> Upon the crois as general acquitaunce
> To every penitent in ful creaunce;
> And therfore, ladi bright, thou for us praye.
> Thanne shalt thou bothe stinte al his grevaunce,
> And make oure foo to failen of his praye. (lines 57–64)

As Emily Steiner points out, Deguileville's version of this prayer says nothing about a "bille" written in Christ's blood. Like other insular poets of the late fourteenth and early fifteenth centuries, however, Chaucer often incorporated legal documents into his works as occasions for formal poetic invention, "catering to an English predilection not just for the law but also for the law's particular mode of textuality."[44]

Chaucer's enlistment of such a "documentary poetics," as Steiner has termed this mode of legal textualization, functions very differently in "The Complaint unto Pity," a first-person personification allegory that may represent Chaucer's earliest employment of the rhyme royal stanza.[45] The poem's death-obsessed narrator has been searching for Pity for many years in order "to compleyne / Upon the crueltee and tirannye / Of Love, that for my trouthe doth me dye" (lines 5–7). The desire for vengeance upon "Cruelte," however, must go unsatisfied, for when he finally finds "Pitee" she is already dead and "buried in an herte" (line 14). The death of Pity gives Cruelty free rein over the domain of love, though the narrator will seemingly remain the only human being who knows of her death. Much of the poem's gloomy narrative tension results from the subjective isolation of the speaker over against a formidable company of other allegorical figures (none of them mourning) gathered around Pity's hearse: "Bounte parfyt, wel armed and richely, / And fresshe Beaute, Lust, and Jolyte, / Assured Maner, Youthe, and Honeste, / Wisdom, Estaat, Drede, and Gouvernaunce, / Confedred both by bonde and alliaunce" (lines 38–42). As the narrator acknowledges with great regret, this sinister confederacy will hardly prove a sympathetic audience for either his grief or its legal documentation:

> A compleynt had I, writen in myn hond,
> For to have put to Pite as a bille;
> But when I al this companye ther fond,
> That rather wolden al my cause spille
> Then do me help, I held my pleynte stille,
> For to that folk, withouten any fayle,
> Withoute Pitee ther may no bille availe. (lines 42–49)

Crucially, given what is to follow, the narrator is quite emphatic here about the fact that he himself has written the bill (it is "in myn hond"), an official legal complaint to be presented before a juridical body of some sort.

Yet for all this, "The Complaint unto Pity" refuses to transmit the actual document around which the poem as a whole is organized. As the narrator explains, given the impossibility of receiving a fair hearing from the confederacy of personifications, "I have put my complaynt up ageyn, / For to my foes my bille I dar not shewe" (lines 54–55). As the final line preceding the bill insists, the narrator will refuse, not only to divulge the bill's contents to the allegorical assembly, but even to transcribe it word for word for the benefit of his readers. "Th'effect of which seith thus, in wordes fewe" (line 56): all the reader gets, in other words, is an abbreviated paraphrase, a précis of a legal document that wouldn't hold up even in a literary court of law. It comes as something of a surprise after all this to learn of the almost comic simplicity of the speaker's foundational complaint: "My peyne is this, that what so I desire / That have I not, ne nothing lyk therto" (lines 99–100). The bill itself, even as paraphrased by the narrator, does contain some specific legal terminology,[46] though now that cruelty has usurped Pity's "regalye" "[u]nder colour of womanly Beaute" (in other words, now that feminine beauty has displaced surface for substance), the utter fruitlessness of the whole enterprise becomes pathetically clear: no matter what court the speaker ultimately chooses to hear his Bill of Complaint, it will possess no jurisdiction (let alone inclination) to intervene now that Pity rests in her grave.

As such foundational legal conceits suggest, Chaucer was a master metaphorician, a poet always aware of the cultural and formal tension between tenor and vehicle as well as the variety of techniques demanded for the persuasive construction of metaphor, metonymy, and the other rhetorical tropes of comparison and proximity. One of Chaucer's most metaphorically delightful poems of any length is "To Rosemounde," an undated simple ballade to which critics have ascribed a wide variety of dates and motives, from an early experiment in edgy love poetry to a sophisticated and late tribute to Isabelle of Valois, the seven-year-old bride of Richard II who came to London just a few years before the poet's death.[47] Whether occasional or not, "To Rosemounde" is a virtual clinic in the double-edged practice of figurative poetry, beginning with a second-person address to its subject that combines metaphor and metonymy to head-scratching effect: "Madame, ye ben of al beaute shryne / As fer as cercled is the mapamounde" (lines 1–2). The opening metaphor that characterizes Rosemounde as the shrine of all beauty seems initially unproblematic: so great is her beauty that its renown travels "as fer as cercled is the mapamounde." Here, though, subversive metonymy kicks in: we know that by *mapamounde* (or map of the world) Chaucer really means *mounde* or *monde*, French for earth. But of course this is not what the poem actually says: without the implied metonymic leap from the reader, Chaucer is comparing the beauty of Rosemounde to a cartographic artifact approximately the size of a large dining room table. Like her beauty, Rosemounde's voice, too, comes in for some rather insulting comparison: "Your semy voys that ye so smal out twyne," Chaucer describes it, leaving the impression of his beloved squeezing faint words out of her constricted throat. The poem's greatest contribution to the archive of metaphor, though, comes in the form of a simile in the final stanza:

> Nas never pyk walwed in galauntyne
> As I in love am walwed and ywounde,
> For which ful ofte I of myself devyne
> That I am trewe Tristam the secounde. (lines 17–20)

On one hand, the passage seems intended to exploit the unbalanced comparison between the mundane fact of a marinating fish and the earth-shattering love of Tristan and Iseult, one of the defining narratives of the medieval romance tradition. Yet on further reflection, the pike metaphor becomes peculiarly moving for those accustomed to the objectifying clichés that define this genre: for there is no greater intimacy imaginable between a living being and what affects it most intimately than the image of a piece of flesh soaking in a marinade that will suffuse it thoroughly with its flavor, its scent, its color, and its very taste. "To Rosemounde," then, might be understood as a statement about the futility of metaphor itself in the face of love's immensity: anticipating in this respect Shakespeare's famous anti-blazon in Sonnet 120, "My mistress' eyes are nothing like the sun," which defines the beloved's reeking breath, wire-like hair, and other aspects of her physical appearance in a process of metaphorical negation that only confirms her superiority over the poetic conventions that would seek to describe and contain her beauty.

Yet metaphor can also serve in Chaucer's short poems as a powerful argument against the bonds of love, or at least of matrimony (separate categories in medieval culture, it should be remembered). The thirty-two-line "Lenvoy de Chaucer a Bukton," a verse epistle in ballade form written probably in the mid-1390s, deploys a densely metaphorical register to advocate the abandonment of its recipient's plans to marry.[48] Though the poet has agreed "to expresse / The sorwe and wo that is in mariage," he appears hesitant to provide a straightforward polemic against the institution: "I dar not writen of it no wikkednesse, / Lest I myself falle eft in swich dotage" (lines 5–8). Instead Chaucer resorts to the rhetorical trope of *occupatio,* a technique that allows the speaker to say exactly what he claims not to be saying:

> I wol nat seyn how that [marriage] is the cheyne
> Of Sathanas, on which he gnaweth evere,
> But I dar seyn, were he out of his peyne,
> As by his wille he wolde be bounde nevere.
> But thilke doted fool that eft hath levere
> Ycheyned be than out of prison crepe,
> God let him never fro his wo dissevere,
> Ne no man him bewayle, though he wepe. (lines 9–16)

The rhyme scheme sets up a series of rhetorical oppositions: between the "cheyne" of marriage and the "peyne" of Satan, between the eternity of Satan's punishment ("evere") and his desire to escape his prison ("he wolde be bounde nevere"). The overall construction here of the hellishness of marriage is reinforced through a careful invocation of the Wife of Bath, who herself functions as a kind of metaphor in "Bukton" for the complexity of marriage as both institution and relationship. The poem's avowed theme ("the sorwe and wo that is in mariage") precisely echoes the opening lines of the *Wife of Bath's Prologue:* "Experience, though noon auctoritee / Were in this world, is right ynogh for me / To speke of wo that is in mariage" (3.1–3). In the envoy, moreover, Chaucer explicitly recommends this text as follow-up reading for the audience of "Bukton":

> The Wyf of Bathe I pray yow that ye rede
> Of this matere that we have on honde.
> God graunte yow your lyf frely to lede
> In fredam, for ful hard is to be bonde (lines 29–32)

The opposition of freedom and bondage is common in medieval antimatrimonial writings, but the directness of these references suggests that the poem's argument against marriage is far from straightforward: indeed, while "Bukton" is clearly addressed to an individual man and thus, by extension, to a male audience steeped in a long tradition of misogynist writings against marriage, its avowed intertext is written in the voice of the Chaucerian character who argues most powerfully and directly against this same tradition.

"Lenvoy de Chaucer a Scogan" provides an interesting contrast. One of Chaucer's most consistently admired poems, this verse epistle is addressed to Henry Scogan, who served in the royal household and wrote a "moral balade" that incorporates the text of Chaucer's "Gentilesse." Unlike Bukton, on the brink of a disastrous commitment, Scogan has severed his ties with his prospective lover and indeed with love in general, "in blaspheme of the goddis" (line 15). The poem begins in a resolutely apocalyptic tone that implicates both the pagan gods and the speaker, who bewails a near-death experience brought on by the sundering of divine law:

Tobroken been the statutz hye in hevene
That creat were eternally to dure,
Syth that I see the bryghte goddis sevene
Mowe wepe and wayle, and passioun endure,
As may in erthe a mortal creature.
Allas, fro whennes may thys thing procede,
Of which errour I deye almost for drede? (lines 1–7)

The hyperbole is humorous and deliberate, as Scogan's abandonment of the domain of love threatens to drown the human race in the tears of its forsaken goddess: "Now so wepith Venus in hir spere / That with hir teeres she wol drenche us here" (lines 11–12). Without love, of course, poetry itself will be useless as its vehicle, a notion that leads Chaucer to bemoan his own unfitness as a man "hoor and rounde of shap" (that is, old and fat) for either love or its literary performance:

Thynke I never of slep to wake my muse,
That rusteth in my shethe stille in pees.
While I was yong, I put hir forth in prees;
But al shal passe that men prose or ryme;
Take every man hys turn, as for his tyme. (lines 38–42)[49]

Even here, though, the grammar of abjection confuses the conceit. The pronoun "that" in line 41 works with two antecedents at once: both the matter that men turn into prose and rhyme, *and* the prose and rhyme itself, "shal passe," leaving the world possessed neither of love nor of its literary incarnation. The "sheathed muse," as Chaucer characterizes the sword of his own abandoned artistry, rests in its scabbard even as it makes a last, rusty attempt to parry the thrust of "thilke rebel word that thow hast spoken" (line 23).

This "rebel word," obviously, is *no*. Scogan's refusal to say yes to love embodies the defining motivation of practically all lyric poetry, and certainly of Chaucer's: that is, to name and attempt to overcome a site or mode of resistance to the imagined fulfillment of the speaker's desire. This resistance takes many forms in Chaucer's short poems: the failure of another to return the speaker's love, the fickleness of Fortune in sundering the speaker from wealth and happiness, the difficulty of restraining Cruelty in the absence of Pity, even the constraints of a particular language in finding enough high-quality rhymes to squeeze into a French poetic form. As far as we know, not one of Chaucer's lyric poems ever got what it asked for, but of course this is part of the point. Unlike narrative poetry, lyric poetry rarely provides resolution. Even those Chaucerian lyrics tied most definitively to specific historical events and actors — "To His Purse," for example, a simple ballade that follows a densely metaphorical construction of the author's empty purse as his "lady dere" with an injunction to the newly crowned Lancastrian King Henry IV to "alle our harmes amende" (line 25); or Chaucer's "Wordes unto Adam, His Owne Scriveyn," a single rhyme royal stanza that presents itself as a tongue-lashing of a hapless scribe whose "negligence" leads to the sloppy presentation of the author's works in manuscript — cannot be comprehended in relation to their moments of production without some attention to the formal legibility they assume specifically as poetic artifacts. To return to form, then, is not to deny the status of Chaucer's lyric utterances as historical and ideological productions in the strictest of senses: the "Words unto Adam" cast in miniature the sexual politics of medieval textual culture, while "To His Purse" represents a subtle encapsulation of the forces that gave rise to the Lancastrian claim to the English throne.[50] It may be precisely the historical intimacy of ideology and form, in fact, that lies behind one of the most significant choices Chaucer made as a writer of literature: his decision *not* to become primarily a lyric poet — or, rather, his decision to stake his career and reputation on the production of narrative rather than lyric. In a certain sense, to consider Chaucer from the perspective of the poet he did not become reveals the lyric eccentricity of his oeuvre itself: a corpus of poetry and prose continually inspired by a lyric impulse that its author could neither fully recognize nor ever resolve.

NOTES

1. Wimsatt, *Chaucer and His French Contemporaries,* ix.

2. A helpful overview of Chaucer's lyric poetry that is highly recommended for students and scholars at all levels coming to these works for the first time is Ruud, *"Many a song and many a lecherous lay."*

3. Hollander, *Rhyme's Reason;* Adams, *Poetic Designs.*

4. On Chaucer's *Boece,* see the essay collection edited by Minnis, *Chaucer's Boece and the Medieval Tradition of Boethius.*

5. One of the most rigorous treatments of this question is Eckhardt, "Medieval Prosimetrum Genre (from Boethius to *Boece*)."

6. See Hannah and Lawlor, introduction to *Boece,* in *Riverside Chaucer,* 396–97.

7. Boethius, *Consolation of Philosophy,* 2m2, trans. Cooper.

8. The comments on meter appear in O'Donnell, ed., *Boethius' Consolation Philosophiae.*

9. A dated but still useful study is Boyd, *Chaucer and the Liturgy;* a more critical approach to Chaucer and liturgy is adopted in Zieman, "Chaucer's 'Voys.' "

10. On the historical implications of Chaucer's relationship to his Italian sources, see James Simpson's chapter, "Chaucer as a European Writer," in this Companion, as well as Wallace, *Chaucerian Polity.*

11. The most in-depth treatments of Chaucer's lyric insertions into his larger narratives can be found in Payne, *Key of Remembrance,* and especially Stillinger, *Song of Troilus,* a book that contains many provocative insights into the *Canticus Troili* and its implications for Chaucer's partially effaced identity as a lyric poet.

12. Petrarch, Sonnet 132, "S' amor non è," ed. and trans. Durling, *Petrarch's Lyric Poems,* 270–71.

13. See the notes to *Troilus and Criseyde* 1.400–420, in the *Riverside Chaucer,* 1028.

14. The most generous answer to this question has been Wimsatt's suggestion that Chaucer is translating the Petrarchan sonnet into a three-stanza ballade (*Chaucer and His French Contemporaries,* xiii), though given the lack of through-rhyming, refrain, and envoy in the *Canticus Troili,* this conclusion seems questionable at best.

15. Patterson, *Negotiating the Past,* 147. See also Pace, "Cotton Otho A. XVIII," esp. 306–8 and n. 46.

16. Quoted from Patterson's transcription of the relevant passage in *Negotiating the Past,* 123.

17. The standard study of Middle English religious lyric is Woolf, *English Religious Lyric in the Middle Ages.*

18. "Sumer is icumen in," in Brown, ed., *English Lyrics of the Thirteenth Century,* 13.

19. On Chaucer's presumptive familiarity with Deschamps's notion of "natural music," see Wimsatt, *Chaucer and His French Contemporaries.*

20. Davis, "Language and Versification," in the *Riverside Chaucer,* xliii.

21. "The Blessed Virgin to Her Son on the Cross," no. 128 in Brown, ed., *Religious Lyrics of the Fourteenth Century,* 228. The version here is from Oxford, Balliol MS 149; a very similar poem appears in Worcester Cathedral F.10, fol. 25a, in octosyllabic and variant couplets.

22. On this debt, see Wimsatt, *Chaucer and His French Contemporaries.*

23. There is a group of French lyrics attributed to a certain "Ch" that has been edited by Wimsatt, *Chaucer and the Poems of "Ch,"* though any attribution of these lyrics to Chaucer will have to remain suggestive unless further evidence is found for his authorship.

24. Importantly, in following the *Riverside Chaucer*'s text of this poem, I am accepting Skeat's sensible reconstruction of the form; see the note to these lines on 1002.

25. On Chaucer's relationship to Dante, see Taylor, *Chaucer Reads "The Divine Comedy."*

26. The most important recent studies of "The Complaint of Mars" include Patterson, "Writing Amorous Wrongs," and Dean, "Mars the Exegete."

27. Stanzaic variation in the Middle English lyric and narrative-poetic tradition has not been given the attention it deserves, though a richly learned approach to the possibilities of such study may be found in Fein, "Twelve-Line Stanza Forms."

28. The Chaucerian *aube* (particularly in the *Troilus,* though with some reference to the lyric poems) has been treated in Kaske, "*Aube* in Chaucer's *Troilus.*"

29. See Scattergood, "Short Poems," in Minnis et al., eds., *Shorter Poems,* 467, and Wimsatt, *Chaucer and His French Contemporaries,* 119–23.

30. The most sensitive treatment of the poem's gendered constructions in relation to its sources is Phillips, "*Complaint of Venus.*" On the feminization of men in Chaucer more generally (though without reference to this particular lyric), see Hansen, *Chaucer and the Fictions of Gender.*

31. See the comment in the textual notes in the *Riverside Chaucer,* 1187.

32. Davenport, "Ballades, French and English, and Chaucer's 'Scarcity' of Rhyme," argues persuasively that Chaucer's talk of the scarcity of English rhymes here is disin-

genuous and that the ballades in general represent in part deft experiments in the richness of English as a rhyming poetic language.

33. A useful overview of the tone and thematics of the Boethian group is Chance, "Chaucerian Irony in the Boethian Short Poems."

34. On the contrast between the stoicism of lyrics such as "Truth" and the view of the church in the *Canterbury Tales,* see Aers, *Faith, Ethics, and Church.*

35. On Vache and Chaucer, see David, "Truth about 'Vache.' "

36. Green, *Crisis of Truth,* 5.

37. See Saul, "Chaucer and Gentility," 41–55.

38. See Justice, *Writing and Rebellion,* 108–9.

39. Strohm, *Hochon's Arrow,* 57–74. Compare Norton-Smith, "Textual Tradition, Monarchy, and Chaucer's *Lak of Stedfastnes.*"

40. The quotation comes from Scattergood, "Short Poems," 489.

41. See the helpful overview of the poem's formal and thematic relationship to Boethius in Schmidt, "Chaucer and the Golden Age." The most important historicist work on the poem is Galloway, "Chaucer's *Former Age* and the Fourteenth-Century Anthropology of Craft."

42. On "Fortune," see Norton-Smith, "Chaucer's Boethius and Fortune"; of the many eccentric suggestions critics have made regarding the poem's topicality, the most amusing is that "Fortune" was written in the aftermath of a beating and robbery Chaucer received at the hands of thieves; see Margaret Galway, "Chaucer among Thieves."

43. "An ABC" is much more than a translation, as William A. Quinn demonstrates amply in "Chaucer's Problematic *Priere.*"

44. Steiner, *Documentary Culture and the Making of Medieval English Literature,* 49.

45. Prospective scholars of this poem should be aware of the numerous misstatements in the *Riverside Chaucer*'s Explanatory Notes to "The Complaint unto Pity" (and to other of the short poems as well); on 1077, for example, there are several egregious factual errors concerning the most basic matters of the poem's meter, voice, and form. For the short poems more generally (though not, unfortunately, "Pity," which was to be included along with the other complaints in a second part that has never appeared), much more reliable are the comprehensive notes in Pace and David's variorum edition, *The Minor Poems.*

46. On the poem's legal terminology (e.g., "Sheweth" at line 59; the more generic term "complaint" is also a designation for a legal document that would be presented before a legal body), see Nolan, "Structural Sophistication in the *Complaint unto Pity.*"

47. There have been few studies of this lyric; a short but provocative reading of the poem is Robbins, "Chaucer's *To Rosemounde.*" On the poem's parodic elements, see Stemmler, "Chaucer's Ballade 'To Rosemounde' — A Parody?"

48. A fascinating consideration of this poem's relation to biblical exegesis is Besserman, "Chaucer's Envoy to Bukton."

49. The reference to Chaucer's advanced age seems to me more self-deprecatingly humorous than serious, though many critics have taken it as a mark of the poem's late date; see, e.g., Wimsatt, *Chaucer and His French Contemporaries,* 96.

50. On "Chaucer's Wordes," see the extremely influential interpretation in Dinshaw, *Chaucer's Sexual Poetics,* and on "To His Purse," see Strohm, *Hochon's Arrow,* 75–94.

7

Troilus and Criseyde

JENNIFER SUMMIT

Although the *Canterbury Tales* is Chaucer's best-known work today, in the centuries following his death many readers believed Chaucer's greatest work to have been *Troilus and Criseyde*.[1] For Sir Philip Sidney, the poem confirmed Chaucer's rank as England's first great author: "Chaucer, undoubtedly did excellently in hys *Troylus and Cresseid*; of whom, truly I know not, whether to mervaile more, either that he in that mistie time, could see so clearly, or that wee in this cleare age, walke so stumblingly after him."[2] Sidney's judgment reflects Chaucer's ambitions for the poem, which are visible throughout: in its classical subject matter and appeals to literary tradition, its attention to literary performances in embedded lyrics and other literary forms, and its self-conscious adaptation of such classical literary devices as the Proem, or invocation of the muses. When, at the poem's end, Chaucer commends the work to "Ovide, Omer, Lucan, and Stace" (5.1792), it would be the first time an English writer dared to place his work among the classical greats. Yet for all its literary ambition, *Troilus and Criseyde* is at the same time deeply aware of and anxious about the risks that such ambition involves — the risks of meeting not acclaim but disapproval, misunderstanding, or blame. Moving between these two poles of ambition and anxiety, *Troilus and Criseyde* is profoundly concerned with the problems of literary production — what it means to write fiction, to take a place in literary history, to aspire to literary immortality as well as to commit words to the uncertain media of manuscript culture, ink and parchment. In its self-conscious representation of texts and textuality, *Troilus and Criseyde* offers a virtual library of literary genres, including not only source texts that are embedded within it but also the texts of songs, letters, and books that appear throughout the poem and are continually read, written, and passed between characters, foregrounding literacy as one of Chaucer's primary concerns.[3]

As well as establishing its author's literary ambition and interest in the acts and meanings of textual production, *Troilus and Criseyde* launched Chaucer's reputation as a poet with an abiding interest in what we could call, following Jill Mann, "the woman question"—a focus, shared by many late-medieval writers, on the roles and nature of women that runs throughout *Troilus and Criseyde* and persists in Chaucer's later work like the *Legend of Good Women* and the *Wife of Bath's Tale*.[4] Chaucer did not invent Criseyde but inherited her from his sources, in which she is an example of female inconstancy, fickleness, and treachery in love. But in representing Criseyde anew, Chaucer not only humanizes her by making her a complex individual who faces difficult choices, he also examines the very conditions of medieval misogyny that shaped her literary history, asking why and how women become the objects of so many narratives and legends that debase them. In so doing, Chaucer both addresses and transforms the inheritance of medieval misogyny that made "the woman question" an enduring subject of debate in the Middle Ages.[5]

In *Troilus and Criseyde* these two topics, literary production and "the woman question," come together and inform each other. The poem frequently encodes questions of sexual ethics as problems of textual interpretation or storytelling, endowing acts of reading and writing with erotic or gendered significance.[6] As the poem repeatedly suggests, texts influence how men and women see themselves in the world. So much is evident in the first scene in which Pandarus and Criseyde meet in the poem: Criseyde sits with several of her female attendants while "a mayden redden hem the geste / Of the siege of Thebes" (2.83–84), which appears to be the *Thebaid* by Statius, one of the classical *auctores* to whom Chaucer commends his poem, along with Ovid, Homer, and Lucan, at its conclusion. Since the *Thebaid*'s subject, the fall of Thebes, was believed to presage and parallel that of Troy, Criseyde is proleptically reading what is in essence her own story.[7] As she could learn from the book, that story of wartime violence and loss will end tragically, a lesson that Chaucer shows to have special significance for women by setting it in this female scene of reading. Statius's story is unusually attuned to women's heightened vulnerability during wartime, as Criseyde—a woman living in a besieged city without male protection—is certainly aware.[8] Yet Pandarus is determined to distract Criseyde from her grim subject; "Do wey youre book, rys up, and lat us daunce" (2.111), he directs her, attempting to turn her attention instead to Troilus's suit. When Pandarus presents it to her, he does so with all the literary self-consciousness of an expert storyteller:

> Than thought he thus, "If I my tale endite
> Aught harde, or make a proces any whyle,
> She shal no savour have therin but lite,
> And trowe I wolde hire in my wil bigyle." (2.267–70)

For Pandarus, winning Criseyde for Troilus means convincing her to give up one text—the "book" she reads with her women—for another, the "tale" of love into which he hopes to "bigyle" her to enter. If both Criseyde and Pandarus experience their lives in Troy through the mediation of literary texts, those texts are decidedly different in the perspectives on both gender and genre that they offer. Where the *Thebaid* illuminates the brutal effects of war on women, Pandarus's "tale" would subsume that story—and, by extension, women's wartime experiences—under the courtly conventions of romantic love.

The poem's concern with gender also informs a related concern: the definition of personhood, the question of what makes individuals. In this, *Troilus and Criseyde* participates in a late-medieval preoccupation with inwardness, and a related sense of the self as a private and complex entity, reflected in the poem's preoccupation with its characters' "entente."[9] Some of the richest criticism on *Troilus and Criseyde* has employed the insights of psychoanalysis to illuminate how Chaucer constructs selves through textual, architectural, and other symbolic devices.[10] At the same time (and as these studies demonstrate), the Chaucerian self is a deeply social entity, as Criseyde herself demonstrates; constantly bound by social, political, and historical circumstances beyond her control, Criseyde offers a medieval corrective to the modern notion of the self as an autonomous agent.

Sources

The selves in *Troilus and Criseyde* are above all the products of narratives. This is true, not only of Criseyde, who is written by the misogynist texts that make up her own literary history, but also of Troilus, who variously finds himself written by the texts of courtly love traditions or by those of epic that form the literary context of the Trojan War. As the literary histories of *Troilus and Criseyde* witness, Chaucer drew on numerous sources for his poem. The story of the Trojan War was already well known to Chaucer's readers; indeed, following Geoffrey of Monmouth's *Historia Regum Britanniae* (History of the kings of England), in late medieval England, British history was seen as an outgrowth of Trojan history, and London itself was sometimes called "New Troy." This identification suggested that London inherited not only Troy's status as an ancient civilization but also its vulnerability; as Troy fell, so might London (a fear that became increasingly palpable under the shaky and doomed reign of Richard II). Telling a story about the fall of Troy, then, meant that Chaucer was also telling a story about his own place and time.[11]

Where the Trojan matter grounds the poem in history, Chaucer chooses to focus on the love story of Troilus and Criseyde, a focus that has struck some of his readers as an evasion of the political and historical implications of the Trojan War. It would be inaccurate to say, however, that the Trojan War disappears from the poem, since it enters and reenters the story in key moments to comment on the activities of the lovers. If we are never able to forget that Troilus is bound to the history of Troy itself (as his very name implies, along with his identification in line 2 as "kyng Priamus sone of Troye"), that history also circumscribes Criseyde's life in both direct and indirect ways. When the story is introduced in the poem's opening stanzas, we are reminded that the war itself is the result of illicit love, culminating in Helen of Troy's "ravysshyng" (1.62). The related question of whether she was carried away by force against her will or whether she consented to her "ravishment" by Paris frames the story of Criseyde, for whom the story of female consent and intention will likewise be central and unresolved. It also leaves us with the distinct impression that history will repeat itself, that this is a story that has already been written both in literary fiction and in historical fact.

Chaucer draws the story of Troilus and Criseyde's love affair from a number of sources. Homer's *Iliad* mentions Briseis, a beautiful widow who becomes Achilles' slave and lover and is later demanded by Agamemnon in an exchange of prisoners. That story reached medieval readers through Ovid's *Heroides*, which features Briseis's complaint to Achilles and stresses her love for the man she has been forced to leave. Ovid's *Remedia Amoris* — a text also well known in the Middle Ages — takes a more cynical view of Briseis, suggesting (as the *Iliad* and *Heroides* do not) that Briseis became Agamemnon's lover following her trade.[12] From this line of literary inheritance came the basic outlines of Criseyde's story as well as its central paradox, as Chaucer receives and develops it: Criseyde is both a woman traded involuntarily between men and one of dubious constancy, whose affections are transferred as easily as is her physical person.

The story of Briseis is also mentioned in Dares the Phrygian's *De Excidio Troiae Historia*, which, together with Dictys of Crete's *Ephemeridos Belli*

Troiani Libri, was considered an eye-witness account of the Trojan War. But it was in later medieval works that the love story of Troilus and Criseyde took shape. Benoît de Sainte-Maure's *Roman de Troie* (c. 1165) expands on Dares' account by inventing a romance between Briseida and Troilus, as well as her betrayal of Troilus for Diomede. For Benoit, Briseida becomes an example of female fickleness in love, a point that was expanded in a later version of the story by Guido de Columnis, *Historia Destructionis Troiae* (1287), which exemplified in Briseida the misogynist assertion that "all women naturally tend to lack any kind of firm constancy."[13]

Above all Chaucer's sources, the one that has the most direct impact on *Troilus and Criseyde* is Giovanni Boccaccio's *Il Filostrato* (c. 1335), whose story of Troiolo and Criseida Chaucer follows closely in what Barry Windeatt calls a process of "composition through adaptive translation."[14] Although Chaucer's text appears in places to be a close translation of Boccaccio's, it also departs from and develops its source-text in ways that make *Troilus and Criseyde* a distinct and original work on both the broad level of the plot and finer details of style. Following *Il Filostrato,* the story of *Troilus and Criseyde* takes the love affair as its focus and develops the character of Pandarus (Pandaro in Boccaccio) and the central drama of Criseyde's betrayal. But the differences between Chaucer's and Boccaccio's texts are significant: whereas Boccaccio's Pandaro is Criseida's cousin, Chaucer's Pandarus is Criseyde's uncle and thus a male relative who should be responsible for her protection in Troy. In Chaucer's hands, Troilus becomes more uncertain and courtly, while Criseyde is likewise given a more complex inner life than is Boccaccio's Criseida, whose vanity and inconstancy recall earlier representations of the character.[15] Chaucer's adaptive use of Boccaccio is also visible on the stanzaic level. To take one symptomatic example: early in the story, while Troilus is languishing in love for Criseyde, both Chaucer's and Boccaccio's narrators question whether Criseyde is aware of Troilus's suffering. Boccaccio reads thus:

> E qual si fosse non è assai certo:
> O che Criseida non se n'accorgesse
> Per l'operar di lui ch'era coverto,
> O che di ciò conoscer s'infignesse;
> Ma questo n' assai chiaro ed aperto:
> Che nïente pareva le calesse
> Di Troilo e dell'amor che le portava
> Ma come non amata dura stava.[16]

[And the true state of things is not very clear: whether Criseida because of his discretion perceived nothing of this, or whether she was pretending not to understand. But this much is clear and obvious: that she seemed to care nothing for Troilo and the love he had for her, but remained impervious, as if untouched by love.][17]

The parallel passage in Chaucer's text shows both clear similarities to its Boccaccian source and telling departures from it:

> But how it was, certeyn, kan I nat seye,
> If that his lady understood nat this,
> Or feynede hire she nyste, oon of the tweye;
> But wel I rede that, by no manere weye,
> Ne semed it that she of hym roughte,
> Or of his peyne, or whatsoevere he thoughte. (1.492–497)

Chaucer's stanza compresses Boccaccio's treatment of Criseyde's knowledge, in part necessitated by Chaucer's use of the seven-line rhyme royal stanza, which is one line shorter than Boccaccio's eight-line ottava[18] — and in the process drops Boccaccio's observation about Troilus's covert love: "Per l'operar di lui ch'era coverto" (because of his discretion). The effect is to shift the focus from Troilus's actions and to heighten the focus on Criseyde's knowledge and intentions: Did Criseyde not know of Troilus's suffering or only pretend not to know? In Chaucer, however, the question of who knew what at what point — and by extension, the broader question of how individuals can ever know, or express, their own or others' inner knowledge or intentions — becomes layered with complexity. Where Boccaccio speaks from the lofty perspective of what is "clear and obvious" (chiaro ed aperto), Chaucer characteristically injects a first-person narrator into the scene, shifting responsibility for the state of uncertainty that Boccaccio diagnoses as a general problem ("E qual si fosse non e assai certo"; And the true state of things is not very clear) to the narrator, who pins the problem of uncertainty onto himself: "But how it was, certeyn, kan I nat seye." Similarly, Chaucer translates Boccaccio's omniscient statement of clarity, "ma questo n'e assai chairo ed aperto" (But this much is clear and obvious), into a first-person statement of subjective knowledge, "But wel I rede that." The assertion foregrounds the extent to which this narrator draws conclusions — or fails to — on the basis of what he is able to "rede" — that is, to perceive generally or, more specifically, to read in his sources such as Boccaccio. And as we discover both on a microcosmic level in this stanza as well as the larger level of the poem as a whole, the process of reading is always fraught with uncertainty.

Chaucer's transformation of this stanza will have broader interpretive ramifications for his poem. In Boccaccio's version of the stanza, Criseida is an object of subtle but indisputable blame: the fact that she may not even know that Troilus is suffering out of love for her does not mitigate her implied guilt, in that "she seemed to care nothing for Troilo and the love he had for her, but remained impervious, as if untouched by love" (Che niente pareva le calesse / Di Troilo e dell'amor che le portava / Ma come non amata dura stava). Chaucer's condensed retelling drops Boccaccio's final, reproachful line, instead underscoring the uncertainty of "seemed" ("ne semed it") and thus highlighting the problem of knowability that will become a central concern in the poem. Chaucer's subtle but calculated departures from his source in this stanza introduce *in parvo* an interpretive crux that will loom large in the poem that follows: first, by raising the question of Criseyde's interiority and knowledge as an important problem, but one that will remain essentially opaque; and second, by linking this opacity — and, by extension, the opacity of all human motives in the poem — to the instabilities of textual interpretation and of translated sources.

Chaucer continually draws attention to his indebtedness to literary sources; "For as myn auctour seyde, so sey I" (2.18), he claims frequently, showing a deference to literary authority that was conventional for medieval writers.[19] Yet the "auctour" he names directly is not Boccaccio — as we might expect of the source that most clearly shaped his own work — but "myn auctour called Lollius" (1.394). This and other references have led generations of Chaucer's readers to attempt to track down the identity of "Lollius," of whom no work or independent literary identity survives. Instead, the attribution seems likely to be a deliberate red herring, meant to ironize the rituals of citation that were central to the establishment of medieval literary authority.[20] In a book as supremely embedded in literary traditions as *Troilus and Criseyde*, the references to Lollius heighten the fact that this is a story about storytelling, beginning with the very sources from which the poem claims to derive.

Book 1

Narrator. The opening stanzas of the poem reinforce the sense that Chaucer's narrator is merely transcribing a story that is already well known and whose end is predetermined. We are told from the outset that the story will end badly, as Troilus is destined to fall "fro wo to wele, and after out of joie" (1.4), a line that invokes the medieval wheel of fortune in order to reinforce the sense of history's circularity. Moreover, the narrator — who becomes a central character in his own right — constantly stresses his own passivity in the writing process, claiming the role of mere transcriber of the story, rather than its inventor. When he refers to "thise woful vers, that wepen as I write" (1.7), the narrator imagines the verses themselves weeping (as indicated by his use of the plural "wepen"), thus giving the verses their own life independent of him. Sounding much like the medieval female mystics who claimed to be the media, rather than originators, of texts written through them by God, the narrator refers to himself merely as a "sorwful instrument" (1.10) who is remarkably passive in the act of writing. This impression is reinforced by his own apparent lack of erotic experience. Presenting himself as "I, that God of Loves servantz serve" (1.15), the narrator insists that he is excluded from love "for myn unliklynesse" (1.16), a characteristically opaque statement that has led critics variously to conclude that he is referring to his impotence, class, or age, which disqualify him from participating in the arts of love. The effect is a deliberate shift from the model of Boccaccio, who addressed his poem to a female beloved, to suggest instead that writing is taking the place of erotic experience — that for those who can't love, writing is a form of sublimation. The result is a narrator who promises to write on behalf of lovers — to "helpeth lovers, as I kan, to pleyne" (1.11) and "write hire wo" (1.49), as if love is invariably tragic — but also one whose experience of love seems to come only through books.

Criseyde. If the narrator knows love only through books, Criseyde, as Chaucer inherited her, was a creature of books, since her character had already been firmly established in literary tradition. Chaucer's Criseyde grows into awareness that she is destined to be a figment of literary history, as she will lament at the poem's end. But even while Chaucer explores, through Criseyde, his own literary inheritance, he departs from his sources to illuminate the complexities of Criseyde's social standing and the choices she faces. In the process, he balances the stock characterization of female treachery that he inherited from the medieval debates over "the woman question" with a much more layered consideration of women's place in medieval society.

As a widow, Criseyde would have been recognized by medieval readers as occupying a contradictory place in her world. Widows, as medieval historians note, were able to own and control property in their own names, unlike unmarried maidens or married wives (without special dispensation). Their relative independence in the economic sphere sometimes translated into sexual licentiousness in the popular mind (as witnessed by Chaucer's other well-known widow, the Wife of Bath). Yet if widows enjoyed greater financial autonomy than other women, that autonomy was circumscribed by a lesser degree of social freedom, as they lived without male protection and subsequently became vulnerable to a greater degree of social scrutiny and criticism.[21]

And Criseyde is especially vulnerable: the first thing we learn about her is that her father, Calchas, has abandoned her and Troy for the Greek side after learning that Troy was doomed. Calchas's treachery leaves his daughter in a perilous position when the enraged Trojans declare that "he and al his kyn at-ones / Ben worthi for to brennen, fel and bones" (1.91); since Criseyde is Calchas's nearest kin left in Troy, as far as we can tell, this threat is aimed directly at her. As a widow lacking any other male protection, Criseyde throws herself at the feet of Hector, Troy's governor, whose assurance that "youre body shal men save" (1.122) promises Criseyde the protection she seeks. But by emphasizing the vulnerability of her physical body, Hector's remark also disconcertingly underscores the special dangers that she faces as a woman alone — of rape, possibly, but also of mistreatment by the same male protectors like Hector, whose mercy appears to be inspired by his attraction to that body, when he privately notes "that she was so fair a creature" (1.115).

Criseyde's beauty becomes a source of danger both to her and to those who observe it. She is first described as "an hevenyssh perfit creature, / That down were sent in scornynge of nature" (1.104–5), leading to the expectation that she will be punished for scorning nature, just as Troilus later will be punished for rejecting "the lawe of kynde" (1.239) when he initially resists falling in love. In a poem in which characters seem continually controlled by outside forces, Criseyde would appear to be the instrument supernaturally selected for Troilus's punishment, who will later wonder, sacrilegiously, "wheither god-desse or woman, iwis, / She be, I not" (1.425–26). If Criseyde appears to be "scornynge of nature" in her first appearance in the poem, she projects scorn-fulness in the first scene in which Troilus glimpses her, when she is described as "somedel deignous" (haughty or disdainful) (1.290). Similarly scornful is her "askaunce" look, which seems to ask "what, may I nat stonden here?" (1.292). But there are good reasons why she, as a widow whose protection is still tenuous, might worry about her right to stand alone in a public gathering; and as will be true elsewhere in the narrative, here her apparent assertion of self-confidence is also an expression of her vulnerability.

Troilus. Following a convention for male literary lovers set by Guillaume de Lorris's *Roman de la Rose,* Troilus technically falls in love before setting eyes on Criseyde, when the God of Love shoots his arrow into Troilus's heart long before Criseyde's initial appearance. When he does spy Criseyde, Troilus ap-pears to become an archer like the God of Love, sending his look into the crowd like an arrow: "thorugh a route / His eye percede, and so depe it wente, / Til on Criseyde it smot, and ther it stente" (1.271–73). The language of piercing ("percede") and hitting ("smot") seems to fit the pattern of postmod-ern feminist theories of the cinematic gaze, in which the male viewer ag-gressively pierces the female object in the act of looking at her.[22] But this scene reminds us that medieval theories of masculinity differ from, and demand modification of, modern critical paradigms. Troilus, the piercer, is already pierced himself by love's arrow. Moreover, his piercing gaze rebounds, so that he is himself pierced by the image of Criseyde: "in his herte botme gan to stiken / Of hir his fixe and depe impressioun" (1.297–98), he is "right with hire look thorugh-shoten and thorugh-darted" (1.325). Love plunges Troilus into a state of physical and mental vulnerability.

Troilus's experience of love is consistent with medieval conventions of love-sickness, which was believed to afflict mostly young men of high social standing not only in literature but also in actuality: in the mid-fourteenth century, for example, Henry of Lancaster persuaded friends that he would die unless he received their aid in securing his beloved's attention.[23] Similarly, Troilus — like, apparently, Criseyde — believes that the inevitable end of his lovesickness is death. According to conventions established by *fin amors* (or "courtly love"), love inverted the power relations between men and women, giving women a unique degree of control over their lover's very life and death, while making the male lover, in the words of Mary Wack, "passive, helpless, and vulnerable."[24]

Troilus's vulnerability (a word whose literal meaning, wound-ability, is especially apt for Troilus, who is continually described as wounded in both body and spirit) manifests his tortured subjectivity; here and throughout the narrative, he responds to his wounding by withdrawing to his chamber and reflecting on his pain. The scene following Troilus's first encounter with Criseyde is noteworthy for several reasons. First, it offers the historically significant representation of a character's inner life and subjectivity, signaling one of the poem's abiding interests in problems of the private self; and second, it locates this private self as the site of poetic production, since Troilus's sequestration inspires the *Canticus Troili*, a Petrarchan lyric whose skill and beauty were sufficiently admired in the Middle Ages to lead to its circulation independently of *Troilus and Criseyde*.[25] The lyric, like Petrarch's original, expresses conventional experiences of the male lover: but a comparison with Boccaccio's original text reveals it to be a particularly Troilian representation of love. In a parallel scene, Boccaccio's Troiolo withdraws to his chamber to utter a short, lyrical praise of his lady; in contrast, Troilus's lyric focuses entirely on his own, inner experience of love: "If no love is, O God, what fele I so?" (1.400). Following a lengthy anatomy of his own feelings, Troilus's admission that he doesn't know whether Criseyde is a "goddesse or womman" (1.425) confirms the impression that, in Troilus's experience of it, love is an entirely inner state, to which Criseyde herself becomes almost extraneous.[26]

Pandarus. Chaucer's representation of Troilus's friend Pandarus also departs from his source. In contrast to Boccaccio's Pandare, who is Criseyde's cousin, Chaucer's Pandarus becomes Criseyde's uncle; the character who would therefore seem to be most responsible for Criseyde's protection in her father's absence takes on a more sinister role as he devotes himself to helping his friend win her love. In both Boccaccio and Chaucer, Pandarus has been unlucky in love himself, but he nonetheless offers his assistance to his friend with a revealing choice of metaphors; in Boccaccio's text, Pandaro assures Troilo:

> Spesse volte avvene
> Che quei sé non sa guardar dal tosco,
> Altrui per buon consignlio salvo tene,
> E già veduto s'è andare il losco
> Dove l'alluminato non va bene.[27]

> [It often happens that those who cannot protect themselves from a poison may save others through timely warning — and a squint-eyed man has indeed been known to walk where one with good sight cannot easily go.][28]

In contrast to Pandaro, whose metaphors suggest that he sees himself giving charitable aid to one who is helpless, Chaucer's Pandarus reflects on his position with a strikingly different metaphor, observing that "a wheston is no kervyng instrument / But yet it maketh sharppe kervyng tolis" (1.631–32). In his choice of the "wheston" (whetstone) image, Pandarus reveals how his views of the masculine role in love differ from Troilus's more traditional courtly attitude. If Troilus experiences love as one who is "thorugh-shoten and thorugh-darted," or the object of piercing, Pandarus offers to turn him into a knife, a piercing agent. His subsequent reflections on love reveal a view of the male lover as an active subject whose aggressivity in pursuing his beloved will not stop at violence. Although Troilus's private deliberations maintain no hope of resolution to his lovesickness beyond endless languishing and death, Pandarus represents a view of love that is a spur to action; as he famously exhorts Troilus, "unknewe, unkist" (1.809).[29]

Pandarus's investment in Troilus's love affair is also disconcertingly self-serving: the affair between Troilus and Criseyde, Pandarus asserts, will bring pleasure not only to the lovers but also to himself: "And so we may be gladed alle three" (1.994). He similarly inserts himself into the love affair when he pressures Criseyde to accept Troilus's advances not only for Troilus's sake but for his own by putting both men's lives on the line: "If ye late hym deyen, I wol sterve" (2.323), a prospect that appears genuinely alarming to Criseyde. Pandarus's vicarious involvement in Troilus and Criseyde's love affair crosses the boundaries of propriety, reflecting uneasily, by extension, on the narrator's involvement as a similarly instrumental agent.[30] Where Pandarus is unable to love but offers himself as an aid to lovers, he resembles no one so much as the poem's narrator, who is likewise disqualified from loving because of his "unlikliness" but similarly offers himself as an "instrument" to help lovers. As a stand-in for the poet-narrator, Pandarus participates in one of the poem's defining dramas, which concerns the sexual politics and ethics of storytelling. If Pandarus offers an unsavory reflection of the narrator's role in concocting this particular story, also like the narrator, Pandarus seems to have reaped his knowledge of love largely from books: his language, as Troilus notes in annoyance, is characterized by "proverbs" (1.756) and "olde ensaumples" (1.760) lifted from classical sources and other literary commonplaces. Given that Pandarus's chief investment in love appears to lie in the production of language, it is not surprising that Pandarus is the main impetus behind the letter writing that Troilus and Criseyde undertake in Book 2. As Troilus's writing master, Pandarus instructs him not to write "scryvenyssh or craftyly" (2.1026) but to affect a natural style that will inspire Criseyde to write back; in so doing, he shows how the production of love in this most self-conscious of poems is intimately linked to the production of texts.

Book 2

The letters that pass between Troilus and Criseyde represent the meeting place of the two concerns that have been in play throughout the poem, the sexual and the textual; they also engage the poem's related concern with the question of how selves are constituted in and through texts. Pandarus urges Troilus to see his letter as a physical extension of himself: "biblotte it with thi teris ek a lite" (2.1027), he urges him, and Troilus complies, making the letter a physical emissary by kissing it and projecting himself into its place: "letter, a blissful destine / The shapyn is: my lady shal the see!" (2.1091–92). And Pandarus endows the letter with some of the erotic aggression that he wishes its writer would assume, when he delivers the letter to Criseyde "and hente hire faste, / And in hire bosom the letter down he thraste" (2.1154–55). The scene markedly departs from Boccaccio's text, in which Criseyde tucks the letter in her bosom herself; with Chaucer, the letter becomes an instrument of Pandarus's sexual coercion.[31]

If letters show how selves are constituted in language, Troilus's letter reflects how thoroughly he has taken on the literary role of courtly lover:

> First he gan hire his righte lady calle,
> His hertes lif, his lust, his sorwes leche,
> His blisse, and eke thise other termes alle,
> That in swich cas thise loveres alle seche. (2.1065–68)

If the addresses to Criseyde manage to absorb her completely into the literary conventions of the courtly lady ("His hertes lif, his lust, his sorwes leche," and so on), the three opening lines self-referentially repeat "his" five times, driving home the impression that Troilus is his own primary subject. Despite its traffic in courtly commonplaces (as the narrator suggests, in recounting "ek thise other termes alle / That in swich cas thise loveres alle seche," 2.1067–68), the letter nonetheless impresses Criseyde, who becomes a literary critic herself when she "avysed word by word in every lyne, / And fond no lak, she thoughte he koude good" (2.1177–78). In contrast, Criseyde's letter is a study in textual opacity: the narrator hints that he can hardly decipher it when he summarizes "th'effect, as fer as I kan understonde" (2.1220), and Troilus too concludes that the words hide rather than reveal Criseyde's intention: "Al covered she tho wordes under shield" (2.1327). If Troilus's letter is a study in courtly convention, Criseyde's succeeds in saying practically nothing; in its accumulation of negatives and double negatives ("Holden hym in honde / She nolde nought, ne make hireselven bonde / In love" [2.1222–24]), it does not embody its writer so much as it absents her. Accordingly, Troilus and Pandarus read the letter as a space of inky inscrutability: "Have here a light, and loke on al this blake" (2.1326), Pandarus tells Troilus, urging him to examine the text's physicality in the absence of its meaning. Where Troilus writes — and weeps — himself into his text, Criseyde writes her absence. Perhaps this is why Criseyde protests "I nevere dide thing with more peyne / Than writen this" (2.1231–32); writing for her is not an expression of her "entente" but an evacuation of it.

Historically, it was unusual for even literate medieval women to write their own letters; while female literacy rates in the Middle Ages appear to have been higher than once suspected, women of Criseyde's class were more likely to be able to read than write, and even those who could write often preferred to dictate letters through amanuenses.[32] Yet Criseyde is adamant in insisting that "I kan so written" (2.1205), and the letter that Pandarus takes from her to Troilus is all the more valued because it comes "of hire hond" (2.1055). As a writer of letters, Criseyde confirms her association with texts and literacy that runs throughout the poem. Yet, like her letter, the textuality with which she is associated more often represents a failure of signification than a form of self-expression. In Criseyde's first appearance in the poem, she struggles with the perilous dilemma of what to do after her father has deserted Troy, we are told, "as she that nyste what was best to rede" (1.96), a line that identifies her dilemma as an agent with a failure of literacy. In a similar fashion, Troilus will later in the poem praise his lady's eyes, but observes that "the text ful hard is, soth, to fynde!" (3.1357), making Criseyde herself a text that defies interpretation. In a poem that is deeply concerned with problems of literary meaning, Criseyde stands for texts that fail to signify and evade communication.

The obliqueness of Criseyde's letter — as well as her own opacity, to the extent that she is figured as a text herself—reflects the larger problem of her "entente," with which the poem continually grapples.[33] Criticism has reflected the centrality of this problem in its debates about Criseyde: Does she do what she does out of love for Troilus or out of self-interest? Or is her "entente" beside the point, given the limited agency that women in Chaucer's world (and poem) experienced? The question of Criseyde's "entente" becomes a central focus in Book 2, in which Criseyde deliberates over the news of Troilus's love that Pandarus has brought her. If falling in love is a relatively straightforward process for Troilus, shaped by a host of literary precedents for male lovers from the *Roman de la Rose* to Petrarch, Criseyde's private debate reflects the complexity of love from the perspective of the medieval woman, whom contemporary readers were more used to encountering as a beloved object than as a lover with her own experiences, affective responses, and intentions. Like Troilus, Criseyde withdraws into a private chamber to be alone with her thoughts, confirming the poem's association of inwardness and subjectivity with enclosed architectural spaces—which were, as medieval archaeologists have discovered, an innovation of late medieval domestic settings.[34] Alone in "hire closet" (2.599), Criseyde is interrupted by the appearance of Troilus in procession outside her window, a scene that strikingly represents a female gaze by highlighting her visual experience (indeed, the stanzas that describe his appearance relentlessly remind us that we are experiencing Criseyde's point of view, with their repetition of words such as "seen," "see," and "aspien," as when Criseyde remarks, "It was an heven upon hym for to see," 2.637). Criseyde thus becomes an agent with an individual perspective, capable of deriving visual pleasure in her own right. But what does she see? The description of Troilus highlights his woundedness: his helmet is "tohewen" (2.638), his shield is "todasshed" (2.640), and even his horse is bleeding (2.626). The general impression of vulnerability is precisely what captivates Criseyde: "his manhood and his pyne / Made love withinne her for to myne" (2.676–77), we are told in a passage that conflates Troilus's masculinity with his suffering. In her imagination his suffering comes not from the war but from her: "But moost hire favour was, for his distresse / Was al for hire" (2.663). It is hard to escape the impression that Criseyde's enjoyment of Troilus carries a sadistic tinge that is the perfect complement of Troilus's willingness to suffer. This is the first but not the last time when the poem's two main characters superimpose the literary sufferings of the courtly lover for his cruel mistress onto the sufferings of soldiers in battle; the effect is not to obscure the historical background of the Trojan War but to show how characters accommodate it into their inner lives, as war is transformed from a source of fear to an aphrodisiac.

Criseyde experiences love as a loss of will, as she expresses in her pivotal

musing, "Who yaf me drynke?" (2.651). But her deliberations over the implications of love for her life are decidedly practical. Repeatedly, Criseyde
questions what an affair with Troilus would mean for her "estat" (as when she
laments, "myn estat lith in a jupardie," 2.465), a term that can mean both her
immaterial rank and status and her very material worldly belongings and
property.[35] For a widow like Criseyde, both meanings of the word would hold
great significance, since a love affair or marriage could place both her reputation and her property in jeopardy. Criseyde reflects her sensitivity to the pre-
cariousness of her social position when she worries about being vulnerable to
"every wikked tonge" (2.804), stressing the special dangers that language
poses to her security. In the end, language causes Criseyde to "converte"
(2.903). Overhearing a love lyric sung by her niece Antigone, she reflects on
the poetic manifestations of love, asking "is ther swych blisse among / Thise
lovers, as they konne faire endite?" (2.886).[36] As she reveals when she asks
Pandarus of Troilus, "Kan he wel speke of love?" (2.503), Criseyde is drawn to
beautiful language, even when she fears the effects of malicious tongues or
feels betrayed by her attempts to express herself in writing.

If her lengthy deliberations on the subject make it appear that Criseyde
consents to love Troilus out of her own free will, there are signs elsewhere in
the text that her consent is less freely given than we — or Criseyde herself —
might wish to believe. Disturbingly, the scenes of her falling in love are framed
by symbols of rape.[37] At the beginning of Book 2, Pandarus is awakened to his
task of approaching Criseyde by "the swalowe Proigne," who sings "a sorrow-
ful lay" in the early morning (2.64). The reference is to the story of Philomele,
who, after being raped, mutilated, and imprisoned by her brother-in-law
Tereus, appeals to her sister Procne by sending her a tapestry detailing her
betrayal. In Ovid's account of the story, Procne is transformed into a swallow
and Philomele becomes a nightingale. Improbably, Procne's song reminds Pandarus of his duty to Troilus, prompting us to wonder what a story of rape and
betrayal has to do with the unfolding story of Troilus, Criseyde, and Pandarus.
We are again recalled to this story not long after, when Criseyde falls asleep
after her "conversion" to the song of a "nyghtyngale" (2.918) and dreams that
she is visited in her sleep by a white eagle, who tears out her heart and replaces
it with his own. Though she experiences no fear or pain ("nought agroos, ne
nothing smerte," 2.930), the scene nonetheless offers a conventional image of
love ("with herte left for herte," 2.931) as an involuntary violation.[38] With its
images of the heart extracted from the woman's body and exchanged with her
lover's, the dream reenacts Antigone's song, which in similar terms invites the
God of Love "for everemo myn hertes lust to rente" (2.830) and rejoices in
exchanging hearts with her "knyght, / In which myn herte growen is so faste, /

And his in me, that it shal evere laste" (2.871–73). But in Criseyde's dream, Antigone's lyrical praise of love grows monstrous, showing how the language of love can produce both an incitement to seduction and a threat of sexualized violence.

Book 3

Whatever Criseyde believes she consents to, the consummation of her love affair with Troilus in Book 3 makes the question of her consent into a central problem. Determined to bring the lovers together, Pandarus hatches a plot that conceives Criseyde as quarry to be caught rather than a consenting partner. Comparing seduction to a hunt, Pandarus promises Troilus, "Lo, hold the at thi triste cloos, and I / Shal wel the deer unto thi bowe dryve" (2.1534–35). In so doing, he initiates a pun between "triste," which in Chaucer's Middle English named the place of concealment in which the hunter hides while he entraps his prey, and another meaning of "triste," trust, which Pandarus claims to have won of Criseyde (in making her "so fully . . . thi gentilesse triste," [3.258]).[39] The pun highlights the insignificance of female choice in a world in which "trust" is a "trap."

Book 3 is framed by two bedroom scenes, both elaborately stage-managed by Pandarus; in the first, Troilus feigns illness so that Criseyde can visit him and the lovers can speak for the first time. In the second, Criseyde is put to bed in Pandarus's house, allowing Troilus to surprise her in the night.[40] In their enclosed settings, both scenes recall the "triste" of Pandarus's hunting metaphor as well as developing further the poem's ongoing interest in domestic spaces. The chamber in the first is so small that Criseyde is forced to visit Troilus alone, whereas in the second, Criseyde sleeps in a chamber that she believes to be impermeable but is in fact entered by hidden passageways that allow for Troilus's surprise visit. Given the frequent association in *Troilus and Criseyde* between private spaces and interiority, both rooms could be taken to be spatial embodiments of their subjects; if Troilus finds himself in a room whose privacy is so extreme as to be claustrophobic, Criseyde inhabits one whose privacy is illusory, whose boundaries are all too easily violated.

The two scenes also reverse the two characters' relative positions of agency. In the first, Troilus languishes helplessly in bed like the classic courtly lover; rehearsing familiar courtly topoi, he asks only that Criseyde "wolde somtyme frendly on me see" (3.130), allow him "to don yow my servise" (3.133), and place him "under yowre yerde" (3.137). Troilus thereby appears to yield to Criseyde control over the relationship (indeed, one contemporary meaning of the word "yerde" implies that he is investing Criseyde with an unexpectedly phallic power). But Criseyde responds by reminding Troilus of their unequal social ranks while refusing to be ruled by him nonetheless:

> A kynges sone although ye be, ywys,
> Ye shal namore han sovereignete
> Of me in love, than right in that cas is. (3.170–72)

Criseyde's response cuts through the conventional formulae of courtly love, which nominally place the beloved woman in a position of superior power but, as critics have long pointed out, do so by mystifying and covertly reinforcing men's and women's inequality in medieval society. Her response — kissing him — both exceeds and reverses Troilus's requests. Where he asked only that she behave toward him as the traditionally remote courtly lady was expected to, in accepting his service and delivering correction, Criseyde's kiss translates the affair into a physical realm, signaling her refusal of the traditional courtly lady's distant role.

If Criseyde appears to seize both sexual initiative and an element of control in this first bedroom scene, the second bedroom scene at Pandarus's house reveals her agency to be significantly compromised. Having won Criseyde's "triste" (trust), Pandarus proceeds to turn his own house into a "triste" (trap) to catch Criseyde for Troilus. In a plot whose intricate details again exceed necessity for the sake of "game," Pandarus manages to convince Criseyde to spend the night at his house, only to awaken her by bringing Troilus to her, explaining that Troilus is overcome by jealousy at a rumor that she has been unfaithful to him and is in need of immediate comfort. The ruse reflects the mirror-game of sexual politics in courtly love; while Criseyde is vested with the appearance of control, the plot is arranged in a way that everywhere divests her of it, since it treats her consent as something to be won through trickery.

As many critics have noted, Troilus does not conform to the standards of sexual aggression that are held by modern masculinity: his fear continually forestalls action, and when he is finally in a position to act (as in his bedside scene in Book 3), he swoons.[41] Pandarus continually questions his masculinity: "is this a mannes herte?" (3.1098), he asks Troilus before tearing off his shirt himself. Yet when he finally finds himself in Criseyde's bed, Troilus falls easily into the clichés of masculine sexual aggression: "Now be ye kaught; now is ther but we tweyne! / Now yeldeth yow, for other bote is non!" (3.1207), he exclaims, tinging the scene uncomfortably with the suggestion of rape. But Criseyde's response, "Ne hadde I er now, my swete herte deere, / Ben yolde, ywis, I were now nought here!" (3.1210–11) unexpectedly turns the tables, suggesting that she is only too aware of her situation. Here as elsewhere, the poem questions the extent to which Criseyde knows about and willingly participates in her own seduction. At the same time, her use of the passive voice, "ben yolde," suggests that she knows that the love plot has made her an object rather than an agent.

Pandarus's involvement in Criseyde's seduction has struck more than a few critics as deeply disturbing, and Pandarus himself reflects parallel scruples about the "gamen" (3.250) he has undertaken when he acknowledges that he has become "swich a meene / As maken wommen unto men to comen" (3. 254–55). Yet his awareness of his own morally compromised position doesn't mitigate so much as highlight the problem: that his machinations to bring the lovers together have made him little more than a bawd while compromising his niece for the sake of "game."

Again, Pandarus's unease at the role he plays in bringing Troilus and Criseyde together parallels that of the narrator, who bears ultimate responsibility for Criseyde's treatment. But where Pandarus expresses discomfort with the degree of his own involvement in Criseyde's seduction, the narrator prefers to disclaim responsibility, insisting instead at crucial moments that he is merely repeating his source, or "auctour," and is bound to follow a plot that is not of his making. As A. C. Spearing has noted, these moments of disavowal intrude on some of the poem's most sexually compromising scenes.[42] For example, in the midst of the consummation scene, the narrator announces that he is bound by his source: "I moot, / After myn auctour, tellen hire gladnesse, / As wel as I have told hire hevynesse" (3.1195–97). The point reminds us that this is a literary scene, that the scene of consummation is not so much witnessed as read, and that it represents the coming together not only of the lovers but also of a long tradition of textual sources and influences that collectively bear responsibility for what happens in this particular bedroom.

Another such moment appears in a notorious scene immediately following the consummation, when Pandarus visits Criseyde in bed and unexpectedly "his arm al sodeynly he thriste / Under hire nekke, and at the laste hire kyste" (3.1574–75). With that, we learn, "Pandarus hath fully his entente" (3.1582). What does Pandarus do here, and what, precisely, is his "entente"? Critics have been fiercely divided on the question of what happens, whether it is a scene of incest or sexual assault or whether exploring such a possibility is merely a manifestation of critical prurience.[43] Chaucer's narrator, however, compounds the ambiguity of the scene by disclaiming responsibility for narrating it:

> I passe al that which chargeth nought to seye.
> What! God foryaf his deth, and she al so
> Foryaf, and with here uncle gan to pleye (3.1576–78)

But even this disclaimer raises more questions that it puts to rest: if nothing has happened, why should the narrator be "charged" not to describe it — or, for that matter, should Criseyde need to forgive it? Whatever happens, Pandarus's actions in the bedroom seem coextensive with all the elements of sexual coercion in which his relationship with Criseyde has been framed, starting with his thrusting of Troilus's letter down her bosom. But the specific nature of those actions is left to the reader to imagine. However we interpret this ambiguous scene, the narrative calls attention to the uncomfortable ways in which story-telling — in what it says as well as what it leaves to the imagination — creates webs of complicity between readers and writers that here are implicitly identified with the unsavory machinations of Pandarus.

Book 4

With Book 4 the poem shifts to tragedy, and the narrative further throws Criseyde's "entente" into question as it seeks to assign blame for the turn of events that ensues. Book 4's Proem illustrates this by raising and then obscuring the question of how much responsibility Criseyde holds in the poem's tragic ending. Foreshadowing the story that will follow, the Proem tells us:

> From Troilus she gan hire brighte face
> Awey to writhe, and tok of hym non heede,
> But caste hym clene out of his lady grace,
> And on hire whiel she sette up Diomede. (4.8–11)

It is easy to forget that the narrator is describing Fortune in these lines, and not Criseyde — especially since the terms he uses are echoed in descriptions of Criseyde; "bright," for example, is one of Criseyde's defining characteristics (see 5.465, 516, 669, 1362, 1390, and 1405). If blame for the tragedy initially lands on Fortune, it easily and seamlessly shifts to Criseyde, as the narrator expresses regret that he must recount "how Criseyde Troilus forsook — / Or at the leeste, how that she was unkynde" (4.15–16). In this very recounting, he acknowledges the interpretive ambiguity surrounding the question of what exactly Criseyde did to Troilus. But as with the preceding book, the narrator quickly disclaims any actively interpretive role that he might hold, preferring instead to stress his own passivity in the writing process ("And now my penne, allas, with which I write, / Quaketh for drede of that I moste endite," 4.13–14) and shift blame to his sources: "as writen folk thorugh which it is in mynde" (4.18). Characteristically, the narrator distances himself from the "folk" who bear responsibility for the story — his sources — while suggesting that they, not he, bring about Criseyde's downfall, a narrative event that is tinged with sexual violation:

> Allas, that they sholde evere cause fynde
> To speke hire harm! And if they on hire lye,
> Iwis, hemself sholde han the vilanye. (4.19–21)

Further developing the poem's linkage of storytelling and the violation of women, here "lying" about Criseyde is equated with the sexual offense of lying "on" her.

From Fortune, to Criseyde, to the sources whom the narrator is forced to follow, the short Proem continuously shifts the blame for what we are told will happen: Criseyde will forsake Troilus for Diomede because of a tragic change of heart or "grace." But the blame-shifting that occurs in the book's Proem leaves us unprepared for the fact that this is not in fact what the ensuing narrative recounts.

If Book 4 marks the shift to tragedy, it also signals the reemergence of the Trojan War — until this point a political subtext to the story — with the book's opening lines, which recall us to the wartime scenario in which Troy is besieged by the Greeks "liggyng in oost" (4.28). That scenario now plays a crucial role in the lovers' story when an exchange of prisoners prompts Calchas, Criseyde's father, who has been living with the Greeks, to propose an exchange of the Trojan Antenor for Criseyde, for whom he belatedly experiences a paternal tenderness. The proposal is debated and finally approved by the Trojan parliament, which, by agreeing to send Criseyde to the Greeks, seals the lovers' fate. Thus politics, not Fortune, controls the outcome of this story.

This is emphatically not the way Troilus sees it, however. Despite having been present at the debate, where he might have attempted to influence the proceedings in the other direction, Troilus resigns himself to the inevitability of Criseyde's loss and laments, rather than the contingencies of wartime politics, the cruelty of Fortune. In a series of musings, Troilus contemplates his helplessness in the face of events that he believes to be outside his control; echoing Boethius (though, as critics point out, without the crucial Christian element of faith), he considers the role that providence, predestination, and Fortune play in ordering future events and concludes "we han no fre chois, as thise clerkes rede" (4.980). Criseyde herself arrives at a similar conclusion when she learns the news, likewise blaming Fortune and calling herself an "infortuned wight / And born in a corsed constellacioun" (4.744–45). Like Troilus, Criseyde misrecognizes the real things that circumscribe free will and action in the poem: politics, social class, and gender.

As a woman, Criseyde is considerably less free to act than is Troilus. As David Aers points out, the very idea of the trade reflects Criseyde's lack of free will: "because Criseyde is a woman she has no different status than a prisoner."[44] Unlike Troilus, who as a member of parliament participates in the debate, Criseyde is not consulted about her own exchange, a point that is consistent with her treatment in the rest of the poem. Hector's objection, "We usen here no women for to selle" (4.182), is belied by the terms of exchange with which Criseyde is continually described, not only in this most overt moment, when she is an object in an exchange, but also in the love story itself. Troilus himself laments that the trade forces him to "forgo that I so deere have bought" (4.291) and rues the fact that "I may hire noght purchase" (4.557) once the exchange has been struck — because she has effectively already been "purchased" by another man, his father. Although Troilus rejects Pandarus's advice to "Go ravysshe here!" (4.530), Pandarus's words recall, through the precedent of Helen, that women are already objects of exchange in Troy: "Artow in Troie, and hast non hardyment / To take a womman which that loveth the . . . ?" (4.533–34).

Troilus and Criseyde's contrasting responses to the news of Criseyde's impending exchange reflect their differing perspectives as lovers and as agents. Troilus perceives it as a tragedy that seems exclusively to fall on him: indeed, his lament to Fortune is cast entirely in the first person: "What have I don? What have I thus agylt?" (4.261–62), "how maistow in thyn herte fynde / To ben to me thus cruwel and unkynde?" (4.265–66) and "whi wiltow me fro joie thus deprive?" (4.269). In contrast, Criseyde's lament focuses primarily on Troilus's sorrow rather than her own: "How shal he don, / And ich also?" (4.757–58); as she admits,

> "Grevous to me, God woot, is for to twynne,"
> Quod she, "but yet it harder is to me
> To sen that sorwe which that he is inne." (4.904–6)

Criseyde's impulse to place Troilus's sorrow first may be seen as an admirable trait, a sign of altruism compared to Troilus's more self-centered response; or it can be seen as a sign of her complicity in the notion that his feelings should bear more weight than hers. But her seeming lack of self-interest does raise further the question of her "entente": if she is more concerned with his feelings than with her own, does she act out of love or only because she can't bear to see him suffer?

This question lurks uncomfortably at the end of Book 4, when the lovers discuss possible responses to their separation. Perceiving Troilus to be nearly suicidal with grief, Criseyde proposes that she leave Troy but return again. It is a promise that Criseyde will be blamed for breaking — beginning with Boccaccio, whose Troiolo bitterly laments ever following her "ill-fated advice."[45] But in Chaucer's telling, Criseyde's guilt is mitigated by the fact that the plan is not hers to begin with; rather, it reiterates word for word a suggestion that Pandarus makes to her in their previous meeting, when he advises her to "come ayeyn soon after ye be went." For, he tells her, "Wommen ben wise in short avysement" (4.934–35). Criseyde, vowing to do whatever she can to ease Troilus's pain, recalls Pandarus's advice directly when she tells Troilus, "I am a womman" and thus "I am avysed sodeynly" (4.1261–62), she insists, parroting Pandarus's earlier words: "I shal wel bryngen it aboute / To come ayeyn, soone after that I go" (4.1275–76). It is unclear whether Criseyde actually believes this plan herself or whether it is a promise she makes only to salve Troilus's sorrow in the moment. But it is an instance in which Criseyde both internalizes Pandarus's notion of women ("women ben wise in short avysement") and, in so doing, allows herself to be drafted into a narrative about "women" not of her making.

Book 5

In the final book of *Troilus and Criseyde,* the poem's ongoing concerns about textuality, sexuality, and the possibilities and politics of Criseyde's "entente" come to a culminating point. As the poem brings us to the ending that has been announced from the beginning — Criseyde will leave Troilus and Troilus's story, like that of his city, will end tragically — it also foregrounds the problem it has likewise been setting up from the beginning: the extent to which Criseyde is culpable for that tragedy. From the perspective of Troilus and Pandarus, she is clearly guilty: having promised that she would return to Troilus, she fails to do so. Her prevarication on the subject in the letters she sends to Troilus, moreover, makes her appear all the more blameworthy. Book 5, however, gives us a number of reasons — many entirely plausible — for her failure to return. The first is that she simply has no choice but to remain in the Greek camp; having plotted to convince her father into allowing her to return to Troy to fetch her belongings, Criseyde's plan backfires: "My fader nyl for nothing do me grace / To gon ayeyn, for naught I kan hym queme" (5.694–95). Moreover, her time with the Greeks has given her a new perspective on the war; whereas she had initially believed that her exchange would help bring the war to a fast close and thereby allow her to reunite with Troilus, while living with the Greeks she comes to understand that Troy is doomed and that the war is unlikely to end well. Italian humanists defended Aeneas's decision to leave Troy by asserting that "it is no crime to have fled a city destined by fate to fall."[46] And Criseyde's decision not to return to the city might be excused for similar reasons. Furthermore, as a single woman in the Greek camp, Criseyde is exceptionally vulnerable — a point that Chaucer emphasizes by invoking the image of "Criseyde, / With women few, among the Grekis stronge" (5.687–88). The line follows Boccaccio's original line, "Criseida remained with a few of her ladies amongst the armed men," but Chaucer's decision to substitute "stronge" for "armed" makes them more menacing, by heightening, as Maureen Fries observes, "the ever-present possibility of rape."[47] As Criseyde comes to understand that "she was alone and hadde need / Of frendes help" (5.1026–27), she begins to see the advantages of Diomede's overtures from a practical point of view, just as earlier she had similarly weighed the practical advantages of accepting Troilus's suit.

If Pandarus earlier expresses the opinion that women are entirely interchangeable, the text suggests that Troilus and Diomede are no less interchangeable. They are described in virtually the same terms: Diomede is "Hardy, testif, strong, and chivalrous" (5.802) and "as fresh as braunch in May" (5.844) while Troilus is "Yong, fresh, strong, and hardy as lyoun" (5.830). And Criseyde assesses their relative merits on the same scale: where she initially falls in love with Troilus because of his language, she is similarly attracted to Diomede's "wordes" (5.1024), as well as "his grete estat" (5.1025), which compares favorably to Troilus's. The passages that describe Criseyde's deliberations on Troilus and Diomede, moreover, show a striking similarity, suggesting that Criseyde applies a parallel process of assessing each. When she first considers Troilus's virtues in Book 2, we learn, she

> . . . gan to caste and rollen up and down
> Withinne hire thought his excellent prowesse
> And his estat, and also his renown. (2.659–61)

Similarly, when she considers Diomede, Chaucer depicts her

> Retornyng in hire soule ay up and down
> The wordes of this sodeyn Diomede,
> His grete estat, and perel of the town. (5.1023–25)

Moments like these invite the reader into Criseyde's perspective, both illuminating the practical reasons behind her own decision to "exchange" Troilus for Diomede and suggesting that, all things considered, it is not an unreasonable exchange for her to make. Indeed, given the limitations that the poem's political setting places on Criseyde's actions, we are invited to question whether she has any other choice in the matter: Is someone without free choice able to "betray"?[48] Is Criseyde's error that she didn't return to Troilus or that she ever believed that she was free to do so in the first place?

On the subject of Criseyde's guilt, the narrator becomes increasingly cagey. His immediate source, Boccaccio, leaves no doubts about his judgment of Criseyde, warning his readers to avoid Troiolo's fate, "dying for the sake of a wicked woman."[49] In contrast, Chaucer's narrator points his readers to his sources increasingly throughout the crucial scenes in the book that show

Criseyde beginning to shift her affection from Troilus to Diomede, disclaiming responsibility of judging her himself. Locating Criseyde's actions "in stories elleswhere" (5.1044), the narrator goes out of his way to show that he is not the originator of the story, which he is compelled to tell by his sources: "Ye may hire gilt in other bokes se" (5.1776). In so doing, he develops further the poem's larger concern with the sexual politics of textuality by inviting reflection on the ways in which gender is constructed through the uses of texts.

Men and women, the narrator tells us, use texts differently. This is the message of the final book's opening stanzas, which begin by describing Criseyde in preparation for her transfer to the Greeks:

> For sorwe of which she felt hire herte blede,
> As she that nyste what was best to rede.
> And trewely, as men in bokes rede,
> Men wiste nevere womman han the care,
> Ne was so loth out of a town to fare. (5.17–21)

In this passage, Criseyde's perplexity over the situation in which she finds herself is compared to a failure of textual interpretation, as she is identified with "she that nyste what was best to rede." The passage echoes the earlier moment in Book 1, when Criseyde, faced with the dilemma of her father's desertion, likewise appears, described in exactly the same terms, "as she that nyste what was best to rede" (1.96). In the lines that follow, Criseyde's textual perplexity (and by extension, that of women — the "she" with whom she is identified) is contrasted with men's more bookish experience: "as men in bokes rede." The substance of that reading is men's inability to interpret women's inner states: "men wiste nevere womman han the care." Glossed, the passage tells us that Criseyde was like a woman who didn't know what to make of her situation ("rede"), just as men read in books that men can't understand women's cares. In other words, if women are unable to "read" their situations, men's "reading" yields only the insight that women's inner states are opaque to men. Women's inability to read themselves parallels men's inability to read women.

This knotty passage establishes a concern with women, men, and the uses of texts that will become the consuming interest of Book 5, in which the characters and narrator increasingly turn to texts to make sense of their actions and the story in which they find themselves. Both Troilus and Criseyde come to understand that they are characters in a written narrative and reflect on the textuality of their situation. Troilus is taken by the way in which his tragedy can be read as a piece of literature: "men might a book make of it, like a storie" (5.585), he observes, explaining his predicament by interpolating it into literary history. For Criseyde, by contrast, the process of entering literary history is akin to sexual violation:

> Allas, of me, unto the worldes ende,
> Shal neyther ben ywriten nor ysonge
> No good word, for thise bokes wol me shende.
> O, rolled shal I ben on many a tonge! (5.1058–61)

If Troilus imagines his story becoming literature as a way of making sense of his situation, Criseyde sees herself undone by the same process: literature will not explain but "shende" — ruin — her.

This point is echoed further in Criseyde's ambivalent responses even to textuality that she wields, in the letters she writes. At the end of her final letter to Troilus, she concludes plaintively by excusing herself: "I dar nat, ther I am, wel letters make, / Ne nevere yet ne koude I wel endite" (5.1626–27), she complains, concluding. "Th'entente is al, and nat the letters space" (5.1630). Yet here as elsewhere, Criseyde's "entente" is as opaque as the letters she writes. This passage returns us to the book's opening stanzas, with their lesson that texts render women less, not more, understandable.

Criseyde's fear that she will be ruined by texts is confirmed by the narrator, who similarly equates the dissemination of her story with her punishment: "Hire name, allas, is publysshed so wide / That for her gilt it oughte ynough suffise" (5.1095–96). But if "publishing" Criseyde's name is itself a form of punishment, it is one in which the narrator is an active participant. For all his efforts to disclaim responsibility for blaming Criseyde ("Ye may hire gilt in other bokes se"), passages like this one reveal that the very act of circulating her story in the poem of *Troilus and Criseyde* itself makes the narrator complicit in her literary fate.

In the end, Criseyde's "guilt" remains an open question, though sympathetic readers need not look far for evidence that Criseyde bears less personal responsibility for leaving Troilus than do the myriad external factors that lie outside her control: the decision to trade her, the dangers of wartime, and her own compromised agency as a woman in both Troy and the Greek camp. The process of blaming Criseyde — which the poem invites us to scrutinize — comes about by giving her responsibility for things that are in fact done to her, a process that the narrator both laments and perpetuates. Disclosing that Criseyde was "slydynge of corage" (5.825), the narrator chooses a provocative yet ambiguous term: In what sense is Criseyde "sliding"? As an action, we might note, "sliding" is characterized by a lack of resistance, which is evident in Criseyde's response to her exchange by the Trojans to the Greeks or to Pandarus's attempts to trap her for Troilus; as Carolyn Dinshaw notes, Criseyde's "sliding character functions in her position as that thing passed between men."[50] If Criseyde is "slydynge of corage," it is because her interiority — her "corage" — becomes defined by the set of external actions to which she is subject.

The "sliding" with which Criseyde is identified suggests a condition of circulation — as, in Dinshaw's words, "that thing passed between men" — that will continue as her story is passed down through literary tradition. Just as Criseyde worries about the future reception of her story, the narrator similarly worries about his poem's fate as it enters circulation and therefore an uncertain literary future: Will it find literary fame akin to that of its illustrious predecessors, or will it be blamed, misinterpreted, and subject to misunderstanding? The narrator addresses such concerns in the poem's famous envoy, which bids the poem "Go, litel bok, go litel myn tragedye" (5.1786), and tells it to be "subgit"

> To alle poesye
> And kis the steppes where as thow seest pace
> Virgile, Ovide, Omer, Lucan, and Stace (5.1790–92)

If this envoy indicates, in paying homage to his illustrious classical authors, the height of the poet's literary ambitions, it is followed immediately by a stanza that worries that his poem will meet the opposite fate — not literary immortality but a future of misunderstanding:

> And for ther is so gret diversite
> In Englissh and in writyng of oure tonge,
> So prey I God that non myswrite the,
> Ne the mysmetre for defaute of tonge;
> And red wherso thow be, or elles songe,
> That thow be understonde, God I biseche! (5.1793–98)

The narrator's plea for understanding reflects the volatility of English as a written language at the time that Chaucer was writing; unlike the Latin of Virgil or Ovid, English, as both a written language vulnerable to the uncertainties of manuscript transmission and a spoken language with numerous dialects, was subject to considerable change and instability. Both ultimately compromise the poet's control over the text's later meanings and uses; they also unexpectedly echo concerns expressed most urgently in the poem by Criseyde, for whom change and instability are conditions of being. Throughout *Troilus and Criseyde,* Criseyde is associated with problems of textual production, transmission, and reception; while drawn to the linguistic performances of Troilus, Diomede, or Antigone, Criseyde's letters and identification with texts and as a text herself are riddled with problems of misunderstanding, miswriting, and misuse. By the end of the poem the narrator shows how these problems plague the vernacular poet, who, like Criseyde, has no power to control how he will be "understonde" by contemporary and future readers. In a poem that is populated with writers, readers, and linguistic performers, Criseyde defines a position of textual uncertainty and vulnerability akin to Chaucer's self-representation as a medieval poet.[51]

The poem's ending, in which Troilus ascends to the eighth sphere and laughs at the worldly cares he has left behind, appears to disclaim the very literary aspirations that have underwritten the poem we have just read by dismissing "the forme of olde clerkis speche / In poetrie, if ye hire bokes seche" (5.1854–55). *Troilus and Criseyde*'s ongoing struggles over the uses and misuses of human language and textuality come to a head in the poem's conclusion, which E. T. Donaldson calls "a kind of nervous breakdown in poetry."[52] In its final lines the poem takes a radically different direction, turning instead to a Christian model of eternity that is "uncircumscript, and al maist circumscrive" (5.1865). These lines present an image not only of divine boundlessness but also of writing; where "olde clerkis speche," "poetrie," and "bokes" are all vulnerable to the linguistic and material contingencies of an ever-changing English language and manuscript culture, Christ commands a language that contains all within its limits but is itself unlimited.[53] This final image is both a Christian reminder of the failures of human language and an attempt to disengage with the concerns about textual production and reception that run throughout the poem, reaching a fever pitch in the envoy. If Chaucer's human language means that future readers will "myswrite," "mysmetre" and "[mis]-understonde" the poem (5.1795–98), the ending indicates that the only language that is unbound by these historical and material conditions is outside human control.[54]

With the final lines, the poem invokes the Virgin Mary: "So make us, Jesus, for thi mercy, digne, / For love of mayde and moder thyn benigne" (5.1868–69). If the turn to Christ attempts to resolve — or at least escape — the problems of language that the envoy raises, this closing invocation of the Virgin similarly attempts to disengage from "the woman question" as it forms a parallel preoccupation throughout *Troilus and Criseyde*. In medieval debates on the topic, the Virgin represented the ultimate defense of women, which is why Christine de Pizan selects her to preside over the final book of her *Book of the City of Ladies*, praying to Mary as women's "defender, protector, and guard against all assaults of enemies and of the world."[55] When Chaucer identifies Mary as "mayde and moder" (5.1869), he offers her as an image of femininity to counter medieval stereotypes of women as fickle, lascivious, and sexually debased — stereotypes that shape Criseyde's own literary history. But the attributes with which Chaucer identifies the Virgin, maid and mother, occlude the reality of female sexuality, thus rendering Mary's ideal out of the reach of human women. Just as Christ's language lies outside human abilities, the Virgin similarly represents a model of femininity that is beyond women's attainment. Sexuality and textuality, the two interlinked concerns that run throughout *Troilus and Criseyde,* come together in the end as signs of human fallenness.

NOTES

Author's note: I am grateful to the wonderful students in my fall 2003 Chaucer seminar, especially Claire Bowen and Ruth Kaplan, whose insights and provocative discussion helped shape this chapter.

1. See Spurgeon, *Five Hundred Years of Chaucer Criticism and Allusion,* 1:lxxix, "Table of the Relative Popularity of Chaucer's Poems at Different Times."

2. Sir Philip Sidney, *Apologie for Poetrie;* this and other historical assessments of Chaucer's works are extracted in Brewer, ed., *Chaucer: The Critical Heritage,* 120.

3. As A. C. Spearing notes, "The process and dilemmas of writing are not suppressed [in *Troilus and Criseyde*] but are incorporated into the poem written, so that, even as we read it, we are kept aware of the nature and limits of its art" (*Chaucer: Troilus and Criseyde,* 57); see also Kiser, *Truth and Textuality,* esp. 63–88, and Strohm, *Social Chaucer,* who examines the narrator's self-conscious addresses to a text-using "redere" (56). The valuable collection edited by Shoaf and Cox, *Chaucer's Troilus and Criseyde,* also contains a number of essays on this topic.

4. See Mann, "Chaucer and the 'Woman Question.'" For other feminist perspectives on the poem, in addition to sources cited below, see Hansen, *Chaucer and the Fictions of Gender,* ch. 6; Margherita, "Historicity, Femininity, and Chaucer's *Troilus*"; Robertson, "Public Bodies and Psychic Domains"; and Mann, *Feminizing Chaucer.*

5. That tradition is captured in Blamires et al., eds., *Woman Defamed and Woman Defended.*

6. On this point, see Dinshaw, *Chaucer's Sexual Poetics,* and Cox, *Gender and Language in Chaucer,* on "how Chaucer uses manifestations of gender to articulate a metapoetics" (5).

7. See Wetherbee, *Chaucer and the Poets,* esp. ch. 4, which treats this scene (115–17) and Statius's influence on the poem; Sanok, "Criseyde, Cassandre, and the *Thebaid,*" treats the gendered implications of Chaucer's reading of the *Thebaid.*

8. See Sanok, "Criseyde, Cassandre, and the *Thebaid,*" 44.

9. On the problem of "entente" in *Troilus and Criseyde,* see Patterson, *Chaucer and the Subject of History,* 138–40, and Campbell, "Figuring Criseyde's 'Entente.'" See also Lerer, "The Canterbury Tales," in this *Companion,* which shows how problems of "entente" persist in the *Canterbury Tales.*

10. See Stanbury, "Women's Letters and Private Space in Chaucer," and Fradenburg, *Sacrifice Your Love,* 199–238.

11. Benson, *History of Troy in Middle English Literature;* Federico, *New Troy.*

12. Mapstone, "Origins of Criseyde"; see also Mieszkowski, "Reputation of Criseyde."

13. Havely, ed. and trans., *Chaucer's Boccaccio,* app. B: Guido de Colomnis, *Historia Destructionis Troiae* (excerpts), 184.

14. Windeatt, *Chaucer: Troilus and Criseyde,* 54.

15. A number of sources examine the differences between Chaucer's and Boccaccio's texts: see Gordon, ed. and trans., *Story of Troilus;* Wallace, *Chaucer and the Early Writings of Boccaccio,* chs. 5, 6; Havely, *Chaucer's Boccaccio;* and Windeatt's invaluable parallel-text edition, *Chaucer: Troilus and Criseyde.*

16. Boccaccio's and Chaucer's texts of this passage are cited from Windeatt, *Chaucer: Troilus and Criseyde,* 116.

17. Translation of Boccaccio taken from Havely, *Chaucer's Boccaccio,* 29.

18. On this point, see Wallace, *Chaucer and the Early Writings of Boccaccio.*

19. Minnis, *Medieval Theory of Authorship.*

20. Windeatt similarly suggests: "Chaucer's attribution of *Troilus* to Lollius seems designed both to claim and yet to play with the tradition of attribution to an ancient authority" (*Troilus and Criseyde,* 40).

21. See Hanawalt, "Widows."

22. For a reading of the erotics of gazing in this scene, see Stanbury, "Lover's Gaze in *Troilus and Criseyde.*"

23. See Wack, *Lovesickness in the Middle Ages,* 147.

24. Wack, *Lovesickness in the Middle Ages,* 151.

25. On this and other lyrics in *Troilus and Criseyde,* see Stillinger, *Song of Troilus.*

26. As Wetherbee notes, "The tendency of Troilus's emotions to turn in upon themselves rather than to cause him to actively pursue love is perhaps the most consistent feature of his behavior in the early books of the poem" (*Chaucer and the Poets,* 67).

27. Windeatt, *Geoffrey Chaucer: Troilus and Criseyde,* 124.

28. Havely, *Chaucer's Boccaccio,* 32.

29. For a reading of Troilus and Pandarus's contrasting roles as "the idealistic and the pragmatic," see Wetherbee, *Chaucer and the Poets,* 77.

30. The connection between Pandarus and the narrator has been often noted by critics; see Dinshaw, *Chaucer's Sexual Poetics,* 47–50, for a survey of the criticism and an interpretation of how "Pandarus's actions are in fact thoroughly paralleled to the narrator's . . . and, as a consequence, reading as an activity with a gendered valence is more fully developed in the poem" (47–48). On the literary-historical implications of Pandarus's role as a literary go-between, see Lerer, *Courtly Letters in the Age of Henry VIII.*

31. On the significance of the letters in Book 2 as examples of gendered writing, see Summit, *Lost Property,* 52–59.

32. On medieval women's practices of letter writing, see Cherewatuk and Wiethaus, "Introduction," and Ferrante, *To the Glory of Her Sex.*

33. On this point, see Benson, "Opaque Text of Chaucer's Criseyde."

34. See Stanbury, "Women's Letters and Private Space in Chaucer."

35. Aers, "Criseyde."

36. See Kinney, " 'Who Made This Song?' "

37. As Dinshaw comments, "The story of Philomela in fact haunts *Troilus and Cri-*

seyde" (Chaucer's Sexual Poetics, 82); see also Robertson, "Public Bodies and Psychic Domains," and Rose, "Reading Chaucer Reading Rape." This scene substantiates Mann's more general point that "for Chaucer . . . rape remains a constant touchstone for determining justice between the sexes" (*Feminizing Chaucer,* 36).

38. Hansen notes, "This dream thus evokes and contains, like the poem as a whole, the sexual violence and mutilation that the myth of Procne and Philomela, the song of the swallow and the nightingale, brings to mind and then sets in contrast to Criseyde's story" (*Chaucer and the Fictions of Gender,* 160).

39. See *MED,* s.v. "triste."

40. On the significance of domestic architecture in this scene, see Brody, "Making a Play for Criseyde."

41. Mann, "Troilus' Swoon"; Lees, ed., *Medieval Masculinities;* Beidler, ed., *Masculinities in Chaucer.*

42. See Spearing, *Chaucer: Troilus and Criseyde* and *Medieval Poet as Voyeur,* 136.

43. For a summary and consideration of these critical approaches, see Fehrenbacker, " 'Al that which chargeth nought to seye.' "

44. Aers, "Criseyde," 190.

45. Havely, *Chaucer's Boccaccio,* 89.

46. Kallendorf, *In Praise of Aeneas,* 13.

47. Havely, *Chaucer's Boccaccio,* 82; Fries, " 'Slydynge of Corage,' " 51.

48. This point is explored by Fradenburg in *Sacrifice Your Love.*

49. Havely, *Chaucer's Boccaccio,* 101.

50. Dinshaw, *Chaucer's Sexual Poetics,* 58.

51. On "the special relation to Criseyde and Woman that [Chaucer] claims for the figure of the male author," see Hansen, *Chaucer and the Fictions of Gender,* esp. 185.

52. Donaldson, *Speaking of Chaucer,* 91; similarly, McAlpine finds that "although what has proved to be the enigma of Chaucer's epilogue is usually approached as if it arises from a problem in the nature of love, I believe that it arises chiefly from what Chaucer saw as a problem in the nature of art" (*Genre of "Troilus and Criseyde,"* 237).

53. The line ultimately comes from Dante; for a discussion of its significance, see Wheeler, "Dante, Chaucer, and the Ending of *Troilus and Criseyde,*" esp. 120–21, and Pulsiano, "Redeemed Language and the Ending of *Troilus and Criseyde.*"

54. Donaldson, *Speaking of Chaucer,* 91. Wetherbee finds that "in the final stanzas of the poem the voice we hear is that of a poet who has been finally liberated from the darkness of his long and excessive involvement with the story of Troilus" (*Chaucer and the Poets,* ch. 8, "The Ending of the *Troilus,*" 235ff.).

55. Pizan, *Book of the City of Ladies,* trans. Richards, 218.

8

The Canterbury Tales

SETH LERER

Tantum, cum finges, ne sis manifesta, caveto. — Ovid, Ars Amatoria, *3.801*

Chaucer's *Canterbury Tales* has long been esteemed for its blend of philosophical acumen and psychological insight, its attentions to allegory and character, its sublime aspirations, and its earthy wit. It is, at times, brilliantly funny, poignantly sad, horrifically obscene, and spiritually inspirational. Modern critics have located the *Canterbury Tales* in a range of literary and cultural frameworks: the rise of vernacular writing in the fourteenth century; the politics of authorship and the place of literature in effecting social change; the influence of European literary forms, Christian allegorical modes of reading, and linguistic change on late medieval poetry; the culture of the manuscript and the ways of reading and writing before the invention of print.[1] Chaucer's poem, too, has been explored for its omnivorous command of medieval literary genres: fabliau, hagiography, epic, sermon, beast fable, romance, and theater.[2] It is a poem about men and women, people and God, imagination and reality.[3] Critics of the past century have found nearly everything within its purview: from F. B. Gummere, who in 1900 saw Chaucer's immortality assured by his poem's excellence "in narrative, in humor, [and] in the drawing of characters," to David Wallace, who in 1997 understood the *Canterbury Tales* as operating "within a familiar international framework of magnate militarism and merchant exchange: capital, warfare, and wool."[4] The *Canterbury Tales* is often read and taught in an accepted editorial sequence, based on the famous Ellesmere Manuscript of the poem. We begin with the *General Prologue,* the Tales of the Knight, Miller, Reeve, and Cook, and then move through the various fragments until the final prose sermon of the Parson and Chaucer's Retraction.[5] Although Chaucer may have, in some sense, intended the sections to be read in this order, the *Canterbury Tales,* in fact, survives in a variety of orderings.[6] Both medieval scribes and modern critics have sought to make sense of its associations and its sequences, and it remains one of the most open-ended of major literary works. Some tales may be linked by drama (for example, the opening set, each responding to the other); others through theme (what has come to be known as the "marriage group"); others through generic patterning (the sequence running from the *Shipman's Tale* through the *Nun's Priest's,* that make up Fragment VII); still others by prosodic form (the four tales of idealized female figures told in rhyme royal).[7] The *Canterbury Tales* may be unfinished, but we want it to be complete. We want to discern an overarching pattern, an "idea," as Donald R. Howard put it thirty years ago, embedded in the welter of its fragments, interruptions, editorial manipulations, and scribal mistakes.[8]

Many ideas populate the *Canterbury Tales,* but a few stand out as central to its form and theme. It is a written work whose central fiction is that of oral performance. It pretends to be the record of speeches, but it constantly calls attention to its own textuality. The poem is a pretense, and it takes pretense as its governing concern. Chaucer impersonates the pilgrim voices, much as each of those voices tell stories of impersonation — tales of characters who lie, deceive, delude, take one thing for another, or stage-manage fictions of desire.[9] To *counterfeit* (Middle English *countrefete*) becomes one of the key verbs of the *Canterbury Tales,* whether it be the forging of false capital, the feignings of the word, or the fakery of the bedroom.[10] Money, language, and sex thus emerge as literary themes and social issues at the center of this poem (as they had been at the center of Chaucer's life). Chaucer recognizes that all three are about forms of representation: ways of speaking and presenting a performing self, ways of taking ordinary objects, pieces of the world, or parts of our bodies and investing them with meaning. They are all media of exchange, ways of replacing one thing for another, of creating value in goods, actions, and ideas.[11]

The social expectations of exchange — be it of words, of goods, of vows, of bodies — are all expectations of performance. Life goes on, in the *Canterbury Tales,* before an audience. And each character will play a part. What Chaucer and his fictive tellers learned from manuals of rhetoric, of love, and of poetry were the arts of impersonation. Beware, Ovid had advised his women at the end of the *Art of Love,* that when you fabricate or fake it (*cum finges*) you are not exposed. I take this statement as the epigraph for a chapter that will assess how Chaucer's poem figures forms of performance. My goal is to explore how his narrators, characters, and dramatic interchanges question literary and social selves; how they interrogate language's ability to shape or describe the person and the world; how they explore the *value* (in all senses of that word) of the imagination, both in public space and in private fantasy.

This chapter does not cover every single Canterbury Tale, nor does it address all the possibilities of meaning raised by links, associations, references, and sources of and among each of Chaucer's stories. Instead, it offers guidelines for a student's (and, I hope, a teacher's) understanding of the poem by examining a set of representative performances. It highlights some familiar things (the juxtaposition of the Wife of Bath and the Pardoner, for example, as great speakers and great readers, or misreaders); it calls attention to some features of the poem only recently stressed in criticism and pedagogy (the middle tales of Fragment VII); it devotes space to some personal favorites (the *Squire's Tale,* the *Thopas-Melibee* link). In the end, it argues that the *Canterbury Tales* — in whatever order we, or its previous readers, engage it — for all its politics and history, or its wit and weirdness, is fundamentally about literature itself: the forms it takes and the social purposes we grant to telling stories and attending to our audience's answers.

Word and Deed: The General Prologue

After the pilgrim portraits have been splayed before us, but before the Host announces his intentions in the game of telling tales, Chaucer's narrator frames the purpose of his project. His goal is to retell every tale, to rehearse each word, according to the teller. Fidelity to source remains his primary concern, for if he were to falsify, expand, or invent something and attribute it to someone else, "he moot telle his tale untrewe" (1.736). Plain speaking is the order of the day — "Crist spak hymself ful brode in holy writ" (1.739) — and Plato's authority dovetails with the scriptures to affirm: "The wordes moote be cosyn to the dede" (1.742).

Words should reflect the things they denote.[12] The relation of word and deed echoes a sustaining medieval debate about *verba* and *res.* From Saint Augustine, through Macrobius, Boethius, the scholastics, and the nominalists, philosophers of language and behavior recognized the complexities among intention and expression, word and object. "Every word," Macrobius had argued, "has a true meaning," but the circumstances and intentions of the utterer could possibly impede the true expression of that meaning.[13] Some held that that the speaker's will to say was more important than what was said, and many recognized that words may have effects that writers or speakers did not intend. Here in the real world, words cannot have a one-to-one correspondence to the things they denote or to the wills of their speakers. Instead, there is but a rough association — cousinhood, rather than, say, brotherhood.

Chaucer's narrator recognizes the potential slippages between the utterance and the idea, and Harry Bailly, later in the *Prologue* and throughout the *Canterbury Tales,* adds an additional requirement. Tales should appeal to "sentence" and "solaas." They should instruct as well as entertain, and the pilgrim who tells the tale that brings the two together best, "Shal have a soper at oure aller cost" (1.799). Harry recognizes that the value of a literary performance lies in audience response. Nothing is worse than boring with sententious erudition, preaching without humor, or offending with mere bawdry or vacuous play. Authorial intention and reader response thus come together at the opening of the *Canterbury Tales* to define the scope literary making and its social meaning. The poet has a double duty: to be faithful to a source and to be responsible to a public. Each of the tales' performances will triangulate this set of relationships differently; each will appeal to (or undermine) its source material, please (or offend) an audience. In the process, the tale tellers emerge as vernacular authors, and the poem takes shape as an anthology of the resources, techniques, and theoretical positions at play in late medieval literature.

But it is, first and foremost, the Chaucerian narrator who emerges as the poem's literary voice.

> Whan that Aprill with his shoures soote
> The droghte of March hath perced to the roote,
> And bathed every veyne in swich licour
> Of which vertu engendred is the flour;
> Whan Zephirus eek with his sweete breeth
> Inspired hath in every holt and heeth
> The tendre croppes, and the yonge sonne
> Hath in the Ram his half cours yronne,
> And smale foweles maken melodye,
> That slepen al the nyght with open ye
> (So priketh hem nature in hir corages),
> Than longen folk to goon on pilgrimages,
> And palmeres for to seken straunge strondes,
> To ferne halwes, kowthe in sondry londes;
> And specially from every shires ende
> Of Engelond to Caunterbury they wende,
> The hooly blisful martir for to seke,
> That hem hath holpen whan that they were seeke. (1.1–18)

This passage is many things: an invocation, an exordium, a call for audience attention, and a display of poetic craft. Its line of sight moves from the heavens to the earth, focusing down from the zodiacal empyrean, through the clouds of meteorological reality, to the tops of the trees, to the earth itself. And once we hit the ground, the sentence then moves from the outer to the inner: from the peripheries of "every shires ende / Of Engelond" to the telos of the pilgrimage to Canterbury. Two parallel contractions, one vertical, the other horizontal, bring the world of everyday experience into sharp focus.

That focus, though, is calibrated metrically and lexically, and Chaucer emerges in these opening lines as a linguistic innovator. Words such as *engendred* and *inspired* would have been, by the late fourteenth century, part of the new vocabulary taken from the Romance languages, while words such as *vertu* and *melodye* — long in the Middle English lexicon — appear in distinctive ways. The histories of words come to the fore (*vertu*, for example, appears in all its etymological force from the Latin *vir*, masculine prowess). Figuration takes precedence over denotation (the word *melodye*, for example, evokes, as it did for many in the later fourteenth century, a sense of heavenly bliss or mirth). The Anglo-Saxon and the French contend (the nature that pricks these birds to melody, for example, gets them in their *corages* — their very francophone hearts).[14]

Juxtaposed against these learned and Romance words is an English landscape. *Holt* and *heeth*, two old and here alliterating words, emblematize that landscape into which Zephyr's new winds blow. And against that mythological west wind comes the zodiacal figure of the Ram: not "Aries," but the ordinary animal. The *palmeres* on their *pilgrimages* (both originally Old French terms) "seken straunge strondes / To ferne halwes, knowthe in sondry londes" — every word there, ultimately, from Old English. And, at the sentence's conclusion, the last couplet reaffirms the Englishness of this experience. Though Beckett remains here a *martir* (a French word that entered English almost from the moment of the Norman Conquest), he stands surrounded by English modifiers: *hooly* and *blisful*. Finally, in the last line, we may find a formal reassertion of a native English prosody and idiom. "That hem hath holpen whan that they were seke." The strong alliterations on the *h*-words slow the pace of reading down. They force the performer (for this is, as far as we can tell, a poetry that was read aloud) to articulate, to feel the repetitions, soon to be felt again in the concatenating "that they." Chaucer deploys the resources of his rich vocabulary and his metrics to suggest a politics to literary form. There is a sense of a resurgent English vernacularity here — a poem in decasyllabic couplets that apposes words of English and French origin; a poem in which the alliterative idiom can rear up; a poem in which, for all the learning of astrology or the sophistications of science, there is still an old familiar holt and heeth.

The *General Prologue* is an essay in the arts of language. It establishes Chaucer as a finder of those very "wordes newe" that his narrator would suspect. Language describes the world, but does it shape it? How do the available vocabulary terms configure items into meaningful wholes? How do the techniques of rhetorical description make sense out of landscapes and inhabitants? It is this set of questions that the *Prologue* portraits set out to answer. Each is a model of rhetorical description. The medieval rhetoricians had long seen *descriptio* at the heart of the *artes poeticae*.[15] In describing a person, both the internal and the external attributes should be considered. And those attributes, the rhetoricians argued, should be ordered: for example, from head to toe, from general to specific. But individual descriptions could be amplified. Similes and metaphors could emerge, and within the figurations of *descriptio* could lie miniature narratives: allegories of power, allusions to the classics. The description, then, did more than just present a person to the viewer. It became, at its most elaborate, an anthology of reading: an assembly of the texts, events, and images called to the mind of the rhetorical describer.[16]

At a basic level, Chaucer's portraits conform to the dictates of the rhetoricians. We can see, for example, the tensions between external and internal description in the Knight, whose rusty armor and stained tunic have signaled (at least to some) a moral as well as a physical blot on an otherwise noble character defined by the high-concept words, "trouthe and honour, fredom and curteiseie" (1.46).[17] We can see the physical detail that grants the Prioress her erotic charge, the Wife of Bath her powerful, still sexual charisma, the Pardoner his creepy ambiguity. The Monk and Miller are described so purposefully in terms of the animals they eat or seem like that they become animals themselves: the Monk, a creature all of appetites, the Miller much like the very ram he would win as a prize.

But, at another level, the portraits challenge the idea of mere description, either physical or moral. Many of its characters are made up not of features but of words, of allusions to literary and philosophical works. Best-known among such allusions are the description of the Prioress's table manners, modeled after the advice of La Vieille from the *Roman de la Rose;* the figurations of the Wife of Bath shaped after that same character; and the Pardoner, whose description matches closely that of Faux Semblant from this same source.[18] Other pilgrim portraits seem to hinge their meaning on their wordplay or their rhetoric: the appetitive nature of the Monk is reinforced by metaphors drawn from food ("He yaf nat of that text a pulled hen," for example, 1.177); the beastliness of the Miller is enhanced through simile ("His berd as any sowe or fox was reed," 1.552). Still others make their characters into nothing less than walking texts: the Clerk, described largely in terms of the books he owns; or the Squire, "embrouded" not just in the latest fashions but in threads that make him readable; the Prioress, whose brooch with the "crowned A" and "*Amor vincit omnia*" make her an illustration virtually with her own caption.

How can, Chaucer seems to ask, a reader understand the world without seeing it in terms of books he or she has read? Literature filters experience, words shape the world — a recognition not lost on the Pardoner himself, whose great accomplishment is to create a fiction of his own devotion, to describe pig bones as if they were saint's bones, to convince us, in short, that the things and the people of this world are really something other than they are. "And thus, with feyned flaterye and japes / He made the person and the peple his apes" (1.705–6). He can even remake us.

And so can Chaucer. Central to the *Canterbury Tales* is a larger aesthetic and philosophical question: Does human artistry impose an order on the world of experience, or does it expose a divinely created order already present within it? Tellers and tales, characters and claimants, often try to make sense of a seemingly disordered world. Forms of description, of narration, of analysis seek some way of controlling such a world — whether it be in the crazy logic of the scholars of the *Reeve's Tale,* the authoritarian despotism of the *Clerk's Tale*'s Walter, the magic of the *Franklin's Tale,* or the alchemy of the *Canon's Yeoman*'s. The *General Prologue* approaches the problem of organization — *ordinatio,* in the terms of late medieval bookmen — by ranging the order of the pilgrim portraits by estate: by the social class, moral condition, or profession.[19] We move from the nobility and clergy through the various professions, down through the isolates (the Wife of Bath, a widow traveling alone), the figures of agricultural exchange, to the grotesques. The portrait of the Pardoner closes the string of personal descriptions: exiled to its ending, he remains the enigma that generations of readers have seen in him. But if the Pardoner is the last of the pilgrims to be described, it is the Reeve who is the last on the journey. "And evere he rood the hyndreste of oure route" (1.622). David Wallace explains: "It seems fitting, then, that a rural watchdog should ride with everyone before him as the pilgrimage moves away from the city and into the countryside."[20] But no watchdog, rural or otherwise, can control the *Canterbury Tales.* The narrator and the Host, both of whom seek order in this welter of the classes, will be outmaneuvered by the Miller, who with his loud bagpipes, animalistic body, and wrestling skills can only barely be contained by social or by literary hierarchy.

In keeping with the orderings of power, the Knight is the one who picks the short straw and tells the first tale. "Were it by aventure, or sort, or cas, / The sothe is this: the cut fil to the Knight" (1.844–45). Was it chance, or luck, or destiny? It was of course all three, combined with the literary control of Chaucer himself. The *Canterbury Tales* begins auspiciously, but we should not take its opening at face value. No sooner has it started, than its plan is interrupted, and the fabliau confusions of the Miller quickly displace the epic assurances of the Knight. In that move lies no mere comic relief but the overarching comic purpose of the *Canterbury Tales* as a whole: a set of literary responses, challenges to social orthodoxy that reveal the fundamental inability of anyone to impose order on the world. The Host had warned the pilgrims not to be "rebel to my juggement," (1.833) but that is precisely what ensues. Words lose their meanings or take unexpected resonances; sex rears its many heads; and money emerges as the marker of both social class and literary accomplishment. What is the price we pay for literature? The first string of tales asks and answers that question in ways that define not just the Canterbury project but an idea of literary history itself.

The First Fragment and the Decay of Language

With its classical setting and stately idiom, its long philosophical digressions, and its equally long ekphrastic descriptions, the *Knight's Tale* befits the ideals of its tale teller and the expectations of the Host and his pilgrims for a noble, memorable story. The two cousins, Palamon and Arcite, contest in their love for Emily, while Theseus presides as something of a *magister ludi* over their strife. His solution is to transform their rivalry into a social spectacle by having them compete, along with their invited military supporters, in a great amphitheater. In the end, the gods must adjudicate, and the locus of authority moves from the world of men and women to the realm of imagined deities.[21]

The *Knight's Tale* sets the template for the tales that follow: two men in love with the same woman; a presiding figure of political authority; a sense of the theatricality inherent in amorous and social life; the inexplicability of human outcomes when viewed in this all-too-human world. It is a tale of language taken to its most elaborate, a performance that threatens to escape the control of its teller, as long strings of asides and excuses only call attention to the Knight's self-consciousness about his skills. It is a tale of sexual desire, not just in its simple plotline of competing lovers, but in its complexities of philosophical reflection. Is there a law to love, the poem asks, in good Boethian fashion. What is the quality of female beauty and does it require mastery by man? The poem's sexuality is governed by its opening. Theseus conquers the "regne of Femenye" (1.866) and brings home Hyppolita to wed. The conquest of the Amazons stands as a controlling moment of control: a mastery of sensuality by reason, an extension of political prowess into domestic life.

All of this obviously appeals to the Host (of whom, as we learn throughout the *Tales,* the conquest of domestic, feminine authority remains an unfulfilled dream), and in keeping with his notions of the social order, he turns to the Monk to ask for something "to quite with the Knyghtes tale" (1.3119). *Quiting,* or quitting, or requiting, has many connotations, but at this moment it has a specific sense of repayment. Let us, he seems to ask, pay back the Knight for his tale with another; let us respond within this medium of exchange. But the Host is thwarted by the Miller, whose inebriated interruption transforms the benign sense of requiting into something virulent. In contrast to the stately amphitheatrical displays of the Knight, the Miller is a creature of a wilder kind of theater. He cries in Pilate's voice, in the voice of the ranting figure of the provincial cycle plays.[22] His swearing, "by armes, and by blood and bones" (1.3125), figuratively dismembers the very body of that Christ whom Pilate had accused. The Host is caught between decorum and deceit: between the attempt to order exchange and the workings of those pilgrims who would rend the body into parts, who would (as we will see throughout the poem) peddle false relics, bad deals, or drunken requitals. It's payback time, the Miller seems to say.

The Miller's interruption is the signal moment of the *Canterbury Tales.*[23] It defines its overarching structure, its relationships of teller and tale, of roadside drama to literary performance, of critical interpretation itself. At a basic level, his performance represents what happens to literature in the wrong hands. The triangle of desire in the *Knight's Tale* becomes a comic ménage. Epic becomes fabliau. Nicholas and Absolon both vie for the attentions of the Carpenter's young wife, Alisoun, a kind of barnyard Emilye whose opening description stresses the animalistic in her nature. The amphitheatrical control of Theseus transmutes itself into the stagy manipulations of Nicholas: the pretense about a second flood, the ropes and kneading tubs, the ruses all show the Oxford scholar as a maker of fictions: an antitype of the poet figure himself. And, in lieu of the Knight's high style, we get the everyday colloquialisms of the world of the Miller, replete with popular songs, crass innuendoes, and laughs.

The *Miller's Tale* inaugurates a set of readings and rereadings of the *Knight's Tale,* and it announces the decay of linguistic stability that will control the First Fragment.[24] Not only have we left the stately measures of the Knight's Theban epic, we soon leave verbal sureness all together. Pun and wordplay, malapropism and misstatement abound here. For the Carpenter, faced with the prospect of an apocalyptic drenching, it is "Nowellis flood" (1.3818). The mistake of Noel for Noah distills the entire logic of the tale: a replacement of a story about retribution with a tale about rebirth. It is but one in a whole string of comic inversions that make this, as the Carpenter had put it, "a world . . . ful tikel" (1.3428). Speech descends, at the poem's end, into loud farts and laughs, into Alisoun's "tee hee" instead of Emelye's heavenly singing (see 1.1055). Instead of kissing Alisoun's inviting lips, Absolon finds himself tricked into kissing her "nether eye," and his response articulates his horror at the inversions of gender: "For wel he wiste a womman hath no berd" (1.3737). The brilliance of the *Miller's Tale* rests precisely in this confusion of scatology and eschatology. All the apocalyptic imagery of flood and fire, hell mouth and horror, finds itself reduced to farts and private parts. And the proper response to such theatricalized mockery and play is the laughter of the group. The townsfolk's response to John the Carpenter's experience may well model our own, as we are invited to laugh at this fantasy (1.3840).

The Reeve takes the laughter of the *Miller's Tale* and turns it into spite.[25] He takes the things of everyday life — those things that, in the hands of Nicholas become imaginative props in some stage play of desire — and turns them into bloodless commodities. In the world of the Miller, people are goods and chattels. Alisoun is as much a possession as an object of desire. But in the world of the Reeve, people seem to fade into the background compared to things; indeed, people *are* things. Look at the opening description of the Miller in this tale.

> Pipen he koude and fisshe, and nettes beete,
> And turne coppes, and wel wrastle and sheete;
> Ay by his belt he baar a long panade,
> And of a swerd ful trenchant was the blade.
> A joly poppere baar he in his pouche;
> Ther was no man, for peril, dorste hym touche.
> A Sheffeld thwitel baar he in his hose. (1.3927–33)

We see him accoutered with his pipes, his fishing gear, his nets, his game of "cups," and, of course, his many knives. Simkin the man fades out behind the things he carries. This opening concern with commodities informs, too, the Miller's wife and daughter. The Miller's wife is the daughter and heir of the parson of the town, and her daughter is therefore that parson's heir as well. Illegitimacy of birth matters little here; what matters is the cash. This is a world not of desire but of goods, where value lies only in the inheritance, where miller's mill for money.

In such a world, what value are words? In the *Reeve's Tale* price is everything — except in language. The northernisms of the students render their language crazy and funny, but also inhuman. In his Middle English translation (1385) of the Latin historical work, the *Polychronicon* of Ranulph Higden, John of Trevisa noted: "the contray longage is apeyred, and some useþ strange wlaffyng, chyteryng, harryng and garryng, grisbittyng." And in the North, he notes, "Al þe longage ys so scharp, slyttyng and frotyng, and unschape, þat we Souþeron men may þat langage unneþe understonde. Y trowe þat þat ys bycause þat a buþ ny3 to strange men and aliens þat spekeþ strangelych, and also bycause þat þe kynges of Engelond woneþ alwey fer fram þat contray."[26]

The *Reeve's Tale*'s students sound much like Trevisa's caricatured northerners.[27] Their words and sounds are harsh and unshapely to the southern ear. They speak in the awful onomatopoetics of the bumpkin (for example, "I is as ille a millere as ar ye," 1.4045).

And yet, they are themselves creatures of the word: students of logic, dialectic, and rhetoric. But their skills, like their dialect, only goad the Miller into mockery. When they have been cheated of their grain and their horse shooed off, the Miller invites them to stay with him:

> Myn hous is streit, but ye han lerned art;
> Ye konne by argumentes make a place
> A myle brood of twenty foot of space.
> Lat se now if this place may suffise,
> Or make it rowm with speche, as is youre gise. (1.4122–26)

Can language really remake the world? Can speech make a little room into a hall? Certainly, literary language can — that is the whole point of imaginative fiction. But in the Reeve's world, people speak in ways that violate associations between word and deed. Imagination gives way to nonsense. We are left with proverbs in dialect: "Man sal taa of twa thynges: / Slyk as he fyndes, or taa slyk as he bryngges" (1.4129–30), a statement that is either tautologically meaningless or meaninglessly opaque. Even the Reeve's own reliance on proverbial wisdom fails, as the tale's closing proverb tells us really nothing about the tale itself:

> And therfore this proverbe is seyd ful sooth,
> 'Hym thar nat wene wel that yvele dooth.'
> A gylour shal hymself bigyled be. (1.4319–21)

Of all the things the *Reeve's Tale* is about — the relations between language and the world, the thrill of sexual conquest, the sourness of its narrator, the pettiness of its Miller, the parody of university studenthood — this proverb addresses none. It represents the Reeve's inability to understand his own tale: the fact that, in the end, not only has he reduced a complex narration to a simple aphorism, but that he himself remains the butt of that aphorism. We continue to laugh at the pleasures of the *Miller's Tale,* but we wince at the "choleric" worldview of the Reeve. He has beguiled neither the Miller nor us.

Nor has he seemingly beguiled Chaucer. The following *Cook's Tale* moves us from the rural universities to the London underworld, where language, sex, and money are the base commodities of ruin.[28] The mercantile world of this tale is an emblem, not of ineptitude (the Miller's Carpenter shop) or cheating (the Reeve's Mill), but of the lie itself. The hero of the tale, we are told in its final remaining couplet, "hadde a wyf that heeld for contenance / A shoppe, and swyved for her sustenance" (1.4421–22). The shop is now a front, a lie, and the real business of the *Cook's Tale* is the prostitution of the self.

The fifty-odd lines of the fragmentary *Cook's Tale* may well be the last word in the decay of language that controls the First Fragment. From high style to colloquialism to dialect humor to authorial silence, the *Tales* chart a trajectory of brilliance and of breakdown. They skirt playfully around the patternings of language, sex, and money until, at the end, they bring the three together into what may be a statement of the literary life itself. What does it mean to sell a lie for "sustenance," the poem asks, and perhaps no better answer may be found than in Chaucer's Wife of Bath, who may not *swyve* but who most brilliantly among the Canterbury Pilgrims holds herself "for contenance" and, in the process, reveals women to be the exemplary performers of and in the world.

The Wife of Bath and Her Fantasies

At the close of his little poem known as the "Envoy to Bukton," Chaucer turns from the familiar, singular address to his friend (the "thee" that had controlled the poem's first three stanzas) to speak to his audience more generally. Shifting to the plural "you" form, Chaucer writes for all:

> The Wyf of Bathe I pray yow that ye rede
> Of this matere that we have on honde.
> God graunte yow your lyf frely to lede
> In fredam, for ful hard is to be bonde.[29]

People have been reading the Wife of Bath for more than six hundred years, seeking to apply her lessons and her liveliness to all the matters that they have in hand. Her claims for mastery in marriage, her assertions of female voice and physicality, and her challenge to the hegemonies of male rule, male writing, and male reading have made her one of the most vivid of literary personages and one of the most controversial in the canons of Chaucer criticism. She is a creature of language, sex, and money, an assemblage of literary allusions and social critiques, an affront to all that is conventional or orthodox.

> We wommen han, if that I shal nat lye,
> In this matere a queynte fantasye:

Wayte what thyng we may nat lightly have,
Thereafter wol we crie al day and crave. (3.515–18)

And she goes on:

Greet prees at market maketh deere ware,
And to greet cheep is holde at litel prys:
This knoweth every womman that is wys. (3.522–24)

These lines sum up all the major Chaucerian idioms of the *Tales,* while helping to define the nature of the Wife's performance and her uses and abuses of source matter.[30] The *Wife of Bath's Prologue and Tale* are a "queynte fantasye" of their own: both a curious fantasy and a fantasia on *queynte* (the Middle English word that she, and Chaucer elsewhere, use for "cunt").[31] Throughout her *Prologue,* the Wife exercises the power of the body over the meaning of texts. She willfully misreports, misinterprets, and mistakes authoritative writings. She claims to substitute experience for authority. But most compellingly, she transforms the intellectual production of words and their interpretations into an act of physical procreation: an application of her "instrument" on the world.

At one level, the "queynte fantasye" is a product of her curious or idiosyncratic imagination. It is a performance about performance itself. The Wife makes telling the theme of her story, as she interrupts herself with phrases such as "now wol I speken" (or "tellen") many times throughout the *Prologue* (for example, at lines 193, 452, 480, 503, 563). Through these consistent interruptions she delays her point or ending.[32] She holds her audience captive to an autobiographical fantasy spun out of speech and texts. Such texts are adduced less for what they say than for their sheer throw weight of authority. She offers, as she says at one point, "ensamples mo than ten" (3.179). These are lists for the sake of lists, a vast ranging of allusions, names, quotations, and asides designed to dilate her narration. She imposes herself on the whole world of textual experience, or, to put it another way, to substitute the endless experience of texts for the bounded experience of life. "This is," as the Friar interrupts, "a long preamble of a tale!" (3.831)—a form of oratorical manipulation designed to withhold (especially from the male reader) closure and satisfaction.

But at another level, the "queynte fantasye" becomes a fantasy about the *queynte:* about the many ways of naming human body parts, about the ways in which language can multiply one thing into many different terms. The Wife is a great namer. She gives her own name ("dame Alys," 3.320), that of her fourth husband (Jankyn), her "gossib" (also Alys or Alisoun, 3.530, 548), and herself again in Jankyn's own reported speech ("Deere suster Alisoun," 3.804).

She also names authorities and speakers, places and astrological signs. And she names, and renames, her sexual organs again and again — at times euphemistically, at times with blunt directness: *queynte* (throughout); *quoniam* (3.608); *bele chose* (447, 3.510); *instrument* (3.149); *membres* (3.116); *oure bothe thynges smale* (3.121). Is the word cousin to the deed here? What are the relationships between name and object, between the need to affirm and the demands of decorum?

Such questions were posed and answered by one of the Wife's major source-books for her sexuality, the *Roman de la Rose*.[33] In the course of a discussion between the poem's lover (Amant) and Lady Reason, Amant objects to Lady Reason's bluntness. She has used the word *coilles* ("balls"), which he says, "are not of good repute in the mouth of a courtly maid." And he goes on: "I do not know how you, who are so wise and beautiful, dare name them without at least glossing the word with some more courteous expression as a noble woman should speak."[34] But Lady Reason counters this argument of Amant, claiming that she calls noble things (*nobles choses*) by their proper name (*par plain texte*), without glossing (*sanz metre gloses*), because God made such things with his own hands and they are therefore good.[35]

This is precisely the Wife of Bath's claim early in her *Prologue*. Whatever we may say, God gave us organs of pleasure and reproduction, and we should call them as they are (3.115–34). She constantly renames her organs, not just to revel in the effrontery of bluntness, but to call attention to the ways in which the problem of sexuality is the problem of language. She takes the argument from the *Roman de la Rose* and transforms it into a statement of literary identity. The Wife becomes the sum of her named parts. She aspires to a link between the word and the thing, and yet every time she renames one of those things she calls attention to the slippages of speech and the conventions of denotation. The Wife, for all of her appeals to what the *Roman* would call *plain texte,* is always glossing.

For everything is covered by a gloss, a veil, a curtain of interpretation, and such textile imagery lies at the heart of medieval literary theory. A weaver of wool, a woman riding on her horse dressed in the veritable tonnage of the cloth trade, the Wife combines text and textile: a wordplay that had been recognized throughout the classical and medieval periods as central to the meaning of the Latin verb *texere*. One could weave with words (thus, make texts) or threads (thus, make textiles), and the Wife does both.

Such weavings fill the patterns of her performance. Texts show up, much like textiles, to be sewn up or ripped apart — as, most famously, when she tears out the pages of her fourth husband's, Jankyn's, book of wicked wives. And in her tale itself, with its blend of Arthurian romance and Ovidian mythology, bodies and texts are constantly wrapped up or reaved apart. The knight's rape of the maiden that precipitates the tale's narrative is not very far from the textual rapine worked by the Wife on, say, the tale of Midas told by Ovid in his *Metamorphoses*. Within the fiction of the tale, the knight is brought before the queen, and she agrees to release him of charges if, within a year, he can tell her what women want the most. This challenge then provokes the Wife herself to reflect on female desire, and she adduces Ovid's tale of Midas — which she subtly mis-tells — to argue that women, above all, cannot keep secrets. In Ovid's version, it is Midas's barber who cannot keep to himself the knowledge that Midas has ass's ears.[36] In her version, it is Midas's wife. But she abbreviates her story, cuts it short — indeed, cuts it short in a form as brusque and nearly physical as her ripping out Jankyn's pages. "The remenant of the tale if ye wol heere, / Redeth Ovyde, and there ye may it leere" (3.981–82).

This is a world of remnants, of bits of texts, and textiles, sewn together to make something of a patchwork narrative.[37] The Wife trades in textual remnants, and the cloths and clothing of her characters are, in the end, stripped aside in favor of something apparently more ical. "Cast up the curtyn, looke how that it is." With this line, the old woman of the tale asks her newly mastered knight to see her as she really is. She had given him the answer to the Queen's question, what do women want the most, and in the process had saved him from the execution that awaited him on the charge of rape. Now, at the tale's end, she poses him a choice: Does he want her old and faithful or young and fickle? Forever in her debt, the knight lets her choose, and that is (at least for the Wife) the right answer. For the old hag now becomes both beautiful and true, and she asks him to pull back the curtains of the bed to see her in her beauty.

But just what happens when we cast up the curtain? Should a woman ever be seen in plain sight? Certainly, Ovid did not think so. At the conclusion to his *Ars Amatoria,* Ovid details just how the woman should prepare herself for sex and how, if necessary, she should fake her own enjoyment.

> You, to whom nature has denied the sensation of love, counterfeit
> the sweet bliss with lying sounds. Unhappy the woman for whom
> that place, whereof man and woman ought to have joy alike, is
> dull and unfeeling. Only, when you pretend, see that you are not
> caught; win assurance by your movements and even by your eyes.
> Let your words and panting breath make clear your pleasure; ah, for
> shame! That part of your body has its secret signs. She that after love's
> joys will ask a lover for reward will not wish her prayers to have much
> weight. And let not light into your room by all the windows; it is better
> that much of your body should be hidden.[38]

The windows should be curtained, the *thalamos* (the marriage bed) left in darkness so that much of the body lies hidden. The fantasy behind the *Wife of Bath's Tale* lies precisely in this contradiction: for by casting up the curtain, she reveals a woman who is beautiful and true, a woman not in need of ruses, lies, or cosmetic enhancement. But, of course, for Ovid and for Chaucer, those enhancements are precisely where the power of poetic creativity rests. Ovid shows us the woman as the best of artificers, the master of fiction (note his uses of the word *fingere* here, meaning to craft or shape in artistic or literary terms). *Tantum, cum finges, ne sis manifesta, caveto.* Be sure, he says, when you create this fiction (*finges*), that it may not be revealed. Love is a fiction, and the woman is the artist of desire. Chaucer's Wife of Bath has shaped a *fantasye* of *queynte*: a fiction about sexual identity, female control, and male submission.

But she has also shaped a fantasy about literature. The curtain of the loathly lady's bed is, too, the veil of allegory. Poetry, for medieval literary theorists, was veiled truth, and the reading of a literary work stripped away the fabric of illusion to reveal an inner truth. To cast up the curtain is to strip away the veil of allegory: to reveal the kernel underneath the fair integument of art. Such a move would have been familiar from a range of sources. The medieval romances often turn for their plots on the workings of sorcery. Female figures of powerful magic or social wiles (most famously, Morgan la Fay of the Arthurian tales) manipulate their male superiors. But more than that, magic becomes a theme. The figure of the sorcerer or sorceress (Merlin, Morgan, or others) stands as the fictional counterpart of the real magician in literature: the writer of the story.

Authorship and tale telling are a kind of magic — a way of changing shapes, forms, and personae; a way of enchanting a reader or an audience and transporting them to an imaginary world.[39] In the *Genealogy of the Gentile Gods,* Boccaccio reflects on the nature of poetry, finding in it nothing less than a transformative magic. Poetry, he wrote, "brings forth strange and unheard of creations of the mind; it arranges these meditations in a fixed order, adorns the whole composition with unusual interweaving [*contextu*] of words and thoughts; and thus it veils truth in a fair and fitting garment of fiction" [*uelamento fabuloso atque decenti ueritatem contegere*]. And he continues, "Whatever is composed as under a veil [*sub uelamento componimus*], and thus exquisitely wrought, is poetry and poetry alone."[40]

The Wife of Bath has sought to adorn herself in a fair garment — to present an allegory about love, desire, and interpretation; about what place literature may have in a world, as David Wallace has put it, of "capital, warfare, and wool." The capital is what the Wife imagines as her value, whether it be the land she holds (and accuses Jankyn of trying to murder her for) or the "instruments" she wields. The warfare, constantly ongoing, is the war that breaks out between men and women (a war that, with Jankyn as well, results in hard blows to the body). And the wool, though very real in the Wife's economic world, is figurative, too: the interwoven words and thoughts, the garment of fiction.

The Wife of Bath thus stands as one of Chaucer's most profound challenges to male authorial control. Much like the Miller, she upsets the ordered worlds of textual and sexual understanding. She undermines relationships between the authority of inherited text and their enactment in performed discourse. And she does so by asserting a distinctive, gendered way of reading, as her performance successively garbs and strips away the coverings of artifice and arch self-consciousness that make her an enduring, and still enigmatic, literary creation.

The Literal and the Allegorical:
The Pardoner and His Performances

And so does the Pardoner. From his first appearance in the *General Prologue*, he seems marginal, unusual, disturbing. His long, stringy yellow hair, his beardlessness, his stylishness all conspire to confuse the narrator. "I trowe he were a geldyng or a mare." He thinks him either a eunuch or a homosexual. Whatever he may be, the Pardoner is a creature of the vacuous. There is a scrotal imagery about him: an assembly of empty vessels, bogus bags, misleading purses: wallets full of fake pardons, pillow cases passing themselves off as holy veils, glass jars full of pigs bones he will sell as relics.[41]

Much like the Wife of Bath (with whom he has been frequently compared in Chaucer criticism), the Pardoner compensates for barrenness by speaking. He is a great manipulator of language, a master of "feyned flaterye and japes," who could "wel affile his tonge." He stands as a comparable challenge to Chaucerian authority: a kind of anti-poet, a figure of linguistic trickery in sharp contrast to the narrator's pleas for responsible telling and the cousinage of word and deed. The Pardoner ends the sequence of pilgrim portraits, but he also provokes the narrator's own reflections on his craft. His notions of reportage recast the description of the Pardoner into an ideal: the narrator will not "feyne thyng, or fynde wordes newe," a striking contrast to the feigning of the Pardoner and the "newe jet" of his appearance (a stylistic detail that reflects not merely his attentions to fashion but his affiliations with what Chaucer elsewhere would critique as the "newfangleness" of the deceptive or inconstant).[42]

And like the Wife of Bath as well, the Pardoner comes off as a teller lost in his own tale, a shaper of an autobiographical fiction that gets away from him. Every now and then, the Wife forgets herself (witness, most strikingly, the moment in her *Prologue* when she states: "But now, sire lat me se what I shal seyn. / A ha! By God, I have my tale ageyn," 3. 585–86). But the Pardoner's whole performance is an act of self-forgetting. He seems blithely unaware that he is giving away the whole game of his profession. He begins his *Prologue* by announcing just how he preaches, how he twists the meaning of the scriptures to his own ken, how his own intention "is nat but for to wynne, / And nothyng for correccioun of synne" (6.403–4). The goal of all this talk is money, the "pens" that the unsuspecting folk will pay. He loves to tell old stories, and the one he offers here concerns three drunken fellows at a tavern who, on hearing that "Death" is killing people in the town, vow to kill him off. They meet an old man on the way, who tells them that, indeed, they will find death "up this croked wey" (6.761). But what they find is gold. Conspiring among themselves, betraying one another, they wind up, in the end, only killing each other off (two gang up on the youngest, who has returned from the town with poison for the others, which they unknowingly drink). From this fable the Pardoner spins out a moral against avarice, and then turns to the Canterbury pilgrims to proffer his wares. In trying to sell them relics for indulgences, he approaches the Host, who reacts angrily and violently, and it is left, in the end, for the Knight to orchestrate their reconciliation and keep the pilgrimage, and its tale-telling game, going.

The *Pardoner's Tale* shows ordinary people lost in literature. The rioters take everything too literally. "Death" is not a person, it is a personification (here, resonant with the Black Death, the plague). The Old Man, the crooked way, the tree under which they find the gold — all these are stock icons of the exegetical tradition. Even the tavern of the rioters takes on a figurative cast. It is the world of the inebriated imagination, the site here, as it was throughout medieval literature, of the theatrical, the transgressive, the dreamt.[43] Indeed, these bad pilgrims — drunk, chasing death, and finding gold — relive something of the *Canterbury Tales* experience as a whole. How different, really, is the Tabard from the tavern of the *Pardoner's Tale,* for both are the loci of imagination? And just how different are these rioters, or for that matter the Pardoner himself, from the Miller, who had interrupted the Host's ordered plan because, as he claimed, he was drunk on the Host's own Southwark ale? Are we intoxicated by the Pardoner's words?

Surely, the Pardoner is himself.[44] Palamon in the *Knight's Tale* put it well, echoing Boethius's *Consolation:*

> We faren as he that dronke is as a mous.
> A dronke man woot wel he hath an hous,
> But he noot which the righte wey is thider,
> And to a dronke man the wey is slider. (1.1261–64)[45]

The Pardoner's rioters are similarly lost upon the way, and that remains the larger point about the *Canterbury Tales,* and the Pardoner's place in it. "I wol bothe drynke and eten of a cake" (6.322), the Pardoner had averred before beginning. Drink governs his performance, from this opening avowal to the long tirades against drunkenness in his tale (see 6.551–54). And he concludes: "Thy tonge is lost" (6.557). It is precisely that loss of tongue that the Pardoner fears the most, for he is a creature of that "filed tonge" of his *General Prologue* portrait. The spiritual drunkenness that governs his performance, much like the Miller's, gives us a world full tickle: a world in which words lose their meaning, in which human sounds cannot communicate, in which, in short, the tongue is lost.

That loss of tongue resonates, too, with the controlling images of bodily dismemberment and fragmentation in the Pardoner's performance. Relics are many things, but they are first and foremost body parts. They represent the power of the broken holy body, but in the Pardoner's world they are the bogus bits of animal and cloth — not holy things but fetishes, really, objects of atten- tion that have been invested not with the power to heal but with the power to delude.[46] And body parts litter the landscape of the *Pardoner's Tale.* There are the womb, the belly, the vile stinking cod of his tirade; the face, the nose, the tongue of drunkenness. And there are all the oaths: God's blood, God's wounds, God's nails. These old, familiar medieval oaths trade on the fragmen- tation of the holy body. They dismember the divine into the bits and pieces of the cursed. Oaths are the flip side of relics, then: bits of a holy body spat out, not for healing but for harm. Even the dice played by the rioters takes on this weird corporeality: "bicced bones," parts of another body reshaped for deceit. In this world of fragmentations, no bodies can be whole. The Pardoner's eunuchry is part and parcel of a reliquary landscape, something that the Host knows all too well. For when the Pardoner approaches him for money, he responds in terms perfectly in keeping with the idiom of the tale: cut up the body, break its parts, pull out its balls for relics.

If the Pardoner breaks up the sacred world, and if the Host's retort at the conclusion of his tale threatens to break the Pardoner's body up, as well, then his tale as a whole breaks up and reassembles the entire *Canterbury Tales* into a travesty. We see the review of the *General Prologue* portrait technique in the Pardoner's own self-presentation of his relics (6.335–51). We see the idioms of intention and correction, so central to the narrator's avowals at the close of the *General Prologue* and in the *Prologue* to the *Miller's Tale,* in the Pardoner's repeated claims for his "entente" (6.403–4, 408, 423, 432). The vision, in the *Pardoner's Tale,* of the "cors, . . . carried to his grave" (6.665) and the ensuing speculation by the rioters recalls the Miller's Carpenter and his amazement of "a cors yborn to chirche / That now, on Monday last, I saugh hym wirche"

(1.3429–30). The scene among the rioters when they decide just who will go to town and who will stay echoes the very moment of the *Tales* when the Knight takes the cut and all the pilgrims, in "one assent," agree to the Host's plan:

> Wherfore I rede that cut among us alle
> Be drawe, and lat se where the cut wol falle;
> And he that hath the cut with herte blithe
> Shal renne to the town, and that ful swithe,
>
> . . . .
>
> . . . , and if he wol nat tarie
> Whan it is nyght, we wol this tresor carie,
> By oon assent, where as us thynketh best." (6.793–801)

And, finally, when the Pardoner turns to Host and asks, "Unbokele anon thy purs" (6.945), how can we not recall the Host's joyful pleasure at the end of the *Knight's Tale* and the apparent success of his plan: "Unbokeled is the male"?

These reminiscences help shape the Pardoner's performance as a kind of anti-*Canterbury Tales,* a story of a kind of negative pilgrimage. For, in the poem as a whole, the pretext of the pilgrimage remains a spiritual renewal through participation in the feast of the sacrament.[47] The visit to the shrine of Thomas à Becket is a search for healing in sickness. By contrast, the Pardoner travesties the central eucharistic imagery of the pilgrimage and of the spiritual feast. Instead of wine and wafer, we get cakes and ale. Instead of a reward of supper "at our aller cost," the Pardoner seeks only coin.

Meaning and Intention: The Friar/Summoner, Clerk/Merchant, Squire/Franklin

The tales of the First Fragment and those of the Wife and Pardoner explore the ways in which words become separated from their meanings: how tellers lie, manipulate, or stretch the truth; how the value of words becomes not the gold of meaning but the forgeries of will; and how ruses, fictions, and self-serving autobiographical fantasies become either the goads to sexual conquest or the glib replacements for a sexuality long past or never there. For these tales and their tellers, language, sex, and money govern literary fictions — fictions that also appear as forms of theater, politics, or magic.

These issues govern, too, a clutch of tales that place the act of storytelling in a set of social contexts new to Chaucer's age. Pilgrims such as the Franklin, Squire, and the Merchant were the "new men" of the later fourteenth century.[48] The Franklin has attained his landed security not by inheriting it but by buying it; the Merchant's success lies in the capital economy of urban trade; and the Squire's accomplishments lie not within the martial chivalry of his father, the Knight, but in the courtly artistry of music, poetry, and domestic service. The Friar and the Summoner, too, may represent new figures on the social landscape: men who embody the abuses of the Church, who place personal attainment above spiritual service. And the Clerk, for all the antiquity of his learning, is very much a creature of the late medieval intellectual and social worlds, with his obeisances to the contemporary poet Petrarch and his portrait of Walter as a Lombard despot of the time.[49]

The newness of these new men shapes their literary idiom. They are remarkably self-conscious tale tellers, remarkably concerned with how their tales will reflect on them personally. They all tell tales that hinge on promises and good intentions gone awry. But they preoccupy themselves, as well, with their own intentions: with the promises, in essence, made by every writer to an audience. Their tales become essays in responsibility: reflections on the function of imaginative literature in society and, in turn, how that function has a value in the exchange systems of desire, capital, and language. Each of these tales, too, shares in a literary and dramatic pairing. They enact the *quiting* structure central to the *Canterbury Tales,* but they do so in new ways, challenging the expectations of an audience and taking not so much the plotlines or the characters for reinterpretation (as the First Fragment did) but the broader themes and images of literary power and performance.

After the Wife of Bath has finally completed her performance, the Friar quickly turns from commending her story to defaming the Summoner, a move perfectly in keeping with the social realities of late-fourteenth-century religious politics. The friars and the summoners had, by Chaucer's time, long been the butt of satire.[50] Faux Semblant, in the *Roman de la Rose,* sometimes takes the shape of a friar, and the *General Prologue* portrait of Chaucer's character reveals a creature in keeping with the excesses of mendicancy.[51] He is explicitly concerned with money rather than with souls; his affectations make him very much a worldly man; and in his haunts and dalliances, he knows more of taverns and barmaids than beggars and lepers. But more than just a figure of excess or vice, the Friar is a figure of confession. In a politically and doctrinally challenging move, the mendicant orders were granted papal license, by the late thirteenth century, not just to preach but to hear confession and bury the dead. Such license had divisive effect on the institutions of the medieval Church. For one thing, friars were now in competition with other clergy for the fees and benefits of such service. But, for another, they were threatening the very structures of salvation. Just who was entitled to grant

Catholics the sacrament of confession? Certainly — after the Lateran decree of 1215 and a range of other thirteenth-century ecclesiastical legislation making confession mandatory — confession was not only central to the salvation of the individual's soul. It was a practice, in the words of Rita Copeland, that "invests broad social power and profound spiritual authority in the individual priest, powers that occupy both public and secret spaces."[52]

For Chaucer's *Canterbury Tales,* confessors have access to secret spaces. The confessor is a figure, other than a literary author, who can know something of another's mind. The Friar learns intentions and desires, takes advantage of that knowledge, and, in the course of his tale, questions the very nature of literary impersonation. Confession, in both the Friar's and the Summoner's tales, therefore, appears as nothing other than a form of intellectual intrusion, a breaking into confidence, a reading of another's mind. This is, it seems to me, what makes these tales so powerfully threatening to the social order of their day. They reveal not just the abuses of confessors but the potentially transgressive nature of confession itself.

Like the Friar, the Summoner is both a caricature of ecclesiastical abuse and a character in Chaucer's drama of intention and representation. Summoners had the job of calling defendants to trial in the ecclesiastical courts, but Chaucer's Summoner abuses his position by associating himself with (and, ultimately, getting money from) the very sexual transgressors that the church courts were supposed to punish. But more than just a figure of malpractice, this Summoner, too, is someone who seeks the intentions of others; who dissembles and deludes; and who, with his grotesque appearance and disfigured features, emerges as more a theatrical, than an historical, personage.

Representation and intention form the two poles of their mutually quitting tales.[53] The Friar tells a story of a corrupt Summoner who maintains a ring of spies to let him know just who is abusing, or transgressing, canon law. These spies seek out the harlots and the bawds: they "tolde hym al the secree that they knewe" (3.1341). But this beguiler is himself beguiled. One day, he meets a certain yeoman, strikes up an acquaintance, and learns that this man is also something of a summoner. But this one does not summon men to court; rather, he calls souls to hell. He is a devil, and he teaches his new friend the tricks of his trade. They share much in common: "looke how thou rydest for the same entente, / To wynne good" (3.1452–53). And like the Summoner, he, too, is a creature of impersonation. He does not simply lie but can also feign appearances. These devils, he explains, can take on different shapes and forms: "But whan us liketh we can take us oon, / Or elles make yow seme we been shape" (3.1462–63). "Sometyme we feyne," he says further on, and sometimes such devils can animate the dead and make them rise again.

This devil/Summoner becomes a figure of fiction-making — a character who can take on different voices and personae, one who can bring the dead back to appearance. As such, he is a kind of negative Chaucerian, a fictive creature who, much like the author of the *Canterbury Tales,* can, quite simply, *impersonate.* But unlike Chaucer, who has made it clear that his *entente* is good, this devil seeks only gain. Coming upon a carter, trapped with his horse in the mire, he instructs the Summoner in the proper understanding of intention and expression. The carter damns his horse and cart to hell. But he is only frustrated. It is an expression of the moment, a blast of temporary anger. "It is nat his entente, trust me weel" (3.1556). In the end, as the devil explains, "The carl spak oo thing, but he thoghte another" (3.1568). But when they come upon an angry old woman, cursing out this human Summoner for calling her to court and seeking to extort a mere twelve pence from her penury, word and will are unified. She curses the Summoner to hell, and means it. "Now, Mabely," asks the devil, "Is this youre wyl in ernest that ye seye?" (3.1626–27). It is, and in spite of the Summoner's protestations ("Nay, olde stot, that is nat myn entente," 3.1630), he is carried off to hell.

Of course the pilgrim Summoner cannot abide this calumny. He tells a story of a cheating friar who gets his comeuppance when he puts the touch (as it were) on a poor householder named Thomas.[54] Life is hard at the house: their child has recently died, and the husband and wife are fighting. This friar (after a long exchange involving a whole string of quotations, dubiously applied, to authoritative works on anger, marriage, and good behavior), gives the husband some advice, and then he asks for money. But what Thomas has to donate is, to say the least, unexpected. Getting the friar to reach into his pants, he promises "A thyng that I have hyd in pryvetee" (3.2143). But what the friar finds is but a fart:

> About his tuwel grope there and heere,
> Amydde his hand he leet the frere a fart;
> Ther nys no capul, drawynge in a cart,
> That myghte have lete a fart of swich a soun. (3.2148–51)

This brilliant scene transforms the fabliau flatulence of the *Miller's Tale* into a profound statement about linguistic value and authorial intention. How can this fart be divided up among the friar and his twelve compeers? The lord to whom the friar appeals at the tale's end cannot fathom such a challenge, but the lord's squire has a solution. Let the friar sit in the middle of a cartwheel with twelve spokes, and let his brethren sit at the ends of each of those spokes; when he farts, "the soun of it wol wende, / And eke the stynk, unto the spokes ende" (3.2273–74). It is an ingenious solution, and with it the tale ends.

The *Summoner's Tale* depends for its effect on pun and wordplay. The Summoner, as we knew from the *General Prologue,* is a mangler of language. His Latin comes off garbled, his voice slurry from his drink. So, too, within his tale, his friar speaks a bogus Latin and a silly French. "Deus, hic," that friar's opening greeting (literally, God be here), sounds more like a hiccup than a blessing, and his line about the rich and powerful, we may well hear a similar eruption: "Lo, 'buf!' they seye, 'cor meum eructavit.' " What his heart utters here is not the good word of the opening of Psalm 45 (from which these words are taken), but a meaningless belch (*eructare* can mean to belch up or vomit or, more specifically, to talk drunkenly). And, at the tale's end, when the challenge to divide the fart is made, the lord remarks how this poses a challenge "in arsmetrike" (3.2222): yes, the art of measurement but surely, too, the metrics of the arse.[55]

Words fall apart, as in the *Miller's Tale,* into mere sounds and eructations. The puns here call attention to the instability of language in this human world. But the decay of language in these two tales takes itself a step beyond the bawdry of the Miller or the dialect jokes of the Reeve. The *Friar's Tale* leads its Summoner not to some figurative hell (the furnace of the smith Gervais in the *Miller's Tale,* say) but to a real one.[56] And the imagination of the squire at the close of the Summoner's Tale leads not to sexual fulfillment or poetic justice (as the manipulations of Nicholas or those of the northern clerks did) but to rank offense.

The impersonations of the Friar's and the Summoner's tales transform the benign comedy of fabliau into outright affront. It is not so much that these stories are meaner or more pointed in their satire than the Miller's and the Reeve's. It is that their conception of authorial performance is far more threatening. How can we know, the *Friar's Tale* appears to ask, just who we meet upon the road: a yeoman or a devil? The impersonations of literary performance seem, by this tale's end, barely a hair's breadth away from sin. And when the imposter comes knocking at our door, how should we pay him? Is the poet something of a mendicant, begging for our attention or our patronage? And is a fart a proper payment for a tale? The Friar and the Summoner make us suspect of intruding on authorial intention or on audience response. They query how we may know the "entente" of others — but when someone claims to know that "entente," it appears here as deceit. To go back to Rita Copeland's formulation, what confession does in these tales is not only illustrate the powers that "occupy both public and secret spaces." It illustrates just how, in the wrong hands, the secret space can be made public: how, in other words, interiority can be made open. Such is the power of the priest or friar; but such, too, is the responsibility of the author of our fictions.

The Clerk's and Merchant's tales deal with authorial responsibility, as well, and like the Friar's and the Summoner's, constitute a quitting pair keyed to problems of intention and expression, social decorum and literary success. In response to the Host's aggressive call for a tale, the Clerk is all subjection.[57] "I am under youre yerde," he replies, an image that reifies the physical control the Host has over his charges. Indeed the passivity of the Clerk anticipates that of his fictional Griselda, making his relationship to the Host akin to her relationship to Walter. But so, too, the teller's relationship to authorial source is one of power and subjection. "Frauceys Petrak, the lauriat poete," had taught the Clerk this tale, and Chaucer draws on the story of Griselda told in Petrarch's letter to Boccaccio — a letter in which he announces that he is taking Boccaccio's own version of the tale and translating it. From Boccaccio's Italian to Petrarch's Latin to Chaucer's Middle English, the story of Griselda is a story of translation: a tale of finding something beautiful or valuable and of clothing it anew in different words. Chaucer himself reflects on this process, as the figure of Griselda in his story is herself "translated": literally, moved from one place to another (the etymology of the Latin word *translatio*), but socially transformed, too, from a peasant to a duchess. The imagery of clothing (signaled by the word *array* throughout the tale) reveals Griselda as a kind of literary text. She is a creature of the garments and the dress of the imagination. Clothed and reclothed, her steadfastness in the face of Walter's cruelty is an act not just of patience in adversity but, quite simply, an act: a remarkable performance, a stage show that depends on silence as much as the Wife of Bath's depended on prolixity.[58]

Throughout the *Clerk's Tale*, meaning and intention are the problems. Just what was Walter thinking when he sought "To tempe his wife," to "assay" her steadfastness? He orchestrates a play of disillusion, much as Nicholas in the *Miller's Tale* would organize his ruses. He is a creature of feigning, of secrecy, of hidden motives. When Griselda responds submissively, he fakes displeasure: "Glad was this markys of hire answeryng, / But yet he feyned as he were nat so" (4.512–13). And, when her second child is born and he plans to take this one away, too, the tale's narrator reflects:

> But ther been folk of swich condicion
> That whan they have a certein purpos take,
> They kan nat stynte of hire entencion, ... (4.701–3)

And again: "To tempe his wyf was set al his entente" (4.735).

If the Marquis shields his intentions, Griselda (when she actually does speak) reveals hers. As she announces, towards the tale's conclusion, when she is about to be dismissed in favor of another wife: "I yow yaf myn herte in hool entente" (4.861). She can only barely fathom Walter's motives, when he strips her of her finery and turns her out: "But yet I hope it be nat youre entente / That I smoklees out of youre paleys wente" (4.874–75). When the supposedly new wife appears, and Griselda is beseeched to wait on her, she reaffirms that she would "love yow best with al my trewe entente" (4.973).

It goes on. The revelations at the tale's conclusion — with the children re-united with the mother and Griselda welcomed back into the household — become revelations of intention. And when the tale is done and the Clerk turns back to his audience, he too must say something of his own intent:

> This storie is seyd nat for that wyves sholde
> Folwen Griselde as in humylitee,
> For it were inportable, though they wolde,
> But for that every wight, in his degree,
> Sholde be constant in adversitee
> As was Grisilde; therfore Petrak writeth
> This storie, which with heigh stile he enditeth. (4.1142–48)

This is a statement of *intentio auctoris* — of the formal causes for writing in accordance with the prescriptions of late medieval literary theory.[59] And with this statement — and the following turns to the Canterbury pilgrims, the Wife of Bath, and the general reader — the Clerk, and perhaps Chaucer, make clear that the tale of Griselda may be less a tale of love and patience than a story about reading. Just how are we to take this story? Petrarch was alive to such a question, as he announces in his letter to Boccaccio that he had shown the story to two very different readers.[60] The one, a man from Padua, read it and "When scarcely half-way through the composition, he was suddenly arrested by a burst of tears." The other, a man from Verona, sat stock-still:

> "I too," he said at the end, "would have wept, for the subject certainly
> excites pity, and the style is well adapted to call forth tears, and I am not
> hard-hearted; but I believed, and still believe, that this is all an
> invention. If it were true, what woman, whether of Rome or any other
>   nation, could be
> compared with this Griselda?"[61]

Do we weep, or are we silent? The purpose of the tale is to inspire critical response: to get people talking or, in the world of Chaucerian contestation, to get them quitting.

The *Merchant's Tale* quits the Clerk's in a range of ways, not least by trans-forming its potential for tears into farce. Both of their tales explore the problem of Italian despotism and its literary implications. As David Wallace sees it, these "two tales of Lombard tyranny" both play out a comparable story: "a tyrannical male sees a female body, commands it, takes possession of it." But like the Miller's retelling of the *Knight's Tale,* the Merchant's "performs a humorous critique" of the Clerk's: "The somber, claustrophobic, courtly societies of Theseus and Walter yield to the cheerful, mobile market economies of Alisoun and May."[62] There is a politics to both tales, a question about the power of the ruler and the subjugation of the populace that functions as analogy to the power of the author and the acquiescence of an audience.

The *Merchant's Tale,* however, goes one step further. It questions the commercial value of literature itself. What happens when the older forms of fable, myth, romance, and debate find themselves in the mouth of a creature of commerce? In the *General Prologue,* we are told of the Merchant's skill at "eschaunge"; that he was never in debt; and that his bargains and his borrowings keep him "estatly" in "his governaunce" (dignified in his behavior, but also, of course, estately in his economic self-possession). So it should be no surprise that this Merchant phrases matters of the heart as matters of the marketplace. When January, the tale's aged Lombard knight, thinks of taking a wife, he debates with his friends and with himself and, in the process, imagines a "mirrour, polioohed bryght / . sette in a commune market-place" (4 1582.–83). In his mind, women pass before this mirror much like chattels in a market, and the vision of erotic fantasy — impressed, in the Merchant's words, upon January's soul — becomes a bazaar of desire.

Two central images emerge from this encounter. The first is that of impression. Images impress themselves upon the mind throughout the *Merchant's Tale.* Its characters are like blank slates on which pictures, letters, words are written. Such imagery is central to the medieval inheritance of Stoicism, and nowhere is this more explicit than in Boethius's *Consolation of Philosophy.* In Book 5, metrum 4, of the *Consolation,* Lady Philosophy argues against the Stoic position that the mind is a tabula rasa. Advocating a Platonic notion of identity and learning — that the mind bears with it certain ideas or deep memories of its earlier, precorporeal existence and, therefore, that learning is a form of remembering — she reviews the Stoic position critically. In Chaucer's Middle English translation (complete with his added glosses) the passage reads:

> [The Stoics] wenden that ymages and sensibilities (that is to seyn,
> sensible ymaginaciouns or ellis ymaginaciouns of sensible thingis)
> weren enprientid into soules fro bodyes withoute-forth (as who seith
> that thilke Stoycienis wenden that the sowle had been nakid of itself,
> as a mirour or a clene parchemyn, so that alle figures most first comen
> fro thinges fro withoute into soules, and ben emprientid into soules):
> . . . ryght as we ben wont somtyme by a swift poyntel to fycchen lettres
> emprientid in the smothnesse or in the pleynesse of the table of wex or in
> parchemyn that ne hath no figure ne note in it.[63]

The Merchant's characters are trapped in this discredited Stoic epistemology. Women are like warm wax in the lover's hands (4.1429–30), but so too is the access to that woman's body. May makes a wax impression of the key to January's garden and gives it to Damian, so he may enter there (4.2117–21). Life operates through signs and texts; letters are exchanged between the illicit lovers, to the point where:

> . . . by writyng to and fro
> And privee signes wiste he what she mente
> And she knew eek the fyn of his entente. (4.2104–6)

Intention and expression now become the purview of the secret signs of lover's missives. So, too, when Damian and May are in the garden and will horribly delude poor old, blind January, she signals him through "fynger signes."

> For verraily he knew al hire entente,
> And every signe that she koude make, . . . (4.2212–13)

The *Merchant's Tale* becomes a romance of impression: a story of desire and deceit told through the images of Stoic epistemology.

But it, also, becomes a romance of the garden. The enclosed garden is, throughout medieval literature, the paradise of biblical and exegetical narrative. Throughout the tale, January finds himself in paradises of his own imagining, worlds of desire that he foolishly imagines lead him to a spiritual bliss. The humor of the tale lies in its fabliau-like transformation of the central image of religious devotion into the scene of carnal transgression. The tree in the garden cannot but resonate with the tree in the garden of Eden; and the exegetical afterlife of that tree — from Christ's cross to the illicit pear tree of Augustine's childhood confession — cannot but ring comically at the tale's end. For when January has his sight restored by Pluto, he looks up to see May and Damian coupling in his tree, and May announces: "Was no thyng bet, to make yow to see, / Than strugle with a man upon a tree" (4.2373–74). That struggle transforms an allusion to the Passion — Christ on the cross, the man of sorrows on the tree — into farce.

But it transforms, as well, the easy fabliau humor of the *Miller's Tale* into explicit sexuality. We see much in that tale, as we see in the Reeve's, or for that matter in the Wife's — but we never see real penetration, as we do in the Merchant's. "Ye, algate in it wente!" In the hands of the Merchant, fabliau comedy, stoic epistemology, and mythological romance become pornography. This is a world of the explicit, of saying exactly what happens without gloss or euphemism. Such is the idiom of the Merchant, who would be in no one's debt, who would create a system of exchange that always rests in his favor.

Ladyes, I prey yow that ye be nat wrooth;
I kan nat glose, I am a rude man —
And sodeynly anon this Damyan
Gan pullen up the smok, and in he throng. (4.2350–53)

The Merchant sets out, then, to strip away the ruses of the literary to give us blunt facts. His rudeness, his refusal to gloss, mirrors Damian's brusque way with May. For if we have learned anything throughout the *Canterbury Tales,* it is that poetry is a garment; that texts are woven things, and that the stripping of the veil of allegory, or the casting away of the curtain, is designed to reveal truth — or woman — plain to see. Pull up the smock, cast up the curtain. At the close of the *Merchant's Tale,* much like at the close of the Wife of Bath's, a stripping of a garment or a cloth reveals a hidden truth.

The Merchant would have us see. January in love was blind, and when he becomes truly blind, and then has sight restored, he remains deluded. May convinces him that what he sees is something else, "Ye maze, maze, goode sire" (4.2387), and with this ruse she becomes but another female fiction maker. May tells more than a good lie; she convinces January to see something that is not there — and in the process, like any good author, she avows her good intentions: "I did it in ful good entente" (4.2375). She takes the impressions of his vision and transforms them into allegory (what you see, she says, is not what it means). She takes the language of a Lady Philosophy and turns it into lie. "Ful many a man weneth to seen a thyng, / And it is al another than it semeth." (4.2408–9). It is as if she, too, has taken Ovid's counsel to heart: *Tantum, cum finges, ne sis manifesta, caveto.* Through her writings and her signs, her impressions and counterfeits, May stands as an artist of the erotic, who both keeps her husband and her lover.

The *Merchant's Tale* pushes the fabliau genre to its limits, and it may come as something of a relief (at least in the Ellesmere order of the *Canterbury Tales*) to have the Host turn to the Squire to "sey somwhat of love" (5.2). But the Host's claim, that he knows "theron as muche as any man," must surely be ironic, for all that this young man knows is what he reads in books and in the courtly mannerisms of display and play. It is true that the *General Prologue* tells us that he loves hotter than the nightingale (1.98), but that is probably just a trope. All we see this Squire doing is "syngynge" and "floytynge, all the daye" (1.91). Unlike his father the Knight, whose vast experience contributes to his literary authority, the Squire seems to be a creature of little more than aspiration. Instead of his father's antique epic, rich with philosophical texture, we get an oriental fantasy: a tale set in the realm of Genghis Khan (whom he calls Cambuskyan), full of marvelous machines and talking birds. And if the

Knight seemed prolix in his narrative — his tale full of asides, descriptions, and excuses for his shortcomings — then the Squire seems positively logorrheaic. Scarcely has he begun than he must aver that his "wyl is good," that he must be "excused if I speke amys," and that his "Englissh eek is insufficient."[64]

This opening apology is central to the tale, as it presents a string of characters all measured by their verbal skill and literary intention. The knight who breaks in, early in the story, into Cambuskyan's court is distinguished not so much by his visage or prowess as his verbal skill (5.100–108). And when Canacee, armed with the magic ring that makes the language of the birds accessible to her, talks to the falcon in the second section of the tale, she learns that she has been deceived by a treasonous tercel, a "ypocrite."

> And in this wise he served his entente
> That, save the feend, noon wiste what he ment. (5.521–22)

> Ne koude man, by twenty thousand part,
> Countrefete the sophymes of his art. (5.553–54)

The *Squire's Tale* dramatizes the difficulty, if not the impossibility, of recovering human intention. We have no secret decoder ring to enable us to grasp the meaning and intention of birds, let alone of people. We live neither in the fantasy world of Cambuskyan's marvelous visitors nor in the half-dreams of Canacee's evening strolls.

The Franklin recognizes this. In his world — the all too real world of love and marriage, of commercial travel and commodity exchange, of price and purchase — words often go amiss.

> For *in this world,* certein, there no wight is
> That he ne dooth or seith sometyme amys. (5.779–80, emphases added)

Throughout his tale, intention and meaning contrast with play and feigning. People strive to learn each other's "entente," or to reveal or to conceal their own from others. The Franklin shows us people who are the measure of their wills: characters who plead for judgment based on what they meant rather than what they did.[65]

Look, for example, at the exchange between the merchant's wife, Dorigen, and her suitor, Aurelius. First, we are told that Dorigen knows nothing of Aurelius's desire: "But nothyng wiste she of his entente" (5.959). Then, when he professes his love, Dorigen, dumbfounded, states:

> "Is this youre wyl," quod she, "and sey ye thus?
> Nevere erst," quod she, "ne wiste I what ye mente.
> But now, Aurelie, I knowe youre entente." (5.980–82)

But when Dorigen asks him to remove the rocks that threaten the harbor (and, in turn, her husband's shipbound homecoming) as a way of proving his love, she does so "in pley" (5.988). Here is the crux. Aurelius proffers unmediated "entente." His confession opens his mind to Dorigen. But instead of matching will for will, she offers only game. Her request obviously bases itself on the impossibility of fulfillment (how can the rocks be removed?). But the story seems to say, at one level, that a promise is a promise regardless of the promiser's intention. At least, that is how Dorigen takes it later, when she bewails the Aurelius's successful removal of the rocks.

Both Canacee in the *Squire's Tale* and Dorigen in the Franklin's are made suddenly aware of another's thoughts and wills: the former, by means of a magic ring; the latter, by means of the openness of her interlocutor. For both, enchantment makes intention possible. Magic is an enabling artifice. It permits Canacee to understand the birds, it permits Aurelius to show his love for Dorigen. In one way, it removes the impediments to the successful articulation of intention, whether it is the indecipherable "bird-leden" of the falcon or the irremovable rocks of Brittany.

Like magic, poetry transforms the world, and both the Squire's and the Franklin's tales present the figure of the poet in the guise of a magician. Without ever leaving his study ("ther as his bookes be," 5.1207), the clerk of Orleans shows Aurelius a panoply of fantastic scenes: "Forestes, parkes ful of wilde deer," and "fauconers upon a fair ryver" (see the whole passage, 5.1189–1208). As Boccaccio had put it in the *Genealogy of the Gentile Gods:*

> [Poetry] can arm kings, marshal them for war, launch whole fleets from their docks, nay, counterfeit sky, land, sea, adorn young maidens with flowery garlands, portray human character in its various phases, awake the idle, stimulate the dull, restrain the rash, subdue the criminal, and distinguish excellent men with their proper need of praise.[66]

Without ever leaving a room, magic — or literature — transports us.

In the *Squire's Tale,* fabulous crafted devices become the objects of wonder for a misapprehending public. The mirror that reveals an enemy, the sword that wounds and heals, the ring that reveals any bird's expression, and the steed of brass that travels with the turn of a pin — all provoke little more than open-mouthed inanity.

> Diverse folk diversely they demed;
> As many heedes, as many wittes ther been.
> They murmureden as dooth a swarm of been,
> And made skiles after hir fantasies,

Rhehersynge of thise olde poetries,

. . . .

Of sondry doutes thus they jangle and trete,
As lewed peple demeth comunly
Of thynges that been maad moore subtilly
Than they kan in hir lewednesse comprehende;
They demen gladly to the badder ende. (5.199–224)

All they can do is think in terms of the books they have read or the stories they have heard, finding in the figure of the steed the shape of Pegasus or the Trojan horse (5.207–11). People who cannot understand the craft, the art, the subtlety of "thynges that been maad" are much like readers who cannot see virtue in the literary text (the horse stands still because, at first, "they kan nat the craft," 5.185). The Squire's words, in fact, remain the terms of literary making — *thynges* connoted poems, as well as objects, in Middle English, and *making* itself was the verb used for vernacular poetic creation.[67] The intentions of the craftsman, or the poet, or the teller, may always be badly judged (as Boccaccio noted, especially by those who cannot stand what they cannot explain), as the tale presents a drama of poetic reception as a story of the fantasy of intent.[68]

For the Squire, literature is artifice. He sets out to bedazzle the reader with descriptions of wonderful things, leading only to more wonder. For the Franklin, poetry offers an exercise of the social mind. His magic fosters not the wonder of the Squire but the exercise of *gentilesse* — a distinctively public kind of ethic. He takes his magic, and his poetry, outside the study of the clerk and places it squarely in the outside world. What matters for the Franklin is the way in which people cope with intentions or interpretations. More important for him than the philosophical issues of understanding are the social issues of performance. For a story fraught with problems of private intellection, the *Franklin's Tale* ends with a plea for public communication. His final question, "which was the moste fre," has no one answer. That he asks it at all only contributes to his notion of the social function of literature. Poetry, in his view, gets people talking. Unlike the Squire, whose tale (if it ever finished) would keep us listening all the way to Canterbury, the Franklin generously provides enough controversy to keep us all talking for the rest of the pilgrimage. As Boccaccio had put it, defending literature itself: "If it is a sin to compose stories, it is a sin to converse, which only the truest fool would admit. For nature has not granted us the power of speech unless for purposes of conversation and the exchange of ideas."[69]

But the Franklin is not prepared to admit all speech. In the Ellesmere Manuscript, the Squire barely gets two lines of this third section of his tale under way, when the Franklin bursts in: "In feith, Squier, thow hast thee wel yquit /

And gentilly, I preise wel they wit" (5.673–74). Is it that the young man has gone on far too long or that he is in danger of dramatic indecorum? We know from the *Man of Law's Prologue* that Chaucer wrote no word "Of thilke wikke ensample of Canacee, / That loved her owene brother synfully" (2.78–79). Or did he? The *Squire's Tale* appears to verge in that dangerous direction, as he concludes his second part by noting that he soon will speak of "Cambalo, / That faught in lystes with the bretheren two / For Canacee er that he myghte hire wynne" (5.667–69). For a reader like the Franklin, concerned with maintaining decorum through gentilesse and patience, such a subject matter threatens the control of storytelling.[70] But it also shows us just what happens when literature gets into the hands of one of the "new men" — though, in this case, that new man is a boy. For it is the Squire's boyishness that generates the Franklin's paternalistic comments. "I have a sone," he says, and he avows that he would rather have him be "a man of swich discrecioun / As that ye been" than twenty pounds worth of land (5.682–86). That son, according to the Franklin, is a wastrel: a gambler and a gossip, one to whom "vertu listeth nat entende," one worthy only of rebuke — indeed, a creature more at home in the *Cook's Tale* than in the Squire's or the Franklin's.

The Franklin's quitting of the Squire sustains the problem of intentionality and goodwill that the boy had addressed in his tale. Good sons, like good poets, should "entende" to "vertu"; they should not waste their time in "talken with a page" but should, instead, "comune with any gentil wight." Embedded in this sly rebuke is something of a theory of literary decorum: What are the proper themes of poetry, what should be its intended audience, and how should feeling, eloquence, and discretion govern narratorial performance? His final question, "which was the moste fre?" applies, then, not only to the figures in his tale but to all literary makers — including, of course, the Canterbury Pilgrims. Which one was the most generous, the most giving, the most honest in his or her dealings with the audience? This question, too, lies at the heart of the intentio auctoris: for all our protestations of goodwill or all pleas for forgiveness or indulgence, in the end, there is nobody but us responsible for our words. As Petrarch put it in his letter to Boccaccio that contains his translation of the story of Griselda: "the responsibility for the story rests with the author; that is, with you."[71]

"Now holde youre mouth": The Tales of Fragment VII

As we read on, however, we realize that the responsibility of Chaucer's stories floats somewhere between the author and the audience, the source and the teller. The *Introduction* to the *Man of Law's Tale* dramatizes the problem of responsibility early on. In the Ellesmere Manuscript order, the *Introduction* follows on the aborted *Cook's Tale,* and it reestablishes both the rhythm of the pilgrimage and the social decorum of Chaucer's authorship. Called upon to tell a tale, the Man of Law announces that he cannot come up with a suitable story because Chaucer has written them all. Chaucer's accomplishment embraces all genres and all subjects, he remarks. In particular, he has written well and wisely about women (more tales than even Ovid in his "Episteles," that is, his *Heroides*). He told the tale of Cyex and Alcyone (that is, the *Book of the Duchess*), as well as the collection assembled in the *Legend of Good Women* (which the Man of Law calls "the Seintes Legende of Cupide"). But, as we must recall later when the Franklin interrupts the Squire, he never told the "wikke ensample of Canacee," or any other abominable stories of incest or transgression.

The Man of Law (both in his *Prologue* and his stately, rhyme royal tale of Constance) reasserts Chaucerian decorum and intention after the truncated and transgressive possibilities of the *Cook's Tale.* After interruption, after fragmentation, the *Canterbury Tales* seek (at least in their Ellesmere Manuscript order) a smoothing over and a reassertion of both literary and social authority. In Fragment VII, social interruption governs the dramatic sequence of its stories. There are no real resolutions here, and breakage, errancy, and interruption become themes for pilgrims themselves. Each of their stories dramatizes fiction gone wrong or performance broken.

Fragment VII has long puzzled readers.[72] From the Shipman to the Nun's Priest, it assembles all the possible poetic forms and narrative genres available to Chaucer.

Shipman — fabliau; rhymed couplets
Prioress — miracle of the Virgin; rhyme royal stanzas
Thopas — popular romance; tail-rhyme stanzas
Melibee — moral allegory; prose
Monk — collection of *de casibus* tragedies; eight-line stanzas
Nun's Priest — beast fable; rhymed couplets

Two of these tales are perceived to be so bad that they must be stopped: Chaucer's *Tale of Sir Thopas,* which the Host stanches, and the *Monk's Tale,* which the Knight closes down. One of them, the *Prioress's Tale,* is to modern readers so repugnant (with its explicit anti-Semitism and its grotesque drama of the little boy's slit throat) that many have questioned the seriousness with which Chaucer included it. The *Shipman's Tale,* a bawdy fabliau, is usually assumed to have been intended originally for the Wife of Bath, and there are several remaining inconsistencies in its narrative voice.

With the exception of the universally beloved *Nun's Priest's Tale,* this fragment looks like little more than an assemblage of bad tales, bad tellers, and misplaced false starts yoked together by circumstance. But much recent criticism has found both literary import and important social meaning to these tales. The *Shipman's Tale* has emerged from fabliau conventionalism into a complex statement about language and reality, as its Merchant, Monk, and wife all come together over gold and credit. Its concluding wordplay yokes together *tail*, *tale*, and *tallying* into a synthesis of language, sex, and money: "God us sende / Taillynge ynough unto oure lyves ende."[73] The *Prioress's Tale* has been provocatively reassessed as a cultural statement about the theatricality of Judaism and the rituals of exclusion in late medieval Europe.[74] The *Thopas* and the *Melibee* are now understood to dramatize the problems of orality and writing, *solaas* and *sentence*, central to the fiction of the *Canterbury Tales*.[75] Chaucer's own performances move from a seemingly vacuous recitation (all *solaas*, all speech) to an allegory of moral behavior, rich with philosophical quotations, resonant with allusion to contemporary politics, and deeply challenging to the representation of idealized female authorities. The *Monk's Tale* has been relocated in the ambiance of Chaucer's Italian politics, a response to the tradition of Boccaccio's *De casibus virorum et illustrorum* that comments on the place of poetry, and poets, in the maintenance of despotism.[76] And finally, the *Nun's Priest's Tale*, for all its seemingly transcendent wit, has been read anew as deeply implicated in the events of the Rising of 1381 and, therefore, in the *Canterbury Tales*'s own complex relation to political authority and insurgent vernacular expression.[77]

Fragment VII may be thought of, therefore, as the "literature" fragment: an occasion for exploring, in a systematic way, the problems of intention and expression, performance and audience response, raised throughout the *Tales*. The *Prioress's Tale*, for example, dramatizes just what happens when a performer faces a hostile audience. The little clergeoun of the tale, taught to sing his *Alma redemptoris mater*, walks unsuspectingly through his city's ghetto, and the Jews there, goaded into action by the devil, slit his throat and bury him. He keeps on singing, to the point where the townsfolk can find him, bring him to the church, and witness the miraculous power of the little seed ("greyn") that the Virgin had placed on his tongue. The tale becomes a nightmare of performance. We will never brush away the medieval anti-Semitism that controls it nor fully reconcile the *General Prologue* portrait of the sentimental, yet eroticized, Prioress with her clearly heartfelt storytelling. But we may recognize that Chaucer presses these grotesqueries and ambiguities into the service of another statement about literary activity.

The Prioress's story of the little singer cut off by a hostile audience forms the basis for the *Tale of Sir Thopas*. Chaucer here is reduced to little more than a child: the Host sees him as *elvyssh*, as a *popet* (a little puppet or a doll). And the tale itself recounts the story of Thopas, an "elf-child," doing battle against the monstrous giant Oliphant. Does such a story offer up an allegory of the narrator's relation to the Host? Perhaps so, as the Host monstrously breaks in. "Namooore of this, for goddes dignitee," he cries. His ears ache from what he calls this "rym dogerel." "Thy drasty ryming is nat worth a toord!" (7.930). Much like the little clergeoun, the Chaucerian narrator has been cut off, and the anxiety of interruption had punctuated his tale. "Listeth, lordes," he began the *Thopas,* and this simple opening cliché becomes, by the telling's end, a trope of narratorial unease. Again, he avers, "Yet listeth, lordes, to my tale," at the beginning of the Second Fit, and at the close of that section, he self-consciously announces,

> Loo, lordes myne, heere is a fit!
> If ye wol any moore of it,
>   To telle it wol I fonde. (7.888–90)

And he goes on, "Now holde your mouth, *par charitee*" (7.891), as if to stanch the interruption of an audience that is about to come.

But the Host cannot hold his mouth — nor can Chaucer, who responds to the request for a different kind of story with "a litel thyng in prose." The *Tale of Melibee,* however, is more than just a little thing. It is, as Chaucer calls it in this interchange, a "moral tale vertuous" (7.940), a story inherited from others that he will, admittedly, tell somewhat differently. He apologizes to the audience for adding more proverbs than elsewhere ("To enforce . . . th'effect of my mateere," 7.958). But, as he states, though the words may differ, the "sentence" is the same as that of his sources. Chaucer appeals here to an idea of moral gist or literary substance. But his plea for indulgence ("Blameth me nat," 7.961) differs from that of the *Prologue* to the *Miller's Tale.* There, he had avowed that his responsibility was to report what others said, as accurately as possible. If the audience was offended, it was not his fault, as he was merely passing on the words of others ("Blameth nat me if that ye chese amys," 1.3181). But here he is apologizing for precisely not doing that. His notion of fidelity has shifted from the surface to the substance, from the "tellyng" to the "sentence." For the *Melibee* is not the record of an oral performance but a written text. Twice Chaucer calls it a "tretys," a word reserved in Middle English for a document: a treaty, a letter, a manual. And he states that this tale is not performed but actually written.

> . . . for, as in my sentence,
> Shul ye nowher fynden difference
> Fro the sentence of this tretys lyte
> After the which this murye tale *I write.* (7.961–64; emphasis added)

Chaucer invites his audience to take on the mantle of the textual critic: to align themselves with the expectations of "correccioun" that, for example, governed the appeal to Gower and Strode at the close of *Troilus and Criseyde* and that will inform the Parson's apology at the close of the *Canterbury Tales* (that, being "nat textuell," he would "stonde to correccioun" by members of the audience; 10.55–60). The act of finding difference between Chaucer's version and those currently in circulation requires the perusal of the text. The *Melibee* stands in a genealogy of translated, inherited texts. Its generic affiliations lie with the traditions of material directed at the literate, the learned, and the pedagogically minded.

No accident then, that the *Melibee* begins with an appeal to texts — with a representation of the act of reading paralleling the Chaucerian narrator's own act of textual selection. After the initial attack on Melibee's house, wife, and daughter, and his discovery of the atrocity, Prudence tries to silence her husband's weeping: "This noble wyf Prudence remembred hire upon the sentence of Ovide, in his book that cleped is the Remedie of Love, where as he seith" (7.976). Each subsequent challenge, from Melibee's doubts to the contentions of his counselors to the appearance at the tale's close of the original adversaries, is greeted by a demonstration of Prudence's wide reading. The lesson of the *Melibee,* beyond its specific instructions in patience and virtue, lies in the ability to read both appropriately and, as it were, appropriatively. Prudence demonstrates the ability to match the proverb with the problem. And unlike the Wife of Bath — who would greet textual difference with mangling, misquotation, or, in the case of Jankyn's book of wicked wives, physical violence — Prudence displaces physical confrontation with textual citation.[78]

So, too, I suggest, does Chaucer. He takes refuge in the written. The pitfalls of oral performance — a hostile audience, an interruption, a humiliation — brush themselves aside in favor of the security of the treatise. Much like his Prudence, he greets threat with massive textuality, defusing the Host's verbal violence with a displace of "sentence" that, within the context of the Canterbury fiction, may stand as much as a lesson to the Host himself as to the poem's historical readers.

But it is precisely this ostentatious display of textuality that throws the pervasive oral quality of Fragment VII in relief. From the puns of the *Shipman's Tale* to the noise of the *Nun's Priest's,* the twists of language control these diverse tales. The wordplay on "cosyn" and "cosynage" (kinship and trickery) and the fantastic triple pun on "tailynge" at the *Shipman's Tale's* close present a verbal texture in which we can never be quite sure just what we hear. The Prioress's story reveals the price paid for words spoken without knowledge. "I lerne song; I kan but smal grammeere" (7.536), the older boy says to the clergeoun when asked to expound the meaning of this prayer, affirming that the *Prioress's Tale* is, in some way, a fiction of illiteracy: a story about rote memorization. So, too, after the *Melibee,* the Monk's seemingly oblivious recitation of one tragedy after another gets him in trouble — here, in the curt yet courtly interruption of the Knight. In the *Nun's Priest's Tale,* Aesopic fable dovetails with a compilation of educational materials to produce a story whose moral, as Donald R. Howard aphorized it, tells us to open our eyes and shut our mouths.[79] From the loud rap on the door in the *Shipman's Tale* (7.213), through the ringings of the Prioress's *Alma,* the bobbings of Thopas's horse, the "clinking" of the Monk, and the crowing of Chauntecleer and the unbridled barnyard yelps at the end of the *Nun's Priest's Tale,* this fragment rings in our ears more than any other section of the *Canterbury Tales.*

It rings, too, in the ears of Chaucer's audiences — not just the fictive aching Harry Bailly or the impatient Knight but the historical community of English readers at the close of the fourteenth century. In what is clearly Chaucer's single most explicit reference to contemporary events — the Rising of 1381 — critics have seen a poet struggling with the provocations of social upheaval. The *Nun's Priest's Tale* is many things.[80] It takes the form of a beast fable: Chauntecleer and Pertelote, the talking chickens in the barnyard, find themselves menaced by Reynard the Fox (himself another literary figure drawn from medieval entertainments). It takes as its content a long meditation on dreams and texts: the birds debate the value of dreams and dream lore, and in the process, they illustrate the value (or vacuity) of written *auctores* and the potential abuses of rhetorical display. And it takes as its plot the fall of Chauntecleer: his proud strutting brought low by Reynard's attack, followed by his clever extrication and the massive, noisy riot of the barnyard animals. Throughout the tale, the Nun's Priest — of whom we know absolutely nothing — comments on the nature of literary fiction, the quality of audience response, and the responsibilities of a poetic narrator. The tale remains a summa of Chaucerian artistry, a compilation of the forms, themes, and literary strategies that go into the making of the entire *Canterbury Tales.*

It is about politics, as well. The spring of 1381 had seen revolts throughout the south of England in response to a variety of provocations — the arrogance of Richard II, the greed of millers, and imposition of a poll tax. By mid-June, rebels had reached London. The king holed up in the tower; buildings were burned; the Temple was plundered. Demands were made; some were met, but many were not, and within a few days the rebel leaders (notably Jack Straw, Wat Tyler, and John Ball) were either rounded up, wounded, or executed. The Rising of 1381 (formerly known as the Peasants' Revolt, for we now know that more than peasants were involved) remained in the literary and official imagination long after its rebels were dead. It produced volumes of chronicles and histories, but it also generated poetry.

That is where the *Nun's Priest's Tale* comes in. When Reynard captures Chauntecleer, the barnyard goes berserk:

> Ran Colle oure dogge, and Talbot and Gerland,
> And Malkyn, with a dystaf in hir hand;
> Ran cow and calf, and eek the verray hogges,
> So fered for the berkyng of the dogges
> And shoutyng of the men and wommen eeke
> They ronne so hem thoughte hir herte breeke.
> They yolleden as feendes doon in helle;
> The dokes cryden as men wolde hem quelle;
> The gees for feere flowen over the trees;
> Out of the hyve cam the swarm of bees.
> So hydous was the noyse — a, benedicitee! —
> Certes, he Jakke Straw and his meynee
> Ne made nevere shoutes half so shrille
> Whan that they wolden any Flemyng kille,
> As thilke day was maad upon the fox. (7.3383–97)

In this crazy moment, Chaucer transforms the horror of rebellion into fable comedy. He effectively domesticates the memory of the rising, ensconcing it within the safe place of the fabular imagination; yet the noise remains. That noise, as Steven Justice as persuasively shown, is not just the sound of the people but the poetry of Chaucer's contemporary, John Gower. In his *Vox Clamantis,* Gower had explicitly described the terror of rebellion in animalistic terms. The rebels bray like asses, he says, and he catalogues all their sounds as if they were some wild menagerie of revolt: pigs, boars, dogs, foxes, wolves. Men become beasts, and the specific names that Gower gives these beasts find their comic echo in the finale of the *Nun's Priest's Tale*.[81]

As Justice has argued, Chaucer uses such a moment to critique Gower's literary and political project. The *Vox Clamantis* set itself up as a kind of prophetic complaint against political corruption and social unease. The poem was well under way when the Rising of 1381 broke out, almost literally under his window, and that rising clearly threatened Gower's purpose in his poem. Now he had to disassociate himself from the rebels' criticism of corruption. His voice crying in the wilderness had to be distinguished from the noise of unrestrained rebellion (and, of course, with Gower writing in Latin, he had to distinguish his own measured criticisms from the regional vernacular of the rebels). Chaucer's parody of Gower at the close of the *Nun's Priest's Tale,* therefore, not only presents a different way of dealing with political upheaval in poetic form. It also *quits* Gower: rewrites as directly as any Canterbury pilgrim would a previous tale teller. Like all the quittings of the *Canterbury Tales,* it deflates moral pretense and literary pretentiousness. It stints a sententious teller. It asserts that literary history, in essence, proceeds by interruption.

In this move, the *Nun's Priest's Tale* returns us to the initial interruption of the Miller, which has also been read by recent critics as a thinly veiled allusion to the social forces and the "rural vernacularity" unleashed by the Rising of 1381.[82] The tale's conclusion also sustains the controlling arc of Fragment VII, where tale tellers realize that there may be audiences unprepared or inappropriate for their tellings, where the dangers of oral performance lie precisely in the fear of being shouted down. No creature holds its mouth in the *Nun's Priest's Tale:* not Chauntecleer, who goes on seemingly forever with his catalogue of dream lore, rhetorical self-aggrandizing, his sexual posturing; not Pertelote, who argues with her mate at any opportunity; not Reynard, who flatters unashamedly and whose own mouth becomes, quite literally, the trap for Chauntecleer (and whose inability to keep it closed around his prey leads him to lose it).

Not even the Nun's Priest holds his mouth. He loses no opportunity to comment, with only apparent veracity, on the nature of his tale. "This storie is also trewe, I undertake," he says, "As is the book of Launcelot de Lake, / That wommen holde in ful greet reverence" (7.3211–13). Does this mean that the tale is true or false? Or does it rather mean that this is a form of literature, whose purpose, meaning, and power depend on the reading taste of a public reared on French romance? He disavows the opinions that the birds express: "I wol nat han to do of swich mateere; / My tale is of a cok, as ye may heere" (7.3252). Still, he avows that there is a moral to his story.

> But ye that holden this tale a folye,
> As of a fox, or of a cok and hen,
> Taketh the moralite, goode men.
> For Seint Paul seith that al that writen is,
> To oure doctrine it is ywrite, ywis;
> Taketh the fruyt, and lat the chaf be stille. (7.3438–43)

Unlike the *Miller's Tale,* whose ending dramatizes the group laughter at the story, the *Nun's Priest's Tale* ends with an injunction to an individual reader's response. Just what the fruit and chaff are, or what the morality may be, we are not told. Readers make meaning out of literary texts. Sometimes they mangle it (as, say, the Wife of Bath), but for all the intentions or the will of authors, it is audiences, in the end, who matter. The drama of quitting illustrates what happens when an unintended reader gets ahold of literature. Texts always escape their makers, and no protestations of will or claims to specific intention or interpretation can control how everyone will take a tale. Some weep, some don't, over the story of Griselda. The responsibility for a story may rest with the author; but the social function of literature — the meaning of specific stories, the communal uses of the written word, the political implications of utterances — rests with us.

Quitting the Canterbury Tales

After the noise has died down, we are left (at least in the Ellesmere order) with strings of silences and interruptions, breakdowns and renunciations. The *Prologue* to the *Second Nun's Tale* returns to the rhyme royal stanzas now familiar from the tales of the Man of Law, the Clerk, and Prioress. Her tale, a life of Saint Cecilia, like the others in this metrical form, centers on an idealized woman: a figure of patience in adversity, of miraculous power, or of martyrdom. But it shares also with these other tales a governing preoccupation with relations among word and thing, idea and action. The *Prologue* to the tale rehearses the familiar medieval etymologies for Cecilia's name — an attempt to get at some deeper validation of the human word. And in the tale itself, we see characters approaching truth: through dreams, visions, and angelic visitations.[83]

All of these themes and images would be familiar to a reader of the *Canterbury Tales,* and none on their own singles out the *Second Nun's Tale* for comment. What gives the story overarching meaning, though, is its placement in the Canterbury sequence. There is no geographical or temporal marker in the tale's *Prologue.* We have no information as to where the tale is told, or whether it responds to any other tale or teller. It just seems to happen. Such abruptness clearly challenged medieval scribes and editors. Most of the manuscripts, in fact, place it (with the *Canon's Yeoman's Tale*) between the Franklin's and Physician's tales; one manuscript, the Hengwrt, puts it between the Franklin's and the Clerk's, and eliminates the *Canon's Yeoman's Tale* altogether.[84] In the Ellesmere sequence, however (and in the manuscripts that follow its example), the tale inaugurates the final movement of the poem. It begins a sequence — Second Nun, Canon's Yeoman, Manciple, Parson — fully in keeping with the structures of that manuscript: an initial statement of social orthodoxy, followed by an undermining interruption to that orthodoxy, followed by attempts to correct or constrain that challenge. Such is the pattern of the First Fragment, and it reappears throughout the individuated sequences of the manuscript. The *Second Nun's Tale,* too, makes sense within the Ellesmere ordering as an attempt to reaffirm an orthodoxy broken in a previous sequence. Thus the *Man of Law's Tale* follows the broken *Cook's Tale* at the close of the First Fragment: an assertion of a moral voice that tells a tale in formal, rhyme royal stanzas designed to affirm the truth of female virtue. The *Second Nun's Tale* follows the cacophony of the *Nun's Priest's Tale* in the same way.

But if the Ellesmere manuscript presents continuous attempts to right the literary and the social order, it also reveals the near-impossibility of doing so. The *Man of Law's Tale* gives way to the Wife of Bath. The *Second Nun's Tale* is scarcely over when the Canon and his Yeoman break into the Canterbury pilgrimage, sweating on their horses, arguing among themselves, and ulti- mately so disturbing the pilgrimage that at least one medieval compiler — the one responsible for the Hengwrt Manuscript — did not even include it.[85] If the Second Nun's life of Saint Cecilia is a story about language and desire (here, of course, devotional language and spiritual desire), the Canon's Yeo- man's stories are, again, about the monetary value behind language and desire. I say "stories" because what we have here are really three discrete texts, yoked together. There is the *Prologue,* with its dramatic conflict of the Canon and his Yeoman, the discussion about the nature of alchemy, and the reflections on the linguistic and philosophical implications of that art. There is what Ellesmere then calls the *Pars Prima* of the tale: an autobiographical account of the Yeo- man's life with the Canon and the temptations, and failures, of alchemy. Third, there is the *Pars Secunda,* a narrative about a canon (perhaps a different one) and how he dupes folk through the ruses of his alchemy.[86]

Throughout, these stories ask a question central not just to alchemy but to literature: How can one turn dross into gold? How can one take the detritus of experience and make it into literature? The Yeoman's opening description of his canon makes him into one more fiction-maker of the *Canterbury Tales.* "My lord," he says, "kan swich subtilitee" (8.620), and his prowess could take the road to Canterbury, "al clene turnen up-so-doun, / And pave it al of silver and of gold" (8.625–26). The Miller's world "ful tikel" has become the play- thing for the alchemist. But it is only language that the Canon has, for his Yeoman reveals that behind all his secrets and his "privitee" lies little more than trickery. Much like the Pardoner, who could convince us that pigs' bones were holy relics, so the alchemists of the Yeoman's confession can delude us into thinking that mere dross was gold.

> This false chanoun — the foule feend hym fecche!
> Out of his bosom took a bechen cole,
> In which ful subtilly was maad an hole,
> And therinne put was of silver lemaille

An ounce, and stopped ws, withouten faille,
This hole with wex, to kepe the lemaille in.
And understsondeth that this false gyn
Was nat maad ther, but it was maad bifore; (8.1159–66)

Like the Pardoner, who could make everyone an ape, so, too, the Canon: "Right as hym liste, the preest he made his ape" (8.1313).

Alchemy stands in for the literary imagination here, but with a difference. For, unlike the Pardoner or the Wife of Bath, or unlike Nicholas in the *Miller's Tale* or the devil in the *Friar's Tale,* or the clerk of Orleans in the *Franklin's Tale,* this magician is not here. So angry is he at his Yeoman for revealing his secrets, he runs away with hardly a word before the tale begins. "Syn that my lord is goon," the Yeoman crows, "I wol nat spare; / Swich thyng as that I knowe, I wol declare" (8.718–19). The Yeoman is a student, an apprentice, an imitator. He can reveal his master's "elvysshe craft" but cannot really practice it himself. He tries to organize his knowledge into lists and arguments, but he can only tell things "as they come to mynde, / Though I ne can nat sette hem in hir kynde" (8.788–89). The skills of *ordinatio* fail him, and what we get is but a concatenation of chemicals, instruments, objects, and illusions.

The *Canon's Yeoman's Tale* remains a fiction of imitation. Its teller stands in relation to the master as the imitator stands before the *auctor.* Like the *Clerk's Tale,* it explores the problem of fidelity to source. Like the *General Prologue,* it dramatizes the challenge of organization. But unlike the Clerk, whose fealty to the departed Petrarch is unquestioned, and unlike the Chaucerian narrator, who confidently ranges his descriptions by estate, degree, and physical appearance, the Yeoman remains a traitor and a bore. Again and again, he comments on how bored and tired he is with his recitation. "It dulleth me," "It weerieth me." In spite of all the welter of the world, in spite of promises of gold, the Yeoman is possessed by ennui. And, in the *Pars Secunda* of his tale, when he recounts the story of the priest duped by the canon, he places a price on idiocy itself. "What shal I paye?" the priest asks for this knowledge, and the Canon of the story answers: "Ye shul paye fourty pound, so God me save!" (8.1361).

What shall I pay? Throughout the *Tales,* Chaucer asks this question. Every character, each tale teller, confronts in some way the price or the value of his or her performance or action. "Considereth sires," says the Canon's Yeoman in conclusion to his tale, "how that, in ech estaat, / Bitwixe men and gold ther is debaat" (8.1388–89). The debates of the *Canterbury Tales* fixate not just on gold itself but on the value of the literary imagination: the *pris* of words, the effects of deeds, the cost of loving, living, learning, doing business with the world. Can we ever escape the capital economy, Chaucer seems to ask. For as long as we wander on these human roads, there is a toll to pay.

The *Canon's Yeoman's Tale* inaugurates a quitting of this economic voyage. There is, in its *Prologue,* an unsettling allegorical cast. For, even though its mileage is precise and its topography is accurate, this is a road on which strange characters appear: sweaty, black horsemen, out of breath, seeking to waylay the pilgrimage just before it reaches its conclusion. So, too, in the following *Prologue* to the *Manicple's Tale,* we find another moral waylaying. We may be, as scholars have understood it, at Harbledown, two miles from Canterbury, but the poem's narrator says they are at "Bobbe-up-and-doun."[87] Things have been bobbing up and down throughout the poem — a delightfully colloquial way of expressing the condition of living on the wheel of Lady Fortune. Now the Cook, called on for a tale, is far too drunk to tell one. Unlike the Miller, whose inebriation provoked interruption and a brilliant, undermining performance, the Cook is far too gone to speak. He is a "sory palled goost," a "hevy dronken cors" (9.55, 67). The spirit is unwilling, the flesh is but mere weight. Recall again Arcite's Boethian announcement of the *Knight's Tale:* "We faren as he that dronke is as a mouse." To a drunken man, he says, "the wey is slider." The way is slippery when you have been bobbing up and down. Keep your eyes open and your mouth shut (the besotted Cook had ridden with his open mouth, reeking of bad breath, and his eyes obviously closed, for Harry Bailly has to rouse him: "Awake, thou Cook," 9.15). At the close of the *Canterbury Tales,* there seems to be a need for righting, if not quitting, this jostling voyage.

The Manciple steps in to tell a story about how Phoebus had taught a crow to speak, but that crow betrayed the god, and in punishment, Phoebus blackened its feathers and stripped it of its voice. This crow could "countrefete the speche of every man" (9.134), and when we come upon a line like this one, so late in the *Canterbury Tales,* we should be on the alert for a story about literary impersonation. We are not disappointed. The Manciple recalls the central idioms of the *General Prologue* — right down to Plato's avowal that "The word moot nede accorde with the dede" (9.208); the apologies of the Franklin ("But for I am a man noght textueel, . . ." 9.235); the bluntness of the *Merchant's Tale* ("for on they bed thy wyf I saugh hym swyve," 9.256, says the crow to Phoebus). In anger and despair, Phoebus, the god of music and desire, "brak his mynstralcie, / Bothe harpe, and lute, and gyterne, and sautrie" (9.267–68). The instruments of artistry are gone. The crow is cursed to incomprehensible cawing. "Keep wel thy tonge" is the Manciple's moral, and it may well be Chaucer's, too. For like the ending of the *Nun's Priest's Tale,* ill speech results in social anguish.[88]

We are still on the road, but all the landmarks change. Town names become garbled figurations. The sun is setting. It is, by the occasion of the *Parson's Prologue,* four in the afternoon; the narrator's shadow is eleven feet long; the sun is twenty-nine degrees high. We are, here, in the place of the penultimate, the eleventh hour, "at a thropes end" (10.12), just at the liminal space before arrival.[89] When the Host turns to the Parson, we get no claims for a literary performance, but a disavowal of all things poetic, fictive, feigned. "Thou getest fable noon ytoold for me" (10.31), he shoots back, and he catalogues the possibilities of literary art only to reject them: "I kan nat geeste 'rum, ram, ruf,' by lettre, / Ne, God woot, rym holde I but litel bettre" (10.43–44). This is a pilgrimage now not just to an earthly Canterbury but, in the Parson's exegetical interpretation, to a "Jerusalem celestial." All the competing voices have been silenced. "Oure Hoost hadde the wordes for us alle" (10.67). Assent is universal, and the pilgrims, and perhaps the readers, find themselves transformed from audience to congregation. But the *Parson's Tale* is not so much a sermon as it is a penitential manual, one that takes as its text the prophet Jeremiah's words about the very pathways that the pilgrims take. "Stondeth upon the weyes, and seeth and axeth of olde pathes (that is to seyn, of olde sentences) which is the goode wey, / and walketh in that wey, and ye shal fynde refresshynge for youre soules, etc" (10.76). The way is now not *slider;* we are no longer bobbing up and down. Instead, we are invited to stand on the old paths of old texts and read this moral manual in silence.[90]

Or are we? In Ellesmere, the *Canterbury Tales* ends not with the Parson's but with Chaucer's voice. "Heere taketh the makere of this book his leve." This section, known as the *Retraction,* has long puzzled readers. Could it really be that Chaucer disavows his greatest literary creations? Could it really be that he believes, wholeheartedly, that "Al that is writen is writen for oure doctrine"? Is this a deathbed recantation, a moral guide to rereading the *Tales,* a refutation of all that has gone before?[91]

To me, the voice of the *Retraction* remains the voice of the Chaucerian narrator. It is a pilgrim's voice, responding to the "litel tretys" of the preceding *Parson's Tale.* The scene of the *Retraction* replays, in a different vein, the scene at the close of the *Pardoner's Tale.* There, the false preacher turned to the controller of the game and asked for penance. Here, the maker of the book rises to the invitation of the true priest to "understonde what is the fruyt of penaunce." We need to understand that the *Retraction* operates, still, in the fiction of the *Canterbury Tales.* Its catalogue of Chaucer's works is as voiced (and perhaps ironic) as that of the Man of Law: a set of claims for literary production assessed at a certain moment in a literary drama, pressed into a moral or aesthetic argument. It is the final act of quitting in the *Canterbury*

Tales. Much as the Parson quits the *Tales* — responds to the whole enterprise of fiction making and pays back our patience not with earthly gold but with divine — the narrator quits the entire poem: ends it, pays back, takes his leave. Such is the effect of the Ellesmere ordinatio of the *Canterbury Tales:* a structure that (whether it is or is not ultimately Chaucer's own) affects the reader by framing the stories in a moral structure, a dramatic telos, and a sustained literary fiction.

But for all of this attempt — either by medieval scribes or modern critics — to impose or find an ordinatio in Chaucer's poem, the *Canterbury Tales* remains an interrupted work. Interruption, here, is not an aberration but a guiding principle. For at the heart of Chaucer's poem is the problem of attention, the problem of finishing what one starts out to say, the problem of keeping the interest, the docility, and the benevolence of the audience. What happens if that audience is inattentive, boisterous, or malign? The Parson's quitting of the *Canterbury Tales* may more accurately be seen as a return to the initial dynamic of interruption that has controlled the entire fiction. Just like the Miller, the Parson rejects the order of the Host's control (but unlike the *Miller's Prologue,* the Parson's ends with the assent of the Host and everyone to the Parson's auctoritas — no narratorial apologies here, no invitations to turn the leaf and chose another tale, if one is dissatisfied). The ordinatio of the *Canterbury Tales* is, in the end, not some fixed plan occasionally waylaid by a bumpy road but an ideal that never takes full shape — an ordering that constantly is being stopped, excused, broken, and broken down.

In its structure of quitting and response, the *Canterbury Tales* provides a model for a future literary history. Acts of writing after someone — Chaucer writing after Boccaccio, Spenser writing after Chaucer, and so on — become acts of quitting: ways of recasting inherited material to meet new social contexts or aesthetic expectations. The sequence of quitting thus becomes a sequence of literary history. The Knight-Miller-Reeve-Cook section, or the Friar-Summoner interchange, offers up a version of how literary texts are transformed by later writers. Source material thus becomes a quittable subject: the *Knight's Tale* may be said to "quit" Boccaccio's *Tesseida,* much as the *Tesseida* may be said to quit Statius's *Thebiad.* Translation, too, becomes a form of quitting, and the status of the *Canterbury Tales* as a set of purported translations (for example, in the explicit acknowledgments to Petrarch in the *Clerk's Tale* or to Livy in the *Manciple's Tale*) finds itself transformed, within the poem's larger structure, into forms of literary contestation. When the Canon's Yeoman quits his master, he too shares in this dynamic — though, as I suggested, as an unsuccessful imitator.

Critics have long known, and some have lamented, that the *Canterbury*

Tales is incomplete. Where are the two tales to be told by each pilgrim? Where are the tales of the return journey? Some medieval compilers actually recast the poem to conform to this imagined two-way pilgrimage, while certain later poets felt compelled either to insert themselves into the fiction of the pilgrimage (for example, John Lydgate), fill in the gaps (in the anonymous *Plowman's Tale*), or complete fragments (Edmund Spenser's "finishing" of the *Squire's Tale*). But the idea behind the *Canterbury Tales* is of a potentially limitless sequence of readings and rewritings. The *Parson's Tale* and the *Retraction* offer only one way of closing down the system. Others keep it open. The history of English literature, in many ways, plays out the implications of the *Canterbury Tales,* as we find ourselves reading the world through lenses shaped by older writers or as we find ourselves writing about life in words already deployed by Chaucer and his heirs. In its structure of quitting and response, the *Canterbury Tales* provides a model for a future literary history. But, in its interruptions, incompletions, and rough edges, it reveals that literary history as proceeding, not according to smooth plans or clear goals, but through the fits and starts of life itself. Ours is, as John the Carpenter had noted, a world full tickle. In spite of the attempts of medieval compilators or modern critics to right it, it remains so, gloriously in Chaucer's poem.

NOTES

1. On the rise of vernacular writing, see Justice, *Writing and Rebellion,* and Watson, "The Politics of Middle English Writing." On authorship and social change, see Strohm, *Social Chaucer,* and Patterson, *Chaucer and the Subject of History.* On European literary forms, see Muscatine, *Chaucer and the French Tradition;* Wallace, *Chaucer and the Early Writings of Boccaccio* and *Chaucerian Polity;* Wimsatt, *Chaucer and His French Contemporaries;* and Simpson, "Chaucer as a European Writer," in this *Companion.* On Christian allegory, see Robertson, *A Preface to Chaucer,* and the critique in Patterson, "Historical Criticism and the Development of Chaucer Studies," in his *Negotiating the Past.* On English language change, see Cannon, *Making of Chaucer's English.* On manuscript culture and literacy, see Taylor, "Authors, Scribes, Patrons and Books," and the essays collected in Griffiths and Pearsall, *Book Production and Publishing in Britain.*

2. On fabliau, see Kendrick, *Chaucerian Play.* On hagiography, see the essays in Benson and Robertson, eds., *Chaucer's Religious Tales.* On the uses of the epic inheritance, see Anderson, *Before the "Knight's Tale."* On the sermon, see Patterson, "*Parson's Tale* and the Quitting of the *Canterbury Tales,*" and *Chaucer and the Subject of History,* 367–421. On the beast fable, see Wheatley, *Mastering Aesop.* On romance, see Crane, *Gender and Romance in Chaucer's "Canterbury Tales."* On theater, see Ganim, *Chaucerian Theatricality.*

3. Men and women: Dinshaw, *Chaucer's Sexual Poetics,* and Hansen, *Chaucer and the Fictions of Gender.* People and God: Ellis, *Patterns of Religious Narrative,* and Besserman, *Chaucer's Biblical Poetics.* Imagination and reality: Kolve, *Chaucer and the Imagery of Narrative,* and Koff, *Chaucer and the Art of Storytelling.*

4. Gummere, "Is Chaucer to Be Reckoned as Modern or as a Medieval Poet?"; Wallace, *Chaucerian Polity,* 9.

5. On the Ellesmere Manuscript, see "Textual Notes," in Benson, ed., *Riverside Chaucer,* 1117–22; Owen, *Manuscripts of "The Canterbury Tales";* and Hanna, "Hengwrt Manuscript and the Canon of *The Canterbury Tales,*" 140–55.

6. See Bowers, "*Tale of Beryn* and *The Siege of Thebes.*"

7. The so-called marriage group of tales is usually taken to include those of the Wife of Bath, the Clerk, the Franklin, and the Merchant; the four tales of idealized female figures told in rhyme royal are those of the Man of Law (the tale of Constance), Prioress (a miracle of the Virgin), the Clerk (the story of Griselda), and the Second Nun (the life of Saint Cecilia).

8. Howard, *Idea of the "Canterbury Tales."*

9. See Leicester, Jr., "Art of Impersonation."

10. See Hanning, " 'And countrefete the speche of every man.' "

11. See Shoaf, *Dante, Chaucer, and the Currency of the Word.* For Chaucer's encounters with France and Italy and his exposure to literary and political culture in the European vernaculars, see Wallace, *Chaucerian Polity.* For the accusations of *raptus* by Cecily de Champagne and their echoes in Chaucer's work, see Dinshaw, *Chaucer's Sexual Poetics.* For Chaucer's various positions in the Clerk of the Works office and the office of the Exchequer, and their refractions in his poetry (especially in the *Knight's Tale*), see Lindenbaum, "Smithfield Tournament of 1390." For Chaucer biographies that stress (in various ways) his engagements with the monetary and the sexual worlds of his time, see Howard, *Chaucer: His Life, His Works, His World,* and Pearsall, *Life of Geoffrey Chaucer.*

12. See Taylor, "Chaucer's *Cosyn to the Dede.*"

13. Macrobius, *In Somnium Scipionis,* 20.1, quoted and discussed in Taylor, "Chaucer's *Cosyn to the Dede,*" 317.

14. For the histories, etymologies, and literary uses of these words, see their entries in the *MED.* For a general discussion of Chaucer's status as a linguistic innovator, see Cannon, *Making of Chaucer's English* (who argues that that status is, to a large degree, a self-created, rhetorical pose).

15. See Rita Copeland's contribution to this volume.

16. For the classical history (Cicero and Horace) behind the medieval techniques of description, see the discussions in Nims, ed. and trans., *Geoffrey of Vinsauf: Poetria Nova;* Parr, ed. and trans, *Documentum de Modo et Arte Dictandi et Versificandi;* and the still unsurpassed study of Faral, *Les arts poètiques du XIIe et du XIIIe siècle.*

17. For a controversial approach to the Knight as a mercenary, and thus a challenge to the idealism of his portrait and the orthodoxy of his tale, see Jones, *Chaucer's Knight.*

18. For a convenient assembly of sources from the *Roman de la Rose,* keyed in particular to the Prioress, Wife of Bath, and Pardoner, see Miller, ed., *Chaucer: Sources and Backgrounds,* 251–54, 452–73.

19. See Mann, *Chaucer and Medieval Estates Satire,* and Lambdin and Lambdin, *Chaucer's Pilgrims.* For *ordinatio* and its traditions in late medieval philosophy, theology, and book production, see Parkes, "The Influence of the Concepts of *Ordinatio* and *Compilatio.*"

20. Wallace, *Chaucerian Polity,* 155.

21. The major lines of inquiry on the *Knight's Tale* for the past half-century are defined by Muscatine, *Chaucer and the French Tradition,* 175–90; Howard, *Idea of the "Canterbury Tales,"* 227–37; Patterson, *Chaucer and the Subject of History,* 165–230; Leicester, *Disenchanted Self,* 221–382; and Wallace, *Chaucerian Polity,* 104–24.

22. On the theatricality of the *Miller's Tale* and its allusions to the medieval cycle plays, see Prior, "Parodying Typology," and Ganim, *Chaucerian Theatricality,* 38–41, 188–89. For a general assessment of the theatricality of the First Fragment, see Lerer, "Chaucerian Critique of Medieval Theatricality."

23. For a different, but highly influential, reading of the Miller's interruption and the politics of power in the *Canterbury Tales,* see Patterson, *Chaucer and the Subject of History,* 244–79.

24. For approaches to the thematic and dramatic unity of the First Fragment, see Howard, *Idea of the "Canterbury Tales,"* 227–47; Kolve, *Chaucer and the Imagery of Narrative;* and Hansen, *Chaucer and the Fictions of Gender,* 208–44.

25. For the main lines of criticism of the *Reeve's Tale,* see Kolve, *Chaucer and the Imagery of Narrative,* 217–56, and Wallace, *Chaucerian Polity,* 131–36.

26. The standard edition is still Babington, ed., *Polychronicon Ranuplphi Higden.* I quote from the text as reprinted in Mossé, *Handbook of Middle English,* 286–89.

27. The precision of Chaucer's dialect forms and humor has been debated since Tolkien, "Chaucer as Philologist."

28. The single most important engagement with the fragmentary *Cook's Tale* — locating it in Chaucer's London and reflecting on the absence of that city in the *Canterbury Tales*'s stories as a whole — is Wallace, *Chaucerian Polity,* 156–81.

29. "Lenvoy de Chaucer a Bukton," in Benson, ed., *Riverside Chaucer,* 655–56. For an important study of the early reception history of the Wife of Bath, see Schibanoff, "New Reader and Female Textuality."

30. The main lines of recent criticism can be found in Patterson, " 'For the Wyves love of Bathe' "; Fradenburg, "Wife of Bath's Passing Fancy"; Dinshaw, *Chaucer's Sexual Poetics,* 113–31; Hansen, *Chaucer and the Fictions of Gender,* 26–57; and Leicester, *Disenchanted Self,* 65–158.

31. Chaucer uses the word *queynte* elsewhere, especially in *Troilus and Criseyde,* as the node of a variety of puns and social challenges. For a review of the critical debates surrounding this word, see Dane, "*Queynte.*"

32. On the dilatory strategies of the Wife, see Patterson, " 'For the Wyves love of Bathe.' "

33. See Bloch, *Etymologies and Genealogies,* 137–41.

34. *Le Roman de la Rose,* lines 6928–36.

35. *Le Roman de la Rose,* lines 6957–68.

36. Ovid, *Metamorphoses,* 11.172–93.

37. For evidence of Middle English *remenaunt,* meaning a scrap or end of fabric in the fourteenth and early fifteenth centuries, see *MED,* s.v., "remenaunt," def. 1.h.

38. Ovid, *Ars Amatoria,* 3.797–808.

39. See Bloch, *Etymologies and Genealogies,* 1–6; Rollo, *Glamorous Sorcery;* and Heng, *Empire of Magic.*

40. Boccaccio, *Genealogy of the Gentile Gods,* 14.7, in Osgood, *Boccaccio on Poetry,*

39, 42, and see Osgood's notes on the sources of these arguments, 156–60. For the Latin original, see Reedy, ed., *Boccaccio in Defence of Poetry,* 34, 36.

41. The main lines of criticism include Howard, *Idea of the Canterbury Tales,* 333–71; Patterson, *Chaucer and the Subject of History,* 367–421; Dinshaw, *Chaucer's Sexual Poetics,* 156–84; and Leicester, *Disenchanted Self,* 161–77. For a relocation of the *Pardoner's Tale* in the contexts of late medieval Anglo-Flemish cultural relations (and for a full bibliography of studies on the Pardoner and his performances), see Wallace, "In Flaundres."

42. See the *Squire's Tale:* "Men loven of propre kynde newefangelnesse, / As briddes doon that men in cages fede" (5.610–11); *Anelida and Arcite,* where Arcite's falseness is equated with his "newfanglenesse" (141); and the F-Prologue to the *Legend of Good Women,* where "newfangelnesse" is associated with the inconstancy of the bird known as the "tydif" (F.154).

43. See Cornell, *At Play in the Tavern.*

44. Though perhaps only figuratively speaking. For an account of the Pardoner and his performance that takes such drunkenness literally, see Bowers, " 'Dronkenesse is ful of stryvyng.' "

45. Based on Boethius, *Consolation of Philosophy,* 3.pr.2: "quorum animus etsi caligante memoria tamen bonum suum repetit, sed velut ebrius domum quo tramite revertatur ignorat."

46. For the culture of the relic in the Middle Ages and its literary and social implications, see Bynum, *Fragmentation and Redemption,* 239–97; Geary, *Furta Sacra;* and Vance, "Chaucer's Pardoner."

47. For the pilgrimage tradition behind the frame of the *Canterbury Tales,* see Zacher, *Curiosity and Pilgrimage;* Sumption, *Pilgrimage;* and Lawton, "Chaucer's Two Ways."

48. Middleton, "Chaucer's 'New Men.' "

49. See Wallace, *Chaucerian Polity,* 261–98.

50. Fleming, "Antifraternalism of the *Summoner's Tale.*"

51. See Miller, ed., *Chaucer: Sources and Backgrounds,* 237–68, and more generally Szittya, *Antifraternal Tradition.*

52. Copeland, "Confessional Texts," in Wallace, ed., *Cambridge History,* 392.

53. See Godfrey, "Only Words."

54. For an account of the tale in the contexts of late-fourteenth-century ecclesiastical politics, see Fiona Somerset, " 'As just as is a squyre.' "

55. For a review of criticism of the tale and a relocation of its ending in biblical and liturgical contexts, see Olson, "The End of the *Summoner's Tale.*"

56. For the Satanic imagery at the close of the *Miller's Tale,* see Reiss, "Daun Gervays in the *Miller's Tale,*" and Cornelius Novelli, "Sin, Sight, and Sanctity."

57. For the subjections of the Clerk and his relationship to the Host as analogous to Griselda's relationship to Walter, see Dinshaw, *Chaucer's Sexual Poetics,* 132–55. For the Clerk's performance in the larger contexts of Italian literary politics, see Wallace, *Chaucerian Polity,* 261–98.

58. See Dinshaw, *Chaucer's Sexual Poetics,* 144–48 and 253n.38.

59. See Minnis, *Medieval Theory of Authorship.*

60. Petrarch, *Seniles,* 17.3, reprinted in translation in Miller, ed., *Chaucer: Sources and Backgrounds,* 136–52.

61. In Miller, ed., *Chaucer: Sources and Backgrounds,* 139.

62. Wallace, *Chaucerian Polity,* 294.

63. Chaucer, *Boece,* in *Riverside Chaucer,* 464.

64. See Fyler, "Domesticating the Exotic in the *Squire's Tale,*" and Lawton, *Chaucer's Narrators,* 106–29.

65. See Hansen, *Chaucer and the Fictions of Gender,* 267–92, and Van Dyke, "The Clerk's and Franklin's Subjected Subjects."

66. Osgood, *Boccaccio on Poetry,* 14.7, pp. 39–40.

67. *MED,* s.v., "thing." For *making* as a term of vernacular poetic creation, see Olson, "Making and Poetry."

68. See *Boccaccio on Poetry,* 14.14, pp. 69, 71; Latin in *Boccaccio in Defence of Poetry,* 60–62.

69. Ibid., 47.

70. See Scala, "Canacee and the Chaucer Canon."

71. In Miller, ed., *Chaucer: Sources and Backgrounds,* 139.

72. See Gaylord, "*Sentence* and *solaas* in Fragment VII of the *Canterbury Tales,*" and Patterson, "'What man artow?'" This section of my chapter incorporates and develops material originally presented in Lerer, "'Now holde youre mouth,'" 199–202.

73. See Patterson, *Chaucer and the Subject of History,* 351, 360–62.

74. See Fradenburg, "Criticism, Anti-Semitism, and the *Prioress's Tale,*" and Kruger, "The Bodies of Jews in the Middle Ages."

75. See Patterson, "'What man artow,'" and the review of criticism in Lerer, "'Now holde youre mouth.'"

76. See Wallace, *Chaucerian Polity,* 299–336.

77. See Travis, "Chaucer's Trivial Fox Chase," and Justice, *Writing and Rebellion,* 207–24.

78. See Wallace, *Chaucerian Polity,* 212–46.

79. Howard, *Idea of the Canterbury Tales,* 286.

80. See Bishop, "*Nun's Priest's Tale* and the Liberal Arts," and Travis, "Chaucer's Trivial Fox Chase."

81. Gower, *Vox clamantis* 1.783–98, quoted and discussed in Justice, *Writing and Rebellion,* 212–13, working from Bishop, "*Nun's Priest's Tale.*"

82. Patterson, *Chaucer and the Subject of History,* 244–79; Justice, *Writing and Rebellion,* 225–31; Hanna, "Pilate's Voice / Shirley's Case," in *Pursuing History,* 267–79.

83. See Reames, "Cecilia Legend," and "Sources of the *Second Nun's Tale.*"

84. See Cooper, *The Canterbury Tales,* 357.

85. Blake challenges the authenticity of the *Canon's Yeoman's Tale* based on its absence from the Hengwrt Manuscript. See his *The Textual Tradition,* 48–56, and the critical response in Hanna, *Pursuing History,* 141, 152, 306n.19.

86. See Patterson, "Perpetual Motion," and Harwood, "Chaucer and the Silence of History."

87. See the discussion in the *Riverside Chaucer,* note to 9.2–3, p. 952.

88. See Fradenburg, "Manciple's Servant Tongue."

89. See Howard, *Idea of the Canterbury Tales,* 376–87. For a review of the astrological significance of the *Prologue*'s opening (dating it, perhaps, to Good Friday, April 17, of 1394), see Cooper, *Canterbury Tales,* 394–99.

90. See Patterson, "*The Parson's Tale* and the Quitting of the *Canterbury Tales.*"

91. On the Retraction in its generic inheritance and its reception history, respectively, see Sayce, "Chaucer's Retractions," and Wolfe, "Placing Chaucer's Retraction."

PART **III**

Critical Approaches and Afterlives

9

Chaucer's Influence and Reception

STEPHANIE TRIGG

There was a time, not so long ago, when a topic like "influence and reception" was regarded merely as a minor specialization in the broad field of Chaucer studies. For much of the twentieth century, it seemed more important either to read Chaucer's poetry as the expression of a unique medieval sensibility or to insist on its timeless "relevance" for modernity. Either way, the historical patterns of response to Chaucer's poetry in other centuries, or in other contexts, seemed to be of secondary interest. Similarly, a great deal of philological work was undertaken in this period to purify Chaucer's texts of all scribal traces, in a concerted effort to distinguish the work of the poet from his early copyists, editors, and imitators. As a result, the reception of Chaucer, along with the study of these secondary or derivative texts, was set aside as part of literary history, a discipline that had been displaced from its earlier central position by the growth of interest, over the course of the twentieth century, in the theory and practice of criticism "proper." The past ten or fifteen years, however, we have seen a powerful paradigm shift in the understanding of literary history: in more recent practice, cultural history and the patterns of literary reception have become central to literary studies. There are complex reasons why this shift has taken place, concerned with the ever-changing disciplinary boundaries between literary, historical, and cultural study and, more specifically, with criticism's perpetual capacity to interrogate its own traditions.

This chapter takes for granted that the study of how poets, scholars, and critics have read Chaucer in the past is crucial for our understanding of the scholarly, critical, and cultural forms by which he is mediated for us today. It assumes that we are empowered by a greater and deeper familiarity with those forms. It also assumes that Chaucer's indisputably canonical status is due only in part to the qualities of his poetry; also, and more important, it is something we remake anew, albeit in different ways, every time we pick up a volume of Chaucer, no matter what the context. The more we are familiar with those traditions and the origins and histories of our reading practices, the more we can speak with authority of the importance of medieval literature, and the poetry of Chaucer, for the understanding of "English literature," both as a set of poetic and fictional texts and as a foundational cultural construct. For this, finally, is the contentious burden of this chapter: Chaucer is the originary canonical poet of English literary tradition, and he remains an exemplary figure for the patterns of literary reception and criticism, not just of canonical literature, but of all literature in English.

Poetry and Genealogy:
Chaucer and the Patterns of Literary Influence

English literary studies have traditionally been organized around the figure of the author. Modern critiques of the canon have attempted to shake up these patterns of emphasis on the "great" writers of the past, and the cultural assumptions about masculinity, heterosexuality, whiteness, English-ness, and the aesthetics of writing that sustain them, by drawing our attention to neglected writers from earlier periods (women writers, for example) or the work of different language and cultural groups (the writers of the Caribbean diaspora, perhaps, or of Australian Aboriginal communities). However, it has seemed almost impossible to resist shaping our discussions around the work of individual writers. Most of the institutions of general reading beyond the academy (literary prizes, biographies, writers' festivals) still privilege the individual personality that lies, or seems to lie, behind the books we read, while the traditional defense of literature, that it broadens our experience and hones our sensibilities by putting us in touch with the great minds of the past, still exerts a powerful influence on all readers.

Medieval English literary studies is no exception to these general patterns. For many years, the second half of the fourteenth century was thought of and written about as "the Age of Chaucer." As its most widely read author, Chaucer seemed not only to encapsulate the most representative qualities of this period but to do so in a way that surpassed all its other writers. A cluster of important assumptions lies behind his continued preeminence: (1) Chaucer was the first poet to render the English language as a respectable medium for court poetry; (2) he progressively broke free first from French then from Italian literary and rhetorical models to perfect a native style of English comic realism; (3) in some sense Chaucer also enriched the English language and established the southeast midlands dialect of Middle English as the origin of modern "standard English"; (4) Chaucer not only condensed and encapsulated the literary, cultural, social, and political preoccupations of his age but was also able mysteriously to transcend them; and (5) he inaugurated a line of cultural and literary transmission that passed from Chaucer's to the next great "age," that of Shakespeare.

Some of these critical assumptions can be sustained by linguistic and literary evidence, but they are probably best seen as driven by ideological and cultural forces that find their origin beyond Chaucer studies and, in particular, by the needs of a national literary history that delights in finding evidence of continuity in literary production over the centuries, suitably punctuated by works of individual genius. In *Reform and Cultural Revolution,* his revisionary literary history of the period 1350–1547, for the *Oxford English Literary History,* James Simpson stresses the determining influence of concepts of literary periodization on this construction of genius: "The logic of strict periodization (medieval versus Renaissance) determines the need for an exception to prove the rule. This unnatural exception is invariably Chaucer, who is consistently dragooned as a forerunner of the forces of whatever new ideological order takes control of the field of literary studies."[1] There have been many attempts to break down these structures. In addition to detailed studies of individual writers like William Langland, John Gower, and the *Gawain* poet that set out to discuss their works in terms not generated by Chaucer criticism, J. A. Burrow's *Ricardian Poetry* (1971) sought to define a rather more generalized view of literary style between 1370 and 1400. "Despite its fertility," he writes, "the age of Chaucer and Langland has failed to achieve the full status of a 'literary period.' "[2] Before the establishment of a national literary culture, or the self-conscious "movements" that characterize later literary history, the "Ricardian" poets, in Burrow's formulation, nevertheless share a number of stylistic and thematic concerns and preoccupations. Burrow's book encourages us to read Chaucer's experiments with style and voice as part of a broader fourteenth-century engagement with the vernacular tradition and the attempt to graft a more learned Latinate or European style onto that native "stock."

More recently, Christopher Cannon's *Making of Chaucer's English* (1998) debunks many long-cherished beliefs in Chaucer's linguistic and literary innovation. Central and representative among these is Ian Robinson's claim that

"Chaucer *made* English capable of poetry."[3] Cannon emphasizes the traditional elements in Chaucer's language while analyzing why and how the language of his poetry gives the impression of being more innovative than it is and how this impression came to dominate subsequent commentary for so long.

However, these dominant paradigms that attribute broader linguistic or literary developments to single authors and personalities are extremely durable. They persist, for example, in the very influential writings of Harold Bloom, who has mounted the most vehement defense of the tradition Western canon of "genius." When writing on Chaucer, for example, Bloom seeks to untangle the mystery of his position between Dante and Shakespeare, working on the assumption that literary history can best be explained as a series of paradigm shifts from one individual writer to the next. For Bloom, Chaucer is the genius of pre-Shakespearean character, although this insight depends on collapsing the familiar distinctions drawn so influentially by E. T. Donaldson:[4]

> "We should not separate Chaucer the man, Chaucer the poet, and Chaucer the pilgrim: all combine in one loving ironist whose richest legacy is a roster of literary characters second only to Shakespeare's in the language. In them we can see burgeoning what will become Shakespeare's most original imaginative power: the representation of change within particular dramatic personalities. . . . Chaucer anticipates by centuries the inwardness we associate with the Renaissance and the Reformation: his men and women begin to develop a self-consciousness that only Shakespeare knew how to quicken into self-overhearing, subsequent startlement and the arousal of the will to change."[5]

I quote Bloom at such length in part because he is such an influential critic, writing for a nonspecialist audience (a perspective that is always a good corrective to the more narrow assumptions of any academic discipline), and in part because his view of Chaucer so eloquently captures for a contemporary readership what is in fact a relatively conventional view of our poet's skills: his genius for characterization, his knowing irony, and his uncanny insights into human nature. Bloom goes on, in this passage, to wonder at Chaucer's anticipation, with Shakespeare, of insights into human nature that Sigmund Freud "could do little more than prosify and codify."

What is the history of this view of Chaucer as master of character and master of irony?

The word "master" is not used lightly, here. Some of the first responses to Chaucer use such vocabulary very precisely, to show that Chaucer was seen as, indeed, a master of poetic and rhetorical discourse, inspiring a series of followers and imitators. It is important to acknowledge that before the development of the Romantic aesthetic in the eighteenth century, poetic art was firmly grounded in a set of rhetorical skills, as much as it took its first inspiration from nature, from experience, or from the imagination. This is not to suggest that the rhetorical figure of the muse was not important; indeed, it was a familiar mode in which to begin a poem. But a poet's deployment of that well-rehearsed trope could become a powerful indicator of his originality and inventiveness, from the outset of the work. The invocations to each book of Chaucer's *Troilus and Criseyde* experiment with different formal addresses to the Fury Tisiphone; to Clio, the muse of History; to Venus; to the Erinyes, the three Furies; and to the Parcae, the three Fates. Chaucer's earliest work, the *Book of the Duchess,* also plays with this convention. Here, the sleepless narrator promises an elaborate featherbed, fitted out with black satin sheets, to Morpheus, the god of Sleep, if only he will grant him sleep, only to undercut the dedication with a calculated aside "(Yf I wiste where were hys cave)" (line 262).

Medieval poets draw freely on a range of sources, and Chaucer is no exception: he reworks, translates, imitates, and parodies both his classical models, especially Ovid, and his predecessors in the European vernaculars: the authors of *Le Roman de la Rose,* Guillaume de Machaut and Jean Froissart in French; and Dante, Petrarch, and Boccaccio in Italian and Latin. As many commentators point out, however, Chaucer is the first writer in English to reveal any kind of anxiety about authorship as a mark of originality. His *Troilus and Criseyde* is deeply indebted to Giovanni Boccaccio's *Il Filostrato,* yet he avoids mentioning the Italian poet's name, while his own text is deeply concerned both with its relationship with its source and with the question of future posterity. Chaucer's firm reburial of Petrarch ("He is now deed and nayled in his cheste," 4.29) in the *Clerk's Tale* is equally notable.

Like Petrarch, Chaucer is conscious of his fame and refers to himself as a poet whose works are read by others. Some of these moments appeal to the immediate context of recitation or public performance, such as the frequent appeals to the exquisite sentiments of the noble audience of *Troilus and Criseyde* or to the bourgeois war between men and women in the Clerk's *Envoi* after his tale, and various knowing comments about marriage elsewhere in the *Canterbury Tales.* In a more writerly vein, the *Prologue* to the *Legend of Good Women* is concerned with the reception of *Troilus and Criseyde* and opens up a debate about the poet's courtly responsibility to women. Later in Chaucer's career, he adopts a more mocking, even insouciant attitude to his own posterity, as in the Host's brutal assault on his telling of the tale of Sir Thopas in the *Canterbury Tales* — "Thy drasty rymyng is nat worth a toord!" (7.930) — or in passages of less emphatic tone and register. In the *Introduction* to the *Man of Law's Tale,* the lawyer lists some of the many tales that Chaucer has told so badly — "he kan but lewedly / On metres and on rymyng craftily" (2.47–48). Finally, in the *Retracciouns* that conclude the *Parson's Tale,* for all their famous ambiguity, Chaucer shows how it is possible to move from a narratorial voice within a text to an authorial signature beyond it; to develop an authorial identity that can bring together a series of poems as a distinctive body of work, sealed and brought to finite closure by the imminence of death.

This growing sense of what his own poetic signature might guarantee and the implication of an authorial personality beyond the poetry, combined with the sheer rhetorical and cultural authority audible in a poet who was so able to translate classical and European style and content into English verse, made it easy for other poets to see Chaucer as a master and to adopt the vocabulary of homage in their elegiac verse.

The relationship is not straightforward, of course. It is one thing to identify Chaucer's mastery; another thing to emulate it or to adopt a similar rhetorical stance. Seth Lerer argues, indeed, that Chaucer's poetry is preoccupied with authority, in ways that often dramatize the subjection of readers and poetic imitators. "Throughout his major narratives, Chaucer presents a class of read-ers and writers subjected to the abuse of their audience or subject to the authority of their sources. . . . In such examples as the Clerk's obedience to Petrarch and the Host, the Squire's vain attempts to match his father the Knight, and Adam Scriveyn's garblings of the *Troilus* and *Boece,* Chaucer's inheritors found their personae."[6] Lerer reads the poetry of Sir John de Clanvowe, Thomas Hoccleve, John Lydgate, and others, commentaries by William Cax-ton and John Shirley, and other fifteenth- and sixteenth-century texts to show how these writers rehearse a readerly and writerly dynamic already anticipated and rehearsed in Chaucer's fictional scenes of reading and writing. They are thus doubly subjected to Chaucer's authority and must invent various more or less successful strategies for accommodating or resisting that subjection.

Whatever the specific relations of power and influence among Chaucer, his predecessors, his contemporaries, and his followers, it remains the case that they are relations structured around individual voices and names. In one sense this seems obvious, but it represents a dramatic contrast to earlier English understandings of poetry. Even the alliterative poets of the fourteenth century, contemporaneous with Chaucer, never refer to individual makers and poets but place themselves in relation to older anonymous traditions and styles of poetry, either to affirm their inheritance of that tradition or to lament its passing. Under the influence of Italian humanism, mediated through the poets he loved to imitate and outdo, Chaucer learned to make poetry an issue for individual poets and their posterity, and his followers picked up the theme.

In the English court of the late fourteenth and early fifteenth centuries, there was also a growing culture of royal patronage, which rewarded individual practitioners, not traditions. Under pressure from that competition, individual poetic careers began to take shape, both in rivalry (think of Chaucer's throw-away allusion to Gower in the *Introduction* to the *Man of Law's Tale*) and in companionship (think of Chaucer's appeals to Gower and Ralph Strode at the end of *Troilus and Criseyde*). Chaucer himself had to learn how to negotiate the vagaries of patronage. His *Complaint to His Purse* plays most elegantly with the necessity to please, entertain, and flatter while asking for favor, while his *Prologue* to the *Legend of Good Women* similarly improvises a scene of commission, with Cupid and Alcestis giving the orders, and a proleptic scene of presentation to Richard II's Queen Anne. Gower and Hoccleve both learn from Chaucer how to do this: but these are skills the *Gawain* poet, or even Langland, never really needed or troubled to acquire to anywhere near the same degree. We know, too, that Chaucer practiced this discretion in the turbulent factional politics of Richard's court, where his relatively low profile sits somewhat at odds with the growing authority of his narrative and poetic voice in this period.[7]

The poet who responded most fully to the challenges of that narrative voice was John Lydgate, and it is worth pausing over some of the critical problems raised by the inevitable comparisons between the two poets. Lydgate was only one of many Chaucerian imitators in the fifteenth century, but the dynamic of their relationship is instructive for our concern with the patterns and structures of literary reception.

Lydgate wrote far more than Chaucer, and many more manuscripts survive of his work. His name was frequently paired with Chaucer's (and Gower's) in the fifteenth century, and perhaps most remarkably to modern readers, his poems were often included, over his own name, in early "Complete" editions of Chaucer's works in the sixteenth century, as successive editions collected more and more examples of "Chaucerian" poetry. Modern literary study, however, finds room in its canon for only one major medieval figure, and the reception of Lydgate is a far simpler and shorter story than the reception of Chaucer. The volumes of Chaucer's *Critical Heritage* or Caroline Spurgeon's *Five Hundred Years of Chaucer Criticism and Allusion* are substantial documents in the development of a readerly history of Chaucer, from the praise of his contemporaries and followers, laments for his death, hundreds of imitations, modernizations, and translations, and a considerable body of commentary and elucidation.[8] Lydgate's poetry attracted only a fraction of this attention; although individual works, like the *Fall of Princes*, remained popular and influential in the sixteenth and seventeenth centuries, Lydgate criticism never generated its own affectionate traditions and patterns, as Chaucer's did.

In fact, Chaucer's star rose as Lydgate's fell. When modern critical comparisons are made, they are usually at Lydgate's expense, too, although the nadir of Lydgate's posterity came in 1802, when Joseph Ritson delivered what must be the most damning account of any poet, abusing "this voluminous, prosaick, and driveling monk," a "stupid and disgusting author, who disgraces the name and patronage of his master Chaucer."[9]

In the climate of professional medieval studies in the twentieth century, however, there have been a number of lively discussions about the poetic achievement of John Lydgate, though these discussions are nearly always framed in comparative terms, even in books devoted to Lydgate. Derek Pearsall finds only weak imitation of Chaucer's skill and verve; A. C. Spearing follows Harold Bloom's identification of an oedipal struggle between successive poets but names Lydgate as the weaker poet, unable to shake the influence of his master and capable only of a weak "misreading" of Chaucer, as his poetic father.[10]

When Lydgate writes about Chaucer to commend him, he invokes the idea of the laureate poet:

> And eke my maister Chauser is ygrave
> The noble Rethor, poete of Brytayne
> That worthy was the laurer to haue
> Of poetrye, and the palme atteyne
> That made firste, to distille and rayne
> The golde dewe dropes of speche and eloquence
> Into our tunge, thurgh his excellence (*Life of Our Lady*, lines 1628–34)[11]

Here, and in other poems, Lydgate praises the illumination Chaucer brought to poetry and to England while also voicing his own anxiety about following after him:

> To God I pray, þat he his soule haue,
> After whos help of nede I most3 crave,
> And seke his boke þat is left be-hynde
> Som goodly worde þer-in for to fynde,
> To sette amonge þe crokid lynys rude
> Which I do write; as, by similitude,
> Þe ruby stant, so royal of renoun,
> With-Inne a ryng of copur or latoun,
> So stant þe makyng of hym, dout3les,
> Among oure bokis of englische per3les: (*Troy Book*, lines 4701–10)[12]

It can be tempting to read such verses as measures of Lydgate's sense of his own inferiority or belatedness, to use Bloom's terms. Yet such statements are not necessarily our best guide to Lydgate's feelings about Chaucer, either conscious or unconscious, and it is important to distinguish between what we may call the official discourse of Chaucerian elegy from the actual practice of Chaucerian poetry by his followers. One of the central texts here is Lydgate's *Siege of Thebes,* which is prefaced by a long prologue, in which Lydgate presents himself at Canterbury, twenty years after Chaucer's death, and joins the pilgrims for their return journey to London, riding, himself, in Chaucer's place.

In this prologue, Lydgate seems to attempt to out-Chaucer Chaucer's *General Prologue,* in the complex syntax of his opening sentence, the length of his astrological conceits and his vernal poetics. His tale, too, reaches back further in Theban history than Chaucer's *Knight's Tale,* whose structural position it matches, as the first tale told on the return journey. Both prologue and tale can be read as straightforward homage to Chaucer (though Lydgate avoids mention of the poet's name until the very end of his *Siege*); until, that is, we begin to exercise our own aesthetic judgement on Lydgate's achievement. Derek Pearsall establishes the dominant tone here for modern critics, writing of Lydgate "gambolling in clumsy playfulness after his master."[13] In Pearsall's edition of the *Siege,* this attitude has become so entrenched and habitual that his editorial commentary becomes quite scathing, drawing attention to Lydgate's "often tiresome syntax," and the "distress" caused by Lydgate's frequent use of the headless line. Further, the "desperate editor has to call a halt" and impose a full stop after forty-five lines of Lydgate's opening sentence; and finally, in the most unlikely of these comments, Pearsall suggests that the Host's recommended cure for flatulence (lines 117–18) might reflect Lydgate's concern about his poetry's own long-windedness.[14] In spite of various attempts (several of them Pearsall's own) to appreciate Lydgate's achievement, he remains an easy target for satire. Reading Lydgate's poetry and his critical reception independently of Chaucer's remains a major challenge for medieval English literary criticism.

It is only recently that James Simpson has attempted a radical rethinking of Lydgate's relation to Chaucer, bypassing the poetics of personality and concentrating on the thematic and structural relationships between the texts of the two poets while also reminding us of the specific social and political context in which Lydgate was writing. Simpson suggests that Lydgate often "writes back" to Chaucer, setting Chaucerian narratives in the context of a much longer historical perspective. So, his *Troy Book* paints Chaucer's *Troilus and Criseyde* "back onto the larger historical canvas from which Chaucer's narrative has been scaled down," just as his *Destruction of Thebes* (Simpson's preferred title for the *Siege*) reminds us of the broader context of the events of the *Knight's Tale.* Simpson reads Lydgate as foregrounding his own status as "clerical narrator," using that position "to persuade English knights against imperial mission, and against the dangers of civil war."[15]

Lydgate's politics, however, appeared less dynamic and less urgent to writers of the sixteenth century, no longer content to cluster Lydgate, Chaucer, and Gower together. These three poets had dominated fifteenth-century literary history, but in Simpson's reading, Lydgate falls victim to the tyranny of periodization, becoming representative of the fifteenth century at its most medieval, the dull background against which Chaucer's star shines the more brightly.[16]

This is not to say that the image and representation of Chaucer remained stable or indeed that he was always highly regarded for the same qualities in his poetry. Each age, each writer of a national literary history finds something different in Chaucer to suit the dominant climate and aesthetic sensibility. As I mentioned, the Elizabethan poets loved Chaucer for his Ovidian and courtly love poetry. Edmund Spenser recuperates Chaucer for nostalgic pastoral, figuring him as the "God of shepheards Tityrus," the preeminent poet of unrequited love, in the *Shepheardes Calendar,* while later plundering him for chivalric narrative as he furnishes a conclusion to the *Squire's Tale* in Book 4 of the *Faerie Queene.* Here, Spenser rehearses an earlier elegiac mode, allowing him to lament the death of Chaucer, the "well of English vndefyled," while also stepping in to revive his "labours lost."

Other sixteenth-century writers, less concerned to take up Chaucer's poetic mantle, praised other aspects of his classicism and his philosophical learning. In his influential edition of Chaucer's *Works* in 1598, Thomas Speght included a "letter" from Francis Beaumont, who commends Chaucer's imitations of Homer, Virgil, and Horace, although Beaumont also strikes a new vein in praising Chaucer's imaginative powers: "so may Chaucer rightly be called the pith and sinews of Eloquence, and very life itself of all mirth and pleasant writing. Besides, one gift he hath above other authors, and that is by excellency of his descriptions to possess his readers with a more forcible imagination of seeing that (as it were) done before their eyes which they read, than any other that ever hath written in any tongue."[17] This is a crucial aspect of Chaucerian reception: his capacity to consolidate classical tradition in English while also producing the effect of what we would now call realism. Taking the lead, perhaps, from Chaucer's own pairing of *solaas* and *mirthe,* critics often praise Chaucer's learning and his realism in this way.

In 1700, introducing his translations from selected classical and medieval authors, his *Fables Ancient and Modern,* John Dryden picked up this theme, giving influential voice to the idea of Chaucer's naturalism. Dryden's *Preface* is a powerful document in English literary history, as it formulates a number of assumptions about language, poetry, and criticism that would dominate literary discussions for nearly three hundred years. For Dryden, Chaucer is the "Father of English Poetry." but his language is still marked by imperfection, since "he liv'd in the Infancy of our Poetry. . . . We must be Children before we grow Men."[18] The idea of Chaucer as a father figure is not original to Dryden, but he is the first to generalize the idea of literary paternity across such a long historical perspective. The narrative of masculine generation is also crucial to Dryden's understanding of literary history and the transmission of genius: "Milton was the Poetical Son of Spenser, and Mr. Waller of Fairfax; for we have our Lineal Descents and Clans, as well as other Families; Spencer more than once insinuates, that the Soul of Chaucer was transfus'd into his Body; and that he was begotten by him Two hundred years after his Decease. Milton has acknowledg'd to me, that Spencer was his Original."[19] Such inheritances, however, are held in suspension with a different kind of trope; the communion of poets in a kind of transcendent heavenly company. In Chaucer's case, however, as fits such a cheerfully childlike spirit, this company is envisaged in rather more informal terms: "I see   all the Pilgrims in the *Canterbury Tales,* their Humours, their Features, and the very Dress, as distinctly as if I had supp'd with them at the Tabard in Southwark."[20] This is distinctly reminiscent of Beaumont's praise of Chaucer's realism, while the frequency of appeals to the *Canterbury Tales* and to the convivial scenes of drinking, storytelling, and community also play an important ideological role in the formation of the Chaucerian community of readers and our capacity to imagine ourselves coming into Chaucer's presence.[21]

It is almost impossible to tell the story of Chaucerian reception without tracking this path from one influential (that is, male) writer to the next; and as these quotations from Dryden reveal, the traditions of earlier commentary and criticism establish their own patterns of influence and genealogy. This is particularly the case for Dryden, who combines the dual function of poet and critic and who exerts such a powerful influence on the development of literary criticism more generally. This is exactly my point, though: Chaucer's reception is closely bound up with the development of critical method in English. Writers like Dryden needed to develop a set of attitudes and opinions about the origins of poetry in English in order to write both a persuasive national literary history and to coin a workable and fruitful discourse of literary criticism. The specific features that Dryden identifies in Chaucer—the preeminence of the *Canterbury Tales,* his comic realism, his refinement of the English language, and, above all, his position as an early, and thus imperfect poet—dominated Chaucer studies and the writing of English literary history for nearly 250 years.

Many of Dryden's precise formulations echo through the years, as Ethan Knapp suggests in "Chaucer Criticism and Its Legacies" in this *Companion*. Of the variety of pilgrims assembled at the Tabard, Dryden comments: " 'Tis sufficient to say according to the proverb, that here is God's plenty. We have our forefathers and great-grand-dames all before us, as they were in Chaucer's days; their general characters are still remaining in mankind, and even in England, though they are called by other names than those of Monks, and Friars, and Canons, and Lady Abbesses, and Nuns; for mankind is ever the same, and nothing lost out of Nature, though everything is altered."[22] Just over a hundred years later, in 1809, William Blake echoes Dryden, in his commentary on his own beautiful engraving of Chaucer's pilgrims: "Of Chaucer's characters, as described in his *Canterbury Tales,* some of the names or titles are altered by time, but the characters themselves for ever remain unaltered, and consequently they are the physiognomies of lineaments of universal human life, beyond which Nature never steps. Names alter, things never alter."[23] The assumptions behind these comments remain familiar tropes in Chaucer criticism and are an important feature of Chaucer's canonical status, since one of the important features of canonical literature in English is its alleged timelessness and perpetual human relevance. Chaucer's language and some of his rhetorical structures may seem alien to modern readers, and there is no doubt that his work is also deeply imbued with historical references and contexts of all kinds. Nevertheless, Chaucer's abiding interest in human character enables his critics to lift him out of such difficulties. It is no coincidence that this is one of the qualities his critics persistently identify in the works of Shakespeare, of whom Ben Jonson famously wrote, "He was not of an age, but for all time!"[24] As we saw above, Harold Bloom has recently reminded us of this connection between the two poets. There are exceptions, of course, but English literary criticism and literary history repeatedly foregrounds the capacity to represent human character in all its diversity and its realism as the best measure of its poets.

This emphasis certainly remains a dominant strand in Chaucer criticism, especially in those who write of the *Tales* as a human comedy of character. Dryden's terms are still often repeated uncritically in many student guides to Chaucer. David Williams, for example, writes: "In the *Canterbury Tales* Chaucer shows us the moral struggle of men and women. The characters he created are historically centuries removed, but, through great art, are present here and now."[25] This is not to say that this is the only stream of Chaucer criticism and reception, but it has certainly been one of the most influential, in large part because it is an easy bridge between the more rarefied disciplines of academic literary criticism and the less specialized concerns of a general public or student readership.

As we have seen, Chaucer's rhetorical skills were deeply admired by his contemporaries and followers, while in the Renaissance it was his preeminence in romantic and courtly poetry that was singled out. A host of poets in the eighteenth century took delight in modernizing, or "civilizing" Chaucer's poetics into heroic couplets, with a marked preference for the fabliaux: the tales of the Reeve, Miller, and Shipman dominate Betsy Bowden's collection of such modernizations from the *Canterbury Tales*.[26] It is from this period that Chaucer's reputation for comedy and bawdy humor arises, a reputation that persists well into his modern and contemporary reception. Alexander Pope, for example, translated the *Merchant's Tale* as *January and May* while he was still sixteen or seventeen and returned to Chaucer to translate the *Wife of Bath Her Prologue* several years later, in 1713. Yet he was also drawn to Chaucer's study of reputation and honor and wrote his *Temple of Fame* in 1715.[27]

Another important strand of criticism praises Chaucer's sentiment, piety, and his capacity for pathos, though these qualities are usually also paired with the quality of mirth and humor. Samuel Taylor Coleridge finds the perfect balance of tenderness, sympathy, and masculinity: "I take unceasing delight in Chaucer. His manly cheerfulness is especially delicious to me in my old age. How exquisitely tender he is, and yet how perfectly free from the least touch of sickly melancholy or morbid drooping!"[28] As John Burrow points out, it is in this period that the tales of the Man of Law, the Clerk, and the Prioress come into the foreground, as tales in which "children or ladies suffer extremes of distress."[29] Against the context of much Victorian poetry and fiction, however, Chaucer's poetry seems perhaps less weighty, and it is in this period that Matthew Arnold famously excludes Chaucer from the top rank of English poets (see Knapp's essay in this *Companion*). Arnold compares Chaucer favorably to other medieval romance writers and commends him for making an epoch in English poetry and for "the lovely charm of his diction, the lovely charm of his movement." And yet, "The substance of Chaucer's poetry, his view of things and his criticism of life, has largeness, freedom, shrewdness, benignity; but it has not this high seriousness. Homer's criticism of life has it, Dante's has it, Shakespeare's has it. It is this chiefly which gives to our spirits what they can rest upon; and with the increasing demands of our modern ages upon poetry, this virtue of giving us what we can rest upon will be more and more highly esteemed."[30]

Such a comparison of Chaucer with other poets, regardless of the terms of comparison or the critic's conclusions, now appears as a distinctive marker of criticism written before the development of professional Chaucer studies or outside that specialized discourse. D. S. Brewer closes his volumes of Chaucer's *Critical Heritage* at the year 1933, "marking roughly the end of the tradition of the generally cultivated amateur critic and reader, who shared, usually unconsciously, the general tradition of Neoclassical, Romantic, and Victorian premises about literature, with their social implications."[31] All such dates are necessarily somewhat arbitrary, and as I have suggested, this "tradition" of general commentary on Chaucer does persist in important and influential forms.

It is clear, however, that as English literary studies has become more securely established as an academic and university subject in the twentieth and twenty-first centuries, there has been a dramatic shift in the kinds of criticism produced. As "English" becomes more fully instituted as a scholarly discipline, with all the benefits and constraints of such systems, Chaucer criticism and commentary forecloses on its own history, and reconfigures its issues and debates rather more locally, within the confines of a specialist field.[32]

The Terms of Praise

One of the most tantalizing issues raised by Chaucer's life is the issue of how Chaucer's poetry was received and recognized in his day. The external evidence is slight, and the internal evidence — the witness of the poems — often ambiguous. Certainly there is no surviving evidence beyond the poetry of any formal commission or reward: all the evidence that suggests court context — the *Book of the Duchess,* the scene with Cupid and Alceste in the *Legend of Good Women,* the frontispiece to the Corpus Christi Manuscript of *Troilus and Criseyde* — are deeply conditioned by fictional and imaginative constructs: the best means of soliciting patronage seem to involve the suggestive rehearsal of such scenes in poetic form, whether those works received material or personal support or not. We need to recall, too, that Chaucer depended on patronage for the maintenance of his salary and allowances as a court official, as much or more than he depended on political or royal favor for the furtherance of his poetic art. It is thus often difficult to untangle the evidence that survives about Chaucer's personal and social connections with the court and to weigh their import for his reputation as a poet against his reputation as a courtier and administrator.

Several of Chaucer's contemporaries, however, did recognize his poetic supremacy in his own lifetime. Eustache Deschamps addressed a French *ballade* to "Grant translateur, noble Geffroy Chaucier," praising his philosophical and rhetorical skill. And in their narrative fictions, the English poets Thomas Usk and John Gower both give speeches to Love and Venus, respectively, praising Chaucer as a poet of love. Usk's Love praises "the noble philosophical poete in English" for the poem he made of his servant Troilus, while Gower's Venus sends a special greeting to Chaucer, for

> . . . in the floures of his youth
> In sondri wise, as he wel couthe,
> Of ditees and of songes glade,
> The whiche he for mi sake made,
> The lond fulfild is overal . . .[33]

This is powerful testimony to Chaucer's influence on English poetry. However, Gower's *Confessio Amantis* is a profoundly elegiac, even nostalgic poem, recounting as it does the narrator's retirement from love, dismissed kindly but firmly from her service by Venus. This passage goes on to suggest that Chaucer, too, in his latter age should put aside the poetry of love and record his "shrift," or confession.

This movement *away* from poetry is mirrored in Chaucer's own *Retractions;* it is an important counterpoint to the themes of praise that dominate Chaucerian reception. It is easy to look back and chart this gratifying early interest in the poet we have come to love; but it is important to balance this pleasure with due attention to the intimate associations of poetry with morbidity and loss. As we have seen, literary history often appears as a succession of great poets, straddling the centuries through a sheer aesthetic will to continuity. Before these conventions were fully established, though, and before the great leap from Chaucer to Shakespeare could be anticipated, the dominant feeling in the fifteenth century, on the death of Chaucer, was a profound discontinuity and loss. Paul Strohm writes about the apparent inability of most of his successors to claim any part of his poetic inheritance, while Louise Fradenburg writes more generally about the melancholia and loss that have become structural elements in much of our writing and thinking about Chaucer.[34]

Chaucer's death was not a particularly public one, and he left no will, though these facts are not in themselves as suspicious as Terry Jones and the other authors of *Who Murdered Chaucer?* suggest.[35] Surviving testimony, however, suggests that his death was most intensely mourned among the community of poets and among his readers. There seems to have been quite a rush among his friends to gather the manuscripts of the incomplete *Canterbury Tales* on Chaucer's death and assemble them into a coherent order and sequence.[36]

Thomas Hoccleve was one of the first to strike this note in his *Regement of Princes,* which complains about Chaucer's death with the first immediacy of loss:

> Allas that thow thyn excellent prudence
> In thy bed mortel mightist nat byqwethe!
> What eiled deeth? Allas, why wolde he sle the?
> O deeth, thow didest nat harm singuler

In slaghtre of him, but al this land it smertith.
But nathelees yit hastow no power
His name slee; his hy vertu astertith
Unslayn fro thee, which ay us lyfly hertith
With bookes of his ornat endytyng
That is to al this land enlumynyng. (lines 1965–74)[37]

Consolation for Hoccleve and the nation comes in the forms of the works that will survive the poet's death, the "bookes of his ornat endyting / That is to all this land enlumynyng." Hoccleve encapsulates much of the early praise of Chaucer, whom he commends here for the sweetness of his rhetoric, his science, his "fructuous entendement" ("fruitful significance"), his philosophy, and for being "the first fyndere (poet) of our faire langage." Hoccleve's affection for Chaucer is also evident in his desire to memorialize him by including a portrait of him in the text.

The paired expostulations to Chaucer and to Death appear again in the anonymous *Book of Courtesy,* from 1477, a book of instruction printed by Caxton:

O fader and founder of ornate eloquence,
That enlumened hast alle our Bretayne,
To soone we loste thy laureate scyence.
O lusty lyquour of that fulsom fontayne!
O cursid Deth, why hast thow that poete slayne,
I mene fader Chaucer, maister Galfryde?
Alas the whyle, that ever he from us dyde![38]

As Thomas Prendergast puts it, "The fifteenth-century poetic heirs of Chaucer seem to foreground the absence of his body in order to lay claim to his poetic mantle."[39] Lamenting his death in such full rhetorical flight lays open an absence and fills that space with poetry at the same time. As I suggested earlier, it is a strategy many of these poets learned from Chaucer's emphatic burial of Petrarch.

This thirst for a personal relationship with the poet seems almost insatiable, even now, though it tends to take shape in the discourses of criticism rather than poetry. Linne Mooney's recent identification of Adam Pinkhurst as the copyist to whom Chaucer addresses his famous stanza of complaint seems set to generate a range of nostalgic expressions of desire to have shared this same kind of personal working relationship with Chaucer.[40] Now that we have a name, and perhaps a more authoritative ordering of the *Tales* in the Hengwrt and Ellesmere Manuscripts, it seems even more tempting to imagine a closer personal relationship with the poet, in his own lifetime, rather than simply through his posterity.

Sometimes the loss in these elegies appears personal, as in Hoccleve's case, but as time goes on, the mourning for Chaucer is often generalized through the trope of *ubi sunt*. The dominant text in this regard is William Dunbar's (c. 1456–1515) *Lament for the Makeris,* which groups Chaucer, Gower, and Lydgate briefly in one stanza as all taken by Death, with the echoed refrain, "*Timor mortis conturbat me.*" Other lists and catalogues organize their poets more critically. John Skelton in 1507, for example, made some careful distinctions. He found the poetry of Gower and Lydgate to be worthy in theme and subject matter, but Gower's English is "olde, / And of no value told"; and he writes of Lydgate, "It is dyffuse to fynde / The sentence of his mynde." In contrast,

> Chaucer, that famus clerke,
> His termes were not darke,
> But plesaunt, easy, and playne;
> No worde he wrote in vayne. (*Philip Sparrow,* lines 800–803)[41]

In the fifteenth and sixteenth centuries, Chaucer is praised and emulated on a number of fronts; as love poet, as poetic innovator, as rhetorician, as moral philosopher, as scientist, and as courtier.[42] These terms were rehearsed again and again, especially as the invention of print made it even easier to reproduce the terms of criticism. Poets may have internalized and repeated the terms of praise used by their predecessors, but they had to adapt them into their own narrative contexts of love or elegy. The context of print, however, encouraged the accumulation of prefatory material, increasingly in prose, that could be duplicated and repeated or collected, out of context. The history of Chaucer's *Works* in print is a history of the steady accumulation of Chaucerian texts (by Chaucer and others), *and* the commentaries, dedications, sonnets, and letters that precede them, especially in the editions that follow that of William Thynne in 1532.[43]

Although print culture did not always mark a radical disjunction with manuscript tradition (there was initially little change in the way collections of works were assembled or even in the layout, font, and design of many texts), nevertheless, print was quickly absorbed into and came to represent a more obviously commercial sphere of textual reproduction and circulation. This was not a straightforward transition — print and manuscript competed for cultural supremacy and symbolic capital for several hundred years — but this was a crucial period for the development of Chaucerian critical discourse. Thus, the emerging, if restricted public sphere of print directed Chaucer's texts and the work of his editors and commentators into a commercial context. This movement is signaled most dramatically in the split that becomes apparent between the stream of poetry that laments Chaucer's death while it seeks to fill that void; and the stream of critical prose that commends Chaucer to this new class of readers.

Caxton's prose *Epilogue* to Chaucer's translation of *Boethius* (c. 1478) and his *Prologue* to his second edition of the *Canterbury Tales* (c. 1484), establish the convention of bringing together a critical or scholarly introduction to the work in question, with some discussion of Chaucer's poetics, some biographical information, and perhaps some discussion of the textual tradition, with a general commendation of the work to the reader. Both texts invite the reader to pray for Chaucer's soul, but the tone throughout is formal rather than elegiac, and impersonal rather than personal.

Later editions follow this trend, and although it becomes fashionable to express a love for Chaucer that verges on the sentimental, it is a love that is closely aligned to the humanist love for the classical authors, where love is very precisely conditioned and measured by the scholarly labors of historical recovery. In part as a result of his own classicizing, Chaucer was the medieval English author most susceptible to construction as a humanist author, needing linguistic and cultural explication and commentary, and belonging sufficiently to the past to warrant the antiquarian enterprises of recovery and recuperation. So, if Thomas Speght in 1598 writes of the love for Chaucer he shares with his friends, it is a love that takes the form of the "pains" taken to repair the damage to Chaucer's texts caused by "injurie of time, ignorance of writers, and negligence of Printers."[44] This discourse of scholarly recuperation is very different from the mourning and sense of loss that characterize the responses of the poets Chaucer left behind. As editors and commentators, Caxton, Thynne, Speght, and others cultivated a sense of distance between themselves and Chaucer that permits the articulation of a more critical sensibility than was possible when the burden of poetic tradition and inheritance weighed more heavily on the poets who came immediately after him.

This distance has a marked historicizing effect, however, and many of these sixteenth-century editions develop an extensive apparatus of linguistic commentary, glossary, and textual elucidation. Ironically, Chaucer becomes a canonical English poet through the same critical formation that renders his language inaccessible without special expertise and assistance. Chaucer's linguistic alterity remains a vexed issue throughout his reception history and persists into contemporary debates. Is his language best treated as a minor variant of the "standard" linguistic currency of English poetry, requiring only light editorial treatment, or should it be embraced as distinctively medieval and subject to the rigorous, if somewhat forbidding discourses of philological study?

The story of Chaucer's reception, however, is a history of prevailing ideas of "Chaucer," in the most general sense, as much as it is about the history of his texts. Where "Chaucer" is understood as a historical monument to the complexities of fourteenth-century rhetorical, social, and political life, his works will appear with the full critical and textual apparatus; where he is understood as part of a continuous tradition of English poetry, his work will appear in anthologies and discussions of that tradition with minimal editorial intervention. A similar pattern is legible in the long tradition of supplementing Chaucer's texts: over the course of six hundred years, poets, novelists, and filmmakers revisit Chaucer more and more frequently, though with less and less precision, as his reputation becomes both more secure and more global.

Completions and Supplements

I earlier discussed several Chaucerian texts that play with the possibility of Chaucer recognizing his own authorial signature. This sense of a signature is to be carefully distinguished from a later conception of literary propriety, or the sense of personal ownership that would become so important to issues of legal copyright. In the late fourteenth century, such issues were barely imaginable. This is not to say, however, that late medieval English writing took place in a free-floating world of textual exchange. Although some aspects of medieval textuality are perfectly anonymous, and although poets did borrow freely from each other, Chaucer's poetry demonstrates a strong degree of prescience about the relationship between a poet's name and his works that would come to dominate literary criticism. Indeed, Chaucer's various presentations of himself as author and his relationship with the classical past and his medieval contemporaries were influential factors in the development of later critical practice, in the Renaissance and beyond.

The conclusion to the *Troilus and Criseyde* encapsulates many of these dynamics. Critics have often commented on the way Chaucer attempts to balance a number of competing cultural imperatives in this poem: his narratorial sympathy for Criseyde is established as a personal point of resistance to the narrative he has inherited (but also chosen) of her necessary betrayal and the turning of her story from romance in the first three books, to tragedy in the last two. Similarly, he balances his historical curiosity about the epic world of pagan Troy with his fascination with late medieval domestic and court life, in the sequence of domestic interiors and the long conversations that take place in those settings. One of the great achievements of this poem is to present a flexible narrative perspective while also convincing us that the narrator's voice is a relatively simple one.

In the final hundred or so lines of the poem, Chaucer moves rapidly in and out between these perspectives, shortening and lengthening his focus in an impressive display of narrative control as he gradually "takes leave" of his story. Troilus has deferred as long as possible the dual realization that Criseyde will not return to Troy and that she has accepted the protection of a new lover, Diomede. Chaucer refers us to Dares' fuller account of his military exploits but reminds us that he has set out to write of Troilus in love. He seeks forgiveness from the women in his audience for writing of Criseyde's infidelity, promising to write more cheerfully about faithful women. He also expresses sympathy for all men and women who are betrayed in love but then moves suddenly into a public exhortation to his "litel bok," to take its place in the classically conceived temple of learning, in the company of Virgil, Ovid, Homer, and others. The perspective contracts once more, though, to a proleptic apology for any mistakes in future copies of his English poem, implying that in register, theme, and style Chaucer's poem belongs with the deathless classics but that its language is mutable and uncertain. He then returns to Troilus, to give an account of his death, and in four stanzas effects a dramatic reversal of many of the generic expectations established in the poem, especially in the proems to each book. Troilus's spirit ascends to the "holughnesse of the eighthe spere" and looks down, laughing, on the earthly vanities that mourn for lost love and the loss of his own life. Chaucer then moves out again, bringing the focus back to his own audience, exhorting them to piety and spiritual peace in the universal terms of medieval Christianity. But still, the authorial voice returns, in the dedication of the book to two friends, "moral Gower" and "philosophical Strode," to open up the possibility of dialogue or "correction" of his work, before the final stanza dedicating the work to Jesus.

Shell-like, this conclusion seems to open and close in waves, as the narrative voice both opens up and closes down the meaning and interpretation of the poem. In contrast to many others of Chaucer's poems, *Troilus and Criseyde* does bring its narrative fully to an end, but at the same time it raises a series of questions about audience, reception, literary posterity, and the weight of philosophical and literary tradition. In opening those questions so deftly at the end, Chaucer also throws wide open the question of his narrative voice throughout the poem.

His vision of his little book kissing the steps where the classical poets pass up and down has a lovely doubled effect of humility while also placing the poet firmly in that honored company. Dryden was not slow to pick up on this trope of the heavenly company of poets. In some of its earliest origins, the canon of literary works or authors is very clearly, as feminist critics have often pointed out, a club of male friends. Chaucer's open invitation for others to correct his work functions similarly, as a modest, even penitential request for improvement while also drawing attention to the poem's "moral" and "philosophical" content. Whether deliberately and self-consciously or not, this conclusion sets out many of the directions for literary criticism: the relation between the text and its sources, its inherited traditions, its generic affiliations, its audience, and its posterity, all in questions arrayed neatly around the mysterious figure at the heart of the puzzle: the author.

Neither Gower nor Strode took up the invitation to correct Chaucer's text, but others did. *Troilus and Criseyde* enjoys a substantial afterlife of supplements and modernizations. These can be considered under the dual auspices of Chaucerian reception and of medievalism, as this complex poem is rendered into different forms for different contexts and occasions.

The most dramatic re-visioning of the poem must surely be Robert Henryson's *Testament of Cresseid*. Snuggled into his "oratur" in the northern winter, the narrator of this supplement, written in Chaucer's rhyme royal, summarizes the end of the poem "writtin be worthie Chaucer glorious" (line 41).[45] He then enacts a very Chaucerian moment, inventing "ane vther quair"

> In quhilk I fand the fatall destenie
> Of fair Cresseid, that endit wretchitlie (lines 62–63)

Chaucer was not the only medieval poet to appeal to an unnamed anonymous book, but his *Troilus and Criseyde* represents a most sustained elaboration of this trope. Henryson asks, famously, "Quha wait gif all that Chauceir wrait was trew?" and then glosses this comment and his decision to summarize the matter of this new book:

> Nor I wait nocht gif this narratioun
> Be authoreist, or fenʒeit of the new
> Be sum poeit, throw his inuentioun
> Maid to report the lamentatioun
> And wofull end of this lustie Creisseid,
> And quhat distres scho thoillit, and quhat deid. (lines 65–70)

Henryson begins with the traditional medieval dichotomy between a text that might be either "authorized" or "feigned anew," but the terms of discussion rapidly become more complex: Criseyde's lament is "invented" (in the familiar anglicization of *inventio*) and "made," but it also "reports" her miserable end. Henryson's text thus rehearses a number of late medieval anxieties about composition, originality, and testimony, in stances borrowed from Chaucer's.

In the content of his poem, too, Henryson seems to adopt a quasi-Chaucerian style of amicable sympathy toward Criseyde: "I sall excuse als far furth as I may" his heroine's femininity, her wisdom and her beauty, and her innocent fall at the hands of fortune. But this passage comes just one stanza after he has abused her roundly for becoming so stained "maculait" with her own lust and for going "amang the Greikis air and late, / Sa giglotlike takand thy foull plesance!" (82–83). Henryson goes on to tell a gruesome narration of how Criseyde is soon abandoned by Diomede. Praying at Venus's temple, she faints and dreams of how the planetary gods debate her case and the accusations Cupid brings before Saturn. The vengeful god condemns her to suffer leprosy; and so she must leave her father's house. In a lyrical core, like those that structure Chaucer's poem, she laments the turns and twists of fortune, but she is eventually integrated into the community of lepers. One day Troilus rides into the camp and is stirred deeply by the faint resemblance between this diseased woman and his "awin darling."

Henryson is not the only writer to find that Chaucer's sympathy for Criseyde opens up a space for a less equivocal response to his heroine. Wynkyn de Worde, who printed the poem in 1517, adds three more stanzas, also in rhyme royal, depicting Criseyde as, herself, the goddess Fortune.

> Of feminine gendre the woman most vnkynde
> Dyomede on here whele she hathe set on hye
> The faythe of a woman by her now maye you se.[46]

De Worde then slips easily into the medieval catalogue of faithless women, just as Gawain does, when the plot to trap him is revealed by the Green Knight.

When Shakespeare re-visits the story in his *Troilus and Cressida* he accomplishes something rather more complex with this long classical and medieval tradition. His Cressida is so different from Chaucer's — so much more sexualized, and so much more a public figure — that several commentators have denied Shakespeare even read Chaucer's poem. E. T. Donaldson, however, remarks, "I can think of no literary characters who have been subjected to criticism less cool-headed than Criseyde and Cressida; and when they are treated together they tend to become the two halves of a companion picture, in which the good qualities of the one are exactly balanced by the bad qualities of the other. Criseyde is written up at Cressida's expense, and Cressida is written down to Criseyde's advantage."[47] Donaldson wrote this in 1985, before the full weight of feminist criticism was brought to bear on either Chaucer or Shakespeare. Readers of the present volume are more likely to see the traditional polarization of female qualities and female characters into "good" and "bad," precisely the same move made by Wynkyn de Worde and the *Gawain* poet. It is this pattern that lingers in Jonathan Sidnam's refusal, in the early 1630s, to modernize any more than the first three books of the poem, since it would involve rehearsing "the wanton slipps of this deceitfull Dame."[48]

This problem — how to tell the story of Criseyde's failure to keep faith with Troilus while preserving our sympathy for her as long as possible — drives much of the narrative tension in Chaucer's poem. Those of Chaucer's readers who feel compelled to pick up this complex narrative in order to rewrite it for their own interests tend to flatten this feature, imposing strong and authoritative voices on the narrative, where Chaucer had proceeded by indirection and equivocation, and making comparably harsh judgments on Chaucer's most subtle female character. This reminds us that literary canons are not formed solely through the aesthetic preference for some authors over others. Specific patterns of reading are also involved; and in the case of *Troilus and Criseyde,* those patterns are determinedly antifeminist.

A powerful contrast is found in the variety of response to Chaucer's *Canterbury Tales,* among the many texts that take up the challenge to complete, retell, modernize, and imitate. The variety of response here is far more extensive, more diverse, and less programmatic. This should not surprise us, for two main reasons. The first is pragmatic: because Chaucer's poem remained unfinished at his death, its many gaps and incomplete tales and links between tales invited completion rather than the kind of ideological correction we find in the *Troilus and Criseyde* rewritings. The second reason is more thematic. Chaucer's collection of tales and characters seemed to capture the imagination as an idea, as an inclusive set of possibilities for narrative. The *Tales'* early reception history involves the addition of extra links and stories, woven more or less carefully into Chaucer's pattern. Later, a "Canterbury Tale" became a generic expression for a bawdy tale, sometimes completely detached from any Chaucerian or medieval context. In the twentieth century and in recent years, the springtime opening to the *General Prologue* and the drama of character have both come to prominence, so that the signifiers "Chaucer" or "Canterbury" generate a poetic reprise of that opening (heavily mediated by T. S. Eliot's *Wasteland*) or a collection of stories held together by the idea of travel, the diversity of character, or indeed their medieval setting.[49]

As Norman Blake comments, Chaucer's first copyists and scribes responded quickly and consistently to the idea of the alternation of prologue and tale. Blake insists on the primacy of the Hengwrt Manuscript, suggesting that all the various links, completions, even tales (the *Canon's Yeoman's Prologue and Tale,* for example) not found in this early manuscript are necessarily scribal.[50] Medieval writers, scribes, and editors were not so concerned with Chaucerian authenticity, of course. What seems to have possessed their imagination was the idea of completing such a rich, promising, and productive compendium of stories; it was a wonderful opportunity to stitch in other tales, and to join, somehow, the congenial community of storytellers. Modern Chaucerian critics have often positioned themselves informally as listeners, joining the pilgrimage company to listen and comment on the tales; in contrast, earlier readers positioned themselves as *compilatores,* adding links to connect the tales in sequence, or as storytellers, completing unfinished tales, or inventing characters to join the group to interweave their own tales, much as the Canon and his Yeoman join the pilgrimage. Some manuscripts add short conclusions to the *Cook's Tale;* others substitute the *Tale of Gamelyn* for that story.

Alternatively, the *Ploughman's Tale,* in Christ Church Oxford MS 152, foregrounds a reading of Chaucer as anticlerical satirist and ecclesiastical reformer. Several important supplements respond to the novel idea of the pilgrimage framework and construct elaborate "general prologues" of their own. Lydgate's *Prologue* to his *Siege of Thebes* is discussed above, but in many ways the more curious text is the anonymous *Tale of Beryn,* whose preface constitutes one of the most remarkable narratives of fifteenth-century litera-ture and response to Chaucer. Fascinated with the idea of the pilgrimage as a vehicle for a storytelling competition and with the diversity of Chaucer's char-acters, this poet follows the pilgrims into Canterbury and imagines how they spend the day there. The Knight takes his son to view the city's battlements; the other pilgrims form themselves into groups to go off drinking and sightsee-ing; for their part, the Prioress and the Wife of Bath enjoy a quiet glass of wine with the hostess of the inn where they stay. The *Prologue*'s deepest fascination lies with the Pardoner, however, who is presented here as the only pilgrim intent on sex, with Kit, the barmaid of the inn where they all stay. She and her lover, in collusion with the innkeeper, conspire to spend the Pardoner's money on a meal for themselves. In the end the Pardoner is savagely beaten and spends the night, quite literally, in the dog's kennel. What kind of corrective of Chaucer's homosexual and corrupt Pardoner is taking place here is hard to say exactly, but this is an extensive prologue, quite detailed in its composition and execution. The poem survives in only one manuscript, Northumberland MS 455, whose format also breaks up the customary patterns of tales in their groups, reshaping the work so that it might more closely approximate the plan outlined by Chaucer in his *General Prologue,* whereby the pilgrims will tell two stories each, on both the outward and the return journey. Chaucer's own tales of Thopas and Melibee are separated, for example, so that he tells one on the way to Canterbury and one on the way back. This arrangement more closely approximates Bailly's plan but substantially diminishes the self-reflective ironies we have come to appreciate in Chaucer's parody and the Host's interruption of his telling. Chaucer's voice is further silenced, in that while the *Beryn* author reproduces the Host's chatty introductions and gives him some very "Chaucerian" comments about the spring weather and the birds' song, there is no Chaucerian persona here, recording the pilgrimage.

Not everyone was so intrigued by the idea of the communal pilgrimage, however, or by all the tales. A number of tales from Chaucer's collection are lifted out of their Canterbury context and appear in other manuscript collections of religious tales. Similarly, parts of *Troilus and Criseyde* were recopied in different contexts.[51] The imaginative reach of Chaucer's poetry was a uniquely inspiring starting point for many poets in the fifteenth and sixteenth centuries, but we should acknowledge that many of these supplementary writings, commentaries, and recontextualizations depend on the relatively porous borders between poem and commentary that characterize the textuality of manuscript production. The "openness" of medieval manuscripts facilitates the rearrangement of text and tale or the addition of supplementary conclusions to Chaucer's works. The advent of print only gradually closed down these possibilities. Chaucer's textual history is stabilized for several centuries, however, in Thomas Speght's comprehensive edition of Chaucer's *Works* in 1598, at a time when Tudor poets were beginning to find print an acceptable medium (1598 also saw the publication of Philip Sidney's *Works*, for example). By the end of the sixteenth century, Chaucer has become firmly entrenched as a venerable father figure and as the founder of a thriving national poetic tradition.

Once Chaucer is securely entrenched at the head of this tradition, response to his poetry takes rather different form. As we have seen, commentaries, translations, and modernizations start to dominate the reception of Chaucer, and his texts now seem finite and closed rather than open and inviting new closure.

Conversely, with the development of a professional, academic discourse of Chaucer studies and the emphasis on Chaucer's poetry as an important part of the secondary school syllabus for much of the twentieth century, Chaucer enjoys a much wider currency in this period. Steve Ellis's *Chaucer at Large: The Poet in the Modern Imagination* surveys the extensive afterlife of Chaucer's poetry in the twentieth century, in drama, film, puppetry, fiction, poetry, animation, opera, children's literature, and heritage culture more generally. These reprises of Chaucer range widely in the extent of their familiarity and knowledge of their originals, but most take the form of explorations of the *Canterbury Tales,* the text that has become synonymous, to all intents and purposes, with "Chaucer." It seems likely that many of these examples derive from a familiarity with Chaucer learned at school or university.

This is a good place to end this discussion, then, as it raises a wonderful paradox for students and teachers of Chaucer. In this chapter I have emphasized the importance of the various institutions that govern and guide our reading, writing, and teaching of Chaucer over the centuries since his death. I have also tried to suggest that the historical particulars of Chaucer's case make him an exemplary study for the development of the conditions under which the canon of English literature takes shape. So, given the force and persistence of such traditions, is it possible to untangle the structural force of these conventions from any particular qualities in Chaucer's poetry that make him "great"? Or is it Chaucer's poetry that has defined "greatness" for us before we even open his book?

NOTES

1. Simpson, *1350–1547: Reform and Cultural Revolution,* 43.

2. Burrow, *Ricardian Poetry,* 1.

3. Robinson, *Chaucer and the English Tradition,* 4.

4. Donaldson, "Chaucer the Pilgrim," 1–12.

5. Bloom, *Western Canon,* 112.

6. Lerer, *Chaucer and His Readers,* 3.

7. See in particular Strohm, *Social Chaucer.*

8. Brewer, ed., *Chaucer: The Critical Heritage;* Spurgeon, ed., *Five Hundred Years of Chaucer Criticism.*

9. Ritson, *Bibliographia Poetica,* 87, 88, quoted in Matthews, *Making of Middle English, 1765–1910,* 43–44.

10. Pearsall, *John Lydgate;* Spearing, *Medieval to Renaissance in English Poetry,* 84–88. Of Lydgate's commentary on Oedipus's self-blinding in his *Siege of Thebes,* Spearing remarks, "It would be difficult to imagine a more inept explanation of one of the most haunting myths of Western man; indeed, Lydgate's only tribute to its power is to be found in his apparent determination to defuse it" (86).

11. Lauritis, ed., *John Lydgate's "Life of Our Lady,"* 427.

12. Bergen, ed., *Lydgate's Troy Book,* 279.

13. Pearsall, *John Lydgate,* 66.

14. Pearsall, ed., *Chaucer to Spenser: An Anthology,* 345–48.

15. Simpson, *1350–1547: Reform and Cultural Revolution,* 105.

16. Simpson, *1350–1547: Reform and Cultural Revolution,* 45.

17. Chaucer, *The Works.* The full text of Beaumont's letter also appears in Brewer, ed., *Chaucer: The Critical Heritage,* 1:135–39.

18. Kinsley, ed., *Poems of John Dryden,* 1453.

19. "Preface" to Dryden's *Fables Ancient and Modern,* in Kinsley, ed., *Poems of Dryden,* 1445.

20. "Preface," in Kinsley, ed., *Poems of Dryden,* 1450–51.

21. This is the central theme of my *Congenial Souls.*

22. "Preface," in Kinsley, ed., *Poems of Dryden,* 1455.

23. Blake, *Descriptive Catalogue.*

24. Jonson, "To the Memory of My Beloved," in Donaldson, ed., *Ben Jonson,* 456.

25. Williams, *Canterbury Tales,* 9.

26. Bowden, ed., *Eighteenth-Century Modernizations.*

27. Davis, ed., *Pope: Poetical Works.*

28. "Table Talk," in Brewer, ed., *Chaucer: The Critical Heritage,* 1:289.

29. Burrow, ed., *Geoffrey Chaucer,* 39.

30. Burrow, ed., *Geoffrey Chaucer,* 100.

31. Brewer, ed., *Chaucer: The Critical Heritage,* 1:1; see also the discussion in 2:1–3.

32. For a full and engaging account of changes in medieval English literary studies in this period, see Patterson, *Negotiating the Past.*

33. Gower, *Confessio Amantis,* 8.2943–47.

34. Strohm, "Chaucer's Fifteenth-Century Audience," 5; Fradenburg, " 'Voice Memorial.' "

35. Terry Jones et al., *Who Murdered Chaucer?*

36. See, e.g., Blake, *Textual Tradition.*

37. Hoccleve, *Regiment of Princes.*

38. Burrow, ed., *Geoffrey Chaucer,* 44.

39. Prendergast, *Chaucer's Dead Body,* 26–27.

40. The discovery was announced at the Congress of the New Chaucer Society in Glasgow in July 2004.

41. Skelton, "Philip Sparrow," in Brewer, ed., *Chaucer: The Critical Heritage,* 1:83.

42. The importance of Chaucer for Tudor literary and courtly culture, particularly his *Troilus and Criseyde,* is foregrounded by Lerer in *Courtly Letters in the Age of Henry VIII.*

43. See Brewer's facsimile edition of this edition, which also includes the prefatory material added to the subsequent editions up to the second edition of Thomas Speght's volume in 1602.

44. For fuller discussion, see Trigg, *Congenial Souls,* 132.

45. Fox, ed., *Poems of Robert Henryson,* 113.

46. The full text appears in Trigg, *Congenial Souls,* 119–20.

47. Donaldson, *Swan at the Well,* 86.

48. Wright, ed., *Seventeenth-Century Modernisation,* 86.

49. See Conrad, *To Be Continued,* for the literary trajectory of the *General Prologue* in the twentieth century, and for a comprehensive account of Chaucerian reception, see Ellis, *Chaucer at Large.*

50. These additional texts are usefully gathered by Bowers, *Canterbury Tales.*

51. See, e.g., Patterson's discussion of the fifteenth-century religious treatise for women, *Disce Mori,* which quotes knowingly from *Troilus and Criseyde* in its discussion of romantic love, in *Negotiating the Past,* 115–53.

Chaucer Criticism and Its Legacies

ETHAN KNAPP

This final chapter of the *Companion* considers the treatment of Chaucer in twentieth-century literary criticism.[1] Dividing the history of critical opinion into such periods is often an arbitrary exercise, but in Chaucer's case there is good reason to think of what we might call a long twentieth century as a distinct moment in his critical history. Chaucer has been discussed, described, and criticized in a conversation that goes back to his own lifetime, but the study of Chaucer in the twentieth century has been marked by one significant difference: the fact of its absorption into a university setting. Despite the distance sometimes assumed between medieval studies and more modern literary studies, Chaucer has been central to the curriculum of English studies since they entered the university in the late nineteenth century, and arguably no critical tradition shows more signs of the birth pangs and challenges of modern English studies than does that which surrounds Chaucer. Indeed, the literary study of Chaucer begins with a durable paradox, an anachronism even, deriving from the dual and contradictory roles that he has always been asked to play in English departments.

When we study literature in a university classroom, we take part in a cultural activity that first emerged in the late eighteenth century under the banner of Romanticism. Though the creation of fictive narrative is as old a human activity as can be imagined, it was the Romantic movement that established our notion of literature by reinventing the classical division between poetry and history in such a way as to claim a new significance for the poetic. History remained what it had been: the unembellished narratives of things as they existed and had come to exist. Poetry, by contrast, was newly imbued with a staggering philosophical task: the creation of imaginative visions that would not only create an aura of deep significance around the prosaic objects of the world but would use this symbolic register to trace the unity between the essential world of ideas and the simplest things of experience.[2] Poetry, in short, would create the synthesis between matter and idea that had eluded philosophers and theologians for millennia. However, partly because of these ambitions to reshape what had been an essentially metaphysical question into an artistic one, the proponents of this new art had from the start a complicated relationship with two powerful institutions of the time: the church and the university. For some, such as Samuel Taylor Coleridge, the symbolic power of art was a reflection of divine creation. For others, the claim of poetic imagination was absolute, a Copernican displacement of revelatory vision back to the human.

As the latter of these two notions began to gain purchase in the nineteenth century, this displacement provided the grounds for both powerful claims and some suspicion in regard to the social good that the study of literature might serve. In the early part of the century, with universities and colleges in both the United States and Great Britain still dominated by religious foundations and staffed by many clergymen, literature was often relegated to an extracurricular status. Literature was accepted by analogy with classical poetry and drama as a necessary acquisition of an educated governing class, but at the same time, the sensuality and agnostic philosophy flaunted by this new vernacular tradition barred it from a classroom where poetry was still studied mainly for ethical or rhetorical lessons. As the century wore on, the universities themselves went through a radical, and often traumatic, shift in their sense of mission, diminishing the importance of the moral education of undergraduates and taking from the new German university model an emphasis on science and specialized research. But this new environment, too, generated reason to be suspicious of literature as an object of study. The problem now was not so much an ethical or a theological one as it was a sense that there was no content to the subject, particularly, as the anxiety was often voiced, that there was nothing to examine a student in, and there were no facts to memorize or functions to perform, just—in the famous phrase of the philologist E. A. Freeman—"mere chatter about Shelley."

Literature's successful entry into the university required answers to both of these historical objections (its ethical-theological ambiguity and its questionable status as an object of scientific inquiry) — and the answers given then still shape many of the unspoken assumptions and unreflective practices of the field. As we shall see, it was medieval literature, and Chaucer in particular, that gave the champions of the new English studies their clearest answers to these objections. But in so doing, these early scholars also established an originary split in the field of Chaucer studies. By using Chaucer to substantiate literature as both an ethical pursuit and a fit subject for scientific inquiry, these early scholars created a bifurcated and paradoxical Chaucer who still haunts the critics: on one hand, the distant object of philological and codicological detection and, on the other, the jolly poet who rides alongside us, chuckling in our ear about a people and world that remains familiar and sympathetic to us. In part this is simply to say that Chaucer is still caught up in a question that has never been completely put to rest in English studies: What kind of knowledge do we produce and learn when we do English? Is it historical data or interpretive flourish? But with Chaucer this question is uniquely grounded in the long twentieth century of criticism in the university.

Beginnings: Chaucer and the Birth of English Studies

Although we now think of English as a central part of most higher education, English departments and schools of English studies have in fact emerged only recently as organized disciplines. Poetry has been part of the curriculum since the earliest days of the university, but the current disciplinary structure in which poetry is taxonomically divided into discrete national traditions and then studied for a complex of historical, ethical, and hermeneutic insights is a product of post-Romantic notions of what knowledge literature might produce. In medieval universities, a student would have read the Latin verse of Ovid, Virgil, and Horace as part of the trivium, the group of three verbal arts (grammar, rhetoric, and dialectic) that formed the most important division of the seven traditional liberal arts. These school texts were approached as material for grammatical and rhetorical commentary and were used to improve the students' abilities in the comprehension and composition of Latin. This subordination of interpretive issues to grammatical and rhetorical ones has had a lasting impact on the way poetry (and, later, fictive prose) was taught in the universities. The Renaissance humanists may have changed the canon by elevating the status of Greek literature, but even their fervent educational reforms resulted only in a new balance being struck between the importance of rhetoric compared to grammar and a new emphasis on the tertiary field of textual studies.[3] By later periods even the tentative steps made by humanist pedagogy in incorporating poetics into the curriculum had mainly been withdrawn, so that students in the early-nineteenth-century universities of Britain and the United States would have confronted poetry largely in Greek or Latin and largely as exercises in syntax and oratory.[4]

The sea change that brought a new post-Romantic conception of literature and English studies into British and American universities was first discernable only outside the bounds of the old institutions of higher learning. In the United States, most public discussion of literature in the nineteenth century was sponsored by clubs and literary societies. Under the auspices of the lyceum movement (founded in 1826 and growing rapidly through the 1830s and 1840s), speakers offered up literary history in the shape of talks such as that delivered at the Concord Lyceum in 1843 by Henry David Thoreau under the title of "Homer. Ossian. Chaucer."[5] During the same period, literary clubs sprouted on college campuses across the United States, often in the shape of fraternal and sororal associations that ran literary journals and might own libraries larger than those of their colleges.[6] The topics discussed in these groups were marked by the contemporary enthusiasm for Romantic and idealist notions of literature. Rival societies defined themselves by allegiance with the intellectual leaders of the new movements and did so with a polemical energy abundant enough to trigger schisms, such as that between the "Coleridgeians and anti-Coleridgeians" at Brown University.[7] The societies also sponsored conversation on aesthetic politics, ethics, and poetry, such as the debate by the male literary society at Oberlin College over "the propriety of the Ladies' Literary Society Library owning a copy of Byron."[8]

As the philosophical content of Romanticism had always shadowed the topics of theology, so the institutional forms of these associations, both extra-curricular and civic, often appeared as intriguing doubles to the religious institutions of the period. In the colleges, still often staffed by clergymen and influenced by their sectarian origins, the elaborate governing structures, decorated meeting rooms, and separate libraries of the literary clubs offer an institutional testimony to the separateness of a vernacular literature not yet respectable enough to enter the classroom. Similarly, groups like the lyceums functioned as what one might call an alternative pulpit. The Concord meetings were held at different times in the center schoolhouse, in the Congregational and Unitarian churches, and in the town hall; and the career of their most frequent speaker, Ralph Waldo Emerson, testifies to the ease with which one could leave the church for the lyceum circuit. Organized around a secular pulpit, bonded together by a revered set of texts whose ethical and interpretive implications served as the substance of regular meetings, these groups did much to impart respectability to the developing notion of a canon of vernacular literature, prefiguring Matthew Arnold's famous call for literary studies to take up the mantle for religion in the wake of the church's failure to provide a social cohesion sufficient to overcome class tensions in the industrial age.[9]

Even more clearly anticipating Arnold's position were English experiments with a literary curriculum in the rapidly diversifying educational institutions of the early nineteenth century. As the movement for more utilitarian education resulted in the foundation of new colleges ranging from the London Mechanics' Institute (1823) to University College, London (1826), English literature was often added to the curriculum out of a desire to offer a counterbalance to scientific and technical education. As D. J. Palmer describes the beginnings of this shift, "the attitude to Belles Lettres as a polite acquisition, a mark of social refinement, is transformed to a profounder conception of the moral power of great literature, a belief in its humanizing influence, counteracting malignant forces in a rapidly changing society."[10] In this context, English was to act, as the cliché had it, as "the poor man's classics," imparting the benefits of a cultural education to those without the leisure or institutional support to spend years conjugating Greek verbs. The notion of a poor man's classics was reinforced by trends outside adult education. The movement for the education of women created another proving ground for English, as those who argued in favor of allowing women to enroll in existing institutions often found themselves also needing to argue for the importance of the subjects traditionally associated with women's education, English among them.[11] Equally important in the short term was the inclusion of English as a subject for examination in the civil service exam of the East India Company in 1855, ensuring that English began to make its way into the curriculum simply because of the need to prepare for examination in the subject.[12]

Chaucer's work was surprisingly prominent in these early efforts, particularly in the area of adult education. Indeed, the heightened necessity in these experimental institutions for justifying their curricular choices resulted in a presentation of Chaucer that scorned the genteel appreciative criticism of an earlier era and worked self-consciously to place him within the new social mission of English literature.[13] Though shaped by a long history of readership, our own very particular, literary Chaucer starts to appear in this modern guise in classrooms conditioned by the pressures of a particular vision of English studies in later nineteenth-century England. What was the appeal of Chaucer in these classrooms? Whereas early foundations such as the Mechanics' Institute tended to derive the value of English from a vague combination of basic literacy and civilizing influence, later schools, such as the London Working Men's College (founded 1854), developed more elaborate rationales for the study of English literature. Part of this rationale was derived from a new version of the civilizing function of education, one attuned to an age of growing social democratization. In the words of the Reverend J. Llewelyn Davies, a Christian socialist and early instructor, the college was built upon the belief that "all institutions and history had a Divine purpose. Civilization meant being more civil: the raising of human fellowship to a higher level and power."[14] The complicated ideological mix that went into this notion of "Civilization" combined philanthropical idealism with the hardheaded politics that grew up in the wake of Chartism. The mission of the Working Men's College was to create a space where different classes of men might work, study, and learn together and, by so doing, forge a sense of culture that would overcome the class divisions that had risen so threateningly to the surface during the Chartist controversies. Not coincidentally, one of the leading figures in this project was also an eminent medievalist — namely, F. J. Furnivall, a founder and active supporter of the college and the founder of both the Early English Text Society and the Chaucer Society.

Furnivall's surviving accounts make it clear that he viewed instruction in Middle English literature as an intrinsic part of the political program advocated by the Working Men's College. Furnivall used these texts to cement a utopian vision of communal identity by presenting late medieval poetry as the site on which to discover the genesis of a coherent English national literary tradition, shared by all English men and women regardless of class. Moreover, this sublation of class was also reinforced by a very distinctive pedagogical tactic, namely Furnivall's tendency to emphasize medieval poets' own interests in occupation and, in the polite Victorian dislocation of class, station. Furnivall once commented that he lectured on *Piers Plowman* "because of its sketch of working class men in the fourteenth century," and his surviving lecture notes from 1857 consist of quotations drawn from various medieval texts to elaborate on the portraits of the pilgrims in the *General Prologue* to Chaucer's *Canterbury Tales*.[15] Ever since John Dryden's famous comment that the assemblage of personalities in the *General Prologue* shows "God's Plenty" itself, readers have focused on the depiction of character in Chaucer, especially in the great rogues gallery of the *General Prologue*. William Blake found there "the lineaments of universal human life," and this tradition still perseveres in the illuminated images of the Ellesmere pilgrims that decorate textbooks and the well-enshrined pedagogical trick of using the *General Prologue* portraits as introductions to the tales. As Lee Patterson has argued, this dominant reading of Chaucer as a poet particularly interested in *character* has served to underwrite the poet's essential humanism from Dryden's time down to our own.[16] But Furnivall's use of the *General Prologue* is marked by a significant revision of this humanist tradition, one that suggests a fragmentation of the old humanist confidence under the pressure of new institutional priorities.

Rather than presenting the pilgrimage, as Dryden and Blake had done, as a wondrously self-contained universe, he violates the space of the single text in order to draw in parallel figures from other Middle English texts and, by so doing, to substantiate Chaucer's personalities as sociological types. The figures in the *General Prologue* are thus twinned with others, such as "The Fat Friar" from *Piers Plowman's Creed,* a "Knight" from John Leland's *Itinerary,* and a "Ploughman," "Doctor of Phisic," "Merchant," and others from *Piers Plowman.*[17] We can see the purpose of such a sociological extension set out quite clearly in the study *On Books* (1865) by Furnivall's colleague, principal at the college F. D. Maurice. Maurice suggests of Chaucer that "in his 'Canterbury Tales' he has come directly into contact with the hearts and thoughts, the sufferings and sins, of men and women, and has given the clearest pictures we possess of all the distinctions and occupations in his own day."[18] What we see in Maurice and Furnivall is a yoking of an interest in historically differentiable occupation and distinction very alien to Dryden with an equal measure of his humanism, the mixture serving both to acknowledge class and its history and to subsume these categories in the larger shared realities of "hearts and thoughts," of "sufferings and sins" that were to bind all English men and women into a common national heritage.[19]

While Maurice and Furnivall disseminated this vision of Chaucer as a sociologist manqué, Chaucer and English studies continued to develop along two other parallel tracks, both of which I will deal with rapidly, as they have been well discussed elsewhere. First, like English studies in general, Middle English as a field owes much of its early history to literary clubs and societies. Most important among these, in the fascinating story documented by David Matthews, were those devoted to producing printed editions of the manuscript remains of the medieval past.[20] In a history reaching from the Roxburghe Club (1812) to the Camden Society (1842) to the indefatigable Furnivall's own Early English Text Society (1864), these groups laid the groundwork for modern medieval studies by providing the funding and organization that enabled the production of modern editions and, by so doing, fostering debate about philological history and editorial technique. Meanwhile, as the Early English Text Society printed vast numbers of manuscripts for the first time, German academics began to hone the principles of modern philology and editorial practice. Germany's recent reunification meant that its scholars were particularly interested in developing the philological tools needed to decipher the lost national history that they took to be writ mysteriously in the historical development of the European vernaculars; and the precocious development of the German research university gave the philologists the space in which to pursue such work. In short, because of the dominance of the German school in philology and the historical connections between the English and German languages, it was German scholars such as Julius Zupitza and Bernhard ten Brink who led the way in the nineteenth-century reconstruction both of the English language and of the manuscripts through which its earliest examples survived.[21]

Last, though I have been emphasizing the growth of English studies outside the major universities, we should not neglect the presence of the seeds of change in these institutions. English studies as a discipline had not been accepted yet on a national level in either Britain or the United States, but professorships of English had existed in connection with other disciplines for some time. In the United States the professors tended to be attached to the field of rhetoric, though with the founding of the Johns Hopkins University and the growing influence of the German universities more of these appointments began to go to philologists. In Britain, there were chairs of English literature established at University College in 1828, King's College, London, in 1835, and the discipline expanded rapidly through institutions of adult education, extension schools, and the foundation of new university colleges in the 1870s and 1880s.[22] The crisis point, the moment at which English literature changed from being an isolated, ad hoc pursuit, whose justifications shifted tactically from institution to institution, came in the 1870s, 1880s, and 1890s, with the hard-fought acceptance of English departments and schools into the major national universities of the time, especially Harvard in the United States and Oxford in Britain.

The story of the acceptance of English into these two institutions is similar, though it was a much more controversial and bitter struggle at Oxford. Both universities found themselves under pressure from two directions at this moment: on one hand, they were being urged to accede to the gathering momentum behind calls for the incorporation of English literature into the curriculum; and, on the other hand, they were also being required to undertake general reforms so as to move their universities more into line with the influential German model, leaving behind some of the gentility of their ancient programs in liberal arts in favor of a modern emphasis on research and the production of new knowledge. In some ways these two forces worked in concert to benefit the proponents of English. As the calls for general reform included proposals to reorganize studies (especially at Harvard, where discrete departments were formed), an opportunity was created for the consideration of new subjects, including English. In other ways, however, these two impulses worked at cross-purposes. The German model brought with it a new emphasis on professional rigor and with it a revival of doubts about whether English could be considered a legitimate scientific pursuit.

The claims to respectability for English in the university had traditionally been made through analogy with the classics, through the case that education in English syntax could discipline the mind in the same way as Greek and that English rhetoric and poetics could provide the same civilizing influence as Latin. But as reforms proceeded under the banner of a modern, practical education, study of classics came under attack. Their self-defense took the form of an insistence on the priority of philology in their discipline and a symmetrical devaluation of more "literary" insights. Virgil might exert vaguely beneficial ethical effects on his readers, but the only element of study that made the material appropriate to the university was the historical understanding of linguistic data. The advocates of English lost no time in adapting this argument to their own material (triggering much grumbling among classicists who feared the devaluation of their own discipline), and the rigor of philology finally formed the basis on which English was admitted to full respectability, with the creation of a department at Harvard in 1872 and the establishment of the Oxford School of English in 1893.

The importance of philology at this moment of institutional definition created a split in the sense of what English might be that has never left the discipline. The development of English as a poor man's classics in the nineteenth century had, in practice, little to do with philology and much to do with the post-Romantic notions of the power of literature to act as a secular theology, binding a nation through a shared aesthetic tradition. But the price of admission to Harvard and Oxford was the creation of an uneasy balance between the claims of philology and those of literature. In practice this balance led to an emphasis on early literature as required courses and examinations in Old and Middle English literature ensured rigor. It also meant that instructors were perennially bedeviled by the conflicting demands of these two disciplinary formations. As the committee charged with constructing the first set of examination papers for the Oxford school commented: "The Committee, in drawing up this scheme, have endeavoured to give equal importance in the necessary work to Language and Literature. It is not intended, however, that the subjects should be kept distinct on separate papers. It will be possible for the examiner to ask questions on literature in the paper on Old English books, and questions of grammar in the paper on Shakespeare."[23] The hopes, intentions, and possibilities of this statement give fine expression to the founding breach in English studies. And no figure suited the new formation of English studies better than Chaucer. The long tradition of commentary from Dryden to Furnivall had established his credentials as a fully literary poet, gifted with visionary insight and universal applicability. At the same time, his language and complex manuscript remains meant that he was the perfect object of analysis for philology and *Textkritik*. Chaucer was perhaps uniquely suited to satisfying the contradictory demands of English studies at this moment. He could be literature or language, ideological salve or historical sociology.[24] Indeed, one might even suggest that his canonical centrality was assured by the needs of English studies as they entered the university. As we shall see, the subsequent history of Chaucer criticism in the university testifies both to the continuing instability of this compromise and to the great difficulty of moving beyond its terms.

I turn now to the history of this criticism in the long twentieth century, breaking it down for convenience into three periods: Chaucer Industry (from the 1890s to the 1940s); Chaucer in an Age of Criticism (the 1940s to the 1970s); and Chaucer in Theory (the 1970s to the present). Given the great mass of materials produced on Chaucer in the twentieth century, my treatment is highly selective. Although I touch on many elements of these materials, this account emphasizes one strand of the history, an interesting sequence of returns to the founding problem of Chaucer studies, the disciplinary union of two very different historical trajectories of knowledge production.

Chaucer Industry

Along with Shakespeare, Chaucer was one of the two central canonical figures in the early establishment of English literature. He was the main named author in the early part of the curriculum, and the scholarship around him thus took shape via what Michel Foucault has called the "author-function"—our shared tendency to organize the universe of discourse into clusters of texts bound together by their association with one person, a proper name that anchors them and guarantees a cohesion of meaning by means of a particular structuring of knowledge and sentiments.[25] Shaped by this discursive function, the most pressing tasks of the early days of scholarship on Chaucer in its new academic environs lay in three interlocked questions: Who was this author Chaucer? What texts did he write? And what might these texts mean? Within the horizon of the author function these three questions are really aspects of the same literary and historical quandary. How can we reconstruct the fragmentary documentary remains, poetic and other, associated with this person Chaucer to bring a sense of this poet to presence, and having done so, how can we then guarantee that we understand him correctly?

The first step in this reconstruction was the establishment of reliable texts. By the late nineteenth century there was general agreement that the available editions of Chaucer were inadequate. The main editions available to a reader at that moment were Thomas Tyrwhitt's *Canterbury Tales* (1775; glossary, 1778) and Thomas Wright's *The Canterbury Tales* (1847; vol. 3, 1851). Both editions were handicapped by their exclusion of *Troilus and Criseyde* and of the minor poems that had become increasingly important in discussions of Chaucer. Moreover, editorial technique and knowledge about Chaucer's language, meter, and historical background had increased substantially in the century since these editions had been published, making both their texts and explanatory notes obsolete. Tyrwhitt had consulted more than twenty of the manuscripts of the *Canterbury Tales* and had used them to sort out the order of the tales, but his habit of moving from one manuscript to another, selecting a preferred reading from here or there, produced a patchwork edition that seemed irrational and piecemeal in the light of more modern, systematic methods.[26] Wright's advance on Tyrwhitt had been to adopt a version of the "best-text method," in which an editor chose a single manuscript as the most trustworthy witness and used other manuscripts only to correct clear scribal errors.[27] It was his misfortune, however, to choose a bad best text: MS Harley 7334, an early and attractively produced manuscript but one more corrupted by error than other early exemplars. Wright's edition was much criticized on its appearance, partly for his choice of Harley 7334 and partly because his notes were inadequate in giving the authority for his emendations, but it was reprinted in popular series in both England and America and remained the standard edition for fifty years.[28]

The edition finally to replace Wright was the Clarendon Chaucer, edited by W. W. Skeat and published in 1894, the year following the founding of the Oxford School of English.[29] A. S. G. Edwards has suggested that "Skeat's edition marks the beginning of a new epoch in Chaucer scholarship, signaling the beginning of its Modern Age," and it is hard to exaggerate its importance.[30] In order to provide a comprehensive edition of Chaucer's works, Skeat reexamined the canon as it had been established by Tyrwhitt, finally removing many spurious works, such as the *Assembly of Ladies* and the *Plowman's Tale*. His glossary and commentary are monumental products of the nineteenth-century advances in historical and philological knowledge, and they continue to influence interpretation. Most important, perhaps, Skeat was the first editor to choose the Ellesmere Manuscript as his base text for the *Canterbury Tales,* a decision that has been followed by most major subsequent editions (though recent critical opinion has sometimes urged the superiority of another early manuscript, Hengwrt).

Nevertheless, Skeat's edition also drew criticism. A. W. Pollard, the editor of the competing Globe edition of Chaucer's *Works* (1898), insisted on the superiority of the Globe text as "a *scientific,* not an *eclectic* one."[31] As Charlotte Brewer has argued, this accusation was meant to suggest that Skeat's editorial practice was outdated and imprecise. "Scientific" (or, often, "critical") editing referred here to the method of genealogical recension associated with the

German scholar Karl Lachmann and the tradition he had inaugurated. In this practice an editor first assembled all the known manuscripts into family groups that shared the same accidental errors, then constructed a stemma, or family tree of manuscript groups, that was to show the path by which new changes (new scribal errors) had crept into the succession of manuscripts copied from each other. Having established the relation between manuscripts and the points at which errors had entered the chain, the editor could then backtrack to eliminate these errors and produce a reconstruction of a hypothetical archetype. The final edition might look like no known surviving manuscript of a text, but it was taken to represent the original words of the author more accurately by virtue of this painstaking stripping away of accumulated scribal errors. At the other extreme to Lachmann stood Furnivall and the EETS project. Furnivall distrusted critical editions of this sort, calling them "doctored editions."[32] He preferred to print individual manuscripts as they stood, altering them only in the case of obvious errors, errors that might be spotted by a comparison between manuscripts and by the (cautiously exercised) good sense of the editor. Skeat's practice fell somewhere between these two methods. He worked through the comparison of several of the most important manuscripts but was content in the end to let many of his decisions concerning both the ordering of the tales and the emendations of individual readings evolve out of his own best literary judgment.[33]

In the wake of Skeat's eclectic work, two other important editorial projects aimed to bring the methods of rigorous Lachmannian recension to Chaucer's works, the edition of *The Book of Troilus and Criseyde* by R. K. Root and that of *The Text of the Canterbury Tales* by John Manly and Edith Rickert. A faithful believer in the power of a correctly constructed manuscript stemma to eliminate the need for subjective judgments on the part of the editor, Root faced a steep challenge with the confused relations between the *Troilus* manuscripts. His edition attempted to solve these difficulties through two postulates: first, that many of the differences between manuscripts were the results of revisions by Chaucer himself, of the poem being circulated in two versions; and, second, that remaining conflicts between manuscripts in the same revision group might be resolved by taking the complaints Chaucer makes about the scribe in his "Adam Scriveyn" as a literal comment on the mess made of the *Troilus* fair copy.[34] Despite the ingenuity of his solutions, these shaky postulates doomed Root's text, making it, in Ralph Hanna's words, "the elegant, rationalistic construction of a complete chimera."[35] A similar case, of even greater ambition but equally uncertain results, was the Manly-Rickert edition of *The Text of the Canterbury Tales* (1940). One of the most ambitious editorial projects ever undertaken, Manly and Rickert were determined to discover, via recension, a path back to Chaucer's words cleansed of the literary eclecticism of Skeat's edition. Manly and Rickert's work remains controversial. It was issued in eight volumes, two of the text and six of commentary, and the sheer mass of commentary in these later six volumes, the result of years of labor in describing manuscripts and determining manuscript filiations and textual variations has made them an important resource for later editors. Moreover, their work was more successful than Root's had been at demonstrating successive states of authorial revision.[36] Their text, however, has fared less well. Despite the laborious process of compilation, the text produced seemed quite familiar. With a text quite similar in practice both to Skeat and to what was to become the dominant text for the next generation, that edited by F. N. Robinson, and an apparatus so complex as to bewilder many readers, their edition was sabotaged by its unwieldiness.[37]

Despite the undertakings of Root and Manly-Rickert, the edition that still shapes the Chaucer encountered by modern students is the edition of *The Works of Geoffrey Chaucer* published by F. N. Robinson in 1933. The text was not radical in its editorial practices. Like Skeat, Robinson chose the Ellesmere Manuscript as his base text and edited by emending conservatively, based on comparison with a limited number of other manuscripts and demonstrable errors in grammar, meter, and sense. Robinson's edition became standard by the 1940s not because it presented a Chaucer text so definitive as to end all future editorial researches but because it offered a clear presentation of a familiar text (relying on Ellesmere for the *Canterbury Tales* and so not so different in most readings from Skeat) accompanied by excellent introductions and interpretive notes. As university enrollment exploded after World War II, what was needed was not the mass of textual data presented by Manly and Rickert but the approachable commentaries and reassuring solidity of Robinson's text. His edition was reissued with revisions in 1957, and despite criticisms, mostly centered on its use of Ellesmere, Robinson's edition is the direct ancestor of the text in which most students now read Chaucer, the *Riverside Chaucer*.[38]

But Manly and Rickert's labors were not in vain. In one of the not uncommon ironies of the scholarly world, what began as a subsidiary project became, in retrospect, the most influential of the products of the Chicago research team. Part of their initial plan had been to publish a volume of readings as background material for the *Canterbury Tales* and an updated version of the Chaucer Society's *Life-Records of Chaucer* (1900).[39] In 1927 Edith Rickert arranged for the archivist Lilian Redstone to prepare a list of all Chaucer records that could be found, and between 1927 and 1938 a research team gathered and evaluated these materials, working in tandem with the ongoing progress on *The Text of the Canterbury Tales*. The war and Edith Rickert's death conspired to delay the project until their materials could be taken over by a new pair of editors, Martin Crow and Clair Olson, in 1950, and the whole brought to completion in 1965. It remains the standard source for biographical data on Chaucer.

With the possible exception of the Variorum Chaucer, no scholarly projects of comparable magnitude have been undertaken since these editorial and biographical researches of the first half of the twentieth century. This first period of academic research on Chaucer was a tribute to the model of professionalized research that had been established as the central rationale for the presence of English in the universities. The focus of this research had broadened out slightly, enlarging the philology that captivated the Victorians with an equal emphasis on textual studies and historical contextualization, but its driving force still lay in the same model of knowledge production. Research in English was meant to uncover new historical data, primarily new or more accurate texts and documents and, secondarily, new historical contexts for these texts. All this was necessarily prior both chronologically and epistemologically to interpretive questions.

Nevertheless, interpretive work continued apace — though often with little connection to this outpouring of historical research. It is a striking fact that many of the leading historical scholars of the period such as George Lyman Kittredge, John Livingston Lowes, and John S. P. Tatlock published both fundamental historical research as well as descriptive literary criticism but kept the two endeavors strictly divided into different publications.[40] The philological and lexical intensity of Kittredge's *Observations on the Language of Troilus* (1891) is entirely absent from his *Chaucer and His Poetry* (1915), and his segregation of historical scholarship and literary inquiry is typical of his generation. In Kittredge's case this division of scholarly labor was clearly a metonymic image of a division in his sense of professional loyalties, his attachment to the tradition of Germanic philology that still provided a center of gravity for historical researches coming into conflict with his more belle-lettrist resistance to the professionalized specialization implicit in this model. Kittredge's Germanic connections ran deep. He had studied at the University of Tübingen in the late 1880s with the philologist Eduard Sievers, and one of his first published essays, "Zu *Beowulf* 107 ff.," appeared in the *Beiträge zur Geschichte der deutschen Sprache und Literatur* with the byline, Tübingen, 18 Mai, 1887.[41] In 1913, Kittredge was famously criticized in the *Nation* as a representative of that "Teutonic" scholarship that was suffocating literary sensibilities.[42] But Kittredge also chafed at this identification, especially as World War I created a reaction against "Teutonic" philology. When the Ph.D.

became more common and Kittredge's lack of the credential more anomalous, he is said to have quipped, "Who could have examined me?" suggesting that his breadth of knowledge exceeded that of any of the learned, and excessively specialized, doctors. Most strikingly, his celebrated lecture on *Chaucer and His Poetry* describes Chaucer in terms that seem a thinly covered self-portrait of the wide-ranging literary sensibility at odds with the professional. As he says of Chaucer's era: "In a word, it was a good age to live in, and so Chaucer found it. But, as I have said, it differed from our own in one regard: — the man of intellect read everything he could lay his hands on; he did not confine his interests to his specialty. . . . Chaucer's specialty was mankind."[43] According to members of Kittredge's family, he meant the lectures of *Chaucer and His Poetry* to defend himself against the charges of being Teutonic in his scholarship.[44] Of this Chaucer as alternate-ego (" 'Learned Chaucer' people used to call him, when learning was a title of honor"), Kittredge might well have quipped, "Who could have examined *him?*"

Set apart by this professional fault-line, what then was explored in the literary lectures and studies of the period? It is sometimes said that the literary criticism of the early twentieth century is essentially continuous with that of the late Victorian period, descriptive and appreciative criticism emphasizing Chaucer's humor and accuracy of perception. To some extent this is true, but these topics were transmuted by an interest in opposing certain Victorian criticisms of Chaucer, particularly those of Matthew Arnold. Arnold had thrown down the gauntlet in 1880 with his claim that Chaucer lacked "high seriousness."[45] He returns to Dryden's "here is God's plenty," and allots Chaucer the virtues of a "large, free, sound representation of things," but insists that Chaucer lacks the "seriousness" of a Dante, Shakespeare, or even François Villon. These remarks were taken up by T. S. Eliot and Ezra Pound as part of their own championing of Dante over Chaucer, and the question of "seriousness" thus became a spur for Chaucer criticism from Arnold to the Leavisites of the 1940s.[46]

In this early period, there were two defenses raised against Arnold's charge: a renewed defense of Chaucer's realism and an argument that humor and irony might achieve a higher truth than Arnold's seriousness. We have already seen the development of the praise of Chaucer's realism move from Dryden and Blake's humanism to the more political uses to which it was put in the classrooms of the Working Men's College. It may seem at first odd that Arnold would disparage Chaucer when he was proving so useful to those, like Furnivall, who presented him as the source of just the national culture Arnold wanted to discover through English literature. The dispute here is probably best understood as one over the nature of realism or, better, over the choice of which form of realism was best suited to represent English culture to itself. For Arnold, the representative touchstone of realism was often William Wordsworth, imagined as an exemplary English poet for his ability to heal a shattered culture through the lyric suturing of idea and object, to balance thought and sensual experience without letting either dominate. In comparison, Chaucer's realism was naive, a genial but simple interest in the stuff of the world.

In response to Arnold's criticism we see over and over again in the early twentieth century attempts to redefine Chaucer's realism as either of a piece with that of the Romantics or as an alternate realism possessing its own "seriousness." The attempt to equate Chaucer's poetry with the Romantic (or Naturalist) achievement is discernable in the surprisingly frequent references to Chaucer's "modernity" in critics of this generation. For Kittredge, "he is the most modern of poets," because "the fourteenth century seems less remote than the eighteenth; Geoffrey Chaucer . . . nearer to us than Alexander Pope."[47] For Lowes, drawing a comparison with Leo Tolstoy and Thomas Hardy, "Chaucer was as modern as the moderns, six centuries before their birth."[48] In both of these judgments Chaucer is related to privileged forms of nineteenth-century aesthetics by virtue of his disidentity with the intervening era of classicizing aesthetics. The historical scheme claims an essential similarity between the medieval and modern worlds in order to render Chaucer available as a valid Arnoldian cure for the crisis of modernity. A very different line of argument, taken up by Kittredge and W. P. Ker, worked to rehabilitate Chaucerian realism by devaluing the Romantic lyric self and associating Chaucer instead with novelistic forms. Kittredge and Ker both refer to *Troilus and Criseyde* as the first novel in English literature, by which they mean a work whose interest lies mainly in the psychological portraits of its characters and one whose author maintains an ironic (and certainly non-naive) distance from his characters.[49] With this novelistic analogy, they invoked the traditional emphasis on Chaucer's characters but made character signify not the external sociological accuracy of a Furnivall or the still fundamentally external "lineaments" of a Blake but rather a realism of psychic interiority. It was a realism closer to Virginia Woolf than to Wordsworth. For subsequent critics, the centrality of the novel, modernist and postmodernist, in the twentieth-century curriculum has made this novelistic model an appealing version of Chaucerian realism.

In addition to these arguments about the nature of realism, Chaucer's defenders used a reconsideration of Chaucer's humor and irony as another riposte to Arnold. "Seriousness" was a slippery term in Arnold's characterization, but it clearly suggested something quite different from the jovial pilgrim who was the received image of the poet. Lionel Trilling, for one, suggested that "Arnold does not really mean seriousness at all. He means solemnity; he means the knowledge of how to be 'sick or sorry.' "[50] In response to Arnold's canonization of grave solemnity, the Chaucerians insisted on the importance of a deep and multifaceted irony. The most influential voice in formulating this deeply serious irony was that of Kittredge. Irony, of course, is a complex term with meanings ranging from the simple sense of rhetorical irony (in which one thing is said but something different meant) to Romantic irony (in which irony becomes identical with the capacity of poets to reveal contradictory truths simultaneously — as in Friedrich von Schlegel's influential use of the term) to New Critical irony (in which irony becomes the capacity of language to harness the ceaseless play of paradox that makes a given utterance poetic).[51] Kittredge's innovation was to weave all these senses together and link them to Chaucer's humor, arguing that it was humor rather than poker-faced solemnity that created the most complex vision of the world.[52] Chaucer's irony was the source of his insight into character, for it enabled him to rely on an essentially dramatic structure, eschewing the monologic perspective of the Wordsworthian lyric in favor of the unobstructed variety and direct presentation of his cast of pilgrims. Similarly it was irony, for Kittredge, that meant the end of all the talk of a naive Chaucer. The humorist was not the naive object of our laughter but the sophisticated agent who caused us to laugh; in the mask of this poet we were to see the self-presentation of a Socrates, pretending his own ignorance in order to show us the gap between our pretense of knowledge and the complexity of the world as it is. For Kittredge and the Chaucerians who followed him, this image of the poet was to seem much more profound than Arnold's earnest lyricist.

Chaucer in an Age of Criticism

The next great alteration in English studies came from a movement that had begun in the 1920s but reached the peak of its energy in the period immediately following World War II.[53] In the United States its proponents were the New Critics, and in Britain they were a group organized around the journal *Scrutiny* and the leadership of the critic F. R. Leavis. Both formations shared a number of the same beliefs. Both were fundamentally reactions against just the division of historical knowledge and literary sensibility we have been chronicling, and both thought the solution lay partly in a new emphasis on method in literary studies. This method was to be "close reading," a practice through which the critic might shed the accretions of biography and history that they felt had replaced real literary response and instead confront the text simply through an intense engagement with the dynamics of its language. In effect, it was a claim that literary study itself had now accumulated a sufficiently technical apparatus, a sufficiently scientific method, to enable it to challenge the historians and philologists for the central role in the self-definition of the field of English studies. Along with this new vision of the critical enterprise went a particular vision of cultural history. Both schools revered T. S. Eliot, and both borrowed from him a deep suspicion of the modern world, a sense that modernity was marked by endless commerce and machines, by a fatal division between thought and feeling (Eliot's "dissociation of sensibility"), and by the swamping of literature beneath the flood of mass culture. In literature they found virtues to hold these forces at bay. Cleanth Brooks argued that paradox and irony were fundamental to poetic language and inoculated it against scientific rationality; Leavis argued, much in the spirit of Arnold, that an intense examination of life and ethics and mature judgment in literature could redeem the culture; and all of them looked to an ideal of organicism, both in the lost unities of premodern communities and in the desired formal attributes of the ideal work of art. Most simply, perhaps, both groups insisted on *complexity*. There was nothing simple about literature, and they meant to produce a criticism that would shame both the simplifying ideologies of modernity and steal the claim of difficulty away from the editors and philologists.

This new criticism was slow in reaching Chaucer. Q. D. Leavis commented in 1943 that "there is no good book on Chaucer's poetry."[54] According to Charles Muscatine, one of the early critics to adopt a new critical methodology, "she had not far to look; for in the same issue of *Scrutiny* there appeared the last of a series of articles by John Speirs, which were later to be revised and expanded into his book *Chaucer the Maker* (1951). Raymond Preston's *Chaucer* appeared the following year. Between them—and despite numerous and very British infractions of the scholarly code that keep them still much underappreciated in America—these two critics ushered in the modern Chaucer."[55] Partly because of generic preferences (the New Critics showed a preference for lyric poetry and the Leavisites for the novel), and partly because of the dominance of historical questions in Chaucer studies, new critical studies began to appear in number only in the 1950s. As with the earlier generation, there was, of course, some continuity between the critical interests of these scholars and the Kittredge generation. Nevertheless, the new work contributed several innovations, which we can see in the work of three of the most important representatives of the new critical movement in Chaucer studies.

John Speirs was the house Chaucerian for *Scrutiny,* and three of the four sentences in his sparse acknowledgments are devoted to F. R. and Q. D. Leavis.[56] His study *Chaucer the Maker* was important not for presenting a radical new interpretation of Chaucer but for adapting many relatively traditional thematics in Chaucer criticism in such a way as to insert his work into the Leavisite canon. This was a vital operation of renewal, as significant as Kittredge's defense of Chaucer in the face of Arnold's criticism. Speirs had three main arguments for Chaucer's relevance to the Leavisite project. First, his ostentatious use of the technique of close reading (much of the book consists of great swathes of text punctuated by commentary) provides an elegant, because entirely implicit, demonstration of the sophistication of Chaucer's verse. As the method of close reading was presumed to work only on language of a certain density, simply deploying it in relation to Chaucer would show the Leavisites that he was a poet worth their attention. Second, as was crucial in the context of a Leavisite emphasis on the moral and ethical purposes of literary studies, he revisits the need to "take account . . . of Arnold's charge that Chaucer's poetry lacks 'high seriousness' such as that of Milton."[57] His response to Arnold, however, amounts to a reversal of Kittredge, reverting to the Arnoldian and Leavisite tradition of respecting ethical gravity above humor but contesting Arnold's claim that Chaucer lacks such gravity by rendering Chaucer's humor into a mere surface manifestation of that most serious of virtues, "charity."[58] Most daring, perhaps, Speirs insists on the relevance of Chaucer to contemporary discussions of poetry by drawing persistent connections between his poetic techniques and those of the major modernists, particularly Eliot. His analysis of the *Canterbury Tales* begins with a detailed comparison between its opening and that of the *Waste Land,* and his footnotes expand the comparisons to include W. B. Yeats and D. H. Lawrence as well. His point here is not that Chaucer is another modern but that Chaucer can usefully be elucidated by comparison across the broad range of "authentic poetry."[59] By example, he sets the authority of historical differentiation aside for a moment and relies on the power of the critic to map the world of poetry as an independent, autonomous zone.

While Speirs set an example for the Leavisites, on the other side of the Atlantic E. Talbot Donaldson and Charles Muscatine took up cudgels for the New Criticism. Donaldson shared with Speirs a concern with many of Kittredge's preoccupations — irony, the dramatic presentation of character, and a serious interest in the implications of humor as a mode of art.[60] Donaldson, however, radicalized each of these notions in the service of an expanded, New Critical irony.[61] Most typical was his analysis of "Chaucer the Pilgrim." Quoting Kittredge's famous dictum that "a naïf Collector of Customs would be a paradoxical monster," Donaldson comments that "Kittredge's pronouncement cleared the air, and most of us now accept the proposition that Chaucer was sophisticated as readily as we do the proposition that the whale is a mammal. But unhappily, now that we've got rid of the naïve fiction, it is easy to fall into the opposite sort of mistake. This is to envision, in the *Canterbury Tales,* a highly urbane, literal-historical Chaucer setting out from Southwark on a specific day of a specific year."[62] Donaldson pries apart the realism of the framing narrative in a spirit indebted to the New Critics' detection of literary "fallacies," and he does so in order to correct "a confused notion of Chaucerian irony."[63] Whereas, for Kittredge, the figure of Geoffrey was the authorial presence setting the drama in motion and enlightening us all with his deadpan presentation of his characters, for Donaldson, Geoffrey is just another figure in the drama, a persona for the poet. The implications of this small revision are profound. As the author disappears behind the persona, the irony of the text comes unanchored and spreads into the whole of Chaucer's work. Now *Troilus and Criseyde* too can be said to have a narrator, even though there is no Geoffrey in the text, and with the proliferation of narrators comes the proliferation of the so-called dramatic principle where any one of Chaucer's texts can be read as the slippery product of an author forever hidden behind a succession of character and voices.

As Donaldson revolutionized the understanding of irony, so Charles Muscatine reshaped our understanding of Chaucerian realism. Muscatine's *Chaucer and the French Tradition* argues that the true meaning of realism lies not in a relation to the world but in a relation to a style.[64] For Muscatine, the *Canterbury Tales* was a drama of style, a mixture of high and low, of courtly and bourgeois that Muscatine dubbed "Gothic." By drawing attention to the manipulation of levels of style, Muscatine meant to reaffirm the importance of "realism" in Chaucer, but by redefining it as a purely relational and purely conventional mode, Muscatine hoped to sever this realism permanently from any associated notions of artistic naïveté. This argument was deeply indebted to the New Critical notion of the poem as a purely verbal artifact, freed of any necessary mimetic relation to the world, but Muscatine also meant to make his version of the verbal artifact historically specific, by building it up out of historically variable stylistic registers. It was, and remains, an important and ambitious argument, but it is also marked by a significant irony. Though Muscatine was more cautious than other New Critics about flirtations with a "modern" Chaucer, his main category of analysis is, in retrospect, inescapably linked to a specifically modernist aesthetic. Style, in his sense of an aesthetic ordering of language that implies a distinct relation to the act of representation, comes into artistic prominence with the novels of Flaubert and becomes axiomatic to high modernism. Its most sophisticated critic was the medievalist Erich Auerbach, whose *Mimesis,* a chronicle of the history of literary styles as a narrative of changes in conventions for representing reality from Homer to Virginia Woolf, was itself a deeply modernist text.[65] And, as Fredric Jameson has argued, the disappearance of authorial style (in the wake of the dominance of pastiche) is one of the chief barometers of the transition from modernity to postmodernism.[66] Distinguished for the subtlety of its stylistic registers, Muscatine's Gothic Chaucer fit well into the canons of modernist aesthetic value.

With the Leavisites and New Critics, then, we see the union of a conscious polemical insistence on the skilled critic's ability to operate without the supports of historical data united with an implicit commitment to many of the categories of modernity as the underpinnings of this criticism. Both of these elements sparked fierce opposition among other Chaucerians of this generation. Some reinvigorated rhetoric, as an alternative to the emphasis of the New Criticism on the category of poetry, arguing that the bifurcation between the two was a modern phenomenon and that Chaucer would have thought of himself as equally rhetor and poet.[67] Some continued to work on editorial and linguistic problems, and some turned to intellectual history. But the most distinctive response to the New Criticism was the exegetical method developed by D. W. Robertson, Jr.

Robertson's *Preface to Chaucer* was both an immensely learned assault on the method and aesthetic sympathies of the New Criticism and a programmatic essay in its own right that inspired a school of devotees in its wake. In terms of the tension we have been tracing between the historical and literary wings of medieval studies, Robertson placed himself squarely on the side of history, claiming for his work a strict fidelity to the historical object and avoidance of the subjective and anachronistic impulses that he felt marred the work of modern critics. Robertson insisted repeatedly on the absolute alterity of medieval aesthetics. Medieval poetry had no place for the productive tensions celebrated by the New Critics, nor was it touched by the obsessive interest in personality and psychology that had shaped literature since the Romantics. Indeed, Romanticism is an antinomy to medieval literature in that it celebrates the union of the sensual with the idea. For medieval literature, in Robertson's reading, the point was just the opposite. Robertson drew an interpretive method out of Saint Augustine's guide for interpreting the Bible in *On Christian Doctrine* and suggested that this method was adequate to interpret correctly all medieval literature. After much meditation on apparent ethical contradictions in the Bible (recorded in his *Confessions*), Augustine had come to the conclusion that interpretation of the Bible was not, properly speaking, a hermeneutic activity. It was not a question of finding out the meaning of a mysterious text: Matthew had said that the whole of the law depended on charity, and from this Augustine inferred that "scripture teaches nothing but charity, and condemns nothing but cupidity."[68] In essence, the Bible meant just one thing, said over and over in widely different ways. But if the significance of the text was known in advance, there was still a problem in reconciling those parts of the text whose surface meaning seemed not to concern charity with the knowledge that all the Bible must somehow be able to be construed to this sense.

Augustine's stunning solution to this problem was to open the text to allegorical interpretation: "At the outset you must be very careful lest you take figurative expressions literally. What the Apostle says pertains to this problem: 'For the letter killeth, but the spirit quickeneth.' That is, when that which is said figuratively is taken as though it were literal, it is understood carnally. Nor can anything more appropriately be called the death of the soul than that condition in which the thing which distinguishes us from beasts, which is the understanding, is subjected to the flesh in the pursuit of the letter."[69] The letter became the literal and the spiritual the figurative (or allegorical), and the proper understanding of the Bible (and the ultimate goal of salvation) then became dependent on the reader's ability to set aside the carnality of the letter and discover the sublimation of charity in the text. Having outlined this Augustinian theory of reading, Robertson and his followers began to apply it systematically to Chaucer and other medieval literatures. His argument for its validity was that allegorical interpretation centered on the Bible and guided by traditions of commentary and iconography was so widespread as to have been an inescapable guide to interpretation in the period. And if Chaucer did not always *seem* to be talking about charity, Augustine was there to remind us that the challenge of reading was to avoid the mere carnality of the letter. This exegetical method was criticized for a number of reasons—the questionable applicability of Augustine to the vernacular tradition, the central importance given to Augustine even in fourteenth-century England where there were other hermeneutic models available, and the questionable "historicism" of a method that insists on the universality of one mode of thought across a continent and millennium—but the energy of its practitioners and the sheer productivity of its method (no text meant what it said, so all had to be revisited in the light of commentary traditions) meant that this approach remained influential in American Chaucer criticism for some time.

Chaucer in Theory

So where are we now, at the end of this long twentieth century? And what has become of the compromise between literature and language with which the field began? Thus far we have traced out the history of Chaucer criticism as a somewhat irregular dance, with the very different trajectories of literary and historical inquiry circling, disjoining, and coming together again in a series of different arrangements, from the concatenation of sociology and "hearts and thoughts" at the Working Men's College to the self-divisions of a Kittredge to the battles between New Critical and Exegetical methods. As Lee Patterson has suggested in his well-known analysis of the last of these contests, it sometimes seems that "Chaucer studies . . . circles back almost compulsively to an apparently irrepressible scandal."[70] Whether we choose a descriptive language projecting a sense of originary traumas or Hegelian repetitions, it is in some ways tempting to cast the past few decades as a dialectical continuation of this struggle. As theory increased its influence in the 1980s and 1990s, Chaucerians took up positions pro and con along lines that seemed in many ways reminiscent of these earlier debates. "Theory" itself appeared in many instances as a sort of code-word for the refusal of medieval alterity, for a conviction that the vitality of medieval studies depended on its engagement with the contemporary analytic tools of poststructuralist thought; in essence, among Chaucerians, "theory" often occupied semantic terrain analogous to that which had been held by "criticism" in work such as Speirs. Concerns that this project hijacked the materials of medieval culture in the interest of an imitative and fashionable postmodern agenda were often voiced in an equally familiar lexicon, here drawing on the same accusations of "subjectivity" and "anachronism" that had been used by Exegetes and historians of earlier generations.

But to imagine the recent era as a simple reiterative gesture would be to give too little weight to either the crucial changes in the structures of literary studies in the past decades or to a wave of recent introspective work meditating on the nature of medieval studies and, especially, on the forms of the historiographies that shape the field's sense of itself. Perhaps the most obvious sign of a fundamental shift is the reduction in the sense of Chaucer's unique importance to literary studies as a whole and medieval studies in particular. Chaucer's centrality to the canon and curriculum of early literary studies has yielded to the broader canon of undergraduate education and to a general reduction in the teaching of Old and Middle English in graduate programs. Moreover, the singular prestige of Chaucer within the medieval canon has been eroded by critiques of author-centered studies, some deriving from structuralist historiography and some from more local arguments for the priority of broader cultural categories such as "Ricardian."[71] Although "Chaucerian" work remains a discrete category in professional bibliography and publication, it does so more out of a pragmatic adaptation to traditional curricula than out of a deep sense that this author is exceptional in the way Furnivall would have maintained. (A telling index of this shift in sensibility is the decision made in 1979 to name the journal of the New Chaucer Society, the refoundation of Furnivall's old society, as *Studies in the Age of Chaucer*, a name that broadened the rubric in a way Furnivall would never have accepted.) This leads to a difficult question for us. If certain of the tensions in the history of Chaucer studies were reproduced because of a consistent institutional drive to understand him as somehow both poetically exceptional and linguistically and historically representative, to what extent has this central tension survived the erosion of the importance of individual genius (of everything the moderns meant by style) in literary studies?

Complicating the question further is the matter of literary theory. Along with change in the constitution of Chaucer as an object of study has gone a transformation in the methodologies of literary studies in general. Until the 1960s the dominant methods in English studies were traditional historical scholarship (editing, biography, and the like) and interpretation working in the Leavisite or New Critical modes. With the 1970s came the arrival of literary theory. Usually glossed as a succession of interpretive schools (Marxist, Freudian, Feminist, New Historical, and so on), theory can also be understood to have arisen on the Anglo-American critical scene in a series of waves (provided we think of these not so much as discrete chronological chapters as overlapping and irregular currents). In its first phase, French Structuralism imported the linguistic and anthropological insights of Claude Lévi-Strauss to create a new, antihumanist, interpretive science. For the structuralist, meaning was not the creation of an autonomous human consciousness but a result of deep structuration of systems of language and signification — as the German philosopher Martin Heidegger had put the point in an earlier formulation, man did not speak language, language spoke man. Following immediately, or even simultaneously, was the arrival of Deconstruction, the name given to Jacques Derrida's extension and demolition of the structuralist paradigm. His focus remained on language, specifically textuality, but with an emphasis now on the betrayal of structured meaning by the inevitable movement, play, and deferral of any semiotic system. Meanwhile, at the very moment these French imports were arriving, university campuses were alive in the 1960s and 1970s with the new possibilities and constituencies of a moment of great utopian prospects. Feminism, Marxist critique, African-American studies, the decolonization of the third world, and the beginnings of a Gay and Lesbian movement each issued their own challenges to literary business as usual, sometimes in the form of research to expand canons of authorship and representation, sometimes in challenges to the positivist methodologies that hid any sense of the partisanship of the academic researcher. In the interaction of these political aspirations with the counterdisciplinary methods of the French imports we find the volatile moment of theory.

Charting the impact of the theoretical moment on Chaucer studies is a treacherous project. First, not all Chaucer criticism in this period has been driven by these currents. A great deal of valuable work has been pursued in the last decades in areas constituted very much as they were before the advent of theory. Studies in biography and Chaucer's sources have continued to deepen our sense of Chaucer's engagement with the classical past, with his Italian and French contemporaries, and with the pictorial arts of his time.[72] Similarly, work on Chaucer's language and texts has seen something of a Renaissance recently, spurred by a renewed appreciation for the insufficiency of single printed editions (such as the *Riverside*) to reflect adequately the many divergent manuscript remains of work such as Chaucer's.[73] Even if one were to set aside these relatively traditional avenues of inquiry, both the speed of theoretical fashions and the dizzying array of specialties now on offer make it difficult to map out the sort of neat polemical arrangement that dominated earlier periods. In earlier moments, we saw the continuing impact of the initial bifurcation of English studies resonate in various formations. But is there a comparable division in the field in our moment, or has the model of knowledge production diversified so exponentially as to have left us high and dry in the House of Rumor? Some have suggested that Chaucer studies are currently structured by a division between two models of historical knowledge, between the descendants of a nineteenth-century historicism and a more subjectively (sometimes psychoanalytically) inflected mode of inquiry. But I would like to argue that such an understanding of the field is, in part, a reflexive reiteration of the historical divisions we have seen, both insofar as this conflict is so easily mappable onto its predecessors and also insofar as the search for a dominant dialectical tension is in itself so central a part of the inheritance of nineteenth-century historicism.[74] Whereas earlier conflicts had at stake the validation of different models of literary study through their successful application to the founding figure not just of English poetry but of English studies, more recent innovations in method have been driven invisibly by the dissolution of the century-old compromise between the demands of literary and historical inquiry. By way of substantiating this claim let me offer a brief and all too selective sketch of the influence of four of the most significant theoretical modes to shape the contemporary image of Chaucer: New Historicism, feminism, queer theory, and psychoanalysis.

New Historicism is famously difficult to define, partly because its chief practitioners have a habit of refusing the label, but one can get a good sense of its working method by thinking of it as an old historicism that has been so contaminated by Derridean textuality as to lose any possibility of differentiating between literary texts and historical documents.[75] Documents, which would have been treated by past historicisms as objective testimony, may be read as only so many texts constructed through narrative and rhetorical arrangements, while the poems may be called upon to fill the old role of trustworthy witnesses in the reconstruction of historical data. Thus Paul Strohm, for example, can use Chaucer's lyric to his empty purse to anatomize Lancastrian concerns about the accession of Henry IV or, alternately, can read the primary documents describing Oldcastle's Rebellion as testimony to the utter constructedness of the event they purport to describe.[76] Other major work in the New Historicist vein has used the new fecundity of document and anecdote to supplement an essentially Marxist framework of analysis. In this category we would find Lee Patterson's *Chaucer and the Subject of History* (1991), with its intricately traced dialectic of individual subject and historical fate, David Aers's moving juxtapositions of the Statute of Laborers of 1351 with the text of *Piers Plowman* in his *Community, Gender and Individual Identity* (1988), or the reconstruction of the echoes of continental civic and political discourse that David Wallace performs in his *Chaucerian Polity* (1997). Because the New Historicism draws on so many of the traditional tools of English studies as we have seen them develop, showcasing both the dust of the archive and the bravura of the close reading, its products have not been jarring to established professional expectations. Nevertheless, its impact, though subtle, is potentially far-reaching. As the New Criticism had confidently broadcast the new independence of the critic from the historian, based on the professional rigor of proper close reading, the New Historicist tips the balance even further. If the historical document is denied its traditional difference from the literary and becomes just another text, one might wonder what remains then to the historian. Insofar as the model of textuality underlying the New Historicism is adopted, and with it the implicit claim that history (and philology) have become fully hermeneutic practices, the dialectical balance we have followed may have shifted decisively toward the literary and interpretive side of the equation.

More immediately jarring in its impact, and admirably so, has been feminism. Indeed, of all the new theoretical movements, feminism has had the greatest impact on the contemporary presentation of Chaucer's poetry. The representation of women has been a central topic in Chaucer criticism since at least Kittredge's argument for the "Marriage Group" in the *Canterbury Tales,* but Chaucer's thoughts about gender in early criticism were almost universally characterized as charming, liberal, and gentlemanly—reminiscent, in fact, of the enlightened Victorian outlook of many of these critics. (One thinks of Furnivall rowing with his girls' sculling club.) Feminist analysis of Chaucer has taken this genteel patriarchy as one of its principle targets. Mary Carruthers's landmark essay "The Wife of Bath and the Painting of Lions" (1979) disputes the sentimentality of many prior readings of the Wife of Bath, arguing that the Wife has a better sense of the boundaries between fantasy and practicality than many of the male critics who had written about her. In an Afterword to the essay of 1994, Carruthers reflects that her work "struck a raw nerve among Chaucerians," in part because even male critics putatively sympathetic to feminism found themselves disturbed by the prospect of a female power that was not properly channeled through either authoritative discourse or male agency.[77] Carolyn Dinshaw's *Chaucer's Sexual Poetics* (1989) embedded the consideration of gender into the heart of Chaucer's poetics by arguing that Chaucer often represents himself writing as a woman because the "extraordinary and difficult attempts to envision fully the place of the Other in patriarchal society — to imagine even the pleasures and pains of a woman's body . . . motivate, to a large extent, Chaucer's thematic concerns as well as the very forms and structures of his society."[78] In contrast, Elaine Tuttle Hansen's *Chaucer and the Fictions of Gender* (1992) presents, with some palpable regret but great acuity, a refusal of this feminist Chaucer. Like Dinshaw, Tuttle believes that Chaucer was deeply interested in gender, but his occasional adoption of a self-feminized persona does not convince her of any fundamental sympathy with feminine experience. On the contrary, his experiments with a feminized self-presentation are used to describe the vulnerabilities and marginalizations to which even men were vulnerable. And, as Hansen astutely observes, "representations of the vicissitudes of masculine identity in a patriarchal culture, then, do not necessarily entail abandoning its potential privilege."[79] As with the New Historicism, part of the polemical charge of feminism has come from its renegotiation of the relation between the critic and her object. Though nineteenth-century critics might occasionally have pointed to questionable aesthetic choices or ethical missteps, feminism's opposition to the currents of misogyny in the canon has led inevitably to an emphasis on making explicit the standpoint of the engaged critic.

Similar pressures have shaped the development of queer theory. Queer theory has roots in feminism and in sexuality studies' work on the construction of gender and sexuality, but it also takes much of its energy from AIDS activism and keeps a distance from the straitlaced models of an older gay and lesbian studies. This movement has brought two significant new insights to Chaucerian interpretation: first, a renewed attention to sexuality in the *Canterbury Tales,* especially, but not only, in the portrait of the Pardoner; and, second, a challenging emphasis, inherited from feminist theory but taken, perhaps, even further, on the subjective and affective foundations of any given critical practice. It is an irony entirely in the spirit of queer theory that so much of the scholarship on the Pardoner has been an attempt to fix and identify his sexuality. Monica McAlpine began the most recent round of discussion by identifying him as almost certainly homosexual in "The Pardoner's Homosexuality and How It Matters" (1980). Later essays by Richard Firth Green and C. David Benson persuasively dispute this conclusion, but the most striking thing about the best recent work on the character is how little a factual solution seems to matter.[80] For Steven Kruger, our decision to "reclaim the pardoner" is a necessary commitment of our own intention to "regain for ourselves a piece of the history of homophobia, a sense of the particular medieval voicings of revulsion against persons of queer sexuality."[81] Glenn Burger and Carolyn Dinshaw both focus on the ambiguous physicality of the Pardoner as an invitation to intimacy. For Burger, the fact that we are brought face to face with the Pardoner's kiss at the end of the tale forces us to confront our own immersion in the open secret of his identity.[82] For Dinshaw, the Pardoner is a body that leads her to consider "the touch of the queer," the way her own sexual identity inflects her historical practice by creating a sudden arc of sympathy across manifest historical differences. This is an approach clearly indebted to the impact of so-called standpoint theory in feminism, but we also see something new emerging in queer theory (and in some recent feminist analysis as well). In each of these daring historical constructions we see a careful articulation of the role of affect in the literary historian. The standpoint of the investigator is here important not only because of its ethical differentiation but also because of its usefulness in mapping out the variety of affective responses one might discover in relation to a given text or author.

Finally, this historiographical construction has also been a theme in recent psychoanalytic criticism. The use of psychoanalytic categories seems almost inevitable in a critical tradition so centered on character and dramatic modes, and Freudian and Lacanian psychoanalysis have been used to good effect in analysis of the *Canterbury Tales* and their tellers by such critics as Marshall Leicester.[83] In more recent years, Louise Fradenburg has turned to psychoanalysis to argue that classic nineteenth-century historicism is marked by an institutional repression of the desire of the critic. Where traditional academic historicism would insist on its objectivity and guarantee that objectivity by an ascetic eschewal of error, Fradenburg suggests that "techniques of knowledge production do not negate, but are forms of, desire."[84] Though Fradenburg might resist the suggestion, her work is in some ways best situated as part of the recent boom in studies of the history of Chaucer's readers. From Seth Lerer's work on Chaucer's fifteenth-century readers to David Matthews and Stephanie Trigg on the long history of Chaucer criticism, recent studies have documented both the continuities and drastic shifts in Chaucer's reception.[85] Trigg's study, in particular, works with great psychological subtlety to show the delicate lines of affinity that have shaped critics' imaginative relationship with Chaucer, and in so doing it raises a question of unavoidable importance: If the tradition of academic commentary on Chaucer is underwritten and legitimated by repetitive gestures of identification with him and with his first audience (the "primal scene of reception") does this then threaten to delegitimize the work of the critic whose gender (or race or ethnicity) would bar them from this charmed circle of "congenial souls"?[86] Or does it suggest that the role of the critic may be undergoing a historical mutation, another shift in its relationship to historical *Wissenschaft?*

And with these questions we come perhaps to the most distinctive crux in the recent criticism of Chaucer. Clearly the dialectical tensions of language and literature, of objectivity and standpoints still play across the field of Chaucer studies. But as I suggested above, we should hesitate before allowing these differences to crystallize into the familiar oppositions of Romantic expressionism versus Weberian scientificity. The pressures of our moment need to be thought through within the new conditions of English studies. The older categories that underwrote English studies at its foundation were simultaneously epistemological and ethical: they understood the question of interpretation as one of fidelity to a voice, either a named author or an anonymous document. With the supersession of author-centered curricula and the diffusion of voice into discourse, this ethical situation seems no longer adequate to describe the dilemmas facing the literary critic. What we see in recent critical discourse on Chaucer is arguably an attempt to feel our way into an honest and searching connection in a relation that is no longer governed by the same canons of fidelity. In some cases, it may risk a nostalgic re-creation of older encounters, but it seems quite probable that the creative energy of this search will be the element that typifies our moment for future critics.

NOTES

Author's note: I thank Lisa Kiser and Alastair Minnis for their valuable comments on an earlier version of this essay.

1. Useful surveys of shorter periods in Chaucer criticism include: Benson, "Reader's Guide to Writings on Chaucer"; Brewer, "Criticism of Chaucer in the Twentieth Century"; Pearsall, "Chaucer's Poetry and Its Modern Commentators"; Ridley, "State of Chaucer Studies"; Saunders, "Development of Chaucer Criticism"; and, especially valuable, Patterson, "Historical Criticism and the Development of Chaucer Studies." A stimulating survey of the development of medieval studies in general may be found in Middleton, "Medieval Studies."

2. On the theoretical bases of literary Romanticism, see Lacoue-Labarthe and Nancy, *Literary Absolute.*

3. Percival, "Renaissance Grammar."

4. At Yale College, for example, it was only in 1876 that a course called "English Literature and Disputation" was added to the required freshman courses in Greek, Latin, and mathematics. Scholes, *Rise and Fall of English,* 10.

5. Spurgeon, *Five Hundred Years of Chaucer Criticism and Allusion,* 2:3, 250.

6. Graff, *Professing Literature,* 44.

7. Graff, *Professing Literature,* 46.

8. Graff, *Professing Literature,* 45.

9. As Arnold puts it in his "The Study of Poetry": "The future of poetry is immense, because in poetry, where it is worthy of its high destinies, our race, as time goes on, will find an ever surer and surer stay. There is not a creed which is not shaken, not an accredited dogma which is not shown to be questionable, not a received tradition which does not threaten to dissolve. Our religion has materialized itself in the fact, in the supposed fact; it has attached its emotion to the fact, and now the fact is failing it. But for poetry the idea is everything; the rest is a world of illusion, of divine illusion. Poetry attaches its emotion to the idea; the idea *is* the fact. The strongest part of our religion today is its unconscious poetry" (1–2).

10. Palmer, *Rise of English Studies,* 15.

11. On this point see Baldick's fine study, *Social Mission of English Criticism,* 67–69.

12. Palmer, *Rise of English Studies,* 46–7.

13. I allude here to Baldick's study.

14. Palmer, *Rise of English Studies,* 36.

15. Cited in the biographical sketch by John James Munro in *Frederick James Furnivall,* xxxvi.

16. Patterson, *Chaucer and the Subject of History,* 15–16.

17. Spurgeon, *Five Hundred Years of Chaucer Criticism and Allusion,* 2:3, 37.

18. Spurgeon, *Five Hundred Years of Chaucer Criticism and Allusion,* 2:3, 79.

19. The gender inclusivity of the language is also far from accidental here, and testifies again to the influence of the movement for women's education on men like Furnivall and Maurice. On the complex figuration of gender in Furnivall's writing, see Ward, " 'My Love for Chaucer,' " 44–57.

20. Matthews, *Making of Middle English.*

21. Utz, *Chaucer and the Discourse of German Philology.*

22. Palmer, *Rise of English Studies,* 56.

23. Cited in Palmer, *Rise of English Studies,* 113.

24. For an analysis of a similar tension between the demands of Romanticism and philology in the context of Anglo-Saxon studies, see the fine analysis in Frantzen, *Desire for Origins,* 62–98.

25. Foucault, "What Is an Author?" 113–38. We might note that part of the author function, unobserved by Foucault, is its role in suturing the literary and historical — hence, perhaps, the durability of the author in modern syllabi and research agendas despite the numerous demonstrations of the methodological limitations of the category.

26. Windeatt, "Thomas Tyrwhitt," 117–44. See also Blake, *Textual Tradition of the "Canterbury Tales,"* 9–14.

27. Ross, "Thomas Wright," 145–56. On Harley 7334, see Owen, *Manuscripts of the "Canterbury Tales,"* 9–11.

28. Ross, "Thomas Wright," 154.

29. Skeat was a former curate who was pressed into service as an editor by Furnivall in 1864. Though Skeat had no particular experience working with manuscripts, Furnivall introduced him to Henry Bradshaw, the eminent codicologist and librarian at Cambridge University, and set him to work on an edition of *Lancelot of the Laik*. The edition was such a success that it led Skeat to take on an edition of *Piers Plowman,* to be elected as the first holder of the new Elrington and Bosworth chair in Anglo-Saxon in 1878, and finally to his edition of Chaucer in 1894. See Brewer, *Editing Piers Plowman,* 91–112.

30. Edwards, "Walter Skeat," 171.

31. Cited in Brewer, "Critical, Scientific and Eclectic Editing," 16–17.

32. Cited in Brewer, "Critical, Scientific and Eclectic Editing," 26.

33. Skeat also, as Edwards notes, allowed himself to be swayed by established tradition, retaining the order of the tales from the Chaucer Society's Six-Text Chaucer without generating a convincing rationale for the decision. Edwards, "Walter Skeat," 179–82.

34. "The poet's own draft of his poem, confused it would seem, on many a page by erasures and interlineations, was turned over to a professional scribe, who made from it a fair copy. The copy contained not only the errors which are inevitable in the work of transcription, but others which arose from Adam's failure to understand here and there his employer's final intention, obscured as it was by a tangle of rewritings and blotted lines." Root, *Book of Troilus and Criseyde,* lxxvii.

35. Hanna, "Robert K. Root," 194.

36. Pearsall, "Authorial Revision," 39–48.

37. Pearsall, "Authorial Revision," 39–40.

38. The editor of the *Riverside,* Larry D. Benson, refers to the *Riverside* jokingly in his Introduction as "Robinson Three."

39. The following account is drawn from Crow, Olson, and Manly, *Chaucer Life-Records,* v–xii.

40. On this point see Patterson, "Historical Criticism," 17–18.

41. Hyder, *George Lyman Kittredge,* 39–40.

42. Sherman, "Professor Kittredge and the Teaching of English."

43. Kittredge, *Chaucer and His Poetry,* 9.

44. Hyder, *George Lyman Kittredge,* 140.

45. Brewer, *Chaucer: The Critical Heritage,* 2: 220.

46. See, e.g., Eliot's remarks on Chaucer and Dante in "What Is a Classic?"

47. Kittredge, *Chaucer and His Poetry,* 2.

48. Lowes, *Geoffrey Chaucer,* 149.

49. Kittredge, *Chaucer and His Poetry,* 109.

50. Trilling, *Matthew Arnold,* 341.

51. On the history of irony in Chaucer criticism, see Dane, "Myth of Chaucerian Irony," and Birney, *Essays on Chaucerian Irony.*

52. Dane, "Myth of Chaucerian Irony," 128.

53. I take my title here from an essay by Charles Muscatine, whose "Age of Criticism" is itself an ironic allusion to Randall Jarrell's diatribe of 1952 against the New Criticism.

54. Cited in Muscatine, "Chaucer in an Age of Criticism," 173. Q. D. Leavis was, of course, F. R. Leavis's coauthor and one of the most important members of this critical school.

55. Muscatine, "Chaucer in an Age of Criticism," 173.

56. Speirs, in fact, was the last person to visit F. R. Leavis before he died. MacKillop, *F. R. Leavis,* 409.

57. Speirs, *Chaucer the Maker,* 22.

58. Speirs, *Chaucer the Maker,* 22–24.

59. Speirs, *Chaucer the Maker,* 101.

60. In this context we might also think of the important work of C. S. Lewis, whose *Allegory of Love* influentially turned away from the emphasis on Chaucer's comedy, praising instead his achievement in the realm of courtly love poetry such as *Troilus and Criseyde* and the dream visions. See Lewis, *Allegory of Love.*

61. Patterson, "Historical Criticism," 20.

62. Donaldson, "Chaucer the Pilgrim," 2.

63. On the similarity of this argument to the detection of fallacies, see Dane, "Myth of Chaucerian Irony," 129.

64. Muscatine, *Chaucer and the French Tradition.*

65. Auerbach, *Mimesis.* On Auerbach's modernity, see the essays in Lerer, *Literary History and the Challenge of Philology.* On Muscatine's debt to Auerbach, see Patterson, "Historical Criticism," 24.

66. Jameson, "Cultural Logic of Late Capitalism."

67. Payne, *Key of Remembrance.*

68. Cited in Robertson, *Preface to Chaucer,* 295.

69. Robertson, *Preface to Chaucer,* 302.

70. Patterson, "Historical Criticism," 5.

71. A term first proposed in its current usage by John Burrow, *Ricardian Poetry.*

72. For biography, see Pearsall, *Life of Geoffrey Chaucer.* For the classical past, see Baswell, *Virgil in Medieval England;* Fyler, *Chaucer and Ovid;* Kiser, *Telling Classical Tales;* Minnis, *Chaucer and Pagan Antiquity;* and Wetherbee, *Chaucer and the Poets.* For Italy, see Boitani, ed., *Chaucer and the Italian Trecento;* Stillinger, *Song of Troilus;* Taylor, *Chaucer Reads the "Divine Comedy";* Thompson, *Chaucer, Boccaccio, and the Debate of Love;* and Wallace, *Chaucer and the Early Writings of Boccaccio.* On France, see Wimsatt, *Chaucer and His French Contemporaries.* And on visual art, see Kolve, *Chaucer and the Imagery of Narrative.*

73. On language, see Burnley, *Language of Chaucer;* Cannon, *Making of Chaucer's English;* and Sandved, *Introduction to Chaucerian English.* On texts, see Blake, *Textual Tradition;* Hanna, *Pursuing History;* and Owen, *Manuscripts of the "Canterbury Tales."* One should also note that this renewed interest in the texts has been encouraged in the past ten years by the capacity of electronic media to represent manuscript in ways impossible to print, such as the hypertext link, modes that promise to bring the diversity of manuscript culture into the classroom as never before.

74. Thomas Hahn touches on a similar point in "The Premodern Text and the Postmodern Reader," 6.

75. See, e.g., White, "Narrative in Contemporary Historical Theory."

76. See Strohm, "Saving the Appearances," and *England's Empty Throne,* 65–86.

77. Carruthers, "The Wife of Bath and the Painting of Lions," 22–53.

78. Dinshaw, *Chaucer's Sexual Poetics.*

79. Hansen, *Chaucer and the Fictions of Gender.*

80. Benson, "Chaucer's Pardoner," Green, "Pardoner's Pants."

81. Kruger, "Claiming the Pardoner," 166.

82. Burger, *Chaucer's Queer Nation,* 139–59.

83. Leicester, *Disenchanted Self.*

84. Fradenburg, *Sacrifice Your Love.*

85. Lerer, *Chaucer and His Readers;* Matthews, *Making of Middle English;* Trigg, *Congenial Souls.* See also Trigg's chapter, "Chaucer's Influence and Reception," in this *Companion.*

86. On this point see also Dinshaw, "New Approaches to Chaucer."

PART IV

Appendixes

Appendix 1
Chronology: Major Dates and Events in Chaucer's Life and Times

1340   Geoffrey Chaucer probably born.

1348   Black Plague hits England.

1357   First recorded mention of Chaucer in the household of the Countess of Ulster, wife of Prince Lionel.

1359   Chaucer attends the wedding of John of Gaunt and Blanche of Lancaster; John of Gaunt becomes Duke of Lancaster; Chaucer serves in French war under Prince Lionel.

1360   Chaucer captured in France and ransomed by King Edward III.

1366   Chaucer travels to Spain; first mention of Phillipa Chaucer (his wife and the sister of John of Gaunt's mistress).

1367   Chaucer enters the service of Edward III.

1368   Death of Blanche of Lancaster; Chaucer is believed to have written the *Book of the Duchess* to commemorate her.

1370   Chaucer departs on mission to France with John of Gaunt.

1372   Phillipa's sister, Katherine Swynford, bears a son to John of Gaunt. Chaucer leaves for Italy.

1373   Chaucer returns to England; likely date of the birth of Thomas Chaucer, Chaucer's first son.

1370s   Chaucer is probably writing the *Parliament of Fowls* and short ballads and lyric poems during this decade.

1377   Chaucer again in France; death of Edward III and ascension of Richard II (then age ten) to the throne.

1378   Chaucer in France and again to Italy.

1380   May 1, Chaucer released from the charge of *raptus* by Cecily of Chaumpaigne.

1380s   Chaucer probably begins writing the *Canterbury Tales;* probably writes *Troilus and Criseyde* and translates Boethius's *Consolation of Philosophy;* writes short poems to his friends.

1381   The Rising of 1381 (also known as the Peasants' Revolt), from late May to early June. The uprising of agricultural workers and some small craftsmen against royal authority, especially in regards to taxation, was the defining political upheaval of Chaucer's time.

1385   Chaucer appointed justice of the peace for Kent.

1386   Chaucer reappointed justice of the peace; elected member of Parliament from Kent.

1389   Richard II reaches his majority and assumes full power as king; Chaucer named clerk of the king's works.

1390   Chaucer receives commissions as clerk of the works, among others, to build scaffolding for a tournament at Smithfield, London.

1390s   Chaucer writes the rest of the surviving *Canterbury Tales;* writes short poems to his friends. Throughout the decade, Chaucer receives a series of annuities for various services rendered to the king.

1391   Chaucer no longer clerk of the works.

1396   John of Gaunt marries Katherine Swynford, Chaucer's sister-in-law.

1399   Richard II deposed by Henry Bolingbroke, who becomes Henry IV. Chaucer writes a short poem to Henry IV (known as the *Complaint to His Purse*). Henry doubles Chaucer's annuity to forty pounds. Chaucer signs a fifty-three-year lease on a tenement near Westminster Abbey.

1400   Chaucer dies. October 25 is cited as the date of his death on his tombstone in Westminster Abbey (NB: this stone was erected in 1556).

1410s–1420s   Earliest surviving manuscripts of the *Canterbury Tales* are produced.

1478/79   First printed publication of Chaucer's poetry by William Caxton.

1484   Caxton reprints the *Canterbury Tales* in an improved edition.

1532   First edition of the *Works* of Geoffrey Chaucer, edited by William Thynne, the first printed complete works of an English poet.

Appendix 2
Guides to the
Textual Study of Chaucer

Facsimiles of Manuscripts and Early Printed Books
Containing Chaucer's Works

THE CANTERBURY TALES

The Ellesmere Manuscript, Huntington Library, San Marino, CA, MS Ellesmere 26
C 9. Available in the following facsimiles: Ralph Hanna III, *The Ellesmere Man-
sucript of Chaucer's Canterbury Tales: A Working Facsimile* (Cambridge: D. S.
Brewer, 1989); Daniel Woodward and Martin Stevens, *The Canterbury Tales (ca.
1410): The New Ellesmere Chaucer Facsimile* (San Marino, CA: Huntington
Library, 1995).

The Hengwrt Manuscript, National Library of Wales, Aberystwyth, MS Peniarth
392D. Available in facsimile: Paul G. Ruggiers, *The Canterbury Tales: A Facsimile and Transcription of the Hengwrt Manuscript* (Norman: University of
Oklahoma Press, 1979).

TROILUS AND CRISEYDE

Corpus Christi College, Cambridge, MS 61. Available in facsimile: M. B. Parkes and
Elizabeth Salter, *Troilus and Criseyde: A Facsimile of Corpus Christi College
Cambridge MS 61* (Cambridge: D. S. Brewer, 1978).

St. John's College, Cambridge, MS L.1. Available in facsimile: Richard Beadle and
Jeremy Griffiths, *St. John's College Cambridge, MS L.1: A Facsimile* (Norman:
University of Oklahoma Press, 1983).

THE DREAM POEMS AND LYRICS

Pamela Robinson, *Manuscript Bodley 638: A Facsimile* (Norman, OK: Pilgrim Books, 1981).

Pamela Robinson, *Minor Poems: A Facsimile of MS Tanner 346* (Norman, OK: Pilgrim Books, 1980).

John Norton-Smith, *Bodleian Library MS Fairfax 16* (London: Scolar Press, 1979).

M. B. Parkes and Richard Beadle, *Poetical Works: A Facsimile of Cambridge University Library MS Gg.4.27*, 3 vols. (Cambridge: Brewer, 1979–80).

A. S. G. Edwards, *Magdalene College, Cambridge MS Pepys 2006* (Norman, OK: Pilgrim Books, 1985).

Early Printed Editions of Chaucer's Work

English books printed between 1475 and 1640 are referred to by their STC number, the number in the alphabetically arranged catalogue of A. W. Pollard and G. R. Redgrave, *A Short-Title Catalogue of Books Printed in England, Scotland, and Ireland and of English Books Printed Abroad, 1475–1640*, revised and enlarged by W. A. Jacobs, F. S. Ferguson, and Katherine F. Panzer, 3 vols. (London: Bibliographical Society, 1976, 1986, 1992). Many of these books are available in digitized reproduction on Early English Books Online, http://eebo.chadwyck.com/home and on microfilm. Some of the most important early printings of Chaucer's work include the following (arranged by printer):

William Caxton: *The Canterbury Tales,* 1478 (STC 5082), and 1483 (STC 5083); *Troilus and Criseyde,* 1483 (STC 5094); *The House of Fame,* 1483 (STC 5087); *Anelida and Arcite,* 1477 (STC 5090); *The Temple of Brass* [that is, *The Parlement of Foules*], 1477 (STC 5091).

Wynkyn de Worde: *The Canterbury Tales,* 1498 (STC 5085); *Troilus and Criseyde,* 1517 (STC 5095).

Richard Pynson: *The Canterbury Tales,* 1492 (STC 5084), and again in 1526 (STC 5086); *Troilus and Criseyde,* 1526 (STC 5096); *The House of Fame* and *The Parlement of Foules* [together with other non-Chaucerian pieces], 1526 (STC 5088).

William Thynne: *Geoffrey Chaucer, The Works,* 1532 (STC 5068).

Derek Brewer prepared a facsimile edition of Thynne's volume together with additional texts in *Geoffrey Chaucer, The Works, 1532: With Supplementary Materials from the Editions of 1542, 1561, 1598, and 1602* (Menston, UK: Scolar Press, 1969).

Appendix 3
The Canterbury Tales: Order and Pattern

A. *The route from London to Canterbury (schematic):*

London
    Southwark
        Deptford
            Greenwich
                Dartford
                    Rochester
                        Sittingbourne
                          Ospringe
                            Boughton-under-Blee
                              Harble down ["Bobbe-up-
                                and-down"]
                              Canterbury

B. *The order of the pilgrim portraits in the* General Prologue

THE NOBILITY

Knight
Squire
Yeoman

THE CLERGY

Prioress
Nun and three priests
Monk
Friar

THE PROFESSIONALS

Merchant
Clerk
Franklin
Haberdasher, Carpenter, Weaver, Dyer, Rug weaver
Cook
Shipman
Doctor

THE WIDOW

Wife of Bath

THE SPIRITUAL BROTHERS

Parson
Plowman

THE PRODUCERS AND DISTRIBUTORS OF AGRICULTURAL GOODS AND SERVICES

Miller
Manciple
Reeve

THE GROTESQUES, OR CARNAL "BROTHERS"

Summoner
Pardoner

THE CONTROLLERS

Narrator
Host

C. The Order of the Tales in the Ellesmere Manuscript

General Prologue, Knight's Tale, Miller's Tale, Reeve's Tale, Cook's Tale, Man of Law's Prologue and Tale, Wife of Bath's Prologue and Tale, Friar's Tale, Summoner's Tale, Clerk's Tale, Merchant's Tale, Squire's Tale, Franklin's Tale, Physician's Tale, Pardoner's Prologue and Tale, Shipman's Tale, Prioress's Tale, Tale of Sir Thopas, Thopas-Melibee Link, Tale of Melibee, Monk's Tale, Nun's Priest's Tale, Second

Nun's Tale, Canon's Yeoman's Tale, Manciple's Prologue and Tale, Parson's Prologue and Tale, Retraction

D. The Order of the Tales in the Hengwrt Manuscript

General Prologue, Knight's Tale, Miller's Tale, Cook's Tale, Wife of Bath's Prologue and Tale, Friar's Tale, Summoner's Tale, Man of Law's Prologue and Tale, Squire's Tale, Merchant's Tale, Franklin's Tale, Second Nun's Tale, Clerk's Tale, Physician's Tale, Pardoner's Prologue and Tale, Shipman's Tale, Prioress's Tale, Tale of Sir Thopas, Thopas-Melibee Link, Tale of Melibee, Monk's Tale, Nun's Priest's Tale, Manciple's Prologue and Tale, Parson's Prologue and Tale, Retraction

Appendix 4
Maps

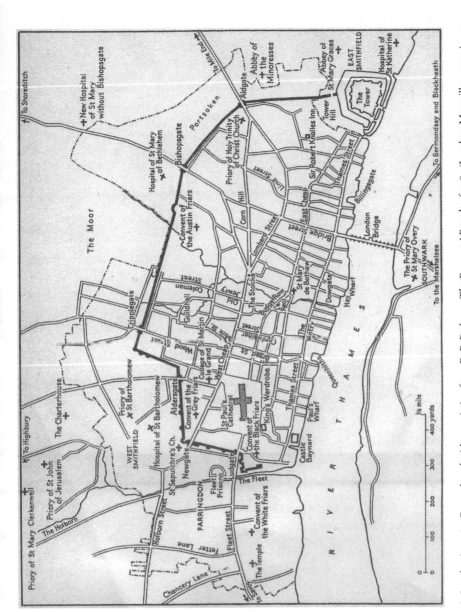

A. London in 1381. Reproduced with permission from R. B. Dobson, *The Peasants' Revolt of 1381* (London: Macmillan, 1970), 152.

B. The spread of Lollardy in England and Scotland. The darkly shaded areas are those with evidence of Lollard activity before 1399. The lightly shaded areas are those with evidence of Lollard activity after 1399. Adapted from G. M. Trevelyan, *England in the Age of Wycliffe* (London: Longmans, 1948).

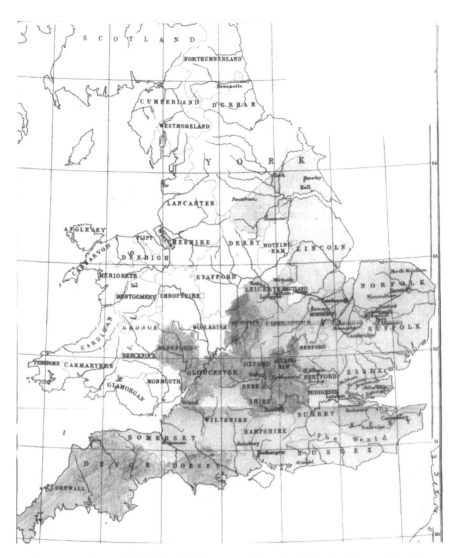

C. The Rising of 1381. The lightly shaded areas are those for which there is recorded evidence of activity. The darkly shaded areas are those for which there is indirect evidence of activity. Adapted from G. M. Trevelyan, *England in the Age of Wycliffe* (London: Longmans, 1948).

Bibliography

Lerer, Introduction

Ahern, John. "Binding the Book: Hermeneutics and Manuscript Production in *Paradiso* 33." *PMLA* 97 (1982): 800–809.

Baugh, A. C., and Thomas Cable. *A History of the English Language.* 5th ed. Englewood Cliffs, NJ: Prentice Hall, 2002.

Bennett, J. A. W., and G. V. Smithers, eds. *Early Middle English Verse and Prose.* With a glossary by Norman Davis. 2nd ed. Oxford: Clarendon Press, 1968.

Bevington, David, ed. *Medieval Drama.* Boston: Houghton Mifflin, 1975.

Blake, N. F. *The Canterbury Tales Edited from the Hengwrt Manuscript.* London: Arnold, 1980.

Boffey, Julia, and John J. Thompson. "Anthologies and Miscellanies: Production and Choice of Texts." In Griffiths and Pearsall, eds., *Book-Production and Publishing,* 279–316.

Boitani, Piero, and Jill Mann, eds. *The Cambridge Companion to Chaucer.* 2nd ed. Cambridge: Cambridge University Press, 2004.

Brewer, Derek. *A New Introduction to Chaucer.* 2nd ed. London: Longman, 1998.

Brown, Peter, ed. *A Companion to Chaucer.* Oxford: Blackwell, 2000.

Cannon, Christopher. *The Making of Chaucer's English: A Study of Words.* Cambridge: Cambridge University Press, 1998.

Clark, Cecily. *The Peterborough Chronicle, 1070–1154.* 2nd ed. Oxford: Clarendon Press, 1970.

Cooper, Helen. *The Canterbury Tales.* Oxford Guides to Chaucer. Oxford: Oxford University Press, 1989.

Copeland, Rita. *Pedagogy, Intellectuals, and Dissent in the Later Middle Ages: Lollardy and Ideas of Learning.* Cambridge: Cambridge University Press, 2001.

Crane, Susan. *Gender and Romance in Chaucer's "Canterbury Tales."* Princeton, NJ: Princeton University Press, 1994.

Dinshaw, Carolyn. *Chaucer's Sexual Poetics.* Madison: University of Wisconsin Press, 1989.

———. *Getting Medieval: Sexualities and Communities, Pre- and Postmodern.* Durham, NC: Duke University Press, 1999.

Doyle, A. I., and M. B. Parkes. "The Production of Copies of the *Canterbury Tales* and the *Confessio Amantis* in the Early Fifteenth Century." In M. B. Parkes and A. G. Watson, eds., *Medieval Scribes, Manuscripts, and Libraries: Essays Presented to N. R. Ker,* 163–210. London: Scolar Press, 1978.

Fisher, John Hurt. "A Language Policy for Lancastrian England." *PMLA* 107 (1992): 1168–80.

———. *The Emergence of Standard English.* Lexington: University of Kentucky Press, 1996.

Fradenburg, L. O. Aranye. *Sacrifice Your Love: Psychoanalysis, Historicism, Chaucer.* Minneapolis: University of Minnesota Press, 2002.

———. "The Wife of Bath's Passing Fancy." *SAC* 8 (1986): 31–58.

Grady, Frank. "Chaucer Reading Langland: *The House of Fame.*" *SAC* 18 (1996): 3–23.

Gray, Douglas, ed. *The Oxford Companion to Chaucer.* Oxford: Oxford University Press, 2004.

Griffiths, J. J., and Derek Pearsall, eds. *Book-Production and Publishing in Britain, 1375–1475.* Cambridge: Cambridge University Press, 1989.

Hanna, Ralph III. *Pursuing History: Middle English Manuscripts and Their Texts.* Stanford, CA: Stanford University Press, 1996.

Hansen, Elaine Tuttle. *Chaucer and the Fictions of Gender.* Berkeley: University of California Press, 1992.

Huot, Sylvia. *From Song to Book.* Ithaca, NY: Cornell University Press, 1987.

Justice, Steven V. *Writing and Rebellion: England in 1381.* Berkeley: University of California Press, 1994.

Kuskin, William. *Symbolic Caxton.* Notre Dame, IN: Notre Dame University Press, 2006.

Lerer, Seth. *Chaucer and His Readers: Imagining the Author in Late-Medieval England.* Princeton, NJ: Princeton University Press, 1993.

———. *Courtly Letters in the Age of Henry VIII: Literary Culture and the Arts of Deceit.* Cambridge: Cambridge University Press, 1997.

———. "Medieval English Literature and the Idea of the Anthology." *PMLA* 118(2003): 1251–67.

———. "William Caxton." In *CHMEL,* 720–38.

Mann, Jill. *Geoffrey Chaucer: Feminist Readings.* London: Routledge, 1991.

Minnis, Alastair, et al. *The Shorter Poems.* Oxford Guides to Chaucer. Oxford: Oxford University Press, 1995.

Parkes, M. B. *English Cursive Book Hands, 1250–1500.* 2nd ed. Berkeley: University of California Press, 1980.

Patterson, Lee. *Chaucer and the Subject of History.* Madison: University of Wisconsin Press, 1991.

——. *Negotiating the Past: The Historical Study of Medieval Literature.* Madison: University of Wisconsin Press, 1987.

Pearsall, Derek. *The Life of Geoffrey Chaucer: A Critical Biography.* Oxford: Blackwell, 1992.

——. *Old and Middle English Poetry.* London: Routledge, 1977.

Ruggiers, Paul G., ed. *Editing Chaucer: The Great Tradition.* Norman: University of Oklahoma Press, 1988.

Stanley, E. G., ed. *The Owl and the Nightingale.* London: Nelson, 1960.

Strohm, Paul. *Hochon's Arrow: The Social Imagination of Fourteenth-Century Texts.* Princeton, NJ: Princeton University Press, 1994.

——. *Social Chaucer.* Cambridge, MA: Harvard University Press, 1989.

Taylor, Andrew. "Authors, Scribes, Patrons, and Books." In Jocelyn Wogan-Browne et al., eds., *Idea of the Vernacular,* 353–65.

Turville-Petre, Thorlac. *England the Nation: Language, Literature, and National Identity, 1260–1340.* Oxford: Clarendon Press, 1995.

Wallace, David. *Chaucerian Polity: Absolutist Lineages and Associational Forms in England and Italy.* Stanford, CA: Stanford University Press, 1997.

Watson, Nicholas. "The Composition of Julian of Norwich's *Revelation of Love.*" *Speculum* 68 (1993): 637–83.

——. "The Middle English Mystics." In *CHMEL,* 539–65.

——. "The Politics of Middle English Writing." In Jocelyn Wogan-Browne et al., *Idea of the Vernacular,* 331–52.

Wetherbee, Winthrop. *The Canterbury Tales.* Cambridge: Cambridge University Press, 1990.

Windeatt, Barry. *Troilus and Criseyde.* Oxford Guides to Chaucer. Oxford: Oxford University Press, 1992.

Wogan-Browne, Jocelyn, et al., eds. *The Idea of the Vernacular: An Anthology of Middle English Literary Theory, 1280–1520.* University Park, PA: Pennsylvania State University Press, 1999.

Chapter 1: Cannon, The Lives of Geoffrey Chaucer

Boffey, Julia. "Middle English Lives." *CHMEL,* 610–34.

Brewer, D. S. *Chaucer.* London: Longmans, 1953.

——. "Class Distinction in Chaucer." *Speculum* 43 (1968): 290–305.

——, ed. *Chaucer: The Critical Heritage.* 2 vols. London: Routledge, 1978.

Burrow, John. *Ricardian Poetry.* London: Routledge and Kegan Paul, 1971.

Cannon, Christopher. "Chaucer and Rape: Uncertain Certainties." *SAC* 22 (2000): 67–92.

Chesterton, G. K. *Chaucer.* London: Faber and Faber, 1932.

Crow, Martin M., and Clair C. Olson, eds. *Chaucer Life-Records.* Oxford: Clarendon Press, 1966.

Dinshaw, Carolyn. *Chaucer's Sexual Poetics.* Madison: University of Wisconsin Press, 1989.

Donaldson, E. Talbot. "Chaucer the Pilgrim." In Donaldson, *Speaking of Chaucer,* 1–12. Durham, NC: Labyrinth Press, 1983; orig. publ. London: Athlone, 1970.

Gardner, John. *The Life and Times of Chaucer.* London: Cape, 1977.

Godwin, William. *The Life of Geoffrey Chaucer, the Early English Poet.* 2 vols. London: Phillips, 1803.

Green, Richard Firth. *Poets and Princepleasers: Literature and the English Court in the Late Middle Ages.* Toronto: University of Toronto Press, 1980.

Hoccleve, Thomas. *The Regiment of Princes.* Ed. Charles R. Blyth. Kalamazoo, MI: Medieval Institute Publications, 1999.

Howard, Donald R. *Chaucer: His Life, His Works, His World.* New York: Dutton, 1987.

———. "Chaucer the Man." *PMLA* 80 (1965): 337–43.

Hulbert, James Root. *Chaucer's Official Life.* Menasha, WI: Collegiate Press, 1912; rpt. New York: Phaeton Press, 1970.

Kane, George. *The Autobiographical Fallacy in Chaucer and Langland Studies.* London: H. K. Lewis, 1965.

Langland, William. *Piers Plowman: An Edition of the C-text.* Ed. Derek Pearsall. London: Edward Arnold, 1978.

———. *The Vision of Piers Plowman: A Complete Edition of the B-text.* Ed. A. V. C. Schmidt. London: Dent, 1978.

Lounsbury, T. R. *Studies in Chaucer: His Life and Writings.* 3 vols. New York: Harper and Brothers, 1892.

Lowes, John Livingston. *Geoffrey Chaucer.* Cambridge: Riverside Press, 1934.

Lukács, Georg. *History and Class Consciousness: Studies in Marxist Dialectics.* Trans. Rodney Livingstone. London: Merlin, 1968.

Mann, Jill. *Chaucer and Medieval Estates Satire: The Literature of Social Classes and the "General Prologue" to the "Canterbury Tales."* Cambridge: Cambridge University Press, 1973.

Middleton, Anne. "William Langland's 'Kynde Name': Authorial Signature and Social Identity in Late-Fourteenth-Century England." In Lee Patterson, ed., *Literary Practice and Social Change,* 15–82. Berkeley: University of California Press, 1990.

———. "The Idea of Public Poetry in the Reign of Richard II." *Speculum* 53 (1978): 94–114.

Pearsall, Derek. "Chaucer's Tomb: The Politics of Reburial." *Medium Aevum* 64 (1995): 51–73.

———. *John Lydgate.* London: Routledge and Kegan Paul, 1970.

———. *The Life of Geoffrey Chaucer: A Critical Biography.* Oxford: Blackwell, 1992.

Plucknett, T. F. T. "Chaucer's Escapade." *Law Quarterly Review* 64 (1948): 33–36.

Simpson, James. "Ethics and Interpretation: Reading Wills in Chaucer's *Legend of Good Women.*" *SAC* 20 (1998): 73–100.

Skeat, W. W. "Life of Chaucer." In W. W. Skeat, ed., *The Complete Works of Geoffrey Chaucer,* 6 vols., 1:ix–lxi. Oxford: Clarendon Press, 1894.

Spearing, A. C. "'Al This Mene I Be Love.'" *SAC, Proceedings* 2 (1986): 160–77.

Speght, Thomas. "Chaucer's Life." In Speght, ed., *The Workes of Our Antient and Lerned English Poet, Geffrey Chaucer, Newly Printed.* London, 1598.

Strohm, Paul. "Middle English Narrative Genres." *Genre* 13 (1980): 379–88.

———. "Politics and Poetics: Usk and Chaucer in the 1380's." In Lee Patterson, ed.,

Literary Practice and Social Change in Britain, 1380–1530, 83–112. Berkeley: University of California Press, 1990.

——. "*Passioun, Lyf, Miracle, Legende:* Some Generic Terms in Middle English Narrative." *Chaucer Review* 10 (1975): 62–75, 154–71.

——. *Social Chaucer.* Cambridge, MA: Harvard University Press, 1989.

Thompson, E. P. *The Making of the English Working Class.* London: Victor Gollancz, 1963.

Thrupp, Sylvia L. *The Merchant Class of Medieval London, 1300–1500.* Chicago: University of Chicago Press, 1948.

Usk, Thomas. *The Testament of Love.* Ed. R. Allen Shoaf. Kalamazoo, MI: Medieval Institute Publications, 1998.

Weber, Max. *From Max Weber: Essays in Sociology.* Ed. and trans. H. H. Gerth and C. Wright Mills. London: Routledge and Kegan Paul, 1948.

Wimsatt, James. *Chaucer and the Poems of "Ch" in University of Pennsylvania MS French 15.* Chaucer Studies 9. Cambridge: D. S. Brewer, 1982.

Chapter 2: *Simpson,* Chaucer as a European Writer

Anderson, David. *Before the "Knight's Tale": Imitation of Classical Epic in Boccaccio's "Teseida."* Philadelphia: University of Pennsylvania Press, 1988.

Beidler, Peter G. "*The Reeve's Tale.*" In Correale and Hamel, eds., *Sources and Analogues of the "Canterbury Tales,"* 56–67.

Boitani, Piero, ed. *Chaucer and the Italian Trecento.* Cambridge: Cambridge University Press, 1983.

Calabrese, Michael A. *Chaucer's Ovidian Arts of Love.* Gainesville: University Press of Florida, 1994.

Cook, James Wyatt, trans. *Petrarch's Songbook, Rerum vulgarium fragmenta.* Italian text ed. Gianfranco Contini. Binghamton, NY: MRTS, 1995.

Cooper, Helen. "The Frame." In Correale and Hamel, eds., *Sources and Analogues of the "Canterbury Tales,"* 7–13.

Copeland, Rita. *Rhetoric, Hermeneutics and Translation in the Middle Ages: Academic Traditions and Vernacular Texts.* Cambridge: Cambridge University Press, 1991.

Correale, Robert M., and Mary Hamel, eds. *Sources and Analogues of the "Canterbury Tales."* Vol. 1. Cambridge: D. S. Brewer, 2002.

Crane, Susan. "Anglo-Norman Cultures in England, 1066–1460." *CHMEL,* 35–60.

Curtius, Ernst Robert. *European Literature and the Latin Middle Ages.* Trans. Willard R. Trask. London: Routledge and Kegan Paul, 1953.

Dimmick, Jeremy. "Ovid in the Middle Ages: Authority and Poetry." In Philip Hardie, ed., *The Cambridge Companion to Ovid,* 264–87. Cambridge: Cambridge University Press, 2002.

Edwards, Robert R. *Chaucer and Boccaccio: Antiquity and Modernity.* Basingstoke, UK: Palgrave, 2002.

——. "*The Franklin's Tale.*" In Correale and Hamel, eds., *Sources and Analogues of the "Canterbury Tales,"* 220–45.

Fisher, John H. "A Language Policy for Lancastrian England." *PMLA* 107 (1992): 1168–80.

Fyler, John M. *Chaucer and Ovid.* New Haven and London: Yale University Press, 1979.

Havely, N. R., ed. and trans. *Chaucer's Boccaccio: Sources of "Troilus" and the "Knight's" and "Franklin's Tales."* Cambridge: D. S. Brewer, 1980.

Hines, John. *The Fabliau in English.* London: Longman, 1993.

Hoccleve, Thomas. *The Regiment of Princes.* Ed. Charles R. Blyth. Kalamazoo, MI: Medieval Institute Publications, 1999.

Kibler, William, trans. *Chrétien de Troyes, Arthurian Romances.* London: Penguin, 1991.

Koff, Leonard Michael, and Brenda Deen Schildgen, eds. *The "Decameron" and the "Canterbury Tales": New Essays on an Old Question.* Madison, WI: Associated University Presses, 2000.

Lewis, C. S. "What Chaucer Really Did to *Il Filostrato.*" In C. David Benson, ed., *Critical Essays on Chaucer's 'Troilus and Criseyde' and His Major Early Poems,* 8–22. 1932; rpt. Milton Keynes: Open University Press, 1991.

Mann, Jill. "Parents and Children in the *Canterbury Tales.*" In *Literature in Fourteenth-Century England: The J. A. W. Bennett Memorial Lectures,* 165–83. Tübingen: Gunter Narr Verlag, 1983.

Miller, F. J., ed. *Ovid: Metamorphoses.* Rev. G. P. Goold. Cambridge, MA: Harvard University Press, 1974.

Minnis, Alastair J. *"Magister Amoris": The "Roman de la Rose" and Vernacular Hermeneutics.* Oxford: Oxford University Press, 2001.

———, and A. B. Scott, eds. *Medieval Literary Theory and Criticism, c. 1100–c. 1375: The Commentary Tradition.* Oxford: Clarendon Press, 1988.

Muscatine, Charles. *Chaucer and the French Tradition: A Study in Style and Meaning.* Berkeley: University of California Press, 1957.

Nims, Margaret F., trans. *Geoffrey of Vinsauf, Poetria Nova.* Toronto: Pontifical Institute of Medieval Studies, 1967.

Nolan, Barbara. *Chaucer and the Tradition of the Roman Antique.* Cambridge: Cambridge University Press, 1992.

Patterson, Lee. *Chaucer and the Subject of History.* London: Routledge, 1991.

Pearsall, Derek. "Chaucer and Englishness." *Publications of the British Academy* 101 (1999): 77–99.

———. *The Life of Geoffrey Chaucer: A Critical Biography.* Oxford: Blackwell, 1992.

Rebholz, R. A., ed. *Sir Thomas Wyatt: The Complete Poems.* London: Penguin, 1978.

Salter, Elizabeth. "Chaucer and Internationalism." In Derek Pearsall and Nicolette Zeeman, eds., *English and International: Studies in the Literature, Art and Patronage of Medieval England,* 239–44. Cambridge: Cambridge University Press, 1988.

Sapegno, Natalino, ed. *Dante Alighieri, La Divina Commedia.* Florence: Nuova Italia, 1955.

Schless, Howard H. *Chaucer and Dante: A Revaluation.* Norman, OK: Pilgrim Books, 1984.

Showerman, Grant, trans. *Ovid: Heroides and Amores.* Rev. G. P. Goold. Cambridge, MA: Harvard University Press, 1986.

Simpson, James. "Dante's 'Astripetam Aquilam' and the Theme of Poetic Discretion in the *House of Fame.*" *Essays and Studies,* n.s., 39 (1986): 1–18.

———. "Ethics and Interpretation: Reading Wills in Chaucer's *Legend of Good Women.*" *SAC* 20 (1998): 73–100.

———. *Reform and Cultural Revolution, 1350–1547.* Oxford: Oxford University Press, 2002.

———. *Sciences and the Self in Medieval Poetry: Alan of Lille's "Anticlaudianus" and John Gower's "Confessio Amantis."* Cambridge: Cambridge University Press, 1995.

Strohm, Paul. *Social Chaucer.* Cambridge, MA: Harvard University Press, 1989.

Taylor, Karla. *Chaucer Reads "The Divine Comedy."* Stanford, CA: Stanford University Press, 1989.

———. "Chaucer's Uncommon Voice: Some Contexts for Influence." In Koff and Schildgen, eds., *The "Decameron" and the "Canterbury Tales,"* 47–82.

Wallace, David. *Chaucer and the Early Writings of Boccaccio.* Woodbridge, UK: D. S. Brewer, 1985.

———. *Chaucerian Polity: Absolutist Lineages and Associational Forms in England and Italy.* Stanford, CA: Stanford University Press, 1997.

———. "In Flaundres." *SAC* 19 (1997): 63–91.

———. " 'Whan she translated was': A Chaucerian Critique of the Petrarchan Academy." In Lee Patterson, ed., *Literary Practice and Social Change in Britain, 1380–1530,* 156–215. Berkeley: University of California Press, 1990.

Westrem, Scott D. "Geography and Travel." In Peter Brown, ed., *A Companion to Chaucer,* 195–217. Oxford: Blackwell, 2000.

Wimsatt, James I. *Chaucer and His French Contemporaries: Natural Music in the Fourteenth Century.* Toronto: University of Toronto Press, 1993.

Windeatt, Barry, ed. and trans. *Chaucer's Dream Poetry: Sources and Analogues.* Cambridge: D. S. Brewer, 1982.

———. *Geoffrey Chaucer: Troilus and Criseyde.* London: Longman, 1984.

Chapter 3: *Smith,* Chaucer as an English Writer

Allen, Rosemund. "Date and Provenance of King Horn: Some Interim Reassessments." In Edward Donald Kennedy et al., eds., *Medieval English Studies Presented to George Kane,* 99–126. Wolfeboro: Brewer, 1988.

Anonymous. *Lay le Freine.* In Anne Laskaya and Eve Salisbury, eds., *The Middle English Breton Lays,* 61–87. Kalamazoo, MI: Medieval Institute Publications, 1995.

———. *Sir Degaré.* In Anne Laskaya and Eve Salisbury, eds., *The Middle English Breton Lays,* 89–144. Kalamazoo, MI: Medieval Institute Publications, 1995.

———. *Sir Orfeo.* 2nd ed. Ed. A. J. Bliss. Oxford: Clarendon Press, 1966.

Barney, Stephen A. "Langland's Mighty Line." In Kathleen M. Hewett-Smith, ed., *William Langland's Piers Plowman: A Book of Essays,* 103–17. New York: Routledge, 2001.

Bennett, J. A. W. "Chaucer's Contemporary." In S. S. Hussey, ed., *Piers Plowman: Critical Approaches,* 310–24. London: Methuen, 1969.

Blake, Norman F. "Chaucer and the Alliterative Romances." *Chaucer Review* 3, no. 3 (1969): 163–69.

Brewer, Derek. "The Relationship of Chaucer to the English and European Traditions." In Brewer, ed., *Chaucer and Chaucerians: Critical Studies in Middle English Literature,* 1–38. London: Nelson, 1966.

Burrow, J. A. *Ricardian Poetry: Chaucer, Gower, Langland and the "Gawain" Poet.* London: Routledge, 1971.

Cannon, Christopher. *The Making of Chaucer's English: A Study of Words.* Cambridge: Cambridge University Press, 1998.

Coghill, Nevill. "Two Notes on Piers Plowman: II. Chaucer's Debt to Langland." *Medium Aevum* 4, no.2 (1935): 90.

Cooper, Helen. "Langland's and Chaucer's Prologues." *Yearbook of Langland Studies* 1 (1987): 71–81.

———. *The Canterbury Tales.* Oxford Guides to Chaucer. Oxford: Clarendon Press, 1989.

Crane, Susan. *Insular Romance: Politics, Faith, and Culture in Anglo-Norman and Middle English Literature.* Berkeley: University of California Press, 1986.

Dinshaw, Carolyn. *Chaucer's Sexual Poetics.* Madison: University of Wisconsin Press, 1989.

Dyer, Christopher. "Piers Plowman and Plowmen: A Historical Perspective." *Yearbook of Langland Studies* 8 (1994): 155–76.

Everett, Dorothy. "Chaucer's 'Good Ear.' " *Review of English Studies* 23 (October 1947): 201–8.

Field, Rosalind. "The Anglo-Norman Background to Alliterative Romance." In David Lawton, ed., *Middle English Alliterative Poetry and Its Literary Background,* 54–69. Cambridge: D. S. Brewer, 1982.

Fisher, John. *The Complete Poetry and Prose of Geoffrey Chaucer.* New York: Macmillan, 1977.

Fowler, H. W. *The New Fowler's Modern English Usage.* 3rd ed. Ed. R. W. Burchfield. Oxford: Oxford University Press, 2000.

Gower, John. *Vox Clamantis.* In Eric Stockton, trans., *The Major Latin Works of John Gower,* 47–288. Seattle: University of Washington Press, 1962.

Grady, Frank. "Chaucer Reading Langland: *The House of Fame.*" *SAC* 18 (1996): 3–23.

Hanna, Ralph. "Alliterative Poetry." In David Wallace, ed., *Medieval English Literature,* 488–512. Cambridge: Cambridge University Press, 1999.

———. *London Literature, 1300–1380.* Cambridge: Cambridge University Press, forthcoming.

———. "Reconsidering the Auchinleck Manuscript." In Derek Pearsall, ed., *New Directions in Later Medieval Manuscript Studies,* 91–102. York: York Medieval Press, 2000.

Hoccleve, John. *Hoccleve's Works: The Regement of Princes.* Ed. Frederick J. Furnivall. *EETS NS* 72. London: K. Paul, Trench, Trübner, 1897.

Hudson, Anne. "Piers Plowman and the Peasants' Revolt." *Yearbook of Langland Studies* 8 (1994): 85–106.

Isaacs, Neil D. "Constance in Fourteenth-Century England." *Neuphilologische Mitteilungen* 59 (1958): 260–77.

Kane, George. "Langland and Chaucer: An Obligatory Conjunction." In Donald Rose, ed., *New Perspectives in Chaucer Criticism,* 5–19. Norman, OK: Pilgrim, 1981.

Kean, Patricia M. *Chaucer and the Making of English Poetry.* Vol. 2: *The Art of Narrative.* London: Routledge, 1972.

Kirk, Elizabeth D. "Langland's Plowman and the Re-creation of Fourteenth-Century Religious Metaphor." *Yearbook of Langland Studies* 2 (1988): 1–19.

Knighton, Henry. *Knighton's Chronicle: 1337–1396.* Ed. G. H. Martin. Oxford: Clarendon Press, 1995.

Lerer, Seth. *Chaucer and His Readers.* Princeton, NJ: Princeton University Press, 1993.

Lewis, C. S. *The Allegory of Love.* Oxford: Oxford University Press, 1936.

Loomis, Laura Hibbard. "Sir Thopas." In W. F. Bryan and Germaine Dempste, eds., *Sources and Analogues of Chaucer's Canterbury Tales,* 486–559. Chicago: University of Chicago Press, 1941.

———. "Chaucer and the Auchinleck MS: *Thopas* and *Guy of Warwick.*" In *Essays and Studies in Honor of Carleton Brown,* 111–28. New York: Columbia University Press, 1940.

———. "Chaucer and the Breton Lays of the Auchinleck MS." *Studies in Philology* 38 (1941): 14–33.

Lydgate, John. *A Critical Edition of John Lydgate's "Life of Our Lady."* Ed. Joseph A. Lauritis et al. Duquesne Studies: Philological Series 2. Louvain: Nauwelaerts, 1961.

Mann, Jill. *Chaucer and Medieval Estates Satire: The Literature of Social Classes and the "General Prologue" to the "Canterbury Tales."* Cambridge: Cambridge University Press, 1973.

Middleton, Anne. "Acts of Vagrancy: The C Version 'Autobiography' and the Statute of 1388." In Steven Justice and Kathryn Kerby-Fulton, eds., *Written Work: Langland, Labor, and Authorship,* 208–317. Philadelphia: University of Pennsylvania Press, 1997.

———. "Narration and the Invention of Experience: Episodic Form in *Piers Plowman.*" In Larry D. Benson and Siegfried Wenzel, eds., *The Wisdom of Poetry: Essays in Early English Literature in Honor of Morton W. Bloomfield,* 91–122. Kalamazoo: Western Michigan University, 1982.

Minnis, A. J. *Medieval Theory of Authorship: Scholastic Literary Attitudes in the Later Middle Ages.* 2nd ed. Philadelphia: University of Pennsylvania Press, 1988.

———, et al. *The Shorter Poems.* Oxford Guides to Chaucer. Oxford: Clarendon Press, 1995.

Morgan, M. M. "A Treatise in Cadence." *Modern Language Review* 47 (1952): 156–64.

Muscatine, Charles. "The Canterbury Tales." In Derek Brewer, ed., *Chaucer and Chaucerians: Critical Studies in Middle English Literature,* 88–113. London: Nelson, 1966.

Mustanoja, Tauno. "Chaucer's Prosody." In Beryl Rowland, ed., *Companion to Chaucer Studies,* 80–81. Rev. ed. New York: Oxford University Press, 1979.

Nicholson, Peter. "The Man of Law's Tale: What Chaucer Really Owed to Gower." *Chaucer Review* 26 (1991): 153–74.

Patterson, Lee. " 'What man artow?': Authorial Self-Definition in *The Tale of Sir Thopas* and *The Tale of Melibee.*" *SAC* 11 (1989): 117–75.

———. "Chaucerian Commerce." In Patterson, *Chaucer and the Subject of History,* 322–66. Madison: University of Wisconsin Press, 1991.

Pearsall, Derek. "Chaucer and Englishness." *Proceedings of the British Academy* 101 (2000): 77–99.

Prendergast, Thomas. *Chaucer's Dead Body: From Corpse to Corpus.* New York: Routledge, 2004.

Riddy, Felicity. "Middle English Romance: Family, Marriage, Intimacy." In Roberta Krueger, ed., *The Cambridge Companion to Medieval Romance,* 235–52. Cambridge: Cambridge University Press.

Robertson, D. W. *A Preface to Chaucer.* Princeton, NJ: Princeton University Press, 1962.

Robinson, Ian. *Chaucer and the English Tradition.* Cambridge: Cambridge University Press, 1972.

Salter, Elizabeth. "Chaucer and Internationalism." *SAC* 2 (1980): 71–79.

Schlauch, Margaret. *Chaucer's Constance and Accused Queens.* New York: New York University Press, 1927.

Shonk, Timothy. "A Study of the Auchinleck Manuscript: Bookmen and Bookmaking in the Early Fourteenth Century." *Speculum* 60 (1985): 71–91.

Smedick, L. K. "Cursus in Middle English: *A Talkyng of þe Love of God* Reconsidered." *Mediaeval Studies* 37 (1975): 387–406.

Smith, D. Vance. *Arts of Possession: The Middle English Household Imaginary.* Minneapolis: University of Minnesota Press, 2003.

——. *The Book of the Incipit: Beginnings in the Fourteenth Century.* Minneapolis: University of Minnesota Press, 2001.

Spearing, A. C. *Medieval to Renaissance in English Poetry.* Cambridge: Cambridge University Press, 1985.

Speirs, John. *Chaucer the Maker.* London: Faber, 1951.

Strohm, Paul. "The Origin and Meaning of Middle English *Romaunce.*" *Genre* 10 (1977): 1–28.

——. "Storie, Spelle, Geste, Romaunce, Tragedie: Generic Distinctions in the Middle English Troy Narratives." *Speculum* 46 (1971): 348–59.

Trigg, Stephanie. *Congenial Souls: Reading Chaucer from Medieval to Postmodern.* Minneapolis: University of Minnesota Press, 2002.

Turville-Petre, Thorlac. *The Alliterative Revival.* Cambridge: D. S. Brewer, 1977.

——. "English in the Auchinleck Manuscript." In Turville-Petre, *England the Nation: Language, Literature, and National Identity, 1290–1340,* 108–41. Oxford: Clarendon Press, 1995.

Wallace, David. *Chaucer and the Early Writings of Boccaccio.* Cambridge: D. S. Brewer, 1985.

——. *Chaucerian Polity: Absolutist Lineages and Associational Forms in England and Italy.* Stanford, CA: Stanford University Press, 1997.

Chapter 4: Copeland, Chaucer and Rhetoric

Alford, John. "The Wife of Bath versus the Clerk of Oxford: What Their Rivalry Means." *Chaucer Review* 21 (1986): 108–32.

Ancrene Riwle. Edited by J. R. R. Tolkien. EETS OS 249. London: Oxford University Press, 1962.

Aristotle. *Rhetoric.* Trans. George A. Kennedy. *Aristotle on Rhetoric: A Theory of Civic Discourse.* New York: Oxford University Press, 1991.

Astell, Ann. "The *Translatio* of Chaucer's Pardoner." *Exemplaria* 4 (1992): 411–28.

——. *Chaucer and the Universe of Learning.* Ithaca, NY: Cornell University Press, 1996.

Auerbach, Erich. *Mimesis: The Representation of Reality in Western Literature*. Trans. Willard R. Trask. Princeton, NJ: Princeton University Press, 1953.

Augustine. *De Doctrina Christiana*. Ed. W. M. Green. *Sancta Aureli Augustini Opera*, Corpus Scriptorum Ecclesiasticorum Latinorum 80. Vienna: Hoelder-Pichler-Tempsky, 1963.

——. *On Christian Teaching*. Trans. R. P. H. Green. Oxford: Oxford University Press, 1997.

Bitzer, Lloyd F. "Rhetoric and Public Knowledge." In Don M. Burks, ed., *Rhetoric, Philosophy, and Literature*, 67–93. West Lafayette, IN: Purdue University Press, 1978.

Blumenberg, Hans. "An Anthropological Approach to the Contemporary Significance of Rhetoric." Trans. Robert M. Wallace. In Kenneth Baynes et al., eds., *After Philosophy: End or Transformation*, 429–58. Cambridge, MA: MIT Press, 1987.

Boethius. *De Topicis Differentiis*. Patrologia Latina 64.

——. *De Topicis Differentiis*. Trans. Eleonore Stump. *Boethius' De Topicis Differentiis*. Ithaca, NY: Cornell University Press, 1978.

Boitani, Piero. "'My tale is of a cock': Or, the Problems of Literal Interpretation." In Richard G. Newhauser and John A. Alford, eds., *Literature and Religion in the Later Middle Ages: Philological Studies in Honor of Siegfried Wenzel*, 25–42. Binghamton, NY: Medieval and Renaissance Texts and Studies, 1995

Breisach, Ernst, ed. *Classical Rhetoric and Medieval Historiography*. Kalamazoo, MI: Medieval Institute Publications, 1985.

Burke, Kenneth. *A Rhetoric of Motives*. Berkeley: University of California Press, 1950; rpt. 1969.

Camargo, Martin. "Defining Medieval Rhetoric." In Constant J. Mews et al., *Rhetoric and Renewal in the Latin West, 1100–1540: Essays in Honour of John O. Ward*, 21–34. Turnhout: Brepols, 2003.

——. "Rhetoric." In David Wagner, ed., *The Seven Liberal Arts in the Middle Ages*, 96–124. Bloomington: Indiana University Press, 1983.

——. "Rhetorical Ethos and the *Nun's Priest's Tale*." *Comparative Literature Studies* 33 (1996): 173–86.

——. "Towards a Comprehensive Art of Written Discourse: Geoffrey of Vinsauf and the *Ars Dictaminis*." *Rhetorica* 6 (1988): 167–94.

——. "Where's the Brief: The *Ars Dictaminis* and Reading/Writing between the Lines." *Disputatio* 1 (1996): 1–17.

Carruthers, Mary. *The Book of Memory: A Study of Memory in Medieval Culture*. Cambridge: Cambridge University Press, 1990.

——. *The Craft of Thought: Meditation, Rhetoric, and the Making of Images, 400–1200*. Cambridge: Cambridge University Press, 1998.

Charland, Maurice. "Constitutive Rhetoric." In Sloane, ed., *Encyclopedia of Rhetoric*, 616–19.

Cicero. *De Inventione*. Ed. and trans. H. M. Hubbell. Loeb Classical Library. Cambridge, MA: Harvard University Press, 1949; rpt. 1976.

——. *De Oratore*. Ed. and trans. E. W. Sutton and H. Rackham. 2 vols. Loeb Classical Library. Cambridge, MA: Harvard University Press, 1942; rpt. 1976.

Copeland, Rita. "Lydgate, Hawes, and the Science of Rhetoric in the Late Middle Ages." *Modern Language Quarterly* 53 (1992): 57–82.

——. "Medieval Rhetoric: An Overview." In Sloane, ed., *Encyclopedia of Rhetoric,* 469–79.

——. "The Pardoner's Body and the Disciplining of Rhetoric." In Miri Rubin and Sarah Kay, eds., *Framing Medieval Bodies,* 138–59. Manchester: Manchester University Press, 1994.

——. *Rhetoric, Hermeneutics, and Translation in the Middle Ages: Academic Traditions and Vernacular Texts.* Cambridge: Cambridge University Press, 1991.

——. "Trivium." In Sloane, ed., *Encyclopedia of Rhetoric,* 782–88.

——. "Why Women Can't Read: Medieval Hermeneutics, Statutory Law, and the Lollard Heresy Trials." In Susan S. Heinzelman and Zipporah B. Wiseman, eds., *Representing Women: Law, Literature, and Feminism,* 253–86. Durham, NC: Duke University Press, 1994.

Copeland, Rita, and Ineke Sluiter, eds. and trans. *Medieval Literary Theory: The Grammatical and Rhetorical Traditions.* Oxford: Oxford University Press, forthcoming.

Dionysius of Halicarnassus. *Dionysius of Halicarnassus: The Critical Essays.* 2 vols. Trans. Stephen Usher. Loeb Classical Library. Cambridge, MA: Harvard University Press, 1985.

Faral, Edmond, ed. *Les arts poétiques du XIIe et du XIIIe siècle.* Paris: Champion, 1924; rpt. 1962.

Farrell, Thomas B. "Knowledge, Consensus, and Rhetorical Theory." *Quarterly Journal of Speech* 62 (1976): 1–14.

Geoffrey of Vinsauf. *Poetria Nova.* In Faral, ed., *Les arts poétiques du XIIe et du XIIIe siècle,* 194–262.

——. *The New Poetics (Poetria Nova).* Trans. Jane B. Kopp. In Murphy, *Three Medieval Rhetorical Texts,* 27–108.

Hanna, Ralph, III. "*Compilatio* and the Wife of Bath: Latin Backgrounds, Ricardian Texts." In A. J. Minnis, ed., *Latin and Venacular: Studies in Late-Medieval Texts and Manuscripts,* 1–11. Woodbridge, UK: Boydell and Brewer, 1989.

Hegel, G. W. F. *The Philosophy of History.* Trans. J. Sibree. New York: Dover, 1956.

John of Garland. *Parisiana Poetria.* Ed. and trans. Traugott Lawler. New Haven and London: Yale University Press, 1974.

Jost, Walter, and Michael J. Hyde, eds. *Rhetoric and Hermeneutics in Our Time: A Reader.* New Haven and London: Yale University Press, 1997.

Kahn, Victoria. *Rhetoric, Prudence, and Skepticism in the Renaissance.* Ithaca, NY: Cornell University Press, 1985.

Kelly, Douglas. *The Arts of Poetry and Prose.* Typologie des sources du moyen âge occidental 59. Turnhout: Brepols, 1991.

Kennedy, George A. *Classical Rhetoric and Its Christian and Secular Tradition from Ancient to Modern Times.* 2nd ed. Chapel Hill: University of North Carolina Press, 1999.

Kilwardby, Robert. *De Ortu Scientiarum.* Ed. Albert J. Judy, OP. London: British Academy; and Toronto: Pontifical Institute of Mediaeval Studies, 1976.

Lerer, Seth. *Boethius and Dialogue: Literary Method in the Consolation of Philosophy.* Princeton, NJ: Princeton University Press, 1985.

Manly, J. W. *Chaucer and the Rhetoricians*. London: Oxford University Press, 1926.

Martianus Capella. *De Nuptiis Philologiae et Mercurii*. Ed. Adolf Dick. Leipzig: Teubner, 1925.

———. *The Marriage of Philology and Mercury*. Trans. William Harris Stahl and Richard Johnson. In *Martianus Capella and the Seven Liberal Arts*, vol. 2. New York: Columbia University Press, 1977.

Matthew of Vendôme. *Ars Versificatoria*. Trans. Ernest Gallo, "Matthew of Vendôme: Introductory Treatise on the Art of Poetry," *Transactions of the American Philosophical Society* 118 (1974): 51–92.

———. *Ars Versificatoria*. In Faral, ed., *Les arts poétiques du XIIe et du XIIIe siècle*, 106–93.

McKeon, Richard. "Rhetoric in the Middle Ages." *Speculum* 17 (1942): 3–32.

Murphy, James J. *Rhetoric in the Middle Ages: A History of Rhetorical Theory from Saint Augustine to the Renaissance*. Berkeley: University of California Press, 1974.

———, ed. *Three Medieval Rhetorical Texts*. Berkeley: University of California Press, 1971.

Neel, Jasper. "The Degradation of Rhetoric." In Steven Mailloux, ed., *Rhetoric, Sophistry, Pragmatism*, 61–81. Cambridge: Cambridge University Press, 1995.

Nichols, Stephen G., Jr. *Romanesque Signs: Early Medieval Narrative and Iconography*. New Haven and London: Yale University Press, 1983

Olson, Glending. "Rhetorical Circumstances and the Canterbury Story Telling." *Studies in the Age of Chaucer* 20 (1985): 28–39.

Parker, Patricia. *Literary Fat Ladies: Rhetoric, Gender, Property*. London: Methuen, 1987.

Partner, Nancy F. "The New Cornificius: Medieval History and the Artifice of Words." In Breisach, ed., *Classical Rhetoric and Medieval Historiography*, 5–59.

Patterson, Lee. *Chaucer and the Subject of History*. Madison: University of Wisconsin Press, 1991.

———. "Feminine Rhetoric and the Politics of Subjectivity: La Vieille and the Wife of Bath." In Kevin Brownlee and Sylvia Huot, eds., *Rethinking the "Romance of the Rose": Text, Image, Reception*, 316–58. Philadelphia: University of Pennsylvania Press, 1992.

———. *Negotiating the Past: The Historical Understanding of Medieval Literature*. Madison: University of Wisconsin Press, 1987.

Payne, Robert O. "Chaucer's Realization of Himself as Rhetor." In James J. Murphy, ed., *Medieval Eloquence: Studies in the Theory and Practice of Medieval Rhetoric*, 270–87. Berkeley: University of California Press, 1978.

———. *The Key of Remembrance: A Study of Chaucer's Poetics*. New Haven: Yale University Press for the University of Cincinnati, 1963.

[Pseudo-Cicero]. *Rhetorica ad Herennium*. Trans. Harry Caplan. Loeb Classical Library. Cambridge, MA: Harvard University Press, 1954; rpt. 1977.

Quintilian. *Institutio Oratoria*. 4 vols. Trans. H. E. Butler. Loeb Classical Library. Cambridge, MA: Harvard University Press, 1920; rpt. 1980.

Robertson, D. W. "A Note on the Classical Origin of 'Circumstances' in the Medieval Confessional." *Studies in Philology* 43 (1946): 6–14.

Rorty, Richard. *Philosophy and the Mirror of Nature.* Princeton, NJ: Princeton University Press, 1979.

Schiappa, Edward. *The Beginnings of Rhetorical Theory in Classical Greece.* New Haven and London: Yale University Press, 1999.

———. "Did Plato Coin Rhetorike?" *American Journal of Philology* 111 (1990): 457–70.

Self, Lois S. "Rhetoric and *Phronesis:* The Aristotelian Ideal." *Philosophy and Rhetoric* 12 (1979): 97–129.

Simpson, James. "*Ut pictura poesis:* A Critique of Robert Jordan's *Chaucer and the Shape of Creation.*" In Piero Boitani and Anna Torti, eds., *Interpretation: Medieval and Modern,* 167–87. Cambridge: D. S. Brewer, 1993.

Sloane, Thomas O., ed. *Encyclopedia of Rhetoric.* Oxford: Oxford University Press, 2001.

Steiner, Emily. "Commonalty and Literary Form in the 1370's and 1380's." *New Medieval Literatures* 6 (2003): 199–221.

Strohm, Paul. *Social Chaucer.* Cambridge, MA: Harvard University Press, 1989.

Struever, Nancy. *The Language of History in the Renaissance: Rhetoric and Historical Consciousness in Florentine Humanism.* Princeton, NJ: Princeton University Press, 1970.

Thierry of Chartres. *The Latin Rhetorical Commentaries by Thierry of Chartres.* Ed. Karin Margareta Fredborg. Toronto: Pontifical Institute of Mediaeval Studies, 1988.

Thomas of Chobham. *Summa de Arte Praedicandi.* Ed. Franco Morenzoni. Corpus Christianorum Continuatio Medievalis 82. Turnholt: Brepols, 1988.

Travis, Peter W. "Chaucer's Trivial Fox Chase and the Peasants' Revolt of 1381." *Journal of Medieval and Renaissance Studies* 18 (1988): 195–220.

———. "The *Nun's Priest's Tale* as Grammar-School Primer." *SAC, Proceedings* 1 (1984): 81–91.

Vickers, Brian. *In Defence of Rhetoric.* Oxford: Clarendon Press, 1988.

Vincent of Beauvais. *Speculum Historiale.* Douai, 1624.

Wallace, David. *Chaucerian Polity: Absolutist Lineages and Associational Forms in England and Italy.* Stanford, CA: Stanford University Press, 1997.

Ward, John O. "Some Principles of Rhetorical Historiography in the Twelfth Century." In Breisach, ed., *Classical Rhetoric and Medieval Historiography,* 103–66.

Woods, Marjorie Curry. "Chaucer the Rhetorician: Criseyde and Her Family." *Chaucer Review* 20 (1985): 28–39.

———. "The Teaching of Poetic Composition in the Later Middle Ages." In James J. Murphy, ed., *A Short History of Writing Instruction from Ancient Greece to Modern America,* 123–43. Mahwah, NJ: Hermagoras Press, 2001.

Ziolkowski, Jan. "Grammar." In Sloane, ed., *Encyclopedia of Rhetoric,* 479–82.

Chapter 5: Willams, The Dream Visions

Aers, David. "*The Parliament of Fowls:* Authority, the Knower and the Known." *Chaucer Review* 16 (1981): 1–17.

Anderson, J. J. "The Narrators in *The Book of the Duchess* and *The Parlement of Foules.*" *Chaucer Review* 26 (1992): 219–35.

Augustine. *Confessions*. Translated by William Watts. 2 vols. Loeb Classical Library. Cambridge, MA: Harvard University Press, 1960–61.

Baswell, Christopher. *Virgil in Medieval England: Figuring the "Aeneid" from the Twelfth Century to Chaucer*. Cambridge: Cambridge University Press, 1995.

Bennett, J. A. W. *Chaucer's Book of Fame*. Oxford: Oxford University Press, 1968.

Benson, Larry, and Siegfried Wenzel, ed. *The Wisdom of Poetry: Essays in Early English Literature in Honor of Morton Bloomfield*. Kalamazoo, MI: Medieval Institute Publications, 1982.

Boitani, Piero. *Chaucer and the Imaginary World of Fame*. Cambridge: D. S. Brewer, 1984.

———. *English Medieval Narrative in the Thirteenth and Fourteenth Centuries*. Cambridge: D. S. Brewer, 1982.

———, ed. *Chaucer and the Italian Trecento*. Cambridge: Cambridge University Press, 1983.

Calin, William. *The French Tradition and the Literature of Medieval England*. Toronto: University of Toronto Press, 1994.

Cherniss, M. "The Boethian Dialogue in Chaucer's *The Book of the Duchess*." *Journal of English and Germanic Philology* 68 (1969): 655–65.

Connolly, Margaret. "Chaucer and Chess." *Chaucer Review* 29 (1994): 40–44.

Delany, Sheila. *Chaucer's "House of Fame": The Poetics of Skeptical Fideism*. Jacksonville: University Press of Florida, 1972.

———. *The Naked Text: Chaucer's "Legend of Good Women."* Berkeley: University of California Press, 1994.

Desmond, Marilynn. *Reading Dido: Gender, Textuality, and the Medieval "Aeneid."* Minneapolis: University of Minnesota Press, 1994.

Dinshaw, Carolyn. *Chaucer's Sexual Poetics*. Madison: University of Wisconsin Press, 1989.

Douglas, Gavin. *Eneados*. London, 1553.

Edwards, Robert. *The Dream of Chaucer: Representation and Reflection in the Early Narratives*. Durham, NC: Duke University Press, 1989.

Ellis, Steve. "The Death of the *Book of the Duchess*." *Chaucer Review* 29 (1995): 249–58.

Evans, Ruth. "Chaucer in Cyberspace: Medieval Technologies of Memory and *The House of Fame*." *SAC* 23 (2000): 43–69.

Ferster, Judith. *Chaucer on Interpretation*. Cambridge: Cambridge University Press, 1985.

Fradenburg, Louise. " 'Voice Memorial': Loss and Reparation in Chaucer's Poetry." *Exemplaria* 2 (1990): 169–202.

Frank, Robert W., Jr. *Chaucer and "The Legend of Good Women."* Cambridge, MA: Harvard University Press, 1972.

Fyler, John M. *Chaucer and Ovid*. New Haven and London: Yale University Press, 1979.

Gaylord, Alan T. "Dido at Hunt, Chaucer at Work." *Chaucer Review* 17 (1983): 300–315.

Hardman, Phillippa. "The Book of the Duchess as a Memorial Monument." *Chaucer Review* 28 (1994): 205–15.

Hieatt, Constance B. *The Realism of Dream Visions: The Poetic Exploitation of the Dream-Experience in Chaucer and His Contemporaries.* The Hague: Mouton, 1967.

Kittredge, G. L. "Chaucer's Lollius." *Harvard Studies in Classical Philology* 28 (1917): 47–133.

Kiser, Lisa J. *Telling Classical Tales: Chaucer and "The Legend of Good Women."* Ithaca, NY: Cornell University Press, 1983.

Kruger, Steven F. *Dreaming in the Middle Ages.* Cambridge: Cambridge University Press, 1992.

Leicester, H. M. "The Harmony of Chaucer's *Parlement:* A Dissonant Voice." *Chaucer Review* 9 (1974): 15–33.

Leyerle, John. "Chaucer's Windy Eagle." *University of Toronto Quarterly* 40 (1971): 247–65.

Lorris, Guillaume de, and Jean de Meun. *The Romance of the Rose.* Trans. Charles Dahlberg. Princeton, NJ: Princeton University Press, 1971.

Lynch, Kathryn L. *The High Medieval Dream Vision: Poetry, Philosophy, and Literary Form.* Stanford, CA: Stanford University Press, 1988.

Millet, Bella. "Chaucer, Lollius, and the Medieval Theory of Authorship." *SAC* 1 (1983): 90–103.

Minnis, Alastair. "Chaucer and the *Ovide Moralisé.*" *Medium Aevum* 48 (1979): 254–57.

———, et al. *The Shorter Poems.* Oxford Guides to Chaucer. Oxford: Clarendon Press, 1995.

Morse, Ruth. "Understanding the Man in Black." *Chaucer Review* 15 (1981): 204–8.

Muscatine, Charles. *Poetry and Crisis in the Age of Chaucer.* Notre Dame, IN: Notre Dame University Press, 1972.

Ovid. *Heroides.* Ed. and trans. Grant Showerman. Rev. G. P. Goold. Loeb Classical Library. Cambridge, MA: Harvard University Press, 1978.

Palmer, J. N. N. "The Historical Context of the *Book of the Duchess:* A Revision." *Chaucer Review* 8 (1974): 253–61.

Quinn, William A. *Chaucer's Dream Visions and Shorter Poems.* London: Garland, 1999.

Robertson, Kellie. "Laboring in the God of Love's Garden: Chaucer's Prologue to the *Legend of Good Women.*" *SAC* 24 (2000): 115–47.

St. John, Michael. *Chaucer's Dream Visions: Courtliness and Individual Identity.* Aldershot, UK: Ashgate, 2000.

Simpson, James. "Ethics and Interpretation: Reading Wills in Chaucer's *Legend of Good Women.*" *SAC* 20 (1998): 73–100.

Sklute, Larry M. "The Inconclusive Form of the *Parliament of Fowls.*" *Chaucer Review* 16 (1981): 119–28.

Skeat, W. W. *"The Legend of Good Women" by Geoffrey Chaucer.* 2nd ed. Oxford: Oxford University Press, 1900.

Spearing, A. C. *Medieval Dream Poetry.* Cambridge: Cambridge University Press, 1976.

Steinberg, Glenn A. "Chaucer in the Field of Cultural Production: Humanism, Dante, and *The House of Fame.*" *Chaucer Review* 35 (2000): 182–99.

Travis, Peter W. "White." *SAC* 22 (2000): 1–66.

Wallace, David. *Chaucer and the Early Writings of Boccaccio*. Cambridge: D. S. Brewer, 1985.

———. *Chaucerian Polity: Absolutist Lineages and Associational Forms in England and Italy*. Stanford, CA: Stanford University Press, 1997.

Watkins, John. " 'Neither of idle shewes, nor of false charmes aghast': Transformations of Virgilian Ekphrasis in Chaucer and Spenser." *Journal of Medieval and Renaissance Studies* 23 (1993): 345–63.

Williams, Deanne. *The French Fetish from Chaucer to Shakespeare*. Cambridge: Cambridge University Press, 2004.

Windeatt, Barry A., ed. and trans. *Chaucer's Dream Poetry: Sources and Analogues*. Cambridge: D. S. Brewer, 1982.

Wimsatt, James I. *Chaucer and His French Contemporaries: Natural Music in the Fourteenth Century*. Toronto: University of Toronto Press, 1991.

———. *Chaucer and the Poems of "Ch" in University of Pennsylvania MS French 15*. Chaucer Studies 9. Cambridge: D. S. Brewer, 1982.

———. "The Sources of Chaucer's Seys and Alcyone." *Medium Aevum* 36 (1967): 231–41.

Chapter 6: Holsinger, Lyrics and Short Poems

Adams, Stephen. *Poetic Designs: An Introduction to Meters, Verse Forms, and Figures of Speech*. Peterborough, ON: Broadview Press, 1997.

Aers, David. *Faith, Ethics and Church: Writing in England, 1360–1409*. Cambridge: D. S. Brewer, 2000.

Besserman, Lawrence. "Chaucer's Envoy to Bukton and 'Truth' in Biblical Interpretation: Some Medieval and Modern Contexts." *New Literary History* 22 (1991): 177–97.

"The Blessed Virgin to Her Son on the Cross." In *Religious Lyrics of the Fourteenth Century*, no. 128. 2nd ed. Ed. Carleton Brown. Oxford: Clarendon Press, 1965.

Boethius. *The Consolation of Philosophy*. Trans. W. V. Cooper. London: J. M. Dent, 1902.

———. *The Consolation of Philosophy*. Ed. G. Weinberger. CSEL 67. Vienna, 1935.

Boyd, Beverly. *Chaucer and the Liturgy*. Philadelphia: Dorrance, 1967.

Brown, Carleton, ed. *English Lyrics of the Thirteenth Century*. Oxford: Clarendon Press, 1932.

Chance, Jane. "Chaucerian Irony in the Boethian Short Poems: The Dramatic Tension between Classical and Christian." *Chaucer Review* 20 (1986): 235–45.

Davenport, W. A. "Ballades, French and English, and Chaucer's 'Scarcity' of Rhyme." *Parergon* 18 (2000): 181–201.

David, Alfred. "The Truth about 'Vache.' " *Chaucer Review* 11 (1977): 334–37.

Dean, James M. "Mars the Exegete in Chaucer's *Complaint of Mars*." *Comparative Literature* 41 (1989): 128–40.

Dinshaw, Carolyn. *Chaucer's Sexual Poetics*. Madison: University of Wisconsin Press, 1989.

Durling, Robert M., ed. and trans. *Petrarch's Lyric Poems: The "Rime Sparse" and Other Lyrics*. Cambridge, MA: Harvard University Press, 1976.

Eckhardt, Caroline D. "The Medieval Prosimetrum Genre (from Boethius to *Boece*)." *Genre* 16 (1983): 21–38.

Fein, Susanna Greer. *Moral Love Songs and Laments*. Kalamazoo, MI: Medieval Institute Publications, 1998.

——. "Twelve-Line Stanza Forms in Middle English and the Date of *Pearl*." *Speculum* 72 (1997): 367–96.

Galloway, Andrew. "Chaucer's *Former Age* and the Fourteenth-Century Anthropology of Craft: The Social Logic of a Premodernist Lyric." *ELH* 63 (1996): 535–53.

Galway, Margaret. "Chaucer among Thieves." *Times Literary Supplement*, 20 April 1946, 187.

Green, Richard Firth. *A Crisis of Truth: Literature and Law in Ricardian England*. Philadelphia: University of Pennsylvania Press, 1999.

Hansen, Elaine Tuttle. *Chaucer and the Fictions of Gender*. Berkeley: University of California Press, 1992.

Hollander, John. *Rhyme's Reason: A Guide to English Verse*. New Haven and London: Yale University Press, 1981.

Justice, Steven. *Writing and Rebellion: England in 1381*. Berkeley: University of California Press, 1994.

Kaske, R. E. "The *Aube* in Chaucer's *Troilus*." *Chaucer Criticism* 2 (1963): 167–79.

Minnis, A. J., ed. *Chaucer's Boece and the Medieval Tradition of Boethius*. Cambridge: D. S. Brewer, 1993.

Nolan, Charles J., Jr. "Structural Sophistication in the *Complaint unto Pity*." *Chaucer Review* 13 (1979): 363–72.

Norton-Smith, John. "Chaucer's Boethius and Fortune." *Reading Medieval Studies* 2 (1976): 63–76.

——. "Textual Tradition, Monarchy, and Chaucer's *Lak of Stedfastnes*." *Reading Medieval Studies* 8 (1982): 3–11.

O'Donnell, James J., ed. *Boethius' Consolation Philosophiae*. Bryn Mawr Latin Commentaries, vol. 1. Bryn Mawr, PA: Bryn Mawr College, 1990.

Pace, George B. "Cotton Otho A. XVIII." *Speculum* 26 (1951): 306–16.

——, and Alfred David. *The Minor Poems*. Part 1. Norman: University of Oklahoma Press, 1982.

Payne, Robert O. *The Key of Remembrance: A Study of Chaucer's Poetics*. Westport, CT: Greenwood Press, 1973.

Patterson, Lee. *Negotiating the Past: The Historical Understanding of Medieval Literature*. Madison: University of Wisconsin Press, 1987.

——. "Writing Amorous Wrongs: Chaucer and the Order of Complaint." In James M. Dean and Christian Zacher, eds., *The Idea of Medieval Literature: New Essays on Chaucer and Medieval Culture in Honor of Donald R. Howard*, 55–71. Newark: University of Delaware Press, 1992.

Phillips, Helen. "*The Complaint of Venus*: Chaucer and de Grauson." In Roger Ellis and Ruth Evans, eds., *The Medieval Translator 4*, 6–103. Medieval and Renaissance Texts and Studies, vol. 123. Binghamton, NY: Medieval and Renaissance Texts and Studies, 1994.

Quinn, William A. "Chaucer's Problematic *Priere: An ABC* as Artifact and Critical Issue." *SAC* 23 (2001): 109–41.

Robbins, Rossell Hope. "Chaucer's *To Rosemounde*." *Studies in Literary Imagination* 6 (1971): 73–81.

Ruud, Jay. *"Many a song and many a lecherous lay": Tradition and Individuality in Chaucer's Lyric Poetry.* New York: Garland Press, 1992.

Saul, Nigel. "Chaucer and Gentility." In Barbara A. Hanawalt, ed., *Chaucer's England: Literature in Historical Context,* 41–55. Minneapolis: University of Minnesota Press, 1992.

Scattergood, V. J. "The Short Poems." In A. J. Minnis et al., *The Shorter Poems,* 455–512. Oxford: Clarendon Press, 1995.

Schmidt, A. V. C. "Chaucer and the Golden Age." *Essays in Criticism* 26 (1976): 99–115.

Steiner, Emily. *Documentary Culture and the Making of Medieval English Literature.* Cambridge: Cambridge University Press, 2003.

Stemmler, Theo. "Chaucer's Ballade 'To Rosemounde' — A Parody?" In Richard G. Newhauser and John A. Alford, eds., *Literature and Religion in the Later Middle Ages,* 11–23. Binghamton, NY: Medieval and Renaissance Texts and Studies, 1995.

Stillinger, Thomas C. *The Song of Troilus: Lyric Authority in the Medieval Book.* Philadelphia: University of Pennsylvania Press, 1992.

Strohm, Paul. *Hochon's Arrow: The Social Imagination of Fourteenth-Century Texts.* Princeton, NJ: Princeton University Press, 1992.

Taylor, Karla. *Chaucer Reads "The Divine Comedy."* Stanford, CA: Stanford University Press, 1989.

Wallace, David. *Chaucerian Polity: Absolutist Lineages and Associational Forms in England and Italy.* Stanford, CA: Stanford University Press, 1997.

Wimsatt, James I. *Chaucer and His French Contemporaries: Natural Music in the Fourteenth Century.* Toronto: University of Toronto Press, 1991.

———. *Chaucer and the Poems of "Ch" in University of Pennsylvania MS French 15.* Chaucer Studies 9. Cambridge: D. S. Brewer, 1982.

Woolf, Rosemary. *The English Religious Lyric in the Middle Ages.* Oxford: Clarendon Press, 1968.

Zieman, Katherine. "Chaucer's 'Voys.'" *Representations* 60 (1997): 70–91.

Chapter 7: *Summit,* Troilus and Criseyde

Aers, David. "Criseyde: Woman in Medieval Society." *Chaucer Review* 13 (1978–79): 177–200.

Beidler, Peter G., ed. *Masculinities in Chaucer: Approaches to Maleness in the Canterbury Tales and Troilus and Criseyde.* Cambridge: D. S. Brewer, 1998.

Benson, C. David. *The History of Troy in Middle English Literature.* Cambridge: Cambridge University Press, 1980.

———. "The Opaque Text of Chaucer's Criseyde." In R. A. Shoaf and Catherine S. Cox, eds., *Chaucer's Troilus and Criseyde: "subgit to lle poesye"; Essays in Criticism,* 17–28. Binghamton, NY: Medieval and Renaissance Texts and Studies, 1992.

Blamires, Alcuin, et al., eds. *Woman Defamed and Woman Defended: An Anthology of Medieval Texts.* Oxford: Clarendon Press, 1992.

Brody, Saul N. "Making a Play for Criseyde: The Staging of Pandarus's House in Chaucer's *Troilus and Criseyde*." *Speculum* 73 (1998): 115–40.

Campbell, Jennifer. "Figuring Criseyde's 'Entente': Authority, Narrative, and Chaucer's Use of History." *Chaucer Review* 27 (1993): 342–58.

Cherewatuk, Karen, and Ulrike Wiethaus. "Introduction: Women Writing Letters in the Middle Ages." In Cherewatuk and Wiethaus, eds., *Dear Sister: Medieval Women and the Epistolary Genre,* 1–19. Philadelphia: University of Pennsylvania Press, 1993.

Cox, Catherine S. *Gender and Language in Chaucer.* Gainesville: University of Florida Press, 1997.

Dinshaw, Carolyn. *Chaucer's Sexual Poetics.* Madison: University of Wisconsin Press, 1989.

Donaldson, E. Talbot. *Speaking of Chaucer.* New York: W. W. Norton, 1970.

Federico, Sylvia. *New Troy: Fantasies of Empire in the Late Middle Ages.* Minneapolis: University of Minnesota Press, 2003.

Fehrenbacker, Richard W. " 'Al that which chargeth nought to seye': The Theme of Incest in Troilus and Criseyde." *Exemplaria* 9 (1997): 341–70.

Ferrante, Joan. *To the Glory of Her Sex: Women's Roles in the Composition of Medieval Texts.* Bloomington: Indiana University Press, 1997.

Fradenburg, L. O. Aranye. *Sacrifice Your Love: Psychoanalysis, Historicism, Chaucer.* Minneapolis: University of Minnesota Press, 2002.

Fries, Maureen. " 'Slydynge of Corage': Chaucer's Criseyde as Feminist and Victim." In Arlyn Diamond and Lee R. Edwards, eds., *The Authority of Experience: Essays in Feminist Criticism,* 45–59. Amherst: University of Massachusetts Press, 1977.

Gordon, R. K., ed. and trans. *The Story of Troilus.* 1934; rpt., Toronto: University of Toronto Press, 1978.

Hanawalt, Barbara. "Widows." In David Wallace and Carolyn Dinshaw, eds., *Cambridge Companion to Medieval Women's Writing,* 58–69. Cambridge: Cambridge University Press, 2003.

Hansen, Elaine Tuttle. *Chaucer and the Fictions of Gender.* Berkeley: University of California Press, 1992.

Havely, N. R., ed. and trans. *Chaucer's Boccaccio: Sources of "Troilus" and the "Knight's" and "Franklin's Tales."* Cambridge: D. S. Brewer, 1980.

Kallendorf, Craig. *In Praise of Aeneas: Virgil and Epideictic Rhetoric in the Early Italian Renaissance.* Hanover, NH: University Press of New England, 1989.

Kinney, Clare Regan. " 'Who Made This Song?': The Engendering of Lyric Counterplots in *Troilus and Criseyde.*" *Studies in Philology* 89 (1992): 272–92.

Kiser, Lisa J. *Truth and Textuality in Chaucer's Poetry.* Hanover, NH: University Press of New England, 1991.

Lees, Clare, ed. *Medieval Masculinities: Regarding Men in the Middle Ages.* Minneapolis: University of Minnesota Press, 1994.

Lerer, Seth. *Courtly Letters in the Age of Henry VIII: Literary Culture and the Arts of Deceit.* Cambridge: Cambridge University Press, 1997.

Mann, Jill. "Chaucer and the 'Woman Question.' " In Erik Kooper, ed., *This Noble Craft: Proceedings of the Tenth Research Symposium of the Dutch and Belgian University Teachers of Old and Middle English and Historical Linguistics,* 173–88. Amsterdam: Rodolpi, 1991.

———. *Feminizing Chaucer.* Suffolk, UK: Boydell and Brewer, 2002.

——. "Troilus' Swoon." *Chaucer Review* 14 (1980): 319–35.

Mapstone, Sally. "The Origins of Criseyde." In Jocelyn Wogan-Browne et al., eds., *Medieval Women: Texts and Contexts in Late Medieval Britain*, 131–47. Turnhout, Belgium: Brepols, 2000.

Margherita, Gayle. "Historicity, Femininity, and Chaucer's *Troilus*." *Exemplaria* 6 (1995): 243–69.

McAlpine, Monica E. *The Genre of "Troilus and Criseyde."* Ithaca, NY: Cornell University Press, 1978.

Mieszkowski, Gretchen. "The Reputation of Criseyde, 1155–1500." *Transactions of the Connecticut Academy of Arts and Sciences* 43 (1971): 71–153.

Minnis, A. J. *Medieval Theory of Authorship: Scholastic Literary Attitudes in the Later Middle Ages*. 2nd ed. Philadelphia: University of Pennsylvania Press, 1988.

Patterson, Lee. *Chaucer and the Subject of History*. Madison: University of Wisconsin Press, 1991.

Pizan, Christine de. *The Book of the City of Ladies*. Trans. Earl Jeffrey Richards. New York: Persea Books, 1982.

Pulsiano, Phillip. "Redeemed Language and the Ending of *Troilus and Criseyde*." In Julian N. Wasserman and Lois Roney, eds., *Sign Sentence Discourse: Language in Medieval Thought and Literature*, 153–74. Syracuse, NY: Syracuse University Press, 1989.

Robertson, Elizabeth. "Public Bodies and Psychic Domains: Rape, Consent, and Female Subjectivity in Geoffrey Chaucer's *Troilus and Criseyde*." In Robertson and Christine M. Rose, eds., *Representing Rape in Medieval and Early Modern Literature*, 281–310. New York: Palgrave, 2001.

Rose, Christine M. "Reading Chaucer Reading Rape." In Elizabeth Robertson and Christine M. Rose, eds., *Representing Rape in Medieval and Early Modern Literature*, 21–60. New York: Palgrave, 2001.

Sanok, Catherine. "Criseyde, Cassandre, and the *Thebaid*: Women and the Theban Subtext of Chaucer's *Troilus and Criseyde*." *SAC* 20 (1998): 41–71.

Sidney, Sir Philip. *An Apologie for Poetrie*. In Derek Brewer, ed., *Chaucer: The Critical Heritage*, vol. 1: *1385–1837*, 118–20. London: Routledge and Kegan Paul, 1978.

Spearing, A. C. *Chaucer: Troilus and Criseyde*. London: Arnold, 1976.

——. *The Medieval Poet as Voyeur: Looking and Listening in Medieval Love-Narratives*. Cambridge: Cambridge University Press, 1993.

Spurgeon, Caroline F. E. *Five Hundred Years of Chaucer Criticism and Allusion, 1357–1900*. 3 vols. Cambridge: Cambridge University Press, 1925.

Stanbury, Sarah. "The Lover's Gaze in Troilus and Criseyde." In R. A. Shoaf and Catherine S. Cox, eds., *Chaucer's Troilus and Criseyde: "subgit to alle poesye"; Essays in Criticism*, 224–38. Binghamton, NY: Medieval and Renaissance Texts and Studies, 1992.

——. "Women's Letters and Private Space in Chaucer." *Exemplaria* 6 (1994): 271–85.

Stillinger, Thomas C. *The Song of Troilus: Lyric Authority and the Medieval Book*. Philadelphia: University of Pennsylvania Press, 1992.

Strohm, Paul. *Social Chaucer*. Cambridge, MA: Harvard University Press, 1989.

Summit, Jennifer. *Lost Property: The Woman Writer and English Literary History, 1380–1589*. Chicago: University of Chicago Press, 2000.

Wack, Mary. *Lovesickness in the Middle Ages*. Philadelphia: University of Pennsylvania Press, 1990.

Wallace, David. *Chaucer and the Early Writings of Boccaccio*. Chaucer Studies 22. Woodbridge, Suffolk: Boydell and Brewer, 1985.

Wetherbee, Winthrop. *Chaucer and the Poets: An Essay on "Troilus and Criseyde."* Ithaca, NY: Cornell University Press, 1984.

Wheeler, Bonnie. "Dante, Chaucer, and the Ending of *Troilus and Criseyde*." *Philological Quarterly* 61 (1982): 105–23.

Windeatt, B. A. *Geoffrey Chaucer: Troilus and Criseyde*. London: Longman, 1984.

——. *Troilus and Criseyde*. Oxford Guides to Chaucer. Oxford: Clarendon Press, 1992.

Chapter 8: Lerer, The Canterbury Tales

Anderson, David. *Before the "Knight's Tale": Imitation of Classical Epic in Boccaccio's "Teseida."* Philadelphia: University of Pennsylvania Press, 1988.

Babington, Charles, ed. *Polychronicon Ranulphi Higden Together with the English Translations of John Trevisa and of an Unknown Writer of the Fifteenth Century.* London: Rolls Series, 1865–86.

Benson, C. David, and Elizabeth Robertson, eds. *Chaucer's Religious Tales*. Cambridge: D. S. Brewer, 1990.

Besserman, Lawrence. *Chaucer's Biblical Poetics*. Norman: University of Oklahoma Press, 1998.

Bishop, Ian. "The Nun's Priest's Tale and the Liberal Arts." *Review of English Studies,* n.s., 30 (1979): 257–75.

Blake, N. F. *The Textual Tradition of the "Canterbury Tales."* London: E. Arnold, 1985.

Bloch, R. Howard. *Etymologies and Genealogies: A Literary Anthropology of the French Middle Ages*. Chicago: University of Chicago Press, 1983.

Bowers, John M. " 'Dronkenesse is ful of stryvyng': Alcoholism and Ritual Violence in Chaucer's Pardoner's Tale." *ELH* 57 (1990): 757–84.

——. "*The Tale of Beryn* and *The Siege of Thebes*: Alternate Ideas of *The Canterbury Tales*." *SAC* 7 (1985): 23–50.

Bynum, Carolyn W. *Fragmentation and Redemption: Essays on Gender and the Human Body in Medieval Religion*. New York: Zone Books, 1991.

Cannon, Christopher. *The Making of Chaucer's English: A Study of Words*. Cambridge: Cambridge University Press, 1998.

Cooper, Helen. *The Canterbury Tales*. Oxford Guides to Chaucer. Oxford: Clarendon Press, 1989.

Cornell, Andrew. *At Play in the Tavern: Signs, Coins, and Bodies in the Middle Ages*. Ann Arbor: University of Michigan Press, 1999.

Crane, Susan. *Gender and Romance in Chaucer's "Canterbury Tales."* Princeton, NJ: Princeton University Press, 1994.

Dane, Joseph A. "*Queynte*: Some Rhyme and Some Reason on a Chaucerian Pun." *JEGP* 95 (1996): 497–514.

Dinshaw, Carolyn. *Chaucer's Sexual Poetics*. Madison: University of Wisconsin Press, 1989.

Ellis, Roger. *Patterns of Religious Narrative in the "Canterbury Tales."* London: Croom Helm, 1986.

Faral, Edmond. *Les arts poétiques du XIIe et du XIIIe siècle.* Paris: Presses Universitaires de France, 1924.

Fleming, John V. "The Antifraternalism of the *Summoner's Tale.*" *JEGP* 65 (1966): 688–700.

Fradenburg, Louise O. "Criticism, Anti-Semitism, and the *Prioress's Tale.*" *Exemplaria* 1 (1989): 69–115.

———. "The Manciple's Servant Tongue: Politics and Poetry in the *Canterbury Tales.*" *ELH* 52 (1985): 85–118.

———. "The Wife of Bath's Passing Fancy." *SAC* 8 (1986): 31–58.

Fyler, John. "Domesticating the Exotic in the Squire's Tale." *ELH* 55 (1988): 1–26.

Ganim, John. *Chaucerian Theatricality.* Princeton, NJ: Princeton University Press, 1990.

Gaylord, Alan T. "*Sentence* and *solaas* in Fragment VII of the *Canterbury Tales:* Harry Bailly as Horseback Editor." *PMLA* 82 (1967): 226–35.

Geary, Patrick J. *Furta Sacra: Thefts of Relics in the Central Middle Ages.* Rev. ed. Princeton, NJ: Princeton University Press, 1990.

Griffiths, Jeremy, and Derek Pearsall, eds. *Book Production and Publishing in Britain, 1375–1475.* Cambridge: Cambridge University Press, 1989.

Godfrey, Mary F. "Only Words: Cursing and the Authority of Language in the *Friar's Tale.*" *Exemplaria* 9 (1999): 307–28.

Gummere, F. B. "Is Chaucer to Be Reckoned as a Modern or a Medieval Poet?" *PMLA* 16 (1901): xxxvii–xl.

Hanna, Ralph. "The Hengwrt Manuscript and the Canon of *The Canterbury Tales.*" In Hanna, *Pursuing History,* 140–55.

———. "Pilate's Voice / Shirley's Case." In Hanna, *Pursuing History,* 267–79.

———. *Pursuing History: Middle English Manuscripts and Their Texts.* Stanford, CA: Stanford University Press, 1996.

Hanning, Robert W. " 'And countrefete the speche of every man / He koude, whan he sholde telle a tale': Toward a Lapsarian Poetics for the *Canterbury Tales.*" *SAC* 21 (1999): 27–58.

Hansen, Elaine Tuttle. *Chaucer and the Fictions of Gender.* Berkeley: University of California Press, 1992.

Harwood, Britton J. "Chaucer and the Silence of History: Situating the *Canon's Yeoman's Tale.*" *PMLA* 102 (1987): 338–50.

Heng, Geraldine. *Empire of Magic: Medieval Romance and the Politics of Cultural Fantasy.* New York: Columbia University Press, 2003.

Howard, Donald R. *Chaucer: His Life, His Works, His World.* New York: Dutton, 1987.

———. *The Idea of the "Canterbury Tales."* Berkeley: University of California Press, 1976.

Jones, Terry. *Chaucer's Knight: The Portrait of a Medieval Mercenary.* Baton Rouge: Louisiana State University Press, 1980.

Justice, Steven V. *Writing and Rebellion: England in 1381.* Berkeley: University of California Press, 1993.

Kendrick, Laura. *Chaucerian Play: Comedy and Control in the "Canterbury Tales."* Berkeley: University of California Press, 1988.

Koff, Leonard. *Chaucer and the Art of Storytelling.* Berkeley: University of California Press, 1988.

Kolve, V. A. *Chaucer and the Imagery of Narrative: The First Five "Canterbury Tales."* Stanford, CA: Stanford University Press, 1984.

Kruger, Steven. "The Bodies of Jews in the Middle Ages." In James M. Dean and Christian Zacher, eds., *The Idea of Medieval Literature: New Essays on Chaucer and Medieval Culture in Honor of Donald R. Howard,* 301–23. Newark: University of Delaware Press, 1992.

Lambdin, Laura C., and Robert T. Lambdin. *Chaucer's Pilgrims: An Historical Guide to the Pilgrims in the Canterbury Tales.* New York: Greenwood, 1996.

Lawton, David. "Chaucer's Two Ways: The Pilgrimage Frame of the *Canterbury Tales.*" *SAC* 9 (1987): 3–40.

——. *Chaucer's Narrators.* Woodbridge, UK: D. S. Brewer, 1985.

Leicester, H. Marshall, Jr. "The Art of Impersonation: A General Prologue to the *Canterbury Tales.*" *PMLA* 95 (1980): 213–24.

——. *The Disenchanted Self.* Berkeley: University of California Press, 1990.

Lerer, Seth. "The Chaucerian Critique of Medieval Theatricality." In James J. Paxon et al., eds., *The Performance of Middle English Culture: Essays on Chaucer and the Drama in Honor of Martin Stevens,* 59–76. Woodbridge, UK: D. S. Brewer, 1998.

——. " 'Now holde youre mouth': The Romance of Orality in the *Thopas-Melibee* Section of the *Canterbury Tales.*" In Mark Amodio, ed., *Oral Poetics in Middle English Poetry,* 182–205. New York: Garland, 1994.

Lindenbaum, Sheila. "The Smithfield Tournament of 1390." *Journal of Medieval and Renaissance Studies* 20 (1990): 1–20.

Mann, Jill. *Chaucer and Medieval Estates Satire: The Literature of Social Classes and the "General Prologue" to the "Canterbury Tales."* Cambridge: Cambridge University Press, 1973.

Middleton, Anne. "Chaucer's 'New Men' and the Good of Literature in the *Canterbury Tales.*" In Edward Said, ed., *Literature and Society: Papers from the English Institute, 1978,* 15–56. Baltimore: Johns Hopkins University Press, 1980.

Miller, Robert P., ed. *Chaucer: Sources and Backgrounds.* New York: Oxford University Press, 1977.

Mossé, Fernand. *A Handbook of Middle English.* Trans. James A. Walker. Baltimore: Johns Hopkins University Press, 1952.

Muscatine, Charles. *Chaucer and the French Tradition: A Study in Style and Meaning.* Berkeley: University of California Press, 1957.

Nims, Margaret F., ed. and trans. *Geoffrey of Vinsauf: Poetria Nova.* Toronto: Pontifical Institute of Medieval Studies, 1967.

Novelli, Cornelius. "Sin, Sight, and Sanctity." *Chaucer Review* 33 (1998): 168–75.

Olson, Glending. "Making and Poetry in the Age of Chaucer." *Comparative Literature* 31 (1979): 272–90.

——. "The End of the *Summoner's Tale* and the Uses of Pentecost." *SAC* 21 (1999): 209–45.

Osgood, Charles G. *Boccaccio on Poetry.* Indianapolis, IN: Bobbs-Merrill, 1956.

Ovid. *Ars Amatoria*. Ed. and trans. J. H. Mozley. Cambridge, MA: Harvard University Press, 1957.

Ovid. *Metamorphoses*. Ed. and trans. F. J. Miller, rev. G. P. Goold. Cambridge, MA: Harvard University Press, 1960–64.

Owen, Charles. *The Manuscripts of "The Canterbury Tales."* Cambridge: D. S. Brewer, 1991.

Parkes, M. B."The Influence of the Concepts of *Ordinatio* and *Compilatio on the Development of the Book.*" In J. J. G. Alexander and M. T. Gibson, eds., *Medieval Learning and Literature: Essays Presented to Richard William Hunt*, 35–70. Oxford: Clarendon Press, 1976.

Parr, Roger, ed. and trans. *Documentum de Modo et Arte Dictandi et Versificandi.* Milwaukee, WI: Marquette University Press, 1968.

Patterson, Lee. *Chaucer and the Subject of History.* Madison: University of Wisconsin Press, 1991.

——. "'For the Wyves love of Bathe': Feminine Rhetoric and Poetic Resolution in the *Roman de la Rose* and the *Canterbury Tales.*" *Speculum* 58 (1983): 656–95.

——. *Negotiating the Past.* Madison: University of Wisconsin Press, 1987.

——. "*The Parson's Tale* and the Quitting of the *Canterbury Tales.*" *Traditio* 34 (1978): 331–80.

——. "Perpetual Motion: Alchemy and the Technology of the Self." *SAC* 15 (1993): 25–57.

——. "'What man artow?': Authorial Self-Definition in *The Tale of Sir Thopas* and *The Tale of Melibee.*" *SAC* 11 (1989): 117–75.

Pearsall, Derek. *The Life of Geoffrey Chaucer: A Critical Biography.* Oxford: Blackwell, 1992.

Prior, Sandra Pierson. "Parodying Typology and the Mystery Plays in the *Miller's Tale.*" *Journal of Medieval and Renaissance Studies* 16 (1986): 57–73.

Reames, Sherry L. "The Cecilia Legend as Chaucer Inherited It and Retold It: The Disappearance of an Augustinian Ideal." *Speculum* 55 (1980): 38–57.

——. "The Sources of the *Second Nun's Tale.*" *Modern Philology* 76 (1978): 111–35.

Reedy, Jeremiah, ed. *Boccaccio in Defence of Poetry: Genealogiae Deorum Gentilium Liber XIV.* Toronto: Pontifical Institute of Medieval Studies, 1978.

Reiss, Edmund. "Daun Gervays in the *Miller's Tale.*" *Papers in Language and Literature* 6 (1970): 117–24.

Robertson, D. W. *A Preface to Chaucer: Studies in Medieval Perspectives.* Princeton, NJ: Princeton University Press, 1962.

Rollo, David. *Glamorous Sorcery: Magic and Literacy in the High Middle Ages.* Minneapolis: University of Minnesota Press, 2000.

Le Roman de la Rose. Ed. Daniel Poirion. Paris: Flammarion, 1974.

Sayce, Olive. "Chaucer's Retractions." *Medium Aevum* 40 (1971): 230–48.

Scala, Elizabeth. "Canacee and the Chaucer Canon: Incest and Other Unnarratables." *Chaucer Review* 30 (1996): 15–39.

Schibanoff, Susan. "The New Reader and Female Textuality in Two Early Commentaries on Chaucer." *SAC* 10 (1988): 71–108.

Shoaf, R. A. *Dante, Chaucer, and the Currency of the Word.* Norman, OK: Pilgrim, 1983.

Somerset, Fiona. " 'As just as is a squyre': The Politics of 'lewed translacion' in Chaucer's *Summoner's Tale.*" *SAC* 21 (1999): 187–207.

Strohm, Paul. *Social Chaucer.* Cambridge, MA: Harvard University Press, 1989.

Sumption, Jonathan. *Pilgrimage: An Image of Medieval Religion.* London: Faber and Faber, 1975.

Szittya, Penn R. *The Antifraternal Tradition in Medieval Literature.* Princeton, NJ: Princeton University Press, 1986.

Taylor, Andrew. "Authors, Scribes, Patrons and Books." In Jocelyn Wogan-Browne et al., eds., *The Idea of the Vernacular: An Anthology of Middle English Literary Theory, 1280–1520,*353–65. University Park: Pennsylvania State University Press, 1999.

Taylor, P. B. "Chaucer's *Cosyn to the Dede.*" *Speculum* 57 (1982): 315–27.

Tolkien, J. R. R. "Chaucer as Philologist: *The Reeve's Tale.*" *Transactions of the Philological Society* (1934): 1–70.

Travis, Peter W. "Chaucer's Trivial Fox Chase and the Peasants' Revolt of 1381." *Journal of Medieval and Renaissance Studies* 18 (1988): 195–220.

Van Dyke, Carolyn. "The Clerk's and Franklin's Subjected Subjects." *SAC* 17 (1995): 45–68.

Vance, Eugene. "Chaucer's Pardoner: Relics, Discourse, and Frames of Propriety." *New Literary History* 20 (1989): 723–45.

Wallace, David. *Chaucer and the Early Writings of Boccaccio.* Cambridge: D. S. Brewer, 1985.

——. *Chaucerian Polity: Absolutist Lineages and Associational Forms in England and Italy.* Stanford, CA: Stanford University Press, 1997.

——. "In Flaundres." *SAC* 19 (1997): 63–91.

Watson, Nicholas. "The Politics of Middle English Writing." In Jocelyn Wogan-Browne et al., eds., *The Idea of the Vernacular,* 331–42. University Park: Pennsylvania State University Press, 1999.

Wheatley, Edward. *Mastering Aesop: Medieval Education, Chaucer and His Followers.* Gainesville: University of Florida Press, 2000.

Wimsatt, James I. *Chaucer and His French Contemporaries: Natural Music in the Fourteenth Century.* Toronto: University of Toronto Press, 1991.

Wolfe, Matthew. "Placing Chaucer's Retraction for a Reception of Closure." *Chaucer Review* 33 (1999): 427–31.

Zacher, Christian. *Curiosity and Pilgrimage: The Literature of Discovery in Fourteenth-Century England.* Baltimore: Johns Hopkins University Press, 1976.

Chapter 9: *Trigg,* Chaucer's Influence and Reception

Bergen, Henry, ed. *Lydgate's Troy Book.* EETS NS, 126. London: Kegan Paul, Trench, Trubner, 1906.

Blake, N. F. *The Textual Tradition of the "Canterbury Tales."* London: E. Arnold, 1985.

Blake, William. *Descriptive Catalogue of Pictures, Poetical and Historical Inventions.* Oxford: Woodstock Books, 1990.

Bloom, Harold. *The Western Canon: The Books and Schools of the Ages.* New York: Harcourt, Brace, 1994.

Bowden, Betsy, ed. *Eighteenth-Century Modernizations from "The Canterbury Tales."* Rochester, NY: D. S. Brewer, 1991.

Bowers, John, ed. *The Canterbury Tales: Fifteenth-Century Continuations and Additions.* TEAMS Series. Kalamazoo, MI: Medieval Institute Publications, Western Michigan University, 1992.

Brewer, Derek, ed. *Chaucer: The Critical Heritage.* 2 vols. London: Routledge and Kegan Paul, 1978.

Burrow, J. A. *Ricardian Poetry: Chaucer, Gower, Langland and the Gawain Poet.* London: Routledge and Kegan Paul, 1971.

——, ed. *Geoffrey Chaucer: A Critical Anthology.* Harmondsworth: Penguin, 1969.

Cannon, Christopher. *The Making of Chaucer's English: A Study of Words.* Cambridge: Cambridge University Press, 1998.

Chaucer, Geoffrey. *The Works, 1532: With Supplementary Materials from the Editions of 1542, 1561, 1598, and 1602.* Ed. Derek Brewer. London: Scolar Press, 1969.

Conrad, Peter. *To Be Continued: Four Stories and Their Survival.* Oxford: Clarendon Press, 1995.

Davis, Herbert, ed. *Pope: Poetical Works.* London: Oxford University Press, 1966.

Donaldson, E. Talbot. "Chaucer the Pilgrim." In Donaldson, *Speaking of Chaucer*, 1–12. London: Athlone Press, 1970.

——. *The Swan at the Well: Shakespeare Reading Chaucer.* New Haven and London: Yale University Press, 1985.

Donaldson, Ian, ed. *Ben Jonson.* Oxford Authors. Oxford: Oxford University Press, 1985.

Ellis, Steve. *Chaucer at Large: The Poet in the Modern Imagination.* Minneapolis: Minnesota University Press, 2000.

Fox, Denton, ed. *The Poems of Robert Henryson.* Oxford: Clarendon Press, 1981.

Fradenburg, Louise O. " 'Voice Memorial': Loss and Reparation in Chaucer's Poetry." *Exemplaria* 2 (1990): 169–202.

Gower, John. *Confessio Amantis.* Ed. Russell A. Peck. Toronto: University of Toronto Press in association with the Medieval Academy of America, 1980.

Hoccleve, Thomas. *The Regiment of Princes.* Ed. Charles R. Blyth. Kalamazoo, MI: Medieval Institute Publications, 1999.

Jones, Terry, et al. *Who Murdered Chaucer? A Medieval Mystery.* London: Methuen, 2003.

Kinsley, James, ed. *The Poems of John Dryden.* Vol. 4. Oxford: Clarendon Press, 1958.

Lauritis, Joseph A., ed. *A Critical Edition of John Lydgate's "Life of Our Lady."* Pittsburgh: Duquesne University Press, 1961.

Lerer, Seth. *Chaucer and His Readers: Imagining the Author in Late-Medieval England.* Princeton, NJ: Princeton University Press, 1993.

——. *Courtly Letters in the Age of Henry VIII: Literary Culture and the Arts of Deceit.* Cambridge: Cambridge University Press, 1997.

Matthews, David. *The Making of Middle English, 1765–1910.* Minneapolis: University of Minnesota Press, 1999.

Patterson, Lee. *Negotiating the Past: The Historical Understanding of Medieval Literature.* Madison: University of Wisconsin Press, 1987.

Pearsall, Derek. *John Lydgate*. London: Routledge and Kegan Paul, 1970.

——, ed. *Chaucer to Spenser: An Anthology*. Oxford: Blackwell, 1999.

Prendergast, Thomas A. *Chaucer's Dead Body: From Corpse to Corpus*. New York: Routledge, 2004.

Ritson, Joseph. *Bibliographia Poetica: A Catalogue of English Poets, of the Twelfth, Thirteenth, Fourteenth, Fifteenth and Sixteenth Centurys, with a Short Account of Their Works*. London: C. Roworth, for G. and W. Nicol, 1802.

Robinson, Ian. *Chaucer and the English Tradition*. Cambridge: Cambridge University Press, 1972.

Simpson, James. *1350–1547: Reform and Cultural Revolution*. Vol. 2 of *The Oxford English Literary History*. 13 vols. Oxford: Oxford University Press, 2002.

Spearing, A. C. *Medieval to Renaissance in English Poetry*. Cambridge: Cambridge University Press, 1985.

Spurgeon, Caroline, ed. *Five Hundred Years of Chaucer Criticism and Allusion, 1357–1900*. 3 vols. London: Cambridge University Press, 1925.

Strohm, Paul. "Chaucer's Fifteenth-Century Audience and the Narrowing of the Chaucer Tradition." *SAC* 4 (1982): 3–32.

——. *Social Chaucer*. Cambridge, MA: Harvard University Press, 1989.

Trigg, Stephanie. *Congenial Souls: Reading Chaucer from Medieval to Postmodern*. Minneapolis: University of Minnesota Press, 2002.

Williams, David. *The Canterbury Tales: A Literary Pilgrimage*. Twayne's Masterwork Series. Boston: Twayne, 1987.

Wright, Herbert G., ed. *A Seventeenth-Century Modernisation of the First Three Books of Chaucer's "Troilus and Criseyde."* Bern: Francke Verlag, 1960.

Chapter 10: Knapp, Chaucer Criticism and Its Legacies

Aers, David. *Community, Gender, and Individual Identity: English Writing, 1360–1430*. London: Routledge, 1988.

Arnold, Matthew. "The Study of Poetry." In Arnold, *Essays in Criticism, Second Series*, 1–3. London: Macmillan and Company, 1895.

Auerbach, Erich. *Mimesis: The Representation of Reality in Western Literature*. Trans. Willard R. Trask. Princeton, NJ: Princeton University Press, 1953.

Baldick, Chris. *The Social Mission of English Criticism, 1848–1932*. Oxford: Oxford University Press, 1983.

Baswell, Christopher. *Virgil in Medieval England: Figuring the "Aeneid" from the Twelfth Century to Chaucer*. Cambridge: Cambridge University Press, 1995.

Benson, C. David. "Chaucer's Pardoner: His Sexuality and Modern Critics." *Medievalia* 8 (1985): 351–57.

Benson, L. D. "A Reader's Guide to Writings on Chaucer." In Derek Brewer, ed., *Writers and Their Background: Geoffrey Chaucer*, 321–51. London: G. Bell and Sons, 1974.

Birney, Earle. *Essays on Chaucerian Irony*. Ed. Beryl Rowland. Toronto: University of Toronto Press, 1985.

Blake, N. F. *The Textual Tradition of the "Canterbury Tales."* London: E. Arnold, 1985.

Boitani, Piero, ed. *Chaucer and the Italian Trecento*. Cambridge: Cambridge University Press, 1983.

Brewer, Charlotte. "Critical, Scientific and Eclectic Editing of Chaucer." In Richard Firth Green and Linne R. Mooney, eds., *Interstices: Studies in Late Middle English and Anglo-Latin Texts in Honour of A. G. Rigg*, 15–43. Toronto: University of Toronto Press, 2004.

———. *Editing Piers Plowman: The Evolution of the Text*. Cambridge: Cambridge University Press, 1996.

Brewer, Derek. "The Criticism of Chaucer in the Twentieth Century." In A. C. Cawley, ed., *Chaucer's Mind and Art*, 3–29. New York: Barnes and Noble, 1970.

———, ed. *Chaucer: The Critical Heritage*. 2 vols. London: Routledge and Kegan Paul, 1978.

Burger, Glenn. *Chaucer's Queer Nation*. Minneapolis: University of Minnesota Press, 2003.

Burnley, David. *The Language of Chaucer*. Basingstoke, UK: Macmillan, 1983.

Burrow, J. A. *Ricardian Poetry: Chaucer, Gower, Langland and the "Gawain" Poet*. London: Routledge and Kegan Paul, 1971.

Cannon, Christopher. *The Making of Chaucer's English: A Study of Words*. Cambridge: Cambridge University Press, 1998.

Carruthers, Mary. "The Wife of Bath and the Painting of Lions." In Ruth Evans and Lesley Johnson, eds., *Feminist Readings in Middle English Literature: The Wife of Bath and All Her Sect*, 22–53. London: Routledge, 1994.

Crow, Martin Michael, Clair Colby Olson, and John Matthews Manly. *Chaucer Life-Records*. Austin: University of Texas Press, 1966.

Dane, Joseph A. "The Myth of Chaucerian Irony." *Papers on Language and Literature* 24 (1988): 115–33.

Dinshaw, Carolyn. *Chaucer's Sexual Poetics*. Madison: University of Wisconsin Press, 1989.

Donaldson, E. Talbot. "Chaucer the Pilgrim." In Donaldson, *Speaking of Chaucer*, 1–12. London: Athlone Press, 1970.

Edwards, A. S. G. "Walter Skeat." In Paul G. Ruggiers, ed., *Editing Chaucer: The Great Tradition*, 171–89. Norman, OK: Pilgrim Books, 1984.

Eliot, T. S. *What Is a Classic?* London: Faber and Faber, 1945.

Foucault, Michel. "What Is an Author?" Trans. Donald F. Bouchard and Sherry Simon. In Donald F. Bouchard, ed., *Language, Counter-Memory, Practice: Selected Essays and Interviews*, 113–38. Ithaca, NY: Cornell University Press, 1977.

Fradenburg, L. O. Aranye. *Sacrifice Your Love: Psychoanalysis, Historicism, Chaucer*. Minneapolis: University of Minnesota Press, 2002.

Frantzen, Allen J. *Desire for Origins: New Language, Old English, and Teaching the Tradition*. New Brunswick, NJ: Rutgers University Press, 1990.

Fyler, John M. *Chaucer and Ovid*. New Haven and London: Yale University Press, 1979.

Graff, Gerald. *Professing Literature: An Institutional History*. Chicago: University of Chicago Press, 1987.

Green, Richard F. "The Pardoner's Pants (and Why They Matter)." *SAC* 15 (1993): 131–45.

Hahn, Thomas. "The Premodern Text and the Postmodern Reader." *Exemplaria* 2, no. 1 (1990): 1–21.

Hanna, Ralph. "Robert K. Root." In Paul G. Ruggiers, ed., *Editing Chaucer: The Great Tradition,* 191–206. Norman, OK: Pilgrim Books, 1984.

——. *Pursuing History: Middle English Manuscripts and Their Texts.* Stanford, CA: Stanford University Press, 1996.

Hansen, Elaine Tuttle. *Chaucer and the Fictions of Gender.* Berkeley: University of California Press, 1992.

Hyder, Clyde Kenneth. *George Lyman Kittredge: Teacher and Scholar.* Lawrence: University of Kansas Press, 1962.

Jameson, Fredric. "The Cultural Logic of Late Capitalism." In Jameson, *Postmodernism: Or, the Cultural Logic of Late Capitalism,* 1–54. Durham, NC: Duke University Press, 1991.

Kiser, Lisa J. *Telling Classical Tales: Chaucer and the "Legend of Good Women."* Ithaca, NY: Cornell University Press, 1983.

Kittredge, George Lyman. *Chaucer and His Poetry.* Cambridge, MA: Harvard University Press, 1915.

Kolve, V. A. *Chaucer and the Imagery of Narrative: The First Five Canterbury Tales.* Stanford, CA: Stanford University Press, 1984.

Kruger, Steven F. "Claiming the Pardoner: Toward a Gay Reading of Chaucer's *Pardoner's Tale.*" *Exemplaria* 6 (1994): 150–86.

Lacoue-Labarthe, Philippe, and Jean-Luc Nancy. *The Literary Absolute: The Theory of Literature in German Romanticism.* Trans. Philip Barnard and Cheryl Lester. Albany: State University of New York Press, 1988.

Leicester, H. Marshall. *The Disenchanted Self: Representing the Subject in the "Canterbury Tales."* Berkeley: University of California Press, 1990.

Lerer, Seth. *Chaucer and His Readers: Imagining the Author in Late-Medieval England.* Princeton, NJ: Princeton University Press, 1993.

Lewis, C. S. *The Allegory of Love: A Study in Medieval Tradition.* Oxford: Oxford University Press, 1936.

Lowes, John Livingston. *Geoffrey Chaucer.* Oxford: Clarendon Press, 1934.

MacKillop, Ian. *F. R. Leavis: A Life in Criticism.* New York: St. Martin's Press, 1995.

Matthews, David. *The Making of Middle English, 1765–1910.* Minneapolis: University of Minnesota Press, 1999.

Middleton, Anne. "Medieval Studies." In Stephen Greenblatt and Giles Gunn, eds., *Redrawing the Boundaries,* 12–40. New York: Modern Language Association of America, 1992.

Munro, John James. *Frederick James Furnivall: A Volume of Personal Record.* London: H. Frowde, 1911.

Minnis, A. J. *Chaucer and Pagan Antiquity.* Cambridge: D. S. Brewer, 1982.

Muscatine, Charles. *Chaucer and the French Tradition: A Study in Style and Meaning.* Berkeley: University of California Press, 1957.

——. "Chaucer in an Age of Criticism." *Modern Language Quarterly* 25 (1964): 473–78.

Owen, Charles A. *The Manuscripts of the "Canterbury Tales."* Chaucer Studies 17. Cambridge: D. S. Brewer, 1991.

Palmer, D. J. *The Rise of English Studies: An Account of the Study of English Language and Literature from Its Origins to the Making of the Oxford English School*. London: Published for the University of Hull by the Oxford University Press, 1965.

Patterson, Lee. *Chaucer and the Subject of History*. Madison: University of Wisconsin Press, 1991.

———. "Historical Criticism and the Development of Chaucer Studies." In Patterson, *Negotiating the Past: The Historical Understanding of Medieval Literature*, 3–40. Madison: University of Wisconsin Press, 1987.

Payne, Robert O. *The Key of Remembrance: A Study in Chaucer's Poetics*. New Haven: Yale University Press, 1963.

Pearsall, Derek. "Authorial Revision in Some Late-Medieval English Texts." *Crux and Controversy in Middle English Textual Criticism*. Ed. A. J. Minnis and Charlotte Brewer. Cambridge: D. S. Brewer, 1992. 39–48.

———. "Chaucer's Poetry and Its Modern Commentators: The Necessity of History." In David Aers, ed., *Medieval Literature: Criticism, Ideology and History*, 123–47. Brighton, UK: Harvester, 1986.

———. *The Life of Geoffrey Chaucer: A Critical Biography*. Oxford: Blackwell, 1992.

Percival, W. Keith. "Renaissance Grammar." In Albert Rabil, ed., *Renaissance Humanism: Foundations, Forms, and Legacy*, 67–84. Philadelphia: University of Pennsylvania Press, 1988.

Ridley, Florence. "The State of Chaucer Studies: A Brief Survey." *Studies in the Age of Chaucer* 1 (1979): 3–16.

Robertson, D. W. *A Preface to Chaucer: Studies in Medieval Perspectives*. Princeton, NJ: Princeton University Press, 1962.

Root, Robert Kilburn, ed. *The Book of Troilus and Criseyde*. Princeton, NJ: Princeton University Press, 1926.

Ross, Thomas. "Thomas Wright." In Paul G. Ruggiers, ed., *Editing Chaucer: The Great Tradition*, 145–56. Norman, OK: Pilgrim Books, 1984.

Sandved, Arthur. *Introduction to Chaucerian English*. Cambridge: D. S. Brewer, 1985.

Saunders, Corinne. "The Development of Chaucer Criticism." In Corinne Saunders, ed,, *Chaucer*, 5–22. Blackwell Guides to Criticism. Oxford: Blackwell, 2001.

Scholes, Robert E. *The Rise and Fall of English: Reconstructing English as a Discipline*. New Haven and London: Yale University Press, 1998.

Sherman, Stuart P. "Professor Kittredge and the Teaching of English." *Nation*, Sept. 11, 1913, 227–30.

Speirs, John. *Chaucer the Maker*. London: Faber and Faber, 1951.

Spurgeon, Caroline Frances Eleanor. *Five Hundred Years of Chaucer Criticism and Allusion, 1357–1900*. 3 vols. Cambridge: Cambridge University Press, 1925.

Stillinger, Thomas C. *The Song of Troilus: Lyric Authority in the Medieval Book*. Philadelphia: University of Pennsylvania Press, 1992.

Strohm, Paul. *England's Empty Throne*. New Haven and London: Yale University Press, 1998.

———. "Saving the Appearances: Chaucer's 'Purse' and the Fabrication of the Lancastrian Claim." *Hochon's Arrow*, 75–94. Princeton, NJ: Princeton University Press, 1992.

Taylor, Karla. *Chaucer Reads the "Divine Comedy."* Stanford, CA: Stanford University Press, 1989.

Thompson, N. S. *Chaucer, Boccaccio, and the Debate of Love: A Comparative Study of the "Decameron" and the "Canterbury Tales."* Oxford: Oxford University Press, 1996.

Trigg, Stephanie. *Congenial Souls: Reading Chaucer from Medieval to Postmodern.* Minneapolis: University of Minnesota Press, 2002.

Trilling, Lionel. *Matthew Arnold.* New York: Columbia University Press, 1949.

Utz, Richard J. *Chaucer and the Discourse of German Philology: A History of Reception and an Annotated Bibliography of Studies, 1793–1948.* Turnhout: Brepols, 2002.

Wallace, David. *Chaucer and the Early Writings of Boccaccio.* Woodbridge, UK: D. S. Brewer, 1985.

———. *Chaucerian Polity: Absolutist Lineages and Associational Forms in England and Italy.* Stanford, CA: Stanford University Press, 1997.

Ward, Antonia. "'My Love for Chaucer': F. J. Furnivall and Homosociality in the Chaucer Society." In Kathleen Verduin et al., eds., *Medievalism and the Academy,* 1:44–57. Studies in Medievalism 10. Cambridge: D. S. Brewer, 1999.

Wetherbee, Winthrop. *Chaucer and the Poets: An Essay on "Troilus and Criseyde."* Ithaca, NY: Cornell University Press, 1984.

White, Hayden. "The Question of Narrative in Contemporary Historical Theory." In White, *The Content of the Form: Narrative Discourse and Historical Representation,* 25–57. Baltimore: Johns Hopkins University Press, 1987.

Wimsatt, James I. *Chaucer and His French Contemporaries: Natural Music in the Fourteenth Century.* Toronto: University of Toronto Press, 1991.

Windeatt, B. A. "Thomas Tyrwhitt." In Paul G. Ruggiers, ed., *Editing Chaucer: The Great Tradition,* 117–44. Norman, OK: Pilgrim Books, 1984.

Contributors

Seth Lerer is the Avalon Foundation Professor in Humanities and Professor of English and Comparative Literature at Stanford University. His many publications include *Chaucer and His Readers: Imagining the Author in Late-Medieval England* (Princeton, 1993), *Courtly Letters in the Age of Henry VIII: Literary Culture and the Arts of Deceit* (Cambridge, 1997), and *Error and the Academic Self: The Scholarly Imagination, Medieval to Modern* (Columbia, 2002).

Christopher Cannon is Reader in English at Cambridge University and Fellow of Girton College. He is the author of *The Making of Chaucer's English: A Study of Words* (Cambridge, 1998) and *The Grounds of English Literature* (Oxford, 2004).

James Simpson is Professor of English at Harvard University and formerly Professor of Medieval and Renaissance English Literature at Cambridge University. His most recent book is *Reform and Cultural Revolution,* volume 2 in the new *Oxford History of English Literature* (Oxford, 2002).

D. Vance Smith is Associate Professor of English at Princeton University and the author of *The Book of the Incipit: Beginnings in the Fourteenth Century* (Minnesota, 2001) and *Arts of Possession: The Middle English Household Imaginary* (Minnesota, 2003).

Rita Copeland is Professor of Classics and Comparative Literature at the University of Pennsylvania. Her publications include *Rhetoric, Hermeneutics, and Translation in the Middle Ages: Academic Traditions and Vernacular Texts* (Cambridge, 1991) and *Pedagogy, Intellectuals, and Dissent in the Later Middle Ages: Lollardy and Ideas of Learning* (Cambridge, 2001).

Deanne Williams is Associate Professor of English at York University in Canada and the author of *The French Fetish from Chaucer to Shakespeare* (Cambridge, 2004).

Bruce Holsinger is Professor of English at the University of Virginia. His *Music, Body, and Desire in Medieval Culture: Hildegard of Bingen to Chaucer* (Stanford, 2001) received the Modern Language Association's Prize for best first book.

Jennifer Summit is Associate Professor of English at Stanford University. Her *Lost Property: The Woman Writer and English Literary History, 1380–1589* (Chicago, 2000) received honorable mention for the Modern Language Association's Prize for best first book.

Stephanie Trigg is Senior Lecturer in English at the University of Melbourne, Australia. Her most recent book is *Congenial Souls: Reading for Chaucer from Medieval to Postmodern* (Minnesota, 2002).

Ethan Knapp is Associate Professor of English at the Ohio State University and the author of *The Bureaucratic Muse: Thomas Hoccleve and the Literature of Late Medieval England* (Pennsylvania State, 2001).

Index